Beginning Behavioral Research

A Conceptual Primer

THIRD EDITION

RALPH L. ROSNOW
Temple University

ROBERT ROSENTHAL
Harvard University

PRENTICE HALL
Upper Saddle River NJ 07458

Library of Congress Cataloging-in-Publication Data

Rosnow, Ralph L.
    Beginning behavioral research : a conceptual primer / Ralph L.
Rosnow, Robert Rosenthal. — 3rd ed.
      p.   cm.
    Includes bibliographical references and indexes.
    ISBN 0-13-791542-X (case)
    1. Psychology—Research—Methodology. 2. Social sciences—
Research—Methodology. I. Rosenthal, Robert.
II. Title.
BF76.5.R64 1998
300'.7'2—dc21
                                98-20614
                                    CIP

Editor-in-chief: *Nancy Roberts*
Acquisitions Editor: *Jennifer Gilliland*
Assistant Editor: *Anita Castro*
Director of Production and Manufacturing: *Barbara Kittle*
Managing Editor: *Bonnie Biller*
Project Manager: *Shelly Kupperman*
Manufacturing Manager: *Nick Sklitsis*
Prepress and Manufacturing Buyer: *Tricia Kenny*
Art Director: *Anne Bonanno Nieglos*
Interior/Cover Designer: *Amy Rosen*
Line Art Coordinator: *Guy Ruggiero*
Marketing Manager: *Mike Alread*
Cover Art: *Elsa Warnick/Stockworks*. Hand Holding
        Magnifying Glass Over Crowd/*Stockworks*

This book was set 10/12 Galliard Roman by the Clarinda Company (Atlantic)
and bound by R.R. Donnelley & Sons (Harrisonburg).
The cover was printed by Phoenix Color Corporation.

Printed in the United States of America

10 9 8 7 6 5 4

ISBN 0-13-791542-X

Prentice-Hall International (UK) Limited, *London*
Prentice-Hall of Australia Pty. Limited, *Sydney*
Prentice-Hall Canada Inc., *Toronto*
Prentice-Hall Hispanoamericana, S. A. *Mexico*
Prentice-Hall of India Private Limited, *New Delhi*
Prentice-Hall of Japan, Inc., *Tokyo*
Simon & Schuster Asia Pte, Ltd., *Singapore*
Editora Prentice-Hall do Brasil, Ltda., *Rio de Janeiro*

To our students and colleagues
in research methods
past, present, and future

Contents

3 Ethical Considerations 57

PART II OBSERVATION AND MEASUREMENT

6   Reliability and Validity   134

PART III   DESIGN AND IMPLEMENTATION

7   The Logic of Randomized Experiments   156

8 The Role of Quasi-Experimental Designs   180

9 Survey Designs and Subject Recruitment   203

PART IV DESCRIBING AND HYPOTHESIS TESTING

10 Summarizing the Data   228

11 Examining Relationships   249

12   Statistical Significance and Practical Importance   267

PART V   STATISTICAL DECISION MAKING

13   The t Test   288

14   The F Test   305

15   Chi-Square   328

Preface

Beginning Behavioral Research was originally conceived as an undergraduate text for students who, as part of an introductory course in research methods, are required to plan an empirical study, to analyze and interpret data, and to report findings and conclusions. It is also intended to encourage students to be analytical and critical not only in interpreting research findings but also in seeing what is behind the claims and conclusions in news reports of scientific results. While the primary emphasis is on behavioral and social research, we make an effort to connect these disciplines with the empirical reasoning used in other fields in order to underscore the unity of science. We have been pleasantly surprised to learn that the text has also been successfully used in ways that go far beyond its original purpose. For example, it has been used in undergraduate courses in which the production of a research project was not a major goal, as well as by master's and doctoral students to slip into our advanced text, *Essentials of Behavioral Research* (1991). Lecturers at the University of South Africa (Unisa) have used *Beginning Behavioral Research* to teach psychological research to several thousand students in their distance learning program. We are gratified that the book has been found useful by so many.

Organization

As in earlier editions, the material in this edition is presented in a linear sequence corresponding to the steps involved in conducting an empirical research study and analyzing and reporting the results. The reader is led step by step through the following process:

1. **Crafting a testable idea for research**
   Understanding empirical reasoning, the scientific method, levels of empirical investigation, and the scientific outlook (Chapter 1); creating, shaping, and polishing a research idea, and conducting a search of the literature (Chapter 2); weighing and balancing ethical considerations, and preparing a proposal for an ethics review (Chapter 3)

2. **Choosing methods of data collection and measurement**
   Knowing what methods are available for watching and recording behavior in laboratory and field research, using archival data and outside observers (Chapter 4); collecting data in which the subjects describe their own behavior or state of mind (Chapter 5); assessing the reliability and validity of measuring instruments and research designs (Chapter 6)

3. **Designing and implementing the research study**
   Designing a randomized experiment while controlling for artifacts and other threats to validity (Chapter 7); using time-series, *N*-of-1, longitudinal, correlational, and other designs (Chapter 8); surveying opinions and behavior, controlling for self-selection bias, and pilot-testing the instruments (Chapter 9)

4. **Approaching the research data**
   Using graphics and statistical summary procedures to develop an overall picture of the results (Chapter 10); identifying relationships (Chapter 11); testing hypotheses, estimating effect size, creating a confidence interval around the obtained effect, using the BESD to interpret practical importance, and doing a power analysis (Chapter 12)

5. **Testing hypotheses and exploring the results**
   Using t to compare two independent or two correlated conditions (Chapter 13); computing F in one-way and two-way designs, examining the simple effects, and interpreting an obtained interaction (Chapter 14); analyzing smaller and larger tables of counts by the chi-square and other procedures (Chapter 15)

6. **Comparing and combining results of independent studies, doing a file drawer analysis** (optional Appendix C)

7. **Reporting the research project** (Appendix A)

Our Approach

In our long experience of teaching research methods (over 60 years and several thousand students between the two of us), we have noted the questions and uncertainties of undergraduate students engaged in empirical research for the first time. The vast majority have not planned to pursue a career in research, but most of them have recognized the vitality and ubiquitousness of scientific research in their daily lives. So we have tried to anticipate and confront questions and uncertainties from their perspective not as potential professional producers of research, but as consumers of scientific results. It is essential for educated consumers to understand the utility and limitations of research as well as the fundamental differences between scientific and pseudoscientific claims of truth. Our aim in chronicling a wide range of older and newer research studies is to show the continuity of science. Once students have mastered this material, they should be able to understand more deeply what scientists mean when they proclaim that they have found something or not found something to be true.

Instructors who know our earlier work will recognize that this book—as well as our advanced text—grew out of a 117-page paperback book that we wrote many years ago: *Primer of Methods for the Behavioral Sciences* (Rosenthal & Rosnow, 1975a). Over the intervening period, we have had an opportunity to develop and refine that material. Most of our undergraduate students have been psychology majors required to take a research methods course as part of their concentration, but a substantial number have been in fields as diverse as communications, computer science, physical education, mathematics, statistics, accounting, nursing, biology, education, sociology, marketing, and even English, art, and theology. Whether they took this course as part of their major or as an elective, many dreaded the thought of having to wrestle again with statistics. On the assumption that few readers have total recall of statistics or will come away from a statistics course with an intuitive understanding of what was taught, we describe basic aspects of data analysis procedures, purposely avoiding the use of any mathematics beyond the high school level. We focus on the most popular procedures, and also on convenient methods that can later be used outside the research methods course to examine the practical importance of a set of results.

Most students with no college training in statistics should find that they can master basic data-analytic skills by reading the chapters and repeating the exercises in the order in which they are presented. In this age of the computer, the speediest method of doing complex calculations is with the aid of a computer, yet as statistician John W. Tukey noted, much can be learned by simply changing our point of view and examining the data in different ways (e.g., exploring for moderator variables by using the stem-and-leaf procedure). Our philosophy of data analysis is to treat statistics (in Chapters 10–15 and Appendix C) by showing, through intuitive reasoning and simple examples, what the results tell us. Instructors who plan to teach students to perform their main calculations on a computer will find that our emphasis on the concrete and arithmetical aspects of data analysis will complement any statistics package they choose. We also describe useful data-analytic procedures that are not typically found in basic computer packages (e.g., the effect size correlation and the confidence interval around the effect, the method of standardizing the margins in chi-square tables, the isolation of interaction residuals, the detective-like probing of reported data for an unreported effect size, and the file drawer method of assessing robustness of an overall p value in meta-analysis).

Instructors familiar with *Essentials of Behavioral Research* will recognize that *Beginning Behavioral Research* can be used for students up to, but just below, the level of *Essentials,* and that the conceptual and philosophical treatment of methods and data analysis is similar in both texts. We again emphasize the utility of the Pearson r as an effect size measure that can be conveniently interpreted as an index of practical importance. We also introduce students to statistical power analysis in a way that many should be able to apply in their individual studies. The chapter on ethics is intended to raise questions that project well beyond this book. Students interested in advanced or more detailed analyses of the topics treated here will find discussions in *Essentials.* In both texts, we have sought to communicate the richness, diversity, and excitement (as well as the basic or advanced technical aspects) of human subjects research that we ourselves find so challenging and stimulating.

Special Features and Additions

In an effort to make this book more useful and more user-friendly to a wide variety of students, we have incorporated a number of pedagogical devices. Each chapter begins with a set of *preview questions,* which readers can refer to as they progress. *Box discussions* highlight and enliven concepts with practical examples and illustrations. Each chapter concludes with a *summary* of the main ideas, followed by a list of *key terms* pegged to particular pages, and finally a number of *review questions* to stimulate thought and discussion—both multiple-choice (new to this edition) and discussion questions, with the answers on pages 343–61. A revised *glossary* at the end of the book lists and defines all the key terms and notes the primary chapter(s) or appendix where each term is discussed. The Instructor's Manual, developed by David B. Strohmetz of Monmouth University, contains class-tested exercises, teaching tips, handout questions, and other ideas that complement each chapter and that can be used to stimulate discussion.

We again informally asked a number of instructors whether they preferred the sample report in Appendix A to be in the format of a journal submission (i.e., including compositor's notes and so on) or in the style of a term paper (i.e., with an appendix containing the student's raw data and calculations). Previously the responses had been about evenly split, but this time they favored the term paper a little more than the journal submission format. Nevertheless, we again show both formats, one based on the American Psychological Association's (1994) publication manual and the other based on Rosnow and Rosnow's (1998) guide to writing research reports and essays. Both sample reports follow the APA style in reference citations, nonsexist language, and other practical considerations.

Instructors familiar with the previous edition will find new boxes, new illustrative cases drawn from different areas of behavioral and social science, further polishing of statistical and other technical material, and, we hope, elimination of unnecessary redundancy. There is a new chapter on ethics, which takes as its point of departure an available draft (1996) of guidelines for researchers studying human behavior (American Psychological Association, 1997.) The chapters on randomized and quasi-experimental designs have been revised in response to comments that we have received from instructors. New to the statistical chapters is a discussion of the confidence interval of the effect size r, which was recommended in a number of recent articles (e.g., Cohen, 1994; Rosnow & Rosenthal, 1996a). We focus on the 95% interval but also show how to create and interpret a narrower or wider band. Instructors will find that our discussion of data analysis is consistent with the recommendations of the recent APA Task Force on Statistical Inference. While we do not focus on psychological constructivism or postmodernism in philosophy of science, there is a box on the former and a strong flavor of the latter in our discussion of aesthetics, visualizations, hidden presuppositions, and so forth. Students interested in broader aspects of the latter might be directed to A. I. Miller's *Insights of Genius: Imagery and Creativity in Science and Art* (Springer-Verlag, 1996) or, if interested in aspects of epistemological issues as viewed by practitioners of behavioral research, to R. L. Rosnow and M. Georgoudi's *Contextualism and Understanding in Behavioral Science* (Praeger, 1986).

Acknowledgments

We have benefited once again from working with David Strohmetz, who prepared the Instructor's Manual; Margaret Ritchie, who did the copy editing; and Mary Lu Rosenthal, who prepared the indexes. We are grateful for their creative, elegant, and helpful assistance. We thank Bruce Rind for again allowing us to include an edited version of his work in Appendix A and Steven Stern for his tips on using PsycLIT. We thank Martin Terre Blanche, René Van Eeden, Fred Van Staden, and Vivien Willers (all at the University of South Africa) for writing and perfecting the hundreds of test items that are available for use with this text. We thank Robert E. Lana for permission to borrow or adapt ideas from *Introduction to Contemporary Psychology* (Lana & Rosnow, 1972). We thank a long line of teaching assistants and students at Temple University and Harvard University for their valuable comments on and criticisms of the lectures, handouts, drafts, and earlier editions on which this third edition was based. The first edition of this book was published by Macmillan Publishing Company, which was absorbed by Prentice Hall, and we thank the following consultants of these publishers for their constructive feedback: Bernard C. Beins, Ithaca College; Patricia R. DeLucia, Texas Tech University; Paul W. Foos, University of North Carolina at Charlotte; Allan J. Kimmel, American University of Paris; John W. Webster, Towson State University; Paul J. Wellman, Texas A & M University; and Jon L. Williams, Kenyon College. Additional valuable feedback was provided by an unusual trio of reviewers for *Contemporary Psychology* (1997, *42*, 835–837). Three members of the academic community of Southern Illinois University each wrote a separate review of the second edition. In an act of unusual and creative packaging, one review was written by a professor, Jack McKillip; one was written by a graduate student, Kristin Duppong; and one was written by an undergraduate student, Laurel J. Tinsley, with only a minor in psychology. We thank them all for their ingenuity and for their helpfulness to us in preparing this third edition. We also thank Jennifer Gilliland, Bill Webber, and others at Prentice Hall for their editorial support. And finally, we thank Mimi Rosnow and Mary Lu Rosenthal for counseling us in ways too numerous to mention.

Certain tables, figures, and passages (specifically noted in the text) have by permission been reproduced in part or in their entirety, for which we thank the following authors, representatives, and publishers: E. Earl Baughman; Leonard Berkowitz; Jacob Cohen; Mihaly Csikszentmihalyi; J. A. Hagenaars; R. Vance Hall; Howard Kahane; Paul Slovic; Alan Sockloff; Laurence Steinberg; Robert Weisberg; Academic Press; American Association for the Advancement of Science; American Psychological Association; American Sociological Association; American Statistical Association; Biometrika Trustees of the Imperial College of Science, Technology and Medicine; Brooks/Cole Publishing Company; Cambridge University Press; Elsevier Science Publishers; Lawrence Erlbaum Associates, Inc.; HarperCollins Publishers; Helen Dwight Reid Educational Foundation and Heldref Publications; Holt, Rinehart & Winston; Houghton Mifflin Company; Iowa State University Press; *Journal of Applied Behavior Analysis;* McGraw-Hill, Inc.; W. W. Norton & Company, Inc.; Oxford University Press; Pergamon Press; The Rand Corporation; Sussex Publishers, Inc. and *Psychology Today Magazine;* The University of Chicago Press; Wadsworth Publishing Company; and John Wiley & Sons, Inc. We are also grateful to the Longman Group UK Ltd., on behalf of the Literary Executor of the late Sir Ronald Fisher, F.R.S., and Dr. Frank Yates, F.R.S., for permission to reprint Table V from *Statistical Tables for Biological, Agricultural, and Medical Research* (6th ed., 1974).

This is our 12th book together in a collaboration that began over 30 years ago, and the beat goes on!

Ralph L. Rosnow
Robert Rosenthal

1 The Scientific Outlook

Why Study Research Methods?

Reading, 'riting, and 'rithmetic—the three R's—are viewed as the fundamentals of education. Beginning in grade school, we are taught these basic skills, and it is not hard to figure out why they are considered important. A fourth R, "researching" (i.e., exploring a problem systematically), is now regarded as another crucial skill for any educated person (Hult, 1996). In high school, for example, you were introduced to the processes involved in "researching" a term paper. In college science courses, the term *researching* implies using what is traditionally called the **scientific method** to explore a problem. Although this "method" transcends all scientific fields, its applications vary from one discipline to another. Scientists in fields as varied as psychology, biomedicine, education, communication research, economics, sociology, anthropology, physics, biology, chemistry, and other disciplines—all use this method. However, you may be wondering why you need to know the scientific method or study techniques of research if you do not plan to become a scientist. There are at least six good reasons.

PREVIEW QUESTIONS

▮ What is the value of studying the scientific method and the fourth R—*researching?*

▮ What "methods" do people use to explain events in the psychological world in which they live?

▮ What is meant by the term *empirical reasoning?*

▮ Why do scientists in all disciplines consider "the scientific method" a misnomer?

▮ What, then, is the nature of the scientific outlook, and what distinguishes it from other outlooks?

▮ How do the behavioral sciences fit into the constellation of sciences?

▮ What are the objectives of descriptive, relational, and experimental research in behavioral science?

▮ What are the nine components of a "scientific attitude"?

One reason is that our way of life is largely the creation of science, and we enhance our understanding of the full range of its influence on our lives by learning about the techniques used by scientists to open up the world to scrutiny and investigation. By analogy, viewing paintings, drawings, and sculpture in a museum becomes more meaningful when we know something about the techniques and creative ideas involved in producing the works of art. Similarly, reading that a public opinion survey shows that candidate so-and-so is ahead but with a particular margin of error, or that scientists in the area of child development have discovered a way of fostering language acquisition skills in young children, or that researchers have found a cure for some illness or have announced a new dietary supplement for increasing longevity has more meaning when we understand how the scientific conclusions were reached.

Besides providing a richer appreciation of the information that science brings to modern life, a second reason for studying research methods is that *not* having a clear understanding of how scientists cast and address questions sometimes costs us dearly. Doctors, teachers, lawyers, the clergy, politicians, the police—these people also have an influence on our daily lives, and everyone seems to know how women and men in these fields go about their work. But few people have even a vague idea of how scientists create and test hypotheses that enlarge our understanding of the world. As a consequence, people often succumb to misleading allegations based on supposedly scientific research. Becoming familiar with the nature of **empirical reasoning** (i.e., a use of logic that is aided by controlled observation and measurement)—especially by designing and carrying out a research study under the watchful eye of an experienced guide—can teach us the difference between good science and **pseudoscience** (i.e., bogus claims masquerading as scientific fact).

A third reason for studying science and the techniques of research, particularly in the context of behavioral and social science, is to acquire information and skills we can use later. For example, by learning about the logic of an "N-of-1 design," we develop a skill that we may use outside the laboratory to test simple causal hypotheses by using empirical reasoning. Learning how professional pollsters properly sample opinions, and how they avoid certain pitfalls in asking people what they feel or think, we learn other skills that we can apply to other real-life questions. The same is true of other information and skills that you will learn, including sharpening your powers of causal reasoning and improving your data-analytic abilities. Not only will you be able to think of probing questions to ask about the basis of sensational claims, but you will often be able to evaluate them independently once you understand certain basic ideas of causal inference, the use of control conditions, and the use of statistical tests and effect sizes to make numerical conjectures.

A fourth reason for studying and doing research is to learn about the limits of empirical methods and why generalizations—including all scientific generalizations—are said to be based partly on a "leap of faith." For example, if physicists were to insist that the only acceptable claims are those based on direct observations, they would be unable to accept the venerable laws of mechanics. Newton's first law of motion tells us that a body not acted on by any force will continue in a state of rest or uniform motion in a straight line forever. No human being has ever seen a "body not acted on by any force" (e.g., friction or gravity), much less observed its "motion in a straight line forever" (M. R. Cohen, 1959). Yet this basic law is accepted as one of science's most fundamental generalizations. You will see that the empirical methods used in behavioral and social science also have limits, such as those derived from studying human beings who are aware they are being observed for scientific purposes (see Box 1.1). We will have more to say about this problem later in the book, where we describe techniques that experimenting psychologists and others who do human subjects research (e.g., medical researchers) use to address this problem. These techniques are also limited, but despite the intrinsic limits, psychologists and others use the scientific method to formulate powerful generalizations about how and why people feel, think, and behave as they do.

Box 1.1   ## The Hawthorne Effect

The fact that a person is being studied experimentally sometimes affects how the person behaves even more than the experimental manipulation does. This conclusion, known as the **Hawthorne effect,** grew out of a series of human factors experiments performed between 1924 and 1932 by a group of industrial researchers at the Hawthorne Works of the Western Electric Company in Cicero, Illinois (Roethlisberger & Dickson, 1939). The experiments were designed to study how workers' productivity and job satisfaction might be affected by workplace conditions (lighting, temperature, rest periods, and so on). Although the results, in retrospect, have proved difficult to unravel because of design ambiguities and irregularities (J. G. Adair, 1984; Bramel & Friend, 1981; Franke & Kaul, 1978; Gillespie, 1988; Parsons, 1974; Schlaifer, 1980; Sommer, 1968), they are often cited in support of the argument that typical subjects in psychological experiments are sensitive and accommodating to inadvertent task-orienting cues. Later, we will describe research on the "social psychology of the experiment" demonstrating that this idea is not far off the mark. Therefore, how subjects in an experiment perceived the experiment (including any inadvertent cues) is valuable information to be taken into consideration when the experimenter interprets the results.

A fifth reason for studying research methods is that the same factors viewed as "nuisance variables" in many studies can tell us something about ourselves and others (McGuire, 1969). Later, for example, when you learn about nonresponse bias, you will also learn about the characteristics of people who volunteer for research participation and about the conditions that promote this behavior. Thinking about research ethics in science forces us to confront our own moral presuppositions. Learning about the "good subject" and about evaluation apprehension gives further insights into human motivation. And learning about how scientists come up with research ideas may stimulate our own creative thinking.

A final reason for studying and doing research is that some of you will find this enterprise so much fun and so absorbing that you may want to make a career of it!

Peirce's Methods of "Fixing Belief"

Of course, the scientific method is not the only strategy that people use to explain or make sense of things. Philosophers, novelists, theologians, and many others also seek to give us a coherent picture of our world, but they do not use the scientific method to organize their ideas and give us information. What distinguishes the various strategies that people use to formulate a sense of understanding and belief? Charles Sanders Peirce (1839–1914), an American philosopher whose work had a strong influence on William James, the founder of experimental psychology in the United States, suggested an answer to this question. Peirce (pronounced "purse") described four distinct strategies for what he called "the fixation of belief," by which he meant the formulation of strongly held beliefs: (1) tenacity, (2) authority, (3) a priori method, and (4) the scientific method. He argued that each strategy, although limited in some ways, essentially contains a formula or guiding principle that, once it becomes inculcated as a "habit of mind," influences whether a person will believe one thing rather than another, or reach one conclusion rather than another, in a given situation (Peirce, 1966).

Peirce theorized that the most primitive approach of all is the **method of tenacity,** by which people cling stubbornly (tenaciously) to beliefs or claims just because they seem obvious or make "common sense." The problem, Peirce noted, is that holding one's ground is sometimes based on an illusion. Like an ostrich that buries its head in the sand, stubborn people who cling to false ideas go through life systematically excluding anything that might change their minds. It sometimes seems that a whole society has fallen victim to a false idea, and it is not easy to shake beliefs loose or to open closed minds. For example, for centuries, people considered it obvious that the earth was fixed and immobile, and that it was at the center of the universe. Elaborate explanations using myths to embellish this strongly held belief persisted until it was finally swept away by what one author called the "witness of the naked eye" (Boorstein, 1985, p. 305), by which he meant empirical astronomy.

In our own time, we recognize that the method of tenacity still has a pernicious hold on many people's beliefs. Peirce thought that strong beliefs are like the cadence that closes a musical phrase in a symphony (see also Box 1.2). However, in the case of some beliefs, this closure is based on what social psychologists call a *false consensus* (Ross, Greene, & House, 1977). The term means that individuals have a tendency to overestimate the extent to which others believe the same thing. Dismissing alternative arguments as deviant, people convince themselves that their own beliefs *must* be the correct ones (Sherman, Presson, & Chassin, 1984). False consensus can be brought about by a host of factors, such as when people keep out of view all that might change their minds or when they seek out information that is consistent with their own prejudices about how the world *should* be understood (Marks & Miller, 1987).

> **Box 1.2   The UFO Myth**
>
> Myth, folklore, and superstition are other examples of the method of tenacity's powerful hold on beliefs that endure for centuries. For example, the noted Swiss psychiatrist and psychologist Carl G. Jung—one of Sigmund Freud's students—theorized about the old rumor of "flying saucers," unidentified flying objects (UFOs) piloted by some extraterrestrial (Jung, 1910, 1959). This belief, a recurrent theme for centuries, usually takes one of two forms: It is claimed either that benevolent superior beings from another planet have come to save humanity (represented in the 1951 movie *The Day the Earth Stood Still*), or that menacing creatures threaten all humanity and will therefore unify people who have diverse ideologies to stand against a common foe (represented in the 1996 movie *Independence Day*). Jung theorized that such claims are merely an expression of people's fears and uncertainties about the world situation and their wish for a redeeming supernatural force.

A second strategy—which Peirce viewed as at least minimally superior to the method of tenacity—is the **method of authority.** In this case, certain claims (some true and others false) are accepted because someone in a position of authority *says* they are true. Peirce noted that false accusations of witchcraft resulted in atrocities of the most horrible kind, as people obeyed the word of authority to carry out their cruelties. A somewhat more benign case occurred in the 15th century, when Nicolaus Copernicus was asked by the Pope to help with calendar reform. Copernicus deduced that the sun, not the earth, was the center of our universe. However, that idea, being at odds not only with "common sense" but also with the authority of ecclesiastical doctrine, was rejected by the Church. It was not until the 16th and 17th centuries, and the revolutionary thinking of Galileo and Newton, that there was a successful intellectual uprising against the strictures of ecclesiastical authority.

Again, we do not need to look very far to find examples of the method of authority's benevolent or malevolent influence in our daily lives. On the positive side, civilized society would cease to exist without people's willingness to obey laws and to carry out reasonable orders. As discussed later, researchers are subject to the benevolent authority of a constantly evolving "social contract" between science and society concerning what is ethically permissible in research. Other examples on the benevolent side are the physician who prescribes a drug or regimen to cure an illness, the electrician who advises replacing wiring that is about to blow out, and the mechanic who informs us that the spark plugs in our car are shot and need replacing; we depend on their honesty and the authority of their expertise. On the negative side are unscrupulous people who use fakery and showy methods to prey on human weaknesses, such as medical quacks, food faddists, faith healers, TV psychics, cult leaders, and eccentric sexual theorists (M. Gardner, 1957; Shermer, 1997). Let the buyer beware, however, for the authority of these hucksters is in the eyes of their victims.

In a third approach, which Peirce called the **a priori method,** we use our individual powers of pure reason and logic to know and explain our world. This method—which Peirce (1966) characterized as "far more intellectual and respectable from the point of view of reason" than either of the previous two (p. 106)—has proved itself quite robust in the hands of mathematicians and philosophers. It is sometimes an effective defense against hucksters who depend on gullibility. We can approach their dubious claims with a questioning mind that, as one writer put it, resists "being overly impressed" even if the evidence seems to be immediately before us (Gilovich, 1991, p. 187). For example, suppose someone repeats a sensational rumor and we are not sure whether to believe it; we might ask how the story originated. Although the immediate source of the story may be quite credible, we may question the trustworthiness of the person with whom it originated. When we are told rumors described to us as being secondhand, we may question whether they are not thirdhand or even more distant from the original source (Allport & Postman, 1947; Gilovich, 1991; Rosnow & Fine, 1976).

However, Peirce also recognized that the a priori method is constrained by the limits of pure reason. Suppose you claim that A causes B, and I disagree. Do we just have to let it go at that? What we need, he argued, is a way of drawing on nature to help us resolve matters of disagreement. In other words, we may use the scientific method, by which we attempt to draw on independent realities to evaluate claims rather than depend on reason alone. In behavioral science, as a leading researcher once stated, we use the scientific method to help us sort out what we know about human nature from what we only think we know (Milgram, 1977). However, the term *scientific method* is a misnomer, because this "method" is not synonymous with any single, fixed procedure (see Box 1.3). It is better to think of the scientific method as a philosophical *outlook,* in the abstract way that Peirce seemed to conceptualize it. How, then, can we distinguish it from Peirce's other strategies for "fixing belief"? One answer is that the scientific method, more than any other method, is characterized by **empirical reasoning.**

Box 1.3   **The Law of the Instrument**

Although there is no such thing as *the* scientific method, some brilliant discovery or achievement may make it seem that the particular method employed has more prestige than other methods, even in applications to which it has no special appropriateness. Such a situation was called the "law of the instrument" by the philosopher Abraham Kaplan (1964). He used an analogy to define the principle: Give a young child a hammer, and the child will find that everything needs pounding. Kaplan explained that some empirical and data-analytic methods seem to acquire a prepotency over others simply because they are successful in some tasks, not because they are intrinsically superior.

What Is Empirical Reasoning?

In its dictionary definition, **empirical** refers to the use of experience or observation. In the context of the scientific method, empirical reasoning relies not on armchair theorizing, political persuasiveness, or personal position but (as noted previously) on controlled observation and measurement. As one scientist noted, when trying to unlock a door with a set of previously untried keys, a person says, "If this key fits the lock, then the lock will spring when I turn the key" (Conant, 1957, p. xii). The same is true in empirical science. The scientist has a choice of "keys" (i.e., empirical methods), decides on one, and then says in essence, "Let's try it." Thus the scientific method calls for a reliance on techniques that are available to *anyone* who is skilled enough to use them to open up the world for scrutiny and investigation. In fact, it is this primary dependence on empirical reasoning that connects scientists working in different fields, even though they use quite different empirical methods in their research. We will have more to say about the basic kinds of empirical strategies used in behavioral and social research, but let us pause for a moment to sample how empirical reasoning has been applied in the past and in the present to a variety of real-world problems.

Our first example comes not from behavioral science but from physics, although the use of empirical reasoning could just as well be illustrated in other disciplines. This particular example involved the investigation of the space shuttle *Challenger's* dramatically televised accident on January 28, 1986, in which seven people lost their lives. A panel of experts and other authorities was convened to look into the disaster and to figure out what had caused it. One member of the panel was Richard P. Feynman, a noted physicist, who thought of a way to demonstrate what had gone wrong in the frigid weather on the day of the launch. The rocket that boosted the shuttle contained two rubber seals in the form of rings, called *O-rings,* that were expected to be resilient but had not actually been tested in freezing temperature. A lack of resilience of the O-rings when it was freezing would explain why the rocket exploded the moment it was ignited. That is, highly inflammable fuel leaked through the seals, then caught fire and exploded.

At the end of an exhausting day of listening to testimony and arguments, Feynman (1988) had a sudden inspiration when he returned to his hotel room:

> I'm feeling lousy and I'm eating dinner; I look at the table, and there's a glass of ice water. I say to myself, "Damn it, *I* can find out about the rubber *without* having NASA [National Aeronautics and Space Administration] send notes back and forth: I just have to *try* it! All I have to do is get a sample of the rubber." (p. 146)

Early the next day, Feynman went to a hardware store, where he bought screwdrivers, pliers, and the smallest C-clamp he could find. He then went to NASA and used the screwdriver to peel away a sample of the rubber used in the O-rings. When the hearings resumed, he used the pliers to squash the rubber, which he then clamped and placed in a glass of ice water. When he removed the rubber and undid the clamp, the rubber did not spring back. In other words, for more than a few seconds, there was no resilience in the rubber when it was at a temperature of 32°F. Feynman thus figured out a way to make his argument by using empirical reasoning.

Empirical Reasoning in Behavioral Science

Empirical reasoning entered into behavioral science during the late 19th century, when the creative advances inspired by the earlier applications of the scientific method in physics and biology led to the development of psychology as a science. In Leipzig, Wilhelm Wundt (1832–1920), trained in medicine and experimental physiology, developed the first formal experimental laboratory to study psychological behavior. Around the same time, William James (1843–1910), who had a background in philosophy and physiology, announced a graduate course at Harvard University in which the students participated in psychological experiments that James arranged. To be sure, psychological science is not practiced only in the laboratory. In Britain, another pioneering behavioral scientist, Francis Galton (1822–1911), was demonstrating the application of empirical reasoning to questions that had been thought to lie completely outside its application (Forrest, 1974).

In one of his numerous investigations, Galton decided to see whether there might be empirical grounds for believing that prayers are answered. Of course, the sincerity of all prayers is not equal. However, Galton thought, one way to get at this problem was to look at something prayed for with tremendous frequency. In England, the health and longevity of the royal family is prayed for weekly or even daily nationwide. Galton wondered: Do members of the royal family therefore live longer than individuals of humbler birth? In 1872, he published the results of his inquiry. What he found, after a painstaking gathering and analysis of actuarial data, was that, of 97 members of royal families, the mean age attained by males had been 64.04 years. Compared to 945 members of the clergy who had lived to a mean age of 69.49, 294 lawyers who had lived to 68.14, 244 physicians who had lived to 68.14, and so forth, the members of the royal family had actually fared worse than he expected based on the many prayers on their behalf.

Of course, Galton did not reject the hypothesis that prayer has a powerful effect in other ways, such as by strengthening people's resolution to face hardships and by bringing serenity in distress. Galton's empirical reasoning, as one scientist noted, was scientific in the context in which he examined this question (Medawar, 1969). Let us look at two more behavioral science examples before moving on—one in developmental psychology and the other in social psychology—both involving the *experimental* application of controlled observation and measurement to the study of human suggestibility.

Stephen J. Ceci, a developmental psychologist at Cornell University, was interested in the accuracy of children's eyewitness testimony. To study this problem in a real-life setting, he and his coworkers designed a simple demonstration experiment in which a character named "Sam Stone" was described to 3- to 6-year-olds as someone who was very clumsy and broke things (Ceci & Bruck, 1993, 1995; Ceci, Leichtman, & White, 1995). Then, a person identified as Sam Stone visited the children's nursery school, where he chatted briefly with them during a storytelling session—but did not behave clumsily or break anything. The next day, the children were shown a ripped book and a soiled teddy bear and were asked if they knew how the objects had been damaged. Over the course of the next 10 weeks, the children were reinterviewed.

Each time, they were asked two leading questions such as "I wonder whether Sam Stone was wearing long pants or short pants when he ripped the book?" or "I wonder if Sam Stone got the teddy bear dirty on purpose or by accident?"

What the researchers observed—and videotaped so that others could see for themselves—was that the planted stereotype of Sam Stone carried over into the children's eyewitness reports. When asked, 72% of the 3- to 4-year-olds said that Sam Stone had ruined either the book or the teddy bear, and 45% of these children claimed they had actually seen him do it (and then embellished their accounts with other details). Ceci used a comparison condition (called a **control group**) against which to evaluate the effect of his experimental manipulation. The control group received the suggestive interviews but no planted stereotypical information about Sam Stone. As we would predict, they made fewer false claims than the children in whom the stereotype had been planted.

Our final example involves a classic experiment by Solomon Asch (1952) in the field of social psychology. Asch was interested in conformity and the reason why people go along with some consensual beliefs. In this research, a subject arrived at the psychology laboratory along with several others who were accomplices of the experimenter. Once seated together at the same table, all of the participants were told by the experimenter that they would be asked to make judgments about the length of several lines. Each person was to judge which of three lines was closest in length to a standard line. The accomplices always stated their judgments first, after which the subject expressed an opinion. The accomplices, acting in collusion with the experimenter, sometimes gave obviously incorrect judgments, but they were unanimous in their responses. One third of the subjects, Asch found, gave the same opinion as the accomplices in the study. When interviewed later, the subjects gave three distinct reasons for yielding to the apparent pressure exerted by the incorrect majority: (1) unawareness of being incorrect; (2) doubts about their own perceptions and lack of confidence in them; and (3) a wish to appear the same as the majority. Thus, using controlled experimental observation, Asch not only produced conformity in the laboratory but also observed that going along with a consensus may come about for a variety of reasons (see Box 1.4).

The Rhetoric of Science

Although the scientific method is uniquely identified by its reliance on observation and measurement, it shares some features with other strategies of explanation. One feature of all methods of explanation is that conclusions are expressed in the accepted **rhetoric** (or informative and persuasive language) of the area they represent (A. G. Gross, 1990; Pera & Shea, 1991). As in learning a new language, one must be familiar with the linguistic and grammatical mode of a particular discipline in order to understand what people in that field are talking about. In other words, psychologists talk like psychologists, philosophers like philosophers, lawyers like lawyers, theologians like theologians, physicians like physicians, police like police, and so on.

In particular, the rhetoric of empirical science traditionally takes the form of written reports. Scientists in all fields believe in the importance of reporting their research

---

Box 1.4 **Inferential Validity**

We use the term **inferential validity** to refer to the notion that causal inferences made in psychological laboratories about real-life experiences are applicable to the experiences (Rosnow, 1991; Rosnow & Aiken, 1973). For example, Asch's studies showed that, at least in the psychological laboratory, subjects can be pressured into making ridiculous perceptual judgments. But is the finding applicable outside the experimental laboratory? Allen Funt, who for years produced the popular television show *Candid Camera,* showed that the answer to our question is yes. His 1970 film, *What Do You Say to a Naked Lady?,* contained a sequence that closely follows the Asch findings. A man serving as the subject of the demonstration is sent to a waiting room in which three accomplices are seated. After a few minutes the accomplices stand and remove their shirts, then their shoes and socks. Soon they have all stripped down to their shorts—and, remarkably enough, so has the subject of the demonstration.

---

as completely and as soon as possible so that others can **replicate** (repeat) the research for themselves. As one scientist put it:

> It is not necessary for the plumber to write about pipes, nor is it necessary for the lawyer to write about cases [except for the writing of "briefs"], but the research scientist, perhaps uniquely among the trades and professions, must provide a written document showing what he or she did, why it was done, how it was done, and what was learned from it (R. A. Day, 1983, p. x).

In behavioral science, the style of the research report has evolved over many years, and it serves several purposes: First, it allows busy readers to read reports more easily because they conform to similar publishing procedures. Second, it contains notes that are important to compositors and editors, such as telling them where tables and figures belong in the printed article. Third, it enables the researchers to organize their thoughts as they summarize their project for others (see Box 1.5).

Previously, we alluded to another characteristic of science: It is limited in certain ways. For example, it is limited by ethical guidelines that are consistent with current moral sensitivities (e.g., Kimmel,1996; Sieber,1982a, 1982b). Science is also constrained by our limited cognitive capacity as human beings to perceive and process all of the rich and disorderly world in which we live. An analogy suggested by Robert Lana (1991) is relevant: We can bend our arms forward at the elbow, but not backward; nature has imposed a limit on how far the human forearm can be bent. By the same token, the rhetoric of science enables us to bend our scientific observations into prose, but nature has imposed a limit on our cognitive capacity to evaluate and communicate all of the world's richness of information. Philosophers call this the *tacit dimension* of knowledge, which means that we frequently *know* more than we can *say* (Polanyi, 1966).

Box 1.5	**Writing Scientific Reports**

Well-written scientific reports imply a logical progression in thought. If you turn to Appendix A (pp. 392–406), you will see how a student's research report might look if it were submitted to a scientific journal that followed the style prescribed by the *Publication Manual of the American Psychological Association* (American Psychological Association, 1994). Appendix A also shows the same research written up as a term paper for a course requirement (pp. 374–391). Although there are a few stylistic differences between the two versions (e.g., the different cover pages and the use of an appendix for reporting calculations in the course report), they both use a basic structure that is used in almost all reports in behavioral science. It consists of an abstract, an introduction, a methods section, a results section, a discussion section, and a list of the references that are cited in the manuscript.

Other Shared Features of the Scientific Method

Besides using empirical reasoning and a specialized language, scientists—indeed, all of us (Bauer & Johnson-Laird, 1993; Johnson-Laird, 1983; Johnson-Laird & Byrne, 1991)—use **mental imagery.** In fact, the history of ideas teaches us that, to be influential, good scientific theories must reflect a way of thinking that includes images. We will have more to say about the nature of theories, but it will suffice here to note that theories have to be perceptible in a way that can be seen as "making sense"—that is, given accepted beliefs. In the same way that Michelangelo began with a mental image in creating his *Pietà,* so did Isaac Newton in developing his laws of motion, and so do behavioral scientists in constructing their scientific theories (e.g., Nisbet, 1976). The annals of science are full of such visualizations (e.g., A. I. Miller, 1986; Randhawa & Coffman, 1978). The reaction to failures in perceptibility is often "I just don't see it!"

A legendary case in modern science occurred when the quantum theorists in physics found it hard to convince the physical determinists among them that, given a very great many atoms, all capable of certain definite changes, we can tell what proportion of atoms will undergo each change but cannot tell which particular changes any given atom will undergo. God "does not play dice with the world" is the way Albert Einstein responded (Jammer, 1966, p. 358). It seems that he could not see (or at least accept) that, at the level of simple atomic processes, activity may be ruled by blind chance (Clark, 1971; Jammer, 1966). Only after mainstream modern physicists were able to accept as "perceptible" the generalizations proposed by quantum theorists did those principles enter the textbooks as a precise model of knowledge.

Finally, although it would be wrong to claim that art is simply the same thing as science, a characteristic of both is the role of **aesthetics** (i.e., having a sense of the beautiful). The chemist Primo Levi (1984) told how, as a young student, he was first struck by the fact that "Mendeleev's Periodic Table. . . was poetry, loftier and more solemn than all the poetry we had swallowed" (p. 1). Scientists and philosophers have long been aware of the basic similarity of the creative act found in the arts and poetry to that found in the sciences (Chandrasekhar, 1987; Garfield, 1989a, 1989b; Nisbet, 1976; Wechler, 1978). "Beauty is truth, truth beauty," the poet John Keats wrote in his "Ode on a Grecian Urn," which is as much a visual metaphor of value in science as it is in art and poetry (Gombrich, 1963). Twenty-five hundred years ago, Plato likened the creative work of the astronomer to that of the painter. In your reading, you will find words such as *beautiful* and *elegant* used to describe the precision and accuracy of scientific laws, equations, theories, and so on. Behavioral scientists, like all scientists, love intellectual beauty and strive for it as they attempt to envisage some aspect of the psychological world. There may be no greater praise of a colleague's work than to say of it that the experiment or the set of findings is "just beautiful."

Thus the scientific method is characterized not only by careful observation and measurement, but by the accepted language in a given discipline, by perceptible images, and by the aesthetic acceptability of those images. But for scientists, the essential criteria are always observation and measurement. In other words, the scientific method rests not just on the rhetorical force of arguments, the visual force of imagination, or the aesthetic force of beauty, but primarily on subjecting plausible ideas to empirical confrontation.

What Is Behavioral Science?

The examples that we have mentioned cover a wide range of disciplines, including psychology, physics, and astronomy. However, this book is not just a trip into the realm of science in general; it is a journey into the domain of behavioral (and social) science in particular. **Behavior** is what you do and how you act; **behavioral science** (as well as *social science*) is an "umbrella" term that also includes cognitive and emotional functioning. The range of interests of behavioral and social scientists covers the study of early primitive humans, humans as political animals, economic animals, social animals, talking animals, and logicians. These aspects of human nature are the concern of psychologists (e.g., clinical, cognitive, counseling, developmental, educational, experimental, industrial-organizational, and social), mass communication researchers, sociologists, physical and cultural anthropologists, economists, psycholinguists, behavioral biologists, neuroscientists, and even some statisticians. But no matter what the preferred label, the objective in all areas of behavioral and social science is the same: to describe and explain how and why people behave as they do, including how and why they feel and think as they do (Kimble, 1989).

For many purposes, it may make little difference whether we can distinguish among those various areas; there are differences nonetheless. For instance, the experimental psychologists use laboratory instruments and techniques to study human experiences in controlled settings. The social and industrial-organizational psychologists, particularly those trained in a psychology graduate program, frequently conduct experiments, but they are likely to be performed in a field setting as well as in a laboratory setting. By contrast, the sociologists are more likely to perform survey studies in the field or to do ethnographic and participant-observer research (described later). Nonetheless, many behavioral researchers borrow from one another's storehouse of methods. Thus sociologists also conduct experiments and social psychologists also perform survey and participant-observer studies. The point is that, in spite of the fences separating different departments in colleges and universities, the boundary lines in behavioral and social science are by no means rigid.

We mentioned that behavioral and social scientists study real-life problems not only in naturalistic settings (e.g., Galton's and Ceci's studies) but in the laboratory as well. For example, in the area known as **psychophysics** (i.e., the study of the relationship between physical stimuli and our experience of them), experimenting psychologists working in the laboratory discovered many years ago that the amount by which stimulus intensity must be increased to cause a noticeable change in the perception of the stimulus is a constant proportion of the intensity of the original stimulus. Following this line of reasoning, they showed that it is possible to write a mathematical statement of the theoretical relationship between the intensity of a stimulus and the intensity of a sensation, a statement that can then be applied to a range of real-life situations. If, say, your dormitory room is lighted by a 100-watt bulb, and if 15 watts of light must be added before you can detect a difference in the amount of the light, then in a room with a 50-watt bulb, 7.5 watts must be added before the difference is detectable.

The philosopher Hans Reichenbach noted that scientists explain things by "concatenations of evidence." Reichenbach's point also applies to behavioral and social scientists. In many areas, research has evolved since the early 1970s to embrace what we call **methodological pluralism** and **theoretical ecumenism,** that is, the use of multiple methods of controlled observation and more than one theoretical explanation (Houts, Cook, & Shadish, 1986; Jaeger & Rosnow, 1988; Rosnow, 1981, 1986). Thus we now see many **interdisciplinary** research projects, as researchers in different disciplines strive to develop a more complete and integrated picture of human nature. Sometimes a whole new field is created when researchers combine the methods and theories of different disciplines. Current examples include behavioral medicine, mathematical psychology, psychobiology, ethnopsychology, psycholinguistics, psychological anthropology, and, perhaps most broadly, neuroscience (see also Box 1.6).

Box 1.6   ## The Interdisciplinary Science of Communication Research

A specific example of interdisciplinary science is the hybrid science of communication research. Joshua Meyrowitz (1985), a noted theorist at the University of New Hampshire, observed that our home life "is now a less bounded and unique environment" because of people's access to other places and other people through electronic communication (p. vii). The old notion of disciplining children by sending them to their room takes on a new meaning when the room is equipped with a computer that is hooked up to the Internet. What used to be a restriction becomes a conduit to an uncensored larger world. At the touch of a few keys or the clicking of a mouse, the young person can summon a range of experiences. To examine scientifically the myriad aspects of this situation, social psychologists, communication researchers, developmental psychologists, educational researchers, and many others have joined hands in interdisciplinary research ventures.

Broad Research Approaches

We have touched on a number of research techniques, such as the use of actuarial data to study the efficacy of prayer, the "Sam Stone" manipulation used to study children's eyewitness testimony, the experimental simulation of conformity, and the laboratory investigation of physical stimuli and our perception of them. But even a cursory glance at the many journals in just one discipline, psychology—more than 360 journals according to the American Psychological Association's *Journals in Psychology* (1993)—will reveal that there are countless techniques of empirical inquiry. To give an overview, it is convenient to lump together the specific orientations of behavioral and social research into three broad types: *descriptive, relational,* and *experimental.* Table 1.1 gives illustrations of each type in three general research areas (psycholinguistics, the social psychology of rumor behavior, and methodological research). As

Table 1.1	Descriptive, Relational, and Experimental Conclusions in Three Research Areas

Psycholinguistics
Descriptive: When a 2-year-old child listens to a message spoken by his or her mother and is asked to repeat it, the child typically repeats only part of the message (R. Brown, 1965).
Relational: On the average, frequently used words tend to be shorter than infrequently used words. This statement is called *Zipf's law* (G. A. Miller & Newman, 1958; Zipf, 1935, 1949).
Experimental: When interfering background noise is present, a speaker tends to use more words and fewer abbreviations than when there is no interfering background noise (Heise & Miller, 1951).

Rumor behavior
Descriptive: Of more than 1,000 rumors collected from all over the United States during World War II, approximately two thirds were divisive in their intent—called *wedge-driving rumors* (Knapp, 1944).
Relational: Rumors that forecast unpleasant consequences (known as *dread rumors*) are passed to others with greater frequency than rumors that predict pleasant consequences (known as *wish rumors*) (Rosnow, Esposito, & Gibney, 1987; C. J. Walker & Blaine, 1991).
Experimental: College students who were made to feel anxious required less verbal prodding to repeat a rumor than students who had been told the rumor but were not made to feel anxious (C. J. Walker & Beckerle, 1987).

Methodological research
Descriptive: It has been estimated that perhaps 80 percent of psychological research on normal adults has used college and university students as research participants (Higbee & Wells, 1972; J. Jung, 1969; McNemar, 1946; Schultz, 1969; Sears, 1986; Sieber & Saks, 1989; Smart, 1966).
Relational: Individuals who volunteer to participate in research are usually higher than nonvolunteers in education, social class, intelligence, and the need for social approval (Rosenthal & Rosnow, 1975b; Rosnow & Rosenthal, 1997).
Experimental: Subjects made to experience a conflict between "looking good" and cooperating with the experimenter are likely to try to look good, whereas subjects not made to experience such a conflict are likely to help the experimenter (Rosnow, Goodstadt, Suls, & Gitter, 1973; Sigall, Aronson, & Van Hoose, 1970).

you study these illustrations, you will see that descriptive conclusions tell us *how things are,* relational conclusions tell us *how things are in relation to other things,* and experimental conclusions tell us *how things are and how they got to be that way.*

As you become better acquainted with the literature in your area of interest, you will see that the research usually involves more than one approach, although a given study can usually be described as *primarily* descriptive, relational, or experimental. As a program of research progresses, the investigators may need to alternate among these three types, or they may follow a natural progression from descriptive to relational to experimental studies. The hypothetical case presented in the following paragraphs on instructional research in educational psychology will show more clearly what we mean by a *natural progression* in a program of empirical studies.

Descriptive Research

First, in **descriptive research,** the goal of the investigation is the careful mapping out of a situation or a set of events, that is, describing what is happening behaviorally. Causal explanations are not of direct concern except perhaps speculatively. For example, if we are interested in the study of children's failure in school, we may spend a good deal of time measuring and evaluating the classroom behavior of children who are doing poorly. We would then describe as carefully as possible what we have observed. Our careful observation of failing pupils may lead to some revision of our traditional concepts of classroom failure, to suggestions about factors that may contribute to the development of failure, and perhaps to speculative ideas for the redemption of failure.

This descriptive orientation is usually considered a necessary first step in the development of a program of research because it establishes the foundation of any future undertaking. But it is rarely regarded as sufficient, because sooner or later someone will want to know *why* something happens or *how* what happens is related to other events. If our interest is in children's classroom failure, we are not likely to be satisfied for very long with even the most careful description of that failure. We will want to know the antecedents of the failure and the outcomes of procedures designed to reduce it. Even if we were not motivated directly by the practical implications of knowing the causes and cures of failure, we would believe our understanding to be considerably improved if we knew the conditions that increase and decrease its likelihood. To learn about the increase or decrease of failure, or any other behavior, we must focus on at least two variables at the same time; that is, we must make two sets of observations that can be related to one another.

Relational Research

At this point, the second broad type of approach, **relational research,** begins. Research is relational when two or more variables or conditions are measured and related to one another. As we continue with the classroom example, let us suppose we have noted that the teachers of many of the failing students rarely look at or address them and seldom expose them to new academic information. At this stage, we may have only an impression about the relation between learning failure and teaching behavior. Such impressions are a frequent, and often valuable, by-product of descriptive research, but if they are to be taken seriously, they cannot be left at the impressionistic level for very long.

Because we want to find out whether the researcher's impressions are accurate, we now arrange a series of coordinated observations on a sample of pupils who adequately represent the target population of pupils (i.e., the pupils to whom we would like to generalize our findings). We note whether each pupil in the sample is learning anything or how much the pupil has been learning; we also note to what degree the teacher has been exposing the pupil to the material to be learned. From these coordinated observations, we should be able to make a quantitative statement concerning the relationship, or correlation, between the amount of the pupils' exposure to the material to be learned and the amount of this material they have in fact learned. We then indicate not just (1) whether "X and Y are significantly related" (i.e., whether this nonzero relationship is unlikely to have occurred by chance alone), but also (2) the form or pattern of the relationship (e.g., linear or nonlinear), and (3) the strength of the relationship. Later in this book, we will define and illustrate what these statistical terms mean.

Experimental Research

To carry the example into the third broad approach, **experimental research,** suppose that the pupils exposed to less information are also those who tend to learn less. The discovery of this relationship may tempt us to conclude that children learn less because they are taught less. Such an **ad hoc hypothesis** (i.e., a conjecture or supposition developed "for this" special result), although plausible, is not warranted by the relationship reported. It may be that teachers teach less to those they know to be less able to learn; that is, differences in teaching behavior may be a result of the pupils' learning as much as a determinant of that learning. To pursue this idea, we make further observations that allow us to infer whether differences in the information presented to the pupils, apart from any individual differences among them, have affected the pupils' learning. We can best answer such questions by manipulating the conditions that we believe to be responsible for the effect. In other words, we introduce some change into the situation, or we interrupt or terminate the situation in order to identify some causes.

That is what is generally meant by *experimental research,* the focus of which is the identification of causes (i.e., what leads to what). Relational research only rarely provides such information, and then only under very special conditions. The difference between the degree of focus on a causal explanation in relational and experimental research can be expressed in the difference between the two statements "X is *related* to Y" (relational research) and "X is *responsible* for Y" (experimental research). In our example, teaching is X and learning is Y. Our experiment is designed to reveal the effects of teaching on pupil learning. Let us select a sample of youngsters and, by tossing a coin, or by some other unbiased method of selection, divide them into two equivalent groups. The teachers will give more information to one of these groups (the experimental group) and will give the other group (the control group) less information. We can then assess whether the experimental group has surpassed the control group in learning achievement. If we find this result, we can say that giving the experimental group more information was *responsible* for the outcome.

There might still be a question of what it was about the better procedure that led to the improvement. It is, in fact, characteristic of research that, when a new procedure is shown to be effective, many questions arise about what *specific* aspects of the procedure are producing the benefits. In the case of increased teaching, we may wonder whether the improvement was due to (1) the nature of the additional material; (2) the teacher's increased attention to the pupil while presenting the additional material; (3) any accompanying increases in eye contact, smiles, or warmth; or (4) other possible correlates of increased teaching behavior. In fact, these alternative hypotheses have already been investigated. The results indicate that the amount of new material that teachers present to their pupils is sometimes predictable not so much by the children's learning ability as by the teachers' beliefs or expectations about their pupils' learning ability. The teachers' expectations about the pupils' performance may serve as a "self-fulfilling prophecy," in which the expectations become responsible for the outcome in behavior (Babad, 1993; Raudenbush, 1984; Rosenthal, 1966, 1976, 1985, 1991; Rosenthal & Jacobson, 1968; Rosenthal & Rubin, 1978).

Orienting Attitudes of the Scientist

We have described the scientific method as a philosophical outlook, and to conclude this discussion, we now consider the appropriate attitudes of individual researchers. In common usage, the term **attitude** refers to a kind of "posture of the mind"; it is usually assumed that attitudes give the impetus that leads a person to behave one way and not another (Cacioppo, Gardner, & Berntson, 1997; Eagly & Chaiken, 1993; Kraus, 1991). In behavioral science, and in science in general, several orienting attitudes of researchers are prescribed or expected in all fields (J. A. Hall, 1984). The technical language of different disciplines often makes science seem to be divisive, but at the individual level, there is an attitudinal unity—in our expectations at least.

1. *Enthusiasm.* A wise researcher, the experimental psychologist Edward C. Tolman (1959), best summed up this aspect of the scientist's orienting attitude: "In the end, the only sure criterion is to have fun" (p. 152). He did not mean that the attitude of the scientist is that research is just fun and games without any ethical or societal implications or consequences; he meant that, for individual scientists, doing research is as absorbing as any game that requires skill and concentration and that fills a person with enthusiasm.

2. *Open-mindedness.* Doing good research requires an attitude of open-mindedness. That is, good scientific practice requires that the scientist observe with a keen, attentive, inquisitive, and open mind—because many valuable discoveries are made by accident (called *serendipity* in the next chapter). To practice science, as another writer put it, is to raise incessant questions, both broad and narrow, concerning *all* of our experiences in the world (Koch, 1959, p. 5). Further, an attitude of open-mindedness allows us to learn from our mistakes and from the advice and criticisms of others.

3. *Good sense.* An attitude that values good sense is important in our daily lives and also in scientific practice. For example, one axiom of science is the **principle of the drunkard's search:** A drunkard lost his house key and began searching for it under a street lamp even though he had dropped the key some distance away. Asked why he didn't look where he had dropped it, he replied, "There is more light here." This principle teaches that all the book learning in the world cannot replace good sense in the planning and conduct of research. Much effort is lost when people fail to use good sense and instead look in a convenient place, rather than the most likely place, for the answers to their questions.

4. *Role-taking ability.* Because people study people in behavioral and social science, the unique role of each party in this complex interaction is important to understand (Fletcher, 1995; Rosnow & Rosenthal, 1997). We must, for example, put ourselves in the subjects' place so that we can ferret out any unintended cues that the research procedure may offer the subjects about what the research hypotheses are. Previously we alluded to the "social contract" between science and society; as partners in this agreement, we must be able to take the role of the research consumer. In that role, we must ask ourselves what the practical implications and moral consequences of our research are. To anticipate criticisms when we submit our work for publication, we must also be able to take the role of the critic or objective observer (Maher, 1978; Oleson & Arkin, 1996).

5. *Principled inventiveness.* An orienting attitude that values inventiveness, such as the ability to develop good hypotheses and to recognize uniformity in human nature as well as the differences among individuals, is greatly prized. Inventiveness is also used in finding financial resources, laboratory space, and equipment; in recruiting and scheduling research participants; in responding to emergencies during the conduct of research; in finding new ways to analyze data, if they are called for; and in coming up with convincing interpretations of the results. The purpose of statistical analysis, as one scientist put it, is to "organize a useful argument from quantitative evidence, using a form of principled rhetoric" (Abelson, 1995, p. xiii). This is sound advice. Inventiveness in science should always be principled.

6. *Confidence in one's own judgment.* A famous remark of Newton's was "If I have seen farther, it is by standing on the shoulders of giants" (Merton, 1993). Yet it is also true that great insights come when the scientist, as Tolman (1959) stated, "has been shaken out of his up-until-then approved scientific rules" (p. 93). He added, "Since all the sciences, and especially psychology, are still immersed in such tremendous realms of the uncertain and the unknown, the best that any individual scientist, especially any psychologist, can do seems to be to follow his own gleam and his own bent, however inadequate they may be" (p. 152). In other words, still another prized attitude is confidence in one's own judgment, or as another writer put it, "You have to believe that by the simple application of your own mind to the facts of experience, you can discover the truth—a little part of it anyway" (Regis, 1987, p. 209).

7. *Ability to communicate*. More than one author has joked that writing is an "unnatural act," and it is certainly a statement that any procrastinator would agree with. But the desire and ability to communicate one's results are vital in science because, as implied above, the end of one study may very well be the starting point for another study (Barrass, 1978). In other words, scientists must be able to communicate clearly so that their findings may be known to others (Barrass, 1978).

8. *Consistency and care about details*. Consistency and care about details are particularly vital in reporting research. This is true whether one is preparing a technical article for a journal or a paper to be submitted in a course. Because we never get a second chance to make a first impression, it is essential that our work represent our best effort. Taking pride in one's work provides a constructive attitude toward all aspects of the relentless detail involved in good research. In science, there is no substitute for accuracy and for the hours of care needed to keep complete records, organize and analyze data accurately, state facts precisely, and proofread carefully.

9. *Integrity and honest scholarship*. Finally, an orienting attitude that values integrity and honest scholarship, and that abhors dishonesty and sloppiness, is paramount in all disciplines (e.g., American Association for the Advancement of Science [AAAS], 1988; American Psychological Association [APA], 1973, 1982; Bridgstock, 1982; Koshland, 1988). This is the most vital aspect of good scientific practice. Because dishonesty (e.g., "rigged" experiments or the presentation of faked results) undermines the basic respect of the literature on which the advancement of science depends, it is devastating to science. Safeguarding against dishonesty is the responsibility of each scientist, and it is a duty that is taken very seriously.

Summary of Ideas

1. Six reasons for studying research methods are (a) to provide a richer appreciation of the information that science brings to modern life; (b) to avoid falling prey to hucksters whose claims are based on pseudoscience or bad science; (c) to learn information and skills that are transferable beyond the research setting; (d) to learn that there are limits to science and that generalizations are always based in part on a "leap of faith," (e) to learn something about human nature and therefore about ourselves; and (f) to consider research as a career.

2. The term the *Hawthorne effect* refers to one of the potential limits of research on human subjects: Changes in subjects' behavior are sometimes due to being studied rather than to the experimenter's manipulation; therefore it is prudent to consider subjects' perceptions of the experiment (including any inadvertent task-orienting cues) as a part of any research strategy.

3. Four alternative strategies for the "fixation of belief" (i.e., the formulation of strong beliefs) were characterized by Peirce as (a) the method of tenacity (e.g., belief in UFOs); (b) the method of authority (e.g., the ancient belief that the earth was the center of the universe or, on the positive side, obeying reasonable

laws that are the basis of civilized society); (c) the a priori method (e.g., a mathematician's use of pure reason); and (d) the scientific method.

4. *The scientific method* is a misnomer, in that it is not any single, fixed procedure (e.g., the law of the instrument), but a philosophical outlook as much as an arsenal of research tools (Box 1.3).

5. *Empirical reasoning,* using controlled observation and measurement as an aid to reasoning, is a primary characteristic of the scientific method. Examples in this chapter applied to real-life problems were (a) Feynman's demonstration of the probable cause of the *Challenger* disaster; (b) Galton's actuarial study of prayer; (c) Ceci's experimental study of children's eyewitness testimony; and (d) Asch's use of accomplices in his laboratory demonstration of conformity.

6. *Inferential validity* means that causal inferences made in the psychological laboratory are applicable to the real-life experiences they are meant to represent (e.g., the *Candid Camera* demonstration of the inferential validity of Asch's conformity study).

7. The informative and persuasive language (or *rhetoric*) of science takes the form of written reports of research findings (Appendix A), which conform to an accepted basic structure and allow other scientists to replicate the investigation and corroborate the conclusions.

8. Other features of the scientific method that are shared with other strategies are (a) the use of mental imagery (e.g., Einstein's image of God playing dice with the world) and (b) the perceived beauty of accepted ideas (e.g., the periodic table in chemistry).

9. Behavioral science comprises different fields that all emphasize the use of many different empirical and theoretical methodologies (i.e., *methodological pluralism* and *theoretical ecumenism*) to explain things by "concatenations of evidence." All these fields are concerned with how and why people behave as they do, including how and why people feel and think as they do.

10. To develop a more complete or integrated picture of human nature, *interdisciplinary* fields of behavioral science (e.g., communication research) have arisen.

11. *Descriptive research,* which maps out a situation, tells us "how things are" (e.g., describes children's failure in school; other examples are given in Table 1.1).

12. *Relational research,* which describes the relation between two sets of observations, tells us "how things are in relation to other things" (e.g., describes the relation between student failure and teaching behavior; see other examples in Table 1.1).

13. *Experimental research,* which aims at the identification of causes, tells us "how things are and how they got to be that way" (e.g., in studying the effects of teaching on pupil learning by manipulating the hypothesized causes of student failure; see other examples in Table 1.1).

14. Good scientific practice values (a) enthusiasm, (b) an open mind (e.g., serendipitous discovery), (c) good sense (e.g., not the "drunkard's search"), (d) role-

taking ability, (e) principled inventiveness, (f) self-confidence, (g) communication ability, (h) consistency and carefulness, and, most important, (i) integrity and honest scholarship.

Key Terms

ad hoc hypothesis p. 16	interdisciplinary p. 13
aesthetics p. 11	mental imagery p. 11
a priori method p. 6	method of authority p. 5
attitude p. 17	method of tenacity p. 4
behavior p. 12	methodological pluralism p. 13
behavioral science p. 12	principle of the drunkard's search p. 18
control group p. 9	pseudoscience p. 2
descriptive research p. 15	psychophysics p. 13
empirical p. 7	relational research p. 15
empirical reasoning p. 2	replicate p. 10
experimental research p. 16	rhetoric of science p. 9
Hawthorne effect p. 3	scientific method p. 1
inferential validity p. 10	theoretical ecumenism p. 13

Multiple-Choice Questions for Review (answers are found on page 343)

1. John believes that women are more emotionally expressive than men. When asked why he believes this, John says it is because he has "always" believed it, and because "everybody knows it is true." John is using the (a) method of tenacity; (b) scientific method; (c) a priori method; (d) method of authority.
2. Some philosophers have suggested that we can understand the universe by using only pure reason and logic. These philosophers would advocate using the (a) method of tenacity; (b) scientific method; (c) a priori method; (d) method of authority.
3. Julie believes that everyone dreams every night, because her psychology professor told her this is true. Julie is using the (a) method of tenacity; (b) scientific method; (c) a priori method; (d) method of authority.
4. Dr. Jones believes that psychotherapy is generally very effective in treating mental disorders. She claims that her belief is based on empirical research in which therapy was given to some patients but not others, and in which the degree of mental disorder was carefully measured. Dr. Jones' belief is based on the (a) method of tenacity; (b) scientific method; (c) a priori method; (d) method of authority.
5. Which of the following is the *most* distinctive characteristic of science? (a) empirical inquiry; (b) reason and logic; (c) the rhetoric of science; (d) parsimonious explanation
6. Behavioral science (a) encompasses many scientific disciplines that study behavior; (b) emphasizes multiple methods of observation and explanation; (c) has seen a growth in the number of interdisciplinary fields; (d) all of the above.

7. Which approach to empirical research is generally considered a necessary first step in conducting research but is rarely considered sufficient by itself? (a) relational research; (b) experimental research; (c) descriptive research; (d) none of the above

8. A researcher at the College of the Southwest conducts a research project on the study habits of students. She reports that, on average, college students study 20 hours per week. This is an example of (a) relational research; (b) experimental research; (c) descriptive research; (d) none of the above.

9. Experimental research (a) can support cause-effect conclusions; (b) involves the manipulation of variables; (c) involves randomly assigning subjects to conditions; (d) all of the above.

10. Which of the following is considered an orienting attitude of the scientist? (a) role-taking ability; (b) ability to communicate; (c) principled inventiveness; (d) all of the above

Discussion Questions for Review (answers are found on pages 343–44)

1. Philosopher Charles Sanders Peirce described four approaches to knowledge. What are these approaches? Give an example of a belief based on each approach.

2. This chapter describes four characteristics of the scientific method. What are these characteristics? Can any one of these be considered "more fundamental" than the others?

3. A Wayne State researcher is interested in the effects of children's viewing TV violence on the children's level of aggression on the playground. The amount and type of viewing will be assessed through a standard procedure: TV diaries sent to parents. Aggression will be rated by two judges. The researcher hypothesizes that children who spend more time watching violent TV at home are more aggressive on the playground than their peers who watch relatively little violent TV at home. Of the three general research types (descriptive, relational, and experimental), which type is this?

4. A Wichita State researcher plans to assign fifth-grade children to one of two conditions. Half the children (Group A) will be shown a relatively violent movie at 10:30, and half (Group B) will be shown a nonviolent movie at the same time. Each film will be equally engaging. Two observers will code the children's behavior when both groups are brought back together on the playground for their 11:00 recess. This procedure will continue daily for six weeks. The researcher predicts that Group A will be more aggressive than Group B. What type of research is this?

5. A researcher at the University of New Hampshire wants to measure the prevalence of shyness in the undergraduate community. She administers the well-standardized Shyness Scale to volunteers in a main dining hall, collecting data on a respectable 35% of all undergraduates. What type of research is this?

6. A North Dakota State student wants to study other students' creativity, and he wants to use all three types of research approaches—descriptive, relational, and experimental—in this project. Think of a concrete example of each type that he could use.

7. A student at Foothill College claims that it is not possible to study such nonscientific concepts as prayer because prayer falls in the domain of theology rather than of science. Is the student correct?
8. The chapter described nine orienting attitudes common to scientists. List as many of these attitudes as you can think of, and describe why they are important in scientific research.

2 Strategies of Discovery

The Stages of Discovery

How do scientists get their ideas? Often they find leads by going to the research literature to discover problems that still need probing or questions that have gone unanswered, or they may get ideas from listening to presentations at meetings. Based on what they read or hear, they might be inspired to think of a new way of looking at some phenomenon or even a way of turning the phenomenon on its head. For example, psychologists have long thought that attitudes can shape behavior (e.g., Kraus, 1991), but Daryl Bem (1965, 1972), a Cornell researcher, reversed this relationship when he raised the possibility that reflecting on one's behavior can shape one's attitude. Suppose a politician takes a stand on an issue for the sake of expediency and, after defending it repeatedly, thinks to himself, "I guess I really believe this." The politician's self-perception has produced a change in his attitude. Or suppose you wolf down a sandwich, and *then* it occurs to you, "Gee, I must have been starving" (Brehm & Kassin, 1996). Bem designed and conducted experiments to test and confirm what he called "self-perception theory."

PREVIEW QUESTIONS

▌ What is the role of "discovery," and how is it distinguished from "justification"?

▌ In the initial thinking stage, where do good research ideas come from?

▌ How can I use the library to help sharpen my ideas during the plausibility stage?

▌ How can I use PsycLIT and other computerized systems to run a literature search on a reference database?

▌ What are accidental plagiarism and lazy writing, and how can they be avoided?

▌ How should I go about defining concepts and variables?

▌ What is the distinction usually made between hypotheses and theories?

▌ In the final stage of the discovery process, what constitutes an "acceptable" scientific hypothesis?

▌ What is the purpose of a construct?

▌ What is meant by *independent variable* and *dependent variable*?

▌ How might an exploratory insight take me on a different path of discovery?

Sometimes promising ideas are thrust on us by circumstances (see also Box 2.1). Ronald Ley, an experimental psychologist at SUNY-Albany, was on a transatlantic flight after having completed three years of work for a book about the activities of Wolfgang Köhler (the founder of Gestalt psychology) during World War I. Köhler was long presumed only to be researching animal behavior on Tenerife, an island off the coast of Africa, but Ley's research led him to conclude that Köhler had been a spy for the German military and that the work had been a cover for his activities (Ley, 1990). On his flight back to the United States, Ley was reflecting on his three-year odyssey when his thoughts were interrupted by the passenger sitting next to him, a middle-aged woman who had told him earlier about her anxieties about flying. Suddenly her chest heaved as she sat with her mouth open, gasping for air. In the moment before he turned to help, Ley thought about the role of hyperventilation in panic disorder. Is it possible, he began to think, that the effects of stress-induced hyperventilation are an *antecedent* as well as a consequence of anxiety? Later on, using this insight as his point of departure, he began a program of investigation on panic disorder (Ley, 1993).

Box 2.1   **Keeping Our Eyes and Minds Open**

Edwin H. Land invented the Polaroid Land Camera after his 3-year-old daughter asked him why a camera could not produce pictures instantly. Thinking about her question while out for a stroll, he suddenly hit on the idea of a camera that would produce developed photographs. In the early 1950s, George deMestral was picking cockleburs from his jacket after a stroll in the Swiss countryside when he got the idea for Velcro fasteners (Roberts, 1989). He noticed that the cockleburs were covered with hooks that had become embedded in the loops of the fabric of his jacket, and he wondered if there might be a way to create something useful out of a nuisance. These examples illustrate the payoff potential of simply keeping our eyes and minds open to exciting new possibilities thrust on us by circumstances.

In this chapter, we examine what goes on during the initial phase of research, in which the scientist comes up with an idea and crystallizes it into a **working hypothesis** (i.e., a testable supposition or conjecture). The traditional name for this phase is **discovery** (Reichenbach, 1938), a term intended to capture the idea of the scientist as a kind of "Christopher Columbus" who is venturing into the unknown. In later chapters, we discuss what goes on in the second phase of the research process, called **justification** (Reichenbach, 1938), in which scientists test their hypotheses and logically defend their conclusions, usually with the aid of statistics. It is convenient to separate the discovery process into three stages: initial thinking, plausibility, and acceptability (Kordig, 1978).

We illustrate the first stage by discussing six broad scenarios in which ideas have sprung up in psychology (McGuire, 1973). Once you have a promising idea, you need to shape and polish it into a good hypothesis in the plausibility stage. We describe what criteria you need to keep in mind and also how you can use the resources of your college library to get started in your literature search. We also discuss *plagiarism* and how to avoid it, including the "accidental" kind. It is also important to understand the distinctions between a number of basic terms, such as *hypotheses, theories,* and *independent* and *dependent variables,* all of which are discussed in this chapter and are required for the acceptability stage. Finally, we examine how a novel exploratory insight might take you on a quite different path of discovery, because no absolute rule says that you *must* follow a traditional path. Such a rule, in fact, would be the antithesis of the advice given to scientists by Tolman (Chapter 1), when he recommended that each researcher "follow his own gleam and his own bent."

The Initial Thinking Stage

While not an exhaustive list (cf. Leong & Pfaltzgraff, 1996), the six scenarios for ideas in the **initial thinking stage** give a flavor of the wide range of possibilities: (1) the use of an intensive case study; (2) the effort to make sense of a paradoxical incident; (3) the use of metaphors; (4) the attempt to resolve conflicting results; (5) the effort to improve on older ideas; and (6) the exploitation of unexpected observations (serendipity).

Using an Intensive Case Study

In the first illustrative scenario, psychologists, sociologists, psychiatrists, and others have used interviewing, testing, and other potentially informative methods to gather information for **intensive case studies.** Although the term *case* is shrouded in ambiguity (Ragin & Becker, 1992), it generally refers to objects of study sharing features that allow researchers to treat the objects as particular instances of some named phenomenon (Ragin, 1992). Anthropologists often describe studies of particular cultures as case studies, because each culture is thought to have an internal consistency, broadly speaking (Platt, 1992). However, a case study might also be a qualitative analysis of a person's behavior (e.g., a clinical case study), or it might be what we define later in the book as "*N*-of-1" and "single-case" studies in behavior modification. The "1" might refer to the modification of a person's behavior, or the study might be of a larger unit (e.g., a Little League team or a community).

By *intensive case study,* we simply mean that the analysis is characterized by meticulous records and sharp discriminations rather than by the usual casual discriminations and inferences that are associated with our daily encounters with "cases" (e.g., at the office, at school, or at home). Investigators who choose this approach might use archival material, or they might describe or record what actually happens when people do something, or report about what they or others have done. Intensive case studies are widely used in educational research, policymaking studies, organizational and management studies, city and regional planning, and many other situations that call for descriptive or relational information (Merriam, 1991; Yin, 1989).

Going back to the classic work of Sigmund Freud (1856–1939), the intensive case study has been used on an individual basis by psychoanalytically inclined researchers to generate ideas about human motivation and subsequent behavior. Freud developed and tested many of his ideas by using the **free association method** (i.e., the subject tells whatever passes through his or her mind) to tease out the concealed psychological bases of people's neurotic symptoms that apparently had no organic cause. For example, using information from individual cases, and from fellow psychiatrists, Freud formulated his theory of motivation. Countless examples of intensive case studies of individual patients (or *clients*, as clinical and counseling psychologists usually call them) have helped to enrich our understanding of the etiology (i.e., the causes) of psychological disorders. Some of these ideas have in turn spawned research in such diverse areas of behavioral science as memory, animal behavior, and cognitive development, among others (Kazdin, 1980, 1992).

An intensive case study of a quite different kind was done by Perry London, a clinical psychologist. A book about the trial of a notorious Nazi criminal (Arendt, 1963) had generated considerable interest in developing an understanding of the character traits and motivations of Christians who saved Jews from the horrors perpetrated by the Nazis during World War II. London and his colleagues carried out intensive case studies of 27 rescuers and 42 rescued people by tape-recording and analyzing interviews with each of them. Because the respondents were not a random sample, the researchers could not generalize from this group of rescuers to the majority of those who aided Jews during World War II. At best, then, the case study could be used only to generate some tentative hypotheses, or as London (1970) described it, "The lacunae in our data are so great that we cannot even conjecture about the generality of our hypotheses" (p. 259).

Nonetheless a number of valuable leads came out of this work. Among London's results was the finding that the behavior of *these* rescuers could not be boiled down to any simplistic definition. Some of them had been well compensated for their efforts, others had spent fortunes and had been left destitute, and still others had started out with little and had shared their meager resources with the rescued. Motives were even harder to pin down. Some of the rescuers were fanatically religious, and others were atheists; some of the rescuers had deep affiliations with the Jewish community, and others were anti-Semites. Three promising clues emerged as the basis of a plausible hypothesis to be evaluated more critically at a later time. First, almost all the rescuers interviewed possessed a spirit of adventure. Second, they also had an intense identification with a parental model of moral conduct. Third, they appeared to be socially marginal in the German culture. London (1970, p. 249) envisioned a scenario in which a zest for adventure and chance had been important in the initiation of the rescue behavior, but what gave the rescuers the impetus and endurance to do what they did was their strong identification with a very moralistic model and the experience of social marginality.

A classic example of an intensive case study in experimental psychology was the work of Hermann Ebbinghaus (1850–1909), another of the early pioneers in the development of scientific psychology. Using himself as the case studied, Ebbinghaus developed theoretical curves to describe the rates at which information is actually learned and forgotten. To do this, he carefully measured his own ability to learn and relearn thousands of so-called nonsense syllables, each consisting of a random combination of two consonants and a middle vowel, pronounceable as words but uniformly lacking in meaning (e.g., *xot, bok, lum, zat*). With himself as the sole subject, he first recorded how long it took him to master a list of nonsense syllables. He waited until he had forgotten the syllables and then relearned the list. He then repeated the procedure, each time making a careful record of his learning and forgetting (Ebbinghaus, 1885).

Making Sense of a Paradoxical Incident

We mentioned earlier that some research questions are thrust on us by circumstances, which is often the case in the second general scenario: the attempt to make sense of a **paradoxical incident** (i.e., an event that seems contradictory). Social psychologists Bibb Latané and John Darley were puzzled by contradictory aspects of the circumstances surrounding a lurid murder in Queens, New York. A nurse was coming home from work at 3 A.M. when she was attacked by a man who stabbed her repeatedly. When they heard her cries of terror, more than three dozen of her neighbors came to their windows to see what was happening. According to Latané and Darley, none of the neighbors went to her aid, even though it took the stalker over half an hour to murder her. The social psychologists were struck by the paradox that, even though there were so many witnesses, none had bothered to call the police. They wondered whether *so many* people failed to intervene because each believed someone else was likely to. Latané and Darley developed their hypothesis—which they called the "diffusion of responsibility"—predicting that the more the witnesses to an emergency, the less likely it is that any one of them will offer help.

The researchers then proceeded to test their diffusion-of-responsibility hypothesis in a series of experiments (Latané & Darley, 1970). For example, in a study at Columbia University, they demonstrated that the larger the number of students present, the less likely any of them was to volunteer to help in an emergency. The students in this experiment had agreed to take part in a discussion of problems related to life at an urban university. As the discussion progressed, a stream of smoke began to puff into the room through a wall vent. The researchers found that, when one student was in the room, she or he was about twice as likely to report the emergency as when the student was in the room with as few as three others. Instead of reporting the emergency, students in a group tended to be passive and to dismiss their fears through rationalization (Latané & Darley, 1968). In a similar study with introductory psychology students at New York University, who had also agreed to take part in a discussion group, each was much more likely to report a (simulated) epileptic seizure that he or she happened to hear if alone than if he or she believed that others were also aware of the emergency (Darley & Latané, 1968).

Using Metaphors and Analogies

A third general scenario calls for the use of **metaphorical themes** that allow a particular view of the world. In Chapter 1, we spoke of the mental imagery that is characteristic of scientific (indeed all) beliefs; an example is how metaphors are used. In common parlance, a **metaphor** is a word or phrase applied to something it does not literally denote. "Her life was an uphill climb" and "He is between a rock and a hard place" are metaphors: Each suggests an analogy (a comparison) with another situation. Whether used in everyday speech, in psychotherapy, or in science, such comparisons allow us to see new connections by making us think about one thing in terms of another (Billow, 1977; Gentner & Markman, 1997; Gigerenzer, 1991; Holyoak & Thagard, 1997; Kolodner, 1997). For example, it has been suggested that cognitive, psychoanalytic, and even behavior therapists often use metaphoric strategies to help people achieve insights or behavioral goals (Barker, 1996). The history of science, including behavioral science (Leary, 1990; Weiner, 1991), is replete with fascinating metaphors and analogies that have been applied to a wide variety of phenomena (see, for example, Box 2.2).

Box 2.2   **The Spiral in Nature and Analogy**

A favorite analogy is the spiral, because it seems to have such a prominent place in nature. For example, economists speak of "inflationary spirals," and in football, we have the phenomenon of "spiral passes." A noted developmental psychologist, Heinz Werner, proposed a "psychogenetic principle of spirality," which he derived from an earlier philosophical analogy about the unfolding of historical events (Werner & Kaplan, 1963). In nature, of course, there are many examples of spirality: Storms that arise in the Northern Hemisphere typically display a counterclockwise spiral rotation, while those that arise in the Southern Hemisphere typically display a clockwise rotation. Human hair forms a spiral that is generally clockwise in men and counterclockwise in women. Spiral forms are also found in pinecones and other varieties of plants. One author told of a researcher who blindfolded a right-handed friend and told him to walk a straight line across a country field; the man walked in a clockwise spiral—until he stumbled on a tree stump (Robin, 1993).

In the field of social psychology, an inoculation metaphor was used as the basis of work by William J. McGuire (1964), a professor at Yale University who developed techniques for inducing resistance to propaganda messages. He began with the assumption that some beliefs are so widely accepted in American society that they are almost truisms (e.g., "Mental illness is not contagious," "It's a good idea to brush your teeth after every meal," and "Cigarette smoking is bad for your health"). Using the inoculation metaphor as his point of departure, McGuire reasoned that such beliefs can be easily modified by well-designed propaganda for two reasons. First, recipients of propaganda attacking cultural truisms, seldom having been called on to defend their beliefs, are unpracticed in mustering a defense. Second, they are not motivated to develop a defense because they probably view such beliefs as established and unassailable.

In other words, McGuire's tentative idea was that cultural truisms exist in a kind of "germ-free" environment. Because they are so seldom attacked, the individual is especially vulnerable to their reversal when faced with massive, effective propaganda. This belief in a truism, McGuire reasoned, can be likened to being unvaccinated for smallpox. The person brought up in a germ-free environment and appearing vigorously healthy may be highly vulnerable to a massive viral attack if he or she has not been vaccinated. On the other hand, a weakened dose of the smallpox virus stimulates the person's defenses so that he or she can later overcome a massive attack. Generalizing from this metaphor, it follows that, to immunize people against massive propaganda, one exposes them to some of the propaganda in advance, so that they can build up their defenses by rehearsing arguments against the propaganda. Exposing them to too much preliminary propaganda may produce the opposite effect, causing them to reverse their attitude. The problem, which McGuire worked out in his empirical research, is to establish the precise amount of "live virus" in an "inoculation" that, without giving the subjects the "disease," will help build a defense against a future massive attack of the same "virus."

Resolving Conflicting Results

In a fourth general scenario, the scientist comes up with an insight by trying to **account for conflicting results.** In some instances it is even possible to argue that both sides are right, a strategy used by experimental psychologists Marshall B. Jones and Robert S. Fennell (1965). During the 1940s, there was a protracted dispute between Clark L. Hull and Edward C. Tolman concerning the nature of animal learning. Hull, inspired by Pavlov's research on conditioned reflexes, had developed a systematic behavior theory that asserted that the stimulus (S) affects the organism (O), but that the resulting response (R) depends on O as well as on S. According to this "S-O-R model," learning is a process in which S-R connections are automatically strengthened only because they occur in association with reinforcement. On the other hand, Tolman's "S-S model" stressed the cognitive nature of learning: Behavior is goal-directed and makes use of environmental supports, but this process is a discontinuous one that depends on exploratory behaviors from which the animal learns what leads to what. Docility, Tolman argued, is thus a mark of purpose, because the animal is learning by acquiring expectations and forming "cognitive maps."

Not only were there distinct theoretical and methodological differences between the two camps, but they also used different strains of selectively bred rats. The Tolmanians, centered at the University of California, used a strain of rats that had been selectively bred by the mating of wild males and laboratory albino females. The Hullians, at Yale under Hull's direction and a second camp at the University of Iowa under Kenneth W. Spence, used another strain of rats that had originally been bred for nonemotionality. It occurred to Jones and Fennell that genetic differences might explain the different results obtained by the Tolmanians and the Hullians, as the two strains of rats had been separated for over 30 years (during which time they had been differently and selectively bred). To test this idea, Jones and Fennell used rats from both strains to duplicate the animal learning experiments by the Tolmanians and the Hullians. The Hullian rats, in the words of Jones and Fennell (1965), "popped out of the start box, ambled down the runway, around the turn, and into the goal box," while the Tolman rats "seemed almost oblivious to their environment." In other words, it seems that Hull and Tolman were both right (see also Box 2.3).

Box 2.3   **The Dayyan's Decree**

Jones and Fennell's resolution of the Tolman-Hull conflict is reminiscent of a Yiddish anecdote and its reincarnation as a maxim of modern science, which we call the **dayyan's decree** (Rosnow & Rosenthal, 1996b). A dayyan, or rabbinical judge, was asked by a couple to mediate a conflict in which they were embroiled. The woman told her side, and the dayyan commented, "You are right." Then the man told his side, and the dayyan said, "You are right." A young student, who happened to overhear the conversations, meekly pointed out to the dayyan, "Surely, sir, they both can't be a hundred percent right." To which the dayyan replied, "You are right, too."

The lesson of the dayyan's decree is not to foreclose on the possibility of more than one right answer. In modern science, the physicist Neils Bohr stated that "the opposite of a great truth is also true," while psychologists Donald T. Campbell and Julian C. Stanley (1963) put it this way:

> When one finds, for example, that competent observers advocate strongly divergent points of view, it seems likely on a priori grounds that both have observed something valid about the natural situation, and that both represent a part of the truth. (p. 3)

Of course, even when all agree, this is no certain proof of accuracy or precision. In science, tests for accuracy and precision always include an empirical confrontation.

Another example of how scientists sometimes come up with an innovative hypothesis by trying to account for conflicting results is illustrated by the work of Robert Zajonc (pronounced "zy-ence," rhymes with *science*), a social psychologist at Stanford University. He proposed a hypothesis that he termed "social facilitation" (Zajonc, 1965) to account for some conflicting published data: Some reports indicated that performance in humans and animals improved when passive observers were present, whereas other reports showed performance becoming poorer in the presence of others. For instance, in one experiment, subjects were required to learn a list of nonsense syllables, either alone or in the presence of others. The number of trials needed to learn the list was the criterion variable. Those subjects who learned the list alone averaged more than 9 trials, and those who learned the syllables before an audience averaged more than 11 trials (Pessin, 1933). In other experiments, subjects who performed a familiar task in groups did better than when they performed the task alone (Bergum & Lehr, 1963). It seemed that the presence of others enhanced performance on some tasks but not on others.

How could these seemingly inconsistent results be explained? One important finding in experimental psychology is that a high drive level causes people to give the dominant response to a stimulus. When the task is familiar and well learned, the dominant response will probably be correct; when the task is novel and the correct responses are unknown or not well learned, the dominant response will probably be incorrect. Zajonc started with the idea that the presence of others serves to increase the individual's drive level and that this increase leads to dominant responses. Therefore, Zajonc reasoned, the presence of others must inhibit learning new responses but facilitate the performance of well-learned responses. If this is true, then it follows that students should study alone, preferably in an isolated cubicle, and then (once they have learned the correct responses) take examinations with many other students on a stage before a large audience (see also Box 2.4).

Box 2.4   Intuition and Role-Taking Ability

Zajonc also intuitively recognized some plausible limitations on his social facilitation hypothesis. For example, when confronted with a highly complex and ambiguous problem to which the answer is not immediately apparent or well learned, we should expect to solve the problem more quickly alone than in a group. On the other hand, if a problem is one whose solution will be easily recognized when suggested by others, groups would probably fare better in solving it than isolated individuals because the correct response is likely to be given by someone in the group. This example not only illustrates the fourth possible scenario but also shows how good intuition and role-taking ability—two of the orienting attitudes listed in Chapter 1—help to move an initial idea forward.

Improving on Older Ideas

A fifth illustrative scenario involves trying to **improve on an influential older idea**. For example, one of many contributions by the noted experimentalist B. F. Skinner was to show that it is possible to look at two sets of older ideas in a new light, those of the Russian physiologist Ivan Pavlov and those of the American psychologist E. L. Thorndike. In the 1930s, Skinner's clear distinction between Pavlov's and Thorndike's ideas of conditioning opened the way to a long series of classic studies by Skinner and others (e.g., Ferster & Skinner, 1957; Skinner, 1938, 1980, 1987).

Pavlov had done pioneering work on classical conditioning. In the experimental procedure that produces this type of conditioning, a neutral stimulus is paired with one that always brings about some desired behavior or response. Suppose we, like Pavlov, wish to condition a hungry dog to salivate at the sound of a bell. After the animal becomes accustomed to the apparatus, we sound the bell to make sure that the dog does not automatically salivate to it. The dog pricks up its ears or barks, but it does not salivate. We now know that the bell will not cause the animal to respond as it does to food. The next step is to ring the bell and present meat to the dog. If we do this a number of times, we find that the dog begins to salivate at the sound of the bell, before we present the meat.

In contrast, E. L. Thorndike, who experimented at about the same time as Pavlov, in the early 1900s, worked with what he called "trial-and-error learning." For example, he studied how cats learned to escape from a puzzle box to gain food. He was convinced that the cats did not reason out a solution. Instead, he thought that their getting out and eating the food he provided somehow strengthened the connection between successful escape movements and the actual escape.

Skinner recognized a clear distinction between Pavlov's and Thorndike's types of conditioning. Skinner perceived that, in Pavlovian conditioning, the major factor is the stimulus that precedes the response. The response is elicited reflexively. In Thorndike's trial-and-error conditioning, the major factor is the stimulus consequence (i.e., the reinforcement of escaping from the puzzle box), which follows the response. Skinner focused his own work on the latter type of conditioning, called *operant* or *instrumental.* In operant conditioning, first, the organism responds to a stimulus, and then something is done that will either increase or decrease the probability of its making the same response again. Say that we wish to train a dog to sit on command, and we prepare the animal by withholding food for a time. An operant-conditioning procedure requires that we reward the dog *after* it sits (or approximates sitting) following the command. The work on operant conditioning, in turn, paved the way for applications in the military, in educational institutions, and in the treatment of behavior disorders. In his novel, *Walden II,* Skinner (1948b) viewed a whole society organized according to known principles of conditioning.

Another classic illustration of this fifth possible scenario was Stanley Milgram's series of experiments on how far people will go in subjecting another person to pain at the order of an authority figure (Milgram, 1974). We will have more to say about this research in the next chapter, but it will suffice here to note that Milgram came up with the idea for his studies as a way of improving on Asch's earlier conformity experiments (discussed in Chapter 1). Milgram (1977) explained that he wanted to make the work done by Asch "more humanly significant" (p. 12). Asch had designed his investigation to determine under what conditions people will remain independent of their groups and when they will conform. It will be recalled that Asch used accomplices to influence an individual subject's expressed judgment concerning which of three lines was closest in length to a standard line.

Milgram (1977) recalled the moment when he suddenly hit on the idea for his own experiments:

> I was dissatisfied that the test of conformity was judgments about *lines.* I wondered whether groups could pressure a person into performing an act whose human import was more readily apparent, perhaps behaving aggressively toward another person, say by administering increasingly severe shocks to him. But to study the group effect you would also need an experimental control; you'd have to know how the subject performed without any group pressure. At that instant, my thought shifted, zeroing in on this experimental control. Just how far *would* a person go under the experimenter's orders? It was an incandescent moment, the fusion of a general idea on obedience with a specific technical procedure. Within a few minutes, dozens of ideas on relevant variables emerged, and the only problem was to get them all down on paper. (p. 12)

Exploiting Serendipity

Serendipity, which refers to the faculty for making lucky discoveries, is a sixth possible scenario (see also Box 2.5). The origin of the term derives from Serendip, an ancient name for Ceylon, now known as Sri Lanka, because of a fairy tale about "The Three Princes of Serendip," who constantly made lucky discoveries (Evans, 1993). For example, without his chance encounter with cockleburs, George deMestral might never have invented the Velcro fastener (Box 2.1). The story of how Isaac Newton came up with the idea of using prisms to study optics is another famous case of serendipity. Newton was using a refracting telescope to magnify the viewed object, but fringes of color at the ends of the telescope would sometimes obscure the field of vision. It occurred to him that the edges of lenses acted like prisms and this is what was responsible for the aberrations of color around the image of the object. He immediately saw a way of using prisms to study how they refracted the incoming light (Roberts, 1989; Robin, 1993).

Box 2.5   Serendipity in the Art World

One day in May 1984, a young artist named J. S. G. Boggs was sitting in a Chicago diner having a doughnut and coffee and doodling on a napkin. As the waitress kept refilling his cup, the doodle evolved into an abstracted one-dollar bill. Fascinated, the waitress asked if she could buy it, causing Boggs to wonder why anyone would want a greasy napkin covered with coffee stains and perspiration. "Tell you what," he said, "I'll pay you for my doughnut and coffee with this drawing." To his astonishment she took the "dollar" and gave him a dime's change! Inspired by this serendipitous incident, Boggs began using colored ink and pencils to launch a career of drawing fairly exact representations of existing denominations of actual currency, and then photocopying them and successfully "spending" them in a kind of artistic performance for goods and services (Weschler, 1988). That is, he always insists on receiving a receipt and change in real money; he then sells the change and receipts to collectors, who in turn track down the people who accepted the art currency. The performance ends when all the elements are encased in a frame on the collector's wall.

The story does not end here, however. According to an article in The *New York Times* (December 6, 1992), Boggs suddenly found himself under the scrutiny of the law in several countries. In 1987, he was tried in England on charges of producing counterfeit British currency. When he was found not guilty, he paid his lawyers in drawings. He was also prosecuted in Australia and, this time, was found not guilty and awarded $20,000 in damages. In the United States, the Secret Service seized some of his work, calling it "counterfeit money." They also searched his office and stopped him as he was leaving his apartment one day to attend a ceremony where he planned to announce a new project to print $1 million in his own bills. Boggs was quoted in the *Times:* "They said I was a counterfeiter; they don't understand the difference between art and crime."

Like many other behavioral and social researchers, both of us have also benefited from the role of serendipity in our research. In Chapter 1, we noted the finding that teachers' expectations about their pupils' performance can sometimes serve as a "self-fulfilling prophecy," in which the expectations become responsible for the outcome in behavior (Babad, 1993; Raudenbush, 1984; Rosenthal, 1966, 1976, 1985, 1991; Rosenthal & Jacobson, 1968; Rosenthal & Rubin, 1978). Later in the book, we will discuss the further implications of self-fulfilling prophecies in behavioral research, since some prophecy of how the investigation will turn out (e.g., the scientist's hypothesis) is virtually a constant in behavioral research. The systematic study of this phenomenon (called **expectancy bias**) started in the late 1950s and had a lot to do with serendipity. The idea for a series of studies of expectancy effects was inspired by a serendipitous result in Rosenthal's dissertation research. It led to a frantic search of the literature for an explanation and to the term *unconscious experimenter bias,* which evolved into the concept of experimenter expectancy bias and, subsequently, into a series of studies, beginning at the University of North Dakota (with Kermit L. Fode), of how experimenters' hypotheses can unwittingly influence their results (Rosenthal, 1993).

Rosnow's brush with serendipity occurred in 1969, when the Beatles were at the height of their popularity and a rumor concerning them began to circulate. According to the rumor, Paul McCartney of the Beatles had been decapitated in an automobile accident and replaced by a double. The basic core of the story—which was a preposterous fiction—swept across U.S. colleges and universities with numerous variants and deviations (Rosnow & Fine, 1974, 1976). What made this rumor theoretically interesting was that it was behaving not at all like the rumors that had been previously dissected by psychologists and sociologists. The standard text on the subject in psychology (Allport & Postman, 1947) stated that, because of the porosity of human memory, rumors *always* become shorter. The McCartney rumor was not shrinking, however; it was growing by leaps and bounds as each person improvised details.

This serendipitous event opened the way to further research and new hypotheses that both challenged and built on aspects of the traditional theory of rumor (Rosnow, 1980, 1988, 1991), which were tested in relational and experimental studies. According to current theory, the spread of rumors is usually an attempt to deal with anxieties and uncertainties by generating and passing stories that explain things and provide a rationale for behavior. Using the metaphor of a revolver, the process of rumor generation and transmission has been compared to loading and firing the gun (Rosnow, 1991). The "gun" is analogous to the public, and the "bullet" is analogous to the rumor, which is loaded in an atmosphere of anxiety and uncertainty. The trigger is pulled when people believe the "bullet" will hit the mark, in the same way that a rumor is more likely to be transmitted if the teller perceives it as credible (i.e., likely to be true). But when anxiety is intense, passing a wild rumor is like a "shot in the dark," because stressed-out people may be less likely to think carefully about the rumors they pass (Rosnow, 1991). Using this empirically grounded model, researchers have outlined procedures that can be implemented for handling potentially damaging rumors in organizations (DiFonzo, Bordia, & Rosnow, 1994).

The Plausibility Stage

Focusing and Assessing Ideas

Although many innovative ideas in science originate from intuitions and an inquisitive nature, we have also seen how reason and logical thought (i.e., Peirce's a priori method) enter into this initial thinking process. They play an even more deliberate role in the second phase of discovery: the **plausibility stage.** The scientist asks himself or herself whether the initial idea will measure up in, or is worthy of, actual testing, that is, whether there are plausible reasons to support the feasibility of the idea. To help them in this deliberative effort, scientists customarily turn to the relevant literature and also discuss their ideas with colleagues with common interests. In this way, they focus and assess their ideas and decide whether they are really worth pursuing.

As you approach this task of focusing and assessing your ideas, you can also look for the most relevant work related to your initial idea and then make detailed notes and analyses, being careful to document the page numbers of any quotations. You might also keep in mind the advice given by the philosopher Francis Bacon more than 350 years ago:

> Read not to contradict and confute; nor to believe and take for granted . . . but to weigh and consider. Some books are to be tasted, others to be swallowed, and some few to be chewed and digested; that is, some books are to be read only in parts; others to be read, but not curiously; and some few to be read wholly, and with diligence and attention. (from Bacon's "Of Studies," originally published in 1625; see Vickers, 1996, p. 438)

Whether you are using a laptop computer or index cards, a good strategy is to write down each useful idea and quote (on a separate card, if you use index cards) with an exact citation: author and year, title of publication, source of publication, and page numbers. Not only will having detailed notes pay off as you start pulling your analyses and quotes together to use as background material for your writing, but it will also help you avoid committing plagiarism accidentally. The term **plagiarism** comes from a Latin word meaning "kidnapper," and to plagiarize means to kidnap another person's idea or work and then to pass it off as one's own. **Accidental plagiarism** occurs when one copies someone else's work but forgets to credit it or to put it in quotes.

Avoiding Plagiarism and Lazy Writing

Of course, you can use other people's ideas or work in your writing, but you must always give the author of that material full credit for originality and not misrepresent (intentionally or accidentally) that material as your own original work. For example, suppose a student did a study on cognitive dissonance and then turned in a report that, without a citation, contained the following passage in the introduction:

> Dissonance—that is, the existence of nonfitting relations among cognitions—is a motivating factor in its own right. By *cognition* is generally meant any knowledge, opinion, or belief about the environment, about oneself, or about one's behavior.

Cognitive dissonance can be seen as an antecedent condition that leads to activity oriented toward dissonance reduction, just as hunger leads to activity oriented toward hunger reduction.

The student has cheated by committing plagiarism and will pay the consequences: an F in the course. The reason is that, except for a changed word here and there, the student has lifted this passage directly from Leon Festinger's *Theory of Cognitive Dissonance* (1957). On page 5, Festinger wrote:

> In short, I am proposing that dissonance, that is, the existence of nonfitting relations among cognitions, is a motivating factor in its own right. By the term *cognition,* here and in the remainder of the book, I mean any knowledge, opinion, or belief about the environment, about oneself, or about one's behavior. Cognitive dissonance can be seen as an antecedent condition which leads to activity oriented toward dissonance reduction just as hunger leads to activity oriented toward hunger reduction.

How might the student have used Festinger's work without falling into plagiarism? The student would simply indicate what is his or hers and what is Festinger's. For example, this student could have written:

> In his book *A Theory of Cognitive Dissonance* (1957), Festinger described cognition as "any knowledge, opinion, or belief about the environment, about oneself, or about one's behavior" and defined cognitive dissonance as "the existence of nonfitting relations among cognitions" (p. 5). He added, "Cognitive dissonance can be seen as an antecedent condition which leads to activity oriented toward dissonance reduction" (p. 5).

Incidentally, some students, on hearing that cited material is not construed by definition as plagiarism, submit papers that are saturated with quoted material. However, such papers are viewed by instructors as **lazy writing.** Although the penalty for lazy writing is not as severe as that for plagiarism, often it means a reduced grade. You may need to quote or paraphrase some material (with a citation, of course), but your written work is expected to result from your own individual effort. Quoting a simple sentence that can easily be paraphrased signals lazy writing (Rosnow & Rosnow, 1998).

Searching the Literature

In psychology, some of the favorite strategies for finding reference material include reading review articles and monographs, consulting with people who share a similar interest, and looking up relevant references in journal articles (H. M. Cooper, 1985). These are also good ways for you to get started, and, of course, you should ask your instructor whether your idea seems worth pursuing. If you need to do an exhaustive literature review (e.g., for a thesis), then you will also have to turn up hard-to-find material (called the **fugitive literature**). This includes unpublished manuscripts and technical reports, presentations at meetings and conferences, and so on. You will find tips on how to track down such elusive material in an informative chapter by MaryLu C. Rosenthal (1994).

Whatever the objective of your search, you should start by spending an afternoon simply perusing the variety of reference materials available in your college's or university's library. You will find, for example, resources called *abstracts*, which contain summaries or brief descriptions of books, articles, and other relevant material. You will also find useful dictionaries (such as the *Oxford English Dictionary*, which gives the origin and evolution of words in the English language), encyclopedias, handbooks, and, of course, shelves of textbooks and journals. Browsing through the library's shelves (if that is permitted) is also a good way to make serendipitous discoveries of potential quotes.

The reference for abstracts that is best known in psychology is *Psychological Abstracts*, a monthly periodical that gives brief descriptions of thousands of works in this and related fields. Figure 2.1 shows sample material from this periodical, and we see that each abstract begins with a code number, so that we can easily find it again by going back to this volume (Volume 77) and issue (Number 2) of the *Psychological Abstracts* and looking up this code number. The author's name is then listed; if there are many authors, the first author's name is followed by *et al.* (an abbreviation for *et alia*, "and others"). The first author's institutional affiliation is given next, followed by the work's title and the journal (or other) source where the work appeared. If the work was written in a foreign language, the original title is followed by the translated title. A synopsis (summary or abstract) of the work follows (see also Box 2.6).

Box 2.6   ## Don't Stop with the Abstract

You should not stop with the abstract, even if it was written by the original author of the work, but go to the work itself and read it. This advice applies even to a summary of a classic work that you find consistently cited and described by many authors. Mark Twain once defined a classic as "a book which people praise and don't read." Ironically, in the area of eyewitness testimony research, classic demonstration studies of information distortion have been misreported in published works for years (Treadway & McCloskey, 1989). It seems that many researchers in this area never bothered to read the original work and instead copied one another's erroneous descriptions of it.

PsycLIT and Machine-Readable Databases

If you need more than just a few key studies, or if your aim is to compile a comprehensive bibliography, your best bet is to start by using **PsycLIT.** This is a computerized database that is purchased by libraries from the American Psychological Association (APA). PsycLIT stores information contained in the *Psychological Abstracts*, and this information is updated quarterly by the APA. Using PsycLIT is faster and more fun than doing a by-hand search of the *Psychological Abstracts*, and you will find that doing a computerized literature search will become easier as your experience grows. But even inexperienced users will find PsycLIT friendly and time-saving.

3460. **Yakimoff, Naum; Lánský, P. & Radil, T.** (Bulgarian Academy of Sciences, Inst of Physiology, Sofia, Bulgaria) **Systematic error in estimating the orientation of random dot patterns.** 23rd Conference of the Higher Nervous Functions (1987, Mariánské Lázně, Czechoslovakia). *Activitas Nervosa Superior,* 1988(Dec), Vol 30(4), 275–276. —A systematic deviation in 10 Ss' estimations of orientation of dot patterns toward visual meridia provided evidence for at least 2 visual axes, other than horizontal and vertical, that might be accepted as standards for obliqueness.

3815. **Cornell, Carole E.; Rodin, Judith & Weingarten, Harvey.** (U Florida, Gainesville) **Stimulus-induced eating when satiated.** *Physiology & Behavior,* 1989(Apr), Vol 45(4), 695–704. —Two studies investigated factors that promote the desire for food when satiated. In Study 1, 20 Ss (aged 16–33 yrs) tested under conditions of either hunger or satiety, were exposed to 1 of 2 palatable foods (pizza or ice cream) and then given more of that food to eat. Operationally-satiated Ss still ate pizza or ice cream, and the sight of these foods enhanced reported desire for them. The amount of these foods consumed was predicted by the Ss' self-reported desire for the food. In Study 2, 28 males (aged 16–28 yrs) were fed to satiety, then primed with either pizza or ice cream (or not primed at all) and then given both pizza and ice cream to eat. Results suggest that a brief taste of a desirable food enhanced its intake relative to the other, equally-preferred food.

4282. **Taylor, Ronald L.** (U Connecticut, Storrs) **Black youth in crisis.** Special Issue: Black America in the 1980s. *Humboldt Journal of Social Relations,* 1987(Fal–Win–Spr–Sum), Vol 14(1–2), 106–133. —Reviews major social indicators that highlight the negative trends among Black adolescents and young adults during the past 2 decades and underscores the need for corrective action. These negative trends include the growth in single-parent families with children under 18 yrs, the significant differences between Black and White youths in the rate of delayed education and in nonattendance, the dramatic increase in the unemployment of Black youth, the disproportionate representation of Black youth in arrest statistics on crime and delinquency, and the continued rise in out-of-wedlock childbearing among Black teens. Programs and policies designed to reverse these negative developments are discussed.

4451. **Hammer, Torild & Vaglum, Per.** (U Oslo, Norway) **The increase in alcohol consumption among women: A phenomenon related to accessibility or stress? A general population study.** *British Journal of Addiction,* 1989(Jul), Vol 84(7), 767–775. —Explored the relative importance of accessibility and stress variables in explaining the increasing level of women's alcohol consumption. Survey data from 3,997 Norwegian women (aged 16+ yrs) and their husbands indicate that population density and husbands' alcohol consumption had a significant impact on women's consumption. Employment among women was not significantly related to their alchohol use when controlling for the husband's consumption. Stress variables had no significant influence on consumption when controlling for accessibility variables. Accessibility variables with a close relationship to lifestyle had a greater impact on consumption than general accessibility to alcoholic beverages.

6383. **Lynn, Michael.** (U Missouri, Columbia) **Scarcity effects on desirability: Mediated by assumed expensiveness?** *Journal of Economic Psychology,* 1989(Jun), Vol 10(2), 257–274. —Conducted 2 studies to examine whether scarcity effects on desirability are due to a tendency for people to assume that scarce things cost more. Study 1, with 392 undergraduates, found that scarcity increased the desirability of art prints only when Ss had been primed to think about the expensiveness of art prints in general. Findings from Study 2, with 171 undergraduates, further supported the hypothesis by finding that scarcity enhanced the desirability of wine only when Ss did not know how much the wine cost. Economic and marketing implications are discussed.

FIGURE 2.1 **Sample abstracts from *Psychological Abstracts*.**
Source: Reproduced from *Psychological Abstracts,* Vol. 77, No. 2; reprinted with permission of the American Psychological Association, publisher of *Psychological Abstracts,* all rights reserved.

If your library also has PsycLIT's *Quick Reference Guide,* you will find that it is a very useful summary of the commands used by PsycLIT and also shows how to define a search. To get you started once you have PsycLIT on the computer screen, you can press the F3 key to display a list of topics or the F1 key to get help with the retrieval software. If the terminal is equipped with a printer, you can press the F6 key to display a menu that will allow you to make a printed copy of your results. You will find other tips in Box 2.7 and some further hints in Rosnow and Rosnow's *Writing Papers in Psychology* (1998).

Box 2.7 **Practice Tips on Using PsycLIT**

Steven E. Stern, who teaches at the University of Pittsburgh at Johnstown, offers his students the following practice tips to get them started on PsycLIT:

- Pressing the F2 key on your keyboard puts the word *Find* on the screen; you now tell the computer what you want it to find.

- Try using the following abbreviations in your search: AU, personal author(s); DE, descriptors; JN, journal name; PO, population.

- For example, suppose you are doing research on prejudice. At the "Find" prompt, type "prejudice in DE" (don't type the quotes). You have told the computer to find citations where prejudice is important enough to be listed as a descriptor of the title or synopsis.

- Suppose you are studying aggression and want to find out what a leading researcher has published. Type "Bandura in AU" (again, always without the quotes), which instructs the computer to look for work *by* Bandura but not for work that merely *refers* to Bandura.

- Suppose you want studies on attribution but your library takes only one journal in social psychology, the APA's *Journal of Personality and Social Psychology.* Type "attribution and (journal-of-personality-and-social-psychology in JN)," which tells the computer to narrow its search; the hyphenated title suggests how the journal field is entered in the database.

- Suppose you wanted studies using humans. Typing "human in PO" (population) roots out any studies using animals ("animal in PO" does just the opposite).

- Now press the F5 key, which is the "Index" key. If you type in a term or name, the computer will list all words that are alphabetically close.

- Pressing the F9 key brings up the "Thesaurus" prompt, and by entering a term, you elicit synonymous or related terms. For example, type "hallucination" after the "Thesaurus" prompt, and see what it turns up.

- Notice that there is something called "ISBN#" which comes with every citation; it stands for International Standard Book Number. If you cannot find what you want in your college library, you can report this code number and ask whether your library can borrow what you need from another library.

Table 2.1	Five Relevant Databases Available on Computers
Database	Coverage
ABI/Inform	Business and personnel management, finance, consumer information, advertising
ERIC	Educational Resources Information Center; includes references from preschool to the postdoctoral level
MEDLINE	References in medicine, biomedicine, and related fields
PsycINFO	The parent file of PsycLIT, this is the most comprehensive source of references in all areas of psychology
Social Work Abstracts	Social work references, including substance abuse literature and family and mental health literature

In fact, there are many useful collections of abstracts besides the *Psychological Abstracts,* and many of them are also accessible by computer. Table 2.1 lists some of them. You will find, for example, that ERIC (Educational Resources Information Center) is another relevant database. Although your library may not subscribe to all of them, there are abstracts and indexes for just about every discipline and area of interest (e.g., *Biological Abstracts, Art Index, Abridged Index Medicus,* and *Humanities Index)*. If you would like to learn more about reference databases in the behavioral sciences, see the reviews by M. C. Rosenthal (1985) and J. G. Reed and Baxter (1994).

Defining Terms and Variables

As you study the material you have gathered, think carefully about the plausibility of your initial idea in the context of the published work. Does the idea still make sense to you in view of what experts have written about the subject? We return to this question later, when we consider the "payoff potential" of the working hypothesis. At this juncture, you will also need to think about naming and defining the things you want to study, because calling a thing by its precise name "is the beginning of understanding" (Hoover & Donovan, 1995, p. 19). For example, if you wanted to study rumormongering, it would make a difference whether you defined it as a collective enterprise (i.e., as sociologists usually envision it, such as Shibutani, 1966) or as a message chain in which the links are individuals (i.e., as it was traditionally envisioned by psychologists Allport & Postman, 1947). As another example, Hoover and Donovan (1995) noted, "It makes a great deal of difference whether an illness is conceived of as caused by the Evil spirit or by bacteria on a binge" (p. 19).

Researchers usually distinguish between two types of definitions, called *operational* and *theoretical.* First, **operational definitions** "link concepts to observable events" (Stanovich, 1986, p. 42). That is, this type of definition identifies terms on the basis of the empirical conditions (i.e., operations) used to measure or to manipulate them. For example, an experimental psychologist may define hunger operationally (empirically) by using laboratory equipment to measure stomach contractions. A social psychologist may define prejudice operationally by using a person's score on an attitude questionnaire. A developmental psychologist may define frustration operationally by stopping a child from playing with a set of attractive new toys.

In another example, a team of clinical psychologists (Kendall, Howard, & Hays, 1989) had college students and inpatients at a psychiatric institution respond to an inventory of "thoughts" by indicating how frequently, if at all, each thought had occurred to them over the past week. Some thoughts listed were positive ("I feel very happy" and "This is super!"); others were negative ("My life is a mess" and "There must be something wrong with me"). The researchers used simple statistics to compare their results with previous data and thus developed a way of empirically defining the concept of *clinical depression* in terms of reportable events (i.e., positive and negative thoughts).

Next, **theoretical definitions** (also called **conceptual definitions**) assign the meaning of terms more abstractly or generally, as in defining *hunger* by a connection between the feeling of being hungry and the experience of certain internal and external cues. The social psychologist may conceptualize *prejudice* as "an attitudinal disposition to hasty or premature judgment." The developmental psychologist may conceptualize *frustration* as "the condition that exists when people feel their goals are blocked by internal or external barriers." In their research, the team of clinical investigators mentioned above (Kendall et al., 1989) conceptualized *clinical depression* simply as "a preponderance of negative thinking." Their empirical findings were, in fact, consistent with this theoretical picture: People who had been clinically defined as depressed reported a high proportion of negative thoughts and a low proportion of positive thoughts.

How can you get started in your quest for good operational and theoretical definitions of the things you want to study? Before you find yourself reinventing the wheel, you might look in standard references to see how others have conceptualized the same things. For example, you will find psychological terms and concepts defined in V. S. Ramachandran's *Encyclopedia of Human Behavior* (1994), R. Harré and R. Lamb's *Encyclopedic Dictionary of Psychology* (1983), B. B. Wolman's *International Encyclopedia of Psychiatry, Psychology, Psychoanalysis, and Neurology* (1977), and R. J. Corsini's *Encyclopedia of Psychology* (1984). Once you have located any of these encyclopedias, you should find others nearby. Other useful encyclopedic works outside psychology are the *International Encyclopedia of the Social Sciences* (1968, 18 vols.), *The Encyclopedia of Education* (1971, 10 vols.), and the *International Encyclopedia of Communications* (1989, 4 vols.).

A Summary Illustration

Before we move on, let us illustrate with a concrete example what we have discussed so far (i.e., coming up with an idea, then doing a literature search, and finally defining the idea operationally and theoretically). Suppose we are interested in studying what we view as a particular aspect of intelligence that is different from being "book smart" (i.e., academic intelligence). We know that people from different countries and cultures have different ideas about intelligence, but all seem to view "dealing with other people" as an aspect of intelligence. In our society, for example, we speak of some people as being "street smart" (i.e., astute in the ways of the world) and others as having "business savvy" or "political sense." All of these qualities seem to use social skills, such as being able to read others' motives or intentions. Given this crude conception, where do we go next?

Because every scientific idea has a lineage, the next step is to do a literature search to find out how experts in this area may have viewed intelligence as encompassing multiple abilities. This search, let us say, turns up the early work of J. P. Guilford (1967), who envisioned 120 different ways of being intelligent. We have made a promising beginning, but even these 120 ways do not relate specifically to the "intelligence" we have in mind. It appears that we will have to be more dogged in our literature search. We continue our search by consulting recent texts and handbooks; by searching PsycLIT, ERIC, and other computerized databases; and by asking faculty who work in developmental, educational, and social psychology if they can suggest leads. If we continue in this way, we will eventually hit pay dirt by turning up a large body of more recent work on "multiple intelligences" by developmental, educational, and social psychologists (e.g., Cantor & Kihlstrom, 1989; Ceci, 1990, 1996; H. Gardner, 1985, 1993; Sternberg, 1985, 1990; Sternberg & Detterman, 1986; Wyer & Srull, 1989).

All of these researchers stress the existence of intellectual capacities beyond mathematical and language skills. We are interested in only one particular set of skills, which some include in the category of either "social intelligence" (e.g., Cantor & Kihlstrom, 1989; Wyer & Srull, 1989) or "interpersonal intelligence" (H. Gardner, 1985). Gardner (1985) described the core capacity of interpersonal intelligence as "the ability to notice and make distinctions among other individuals and, in particular, their moods, temperaments, motivations, and intentions" (p. 239). This sounds like a good description of what we are interested in, and we also find other conceptual definitions that we might be able to quote later. Gardner (1985) also stated, for example, that interpersonal intelligence is a system that "turns outward, to other individuals" (p. 239); another leading researcher wrote that it involves "understanding and acting upon one's understanding of others" (Sternberg, 1990, p. 265). All of these descriptions are quite consistent with our idea of socially skilled intelligence.

All we need now is a researchable idea, and we will find many promising leads throughout this work—as well as by watching (and thinking about) how people interact. What interests us most is the idea of levels of interpersonal intelligence. For example, Gardner (1985) envisioned that, in its most elementary form, interpersonal intelligence entails the ability "to discriminate among individuals . . . and to detect their various moods" (p. 239); in its advanced form, it "permits a skilled adult to read the intentions and desires—even when these have been hidden—of many individuals and, potentially, to act upon their knowledge" (p. 239). We cannot study everything, and so we need to narrow our conceptualization. To differentiate what we want to study from the broader conceptualizations of interpersonal and social intelligence, we will name what we want to study "interpersonal acumen" (Rosnow, Skleder, Jaeger, & Rind, 1994). That is, we are interested in a person's ability to discern (*acumen* means "discernment") another's intentions and behavior, and we think there must be "levels" of this ability. We can think of operationally accessible situations that tap interpersonal acumen, such as the ability of teachers to discern their students' motivations to act in certain ways, or the ability of children to discern the mood of a parent, or the ability of salespeople to spot impulse buyers. We still need to connect the theoretical idea of levels of interpersonal acumen with measurable sets of events, but we have made a good beginning.

The Acceptability Stage

Theories and Hypotheses

By reading, thinking, and keeping our eyes and minds open, we find we are able to zero in on researchable ideas and on promising operational and theoretical definitions. We are ready to tackle the final phase of the discovery process, the acceptability stage, in which the scientist accepts the plausibility of the idea and molds it into a testable supposition, or **working hypothesis** (also called an **experimental hypothesis** in experimental research). Before we go on, however, it will be useful to clarify the distinction usually made between **hypotheses** and **theories** (e.g., Lana, 1991; N. Miller & Pollock, 1994; Overton, 1991a, 1991b). Let us look at another example, a classic formulation that is called *social comparison theory.* This theory was developed by Leon Festinger (1954), and, like all scientific theories (cf. Lana, 1991; Overton, 1991b; Rosnow, 1981), it comprises a number of explicit and implicit assumptions.

Most basically, social comparison theory assumes that we all have a need to evaluate our opinions and abilities. We want to know whether we are like or unlike others, or better or worse than they are. For many opinions and abilities, there are objective standards to help us decide where we stand in relation to others. But for many others, such as our opinions about ethnic or racial groups, religion, sex, or environmental pollution, not many objective criteria are immediately available. It follows, Festinger reasoned, that when no immediate objective standard exists, we will attempt to evaluate our opinions and abilities by comparing ourselves to others. He also theorized that the tendency to compare oneself with another person decreases as the expected difference between oneself and another increases. Thus, if you wanted to evaluate your opinions about the existence of God, you would be more likely to compare yourself with another college student than with a member of the clergy. The theory also states that you will be less attracted to groups in which the members' way of thinking is very different from your own than to groups in which the members think more as you do. One reason, according to Festinger, is that people are motivated to elicit feedback (reinforcement) about the legitimacy of their own opinions.

We see what a "theory" can look like, and now let us see what working hypotheses derived from a theory look like. Previously we said that working hypotheses take the form of conjectures or suppositions; their goal is to "select" what the researcher should observe (see Box 2.8). In the case of Festinger's social comparison theory, he and many other researchers have developed their own working hypotheses. Here are a couple of examples that Festinger (1957) articulated: "Given a range of possible persons for comparison, someone close to one's own ability or opinion will be chosen for comparison" (p. 151) and "The existence of a discrepancy in a group with respect to opinions or abilities will lead to action on the part of the members of that group to reduce the discrepancy" (p. 124).

Box 2.8   **"Selecting" What to Observe**

To illustrate this function, Karl Popper (1934, 1963), an eminent philosopher of science, told his students, "Take pencil and paper; carefully observe, and write down what you have observed." They immediately asked *what* it was he wanted them to observe, because a directed observation needs a chosen object, a definite task, an interest, a point of view, and a problem. Popper then explained to them that this was why the scientist develops hypotheses: to give direction to his or her observations, a direction researchers cannot do without.

What does this example teach us about typical theories and hypotheses in the behavioral and social sciences? First, the example illustrates that a hypothesis is basically a conjectural statement or supposition, while a theory is a larger set of such statements in the context of certain assumptions, or presuppositions. Second, we see that hypotheses can be derived from a theory and that they give direction to the researcher's systematic observations. Third, we see that a theory postulates a kind of conceptual pattern, which then serves as a logical framework for the interpretation of the larger meaning of our observations (e.g., Hoover & Donovan, 1995). Finally, it is true of seminal theories that they are constantly evolving as new hypotheses and observations emerge. Such theories are also described as **generative,** because they allow others to generate new hypotheses and observations. Social comparison theory measures up well by this standard (e.g., Suls & Miller, 1977; Wheeler, Martin, & Suls, 1997).

Molding Ideas Into Acceptable Hypotheses

In the **acceptability stage,** the goal is to mold the plausible idea into a working hypothesis that can direct the researcher's observations. To pass muster as an "acceptable" hypothesis, the working hypothesis must satisfy three criteria, which we will call (1) correspondence with reality, (2) coherence and parsimony, and (3) falsifiability.

First, **correspondence with reality** refers to the extent to which the hypothesis agrees with "accepted wisdom" (e.g., respected theory and reliable empirical data). The working hypotheses that correspond most closely to accepted wisdom are generally understood to have a higher "payoff potential" when subjected to empirical testing. That is, such hypotheses are expected to be more easily corroborated than hypotheses that come out of the blue. There is no way, of course, to be absolutely sure that one's working hypothesis will pay off when it is tested. However, the idea is to try to maximize the odds in our favor by ensuring that our hypotheses are consistent with accepted wisdom. We can illustrate this first criterion by the classic proposition "Similarity leads to liking," which in recent years has been most closely associated with the work of Donn Byrne (1971) and his students.

In 1961, Byrne began a series of studies proceeding from what he called the "similarity-attraction principle." Such a principle could be easily seen as quite compatible with accepted wisdom in psychology. For instance, in a classic study, Francis Galton (1869) found that marriage patterns of eminent English men suggested a pattern of "like-to-like" in the women they chose as mates. Similarly, an early test of social comparison theory by Festinger and others (Festinger, Gerard, Hymovitch, Kelley, & Raven, 1952) was also consistent with this principle. The subjects wrote their opinions on a specific social issue and were then given a slip of paper that supposedly contained a summary of the opinions of other group members. Some of the subjects were led to believe that the others in the group held opinions similar to their own, while the remaining subjects were told that the opinions of the others were considerably different. All subjects were then asked to state how much they liked the others in the group. The results showed that those who thought the others held divergent opinions were less attracted to the group.

Byrne (1961) himself cited a number of other studies with similar results, and he pointed out again that we generally seem to be attracted to people who offer us rewards and dislike people who offer us punishment. Byrne reasoned that knowing that someone has attitudes similar to oneself should be perceived as rewarding whereas dissimilarity should be perceived as punishing. These perceptions, he argued, explain why we are attracted to people with attitudes that are similar to our own—the desire for rewards. Thus, by ensuring that his research ideas were quite consistent with accepted wisdom, Byrne had attempted to maximize the payoff potential of finding the hypothesized relationship between similarity and attraction.

We will return to Byrne's idea in a moment, but the second criterion—also used by him in formulating specific hypotheses—is a combination of coherence and parsimony. **Coherence** refers to whether the hypothesis "sticks together" in a logically compelling way; **parsimony** refers to how "sparing" and "frugal" the hypothesis is. Scientists are taught that, to be acceptable, their hypotheses must be logically coherent and only as wordy or complicated as is absolutely necessary. Thus they "cut away" what is superfluous by means of a ruminative and winnowing process that is known as **Occam's razor,** after William of Occam, a 14th-century Franciscan philosopher who insisted that we cut away what is unwieldy. What can be explained in fewer words or on the basis of fewer principles is explained needlessly by more, he argued. A word of caution: Occam's razor is not a description of nature (because nature is often very complicated); it is only a prescription for the wording of acceptable hypotheses. It is important not to cut off too much—"beards" but not "chins." How can you find out whether your hypothesis cuts off too much or does not cut off enough? A straightforward approach is to ask your instructor for critical feedback and suggestions to help you avoid any missteps.

The third criterion used by scientists to evaluate the acceptability of their hypotheses comes from another of Karl Popper's brilliant insights (see again Box 2.8), which he called **falsifiability** (synonymous with *refutability*). Beginning in the 1930s, recognizing that it was possible for those with a fertile imagination to find support for even the most preposterous propositions, Popper put forth the standard of falsifiability as the sine qua non of scientific hypotheses or propositions. Hypotheses that cannot, in principle, be refuted by *any* means are not within the realm of science, he argued (e.g., Popper, 1934, 1961). An example of such a proposition would be "Behavior is a product of the good and evil lying within us." As you peruse the journal literature in your area, you will find many examples of potentially falsifiable hypotheses that guided the research. You will see that scientific hypotheses go out on a limb by stating what should happen (Stanovich, 1986, p. 28), as do Byrne's similarity-attraction and Festinger's social-comparison hypotheses (see also Box 2.9).

Box 2.9	**The Evolution of Knowledge**

Going out on a limb allows other researchers to use your work as a point of departure for further insights. The way that classical rumor theory was a stepping-stone to new ideas is illustrative, and we can expect that current ideas in this area will be an embarkation point for future developments. Byrne's seminal work is also illustrative of the evolutionary nature of scientific knowledge. Milton Rosenbaum (1986a, 1986b), another noted social psychologist, challenged the similarity-attraction paradigm on theoretical and empirical grounds. Rosenbaum argued that, while dissimilarity can lead to repulsion, similarity *never* leads to attraction. In an answer reminiscent of the principle of the dayyan's decree (Box 2.3), Byrne and his coworkers responded by proposing that similarity-attraction and dissimilarity-repulsion are *both* right, depending on the particular stage of a relationship (Byrne, Clore, & Smeaton, 1986). The dispute between Byrne and Rosenbaum is still unresolved, but new results (e.g., Tan & Singh, 1995) imply that the old paradigm may be far more complex than was once thought.

Constructs and Variables

In Chapter 1, we mentioned that the rhetoric of science includes technical terms. Two terms, which refer to key elements of scientists' theories and hypotheses, are *constructs* and *variables*. **Constructs** are theoretical concepts formulated (i.e., constructed) to serve as causal or descriptive explanations. We discuss constructs and their validation more fully later in this book, but an example is the "diffusion of responsibility" construct mentioned earlier. Latané and Darley used this construct (or concept) to explain why each bystander in a group feels that he or she is not chiefly responsible for summoning help, and that others should and will help. As discussed in a later chapter, constructs act as a "theoretical scaffolding" for variables, particularly to relate independent and dependent variables.

A **variable** is an event or condition that the researcher observes or measures or plans to investigate and that is liable to variation (or change). The rhetoric of behavioral and social science recognizes a further distinction between dependent variables and independent variables. The **dependent variable** (usually symbolized as Y) is the "effect" (or outcome) in which the researcher is interested; the **independent variable** (usually symbolized as X) is the presumed "cause," changes in which lead to changes in the dependent variable. For example, in the statement "Jogging makes you feel better," the independent variable (X) is jogging or not jogging, and the dependent variable (Y) is feeling better or not feeling better. It is important to recognize, however, that *any* event or condition may be an independent variable *or* a dependent variable.

It is easy to imagine how some independent variable might be transformed into a dependent variable, and vice versa, because how a variable is labeled depends on its context. For example, in the 1960s, the Kerner Commission studied the roots of racial rioting in the United States. One widely cited conclusion was that "rumors significantly aggravated tensions and disorder in more than 65 percent of the disorders studied" (Kerner et al., 1968, p. 136). Earlier in this chapter, we mentioned that rumors are triggered by a combination of anxiety and uncertainty. In this conceptualization, we see that anxiety and uncertainty are the independent variables, and that rumor is the dependent variable. In the Kerner Commission's conclusion, rumors are the independent variable (i.e., the aggravating condition) and anxiety and uncertainty are the dependent variables (i.e., the aggravated tension). In the blink of an eye, independent and dependent variables have switched places. Thus the causal pattern is no longer linear (cause leads to effect); it now becomes a vicious circle in which rumors can be properly viewed as "causes" one moment and "effects" the next (Rosnow, 1980, 1991).

Examples of Independent Variables

You may ask whether there is an agreed-upon way of classifying independent variables, in the way, for instance, that chemists can turn to the periodic table to see how a particular element is classified. The answer is no. There are, in fact, scores of specific independent and dependent variables in the research literature of the behavioral and social sciences. Broadly speaking, two general categories of independent variables that encompass many specific forms are biological and social variables. To illustrate, we will use the case of eating behavior and note a couple of biological and social independent variables that researchers have examined.

One example of a biological independent variable is seen when blood from a well-fed animal, as compared to the blood of a hungry animal, is injected into another animal that is hungry. The hungry animal stops feeding (Davis, Gallagher, & Ladove, 1967). This finding suggests that a biological independent variable for satiation is somehow carried by the blood: Information about a cell need must be transmitted to a part of the central nervous system that is well supplied with blood and that can control and organize the food-getting activities of the whole animal.

Another independent variable affecting eating behavior was first identified by physicians who observed that tumors in the region of the brain near the hypothalamus and the pituitary gland cause the symptoms (described as Fröhlich's syndrome) of tremendous obesity and atrophy of the genital organs. It was unclear, before classic experiments on animals, whether the syndrome is due to damage of the pituitary or to damage of the hypothalamus by the tumor. When the pituitary gland of normal animals was surgically removed, no obesity resulted, but subsequent damage to the hypothalamus was followed by obesity (Bailey & Bremer, 1921). The status of the hypothalamus, not the pituitary gland, is the independent biological variable involved in the physiological regulation of food intake.

There are also many examples of social independent variables affecting eating behavior. The reason, of course, is that feeding by both humans and other species is strongly affected not only by internal factors but also by many external conditions. Having learned to eat at particular times, for example, clearly affects one's experiences of hunger (e.g., Schachter, 1968), as anyone who has crossed several time zones during an airplane trip can testify. Taste, appearance, and consistency also strongly influence what foods humans prefer and how much food they will eat.

Biological and social independent variables also occur in combinations, or **interactions.** For example, obese humans are highly sensitive to the taste of food. If ice cream is adulterated with quinine in increasing quantities, obese people will refuse it before normal-weight people will refuse it. Obese humans will also eat more of an expensive, good-tasting ice cream than will normal-weight people, but they will not work as hard as normal-weight or underweight people to obtain food (Schachter, 1968).

Examples of Dependent Variables

Dependent variables also have no single classification system in behavioral or social science. Suppose an animal behaviorist wanted to study pain avoidance as a "drive" somewhat different from the appetitive drives of hunger, thirst, and sex. (A *drive* is another example of a construct; it is a theoretical idea referring to the state of readiness of an organism to engage in physiologically connected behavior.) There is no distinct element that is characteristic of pain avoidance and that compares with the drive for food, water, or a mate. What should the researcher choose as the dependent measure?

Imagining yourself quickly withdrawing your hand from a shock-producing stimulus, suggests that measuring the time it takes to withdraw from the stimulus (i.e., the *latency,* or delay, of withdrawal) is a good dependent measure. However, suppose the researcher were interested instead in the pain connected with extreme sexual deprivation. This topic seems more complex than food or water deprivation, though similarities certainly exist. If the subjects were hungry, sexually starved male rats, then the researcher might record their actions as they were faced with choosing between food and a female rat in heat.

In animal learning and conditioning experiments, four broad categories of dependent variables have frequently served as outcome measures: (1) the *direction* of any observed change in behavior; (2) the *amount* of the change; (3) the *ease* with which this change is effected; and (4) the *persistence* of the changes over time. For example, in a learning experiment that consists of teaching a thirsty rat to run through a complex maze toward a thimbleful of water, the measurements might focus on (1) the direction the rat chooses on each trial (i.e., whether it turns toward or away from the water); (2) the amount of change, as reflected in how long the rat persists in the correct response when the water is no longer available at the end of its run; (3) the ease with which the rat reacquires the correct response when the reward is again made available; and (4) how long the correct response persists after it is reacquired and the reward is permanently removed.

We can easily imagine parallels of these dependent variables in a social psychology experiment. A researcher interested in attitude change might, for example, measure participants' reactions to a message treatment or to a no-treatment comparison condition. The independent variable is exposure (experimental group) or nonexposure (control group) to the message. Among the researcher's outcome (dependent) measures would be (1) the direction of each person's attitudinal response (which determines whether the results in the experimental group are in different directions from those in the control condition); (2) the intensity of the new attitude, or how deeply felt it is; (3) the ease with which the subjects are able to express or defend their newly acquired attitude; and (4) how long the new attitude lasts and whether the level of belief diminishes with time.

When you peruse the journal literature in your field, you will see that these examples barely scratch the surface of the many kinds of dependent variables examined by behavioral scientists. For example, cognitive-developmental psychologists Janellen Huttenlocher and Nora Newcombe have studied how infants learn the spatial locations of objects (Huttenlocher & Newcombe, 1984; Huttenlocher, Newcombe, & Sandberg, 1994; Newcombe & Huttenlocher, 1992). The researcher hides toys in a sandbox while the child, seated on the lap of a blindfolded parent, watches. The blindfold is then removed, and (in some conditions) the parent walks with the child to the opposite side of the box, and the child is asked to find the toy. The child's behavior is videotaped, and the dependent measures include whether the child can remember where the toy was hidden and how long it takes the child to respond. Based on observations of several hundred children, these researchers concluded that children as young as 5 months may begin to notice where things are, and that 5-month-olds usually define what an object is by where it is rather than by what it looks like. At 10 months, children begin to draw relationships; at 22 months, they begin locating objects by using other objects as landmarks (see also Box 2.10)

Box 2.10   The Visual Cliff

As a more exotic example from the field of developmental psychology, infants have always fascinated their parents by balancing precariously on the edge of a chair or table in apparent imitation of a tightrope walker. The fascination is usually liberally mixed with fear for the safety of the infant. Obviously, an infant is not yet a fully competent and accurate judge of size and distance in its exploration of the space around it. The child's ability to perceive depth was a subject of intense interest to psychologists Eleanor J. Gibson and Richard D. Walk. These investigators worked with a "visual cliff," a board laid across a large sheet of glass that was raised a foot or more above the floor. A checkerboard pattern covered half the glass. On the other half, the same checkerboard pattern appeared on the floor directly under the glass. The visual cliff was created by the perceptual experience of the difference between the two sides.

In one study, Gibson and Walk (1960) tested infants ranging in age from 6 to 14 months on the visual cliff. Each child was placed on the central board and was called by its mother from the "cliff" side and the "shallow" side successively. Most of the infants moved off the central board onto the glass, and all of these crawled out to the "shallow" side at least once. Only a few of them, however, moved to the glass suspended above the pattern on the floor. Thus most infants would not cross the apparent chasm to their mothers. The dependent variable in this example was crossing versus not crossing the apparent chasm. As a consequence of having developed this not-so-ordinary variable, Gibson and Walk were able to conclude that most human infants discriminate depth as soon as they are able to crawl. The study also illustrates how developmental researchers frequently define the dependent variables in terms of incremental stages or levels of cognitive and behavioral development (e.g., Fischer, Pipp, & Bullock, 1984).

Discovery as Exploration

So far, we have characterized discovery as a linear process of inspiration, library research, and critical rumination. But no rule says the scientist cannot explore by simply keeping his or her eyes and ears open and then developing a very tentative hypothesis to serve as an ad hoc explanation of an observed effect or phenomenon. A prototypical example of this approach in behavioral science was the creative style of Stanley Milgram. In his words, "You try to determine whether particular incidents lead up to the myriad surface phenomena. . . . You generalize from your own experience and formulate a hypothesis" (Milgram, 1977, p. 2).

In fact, Milgram was a master of exploratory discovery. In an interview with Carol Tavris of *Psychology Today* magazine,* he described how the routine incidents that he encountered while commuting to work in Manhattan by train led him to hit on what he called the "familiar stranger" phenomenon and to research questions with societal implications:

> **MILGRAM:** I noticed that there were people at my station whom I had seen for many years but never spoken to, people I came to think of as *familiar strangers*. I found a peculiar tension in this situation, when people treat each other as properties of the environment rather than as individuals to deal with. It happens frequently. Yet there remains a poignancy and discomfort, particularly when there are only two of you at the station: you and someone you have seen daily but never met. A barrier has developed that is not readily broken.
>
> **TAVRIS:** How can you study the phenomenon of the familiar stranger?
>
> **MILGRAM:** Students in my research seminar took pictures of the waiting passengers at one station. They made duplicates of the photographs, numbered each of the faces, then distributed the group photographs the following week to all the passengers at the station. We asked the commuters to indicate those people whom they knew and spoke to, those whom they did not recognize, and those whom they recognized but never spoke to. The commuters filled out the questionnaires on the train and turned them in at Grand Central Station.
>
> Well, we found that the commuters knew an average of 4.5 strangers, and the commuters often had many fantasies about these people. Moreover, there are sociometric stars among familiar strangers. Eighty percent of the commuters recognized one person, although very few had ever spoken to her. She was the visual high point of the station crowd, perhaps because she wore a miniskirt constantly, even in the coldest months.
>
> **TAVRIS:** How do your dealings with familiar strangers differ from those with total strangers?
>
> **MILGRAM:** The familiar-stranger phenomenon is not the absence of a relationship but a special kind of frozen relationship. For example, if you wanted to make a trivial request or get the time of day, you are more likely to ask a total stranger, rather than a person you had seen for many years but had never spoken to. Each

*Reprinted with permission from *Psychology Today Magazine,* Copyright 1974 (Sussex Publishers, Inc.).

of you is aware that a history of noncommunication exists between you, and you both have accepted this as the normal state.

But the relationship between familiar strangers has a latent quality to it that becomes overt on specific occasions. I heard of a case in which a woman fainted in front of her apartment building. Her neighbor, who had seen her for 17 years and never spoken to her, immediately went into action. She felt a special responsibility; she called the ambulance, even went to the hospital with her. The likelihood of speaking to a familiar stranger also increases as you are removed from the scene of routine meeting. If I were strolling in Paris and ran into one of my commuter strangers from Riverdale, we would undoubtedly greet each other for the first time.

And the fact that familiar strangers often talk to each other in times of crisis or emergency raises an interesting question: Is there any way to promote solidarity without having to rely on emergencies and crises? (Milgram, 1977, pp. 3–4)

By simply observing people—keeping his eyes and ears open and coming up with a causal hypothesis to describe the events—Milgram invoked ad hoc hypotheses. Such hypotheses must then stand up to the challenges of empirical testing in order to be absorbed into the scientific literature as valid generalizations (i.e., accepted wisdom)

Summary of Ideas

1. A convenient way to organize our thinking about the scientific method is in terms of (a) a *discovery* phase (in which testable ideas are fashioned) and (b) a *justification* phase (in which the ideas are tested and any conclusions defended). In this chapter, we described three stages in the discovery phase as (a) initial thinking, (b) plausibility, and (c) acceptability.

2. In Stage 1 *(initial thinking)*, some general scenarios that produce good research ideas are (a) an intensive case study (e.g., Freud's studies of neurotic symptoms, London's study of rescuers, and Ebbinghaus's studies with nonsense syllables); (b) a paradoxical incident (e.g., Latané and Darley's studies of bystander intervention); (c) a metaphorical theme (e.g., McGuire's inoculation model of propaganda resistance); (d) a conflicting result (e.g., Jones and Fennell's adjudication of the Tolman-Hull debate and Zajonc's social facilitation hypothesis); (e) an old idea that needs improving (e.g., Skinner's improvement on traditional learning theories and Milgram's refinement of Asch's classic research); and (f) serendipity, or an unexpected observation (e.g., Rosenthal's initial interest in the self-fulfilling nature of expectations, and Rosnow's reexamining rumor theory because of its inconsistency with the Paul McCartney rumor).

3. The *dayyan's decree* is the principle that there may be more than one right answer, and that sometimes two researchers can disagree and yet both be right (e.g., the adjudication of the Tolman-Hull debate).

4. In Stage 2 of discovery *(plausibility)*, reason and logic, aided by the critical reading of relevant work, are used to evaluate initial ideas.

5. Plagiarism means kidnapping another person's idea or work, and it is severely punished. To avoid "accidental plagiarism," it is essential to make careful notes and to cite the sources of any ideas, work, or quotations used in your report. To avoid "lazy writing," avoid repeatedly quoting sentences that can be paraphrased in your own words (and referenced, of course).

6. To look for relevant published work, we may do a by-hand search using *Psychological Abstracts,* or we may use the machine-readable databases in Table 2.1 if we want to save time or need to compile a comprehensive bibliography.

7. PsycLIT is the machine-readable database that is used most often by psychological researchers, and Box 2.7 contains practice tips on using it.

8. Operational and theoretical (or conceptual) definitions are the two primary kinds of definitions used by scientists.

9. Coming up with and focusing on the plausible concept of *interpersonal acumen* provided a summary case illustrating the first two stages of discovery.

10. Theories are sets of statements, possibly including some hypotheses, connected by a logical argument (e.g., Festinger's social-comparison theory). Hypotheses are testable suppositions that may be derived from a theory and that give direction to the researcher's observations. Theories provide conceptual patterns and a framework for the interpretation of the larger meaning of the observations.

11. Basic criteria to be met by scientific hypotheses in Stage 3 of discovery *(acceptability)* are (a) that they correspond with accepted wisdom; (b) that they be coherent and parsimonious; and (c) that they be potentially refutable, or falsifiable (e.g., Byrne's similarity-leads-to-attraction hypothesis, or Rosenbaum's dissimilarity-leads-to-repulsion hypothesis).

12. Constructs are explanatory concepts (e.g., *diffusion of responsibility)* that provide a theoretical connection between variables, whereas variables are what the researcher observes or measures (and are liable to variation).

13. The independent variable *(X)* refers to the status of the determining event or condition (e.g., eliciting and emitting variables of aggression, or physiological and social variables of eating behavior); such events or conditions may also occur in combinations *(interactions)*.

14. The dependent variable *(Y)* refers to the status of the effect or consequence (e.g., direction, amount, ease, and persistence of changes in behavior). However, like independent variables, dependent variables occur in infinite variety (e.g., locating toys in a sandbox or crossing a "visual cliff" in studies of young children).

15. In exploratory discovery, the idea is to keep one's eyes and ears open and to develop plausible ad hoc hypotheses as your observations progress (e.g., Milgram's insights about "familiar strangers").

Key Terms

acceptability stage p. 45	coherence p. 46
accidental plagiarism p. 36	conceptual definitions p. 42
accounting for conflicting results p. 30	constructs p. 47

Multiple-Choice Questions for Review (answers are found on page 344)

1. Paul has suffered brain damage in a car accident. Dr. Kern studies Paul inten-sively, giving him many clinical interviews and tests to measure his cognitive functioning. Based on his work with Paul, Dr. Kern comes up with a scientific theory of brain functioning. Dr. Kern's theory has come about through the process of (a) serendipity; (b) the use of metaphors; (c) an intensive case study; (d) examining a paradoxical incident.

2. A professor at the University of Colorado is interested in studying dynamics in small groups (typically consisting of two to five people). She begins by thinking that people in small groups relate to each other much as the governments of large countries relate to each other. She develops hypotheses about small-group dynamics by thinking about how people in small groups are similar to diplomats at the United Nations. Her hypothesis has come about through the process of (a) attempting to resolve conflicting results; (b) improving on older ideas; (c) the use of metaphors; (d) serendipity.

3. A researcher at Monmouth University conducts a study of high school students and finds there is no relationship between the amount of time spent watching TV and grade point average. A researcher at Emporia University conducts a study of elementary school students, and finds that those who watch a lot of TV tend to have very low grades. A third researcher, from Providence College, now develops a new theory stating that the relationship between watching TV and grade point average depends on other variables, including the age of the subject. This third researcher's theory has come about through the process of (a) serendipity; (b) the use of metaphors; (c) attempting to resolve conflicting results; (d) exam-ining intensive case studies.

4. A medical researcher at Johns Hopkins University sets out to find a new treatment for cancerous brain tumors. She accidentally discovers a treatment for Parkinson's disease, a disease that is totally unrelated to cancer. Her new discovery has come about through the process of (a) improving on older ideas; (b) the use of metaphors; (c) examining intensive case studies; (d) serendipity.

5. Which of the following is true about plagiarism? (a) It is illegal. (b) It can be accidental. (c) One can avoid it by taking careful notes. (d) All of the above.

6. "Intelligence can be defined as a person's general ability to adapt to his or her environment." This is an example of (a) an operational definition; (b) a theoretical definition; (c) a dimensional definition; (d) none of the above.

7. "Intelligence can be defined as a person's score on the WAIS (Wechsler Adult Intelligence Scale)." This is an example of (a) an operational definition; (b) a theoretical definition; (c) a dimensional definition; (d) none of the above.

8. _____ is to operational definition as _____ is to theoretical definition. (a) Construct; variable; (b) Coherence; parsimony; (c) Parsimony; coherence; (d) Variable; construct

9. Dr. Gomez conducts an experiment with two groups of subjects. Half the subjects are given 1 ounce of alcohol; the other half are given 4 ounces of alcohol. He then gives all subjects a test of physical and motor coordination. In this experiment, the test of physical and motor coordination is the _____ variable. (a) control; (b) dependent; (c) independent; (d) none of the above

10. In Dr. Gomez's experiment, the amount of alcohol is the _____ variable. (a) control; (b) dependent; (c) independent; (d) none of the above

Discussion Questions for Review (answers are found on pages 344–45)

1. A Northern Illinois University student wants to see whether self-esteem affects academic performance. He asks 30 randomly selected students from his dormitory to fill out a self-esteem measure, and he divides them into groups having high and low self-esteem on the basis of their test scores. He then compares the self-reported grade point average (GPA) of the two groups and concludes that high self-esteem does lead to a higher GPA. How has he operationalized his independent and dependent variables? If he finds these variables to be highly related, how well justified will he be in claiming that self-esteem affects academic performance?

2. A Virginia Tech student is interested in the personality trait of extraversion. Give an example of both an operational and a theoretical definition of this construct that she can use.

3. A friend tells a George Washington University student that astrology is a science and reminds her that no less than a recent president of the United States consulted an astrologer. How should the student respond to her friend? Can you think of a way for her to do an empirical study to test her friend's assertion?

4. A San Diego State student is interested in studying revenge. Can you devise a causal hypothesis for her to test? How can you assess your hypothesis on scientific grounds of acceptability before passing it to her?

5. A "wolf boy" was discovered in Alaska and brought to a learned doctor for study. The doctor conducted many exploratory tests to determine the boy's reactions. The doctor slammed the door, and though everyone else flinched, the boy remained calm and unmoving. The doctor called out to his secretary, who was taking notes, "Write: Does not respond to noise." A nurse who was looking after the boy protested, "But, sir, I have seen the boy startle at the sound of a cracking nut in the forest 30 feet away!" The doctor paused and then instructed his secretary, "Write: Does not respond to *significant* noise." How was the doctor's explanatory observation flawed? How would you propose to study the wolf boy?

3 Ethical Considerations

What Are Ethical Guidelines?

You have learned that there are three general research approaches—descriptive, relational, and experimental—and that any single study may be focused on one objective of these three types (i.e., to describe, to identify relationships, or to infer causality), or it might have more than one objective. We showed that, within these three types, there are a great many different strategies and options, but we have given only a flavor of them so far. (Beginning in Chapter 4, we will examine a number of these alternatives in more detail.) We have also discussed the "discovery" process, the goal of which is to develop "risky" (i.e., falsifiable) hypotheses that direct the researcher's observations and data analysis. Once your instructor is satisfied that your research question is worth studying and can be formulated in a scientifically meaningful way, it is time to think more carefully about the ethics of the empirical strategy that you will propose.

The term **ethics** (from the Greek *ethos,* meaning "character" or "disposition") refers to the values by which we morally (from the Latin *moralis,* meaning "custom" or "manner") evaluate the character or conduct of a

PREVIEW QUESTIONS

- What is the role of ethical guidelines in behavioral and social research?
- What are the five broad principles discussed here?
- What is an informed consent agreement, and when am I expected to use it?
- How does the review process operate, and how can I prepare for an ethics review?
- What are some ethical dilemmas in research with human participants?
- Why do some design problems raise ethical concerns and not just methodological concerns?
- Is active or passive deception ever justified in behavioral or social research?
- What is the purpose of debriefing, and how do I go about it?
- What are the issues in the debate about animal research, and how is such research governed by ethical rules?

person. As the term is used in science, *ethics* refers to the values by which we judge the conduct of individual researchers and the morality of the research strategies they use. To help us in this process, we consult **ethical guidelines,** that is, explicit and implicit specifications that are relevant when the researcher's question "Should I conduct this study?" involves a moral issue (Kimmel, 1996, p. 5). Guidelines that have figured most prominently in the decision making of many behavioral and social scientists were originally created and adopted by the American Psychological Association (1973, 1982) and have been updated by a task force consisting of members of the APS (American Psychological Society) and members of the APA (American Psychological Association, 1997). The conceptual framework of the ideas discussed by this group to guide researchers and protect participants has its roots in a document called *The Belmont Report* and in more recent government directives (see Box 3.1).

Box 3.1   **The Belmont Report**

The **Belmont Report** was developed in 1974 by a national commission that was given the task of formulating guidelines that would protect the rights and welfare of participants in biomedical and behavioral research. Prior to this work, there had been safeguards to protect subjects in medical research, but serious violations had occurred nonetheless. For example, in a notorious study done by the U.S. Public Health Service from 1932 to 1973, the course of syphilis in more than 400 low-income African-American men in Tuskegee, Alabama, had been monitored without the researchers' informing the men they had syphilis or giving them penicillin when it was discovered in 1943. Although given free health care and a free annual medical exam, they were told that they would be dropped from the study if they sought treatment elsewhere. The study was finally terminated after details were made public by an Associated Press reporter, although not until the disease had progressed in its predictable form without treatment and the men had experienced skeletal, cardiovascular, and central nervous system damage and, in some cases, death (J. H. Jones, 1993). The report takes its name from the discussions that were held at the Smithsonian Institution's Belmont Conference Center (National Commission for the Protection of Human Subjects of Biomedical and Behavioral Research, 1979).

No set of ethical guidelines can anticipate every possible case, but the idea of an ethics code is to have an agreed-upon focal point from which to examine "matters of right or wrong, ought or ought not, a good action or a bad one" (Kimmel, 1996, p. 5). In this chapter, we examine some of the implications of five broad principles that define the basic framework of the code: (1) respect for persons and their autonomy; (2) beneficence and nonmaleficence; (3) justice; (4) trust; and (5) fidelity and scientific integrity. These principles might be conceptualized as a kind of "social contract" of do's and don'ts. In general, they remind us of our responsibility *not to do* harm to participants and *to do* potentially beneficial research in a way that will produce valid results (Rosnow, 1997). Your research proposal will need to be approved, and we will give a flavor of the review process in which the costs (risks) and benefits of proposed research are judged (see also Box 3.2). We will also have something to say about the ethics of animal experimentation, although the main purpose of this chapter is to sharpen your intuitions about the ethics of research with human participants.

| **Box 3.2** | **Treading on Thin Moral Ice** |

Philosopher John Atwell (1981) noted that all research with human subjects treads "on thin moral ice" because researchers "are constantly in danger of violating someone's basic rights, if only the right of privacy" (p. 89). Mindful of this situation, ethicists and scientists (e.g., Blanck et al., 1992; Kimmel, 1981, 1988, 1991, 1996; Parloff, 1995; Rosenthal, 1994b; Rosnow, Rotheram-Borus, Ceci, Blanck, & Koocher, 1993; Schuler, 1982; Sieber, 1982a, 1982b, 1983, 1992) have raised and debated difficult questions, such as:

1. Is it right to withhold information from subjects if I think that a full disclosure will bias their responses?
2. Am I justified in misleading subjects by using a deception if it is necessary to study an important issue?
3. Is it permissible for me to invade the privacy of subjects if there is no other way to gather essential facts?

Principle I. Respect for Persons and Their Autonomy

Autonomy means "independence" and, in the context of research ethics, refers specifically to a prospective subject's right as well as ability "to choose" whether to participate in the study or to continue in the study. Our ethical and legal responsibility is to ensure that potential participants know what they will be getting into, and that they are free to decide whether or not to participate. In practice, the way this works is to tell them about the study and then to obtain their written agreement to participate (called **informed consent**). There are, however, situations in which obtaining the informed consent of prospective subjects is either unnecessary or impossible (e.g., research that uses public records and some field experiments). A tipping study by a team of social psychologists is illustrative (Rind & Bordia, 1996). They had servers in a restaurant-diner either draw or not draw a happy face on the back of customer checks before delivering them. The social psychologists explained the study to the servers and the owner of the restaurant and obtained their consent to proceed. Clearly, it would have been impossible, however, to inform the subjects (i.e., the customers) of their participation without destroying the credibility of the manipulation and rendering the experiment meaningless. (Incidentally, the results were that the happy face increased tips for the female server, but did not increase tips for the male server.)

In most cases, however, informed consent is a requirement of the research procedure. The prospective subjects are given a form that describes (1) the nature of the study; (2) any potential risk or inconvenience to them; (3) the procedure for ensuring the confidentiality of the data; and (4) the voluntary nature of their participation and their freedom to withdraw at any time without prejudice or consequence. The prospective subject is asked to sign the form in order to indicate that he or she understands the study and is willing to participate. Figure 3.1 shows in Section A an example of the consent portion of an informed-consent agreement and, in Section B, that the subject may be asked about being "debriefed" after the study is completed. (We will return to debriefing later in this chapter.)

However, even when acting with the best moral intentions, researchers may inadvertently transgress. Because of increased scrutiny by regulatory committees, the disclosure procedure in some studies has become so detailed and cumbersome that it could defeat the purpose for which it was intended (Imber et al., 1986). If subjects are confused by the form, we cannot be said to have complied with the spirit of the law. Some subjects may also mistakenly assume that they have relinquished their legal right to sue the researcher for negligence by signing an informed-consent agreement

Instructions to participant: Please print and then sign your name in the space provided in Section A before you participate in this study. Once the study is over and you have been debriefed, you will be asked to initial the three statements listed in Section B to indicate your agreement.

Section A
I, ———————————————————, voluntarily give my consent to participate in this project. I have been informed about, and feel that I understand, the basic nature of the project.
I understand that I may leave at any time and that my anonymity will be protected.

————————————————   ————————————————
Signature of Research Participant   Date

Section B
Please initial each of the following statements once the study has been completed and you have been debriefed:
——— I have been debriefed.
——— I was not forced to stay to complete the study.
——— All my questions have been answered satisfactorily.

Figure 3.1 **Example of the written-consent portion of the informed-consent agreement.**

(Mann, 1994). In fact, the right to sue is protected by federal regulations on the use of human subjects (U.S. Department of Health and Human Services, 1983, 45, CFR 46.115).

Suppose the prospective subjects have a limited or diminished capacity to understand the consent agreement. For example, children may have difficulty understanding the nature of the research, particularly if they are young or are feeling anxious (e.g., Dorn, Susman, & Fletcher, 1995; Susman, Dorn, & Fletcher, 1992). Whenever children or adolescents are used as subjects, the researcher is required to obtain parental consent before proceeding and is not permitted to make appeals to children to participate before parental consent is obtained (Scott-Jones & Rosnow, 1998). If the children do not live with their parents (e.g., are wards of some agency), the researcher can speak with an advocate who is appointed to act in the best interests of the child in the consent process. Once the informed consent of the parent or advocate has been obtained, the researcher asks the child on the day of the study whether he or she wishes to participate—assuming the child is mature enough to be asked about participation (see also Box 3.3).

Box 3.3   ## Freedom of Choice for Psych 1 Students

Freedom of choice must also be factored in when students in college or university classes are required to participate in a certain number of hours of research. Introductory psychology students are used frequently in studies by psychologists because such students are so readily available. They must be given a choice whether to participate in the study or to select some alternative requirement, and there must be an educational benefit to the students for participating in the research (e.g., a deeper understanding of the research process and, presumably, the results they are learning about in the course). To prevent coercion or the appearance of coercion, the alternative requirement must be educational and no more difficult than the research participation (e.g., reading one or more journal papers or attending a special lecture).

Principle II. Beneficence and Nonmaleficence

Beneficence means "doing good"; **nonmaleficence** means "not doing harm." This second principle means that, just as in the Hippocratic oath that doctors take, behavioral and social researchers must agree to "do no harm." In addition, the researchers are expected to maximize the benefits of their studies. The researcher submits a proposal of the planned research to a panel of evaluators, called an **institutional review board** (**IRB**), which provides an oversight mechanism by examining the costs (or risks) and benefits of the proposed study. Studies that are classified by the IRB as of **minimal risk** (i.e., the likelihood and extent of harm to subjects is no greater than that typically experienced in everyday life) are usually eligible for an **expedited review**, which means they can be evaluated without undue delay. Student projects in courses typically fall in the minimal risk category and can often be evaluated by the instructor acting on behalf of (and with the permission of) the IRB. Studies involving more than minimal risk raise a red flag that signals the need for a more detailed **cost-benefit analysis** by the IRB.

Figure 3.2 shows a **decision-plane model** that helps us conceptualize how this process is designed to work ideally. Based on their review of a detailed description of the proposed study, and on the responses that researchers give to specific questions, the IRB considers all aspects of the study that may have risk-benefit implications. The specific questions that researchers must answer vary from one institution to another, but Table 3.1 will give you a sense of these questions. We presume you will have to address similar questions regarding your own proposed study. However, your answers may not have to be submitted to an IRB; they may instead be evaluated by your instructor or by a surrogate ethics review panel (e.g., a group consisting of your fellow students).

Basically, the costs and benefits of doing a particular study are evaluated on scales of *perceived* methodological and societal values or interests. That is, this evaluation depends on how members of IRBs choose to define costs and benefits in a given situation. Their evaluation of the costs of doing the research may include annoyances or inconveniences to the subjects, institutional time, expenditures of money and effort, the loss of privacy, and so on, whereas their evaluation of the benefits of doing the research may include educational or psychological advantages to the subjects, to other people at other times and places, to the advancement of scientific knowledge, and so on. Studies that are well thought out and are of minimal risk, and that address compelling issues, will be judged to be more beneficial than studies that are not well thought out, involve physical or psychological risks, or address trivial issues. In Figure 3.2, studies falling in the area labeled A *are not* approved because the costs are high and the benefits low; studies falling in the D area *are* approved because the benefits

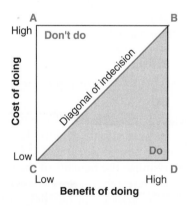

Figure 3.2 **Representation of an idealized cost-benefit ethical evaluation.**
Studies falling at A are not carried out; studies falling at D are carried out; and studies falling along the B–C diagonal are too hard to decide about and thus require further information.

Table 3.1   Sample Questions for Ethics Review

Investigator
1. Who is the primary investigator, and who is supervising the study?
2. Will anyone be assisting you in this investigation?
3. Have you or the others whose names are listed above had any experience with this kind of research?

Nature of the study
4. What is the purpose of this research? That is, what is it about?
5. What will the research participants be asked to do, or what will be done to them?
6. Will deception be used? If the answer is yes, why is it necessary?
7. What is the nature of the deception, and when will the debriefing (dehoaxing) take place?
8. Will the subjects risk any harm—physical, psychological, legal, or social—by participating in this research?
9. If there are any risks, how do you justify them? How will you minimize the risks?

Research participants
10. How will you recruit the research participants? Will you be offering an incentive?
11. How do you plan to explain the research to your potential subjects and obtain their informed consent? How will you make clear that they can quit the study at any time?
12. What should be the general characteristics of your research participants (e.g., age range, sex, institutional affiliation, and the projected number of subjects)?
13. What, if any, are the special characteristics you need in your research participants (e.g. children, pregnant women, racial or ethnic minorities, mentally retarded persons, prisoners, or alcoholics)?
14. Are other institutions or individuals cooperating in or cosponsoring the study?
15. Do the subjects have to be in a particular mental or physical state to participate usefully?

Material
16. If electrical or mechanical equipment will be used, how has it been checked for safety?
17. What standardized tests, if any, will be used? What information will be provided to the subjects about their scores on these tests?

Confidentiality
18. What procedure will you use to ensure the confidentiality of the data?

Debriefing
19. How do you plan to debrief the subjects?

---

are high and the costs low. Studies falling along the B–C diagonal (the "diagonal of indecision") are too hard to decide about and are returned for changes or further information.

A limitation of this idealized assessment is that it focuses only on the costs and benefits of "doing" research and ignores the costs of "not doing" research. That is, it is oblivious to whether not doing a potentially important study is also subject to evaluation on moral grounds. Because of this limitation, it can be argued that IRBs are held to a less rigorous standard of accountability than that required of the researchers (Haywood, 1976; Rosnow, 1997). Bureaucrats and pressure groups sometimes also impede the pursuit of important societal questions (Brooks-Gunn & Rotheram-Borus, 1994). For example, a recent case involving a sexual survey of adolescents was terminated prematurely on the grounds that it violated community norms. However, stopping this research meant that the community was deprived of data needed to address health problems of general concern (Wilcox & Gardner, 1993). Another problem is that the IRB may ignore potential benefits altogether and simply use a risk analysis as the basis of its decision.

Not surprisingly, given the subjectivity of an ethical review, there may be considerable variability in the decision making of different IRBs. Getting a socially sensitive proposal approved is often a matter of the luck of drawing a particular group of IRB members whose values happen to be congruent with the values of the researchers (Ceci, Peters, & Plotkin, 1985; Kimmel, 1991). Nonetheless, the reality of the situation is not a valid excuse for researchers to "play it safe," since, as Atwell said (Box 3.2), research with human subjects *always* treads "on thin moral ice." This is also why it is important to improve our understanding of dilemmas that are intrinsic in research with human participants. The scientist whose research might reduce violence or prejudice, but who plays it safe by not proposing the study because it involves deception or an invasion of privacy, has not solved the ethical problem but has merely traded one moral problem for another. If there is no reasonable alternative to using deception or invading people's privacy, then the task might be to try to persuade the IRB of the costs of *not doing* a potentially important study.

Principle III. Justice

The spirit of the third principle is that the burdens as well as the benefits of research should be distributed fairly. The men who participated in the Tuskegee study (Box 3.1) could not have benefited in any significant way, and they alone bore the awful burdens as well. Based on the model in Figure 3.2, this study would clearly fall at A. But suppose it had been an experiment to test the effectiveness of a new drug to cure syphilis (e.g., penicillin), and the strategy was to give half the men at random the new drug and the other half a fake "pill" masquerading as the real thing (i.e., a **placebo**). Do you think it is acceptable to deprive some people (e.g., those in the control group) of the potential benefits of a life-saving drug? One alternative that has been used is to give the control group the best available medicine, so that the comparison is between the new drug and the best available option.

Justice also implies **fair-mindedness,** or impartiality, but this is a matter of perception and personal judgment. Even if the objective is desirable, some people might perceive the study as unfair. For example, in the 1970s, there was a field experiment—known as the **Rushton study**—that was designed to improve the quality of work life in a mining operation owned by the Rushton Mining Company in Pennsylvania

(Blumberg & Pringle, 1983). After months of careful preparation by the researchers and the managers of the mine, an appeal was made for volunteers for a work group that would have direct responsibility for the production in one section of the mine. The experiment called for the workers in this group to abandon their traditional roles and to coordinate their own activities after extensive training in safety laws, good mining practices, and job safety analysis. They were also given the top-rate wages, those paid for the highest skilled job classification in that section. Not surprisingly, they were enthusiastic proponents of "our way of working."

Unfortunately, trouble soon reared its head. Workers in the rest of the mine (who were the "control" group) were resentful of the "injustice" of the situation: "Why should inexperienced volunteers receive special treatment and higher pay than other miners with many more years on the job?" Rumors circulated through the mine that the volunteers were "riding the gravy train" and being "spoon-fed," and that the project was a "communist plot" because all the volunteers received the same rate and the company was "making out" at their expense. As a consequence, the study had to be terminated prematurely. Yet, is it reasonable to expect that *full justice* can be achieved in any research situation? As life itself reminds us (see Box 3.4), the principle of justice is an ideal that is unlikely to be fully achieved in a world that is never fully just (APA, in press). Although conscious of the foibles of human nature, behavioral researchers must do the best they can to be just in an imperfect world.

Box 3.4	**Unfairness in Daily Life**

It is not always easy to distribute benefits and burdens equally. For example, a drug company announces a new medicine that slows the course of multiple sclerosis, but the company is unable to produce enough of the new medicine to treat everyone who wants it (Lewin, 1994). The ethical question is how to select people for treatment. The company's answer is to have people register for a lottery and then to draw names at random as the medicine becomes available. Each person in the lottery has the same likelihood of being chosen—in the same way, for example, that a lottery may be used in wartime to select conscripts for the military. Is this a "just" procedure because everyone has an *equal chance* of being selected for life or death? Suppose people were selected to receive the new medicine not randomly, but on the grounds of who is most likely to benefit from it. Similarly, suppose that conscripts for the military were selected on the basis of who is the biggest and strongest (Broome, 1984). Which approach, in your view, is *more ethical*—a random lottery or selection on the basis of who is more likely to benefit or survive?

Principle IV. Trust

This fourth principle refers to the establishment of a relationship of trust with the participants in the research. It is based on the assumption that subjects are told what they are getting into (i.e., informed consent) and that nothing is done to jeopardize this trust. And yet we asked earlier, "Is it right to withhold information from subjects if I think that a full disclosure will bias their responses?" To deal with this situation, researchers **debrief** the subjects after their participation in the study, and we describe debriefing later in this chapter. Another way to establish trust is to maintain the confidentiality of the subjects' disclosures. **Confidentiality** means that subjects' disclosures are protected against unwarranted access; it is a way of ensuring subjects' privacy and may also be a way of improving the data they provide. That is, confidentiality should lead to more open and honest responses by the research participants (e.g., Esposito, Agard, & Rosnow, 1984).

To maintain confidentiality in your research, you need to set in place procedures for protecting your data. For example, you can devise a coding system in which the names of your subjects are represented by a sequence of numbers that it is impossible for anyone else to identify. In cases in which subjects respond anonymously and are not asked to give any information that would identify them, their privacy is obviously protected. In government-funded biomedical and behavioral research, it is sometimes possible for the researcher to obtain a **certificate of confidentiality,** which is a formal agreement that requires the researcher to keep the data confidential (and thus exempts the data from subpoena). The extent to which such a certificate can actually provide legal protection has not been established in the courts, however, and is complicated by the existence of laws that require the reporting of certain sensitive information.

For example, the Child Abuse and Prevention and Treatment Act of 1974 and its revisions and amendments mandated that each state pass laws to require the reporting of child abuse and neglect. The nature and wording of such statutes was left to the discretion of the states, but the lists of people who are now obligated to report suspected cases in each state has expanded over the years (Liss, 1994). Suppose you are a member of a group of developmental researchers that is studying child abuse. You want to protect the confidentiality of your participants, but your legal responsibility is to report suspected cases of child abuse. Reporting a suspected culprit means violating the trust you established with the participants when you promised to hold their disclosures confidential, and you will also lose valuable research subjects (neither a happy nor an admirable thought). It is also possible that charges of abuse will not be proved, but this possibility does not excuse you from your legal responsibility (Liss, 1994).

Principle V. Fidelity and Scientific Integrity

The goal of the fifth principle is to foster scientific advances that promulgate valid knowledge. In other words, the pursuit of valid knowledge is an ethical objective, which means that ethics and scientific quality (e.g., the quality of the design and data analysis, and of the interpretation and representation of the results) are presumed to be interrelated (Rosenthal, 1994b). Poor-quality research is an ethical problem because it is wasteful of resources and can be misleading (and even potentially damaging) to society. Even something as seemingly innocent as implying a causal relationship where the data do not support it might be viewed as an "ethical issue" and not just a design issue.

Imagine you are serving on an IRB that receives a proposal for a study that, according to the researchers' own statement, "will test whether private schools improve children's intellectual functioning more than public schools do." Children from randomly selected private and public schools will be tested extensively, and the hypothesis will be tested by a comparison of the scores earned by students from private and public schools. The research raises ethical problems because it is clear that the proposed design does not permit reasonable causal inference. It is quite possible that differences in "intellectual functioning" are due to intrinsic differences in the different populations of the two schools. To study the question experimentally, the researchers would have to randomly assign children to private or public schools—an ethical and practical absurdity. However, the ethical problem of the proposed design is not only wasted resources (i.e., money will be wasted, and people's time will be taken from potentially more beneficial educational experiences); the study could also lead to unwarranted and inaccurate conclusions that might be damaging to the society that supports the research. Interestingly, if the researchers set out to learn only whether there are *performance differences* between students in private and public schools, their original design would be perfectly appropriate (Rosenthal, 1994b).

Deception

Another example of the interrelationship between ethics and scientific integrity involves the use of deception. Although its use is considered an ethical problem in behavioral science, deception (e.g., hidden cameras and hidden microphones) is often used by investigative journalists (see also Box 3.5). For example, CBS-TV's news program *60 Minutes* used an elaborate deception to study claims made by polygraph examiners (Saxe, 1991). Supposedly representing a photography magazine owned by CBS, the *60 Minutes* people selected four polygraph examiners randomly from the telephone directory and asked each to identify which of the magazine's employees had stolen more than $500 worth of camera equipment. No one had actually stolen anything, but a different person was "fingered" by the *60 Minutes* staff for each

---

Box 3.5   ## Go Directly to Jail

Deception is also used by defense lawyers who manipulate the truth in court on behalf of their clients, and by police who use sting operations to capture fugitives. In a recent case, the New York City police used an elaborate deception to capture 261 fugitives (M. Cooper, 1997). One of the captured fugitives, who had been arrested for selling marijuana, had skipped his court date and fled to New Mexico. He was sent an official-looking letter informing him there was a check for $6,000 waiting for him to pick up in the Bronx office of the "State of New York Division of Abandoned and Unclaimed Funds." When he showed up, after traveling 2,025 miles by bus, he was handed a check marked "Go Directly to Jail. Do not pass go, do not collect $200." He was then searched, handcuffed, and booked.

polygrapher. The "culprits" were confederates who were paid $50 by the program staff if they could convince the polygrapher of their innocence. A hidden camera filmed the testing situation without the polygraphers' knowing they were being recorded. The film record showed each polygraph examiner *trying* to get the "guilty" person to confess. Dramatically, the *60 Minutes* report showed that the polygraphers did not necessarily "read" the psychophysiological polygraph information to make their diagnoses of deception.

Viewed from the perspective of Principles I and V, the moral conflict in the *60 Minutes* case would be between the respect for persons and their autonomy and a duty to scientific integrity (e.g., Kimmel, 1988; Schuler, 1982; Sieber, 1991, 1992). As one psychologist put it, "The demonstration was very clever, but dishonest: CBS lied to the polygraphers. The four polygraphers unwittingly starred in a television drama viewed by millions . . . yet it is hard to think of a way to do this study without deception" (Saxe, 1991, p. 409). Informing the polygraphers that they were research subjects for a *60 Minutes* exposé would have made the study—and no doubt the results—quite different. And yet, were this study to be submitted for approval to an IRB, it is likely that it would be rejected in this form. Would you say that the deception used was justified by the study's purpose (i.e., to expose fraud), or would you say that the end does not justify the means?

In fact, the use of deception has been a particularly knotty problem in behavioral and social science (A. E. Gross & Fleming, 1982; Kelman, 1968; Menges, 1973; Rubin, 1974; I. Silverman, 1977). Some argue that deception in *any* form is morally wrong, while others argue that there are circumstances in which it may be needed to ensure the integrity of the scientific data. In general, two broad types of deception have been used in behavioral and social research; active and passive. In **active deception** (sometimes described as **deception by commission**), the subjects are actively misled, as when they are given false information about the purpose of the research, or when they unwittingly interact with confederates (e.g., Asch's use of confederates who made ridiculous perceptual judgments), or when they are secretly given a placebo. In **passive deception** (sometimes described as **deception by omission**) certain information is withheld from the subjects, as when they are not informed of the meaning of their responses when they are given a projective test or when they are not told the full details of the study (Arellano-Galdames, 1972). In order to be allowed to use a deception, researchers must have no acceptable alternative, and its proposed use must be approved by an IRB. A famous controversy concerning the use of deception involved Stanley Milgram's (1974) work on obedience.

Milgram's Use of Deception

In contrast to Asch's studies (although stimulated in part by them), **Milgram's experiments** sparked ethical debate both inside and outside behavioral and social science from the moment they were reported. He did not make the decision to perform these experiments lightly; he had important societal and scientific questions in mind. His interest in this research stemmed from his profound dismay about the horrifying effects of blind obedience to Nazi commands in World War II. During that nightmarish period, the unthinkable became a reality when millions of innocent men, women, and children were systematically slaughtered in gas chambers. Milgram's purpose in performing his experiments was to study the psychological mechanism that links blind obedience to destructive behavior. In particular, he wanted to determine how far *ordinary adults* will go in carrying out the orders of a legitimate authority to act against a third person.

Milgram tricked volunteer subjects, placed in the role of the "teacher," into believing that they would be giving varying degrees of painful electric shock to a third person (the "learner") each time the learner made a mistake in a certain task. Milgram also varied the distance between the teacher and the learner, to see whether the teacher would be less ruthless in administering the electric shocks as he or she got closer and the learner pressed the teacher to quit. The results were, to Milgram as well as to others, almost beyond belief. A great many subjects (the "teachers") unhesitatingly obeyed the experimenter's "Please continue" or "You have no choice, you must go on" and continued to increase the level of the shocks no matter how much the learner pleaded with the "teacher" to stop. What particularly surprised Milgram was that no one ever walked out of the laboratory in disgust or protest. This remarkable obedience was seen time and time again in several universities where the experiment was repeated. "It is the extreme willingness of adults to go to almost any lengths on the command of an authority that constitutes the chief finding of the study and the fact most urgently demanding explanation," Milgram wrote (1974, p. 5).

Although the "learner" in these studies was a confederate of Milgram's and no actual shocks were transmitted by the "teacher," concerns about ethics and values arose and have dogged these studies ever since they were first reported. Diane Baumrind (1964), a prominent developmental psychologist, quoted descriptions by Milgram of the reactions of some of his participants—such as "a twitching, stuttering wreck, who was rapidly approaching a point of nervous collapse" (Milgram, 1963, p. 377)—and argued that once he had seen how stressful his deception was, Milgram should have terminated the experiments. She insisted that there was "no rational basis" for ever using this kind of manipulation, unless perhaps the participants were made fully aware of the psychological dangers to themselves and unless effective steps were taken to ensure the restoration of their well-being afterward.

Milgram responded that the chief horror was not that a stressful deception was carried out, but that the subjects obeyed. The signs of extreme tension that appeared in some subjects were quite unexpected, but his intention had not been simply to create anxiety, he stated. Indeed, before carrying out the research, he had asked professional colleagues about their expectations, and none of the experts had anticipated the blind obedience that resulted. Like those experts, he had thought the subjects would refuse to follow orders. Moreover, he was skeptical about whether there had been any injurious effects on the subjects, in spite of the dramatic appearance of anxiety in some of them. To ensure that the subjects would not feel worse after the experiment than before, he had taken elaborate precautions to debrief them. They were given an opportunity for a friendly reconciliation with the "learner" after the experiment and were shown that the "learner" had not received dangerous electric shocks but had only pretended to receive them.

To discover any long-range negative effects, Milgram also sent questionnaires to the subjects to elicit their reactions after they had read a full report of his investigation.

Less than 1% of those who received this questionnaire said they regretted having participated; 15% were neutral or ambivalent, and over 80% said they were glad to have participated. Milgram regarded the results as providing a moral justification for his research:

> The central moral justification for allowing my experiment is that it was judged acceptable by those who took part in it. Criticism of the experiment that does not take account of the tolerant reaction of the participants has always seemed to me hollow. This applies particularly to criticism centering on the use of false illusion (or "deception," as the critics prefer to say) that fails to relate this detail to the central fact that subjects find the device acceptable. The participants, rather than the external critics, must be the ultimate source of judgment in these matters. (Milgram, 1977, p. 93)

Is Deception Ever Justified?

In arguing that research participants, not the experimenter, are the ultimate arbiters of whether a particular deception is morally acceptable, Milgram was speaking before the advent of IRBs. In fact, *when* Milgram did his work, it was well within the norms of deception then in use. It might now be impossible to get this classic design approved by a review committee. But suppose the study has never been done, and it is you who wants to do it. The IRB rejects your proposal and responds that the use of deception in any form is unacceptable. "Be open and honest with your subjects, and have them sign an informed consent agreement that indicates they fully understand what the research is about," the IRB admonishes you. Is getting rid of the deception a reasonable requirement in this case, or could it present you with a further ethical dilemma?

Before you answer, imagine an experiment like Milgram's in which the experimenter greeted the subjects by saying something like the following:

> Hello. Today we are going to do a study on blind obedience to a malevolent authority, particularly emphasizing the effects of physical distance from the victim on willingness to inflict pain on her or him. You will be in the "close" condition, which means that you are expected to be somewhat less ruthless in your behavior. In addition, you will be asked to fill out a test of your fascist tendencies because we believe there is a positive relation between scores on our fascism test and blind obedience to an authority who requests that we hurt others. Any questions?

A completely open and honest statement to a research subject of the intention of the experiment might involve a briefing of this kind, but would it result in fewer problems? Clearly, such a briefing would be absurd if you were serious in your wish to learn about blind obedience to authority. If subjects had full information about your experimental purpose, plans, procedures, and hypotheses, it seems unlikely they would behave as Milgram's subjects did. They might instead base their behavior on what they *think* the world is like or what they believe *you* think the world is like. In other words, it is hard to imagine how this experiment could be performed without deception.

This is not to say that any scientists would advocate the use of deception merely for its own sake. At the same time, however, there may be few researchers who feel that they can do entirely without certain minimal-risk deceptions. Certainly no behavioral or social scientist would seriously advocate giving up the study of prejudice or discrimination. However, if all measures of prejudice and discrimination had to be openly labeled, it would hardly be worth the effort of continuing this research. Furthermore, if the research *were* continued, the results would be misleading—and would thus also present an ethical dilemma. The point is that adopting a rigid moral orientation that decries deception as wrong would mean banishing *all forms* of deception or producing misleading results in some cases. Surely, most people—scientists included—would be willing to weigh and measure "sins" of commission and omission resulting from the use of deception, and to judge some to be larger than others.

For example, refraining from telling a subject that an "experiment in the learning of verbal materials is designed to show whether earlier, later, or intermediate material is better remembered" does not seem a particularly troublesome deception. The reason most of us would probably not view this deception with alarm seems, on first glance, that it involves an omission (a passive deception) rather than a commission (an active deception). A truth is left unspoken; a lie is not told. But what if the same experiment were presented as a "study of the effects of the meaningfulness of verbal material on retention or recall"? That is a direct lie, designed to misdirect the subject's attention from a crucial aspect of the experimental treatment to another factor that really does not interest the scientist. Even this change, however, does not seem to make the deception awful, although the "sin" is now one of commission and the scientist has not withheld information from, but actively lied to, the subject.

In other words, it does not seem that the active or passive style of a deception is its measure. Instead, its probable effect on the subject is what is significant. Very few people would care whether subjects focused on a noncrucial aspect of verbal material rather than on a crucial aspect of the experimental treatment, because this deception seems to have no consequence (positive or negative). It is not simply deception so much as it is potentially *harmful* deception that we would like to minimize. But how shall we decide what is potentially harmful? Does it come down to personal opinion, and if so, whose opinions should prevail?

On the one hand, can we agree that most researchers (and the subjects themselves) would concur that it is not very harmful to tell subjects that a test they are taking anonymously as part of a research project is one of "personal reactions" (which it is) rather than a test of their need for social approval, schizophrenic tendencies, or authoritarianism (which it may also be)? On the other hand, can we also agree that most researchers (and the subjects themselves) would concur that it may be harmful to falsely tell college-age students that a test shows them to be "abnormal" even if they are later told that they have been misled? In other words, individual investigators, their colleagues, IRBs, and, to some extent, ultimately, the general community that supports the research—all must decide whether a particular potentially harmful deception is worth a possible increase in knowledge.

Debriefing Participants

We mentioned previously that Milgram's subjects were given the opportunity to have a friendly reconciliation with the "learner." They were also given an opportunity to engage in an extended discussion with the experimenter about the purpose of the study (i.e., a **debriefing**), and about why it was necessary to use deception (see also Box 3.6). The debriefing session gives researchers an opportunity to remove any misconceptions and anxieties the participants may have, so that their sense of dignity remains intact and they feel that their time has not been wasted (Blanck, Bellack, Rosnow, Rotheram-Borus, & Schooler, 1992; Harris, 1988). If deception has been used, it is also important to remove any "detrimental impact on the participant's feeling of trust in interpersonal relationships" (APA, 1973, p. 77).

Box 3.6 **Debriefing**

The word *debrief* was first used by the British military in World War II to describe the procedure used by Royal Air Force (RAF) interrogators of pilots who had returned from bombing missions. Before the mission, the pilot was "briefed," and after the mission, "debriefed." You can see that the term *debriefing*, when it refers to informing research subjects of the nature and purpose of the deception used in a study is a misnomer; such a session should be called a *briefing session*. However, when researchers use this opportunity to interrogate the subjects about their perceptions, the term *debriefing session* is more appropriate (Harris, 1988).

Previously, we mentioned cases in which obtaining informed consent was either impossible or counterproductive; there are situations in which debriefing may also be impossible or inadvisable. In the next chapter, we describe the unobtrusive observation of anonymous public behavior, a method that requires IRB approval but does not require debriefing. A full debriefing may be inadvisable as well if it could produce stress or be ineffective, for example, when the participants are children, are mentally ill, or are retarded (Blanck et al., 1992). In many instances, however, debriefing is not only ethically essential but can also become beneficial to researchers by providing an opportunity to explore what transpired beneath the surface in the study. Careful interviewing may reveal what each participant thought about the study, thereby providing the researcher with an experiential context within which to interpret the results, and with possible leads for further investigation (Blanck et al., 1992; E. E. Jones & Gerard, 1967).

Milgram's debriefings were unusually extensive—far more so, in fact, than is characteristic in most experiments, or than is felt to be necessary in most studies. But as a result of his having duped the participants into believing that they were administering painful electric shocks to another person, Milgram felt it was necessary to go to elaborate lengths to remove any possible stresses and anxieties. Subjects who had obeyed the experimenter when he told them to keep giving the electric shocks were assured that their behavior was normal and that the conflict or tension they had experienced had been felt by other participants. All subjects were told that they would receive a comprehensive written report at the conclusion of the research; this report detailed the experimental procedures and findings, treating the subjects' own part in the research with dignity. All subjects also received a questionnaire that asked them once again to express their thoughts and feelings about their behavior. A year later, a psychiatrist intensively interviewed 40 of the experimental subjects, to identify any possible injurious effects resulting from the experiment.

Most studies do not require debriefing covering so wide an area or so great a span of time as Milgram's, but the debriefing procedure used should be sufficiently focused to satisfy the subjects about having participated in the study. The following guidelines (Aronson & Carlsmith, 1968; Sieber, 1982a, 1983) may be incorporated into more typical debriefings:

First, if your study involved some form of deception, you should give whatever explanation is needed to reveal the truth about the research and your careful consideration of the use of the deception. You might explain, for example, that science is the search for truth and that it is sometimes necessary to resort to deception to uncover truth. Recall, however, that debriefing may not be advisable in all cases of deception. For example, it was unnecessary to debrief subjects (diners) in the social psychologists' tipping study mentioned previously (Rind & Bordia, 1996).

Second, despite your sincere wish to treat your participants responsibly, some subjects may leave the experiment feeling gullible, as if they have been "had" by a fraudulent procedure. Whatever the deception used, you should clearly explain it to your subjects and at the same time assure them that being taken in does not reflect in any way on their intelligence or character but simply shows the scientific effectiveness or validity of the study's design. You presumably went to some pains to achieve an effective design in order not to waste the subjects' time and effort in your search for truth.

Third, you should proceed gradually and patiently, with the chief aim of "gently unfolding" the details of any deceptions used. A patient discussion will go far to reduce the subjects' negative feelings. Instead of thinking of themselves as "victims," they may more correctly realize that they are "coinvestigators" in the search for truth. If you ask each person what he or she thought of the research situation, you may uncover valuable scientific and theoretical information.

Fourth, never use **double deception,** that is, a second deception in what the research subject thinks is the official debriefing. Double deception can be terribly damaging: Instead of restoring your subjects to the frame of mind in which they entered the study, you are leaving them with a lie.

Also, if any subject wishes to withdraw from the study, you must treat this request with dignity because to do otherwise would be a violation of Principle I.

The Use of Animals in Research

Although the primary focus of this book is on research with human subjects, we did mention in Chapter 2 the Pavlovian conditioning of a dog, Thorndike's studies of cats in puzzle boxes, and the use of rat subjects by the Tolmanians and Hullians. Given the biological continuities between animals and human beings, animals are used as research subjects in about 8% of psychological research (Kimmel, 1996). Arguments for and against the use of animals in experiments have been vigorously debated in recent years (Slife & Rubinstein, 1992) because the very assumption of biological continuity raises ethical dilemmas. That is, it should follow that animals, like humans, must experience some measure of pain and suffering. As a consequence of concerns about the treatment of animals, a great many federal laws and licensing requirements now spell out the responsibilities of researchers and animal facilities to protect the well-being of experimental animals, consistent with advancements made possible by research.

For example, the Animal Welfare Act sets specific standards for the use of animals in research, such as their handling, housing, feeding, and use in studying drugs. Research institutions are also subject to unannounced inspections by the U.S. Department of Agriculture at any time, and if violations are uncovered, the institution's license to run animal facilities may be revoked. Beyond these federal regulations, animal researchers are subject to institutional and professional requirements. Institutions with animal care facilities make a point of underscoring the experimenter's responsibilities, and any proposed animal research also routinely undergoes ethical review. In addition, the APA and other professional and scientific organizations around the world have expanded on the ethical obligations of investigators of animal behavior. For example, the APA insists that researchers make every effort to minimize discomfort, illness, and pain in their experimental animals. Any procedure that subjects animals to pain, stress, or privation may be used only when no alternative procedure is available and the goal of the research is justified by its prospective scientific, educational, or applied value.

Nevertheless the confrontation between those who argue for and those who argue against experiments using animals is often quite heated. One point of disagreement concerns whether the interests of human beings supersede the interests of animals. At one extreme, many animal rights activists argue that animals and humans have equal rights and that benefits to humans are not a justification for animal experimentation. On the other side, it has been argued that animals themselves have often benefited from the research, such as from discoveries in veterinary medicine (e.g., vaccines for deadly diseases) and experimental insights that have helped to preserve some species from extinction (e.g., the wild condor). Scientists point out that the use of animals in a variety of behavioral and biomedical studies has directly benefited humans in a great many ways. Research by behavioral scientists has led to advances in the rehabilitation of persons suffering from spinal cord injuries, in the treatment of disease and eating disorders, in communication with the severely retarded, and in the understanding of alcoholism.

For example, studies by experimental psychologist Michael J. Lewis using rat subjects have produced new theoretical insights into the neurobiological mechanisms of alcoholism and the way that alcohol intake is controlled by processes similar to those that maintain nutritional balance (e.g., Lewis, 1996). Another example of benefits to humans from animal experimentation in behavioral science involved Roger Sperry, who won a Nobel Prize for his work. His experiments with cats and monkeys revealed that severing the fibers connecting the right and left hemispheres of the brain (resulting in a so-called split brain) did not impair a variety of functions, including learning and memory. This important discovery led to a treatment for severe epilepsy and made it possible for people who would have been confined to hospitals to lead a normal life instead (Gazzaniga & LeDoux, 1978; Sperry, 1968).

Animal rights activists argue that enterprising researchers would be forced to think of alternative methods if they were actually *banned* from using animals (see also Box 3.7). In fact, such advances have been made without invoking a ban. It has been possible, for example, to use anthropomorphic "dummies" (e.g., in car crash tests), to simulate tissue and bodily fluids in research situations, to use computer models of human beings, to use lower-order species (e.g., fruit flies in experiments on genetics), and to study animals in their natural habitats (e.g., Dian Fossey's studies of gorillas; Fossey, 1981, 1983) or else in zoos, rather than to breed animals for laboratory research. In a fascinating set of studies, comparative psychologists were able to generate new theoretical insights into the functions of yawning behavior simply by comparing Siamese fighting fish in the lab, lions and baboons in the zoo, and students who kept daily logs of yawning behavior (Baenninger, 1987; Baenninger, Binkley, & Baenninger, 1996; Greco, Baenninger, & Govern, 1993).

Box 3.7   **Another Three Rs**

Some years ago, the British zoologist William M. S. Russell and microbiologist Rex L. Burch made the argument that, given scientists' own interest in the humane treatment of the animals used in research, it would be prudent to search for ways to (1) *reduce* the number of animals used in research, (2) *refine* the experiments so that there was less suffering, and (3) *replace* animals with other procedures whenever possible. Called the **"three Rs principle"** by Russell and Burch (1959), it defines the modern search by researchers who use animal subjects. If you would like to learn more about such alternatives, and about the main arguments pro and con in this debate, see the February 1997 issue of *Scientific American*.

In sum, just as the scientific community recognizes both an ethical and a scientific responsibility for the general welfare of human subjects, it also assumes responsibility for the humane care and treatment of animals used in research. There are laws and ethical guidelines to protect animals in research, and it is also clear that humans and animals have benefited by discoveries made in experiments with animals. Thus, even though there is a heated debate about the use of animals in scientific research, it is clear that society has benefited in terms of biomedical and behavioral advances and that the ethical consciousness of science and society has been raised with regard to the conduct of this research.

Ethical Issues Throughout the Research Process

In this chapter, we have concentrated on the data collection phase of the research process, but ethical guidelines also have implications for all aspects of the research process. As we have tried to show, many of these guidelines, although directed specifically at professional researchers, have implications for students who are conducting research to satisfy a requirement in a methods course. Some ethical rules have implications for the final phase of the process, in which you will be writing up your results (Rosnow & Rosnow, 1998).

First, professional researchers are responsible for making available the data on which their conclusions are based. The implication for students writing research reports is that they are expected to produce all of their raw data as required by the instructor. Second, it is considered unethical to misrepresent original research by publishing it in more than one journal and implying that each report represents a different study. The implication for students is that it is unethical to submit the same work for additional credit in different courses. Third, authors of published articles are expected to give credit where it is due. The implication for the student is that if someone gave you an idea, you should credit that person in a footnote.

Incidentally, if you are still looking for a researchable idea, you might think about doing empirical research on research ethics. There are many questions that could advance our understanding of both research ethics and theoretical issues, and you will find a list of such questions in an article by Stanley, Sieber, and Melton (1987). For example, it would be ethically and theoretically useful to know what techniques increase the comprehension of consent forms. It would also be valuable to know more about the role of confidentiality in fostering open and honest responding. The challenge of questions such as these is to expand our knowledge and improve the ethical nature of our research, so that science and society can both benefit (Rosnow, 1997).

Summary of Ideas

1. Ethical guidelines help us evaluate the moral "rights" and "wrongs" of particular strategies of doing and reporting research.

2. In general, researchers are obliged *not to do* physical or psychological harm to research participants and *to do* research in a way that is most likely to produce valid results of benefit to society.

3. Principle I discussed here (Respect for Persons and Their Autonomy) tells us to respect the freedom of individuals to participate in the study and to be told what they are getting into (i.e., use of the informed-consent agreement).

4. Principle II (beneficence and nonmaleficence) instructs us to maximize the benefits and minimize the risks of the research we do.

5. The review process serves as a control mechanism, and in a proposal for review, the questions to be answered concern many aspects of the research (e.g., the way in which the participants will be recruited, the procedures to be used, confidentiality, and the risks to the subjects).

6. The insufficiency of the idealized decision-plane model used to weigh the costs and benefits of doing research is that it ignores the moral costs of not conducting (or of being prevented from conducting) some potentially valuable studies.

7. Principle III (justice) urges that the benefits and burdens of research be distributed as fairly as possible, although (as is true in life itself) full justice can seldom be achieved.

8. Principle IV (trust) tells researchers not to do anything that will jeopardize their trusting relationship with their subjects and to protect the subjects' disclosures against unwarranted access (i.e., to maintain confidentiality).

9. Principle V (fidelity and scientific integrity) defines the promulgation of valid knowledge as an ethical pursuit.

10. It appears that Milgram had no alternative but to use deception, if the research were to be done at all, because being open and honest with the participants would probably have jeopardized the validity of his results.

11. The measure of the acceptability of deception seems to be its potential to harm participants rather than whether the deception is active or passive.

12. Debriefing subjects after the data have been collected is the final step in the data collection process and is considered essential when there has been a deception or when there is likely to be any residual anxiety.

13. Just as the scientific community has an ethical and scientific responsibility for the general welfare of human subjects, it also assumes responsibility for the humane care and treatment of animals used in research.

14. Ethical guidelines pertain to all aspects of a research project, including writing and submitting the final report.

Key Terms

active deception   p. 68
autonomy   p. 59
Belmont Report   p. 58
beneficence   p. 61
certificate of confidentiality   p. 66
confidentiality   p. 66
cost-benefit analysis   p. 62
debriefing   p. 72
deception by commission   p. 68
deception by omission   p. 68
decision-plane model   p. 62
double deception   p. 73
ethical guidelines   p. 58

ethics   p. 57
expedited review   p. 61
fair-mindedness   p. 64
informed consent   p. 59
institutional review board (IRB)   p. 61
Milgram experiments   p. 68
minimal risk   p. 61
nonmaleficence   p. 61
passive deception   p. 68
placebo   p. 64
Rushton study   p. 64
three Rs of humane animal
   experimentation   p. 75

Multiple-Choice Questions for Review (answers are found on page 345)

1. Which of the following methodological procedures can cause moral conflicts to arise? (a) invasion of privacy; (b) deception; (c) withholding information from research subjects; (d) all of the above

2. Deliberately withholding information from subjects is called _____ ; deliberately misinforming subjects is called _____ . (a) active deception; passive deception; (b) active deception; double deception; (c) double deception; passive deception; (d) passive deception; active deception

3. In the Milgram experiments, which of the following actually received electrical shocks? (a) the "teacher"; (b) the "learner"; (c) both a and b; (d) neither a nor b

4. Ethical questions were raised about the Milgram experiments because (a) the subjects were deceived; (b) some subjects received severe shocks; (c) some subjects were physically injured; (d) all of the above.

5. The Rushton study, conducted in a mining company, raised the ethical issue of (a) deception; (b) fair-mindedness; (c) invasion of privacy; (d) all of the above.

6. The subjects who objected to the Rushton study were (a) in the control group; (b) in the experimental group; (c) in both the experimental and control groups; (d) subjected to severe shocks.

7. According to the decision-plane diagram in the text, if the costs of doing a research project are equal to the benefits of doing the research, the study is said to fall on (a) the diagonal of ambivalence; (b) the diagonal of equality; (c) the diagonal of indecision; (d) none of the above.

8. Research at virtually all colleges and universities has to be approved by (a) the president of the institution; (b) the U.S. government; (c) professors in the psychology department; (d) an IRB.

9. The procedure of disclosing the full purpose of a study after subjects have participated is called (a) debriefing; (b) peer review; (c) the Milgram procedure; (d) double deception.

10. Which of the following help ensure that animals used as subjects in research are treated ethically? (a) federal laws; (b) professional codes of ethics; (c) institutional (e.g., university) policies; (d) all of the above

Discussion Questions for Review (answers are found on page 345)

1. A study proposal is submitted to the Tufts University Human Subjects Committee for review. The researchers plan to administer a two-hour-long questionnaire to people hanging out on the street in the red light district. The questionnaire contains questions on these people's lifestyles and attitudes toward criminal behavior. What are some potential costs to the subjects for their participation in the study?

2. A University of Richmond student is interested in studying helping behavior. She designs an experiment to take place in a corner drugstore. Enlisting the aid of the owner, the student has confederates, varying in age and manner of dress, commit a robbery at the store. Another confederate, posing as a customer, observes the real customers, noting who helps, what they do, how long it takes, and so on. What are some ethical problems in this research? What costs and benefits would you consider in deciding whether this project should be done?

3. A UCLA student wants to run a study in which he will deceive subjects into believing that they have done poorly on a test of their sensitivity to others. At the end of the experimental session, he plans to pay the subjects, thank them for participating, and tell them they can call him later if they have questions about the study. How does the student's plan fail in his ethical responsibilities to the subjects? What should he do?

4. A review panel tells a student at SMU that, in their view, his proposed study falls on the "diagonal of indecision." What do they mean, and what are the implications for the student?

5. An Arlington student proposes to replicate Asch's experiment with Texas students. His IRB requires an informed-consent agreement from his subjects. What does this mean, and what are the implications for the student?

6. A Whittier College student is interested in conducting a study of the effects of various financial incentive programs in a large organization. Because her research involves no deception or invasion of privacy, she tells her adviser that no ethical issues are raised by her research. The adviser's reply is "Remember the Rushton study!" What does she mean?

4 Systematic Observational Methods

PREVIEW QUESTIONS

▌ How does systematic observation in behavioral and social science differ from everyday observation?

▌ What is the purpose of methodological triangulation?

▌ What is naturalistic observation?

▌ How do social scientists simultaneously participate and observe?

▌ What is ethnomethodology, and what substantive questions can organize its "sense-making" objective?

▌ How is content analysis used to impose structure on archival data?

▌ What is the role of laboratory experimentation in behavioral and social science?

▌ What is meant by *rival hypotheses?*

▌ How do behavioral and social scientists do experiments in naturalistic settings?

▌ What is the distinction between reactive and nonreactive observation?

▌ What is meant by *unobtrusive observation,* and how do researchers go about it?

▌ How are judges or raters used to code behavior, and how are they chosen?

The Researcher as Observer

For scientists everywhere, the world is a cornucopia filled with fascinating questions waiting to be addressed by systematic observational methods. The term **systematic observation** simply means that what the scientist observes or records is guided by or influenced by preexisting questions or hypotheses (as contrasted with the more casual and haphazard nature of most of our everyday observations). In Chapter 2, we discussed some of the strategies of "discovery" used by scientists to generate their research questions or hypotheses. We also mentioned the term **justification,** which refers to the process in which scientists test, confirm, and defend their scientific explanations, interpretations, and conclusions. We noted that successful justification in science calls for resourcefulness and access to multiple research methods, and in this chapter, we will examine some observational methods used by scientists to address research questions from the perspective of a "let's try it and see" attitude (see Box 4.1).

We also mentioned that the reason for multiple methods is that all are limited in some ways, and that therefore the use of only

| Box 4.1 | Does Anything Go? |

Paul Feyerabend (1988), a philosopher of science, described how the scientific method often depends on researchers' bending or breaking rules and doing whatever works. As Feyerabend put it, "Not every discovery can be accounted for in the same manner, and procedures that paid off in the past may create havoc when imposed on the future. Successful research . . . relies now on one trick, now on another" (p. 1). Feyerabend's description has been called the **anything-goes view of science,** but it does not mean that there are no reliable criteria for evaluating good science and weeding out bad science or pseudo-science. All it means is that doing research *does* involve a "let's try it and see" attitude. The scientist experiments with one procedure and then another before deciding that a theoretical prediction is correct or should be junked. The challenge is to find (or create) and properly implement procedures that address the theoretical question or hypothesis of interest.

a single method will confine our observations. However, by using multiple methods (called *methodological pluralism* in Chapter 1), each of which restricts us in some different way, we attempt to obtain a more coherent view of the pattern of interest. The approach of zeroing in on a pattern by using multiple but imperfect perspectives is referred to as **methodological triangulation** in behavioral science (Campbell & Fiske, 1959). A convergence, or triangulation, of the findings of methodologically varying studies lends credence to the theory pattern (e.g., Crano, 1981). In this chapter, we will sample a range of qualitative and quantitative observational methods used in behavioral and social science. In general, **qualitative methods** are those in which the observed data exist in a nonnumerical form, such as reports of conversations in participant-observer research and ethnographic research. **Quantitative methods** are those in which the observed data exist in a numerical form, such as observers' or judges' ratings.

Within each of these two broad categories of observational (and also *self-report methods,* discussed in the next chapter) lie many possible strategies and applications. For example, in recent years, we have seen a burgeoning literature on qualitative methodology in fields such as organizational management, social psychology, anthropology, social work, aging, and family studies (e.g., H. R. Bernard, 1994; Crabtree & Miller, 1992; Denzin & Lincoln, 1994; Gilgun, Daly, & Handel, 1992; Gubrium & Sankar, 1993; Morse, 1993; Riessman, 1993; D. Silverman, 1993). We will first briefly define the use of naturalistic observation and then turn to more detailed examples in participant-observer research and ethnographic research. We will give a flavor of the advantages and the limitations of both approaches and a flavor of the procedures used. In many cases, it is possible—and even advisable—to use qualitative *and* quantitative perspectives to enrich our understanding of the problem studied. We will also describe the nature of nonreactive research and several categories of unobtrusive observation (i.e., situations in which people are unaware of being observed or studied), and finally we will list alternative ways to choose judges or raters to code behavior.

Naturalistic Observation

Observation of behavior in its natural state is known as **naturalistic observation.** In fact, a number of specific approaches fall within this category, including participant-observer research and ethnographic research in social science and the naturalistic methods used by students of animal behavior. These scientists go by different names. For example, social scientists who use naturalistic observation to study human behavior include sociologists, social psychologists, and anthropologists, while behavioral scientists who use naturalistic observation to study animal behavior include ethologists (who are interested in the biological study of behavior) and comparative psychologists. There is a considerable amount of overlap in the methods used within each scientific arena, and it is sometimes hard to distinguish one type of scientist from another. Nonetheless, there are disputes between and within fields, often because of the specialized orientations of these researchers and where they choose to collect their observational data. For example, one researcher made the generalization that, when performing ethnographic research, "anthropologists go elsewhere to practice their trade while sociologists stay at home" (Van Maanen, 1988, p. 21).

Illustrative of the comparative psychological approach is the work of Ronald Baenninger and his coworkers, who, in one study, systematically observed and recorded the actions of a troop of baboons when it encountered a cheetah drinking from an East African river (Baenninger, Estes, & Baldwin, 1977). Animal behaviorists had claimed that adult male baboons actively defend their troops against predators, but there were few accepted records of this behavior at the time of the study by Baenninger and his associates. Naturalistic observations made by these researchers dispelled any doubts about the reality of the baboons' defensive behavior. As the researchers watched, they recorded that two male members of the baboon troop continued to harass the cheetah until they had successfully chased it far away from the main body of the troop.

Before we turn to the use of naturalistic observation in social science research, it is useful to understand the advantages of this approach, which is also used in many specialized areas. Karl E. Weick (1968), an organizational psychologist, listed a number of useful characteristics of naturalistic observation in both basic and applied settings. First, it enables us to watch events in their "wholeness" (see Box 4.2), thereby giving us a sense of the relevant variables during the preliminary stage of an investigation. Second, it allows us to watch fleeting events that may not be easily or realistically captured or simulated in the experimental laboratory. Third, it permits us to record events *as* they occur, so that we need not rely only on public records of past events made by nonscientists, or on people's memories. Fourth, it allows us to explore the generalizability of laboratory findings in order to see whether changing the context changes the phenomenon. Fifth, it allows us to observe events that may be too risky or dangerous to create in the laboratory.

Box 4.2   ## The Look

An analogy by the philosopher Jean-Paul Sartre (1956) underscores the idea that we need to use different vantage points to watch events in their "wholeness." Sartre reminds us that, when we observe someone who is looking back at us, it is hard for us to apprehend the "watcher" behind the "look" at the same time that we focus on the person's appearance. The more we stare at the appearance, the less likely we are to perceive the personality behind it. The personality is neutralized—put out of play—by a human consciousness requiring that certain elements be disconnected. To glimpse the whole person, we shift our concentration back and forth, attending first to the appearance and then to the personality. In a similar way, behavioral and social scientists can shift their perspective back and forth by using multiple methods, each of which is limited in some ways, but which together allow us to catch a glimpse of the whole.

Participant-Observer Research

Two popular uses of naturalistic observation in social science are participant-observer research and ethnographic research, and we will now describe each of these in turn. First, the term **participant-observer research** is actually somewhat ambiguous in its current usage in social science; it is sometimes used interchangeably with *fieldwork* and *field observation,* although both are also characteristic of other forms of naturalistic observation, including ethnography (Judd, Smith, & Kidder, 1991; Spradley, 1970, 1980). Sometimes it is hard to distinguish participant-observer research from the reporting methods used by investigative journalists, but one difference is that the social scientist is usually not under the extreme time pressure of the news reporter. Because there is no instant deadline to meet, the social scientist can patiently and methodically plumb aspects of the situation to his or her heart's content. A second difference is that, whereas the investigative reporter's agenda may be to prove a point or to make a story, the social scientist allows nature (in this case, human nature) to tell its own tale. That is, the social scientist does not approach the task with a fixed set of conclusions based on a story idea or agenda but allows the observed events to shape the conclusions that he or she reaches.

The methodology of participant-observer research is currently in a state of flux, whereas other naturalistic approaches (e.g., ethnographic research and field experimentation) use a relatively standardized methodology. For example, in the case of animal research in the field (such as Baenninger's study), prescribed naturalistic methods of collecting and handling data have evolved over many years (e.g., Martin & Bateson, 1993). Because of the nonstandardized nature of participant-observer research, it is especially susceptible to criticisms of **interpreter biases.** That is, the researcher's interpretation of the observational records may be unwittingly biased or slanted (Rosenthal, 1976; Rosnow & Rosenthal, 1997). In a similar vein, sample sizes have in the past been reported in a rather casual way in many participant-observer studies, possibly because the sampling was **opportunistic** (i.e., no special sampling procedure was used and only convenience was the criterion in choosing a sample) and quantitative methods were not used. This vagueness in methodology may be changing, however, as users of participant observation begin to pool their ideas about what should be a set of acceptable practices (e.g., D. Silverman, 1993; Spradley, 1980).

Basically, social scientists who use this approach watch and record what people do and say. What the researcher looks for is material that is sufficiently rich in content to reveal consistent themes. The researcher may use a tape recorder or make field notes largely from memory (Judd et al., 1991, p. 320). As in all methods of systematic observation, the researcher is usually guided by specific research questions or hypotheses, so that the observation is not haphazard but theoretically selective. Whereas in laboratory research the experimenter makes a concerted effort *not* to intercede in the lives of the people he or she studies (except, of course, for the intercessions that define the independent variables), the opposite is true in participant-observer research. As the name implies, the participant observer interjects himself or herself into an actual social situation in an effort to draw out and document people's reactions.

An interesting example of participant-observer research is a study by Louise H. Kidder (1972), a social psychologist who has helped focus attention on this method in her field (see Judd et al., 1991). In this study, she investigated the steps that a group of clinical psychologists went through at a three-day hypnosis workshop, during which they gradually learned to become hypnotized. Using a tape recorder and written notes to make a permanent record of her observations, Kidder kept verbatim accounts of the interactions between the experienced hypnotists and the psychologists. What she selectively recorded was guided by two research questions: (1) How do skeptics become convinced that they have been hypnotized? And (2) does becoming convinced reflect a change in the subject's definition of hypnosis, a change in the subject's definition of his or her own experience, or both? Kidder's interest in these questions was reinforced by the vagueness and ambiguity she perceived in the reactions of most participants coming out of hypnosis for the first time: "How do I know if I was hypnotized?" or "I still don't consider it an experience any different from others" (p. 317).

At one point, for example, Kidder observed and recorded the interaction between a "guest subject" (who had been brought into the workshop to be hypnotized by one of the experts) and several of the other participants, who were given an opportunity to interview the guest subject:

QUESTION: How did it feel?
ANSWER: Just very good. Very, very relaxed.
QUESTION: Have you felt anything like this before?
ANSWER: Yeah, well it's sort of like smoking grass. The first few times I used it I just fell asleep.
QUESTION: I want to ask what other experiences it was like.
ANSWER: It's like being very tired. Or like sitting in an airport and feeling tired and hearing other people around you talking—sort of hazy. (p. 321)

Kidder reported that the experts gave a great deal of feedback to the participants, seemingly manipulating the participants' attitudes, just as they might be shaped in a conditioning study. Her interpretation was that, by the last session, most of the participants had learned how to *behave* like good hypnotic subjects and had come to accept the experts' definitions of hypnosis and new definitions of their own feelings. She inferred that becoming hypnotized is similar to a social interaction and that those persons who are most hypnotizable proceed through the learning cycle more rapidly than others. In effect, Kidder's interpretation was that they learn to notice new sensations and to *feel* that maybe they have been hypnotized, whereas some people never go beyond the "I-don't-think-I was hypnotized state" (p. 322). While not a substitute for a more tightly controlled study, Kidder's conversational records flesh out her explanation of how people learn to become hypnotized.

Ethnographic Research

Ethnographic research, which is usually focused on a culture, can be seen as a more standardized variant of participant-observer research. Traditionally the objective of ethnographic research is to document the customs, habits, and actions of a group of people in its own cultural setting. Ethnographers do interviewing as well as make field notes of behavior and conversations in their effort to explore how people in a cultural setting "make sense" of things—also called **sense making.** In particular, the ethnographer is concerned with how people invoke or impose meaning on a situation (see also Box 4.3). To address this question, the ethnographer has to balance two orientations: first, the significant characteristics of the situation (gleaned from first impressions) and, second, the concerns and perspectives of those present in the setting (Emerson, Fretz, & Shaw, 1995). Although used primarily by sociologists and anthropologists to study cultures, ethnographic methods (also called **ethnomethodology**) have been borrowed by researchers in other fields. For example, one organizational researcher made an ethnographic study of how people assigned blame in a public inquiry concerning a fatal pipeline accident (Gephart, 1993).

Box 4.3   **Sense Making and the Social Constructionist View**

The search for meaning in ambiguous circumstances, particularly when the situation is stressful or threatening in some way, has long been of interest to psychologists working in different areas (e.g., Park & Folkman, 1997; Rosnow, 1980, 1991; Weick, 1995). An extreme variation on the sense-making thesis is that *no* social situations have intrinsic meaning, but that all have meaning imposed on them. This thesis was called **social constructionism** by Kenneth J. Gergen (1985), a noted social psychologist at Swarthmore College, who articulated this theme in a way that challenges the traditional role of even empirical observation in science. In his argument that there are few, if any, objective foundations for any knowledge, which instead depends on "communities of shared intelligibility" (p. 273), he has been accused by critics of encouraging a profoundly relativistic view that is antiscientific. Gergen, on the other hand, believes that social constructionism will forge a better understanding of the meaning of all knowledge, including scientific knowledge, by challenging the idea of intrinsic objective foundations.

The qualitative data resulting from this approach are more exhaustive than the selective records that typify participant-observer research. The ethnographer analyzes conversations noted verbatim, extensive field notes, and notes based on memory, perhaps word for word as well as in a more gross way. The ethnographer records many pages of detailed observations, constantly adding his or her own interpretation of the meaning of particular passages. Table 4.1 illustrates the field notes of John Haviland (1977), an anthropologist, who kept meticulous records while living for 10 years in Zinacantan, a small village in Mexico. The table shows excerpts of some of the conversations he tape-recorded and translated, along with his interpretation of each fragment. Haviland was interested in the social-control and sense-making functions of ordinary gossip in this community. He concluded, in general, that gossiping in Zinacantan encouraged spying between households at the same time that it isolated households from one another.

In the early development of ethnography, sociologists and anthropologists had yet to find out how to obtain the most precise and objective results or how to make the most reliable records. But over many years, various techniques have been tested and refined, so that certain procedures are now routinely used in many studies. For example, ethnographers who are interested in describing cultural differences often work in teams insofar as possible, in order to control for any distinctive biases in their classifications and evaluations of events. When the language of the target culture is not the native language of the researchers, they seek out assistance in framing interview questions in the native language of the culture. This approach requires **translation and back-translation,** which means that one bilingual person translates the questions from source to target language, and then another bilingual person translates the questions back into the source language. In this way, the researchers can compare the original with the twice-translated version (i.e., the back-translation) to see whether anything important has been lost in the translation. It is also considered essential to identify the language used for each field note, for example, "investigator's native language," "the language of Group X," or "technical language of social science" (Spradley, 1980).

Haviland's field notes were guided by specific questions. The following are a set of more general questions that were formulated by another leading ethnographer (Goodenough, 1980). Each question is broadly stated, but it may start you thinking about specific questions if you intend to conduct an ethnographic study (or a participant-observer study). After each question, we also indicate how Haviland addressed it in his study of gossiping in Zinacantan:

1. *What is the purpose of the activity?* (For example, what are the goals and their justifications?) In his study, Haviland classified several objectives of gossiping in Zinacantan, which led him to conclude that, despite the actual fences erected between households, the neighbors were constantly scrutinizing one another's dealings.

2. *What procedures are used to perform the activity?* (For example, what are the operations performed, the media or raw materials used, the skills and instruments involved, if any?) In Haviland's study, the medium of gossip was word of mouth; he carefully categorized the linguistic and psychological skills required in gossipmongering in this community.

Table 4.1	Fragments of Zinacanteco Gossip and Their Analysis	
	Examples	Interpretations
	"Didn't I hear that old José was up to some mischief?" "Perhaps, but that never became public knowledge. It was a secret affair." "The magistrate settled the whole business in private." "Yes, when a dispute is settled at the townhall, then a newspaper report goes out to every part of town. . . . Ha ha ha." "Yes, then we all hear about it on the radio. . . . Ha ha ha." "But when the thing is hushed up, then there's nothing on the radio. There are no newspapers. Then we don't hear about it. Ha ha ha."	Shows how some villagers even gossip about gossip.
	"Is it true that old Maria divorced Manuel?" "Yes. She complained that she awoke every morning with a wet skirt. Old Manuel used to piss himself every night, just like a child." "When he was drunk, you mean?" "No, even when he was sober. 'How it stinks!' she said." "Ha ha ha. She spoke right out at the townhall."	Shows how some gossip trades on a separation, but also on a connection, between the public and the private domain.
	"This is what I told him: All right, I'll see how deeply I must go into debt to take this office. But I don't want you to start complaining about it later. If I hear that you have been ridiculing me, saying things like: 'Boy, he is just pretending to be a man; he is just pretending to have money to do ritual service. He stole my office, he took it from me.' . . . If you say such things, please excuse me, but I'll drag you to jail. I'll come looking for you myself. I don't want you to tell stories about me, because you have freely given me your ritual office. If there is no dispute, then I too will behave the same way. I won't gossip about you. I won't ridicule you. I won't say, for example, 'Hah, I am replacing him; he has no shame, acting like a man, asking for religious office when he has no money.' I won't talk like that. 'He wanted to serve Our Lord, but he ran away. I had to take over for him.' I won't say things like that, if we agree to keep silent about it . . ."	Shows a common theme in gossip about shady dealings and how the villagers take pains to ensure that the matter is kept quiet.

Source: Reproduced from "Gossip as Competition in Zinacantan" by J. B. Haviland, 1977, *Journal of Communication, 27,* pp. 186–191. Copyright © 1977; *Journal of Communication,* Oxford University Press. Used with permission of the publisher.

3. *What are the time and space requirements of the activity?* (For example, how much time is needed for each operation, what areas or facilities are required, and are there any obstacles in the way of the activity?) Haviland noted when and where gossiping occurred, as well as what natural obstacles there were to the transmission of information.

4. *What are the personnel requirements of the activity?* (For example, how many actors participate, and what is each person's specialization, if any?) Haviland classified and evaluated the elaborate conversational devices by which certain people in positions of authority protected themselves. In other words, the person's "specialization" was that he or she was someone of authority.

5. *What is the nature of the social organization?* (For example, what are the categories of the actors; their rights, duties, privileges, and powers; and the types of sanctions or restrictions they use?) Haviland classified and evaluated how gossip was used by the villagers to manage their social faces (i.e., how they wanted to appear to others) and at the same time to protect their privacy.

6. *What are the occasions for performance of the activity?* (For example, when is the activity mandatory, permitted, and prohibited, and what is the relationship of the initiator's role to the roles of others?) Haviland noted the occasions that were most and least conducive to gossiping, and he categorized and analyzed the particular role interactions of the gossips within those circumstances.

Content Analysis of Archival Data

Observational methods sometimes involve the use of archival material rather than actual firsthand observation of the behavior. To give you a flavor of the wide variety of archival material that is accessible to researchers, there are (1) actuarial records (e.g., the birth, marriage, and death records in town hall ledgers); (2) political and judicial records (e.g., the voting records of legislators and speeches printed in the *Congressional Record*); (3) other government records (e.g., weather reports, invention records, and crime reports); (4) information from the mass media (e.g., stories, news reports, advertising, and editorials); (5) sales records (e.g., sales at airport bars, sales of trip insurance policies, and decreased sales of airline tickets, all constituting plausible indicators of increased anxiety); (6) industrial and institutional records (sicknesses and absences from the job, complaints and unsolicited commendations from the public, and accident reports); and (7) various other written documents (e.g., diaries and letters of captured soldiers in wartime, letters of protest to large companies, and rumors recorded by rumor control centers).

The use of archival material in social science falls into the category known as **secondary observation,** which means that the observation of the researcher is twice removed from the source. That is, the person who originally recorded the information is once removed from the source, and the researcher is removed from the recorder by another degree. A popular method of decomposing written messages and pictorial documents in archives involves the classification and evaluation of their content, a method known as **content analysis** (see, e.g., Berelson, 1952; Holsti, 1969; Krippendorff, 1980; Rosengren, 1981; Stone, Dunphy, Smith, & Ogilvie, 1966; Weber, 1985). Content analysis calls for the precise, objective classification of material, and we will give an example in a moment. The basic procedure consists of using judges (also called *raters* or *coders*) to count symbols, words, sentences, ideas, or whatever other category of information is of interest.

If you think you might like to do a content analysis, there are three general guidelines to keep in mind (Berelson, 1954):

1. It is important that the analysis of content be consistent among the judges; that is, the different coders should produce close to the same results. If each of the categories and units of analysis is carefully defined, and if the judges are properly trained, the **intercoder reliability** (i.e., the consistency among the judges who do the coding or rating) should be satisfactorily high. We will have more to say about how to choose judges later in this chapter.

2. It is essential that the specific categories and units be relevant to the questions or hypotheses of the study. In choosing categories for written records, for example, it is a good idea to ask, "What is the communication about?" and "How is it said?" These questions will help to focus the analysis on the substance (the *what*) and the form (the *how*) of the subject matter. It is often a good idea to consider several different units of analysis before settling on any one unit. For example, we might consider coding words and word compounds (or phrases) or perhaps themes (or assertions).

3. And finally, it is important to decide on a good sampling procedure. Because content analysis is so time-consuming, one must be sure that the materials to be analyzed are representative enough to justify the effort. We will have more to say about different sampling plans later in this book, including approaches that call for (a) random sampling from listings of all relevant units; (b) stratified samples, which break up units into subgroups and sample from them; and (c) systematic samples, which involve selecting every *n*th unit of a list.

As we said before, all methods have intrinsic limitations, and content analysis is no exception (Weber, 1985). However, it also has four distinct advantages when used properly (Woodrum, 1984). First, developing a coding system and then implementing it requires little more than commonsense logic. Second, content analysis is a "shoestring" methodology in that, although labor-intensive, it does not require much capital investment. Third, it is a "safe" methodology, because the researcher can add necessary information if it is missed or incorrectly coded (if there are changes in what is being measured over time, it is not usually possible to do this in the typical experimental or survey study). Fourth, it forces researchers to scrutinize the material that they are evaluating and classifying by specifying category criteria and assessing their success in measuring qualitative phenomena.

As an illustration of the use of content analysis with pictorial material, Peter B. Crabb and Dawn Bielawski (1994) used this approach in a study of how visual presentations in influential books written for children portrayed female and male roles. Using the basic guidelines listed above, they had to make sure that their analysis was relevant to their question. To ensure the relevance of their content analysis, they chose for their study all picture books that had received prestigious awards (the Caldecott Medal) over a 53-year period, on the assumption that these books had a high profile in libraries and book stores. The books they chose contained 1,613 illustrations, including 416 showing female characters and 1,197 showing male characters. Another guideline noted previously was that it is important to use a good sampling procedure, and Crabb and Bielawski's sampling procedure involved drawing a proportionate sample of 300 representative illustrations of gender and decade.

Before these researchers gave the sample of illustrations to two judges for coding, a coding sheet was developed and the judges were rehearsed in how to use it. After recording the sex of each character shown, the judges coded (1) the depiction of any household tools, such as those used in food preparation, cleaning, repair, and family care; (2) the depiction of any nonhousehold tools, such as those used in construction, agriculture, and transportation; (3) any tools not falling into the above two categories; and (4) other features of the characters using the tools and the situation (e.g., age of character: child, teenager, or adult). The ratings by the two judges were in strong agreement with one another, indicating that there was good intercoder reliability. Turning to the question that inspired their study, the researchers concluded that household tools were generally associated with female characters and that nonhousehold tools were generally associated with male characters. It was also observed that the proportion of male characters using household tools had increased over time, whereas the proportion of female characters using nonhousehold tools had not changed very much over time.

The Laboratory Experiment

The principal advantage of the laboratory experiment is that it allows us to *simulate* (or mimic) a causal relationship in a highly controlled setting in which we can actually manipulate the causal condition (i.e., the independent variable). To illustrate the nature of a laboratory experiment in behavioral science, suppose you want to study why people's ears buzz and tickle as they listen to a hard rock band up close. You could position a loudspeaker next to the subject, manipulate the carefully calibrated sounds, and ask the subject to report the sensations he or she feels. If the subject's ears buzz and tickle, the sound pressure may well be above 120 decibels, which can produce feelings of discomfort, prickling, and pain. After each exposure to such sounds, the sensitivity of the ear may be temporarily reduced. (To find out whether people who have a steady diet of hard rock have hearing difficulties, you could study the minimal audible noise detected by subjects who listen to a lot of hard rock or no hard rock. However, such an investigation would be not an experimental study but a relational study.)

In many cases, doing research in a laboratory setting can be a convenient and effective way of studying a phenomenon of interest in behavioral science (Mook, 1983). However, it is important to proceed with some caution when trying to simulate subtle social phenomena in a laboratory setting. Suppose we wanted to study the effect of frustration on aggression in a controlled laboratory setting. Because it has been theorized that conditions of frustration can make a person display hostile behavior, we might design a study in which two subjects engage in a competitive task and are give an opportunity to administer a mild electric shock to one another. We frustrate one subject by withdrawing some particular desired object and then see whether the person administers shock to the other subject. Does the study have inferential validity (see again Box 1.4 on p. 10)? By means of meta-analysis (described in Appendix C), it was recently shown that studying aggression in the laboratory may yield a faithful representation of certain effects in the real world, but that laboratory simulations of aggression may overestimate the effects of situational variables (e.g., media violence) and underestimate the effects of individual difference variables (C. A. Anderson & Bushman, 1997). (See also Box 4.4.)

| Box 4.4 | **Virtual Reality in the Laboratory?** |

It has been suggested that laboratory simulations of perceptual and social phenomena might be improved by the use of virtual reality technology similar to that found in some arcades (e.g., Biocca & Levy, 1995; Carr & England, 1995; Steuer, 1992). The subject would wear a head-mounted video display and receive tactile, motion, and audio stimulation that is designed to immerse him or her in a "world" that feels the same as the real world. This approach to behavioral experimentation is still in a conceptual stage of development, but it has been used for years by the U.S. military and aerospace programs to train pilots and astronauts. Although the cost of development may be prohibitive for many years, the potential advantages are that (1) subjects might be made to "feel" the same way they do in a real-world setting; (2) naturally occurring variables can be manipulated in a controlled setting; (3) the situation is dynamic (rather than static) in the way that real-world settings are; and (4) we can study questions that may be too sensitive to study in other than passive observational studies or experiments using written vignettes or videotapes (Pierce & Aguinis, 1997).

Later in this book, we will discuss how to anticipate and control for certain experimental design problems. However, it is not too soon for you to begin to sharpen your intuitive skills or for us to give you an idea of what your instructor may expect as you begin to put together a background review of the literature on your research topic or to write the discussion section of your final report. The instructor will expect you to think carefully about flaws in and alternative explanations (also called **rival hypotheses**) for the reported results and about possible ways of improving the studies you review. To get you thinking about rival interpretations, let us look at a couple more examples of laboratory studies (although the process of critical evaluation is typical of the scrutiny given all research studies). This next study focuses on how human beings select from their perceptual environment those objects and events that are significant to them because of their life experience.

Rival Interpretations

Several classic laboratory studies have shown that individuals' personal values affect how they perceive aspects of their environment. In one study, Postman, Bruner, and McGinnies (1948) determined the predominant value attitudes of a group of subjects by having them fill out a questionnaire designed to measure whether their orientation was predominantly aesthetic, theoretical, economic, social, political, or religious. For example, the answers of a person who valued the search for truth above most other things would have received a high "theoretical" score, and a subject whose values were dominated by the usefulness of things would have received a high "economic" score. The "political" subject was concerned about power, the "social" subject about the needs of others, the "aesthetic" subject about criteria of beauty, and the "religious" subject about the meaning of life as it related to her or his conception of God. The subjects in this study were then presented with a series of words through a tachistoscope projector, a device that briefly presents various stimuli by flashing them on a screen for a fraction of a second. The words reflected the six value orientations of the subjects.

On the whole, the subjects tended to identify the words associated with their own value orientation more rapidly than the words not so associated. This interpretation was subsequently challenged by other researchers (Solomon & Howes, 1951), who argued that persons with a specific value orientation may have been exposed to these words in print more often than other individuals (presumably individuals read more literature relevant to *their* own values). Therefore a person oriented to "political" words, for example, would recognize them more rapidly than other words because of their familiarity and not because they were visually perceived more quickly. This criticism paved the way for follow-up studies that were designed to reconcile such differences in interpretation.

Now let us try our own critical evaluation of another study. In the 1960s, when this study was conducted, there were volumes of statistics on the relationship between alcohol use and accident rates, but comparable data for marijuana were unavailable. A laboratory experiment that investigated the effects of drugs on simulated driving performance was ethically acceptable and could be better controlled. What was lost, however, was the actual stress of driving in traffic. In this study (Crancer, Dille, Delay, Wallace, & Haybin, 1969), the effects of marijuana, alcohol, and no drug were compared in two simulated driving tests.

In Test 1, experienced marijuana smokers were tested for 30 minutes after smoking two marijuana cigarettes, and the same subjects were tested when their blood alcohol concentration reached 0.10% (the legally defined intoxication level in 1969), the equivalent of about 6 ounces of 86-proof liquor in a 120-pound subject. In the no-drug control condition, neither marijuana nor alcohol was given. In the driving test, the subject sat in a specially constructed console mock-up of a recent-model car and observed a large screen on which a driver's-eye movie film was projected. Normal and emergency situations on urban and suburban streets appeared on the screen, and the subject was instructed to respond to them by operating the accelerator, brake, turn signals, and steering, and by checking the speedometer. It was possible to make up to 405 errors during the 23-minute film. Test 2 was taken by the subject 2 ½ hours after taking the first test, and Test 3 was taken 1 ½ hours after Test 2. All tests were the same.

The results were revealing, but decidedly ambiguous. Under the effects of alcohol, the subjects did worse than in either the marijuana or no-drug condition. In the alcohol condition over all three tests, they made a mean of 97 errors; they made a mean of 85 errors in the marijuana condition and in the control condition. In the marijuana condition, compared to the control condition, the only bad effect was an increase in speedometer errors. Under the effects of alcohol, there was an increase in all types of errors except steering errors. How many flaws and rival interpretations do you recognize in this study?

One possible flaw is reminiscent of the Hawthorne effect in Chapter 1, in which merely being studied experimentally sometimes affects how a person behaves (see again Box 1.1 on p. 3). In this case, the subjects were experienced marijuana users, were probably motivated to do well in the marijuana condition, and may even have been motivated to do poorly in the alcohol condition. A second possible flaw is that the drug doses may not have been comparable. Two marijuana cigarettes may not have made the subjects nearly as "high" as 6 ounces of 86-proof alcohol; if the alcohol and marijuana treatments had made the subjects equally "high," the resulting errors might have been more nearly equal, and both might have been greater than those accumulated in the no-drug condition. In studies such as this, another possible flaw is that the sequence of the treatments may be a source of confounding. To avoid such a problem, the sequences must be "counterbalanced" (discussed in a later chapter).

The Field Experiment

As we cautioned before, do not get the idea that only laboratory simulation experiments are subject to critical scrutiny for rival hypotheses. The purpose of this exercise was to illustrate the kind of critical evaluation done routinely on all studies. Experimentation is also not limited to the laboratory but can also be done in a naturalistic setting. In such **field experiments,** the researcher evokes behavior by modifying some aspect of the situation or by introducing an experimental variable (i.e., a manipulated independent variable) in a real-world setting. The advantage of this strategy is that it may have more mundane and experimental realism than an analogous laboratory experiment. **Mundane realism** means that the various dimensions of the experiment are very similar to those in the real world, and **experimental realism** refers to the extent to which the subject is drawn into or is affected by the treatment (Aronson & Carlsmith, 1968). The more the manipulation of the independent variable resembles the real-world phenomenon, the greater the mundane realism is. The more involving the manipulation of the independent variable, or the greater the degree to which the subject's attention is "turned on" by the treatment, the more experimental realism there is—which is another potential advantage of virtual reality technology (Box 4.4).

Illustrative of this approach is a field experiment in which one of the authors of this book investigated whether teachers' expectations of their students' intellectual performance may come to serve as self-fulfilling prophecies (Rosenthal & Jacobson, 1968). In the spring of 1964, all the children in a public elementary school in South San Francisco were given a standard nonverbal intelligence test. The test was represented to the teachers as a measure of intellectual "blooming," and approximately 20% of the children (the experimental group) were said to be capable of marked intellectual growth. The difference between these supposed potential bloomers and the other students (the control group) existed solely in the minds of their teachers, because the bloomers had been picked entirely at random. The dependent variable in this study was the children's performance on the same intelligence test after one semester, again after a full academic year, and again after two full academic years.

The overall results revealed that, although the greatest differential gain in total intelligence appeared after one school year, the bloomers clearly held an advantage over the other children, the control subjects, even after two years (see also Box 4.5). To account for this finding, the researchers speculated that the teachers may have been more encouraging and friendly to the children in whom they expected greater gains, and that they perhaps unwittingly motivated the children to greater achievement. The implication is that interpersonal expectations may become self-fulfilling prophecies (Merton, 1948); that is, someone who predicts or expects an event may unwittingly behave in ways that are likely to increase the probability that the event will occur. Because it is plausible that an experimenter's hypothesis may also serve as a self-fulfilling prophecy, the scientist needs to understand this phenomenon and learn how to anticipate and control for it. (We return to this problem in a later chapter.)

Box 4.5	**The Self-Fulfilling Prophecy**

Over time, a picture has gradually emerged of variables that influence the effect of teachers' expectations on their students' intellectual performance. Stephen W. Raudenbush (1984), a professor in the College of Education at Michigan State University, analyzed 18 replications of the Rosenthal and Jacobson experiment. The replications generally involved an experimenter's giving a test of cognitive performance to a sample of students of whom a randomly selected fraction were then identified to their teachers as likely to experience substantial intellectual growth. On a retest of the students, those designated as potential "bloomers" gained more in cognitive performance than did the students of the control group. Raudenbush found the self-fulfilling prophecy to be influenced by the amount of prior contact between the teachers and the students. The beneficial effect was not as likely to occur if the teacher had had prior contact with the student, perhaps because teachers' initial impressions (and prior prophecies) may have hardened by the time they received the expectancy suggestion.

It is occasionally possible to do field experimentation in the area of **evaluation research,** the purpose of which is to determine the efficacy or value of a procedure or intervention used in a real-world setting. Most evaluation research is of the descriptive or relational type, but it has also been done experimentally. A recent example is the work done by a team of clinical psychologists who were interested in evaluating a form of cognitive-behavioral therapy for 9 to 13-year-olds diagnosed with anxiety disorder (Kendall, et al., 1997). The children were randomly assigned to two conditions. Those in one condition (the treatment group) were given the therapeutic intervention, while those in the other condition (called a **wait-list control group**) waited to be given the therapy until after it had been administered to the children in the treatment group. Typical of evaluation research is that a number of observational and self-report measures are used to zero in (triangulate) on the efficacy of the intervention.

Adopting a similar strategy, these researchers found that children in the treatment group, when compared with the wait-list controls, showed the beneficial effects of the therapeutic procedure.

Reactive and Nonreactive Observation

A further distinction is made between **reactive observation** and **nonreactive observation;** the terms are used to differentiate between observations that do (reactive) and those that do not (nonreactive) affect the behavior being observed. The idea of a reactive observation can be viewed as another variation on the Hawthorne effect. For example, in an experiment on therapy for weight control, the initial weigh-in may be a reactive stimulus to weight reduction, even without the therapeutic intervention (Campbell & Stanley, 1963). Any use of **concealed measurement** is illustrative of nonreactive observation, such as using a hidden recording device to eavesdrop on conversations. Another variant involves **partial concealment** (Weick, 1968); the researcher does not conceal the fact that he or she is making observations but does conceal who or what is being observed. For example, in studies of mother-child interaction, the researcher implies that it is the child who is being observed when both the mother *and* the child are being studied (Weick,1968).

A classic example in social psychology of a field investigation that used nonreactive observation was conducted by George W. Hartmann (1936). He examined the role of emotional and rational persuasive communications in an actual voting campaign and election. Hartmann was struck by the fact that much of the persuasive communication to which we are subjected in advertisements and political speeches is designed to appeal more to our emotions than to our reason. The purpose of such communication seems to be to arouse certain needs and to offer simple solutions that, if we adopt them, will supposedly satisfy those needs. Every day, we are bombarded by a host of advertisements on TV, radio, and so forth, each commercial in its own way claiming that it will make us feel better because we will be more sexually appealing or more companionable or more sweet-smelling. Around election time, political commercials become a complex fusion of excitement, resentment, vague enthusiasm, aroused fears, and hopes. While he was working at Columbia University in the 1930s as a postdoctoral fellow, Hartmann decided to test whether emotional or rational advertisements are more persuasive in politics.

During the 1935 statewide election campaign in Pennsylvania, Hartmann's name had been placed on the ballot as a Socialist Party candidate in Allentown. To study the role of emotional and rational messages, he created two political leaflets, one designed to appeal to Allentown voters' reason and the other to appeal to their emotions. The leaflets were distributed in different wards matched on the basis of their size, population density, assessed property valuation, previous voting habits, and socioeconomic status. The nonreactive observation in this study was the objective record of the polls. The results of Hartmann's analysis of these data were that the wards that had received the emotional leaflet increased their Socialist votes more than the wards receiving the rational leaflet. In a more in-depth comparison, Hartmann also found that even the "rational" wards showed a greater increase in Socialist votes than a number of control wards that had received neither leaflet.

Another classic example of a nonreactive measurement uses the "lost-letter" technique, which involves dropping addressed, stamped, but unposted letters in public places. The person who comes across such a letter must decide whether to mail it, disregard it, or destroy it. In the original field experiment that used this technique (Merritt & Fowler, 1948), two kinds of stamped, fully addressed envelopes, one containing a trivial message and the other a lead slug about the size of a half-dollar, were "lost." By recording the return rates, the experimenters attempted to gauge the honesty of various samples of subjects in large cities around the country without the subjects' suspecting that they were participating in an experiment. The result was that fewer letters with slugs than without them were mailed. Variations on this strategy have been used by other researchers, including using lost letters (Milgram, Mann, & Harter, 1965) and lost e-mail on the Internet to study attitudinal responses (Stern & Faber,1997) and using lost post cards to study the spread of rumors (Walker & Blaine, 1991).

Unobtrusive Observation

Hartmann's use of voting behavior and the lost-letter technique are also examples of what is termed **unobtrusive observation**, so called because those being studied are unaware that they are being observed for the purpose of research. Unobtrusive observation, because it involves the use of concealment, causes ethical conflicts, which need to be carefully considered. For example, the threat to privacy is made worse by the lack of permission in this situation and by the fact that debriefing is not typically used. The defense of unobtrusive observation usually assumes that the individuals observed are anonymous, so that their privacy is protected. That is, the behavioral or social scientist's goal (unlike, for example, the investigative reporter's) is not to obtain individually identified information. The code of ethics that governs psychological researchers (see Chapter 3) reminds us that individual researchers are responsible for protecting the dignity of those they study. Thus the ethical obligation of researchers who use unobtrusive observation is to ensure that any information to be published will not damage a person by subjecting him or her to ridicule or scorn.

A major work on unobtrusive observation was written by a team of interdisciplinary authors headed by Eugene J. Webb (Webb, Campbell, Schwartz, & Sechrest, 1966; Webb, Campbell, Schwartz, Sechrest, & Grove, 1981). It is a fascinating gem of a book that contains hundreds of unobtrusive measures collected by Webb and his group. In general, they classified all their measures into four broad categories: (1) archival records, (2) physical traces, (3) simple observations, and (4) contrived observations. Previously, we discussed archival records (see also Box 4.6), and we will conclude this section by giving examples of the other classes described by Webb and his coauthors.

First, **physical traces** include the kind of material evidence that a detective might use as a clue in solving a crime. For example, in one detective case, a car's radio buttons were clues to the driver's geographic location. By studying the commercial station frequencies to which the buttons were turned, the detective could identify the general area where the car had been garaged. In one application of this strategy, a car dealer used radio dial settings in an audience measurement study. The dealer had his

Box 4.6   Behavioral Science Archives

Generally speaking, an **archive** is any relatively permanent depository of data or material, such as a library containing books and journals. For students interested in using behavioral science archives, raw data depositories are available at the Human Relations Area Files at Yale University and elsewhere, the University of Chicago's National Opinion Research Center (NORC), and the University of Michigan's Survey Research Center. The Roper Center of the University of Connecticut, for instance, offers survey data collected by the NORC going back to the early 1950s. Data are available from personal interviews of national samples; these NORC interviews used a standardized questionnaire, the same questions appearing in every survey or according to a rotation pattern. All the data are in the public domain and are readily accessible to researchers for duplication, analysis, and publication without clearance from the NORC. A wide range of variables is tapped, including demographic, sociopsychological, political, and socioeconomic variables. If you are interested in using such data, consult with a librarian about what data are available directly or through interlibrary loan.

mechanics record the position of the dial in all the cars brought in for service. He then used this information to choose the radio stations that would carry his advertising to old and potentially new customers.

Other examples of the use of physical traces include measuring the wear and tear (particularly on the corners of pages) of library books as an unobtrusive measure of what books are actually read (not just books checked out and possibly never opened, never read, or never finished). In another case, the relative popularity of children's museum exhibits was measured unobtrusively. The exhibits had glass fronts, and each evening they were dusted for children's noseprints. Those exhibits with more noseprints on the glass were more frequently or more closely observed, the researchers speculated. The distance of the noseprints from the floor even provided a crude index of the ages of the children. Another example in this category is studying language behavior by analyzing the content of messages that people have composed on floor-sample personal computers in stores.

Second, **simple observation** occurs when one observes events unobtrusively without trying to affect them in any way. For example, Webb's group described a correlation between the methodological and theoretical disposition of psychologists and the length of their hair. The researchers unobtrusively evaluated and classified the hair styles of psychologists at professional meetings and also categorized the research. They reported that the "tough-minded" psychologists had shorter hair than the "tender-minded" psychologists.

Third, in **contrived observation,** the observer introduces some variable of interest into a situation and then unobtrusively observes its effect on behavior. It is what Hartmann did in his field experiment, described earlier. For example, you might estimate the degree of fear induced by a ghost story by observing the shrinking diameter of a circle of seated children. Some investigators have "bugged" cocktail parties and recorded the conversations after introducing some variable of interest (e.g., introducing a stranger or an oddly dressed guest). Before the days of audiotapes, Francis Galton, the pioneering English empiricist mentioned in Chapter 1, carried with him paper in the shape of a cross and a small needle for punching holes in the paper. He used this device to count whatever he was observing at the time; a hole at the head of the cross meant "greater," on an arm "equal," and at the foot "less."

Using Judges as Observers

Except for secondary observations using archival records, we have considered only the researcher himself or herself as the primary observer. Among the other observational "tools" that scientists use in field and laboratory studies are independent **judges** (coders, raters, decoders, etc.) to assist in describing and categorizing ongoing events or existing records of events (film records, narratives, etc.). Judges use **checklists** and **tally sheets** to impose a sense of structure on their observations; as the names imply, these are simply systematic ways of counting (checking off or tallying) the frequency of occurrence of particular acts or events. Earlier we mentioned that Crabb and Bielawski used independent judges to content-analyze a sample of pictures from children's books. In general, researchers choose judges in one of three ways: (1) on the basis of intuition; (2) by consulting the relevant research literature; or (3) by doing pilot testing.

The first approach is to decide intuitively on the type of judges needed (graduate students, community members, college students, clinical psychologists, linguists, mothers, etc.) and then to regard each judge within that sample as equivalent to (or interchangeable with) any other judge within the sample. For example, if you wanted a sample of raters educated at a certain level, you might be content to select college students. If you wanted ratings of nonverbal expressions of neuroses, you would choose as your judges experienced professionals, such as clinical psychologists, psychiatrists, or psychiatric social workers. If you wanted ratings of nonverbal expressions of discomfort in infants, you might select pediatricians, developmental psychologists, or mothers. If you wanted ratings of nonverbal cues of persuasion, you might invite trial lawyers, Fundamentalist ministers, or salespersons. You would also want to make sure that the judges were not relying on stereotypes that might not be accurate (e.g., salespersons recruited to watch people give persuasive messages might rely on stereotypes to tell you which of the nonverbal cues were most persuasive).

A second approach is to consult the relevant research literature, in which case you might do even better by making a special selection of judges. For example, if you wanted to obtain the highest possible general accuracy in judgments of nonverbal cues, your selection of judges might be based on prior research that had identified the specific characteristics of people who are more sensitive to nonverbal cues. This research suggests that, to optimize overall sensitivity to nonverbal cues, you should probably select judges who are (1) female, (2) college-aged, and (as measured by psychological tests) both (3) cognitively complex and (4) psychiatrically unimpaired (Rosenthal, et al., 1979). A recent study has added another characteristic to this list, *field independence,* which means that the person chosen to do the rating is able to impose organization on information and is not entirely dependent on the external or ostensible organization. Field-independent persons, identified by a test designed to measure this characteristic (the Group Embedded Figures Test), tend to be more accurate raters than field-dependent persons (Härtel, 1993).

A third way to select judges is to do a **pilot test** in which you compare all recruits in your pool of potential judges for their accuracy of judgment on some relevant criterion. Suppose you were interested in selecting raters for a study in which they would have to categorize the emotions expressed by participants in encounter groups. You might begin by showing your pool of potential raters pictures of people exhibiting different emotions, such as anger, disgust, fear, happiness, sadness, and surprise. You would ask them to identify the emotion expressed in each picture, score the answers given by them, and then use the most accurate judges in your study.

A Final Note

You have seen from examples that systematic observation provides much of the empirical content of behavioral and social science. We have noted a range of primary and secondary observational methods (e.g., participant observation, ethnography, laboratory experimentation, and field experimentation), yet our discussion barely scratched the surface of what is possible. We will turn our attention in the next chapter to methods in which the observations are directed "inward" rather than "outward."

Summary of Ideas

1. Systematic observation is guided by preexisting questions or hypotheses in descriptive, relational, and experimental research.
2. Feyerabend's "anything-goes view of science" means that doing research *does* involve a "let's try it and see" attitude.
3. Because each qualitative and quantitative method is limited in some ways, behavioral scientists use multiple methods to try to fill in the gaps through triangulation.
4. Naturalistic observation is also done by researchers who study animals in the wild (e.g., the study of how male baboons defend their troops against predators).
5. Sartre's analogy of "the look" underscores the idea that we need to use different vantage points (and methodological pluralism) to observe events in their "wholeness."
6. Participant observers study a social situation from within by watching and recording how people behave and what they talk about (e.g., Kidder's study of participants in a hypnosis workshop).
7. Ethnographic research uses a relatively standardized methodology (ethnomethodology) to study how people in a cultural setting make sense of things (i.e., sense making).
8. Ethnographers are guided by questions about (a) the purpose of the activity being observed; (b) the procedures used to perform the activity; (c) the time and space requirements of the activity; (d) the personnel requirements; (e) the nature

of the activity's social organization; and (f) the occasions for performance (e.g., Haviland's study of gossiping in a small village in Mexico).

9. Content analysis is used in archival research to code and sort secondary observations or, in the case of Crabb and Bielawski's study of gender roles in children's picture books, pictorial representations of behavior.

10. In doing a content analysis, it is important (a) to ensure intercoder reliability; (b) to develop specific, relevant content categories for the judges to code; and (c) to choose a good sampling method.

11. Doing a laboratory experiment generally means testing or trying out something in a tightly controlled setting in order to study causality, and in many cases using a simulation (e.g., the experiment that simulated the effects of marijuana and alcohol use on automobile driving).

12. All research studies, including tightly controlled laboratory experiments, are subject to critical reexamination for potential flaws and rival interpretations (e.g., the study in Number 11 above and the tachistoscopic study of word recognition).

13. Field experiments are a variant of naturalistic observational research (e.g., the experimental study of teachers' expectations as unwitting determinants of their students' intellectual performance and Hartmann's field study of the effects of emotional and rational political communications on voting behavior).

14. Nonreactive observation includes concealed measurement and partial concealment (e.g., Hartmann's study and the lost-letter technique).

15. Unobtrusive observation is nonreactive; examples include (a) archival records, (b) physical traces, (c) simple observation, and (d) contrived observation.

16. When choosing judges to classify events or to rate behavior, we can use (a) intuition; (b) previous results that help us select the most accurate individuals (i.e., college-aged women who are cognitively complex, psychiatrically unimpaired, and field-independent); or (c) pilot testing.

Key Terms

anything-goes view of science (Feyerabend)   p. 81
archive   p. 97
checklists   p. 98
concealed measurement   p. 95
content analysis   p. 88
contrived observation   p. 97
ethnographic research   p. 85
ethnomethodology   p. 85
evaluation research   p. 94
experimental realism   p. 93
field experiments   p. 93
intercoder reliability   p. 89
interpreter biases   p. 83

judges   p. 98
justification   p. 80
methodological triangulation   p. 81
mundane realism   p. 93
naturalistic observation   p. 82
nonreactive observation   p. 95
opportunistic sampling   p. 83
partial concealment   p. 95
participant-observer research   p. 83
physical traces   p. 96
pilot testing   p. 99
qualitative methods   p. 81
quantitative methods   p. 81
reactive observation   p. 95

Multiple-Choice Questions for Review (answers are found on page 346)

1. In a classic study, several social psychologists "joined" a religious cult that be-lieved that the world would soon end. After they were accepted as members of the group, they made careful observations of the behavior of the group. This type of research is known as (a) a field experiment; (b) participant observation; (c) ethnocentric research; (d) back-translation.

2. A student at the University of Hawaii wants to study gossip and rumor among Asian cultures. To conduct the research, interview questions must be translated from English into other languages. To ensure that the translations are accurate, the researcher must use the procedure of (a) ethnographic research; (b) linguistic relativism; (c) back-translation; (d) dual translation.

3. In 1935, social psychologist George Hartmann ran for political office in Pennsylvania. In some areas, he distributed leaflets with an emotional appeal to voters. In other areas, he distributed leaflets with a rational appeal. He then observed the voting records for these different areas. In this study, the type of leaflet was the _____ variable, and the voting records were the _____ variable. (a) independent; experimental; (b) experimental; independent; (c) dependent; independent; (d) independent; dependent

4. Suppose you are conducting an observational study, and you want judges (or raters) who are very sensitive to nonverbal cues. You should choose judges who are (a) psychiatrically unimpaired; (b) college-aged; (c) female; (d) all of the above.

5. A researcher at Montclair State University carefully observes whether or not people lock their car doors when parked in the university's parking lot. The subjects do not realize that they are being observed. This is an example of (a) reactive observation; (b) partial concealment; (c) unobtrusive observation; (d) none of the above.

6. A researcher at Louisiana Tech conducts an observational study of job satisfaction in a large corporation. She tells the research participants that she is studying their behavior but does not tell them what aspect of their behavior she will be observing. This is an example of (a) quasi disclosure; (b) partial concealment; (c) unobtrusive observation; (d) residual disclosure.

7. To determine which classrooms are used most heavily at Drew University, a researcher measures the amount of wear on floor tiles. This is an example of the use of (a) physical traces; (b) simple observations; (c) contrived observations; (d) archival records.

8. A researcher at Colby College observes how far apart people stand from each other at a party. This is an example of the use of (a) physical traces; (b) simple observations; (c) contrived observations; (d) archival records.

9. A researcher at the University of Colorado at Denver reports that marriage rates are associated with the size of the city. She obtained both the marriage rates and the population estimates from government statistics available in the library. This is an example of the use of (a) physical traces; (b) simple observations; (c) contrived observations; (d) archival research.

10. Webb and his colleagues described four types of unobtrusive measures. Which of the following is *not* one these types? (a) physical traces; (b) simple observations; (c) contrived observations; (d) interview schedules.

Discussion Questions for Review (answers are found on page 346)

1. An Iowa State student is given the task of describing two possible uses of archival measures not mentioned in this chapter. Can you suggest some possibilities?

2. An Arizona State student wants to test the hypothesis that people's level of aggression predicts their preference of sports; that is, more aggressive people like more aggressive sports. How might the student test this hypothesis by using non-reactive measures?

3. A Towson State student wants to use content analysis to study the comic pages in the *Baltimore Sun*. Can you think of a particular hypothesis to guide the data collection? What steps would you advise the student to take in carrying out her study?

4. A Fitchburg State College student wants to do a participant-observer study of tourists and local residents in Provincetown. What advice would you give him about systematizing his observations?

5. A student at the University of Massachusetts at Boston wants to illustrate the application of methodological triangulation to the question of whether inhaling cigarette smoke is unhealthy. Can you help by giving an example of a descriptive, a relational, and an experimental study, all addressing the same question?

6. An Ohio State University student has found that teachers' ratings of their students' intellectual ability are highly correlated with the students' IQ test scores and concludes that this correlation reflects the effects of teachers' expectations on students' intellectual performance. What might be a plausible rival hypothesis to that interpretation?

5 Self-Report Methods

Looking Within Oneself

Behavioral scientists not only watch and record, frequently calling on judges (raters or coders) to make systematic observations, but they also often ask research participants to look within themselves and describe their attitudes, feelings, perceptions, beliefs, and so on. Known as the **method of self-report,** this strategy goes back to the formative years of behavioral science. Early psychologists had research participants reflect and verbally report on their sensations and perceptions (called *introspection*). With the development of behavioral methodology, the use of verbal reports by research subjects fell out of favor for many years and was replaced by external observations. However, self-report is used in many fields. For example, when you go to the eye doctor to be fitted for glasses, after you are shown the letter chart you are shown a series of paired letters or images and asked which image you find easier to read or see. When you visit the family doctor, you are asked to tell how you feel. Many behavioral and social scientists also use a variety of self-report methods, including standardized tests of personality to predict behavior (see Box 5.1), attitude and opinion questionnaires, and procedures in

PREVIEW QUESTIONS

- What is the role of self-report methods in behavioral research?
- What are the uses and limits of open-ended and closed measures?
- What are structured and unstructured personality measures?
- What are numerical, graphic, and forced-choice rating scales?
- What are rating errors, and how can they be controlled?
- How are semantic differentials, Likert scales, and Thurstone scales created?
- When is a questionnaire used in research, and how should it be constructed?
- How is an "interview schedule" developed and implemented?
- What is the critical incident technique?
- How are telephone interviews conducted?
- How are "behavioral diaries" used in research?
- What are the advantages and limitations of each of these methods?

which subjects are asked to reflect on their inner feelings or to "think aloud" (Ericsson & Simon, 1993).

Box 5.1   Personality Testing

Psychologists have shown that it is quite possible to predict performance in various occupations from well-constructed measures of normal personality that are given to potential employees in pre-employment screening (Hogan, Hogan, & Roberts, 1996). For example, personality tests are given to prospective draft choices by some National Football League teams to help them judge the draftees. The New York Giants gives its own test to prospective players, including asking them to answer true or false to statements like the following: (1) "When a person 'pads' an income tax report so as to get out of some taxes, it is just as bad as stealing money from the Government," and (2) "I am often said to be hotheaded" (T. W. Smith, 1997, p. 11). Taken together, the prospective player's responses to these and other items are used to create a personality "profile," which can be as informative as the physicals that draftees also take.

In this chapter, we will survey a wide variety of self-report methods, as well as discuss the advantages and limitations of each. Some of these methods are readily available to students, while other methods require supervised training and certification that the person is qualified to use the method. We will mention additional sources of information about what instruments are available to help us assess different characteristics, including dimensions of personality and attitudinal factors. Self-report methods include the use of questionnaires and interviews in survey research, and we will see how these instruments and procedures are developed. We begin this discussion by noting three issues that need to be considered in the use of self-report data, and then we focus on two universal formats (open-ended and closed) of virtually all self-report measures.

Three Basic Considerations

In the collection of self-report data, one important assumption is that what the subjects report is true and not merely a strategy to make themselves "look good." It is not unusual for subjects to feel apprehensive about being evaluated, and when experiencing such **evaluation apprehension,** they may be evasive in their self-reports, particularly when the data asked about are sensitive. Experiments that contain an element of surprise or have an aura of mystery may also arouse evaluation apprehension (Rosenberg, 1969). When we anticipate this reaction, one thing we can do is to assure the subjects that their responses will be held in strict confidence. In some cases, it has been found that an assurance of confidentiality causes the subjects to be more forthcoming in describing themselves (Esposito et al., 1984; Singer, Von Thurn, & Miller, 1995).

A second consideration is that we should not use self-report methods (or undertake any research) without giving careful consideration to the ethical implications (discussed in Chapter 3). When sensitive information may be revealed, it is important to anticipate any potentially risky implications. For example, when studying children and adolescents, what if we learn that the respondent has a suicidal tendency or that the parents are abusing the child (e.g., LaGreca, 1990)? All research in behavioral science must undergo an ethical evaluation, and your instructor will be sensitive to ethical issues and conflicts that may elude you because of inexperience. If you would like to know more about such issues, you will find informative discussions of potential risks and ethical conflicts in Bersoff's *Ethical Conflicts in Psychology* (1995) and Kimmel's *Ethical Issues in Behavioral Research* (1996).

A third issue concerns whether research subjects, even the most well intentioned, *can* provide information that can be considered as objective as other behavioral data. Some critics have challenged the utility of self-report data, arguing that people cannot look within themselves or have a clear sense of themselves apart from the immediate situation (e.g., Nisbett & Wilson, 1977). Others contend that, collected properly and interpreted cautiously, self-report data can enrich our understanding of other results, which are also limited in some ways. This, then, is another justification for methodological triangulation, in which we use more than one perspective to zero in on the phenomenon of interest. It is also why the doctor not only examines you with the help of medical instruments but also routinely asks, "Tell me what hurts."

Open-Ended versus Closed Questions

All of the methods that we describe in this chapter have been used in both basic and applied behavioral research. In fact, few people escape the opportunity to participate in one of these two types of research, although not everyone agrees to participate. For example, suppose you receive the following telephone call:

> Hello, is this _____ ? My name is _____ , and I'm calling from the Survey Institute at Central University. We are conducting a short random survey to determine how people feel about gun control issues so that we can get a true picture of people's attitudes. It will only take about two or three minutes, and we would greatly appreciate your help. May I ask you some questions?

If you answer yes, you will be a participant in a study using self-report data to measure people's behavior or state of mind.

You will be read a series of questions and asked to report how you personally behave, feel, or think (e.g., Lavrakas, 1987). Some of the questions you are asked may be **open-ended,** so called because they offer you an opportunity to express your feelings and impressions quite spontaneously. Other questions, characterized as **closed** (also called *structured, fixed-choice,* or *precoded*), may use a more structured approach, giving you fixed response options such as yes-no or multiple-choice alternatives. Later, we will show how open-ended and closed measures play a role in personality tests, attitude and survey questionnaires, interviews, and behavioral diaries. The rule of thumb is that the method chosen should match the dimensions of interest and the kind of information desired.

When the doctor asks, "How do you feel?" this is an example of an open-ended question. Your answer not only gives the doctor a clue to *what* to observe or measure, but also gives her or him a better sense of how *you* (as an individual) experience things. In the telephone survey, the researcher is also looking for individual responses, although in this case to generalize about similar individuals in some defined population. An example of an open-ended question that the survey researcher might ask would be "How do you feel about the National Rifle Association?" When analyzing the data, the researcher would categorize your responses to this question and correlate the coded data with the responses to other questions.

Like any observational or self-report method, an open-ended format has advantages and disadvantages (Scott, 1968). Advantages of open-ended measures are that (1) they do not lead the research participant by suggesting specific answers; (2) their approach is exploratory, allowing the researcher to find out whether the respondent has anything at all to say; and (3) they invite the research participant to answer in his or her own language, a procedure that sometimes helps to increase rapport. By contrast, disadvantages of open-ended formats are that (1) they are time-consuming for both the researcher (who must code and analyze the responses) and the research participants; (2) they sometimes invite rambling and off-the-mark responses that may never actually touch on the topic the researcher is interested in; and (3) they may be hard to assess for reliability (which is discussed in the next chapter).

An example of a closed (or structured) format would be "How do you feel about a 10-day waiting period for permission to buy a gun? Would you say that you feel strongly in favor, moderately in favor, moderately against, or strongly against this idea?" A response that would not be read to you is "don't know," but if that is your answer, the interviewer will note it down. The advantages and limitations of closed measures are the reverse of those of the open-ended format. For most researchers, the major advantage of a structured format is that, when properly used, it forces respondents' replies into the dimensions of interest to the researcher rather than producing large proportions of irrelevant or uncodable answers (Scott, 1968).

We continue our discussion of self-report measures by focusing on some of the specific instruments used by researchers, clinical and counseling psychologists, school psychologists, and others to get individuals to reveal aspects of their personality, beginning with the use of projective measures.

Projective Measures of Personality

As ideas of personality have developed, from the time of Sigmund Freud to the present, methods of assessing various personality characteristics of individuals, particularly as part of the therapeutic process, have also developed. Much of the early testing of personality characteristics consisted of diagnosing the mental state of the individual by examining that part of the personality relevant to therapy, a process that led to the development of a wide variety of personality measures. The particular configuration of an individual's personality is believed to have profound consequences for her or his social behavior. Although there is disagreement about the factors that are most influential in a given situation, there is theoretical speculation that a small number of factors may transcend cultural differences (McCrae & Costa, 1997). That is, there is presumed to be a human universal in the structure of personality, just as the human skeletal structure is a universal—even though individuals differ from one another in their girth and height, for example (see Box 5.2).

Box 5.2   **The Big Five**

Current thinking in personality assessment generally supports the idea of five broad domains of individual personality, called the **Big Five factors** (Goldberg, 1993; McCrae & Costa, 1997; Wiggins, 1996):

1. *Neuroticism* (N), or the degree of nervousness, moodiness, and temperamentality.
2. *Extraversion* (E), or the degree of talkativeness, assertiveness, and activity.
3. *Openness to experience* (O), or the degree of imagination, curiosity, and creativity.
4. *Agreeableness* (A), or the degree of kindness, trust, and warmth.
5. *Conscientiousness* (C), or the degree of organization, thoroughness, and reliability.

Each factor is presumed to be made up of hundreds, possibly thousands, of specific traits. One way to help us memorize the five factors is the mnemonic phrase "Not Every Organism Acts Consistently," for *NEOAC*.

Measures of the structure of personality take many different forms, including the use of open-ended and closed measures. One of the oldest measures of personality, still frequently used, is the **projective test.** This class of instruments, of which the **Rorschach test** is among the best known and most widely used, uses an unstructured (i.e., open-ended) format. The Rorschach test consists of a set of inkblots on pieces of cardboard; the inkblots are presented to the subject one by one in a standard order, each for as long as the subject likes. The Rorschach is described as open-ended because the researcher instructs the subject to describe *whatever* he or she sees in the blot. The researcher keeps a verbatim record of everything the subject says, also noting any peculiarity of facial expression or bodily movement.

Once the subject has responded to all the cards, the task of scoring begins. Hermann Rorschach, the psychiatrist who developed this instrument, also provided a scoring procedure for the responses, but the scoring method has been modified and explicated by other researchers over the years (e.g., Beck, Beck, Levitt, & Molish, 1961; Exner, 1993; Harrower & Bowers, 1987; Kleinmuntz, 1982; Klopfer & Kelley, 1942). The scoring and analysis procedures call for professionally supervised experience, so that the Rorschach is out of the reach of undergraduate students. However, because it is used by behavioral scientists around the world and you may find references to it in your literature search, you will find an appreciation of its purposes useful. Illustrative of its use in ethnomethodological research was the work done by George A. De Vos, an anthropologist, and L. Bryce Boyer, a psychiatrist. Using a scoring system they developed for cross-cultural studies, these researchers analyzed the verbal responses of Japanese, Algerian Arabs, and Apache Native Americans in order to identify universal concepts and symbols. Used in this way, the Rorschach revealed various adaptive properties of symbolic thinking within and across the cultures studied (De Vos & Boyer, 1989).

Another well-known projective measure is the **Thematic Apperception Test (TAT),** developed by Henry Murray. The TAT is composed of a number of pictures of people in various life contexts. The respondent is asked to make up a story explaining each picture. Because the situations depicted are adaptable to a number of interpretations, a variety of stories is appropriate. The stories the subject tells may reveal one or more themes that disclose certain concerns and personality characteristics. The TAT is a useful tool for studying sense making (discussed in the previous chapter), that is, the meanings that people impose on an event. For example, it was used recently by a team of personality researchers to probe subjects' implicit motives (i.e., enduring nonconscious needs) when they attributed causes to events (Peterson & Ulrey, 1994).

In a classic example of personality research, David McClelland and his coworkers (McClelland, Atkinson, Clark, & Lowell, 1953) used the TAT to map out the personality features of the "need to achieve." The researchers asked college students to construct a story from TAT pictures. As each picture was presented, the student was asked: (1) What is happening? Who are the persons? (2) What has led up to this situation? That is, what has happened in the past? (3) What is being thought? What is wanted? By whom? (4) What will happen? What will be done? Once the students made up their stories about the pictures, they were scored on their need for achievement. The researchers also used other tools of personality measurement to elicit their subjects' level of need for achievement. As a consequence, McClelland and his colleagues were able both to describe the structure and intensity of the need for achievement in each research participant and to develop a model of the situational factors that increase or decrease a need for achievement.

Structured Measures of Personality

In contrast to the Rorschach and the TAT, another widely used personality tool, the **Minnesota Multiphasic Personality Inventory (MMPI),** has a structured (closed) rather than an open-ended format. It contains statements such as "I often cross the street to avoid meeting people," "I am afraid of losing my mind," "I believe I am no more nervous than most others," and "I have a great deal of stomach trouble." The hundreds of such statements in the MMPI were selected after studies had determined which items best discriminated normal individuals and various types of psychiatric patients. Items were also selected to reflect general health, sexual attitudes, emotional states, and so on. From these items, clinical scales were developed, which are related to diagnostic categories such as depression, paranoia, and schizophrenia. Subjects or patients taking the MMPI are usually scored on all scales, and the scores are then compared with those of normal control subjects.

All of the tools described in the remainder of this chapter can be used quite routinely by most students (with the ethical stipulations noted previously), but the

Rorschach, the TAT, and the MMPI call for supervised experience to prevent unintended negative consequences of their use. Gaining access to these three measures also requires certification to the publisher that the user has had such training in testing. Students interested in the standards to which educational and psychological testers are bound will find a detailed account in the most recent edition of the American Psychological Association's *Standards for Educational and Psychological Testing.* The point of describing these tools is that you may find them referred to in your literature search, and knowing more about them will give you a more intuitive sense of the research in which they have been used.

As noted, many other measures of personality are, however, readily accessible to students for their own research. One handy guide to such tools is Robinson, Shaver, and Wrightsman's *Measures of Personality and Social Psychological Attitudes* (1991). This volume contains many tests and information about their scoring, validation, reliability, and use, including measures of subjective well-being, self-esteem, social anxiety, shyness, depression and loneliness, alienation, interpersonal trust, authoritarianism, sex roles, and personal values. In Box 5.2, we defined the Big Five factors, and there are also paper-and-pencil measures of these dimensions of personality (for details, see, e.g., McCrae & Costa, 1997; Wiggins, 1996).

Numerical Scales

Besides purchasing standardized instruments, researchers can also construct their own measures by using simple **rating scales.** By far, the most commonly used rating scales are the numerical, forced-choice, and graphic kinds. Whether you are testing subjects and scoring the results yourself or are using a computer to administer and score rating scales, you will find that they are easy to use and easy to score and have widespread application. Indeed, many standardized tests and measures also incorporate these rating scales. We begin by describing the **numerical scales,** a class of rating scales distinguished by the fact that the respondents work with a sequence of defined numbers. These numbers may be stated for the subject to see and use, or they may be implicit categories (e.g., 1-0 for "yes-no").

To illustrate, here is a question from a 20-item questionnaire that was designed to measure attitudes toward mathematics (Aiken, 1963):

My mind goes blank, and I am unable to think clearly when working with math.
_____ strongly disagree
_____ disagree
_____ undecided
_____ agree
_____ strongly agree

In this example, the numbers are implicit rather than explicit. For instance, we might score *strongly disagree* as −2, *disagree* as −1, *undecided* as 0, *agree* as +1, and *strongly agree* as +2. Alternatively, we might score *strongly disagree* as 1, *disagree* as 2, *undecided* as 3, *agree* as 4, and *strongly agree* as 5 (see also Box 5.3). Either way, we will get equivalent results when we statistically analyze the subjects' responses.

Because there are five response categories in the item above, it can be described as a 5-point numerical scale. Researchers also use more or fewer response categories and use different styles. For example, a team of developmental researchers used several different forms of numerical scales in a machine-scored questionnaire they gave to 6,400 high school students in Wisconsin and northern California (Steinberg, Lamborn, Dornbusch, & Darling, 1992). The purpose of this study was to examine whether student achievement could be best predicted from general parenting practices, parental encouragement of success, or parental involvement in schooling. Shown in Figure 5.1 is a sequence of items that used a 2-point format (Question 24), a 3-point format (25 and 26), a 4-point format (27), and finally a 5-point format (28). The overall finding of this research, incidentally, was that parental involvement was the best predictor and that this relationship was strengthened or weakened by general parenting practices. In other words, if you have terrific parents, it is better to have them involved in your schooling, but if you have bad parents, then it is better not to have them involved.

Box 5.3. ## Nudging the Undecideds

In the item used to measure attitudes toward mathematics, the subject is given the option to respond "undecided" (i.e., a neutral option). Some researchers prefer pushing the respondents to one or the other side rather than giving them the neutral option. Most survey researchers regard neutral responses as a form of missing data that merely reduces their ability to detect statistical differences (Schuman & Presser, 1996). The following item, which simply omits the neutral option, is taken from a 10-item questionnaire that was designed to measure attitudes toward the use of animals in experimental research (Lana, 1959):

Animals in pounds that would normally be destroyed should instead be used in animal experiments.
_____ I agree strongly
_____ I agree moderately
_____ I agree slightly
_____ I disagree slightly
_____ I disagree moderately
_____ I disagree strongly

Before we move on to the next type of scale, there are minimal considerations when we set about to construct a questionnaire (Robinson et al., 1991). One is that the items must adequately sample the "universe of content" that the questionnaire claims to represent. A way to confirm the adequacy of the sampling is to have experts in the content area examine the questionnaire for possible omissions; we have more to say about this consideration (also known as *content validity*) in the next chapter. The second consideration is that the items must be easily understood; that is, they must be written in plain language without any double-talk (ambiguities) or out-of-date expressions. A way to evaluate the clarity of the questionnaire items is to do **pilot testing** with a sample of individuals from the target population and then to use

24. In your family, are there any rules about your watching television?

○ Yes   ○ No

25. How much do your parents TRY to know . . .

	Don't try	Try a little	Try a lot
Who your friends are?	○	○	○
Where you go at night?	○	○	○
How you spend your money?	○	○	○
What you do with your free time?	○	○	○
Where you are most afternoons after school?	○	○	○

26. How much do your parents REALLY know . . .

	Don't know	Know a little	Know a lot
Who your friends are?	○	○	○
Where you go at night?	○	○	○
How you spend your money?	○	○	○
What you do with your free time?	○	○	○
Where you are most afternoons after school?	○	○	○

27. Do your parents have the right to tell you:

	They definitely have the right.	They probably have the right.	They probably do not have the right.	They definitely do not have the right.
How to spend time after school?	○	○	○	○
Who your friends can be?	○	○	○	○
How late you can stay out at night?	○	○	○	○
How to handle your school work?	○	○	○	○

28. Answer this question for the parents or guardians you now live with. How much do your mother (stepmother, guardian) and father (stepfather, guardian) agree with each other on:

	They almost always agree.	They usually agree.	They sometimes agree.	They rarely agree.	Doesn't apply (I live with one parent).
How you should behave	○	○	○	○	○
What to do when you do something wrong	○	○	○	○	○
How hard you should work in school	○	○	○	○	○

Figure 5.1 Consecutive items appearing in a questionnaire used by Steinberg, Lamborn, Dornbusch, and Darling (1992) to study the impact of parenting practices on school achievement in adolescents.

Source: Reprinted by permission of Laurence Steinberg.

content analysis of the subjects' responses to detect difficulties (e.g., Bolton, 1993). The third consideration is whether the subjects are responding to items in the manner intended. Their responses can be checked through some method of **item analysis; we** will have more to say about item analysis when we turn to the major types of attitude scales later in this chapter.

Forced-Choice Scales

A second class of rating scales is called **forced-choice** because the scales "push" subjects into making a definite statement rather than retreating into a neutral (e.g., a "don't know" or an "undecided") category. The sample item in Box 5.3 shows a popular variant of the numerical scale in which the neutral option was omitted. Classic examples of forced-choice items also push responses by presenting equally favorable (or equally unfavorable) alternatives and forcing the respondent to choose among them. Suppose we want subjects to describe themselves in both favorable and unfavorable terms, but we have encountered resistance when we asked them to describe their unfavorable traits. If we ask them, "Which characteristic *best* describes you—honest or intelligent?" we are *forcing* them to choose between two favorable attributes. We may also present two negative choices, of which the subject can reject one, or three negative choices (or three positive choices), so that the subject must select the most descriptive one and the least descriptive one.

As you might surmise, this approach is resisted by some subjects, who object to having to make a choice between equally favorable or equally unfavorable alternatives (Cronbach, 1960). Why use such scales at all, then? The forced-choice approach was developed to overcome a type of response bias called the **halo effect,** which is the tendency to surround some persons with a halo when judging them. There is now controversy surrounding the seriousness of the halo effect and whether it is as ubiquitous as early researchers claimed (Murphy, Jako, & Anhalt, 1993). We will return to the halo effect, but the classic forced-choice format that seems to arouse the least antagonism (and also to produce the most valid results) presents four favorable options and instructs the respondent to select the two *most descriptive* options in this group (Guilford, 1954).

To illustrate, suppose we are interested in testing a new incentive program, which is intended to improve the reward system and morale in a company. To test the effectiveness of the projected program, we plan to expose a sample of workers (i.e., the experimental group) to a one-month treatment condition and to compare their reactions with those of other workers (i.e., the control group) who are not assigned to the condition. The dependent measures will consist of self-ratings, ratings by managers, and nonreactive measures of performance, which we will use to triangulate on the effectiveness of the new program. Among the self-ratings are some forced-choice items, such as:

Circle the *two* characteristics that *best describe* how you feel in your work:

rewarded   relaxed   appreciated   trusting

Our hypothesis is that, if the incentive program has the effect of improving the reward system and morale, the experimental group will be more likely than the control group to circle characteristics such as "rewarded" and "appreciated."

Graphic Scales

Graphic scales are a third basic type of rating scale. Usually a graphic scale is a straight line resembling a thermometer, presented either horizontally or vertically. It can be used as either an observational or a self-report method (just as numerical and forced-choice methods can also be used in both situations). For example, high school teachers might use the following items to rate each student in a class (i.e., an observational method), or each student might be asked to rate himself or herself (i.e., a self-report method):

Unpopular ————————————————————— Popular
Shy ————————————————————— Outgoing
Solitary ————————————————————— Gregarious

The respondent makes a check mark, and we then transform that mark into a number by placing a ruler under the line and reading the number from the ruler. Notice that another characteristic of these items is that they are **bipolar**; that is, the ends of the scale are extreme opposites.

It is much easier, however, to divide the line into segments, transforming the "thermometer scale" into a numerical rating scale (also called a **segmented graphic scale**), as in the following 6-point example:

Unpopular ——— : ——— : ——— : ——— : ——— : ——— Popular
Shy ——— : ——— : ——— : ——— : ——— : ——— Outgoing
Solitary ——— : ——— : ——— : ——— : ——— : ——— Gregarious

Here, we ask the teacher or student to make a decision that reflects only positively or negatively on the person being rated, because a scale with an even number of segments does not allow for an undecided response (see again Box 5.3). This example is, in a way, reminiscent of a forced-choice measure, but it does not force the subject to select only from equally favorable or equally unfavorable choices.

It is important that the respondent really understand what to do on the scale. Particularly when a response category is not labeled with **cue words** (i.e., guiding labels), it is prudent to give the respondent some guiding examples. For instance, we might precede the actual scales with the following sample case if the subjects are to rate themselves:

If you would like to rate yourself *quite closely* to one or the other end of the scale (but not extremely), you should place your check mark as follows:
Unpopular ——— : ——— : ——— : ——— : _✓_ : ——— Popular

or

Unpopular ——— : _✓_ : ——— : ——— : ——— : ——— Popular

Rating Errors and Their Control

The use of numerical, forced-choice, and graphic rating scales (and combinations of these three types) assumes that the respondents are capable of an acceptable degree of rating precision and objectivity. In constructing such measures it is important to think about how to overcome certain **rating errors** (also called **response biases**). We mentioned that the forced-choice method was invented to overcome the halo effect, which is presumed to occur when an observer (e.g., a rater or judge) forms a favorable impression of a person based on one central trait and extends that impression to all of the person's characteristics. For example, a student who is athletic or good-looking may be judged to be more popular than she or he really is. As noted, a numerical scale would allow the respondent simply to pile up favorable ratings, whereas on a forced-choice scale, the respondent is forced to select among equally favorable or equally unfavorable choices.

Recent findings suggest that the halo effect is not as common as once believed, and that it is more likely to occur only in certain specifiable situations (Murphy et al., 1993). For example, it may occur when there is a substantial delay between observation and judgment, so that a rater relies on global impressions rather than on recently observed behavior. Halo effects also seem more apt to occur when the rater is unfamiliar with the person being rated, or when an early judgment involves dimensions that are logically related to the rater's global evaluation of the person. Classic findings suggested other situations in which halo effects may occur, such as when the trait or characteristic to be rated is not easily observed, is not clearly defined, involves relations with other people, and is of some moral importance (Symonds, 1925).

A second type of rating error is **leniency bias,** which occurs when respondents rate someone who is very familiar, or someone with whom they are ego-involved, in an unrealistically positive manner. A possible way to overcome this bias is to give only one unfavorable cue word (e.g., *poor*); the rest of the range is then made up of favorable responses in different degrees (e.g., *fairly good, good, very good, excellent*), as in the following extended scale:

Poor	Fairly good	Good	Very good	Excellent

However, we treat or analyze the cue words numerically so that "Good" is only a 3 on a 5-point scale from "Poor" (scored 1) to "Excellent" (scored 5).

A third type of rating error, **central tendency bias,** occurs when the respondent hesitates to give extreme ratings and instead clusters her or his responses around the center choice. This bias can usually be overcome in the same way that the positive range was expanded in the example above. If, for instance, we wanted to have a range of at least 5 points, we might use a 7-point scale, assuming that some subjects may be reluctant to use the end points in any circumstances. Similarly, if we wanted to have a range of at least 7 points, we might instead use a 9-point scale (see also Box 5.4).

In a fourth type of response bias, the **logical error in rating,** the respondents give similar ratings for variables or traits that they connect as logically related in their own minds but that may not occur together in the target person. This bias is similar to the halo effect in that both erroneously intercorrelate variables or traits that are being rated. The difference is that, in the halo effect, the respondent extends one favorable trait to the person as a whole, whereas in the logical error, the respondent interrelates certain variables or traits irrespective of individuals. The standard way to

---

Box 5.4 **Ceiling and Floor Effects**

Suppose we are using 5-point scales as before-and-after measures (or "tests") in an experiment using a manipulation designed to move the subjects' responses in a given direction. If the subjects make extremely high or extremely low scores on the **pretest** (i.e., the measure taken before the manipulation), there will be a problem if we want to produce further change in that direction. That is, we have a **ceiling effect** or a **floor effect**, which limits the amount of change that can be produced. We could try extending the ends of the scale after pilot-testing it, so that a 5-point scale becomes a 9-point or an 11-point scale. But if we find no changes from pretest to posttest, we must make sure the result is not still due to ceiling or floor effects.

---

overcome a logical error in rating is to construct very precise definitions and to make the instructions as explicit as possible.

In a fifth type of response bias, the **acquiescent response set,** some respondents (called **yea-sayers**) go along with almost any statement. If they are asked whether they agree or disagree with even the most unlikely term, they will almost invariably agree with it. To control for this problem, we would use both anti and pro items. For example, in a questionnaire measuring the person's attitude about the use of animals in medical experiments (called *vivisection research*), we would use both antivivisection items (e.g., "Many times, the same vivisection experiment is performed again and again without conclusive results.") and provivisection items (such as the one in Box 5.3). Yea-sayers can easily be identified (and, under some conditions, eliminated from the sample) by their agreement with both anti and pro items.

These cases give a flavor of response biases or rating errors and their control, although there are other possibilities besides these five (see Box 5.5). Numerical, graphic, and forced-choice rating scales, as noted, are also used in many standardized measures of judgment and attitude. **Standardized** means that certain rules (or

---

Box 5.5 **Socially Desirable Responding**

In the next chapter, we will describe some of the research conducted by Douglas Crowne and David Marlowe on **socially desirable responding.** This type of response bias, which is attributed to what Crowne and Marlowe termed the "need for social approval" (or the "approval motive"), implies that the subject has a tendency to give responses that will make him or her look good. The MMPI, for example, has a set of items (collectively called the **L Scale,** or **Lie Scale**) that were designed to identify respondents who deliberately try to appear socially desirable. Socially desirable responding is frequently viewed as a nuisance variable to be controlled or eliminated in some way (e.g., R. J. Fisher, 1993), but it is also viewed as a personality variable of interest in a wide variety of settings (e.g., Crowne, 1979; Nouri, Blau, & Shahid, 1995; Ones, Viswesvaran, & Reiss, 1996).

standards) must be followed in the development, administration, and scoring of these measures. We turn to three such procedures for developing questionnaires using either a segmented graphic scale, a numerical rating scale, or a simple check-list procedure. If you are doing a literature search in the area of attitudinal research, you are bound to encounter one or more of the following: the semantic differential and the Likert and Thurstone scale methods.

The Semantic Differential

The **semantic differential method,** which uses segmented graphic scales, was originally developed for the study of the connotative meaning of things in everyday life, as opposed to their denotative meaning. **Denotative** refers to the dictionary definition or assigned meaning (e.g., *Canis familiaris* is the denotative definition of *dog*), and **connotative** refers to the subjective or representational meaning, that is, one's own subjective associations (e.g., a warm, furry animal that shows unconditional acceptance of its master). The inventors of this method (Osgood, Suci, & Tannenbaum, 1957) discovered that most things in life (dogs, chairs, continents, ethnic groups, flowers, college majors, and so forth) are perceived in terms of three primary dimensions of subjective (i.e., connotative) meaning, which they named **evaluation, potency, and activity,** and which they defined in terms of bipolar cue words. Osgood and his associates also showed that it is possible to assess such perceptions by using segmented graphic scales with bipolar anchors to tap the full dimension of interest to the researcher.

Suppose we are interested in comparing two music groups, The Who and Pearl Jam, in terms of their respective connotative meanings to samples of different age groups. To tap the evaluative dimension, we could choose from among the following bipolar anchors: *bad-good, unpleasant-pleasant, negative-positive, ugly-beautiful, cruel-kind, unfair-fair,* and *worthless-valuable.* To measure the potency dimension, we could choose from among *weak-strong, light-heavy, small-large, soft-hard,* and *thin-heavy.* For the activity dimension, any of the following could be used: *slow-fast, passive-active,* and *dull-sharp.*

The scales might look as follows—though we will probably want to use more than just these three items—and the instructions to the subjects would be to rate each music group by checking the appropriate space:

Ugly ____ : ____ : ____ : ____ : ____ : ____ : ____ Beautiful
Soft ____ : ____ : ____ : ____ : ____ : ____ : ____ Hard
Dull ____ : ____ : ____ : ____ : ____ : ____ : ____ Sharp

The reason for using more than one scale for each dimension is to increase reliability (discussed in the next chapter). To score the responses, we would assign numbers to the rating, as follows:

Ugly ____ : ____ : ____ : ____ : ____ : ____ : ____ Beautiful
$\quad\quad$ -3 $\quad$ -2 $\quad$ -1 $\quad$ 0 $\quad$ $+1$ $\quad$ $+2$ $\quad$ $+3$

We then might compute a composite index such as a median or mean (described in Chapter 10).

Previously, we noted the importance of ensuring that the subjects understand what each response category signifies, particularly when the segments in graphic scales are unlabeled. In this example, the numbers stand for something like "extremely beautiful music" (+3), "quite beautiful music" (+2), "slightly beautiful music" (+1), "neutral" (0), "slightly ugly music" (−1), "quite ugly music" (−2), and "extremely ugly music" (−3). If these labels make sense to us in terms of the purpose of our study, then the rating scale will do. Figure 5.2 shows a typical set of instructions based on those provided by the inventors of the semantic differential, which we might use in our comparison of music groups. These instructions incorporate a number of sample items to ensure that the respondents understand the meaning of each alternative. If we were actually doing this study, the instructions would appear on the front page of our semantic differential questionnaire.

> The purpose of this questionnaire is to measure the *meanings* of some music groups to various people by having them judge these groups against a set of descriptive scales. We would like you to judge each group on the basis of what the group listed means *to you*. On each page of this booklet, you will find a different group to be judged and beneath it a set of scales. You are to rate the group on each of these scales in order.
>
> If you feel that the group at the top of the page is *very accurately described* by the word at one end of the scale, place your check mark as follows:
>
> Dull ____ : ____ : ____ : ____ : ____ : ____ : _✔_ Sharp
> or
> Dull _✔_ : ____ : ____ : ____ : ____ : ____ : ____ Sharp
>
> If you feel that the group is *quite* (but not extremely) *accurately described* at one end of the scale, place your check mark as follows:
>
> Dull ____ : ____ : ____ : ____ : ____ : _✔_ : ____ Sharp
> or
> Dull ____ : _✔_ : ____ : ____ : ____ : ____ : ____ Sharp
>
> If the group seems *only slightly described* by one end as opposed to the other end (but is not really neutral), place your check mark as follows:
>
> Dull ____ : ____ : ____ : ____ : _✔_ : ____ : ____ Sharp
> or
> Dull ____ : ____ : _✔_ : ____ : ____ : ____ : ____ Sharp
>
> The placement of your check, of course, depends on which of the two ends of the scale seems most descriptive of the music group you are judging. If you see the group as *neutral* on the scale (that is, if both ends of the scale are *equally descriptive* of the group), or if the scale is *completely irrelevant* (that is, unrelated to the group), place your check mark in the middle space:
>
> Dull ____ : ____ : ____ : _✔_ : ____ : ____ : ____ Sharp

Figure 5.2   **Semantic differential instructions.**

The Likert Scale

Another traditional scaling approach popularly known as a **Likert scale** is based on an item analysis method that, in appearance, produces a set of numerical attitude items. That is, numbers are associated with different responses (e.g., "strongly agree," "agree," "undecided," "disagree," and "strongly disagree") to a series of statements. The method of choosing the final set of attitude items was originally called the **summated ratings method** by its inventor (Rensis Likert, 1932). Although most students will not have occasion to use the summated ratings method to develop their own attitude questionnaire, it is useful to understand how questionnaires using this method are constructed in case you decide to use a published one.

Briefly, the first step in using the summated ratings method is to write a large number of statements on the topic of interest. We give these to a sample of subjects from the target population, who indicate their evaluations of each statement, usually by means of a 5-point scale from "strongly agree" to "strongly disagree." We then sort through the data in order to select the best 20 or so statements for the final questionnaire. This sorting consists of finding out the extent to which all of the responses to individual statements are correlated with the total score (the sum of the scores for all the items). Statements that correlate well with (i.e., show a strong relationship to) the total score are then chosen for the final questionnaire. The rationale of the summated ratings method is that statements that have low correlations with the total score will not discriminate those respondents with positive attitudes from those with negative attitudes.

The result of using this method is presented in Figure 5.3, which shows a questionnaire that was pared down to 20 items (Mahler, 1953). Items 2, 4, 6, 9, 10, 11, 14, and 15 (called "pro-socialized medicine" statements by the author of this scale) are in favor of a compulsory health program and against the system of private practice. Items 1, 3, 5, 7, 8, 12, 13, 16, 17, 18, 19, and 20 (called "anti-socialized medicine" statements) are against a compulsory health program and in favor of the system of private practice. In using this attitude scale, we might weight the responses to the pro-socialized-medicine statements from 5 ("strongly agree") to 1 ("strongly disagree"). For the anti-socialized-medicine statements, we would simply reverse this scoring procedure. A person's score is the sum of the responses, a high score indicating an accepting attitude toward a compulsory health program and a low score indicating an unaccepting attitude toward a compulsory health program. The highest and lowest possible scores, then, would be 100 (most strongly in favor of a compulsory health program) and 20 (most strongly against a compulsory health program).

The Thurstone Scale

Another classical item-analysis procedure, developed by L. L. Thurstone (1929, 1929-1934), is the **method of equal-appearing intervals.** It takes its name from the idea that judges, who are asked to sort statements into different piles, can presumably keep the piles psychologically equidistant. The term **Thurstone scale** is ambiguous in some respects because Thurstone also pioneered the development of other scaling

Instructions to Subjects

Please indicate your reaction to the following statements, using these alternatives (circle your choice):

Strongly agree = SA
Agree = A
Undecided = U
Disagree = D
Strongly disagree = SD

1. The quality of medical care under the system of private practice is superior to that under a system of compulsory health insurance.

   SA   A   U   D   SD

2. A compulsory health program will produce a healthier and more productive population.

   SA   A   U   D   SD

3. Under a compulsory health program there would be less incentive for young men and women to become doctors.

   SA   A   U   D   SD

4. A compulsory health program is necessary because it brings the greatest good to the greatest number of people.

   SA   A   U   D   SD

5. Treatment under a compulsory health program would be mechanical and superficial.

   SA   A   U   D   SD

6. A compulsory health program would be a realization of one of the true aims of a democracy.

   SA   A   U   D   SD

7. Compulsory medical care would upset the traditional relationship between the family doctor and the patient.

   SA   A   U   D   SD

8. I feel that I would get better care from a doctor whom I am paying than from a doctor who is being paid by the government.

   SA   A   U   D   SD

9. Despite many practical objections, I feel that compulsory health insurance is a real need of the American people.

   SA   A   U   D   SD

10. A compulsory health program could be administered quite efficiently if the doctors would cooperate.

    SA   A   U   D   SD

11. There is no reason why the traditional relationship between doctor and patient cannot be continued under a compulsory health program.

    SA   A   U   D   SD

12. If a compulsory health program were enacted, politicians would have control over doctors.

    SA   A   U   D   SD

13. The present system of private medical practice is the one best adapted to the liberal philosophy of democracy.

    SA   A   U   D   SD

14. There is no reason why doctors should not be able to work just as well under a compulsory health program as they do now.

    SA   A   U   D   SD

15. More and better care will be obtained under a compulsory program.

    SA   A   U   D   SD

16. The atmosphere of a compulsory health program would destroy the initiative and the ambition of young doctors.

    SA   A   U   D   SD

17. Politicians are trying to force a compulsory health program upon the people without giving them the true facts.

    SA   A   U   D   SD

18. Administrative costs under a compulsory health program would be exorbitant.

    SA   A   U   D   SD

19. Red tape and bureaucratic problems would make a compulsory health program grossly inefficient.

    SA   A   U   D   SD

20. Any system of compulsory insurance would invade the privacy of the individual.

    SA   A   U   D   SD

Figure 5.3 The Socialized Medicine Attitude Scale.

Source: Reproduced from "Attitudes Toward Socialized Medicine" by I. Mahler, 1953, *Journal of Social Psychology,* 38, pp. 273–282. Used by permission of the Helen Dwight Reid Educational Foundation. Published by Heldref Publications, 1319 Eighteenth St., N.W., Washington, D.C. 20036–1802. Copyright © 1953.

methods (which are still frequently used). However, most behavioral and social researchers, when they speak of a "Thurstone attitude scale," mean a questionnaire that has been constructed by the method of equal-appearing intervals. Again, we will describe this method not because you are likely to construct a Thurstone questionnaire for your research, but because you may find examples of attitude or personality measures constructed in this way that you can use in your research (see Box 5.6).

Box 5.6   Useful Source Books

If you are looking for an attitude or personality measure developed by the Likert or Thurstone procedures, you will find many existing measures in the public domain. One good source of such measures is Marvin E. Shaw and Jack M. Wright's *Scales for the Measurement of Attitudes* (1967), which reproduces specific instruments and describes their characteristics (e.g., reliability and validity) and scoring. Another valuable resource is the *Directory of Unpublished Experimental Mental Measures*, (1995, 1996ab), edited by Bert A. Goldman and his colleagues and published by the American Psychological Association. It has descriptions of several thousand psychological instruments that are available for use in a wide variety of research situations, such as measures of educational, psychological, social, and vocational adjustment, and measures of aptitude, attitude, concept meaning, creativity, personality, problem solving, status, and so on.

Briefly, this method also begins with a large number of statements, each typed on a separate slip of paper or an index card. Judges (not the subjects to be given the questionnaire) then sort the statements into 11 piles, numbered from 1 (labeled "most unfavorable statements") to 11 ("most favorable statements"). The judges are allowed to place as many statements as they wish in any pile. A scale value is calculated for each statement, which is the average (usually calculated as the *median*, or midmost value) of the responses of all judges to that particular item. In selecting statements for the final questionnaire, the researcher chooses those that are (1) most consistently rated by the judges and (2) spread relatively evenly along the entire attitude range. Shown in Figure 5.4 is an attitude questionnaire that was developed during World War II by the use of Thurstone's method of equal-appearing intervals (Day & Quackenbush, 1942). In this example, notice that the subjects are asked to respond to each statement three times, once for each type of war. Shaw and Wright (1967) obtained the scale values for these statements (see bottom of page 121) from a sample of 15 women and 35 men (and the reliability of the scale was based on the responses of 326 male students at the University of Mississippi).

We see that the lowest scale value (0.8 for Statement 3) corresponds to the most promilitaristic statement and that the highest scale value (8.4 for Statement 6) corresponds to the most antimilitaristic statement in this set. If we use this scale in research, the attitude score for each referent (defensive war, cooperative war, and aggressive war) is the median of the scale values of the statements that the subject endorses (i.e.,

Instructions to Subjects

This is a study of attitudes toward war. Below you will find a number of statements expressing various degrees of attitudes toward war or tendencies to act in case of war.

In expressing your agreement or disagreement with the statements, please put yourself in three possible situations. First, imagine that the United States had declared a *Defensive War* (war for the purpose of defending the United States in case of an attack). Please indicate in the first set of parentheses, designated by roman numeral I, your agreement, disagreement, or doubt. Put a check mark (✓) if you agree with the statement, put a minus sign (−) if you disagree with the statement, and a question mark (?) if you are in doubt about the statement.

Second, imagine that the United States has declared a *Cooperative War* (war in cooperation with the democratic countries of Europe for the defense of democracy). Go over the statements again and indicate in the second set of parentheses, designated by roman II, your agreement, disagreement, or doubt in a similar way.

Third, imagine that the United States has declared an *Aggressive War* (war for the purpose of gaining more territory). Read the statements again and indicate in the third set of parentheses, designated by roman III, your agreement, disagreement, or doubt by a similar method.

```
 I      II     III
( )    ( )    ( )      1. I would support my country even against my convictions.
( )    ( )    ( )      2. I would immediately attempt to find some technicality on which to evade go-
                          ing to war.
( )    ( )    ( )      3. I would immediately go to war and would do everything in my power to in-
                          fluence others to do the same.
( )    ( )    ( )      4. I would rather be called a coward than go to war.
( )    ( )    ( )      5. I would offer my services in whatever capacity I can.
( )    ( )    ( )      6. I would not only refuse to participate in any way in war but also attempt to in-
                          fluence public opinion against war.
( )    ( )    ( )      7. I would take part in war only to avoid social ostracism.
( )    ( )    ( )      8. I would not go to war unless I were drafted.
( )    ( )    ( )      9. If possible, I would wait a month or two before I would enlist.
( )    ( )    ( )     10. I would go to war only if my friends went to war.
( )    ( )    ( )     11. I would refuse to participate in any way in war.
( )    ( )    ( )     12. I would disregard any possible exemptions and enlist immediately.
( )    ( )    ( )     13. I would not enlist but would give whatever financial aid I could.
```

Figure 5.4 The Attitudes Toward War Scale.

Source: Reproduced from "Attitudes Toward Defensive, Cooperative, and Aggressive War" by D.D. Day and O.F. Quackenbush, 1942, *Journal of Social Psychology, 16*, pp. 11–20. Used by permission of the Helen Dwight Reid Educational Foundation, Heldref Publications, 1319 Eighteenth St., N.W., Washington, D.C. 20036–1802. Copyright © 1942.

Statement	Scale value	Statement	Scale value
1	2.5	8	5.9
2	7.5	9	4.6
3	0.8	10	5.1
4	7.9	11	8.2
5	2.5	12	1.4
6	8.4	13	3.5
7	6.3		

checks) for the referent. The higher the median, the more unfavorable the subject's attitude toward that war referent. For example, if the subject checks Statements 2, 4, 6, and 11 under Roman numeral I, we know that the subject is very strongly opposed to defensive war (median = 8.05, or midway between the scale values of 7.9 for Statement 4 and 8.2 for Statement 11).

Pilot-Testing Your Questionnaire

In developing a questionnaire—as much as in developing an interview (discussed next)—*pilot testing* is absolutely essential. This testing will enable the researcher to determine whether the items are worded properly, for example, whether terms like *approve* and *like* (or *disapprove* and *dislike*) are being used as synonyms or whether there are differences in implication. Suppose that a researcher wants to examine people's perceptions of the quality of a mayor's performance, and this researcher phrases an item as follows: "How do you feel about the mayor? _____ I like him. _____ I dislike him." The item is quite useless because it does not distinguish between liking and approving. It is possible, for example, for people to like someone (or something) without approving of him or her (or it), and vice versa (Bradburn, 1982).

The researcher must also be sure that the way in which the items are worded and presented does not lead the respondent into giving an unrealistically narrow answer. A poor question will produce a very narrow range of responses or will be misunderstood by the respondents. Take the following item: "Do you approve of the way the mayor is handling her duties? _____ Yes. _____ No." One might approve of the way the mayor handled the school crisis but not the snow removal crisis, or might disapprove of the way the mayor handled the strike threat by sanitation workers but not the threatened tax increase.

Thus a number of different items are needed to cover the various issues on which we want an opinion about a mayor's effectiveness, and the issues must be spelled out if we are to prevent any misunderstanding on the part of the respondents. Suppose the school crisis and the sanitation workers' threat both involved union confrontations, but the first was resolved without a strike and the second resulted in a protracted strike. We need a separate question, or set of questions, regarding each situation and whether the respondent approves or disapproves of its handling.

The researcher must also avoid asking **leading questions,** which can constrain responses and produce biased answers: "Do you agree that the mayor has an annoying, confrontational style? _____ Yes. _____ No." The phrasing of the question *leads* (or invites) the respondents to be overly negative or critical. How should such a question be phrased? In coming up with an alternative, the researcher will want to be sure that the new question is not worded so as to produce another meaningless answer: "Do you agree with the mayor's philosophy of city government? _____ Yes. _____ No." What would a yes or no really tell us? We need to do some probing to get meaningful information.

Problems such as these can be identified during the pilot testing and can usually be resolved with rewording or with a set of probing items instead of a single item. The question of whether to use open-ended or more structured items (or a combination of both) can also be answered in pilot testing. Like personality measures, the questionnaires used by many survey researchers come in a variety of open and closed styles. For example, structured questions may take the form of multiple-choice, yes-no, either-or, or acceptable-unacceptable items. A fill-in-the-blank form is useful when more specific responses are sought. Of course, these structured forms are effective only if the material to be covered allows this amount of simplification.

In your pilot testing, think about asking exploratory questions such as "What did the whole item mean to you?" "What was it you had in mind when you said _____ ?" "Consider the same item this way, and tell what you think of it: _____ ," "You said _____ , but would you feel differently if the question read _____ ?" (Converse & Presser, 1986, p. 52). It is also important that the information elicited reflect what the subject *really* feels or believes. As a rule, people have not thought very much about most issues that do not affect them directly; their replies may reflect only a superficial feeling or understanding, or they may try to "put on a good face." Survey researchers often ask the respondent how he or she feels about a topic (e.g., "How *deeply* do you feel about it?"). In this way, they attempt to determine whether the respondent truly believes what he or she has reported (Labaw, 1980). Another useful procedure is to ask subjects to rate their confidence in their answer so that they reveal how much they are guessing.

Interviews versus Questionnaires

We turn next to how to plan a research interview, but it will be instructive if we first note the respective advantages of questionnaires and interviews. In general, questionnaires are convenient to use because (1) they can be administered to large numbers of people (e.g., in mail surveys); (2) they are relatively economical (because a mail survey eliminates travel time and cost); and (3) they provide a type of "anonymity" (in that, instead of meeting the researcher face to face, the respondent sends a mail survey, for example, to an impersonal research center).

However, a **face-to-face interview** has advantages: (1) It provides an opportunity to establish rapport with the subjects and to stimulate the trust and cooperation often needed to probe sensitive areas; (2) it provides an opportunity to help the subjects in their interpretation of the questions; and (3) it allows flexibility in determining the wording and sequence of the questions by giving the researcher greater control over the situation (e.g., by letting the interviewer determine on the spot the amount of probing required).

Just as the researcher who uses a questionnaire needs to do pilot testing, the researcher who uses an **interview schedule** (i.e., a script containing the questions the interviewer will ask in the face-to-face interview) needs to pilot-test it. This pilot testing and all the planning that precedes it, which we discuss next, cover four steps: (1) stating the objective; (2) outlining a recruitment strategy; (3) structuring the interview schedule; and (4) testing it and making appropriate revisions.

Planning and Pilot-Testing the Interview

Step 1.   The objectives of the interview need to be spelled out. What are the questions and hypotheses to be addressed? What kind of data does the researcher need to answer the questions and test the hypotheses? What kinds of subjects will produce the relevant responses? Suppose a researcher's objective is to interview the "opinion leaders" in a community. During the testing phase (Step 4), she or he will have to locate some of the potential interviewees and try out the questions on them. This step requires patience because the researcher may need a long series of interviews with many randomly selected individuals to find the appropriate subjects.

Step 2. Next, the researcher needs to formulate a recruitment strategy, that is, a plan for locating the potential interviewees. Part of this plan will include (a) devising relevant questions and specifying how the replies will be analyzed; (b) pretesting the interview schedule; and (c) recruiting and training the interviewers.

Step 3. The researcher must now structure the interview schedule by (a) checking each item for relevancy; (b) determining ranges of responses for some items; (c) establishing the best sequence of questions; and (d) establishing the best wording of questions:

a. In this third step, each question or item should be examined for its relevance to the research hypotheses or exploratory aims of the study. The interview schedule may require the pruning of Occam's razor (described in Chapter 2) to cut away undesirable or unnecessary items. In addition, the interviews should not be too long; 60–90 minutes seems to be the outermost limit before respondents become bored (cf. Pareek & Rao, 1980).

b. Also, in developing structured items, researchers construct ranges of responses. For example, if we want to know someone's salary, it is better to present ranges of income levels than to ask an exact amount. A potential problem (to which we will return in a moment) is that some questions may make unrealistic demands on the subjects' memory. Even without a range of responses, the subjects may make **false-negative reports** (i.e., they may fail to report information) because of true memory lapses or because of carelessness or an unwillingness to make the effort necessary to give a fuller account of past events (Cannell, Miller & Oksenberg, 1981).

c. Another consideration in this third step is the best sequence of items. Broadly speaking, specific questions seem to be less affected by what preceded them than are general or broadly stated questions (Bradburn, 1982; Schuman & Presser, 1996). And when sensitive topics are to be discussed, it is usually better to ask these sensitive questions at the end of the interview. Some interviewees find questions about their age, education, and income an invasion of privacy. When asked at the beginning of an interview, such questions may interfere with the establishment of trust. However, even when they are asked at the end of the interview, it is helpful to preface such questions with a reassuring statement. In one study, the interviewer stated, "Some of the questions may seem like an invasion of your privacy, so if you'd rather not answer any of the questions, just tell me it's none of my business" (C. Smith, 1980).

d. A final consideration in this third step is to work out the best wording of the items. It is essential that all the subjects readily understand the wording in equivalent ways. The pilot stage (the next step) should show what jargon and expressions are inhibitors and facilitators of communication in the particular circumstances. Especially important is the phrasing of the opening question, which should show the subject immediately that the interviewer is pursuing the stated purpose. Interestingly, research evidence suggests that disclosing as little as possible about the interview in the introduction has no methodological benefits in terms of refusals, rapport, cooperation, or bias (Sobal, 1982). As noted in Chapter 3, we want to be as open and honest as possible in our communications with our subjects, just as we want them to be forthcoming in their responses.

Step 4. The final step before going into the field is to pilot-test the interview schedule and make modifications wherever necessary. At this stage, just as during the actual survey, it is important that the interviewers listen *analytically* to the subjects' responses (Downs, Smeyak, & Martin, 1980). The skilled interviewer does not jump in and interrupt before the subject has developed an idea but is patient, gets the main idea, hears the facts, makes valid inferences, hears details, and demonstrates good listening skills (Weaver, 1972).

The Critical Incident Technique

As in the research questionnaire, a basic consideration in developing an interview schedule is whether to use open-ended or structured questions (see, e.g., Bradburn, 1983; Dohrenwend & Richardson, 1963). Figure 5.5 is an example of a brief interview schedule. This particular schedule was part of a study of children in the rural South (Baughman & Dahlstrom, 1968). As is typical of most interview schedules, some items are more structured than others. The more structured items are 2, 4, and 9, and the most unstructured one is 3.

Of course, open-ended questions can be asked in other ways. For example, the **critical incident technique,** which has special status in clinical and organizational research (Flanagan, 1954), involves asking the subject to give an open-ended description of an observable action. The purpose of the action must be fairly clear to the observer, and the consequences must be sufficiently definite to leave little doubt about its effects. In a recent study, the critical incident technique was used in the United States and India with company managers who were interviewed as part of an investigation of how managers coped with harmful rumors (DiFonzo et al., 1994). The managers were asked to describe as fully and concretely as possible a real situation that was important to their company, in which they had to confront a harmful or a potentially harmful rumor. The resulting narratives revealed some of the circumstances in which rumor control strategies are likely to succeed and which were also found to be consistent with recent empirically based theorizing (Rosnow, 1991).

The critical incident technique is used in questionnaire as well as interview research. For example, a traditional area of research in industrial and organizational psychology is the study of leaders and followers (e.g., House & Aditya, 1997). Edwin P. Hollander, a noted researcher in this area, used the critical incident technique in one aspect of his research (e.g., Elgie, Hollander, & Rice, 1988; Hollander, 1992; Kelly, Julian, & Hollander, 1992). He and his coworkers presented a sequence

MOTHER INTERVIEW SCHEDULE

CHILD'S NAME _____ INTERVIEWER _____

DATE _____

We are interested in spending time with your four-year-old child, _____ . We believe there are many things that children can learn when they are young. There are some things you may be able to tell us about _____ that will help us to know him (her) better.

I will be asking you about what _____ is like and some of the things he (she) may or may not like to do.

1. Could you tell me what X is usually like?

    a. Happy _____   d. Silly _____
    b. Serious _____   e. Other _____
    c. Sad _____

2. Would you describe him (her) as:

    a. Shy _____   h. Needs encouragement _____
    b. Active _____   i. Always in a hurry _____
    c. Careful _____   j. Plays well alone _____
    d. Fearful _____   k. Would rather play by himself (herself) _____
    e. Tries things _____   l. Would rather play with others _____
    f. Shows off _____   m. Does he (she) have to do things just right (just so)? _____
    g. Laughs a lot _____   n. Asks a lot of questions _____

3. Do you have any special concerns about X?

    a. _____
    b. _____

4. Has X had a chance to spend time doing some of these things?

    _____ a. Marking with crayon _____
    _____ b. Marking with a pencil _____
    _____ c. Cutting with scissors _____
    _____ d. Pasting _____
    _____ e. Collecting things _____
    _____ f. Working puzzles _____
    _____ g. Building with blocks or sticks _____
    _____ h. Looking at magazines or catalogs _____

5. Does anyone read story books to him (her)? _____

    (If yes) Does he (she) seem to listen? _____
    (If no) Does he (she) listen to someone tell stories? _____
    Does he (she) seem to enjoy the stories? _____
    What kind does he (she) seem to like most? _____
    Does he (she) ever tell a story that he (she) has heard? _____

    Does he (she) ever make up a story to tell? _____

    Does he (she) ever try to tell a story that he (she) has seen on television? _____

6. Does X get to play with children other than his (her) brothers and sisters? _____

7. Where does he (she) see other children? _____

8. Does he (she) get to spend much time with his (her) daddy? _____

9. Does he (she) like to:

    _____ a. Throw a ball   _____ f. Jump
    _____ b. Run   _____ g. Play games
    _____ c. Climb   _____ h. Make believe (play house, play grown-up)
    _____ d. Dance   _____ i. Other things (list) _____
    _____ e. Sing

10. Does X try to help around the house or farm? _____

Figure 5.5   Example of an interview schedule.

Source: Reproduced from E.E. Baughman and W.G. Dahlstrom, *Negro and White Children: A Psychological Study in the Rural South,* Academic Press, 1968. Used by permission of E.E. Baughman and Academic Press.

of four questions to sketch a profile of bad leadership in organizations (E. P. Hollander, personal communication, May 27, 1992). The first question was

> Think of a group or organization to which you belong, or did belong. Please describe a situation or event there that occurred between you and a superior in which you consider that *bad* leadership was displayed. Try to be as clear as possible in describing the conditions and behavior involved.

Next, the subject was asked:

> Indicate what you found rewarding or not from what that superior did or said as the leader there.

Then the subject was asked:

> What, if anything, was your response?

And the final question in this set was

> What effect did this event have on your relationship with this superior?

Interviews by Telephone

Beginning in the 1960s, various changes in American society led many researchers in the United States to turn to the **telephone interview** and the mail survey as substitutes for face-to-face interviews. Among the changes contributing to this shift were (1) the increased costs of conducting face-to-face interviews (because interviewing is a labor-intensive activity); (2) the invention of random-digit-dialing methods for random sampling of telephone households; and (3) the development of computer-assisted methods of recording responses, in which questions are flashed on a computer screen and the interviewer directly keys in the response for computer scoring (Rossi, Wright, & Anderson, 1983).

Like all methods, telephone interviewing has both advantages and disadvantages (Downs et al., 1980; Lavrakas, 1987; P. V. Miller & Cannell, 1982). Among the advantages are that it allows a quick turnaround (i.e., information can be got more promptly than by face-to-face interview or mail survey). Refusal rates are also usually lower in telephone interviewing (because it is not necessary to allow a stranger into one's home). Among the disadvantages are that interviewing is restricted, first, to households that own a telephone and, then, to those that answer the telephone (instead of having an answering machine or caller ID constantly on duty to screen calls). A further disadvantage is that fewer questions (and less probing questions) can be asked because it is harder to establish rapport than in a face-to-face interview and people are more impatient to conclude a telephone interview.

Generally speaking, whether telephone or face-to-face interviewing is used, the same procedures are followed in developing an interview schedule and training the interviewers. One difference, however, is that telephone interviewers have less time to establish rapport: The subject can always hang up without listening to the introduction. If the subject does not immediately hang up, then a strategy used to foster commitment on the part of the subject is to point out the important goals of the research and to use positive feedback as a means of reinforcing good responding: "Thanks . . . this is the sort of information we are looking for in this research . . . it's important to us to get this information . . . these details are helpful" (P. V. Miller & Cannell, 1982, p. 256).

Memory and the Use of Behavioral Diaries

A problem with the use of self-report measures is that autobiographical questions may yield inaccurate answers when the subjects are asked to rely on memory (e.g., how often they have done something or how much of something they have bought or consumed). Some examples are "How many weeks have you been looking for work?" and "How much have you paid for car repairs over the previous year?" Problems surface because recall is limited (H. B. Bernard & Killworth, 1970, 1980; S. K. Reed, 1988; Webber, 1970; Zechmeister & Nyberg, 1982). Suppose we wanted to study lying in everyday life. If we asked subjects to estimate, for example, the number of "little white lies" they tell each day, the results could hardly be considered valid because of both the porosity of memory and the possible wish to give a socially desirable response.

An innovative tool that attempts to overcome the porosity problem is the **behavioral diary** (e.g., Conrath, 1973; Wickesberg, 1968), a method based on the use of field notes in participant-observer and ethnographic research (discussed in the previous chapter). The basic procedure is to ask the subjects to keep a diary of events at the time they occur. For example, social psychologists Bella M. DePaulo and Deborah A. Kashy, and their coworkers, used tests and behavioral diaries in their studies of the lies that college students tell (DePaulo & Kashy, 1998; DePaulo, Kashy, Kirkendol, Wyer, & Epstein, 1996; Kashy & DePaulo, 1996). The subjects in this research kept meticulous records of their lying. Among the findings were that those who told more lies were more manipulative and more concerned with self-presentation and, not surprisingly, that they told more self-serving lies.

Another study that used this method was conducted by Mihaly Csikszentmihalyi and Reed Larson (1984), who were interested in studying teenagers' day-to-day lives. The subjects in this study were 75 teenagers, who were given beepers and were then signaled at random by the researchers. When the beeper went off, the subject recorded his or her thoughts and feelings at that moment. Figure 5.6 shows a week in the life of one subject. This person had hoped to spend her first year after high school studying abroad but learned that she would not be allowed to go. The scale at the top shows a continuum from bad to good moods, and the zig-zagged line reveals that this subject's mood fluctuated tremendously as she tried to cope with everyday events. Clearly she was happiest when with friends and unhappiest when alone.

The assumption is that such a diary gives more reliable data than questionnaires or interviews that elicit answers to autobiographical questions. To test this assumption, a team of researchers (Conrath, Higgins, & McClean, 1983) collected data from managers and staff personnel in three diverse organizations (a manufacturer of plastic products, an insurance brokerage company, and a large public utility). Each participant was instructed to keep a diary of 100 consecutive interactions, beginning on a

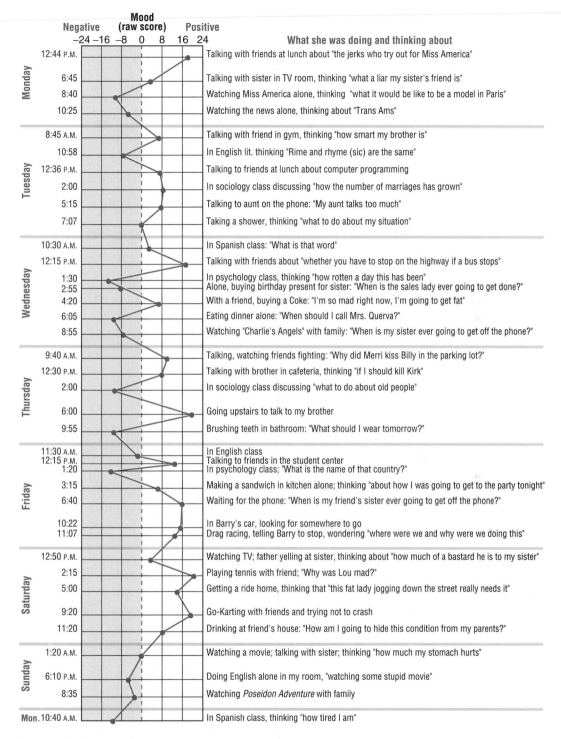

Figure 5.6 The self-recorded diary record of a week in the life of one teenage subject.

Source: Figure 8.4 "The week of Lorraine Monawski" from *Being Adolescent: Conflict and Growth in the Teenage Years* by Mihaly Csikszentmihalyi and Reed Larson. Copyright © 1984 by Basic Books, Inc. Reprinted by permission of Basic Books, a division of HarperCollins Publishers, Inc.

specific date and at a specific time. The instructions were to list the other party to the interaction, the initiator of the activity, the mode of interaction, the elapsed time, and the process involved. The diary was constructed in such a way that the subject could quickly record all this information with no more than four to eight check marks next to particular items. At a later time, each participant was asked to answer a questionnaire covering the same interactions.

The data from all the behavioral diaries and questionnaires were compared afterward. If one person reported talking to particular others, the researchers checked the diaries and questionnaires of those others to see whether they had also reported that activity. In this way, a separate measure of reliability was obtained for the behavioral diary and for the questionnaire data (i.e., concerning the reporting of specific events at the time of the events as opposed to a later time). The results were that the questionnaire data (the recalls from autobiographical memory) were less reliable than the behavioral diary data. In spite of these encouraging results, other researchers have challenged the accuracy of diary information and have argued that the subjects may be overly attentive to events that "stick out" in their minds and may thus underreport other behavior (Maurer, Palmer, & Ashe, 1993)

Summary of Ideas

1. Two forms of self-report measures are those that allow the respondents to express their feelings and impressions quite spontaneously (i.e., *open-ended*) and those that use a fixed response format (i.e., *closed*).

2. The general advantages and limitations of open-ended measures are basically the reverse of the advantages and limitations of closed measures.

3. The Rorschach inkblot test and the TAT operate on the principle that, in the spontaneous responses that come to his or her mind, the respondent will project some unconscious aspect of his or her life experience and emotions onto ambiguous stimuli.

4. The Big Five factors of personality, or NEOAC ("Not Every Organism Acts Consistently"), are (a) neuroticism, (b) extraversion, (c) openness to experience, (d) agreeableness, and (e) conscientiousness.

5. Three kinds of rating scales are the numerical, the forced-choice, and the graphic scales.

6. In a numerical scale, the numbers may be explicit or implicit, but the statements, if any, must always be unambiguous and easily understood.

7. The forced-choice scale was invented to counteract the halo effect (which itself is no longer seen as a very serious or omnipresent problem, however).

8. Graphic scales resemble a thermometer, and they may or may not be segmented.

9. Rating biases include the halo effect, the error of leniency, the error of central tendency, the logical error in rating, and the acquiescent response set.

10. There are specific techniques for dealing with each of these problems as well as with "undecided" responses and the ceiling and floor effects (described in Box 5.4).

11. Socially desirable responding (Box 5.5) is viewed both as a nuisance variable in some cases and as a personality variable of interest in other cases.

12. The semantic differential, which is used to measure connotative meaning, usually focuses on the evaluative, potency, and activity dimensions by means of 7-point graphic scales with bipolar anchors.

13. Item analysis (which is part of the method of summated ratings) is used to construct a Likert scale (e.g., the Socialized Medicine Attitude Scale in Figure 5.3).

14. Thurstone's method of equal-appearing intervals is another method of item analysis used in the construction of attitude scales (e.g., the scale on attitudes toward war in Figure 5.4).

15. The purpose of pilot testing is to enable the researcher to fine-tune the data collection instrument and procedures.

16. The four steps in developing an interview schedule are (a) working out the objective; (b) formulating a general strategy of data collection; (c) writing the questions and establishing the best sequence; and (d) pilot-testing the material.

17. The critical incident technique uses open-ended questions that focus specifically on some observable action or experience.

18. Telephone interviews have both advantages and limitations; in general, they follow the same procedures used in developing any interview schedule.

19. The major advantage of the behavioral diary is that events are recorded as they happen, and there is no need to rely on longer term recall (e.g., the study about lying and the study of teenagers' day-to-day lives).

Key Terms

acquiescent response set   p. 115
behavioral diaries   p. 128
Big Five factors   p. 107
bipolar rating scales   p. 113
ceiling effect   p. 115
central tendency bias   p. 114
closed (structured, fixed-choice, or pre-coded) measures   p. 105
connotative meaning   p. 116
critical incident technique   p. 125
cue words   p. 113
denotative meaning   p. 116
evaluation apprehension   p. 104
evaluation, potency, and activity   p. 116
face-to-face interview   p. 123
false-negative reports   p. 124
floor effect   p. 115
forced-choice scales   p. 112
graphic scales   p. 113

halo effect   p. 112
interview schedule   p. 123
item analysis   p. 112
leading questions   p. 122
leniency bias   p. 114
Lie (L) Scale   p. 115
Likert scale   p. 118
logical error in rating   p. 114
method of equal-appearing intervals   p. 118
method of self-report   p. 103
Minnesota Multiphasic Personality Inventory (MMPI)   p. 108
numerical scales   p. 109
open-ended measures   p. 105
pilot testing   p. 110
pretest   p. 115
projective test   p. 107
rating errors   p. 114

Multiple-Choice Questions for Review (answers are found on page 347)

1. A researcher at Southwestern University decides to use self-report methods in his study of caffeine use. His survey contains the following question: "In the past week, did you drink any coffee? Yes or no." This question is an example of (a) a closed question; (b) an open-ended question; (c) a neutrally worded question; (d) a negatively worded question.

2. A researcher at Baylor is conducting a study about the self-concept of college students. His survey contains the following question: "In your own words, please describe your self-concept. In other words, what kind of person are you?" This question is an example of (a) a negatively worded question; (b) an open-ended question; (c) a neutrally worded question; (d) a closed question.

3. A researcher at Case Western Reserve gives a participant an ambiguous picture of people in a social situation and asks the participant what the people in the picture are doing, what they are thinking, and what they will be doing in the future. This is an example of a (a) closed-format question; (b) reverse-scored question; (c) projective test; (d) none of the above.

4. Some research participants are likely to agree with almost any question that is asked of them. This tendency is generally referred to as (a) an acquiescent response set; (b) an affirmation bias; (c) a nonnegation bias; (d) an affirmation tendency.

5. To avoid problems with the "halo effect," a researcher might want to use (a) forced-choice scales; (b) graphic rating scales; (c) equal-appearing interval scales; (d) segmented graphic scales.

6. Observers often assume that, if a person is physically attractive, he or she also has many other positive qualities, including being intelligent and outgoing. This is an example of (a) the error of central tendency; (b) the halo effect; (c) the error of misperception; (d) none of the above.

7. According to research on the semantic differential method, which of the following is a major dimension of subjective meaning? (a) potency; (b) activity; (c) evaluation; (d) all of the above

8. Which of the following is also known as the method of summated ratings? (a) the semantic differential method; (b) the Thurstone method; (c) the Likert method; (d) the equal-appearing interval method

9. Which of the following is also known as the method of equal-appearing intervals? (a) the semantic differential method; (b) the Thurstone method; (c) the Likert method; (d) the graphic rating method

10. Imagine that you are asked to do the following during an interview: "Describe as fully and concretely as possible a real situation that was important to you in which you acted in some way that was a cover for your true feelings." This is an example of (a) a self-recorded diary; (b) the critical incident technique; (c) the semantic differential method; (d) an interview schedule.

Discussion Questions for Review (answers are found on page 347)

1. An Austin Peay student wants to develop numerical and graphic items to measure attitudes about abortion. What advice would you give him on how to get started?
2. A Central Michigan student is asked by his instructor to tell which rating error each of the following descriptions represents: (a) rating someone you know too positively; (b) tending to respond in an affirmative direction; (c) not using the extremes of a scale; (d) rating a central trait and other traits in the same way. Do you know the answers? Do you also know how to control for each of these errors?
3. A Northwestern University student who has a job selling used cars is thinking about developing a questionnaire to discover the motivations of people who buy and don't buy used cars. What methodological pointers would you give him?
4. A Wheaton College student wants to develop a Thurstone scale to measure attitudes about eliminating final exams for graduating seniors. Describe the steps she will need to take in developing this scale.
5. The student in Question 4 has a boyfriend who is a psychology major at Rhode Island College. He tells her that he is planning to develop a Likert scale to measure the same attitudes. Do you know the difference between these two approaches?
6. A student at the City University of New York wants to use the semantic differential to study people's reactions to certain *New York Times* advertisements. If you were this student, how would you design this instrument?
7. A student at Ohio Wesleyan who is running for student body president reads *The Selling of the President*, in which Joe McGinniss wrote about the use of the semantic differential by advertising researchers who worked for Richard M. Nixon when he began assembling a team for his 1968 presidential campaign. The researchers traveled all through the United States asking people to evaluate the presidential candidates (Nixon, Hubert Humphrey, and George Wallace). They then plotted an "ideal presidential curve" (i.e., a line connecting the points that represented what the researchers thought would be the ideal candidate) and compared the candidates' profiles with this ideal. The Ohio Wesleyan student is also running against two rivals and wonders whether it might be possible to do a similar study. What methodological pointers would you give her?
8. A student at the University of South Africa, a correspondence university, works in a company that wants to study the morale of its employees. The student thinks it might be instructive to ask a sample of the employees one or two critical incident questions. How should they be worded?
9. What is the major advantage of the self-recorded diary over a questionnaire?

6 Reliability and Validity

Random and Systematic Error

Whenever we measure something—whether we are using a ruler to measure physical distance, a scale to measure weight, or a psychological test to measure an individual's personality—our measurements are subject to fluctuations (called **error**). Suppose a grocer weighs the same bunch of grapes a number of times in a row. In an ideal world, the grocer's measurements would give the same result every time he (or someone else) weighed the same bunch of grapes. But no matter how precisely he does it, his measurement will probably come out a bit differently each time it is repeated. In fact, the more careful and precise the repeated measurements, the more detectable will be the chance fluctuations.

For example, the National Bureau of Standards in Washington, D.C., is concerned with checking weights and measures, which it does by comparing measuring instruments with certain standards. One such standard is that for 10 grams, a prototype weight that is owned by the bureau. This prototype, acquired around 1940, has been weighed about once a week ever since. At each weighing, an attempt has been made to control all the factors known to affect the results (e.g., air

PREVIEW QUESTIONS

- What is the difference between random and systematic error?
- When is a measuring instrument said to be temporally stable, and what is the purpose of having alternate forms of a test?
- What is acceptable reliability?
- How are a measuring instrument's item-to-item and composite reliability determined?
- How do these concepts and procedures apply to the reliability of judges?
- What is the meaning of *replication,* and how does replication relate to reliability?
- What is the difference between the content validity and the criterion validity of a measuring instrument?
- What is construct validation, and why is it of paramount importance in instrument construction?
- What do statistical conclusion validity, internal validity, construct validity, and external validity have to do with experimental research?
- When are we interested in the inferential validity of the experiment?

pressure and temperature), but still there have been detectable fluctuations. For instance, one series of five weighings yielded 9.999591 grams, 9.999600 grams, 9.999594 grams, 9.999601 grams, and 9.999598 grams. Although the first four digits are identical, the numbers are nevertheless shaky in the last three digits. As careful and precise as these measurements were, we can clearly see chance fluctuations (i.e., error) at work (Freedman, Pisani, Purves, & Adhikari, 1991, pp. 91–94).

Another name for error of this type—that is, chance fluctuations—is **random error,** which can be distinguished from **systematic error** (also called **bias**). In the previous chapter, it will be recalled that we described several types of systematic error that are associated with biased responding to rating scales (e.g., leniency bias and central tendency bias). The basic difference is that random error tends to push measurements up and down around an exact value, so that the average of all measurements over many trials is very close to the exact value. Systematic error, on the other hand, tends to push measurements in the same direction and causes the average or mean value to be too big or too small. Another way of saying this is that random errors are likely to cancel out, on the average, over repeated measurements; systematic errors do not cancel out but affect all measurements in roughly the same way. The grocer who always weighs grapes with a thumb on the scale will inflate the price of grapes by tacking extra ounces onto the exact weight (a systematic error).

The purpose of this chapter is to expand on the role of measurement fluctuations as they enter into the assessment of reliability and validity. **Reliability,** broadly speaking, refers to consistency or stability, for instance, whether the grocer's measurements can be repeated and confirmed by further competent measurements. **Validity,** broadly speaking, refers to whether the measurements measure what they are supposed (or claim) to measure. In an ideal world, the grocer's measurements would not be contaminated by a thumb on the scale and would consistently give only the true weight of the grapes.

In behavioral research, knowing that a measuring "instrument" (e.g., a personality test, an electroencephalogram for monitoring brain waves, a group of judges, or an attitude questionnaire) is both reliable and valid shortens the time needed to discover the characteristics of what is being measured. If the instrument is not reliable, it is often less likely to be valid, but it can be very reliable without being at all valid. For example, it is possible to imagine that subjects blink their eyes the same number of times a minute under a variety of circumstances (i.e., the measure has high reliability), but under no conditions could one predict the subjects' running speed from their eye-blink rate (i.e., the measure has low validity as a predictor of running speed).

Reliability

Test-Retest Reliability

Suppose we are thinking about using a psychological test or other assessment procedure to operationalize and confront predictions in research. It is important to know the **test-retest reliability** (also called *retest reliability*). The reason is that test-retest reliability gives an estimate of the degree of fluctuation of the instrument, or of the trait it is designed to measure, from one administration to another. To find out the instrument's test-retest reliability, we would administer the test and then readminister the same instrument to the same subjects later (but see Box 6.1). The degree of test-retest reliability can be represented by a **correlation coefficient** between the scores on the test when it is administered at different times. We will have more to say about correlation coefficients in a later chapter, but if you have had a course in statistics, you know that the basic measure of association is the **Pearson r correlation coefficient**.

Box 6.1	**Retesting the Same Subjects Is Sometimes Impossible**

Test-retest reliability requires that the same measure be administered on separate occasions to the same subjects. However, circumstances beyond our control sometimes prevent this from happening, as when subjects are no longer available. A biblical case (which also illustrates the ancient roots of behavioral assessment) involved the Gileadites, who used a one-item ability test to ferret out the Ephraimites who were hiding in their midst (Wainer, 1990). The test was to pronounce the word *shibboleth;* the Ephraimites could not pronounce *sh* (which came out as *s*), and those who failed this test were put to death. Such a test may have cut down on the number of Ephraimites, but it obviously left no opportunity to check on the test's retest reliability.

You will recall that the Pearson r measures the strength of association (i.e., the degree of relatedness) of two variables, such as height and weight. One characteristic of the Pearson r is that it ranges only from -1.0 through 0 to $+1.0$. A value of 0 means that the two variables being correlated have no relation, for example, that taller people are not heavier (or lighter) on average than shorter people. A value of $+1.0$ means that the variables have a perfect positive relation: As scores on one variable increase, there are perfectly predictable increases in the scores on the other variable. A value of -1.0 means the opposite: As the scores on one variable increase, there are perfectly predictable decreases in the scores on the other variable.

Given these characteristics of the Pearson r, what would you want the correlation between the scores at the initial testing and at the retesting to be if you were thinking about using a particular instrument in your research? The answer, of course, is that you would want the Pearson r to be a positive value as high as possible, because the higher the test-retest coefficient, the more "dependable" the test. In other words, the closer the r is to $+1.0$, the more impressive is the measured temporal stability (or dependability) of the instrument.

In actuality, many useful measuring instruments used in behavioral science have test-retest reliabilities substantially lower than 1.0. To give us a feeling for what the test-retest r means, Henry Braun and Howard Wainer (1989, p. 181)—researchers at the Educational Testing Service, the organization that revises and administers the

SAT (Scholastic Assessment Test)—noted some typical reliabilities. For example, the test-retest r on the SAT for essay scores in the humanities is usually between .3 and .6, and for chemistry, it is usually between .6 and .8. If we measured the height of a group of boys at ages 6 and 10 and then correlated these values, the reliability coefficient would usually be greater than .8.

When you look up a standardized test in a sourcebook, you will find references to its test-retest reliability and other useful information (see Box 6.2). For example, for over 50 years the *Mental Measurements Yearbook* (published by Buros Institute of Mental Measurements) has supplied reviews of and background data about thousands of commercially available tests for psychological and educational assessment and research. The test-retest correlations will vary depending not only on the intrinsic reliability of the test, but also on the time interval between the test and the retest. The longer this interval, the more likely the test-retest correlation is to decrease progressively. Thus reports of tests should always tell us the interval over which the test-retest reliability was measured (as well as any other information that might be relevant, such as the nature of the sample on which the reliability was assessed).

Box 6.2   ## Alternate-Form Reliability

If subjects take the same test twice, the test-retest r may be artificially inflated because of their familiarity with the test items. One way of avoiding this problem is by using two forms of the test with different items that measure the same attribute. Not all tests, of course, have alternate forms, but many of the most popular ones do. If the forms are reliable, higher scores on one form should be associated with higher scores on the other. The correlation coefficient is again used to assess the reliability of the two sets of scores—called **alternate-form reliability.**

Internal-Consistency Reliability

Test-retest reliability is concerned with the temporal stability of the test, but we would also be interested in learning about the test's **internal-consistency reliability,** which gives the degree of relatedness of the individual items. One way to find this information would be to give the test to a sample of subjects, then to split the test in half and correlate the scores on the halves with one another (called the **split-half reliability**). For example, we could correlate the scores on the odd-numbered items with scores on the even-numbered items. This process assumes that the odd and even items are, in fact, roughly equivalent in nature. Unlike the test-retest reliability, which gives a correlation coefficient for the entire test, the split-half reliability gives a correlation coefficient of only a half-test (Anastasi & Urbina, 1997). Another difference, of course, is that the test-retest reliability is based on two administrations of the test, and the split-half reliability is based on only one administration of the test.

Suppose you want to assess your fellow students' views of the course in which this book is being used, and you have made up a three-item attitude test to do the job. Your instructor suggests that you look at the "inter-item correlation" and then also check the "overall reliability" of the test and perhaps, if the latter value seems too low, think about adding more items. To find the **inter-item correlation,** you would administer the three-item test to a group of students and then compute the average correlation of each pair of items. That is, you would first correlate Item 1 with Item 2, Item 1 with Item 3, and Item 2 with Item 3. We can symbolize each of these correlations by an r with a subscript indicating the particular items correlated with one another.

Let us say you find $r_{12} = .45$ between Items 1 and 2; $r_{13} = .50$ between Items 1 and 3; and $r_{23} = .55$ between Items 2 and 3. Summing the values gives $.45 + .50 + .55 = 1.50$, and dividing by the number of pairs (i.e., three pairs) gives the mean inter-item (or item-to-item) reliability. This value, more generally symbolized as r_{ii} (the subscript ii stands for "item-to-item," or inter-item, correlation), is computed as $1.50/3 = .50$. This average correlation is an estimate of the reliability of any *single* item on average.

However, the instructor also told you to check the overall reliability of the test (i.e., the reliability of the test as a whole). This reliability, which we call here the **composite reliability,** can be computed from a classic formula created by Spearman and Brown (see also Box 6.3):

$$R^{SB} = \frac{n r_{ii}}{1 + [(n - 1)r_{ii}]}$$

where R^{SB} = the overall (or composite) internal-consistency reliability (i.e., Spearman-Brown correlation); n = the total number of items you plan for your test; and r_{ii} = the average intercorrelation. You set n equal to 3 (because you have a three-item test) and r_{ii} equal to .50. Substituting in the Spearman-Brown formula, you find

$$R^{SB} = \frac{3(.50)}{1 + [(3 - 1).50]} = \frac{1.5}{1 + 1.0} = .75$$

Box 6.3 **Spearman and Brown's "Prophecy Formula"**

More often than we might guess, a discovery is made simultaneously by scientists working quite independently of one another. This was the case in the creation of the Spearman-Brown formula, named after Charles Spearman (1910) and William Brown (1910), whose work appeared simultaneously in the same issue of the *British Journal of Psychology* in 1910. The equation is sometimes referred to as the **Spearman-Brown prophecy formula** because it can be used to predict the effect on the reliability of a test as a whole from changing the length of the test (Walker & Lev, 1953).

If you were to use six items instead of three and the average intercorrelation remained .50, the estimated overall (composite) reliability would be

$$R^{SB} = \frac{6(.50)}{1 + [(6 - 1).50]} = \frac{3.0}{1 + 2.5} = .86$$

What if you wanted to further increase the length of the test, going to nine items? With $n = 9$, you find

$$R^{SB} = \frac{9(.50)}{1 + [(9 - 1).50]} = \frac{4.5}{1 + 4.0} = .90$$

There is not much difference between .90 and .86, but it does seem (as the instructor implied) that you can keep on increasing the overall reliability by steadily adding new, homogeneous items.

When you are using the Spearman-Brown formula, there are some things to keep in mind which affect the overall (composite) reliability. First, adding irrelevant items can detract from the composite reliability (Li, Rosenthal, & Rubin, 1996). Second, adding items of extremely low reliability may also decrease the reliability of the whole test (Wainer & Thissen, 1993). These two considerations pertain to what we had in mind when we assumed that r_{ii} (i.e., the average intercorrelation) remained relatively unchanged as new items were created, because adding irrelevant items or items of dubious reliability would reduce the average intercorrelation and, in turn, the reliability of the test as a whole And finally, there is a practical limit to how long a test can be. Put yourself in the situation of having to take a test of not 9, but 99, items. It would be hard to concentrate after a point because you would begin to feel bored or fatigued. When this happens, the consistency of accurate responding is reduced as the amount of random error increases.

What Is Acceptable Reliability?

What you may need to figure out, and to state in your research proposal, is how many items you feel are optimal to achieve the reliability you want, without making the scale so cumbersome as to give your respondents a headache. Thus an important question becomes: What is an acceptable range of reliability? Unfortunately, there is no simple answer. The acceptable range depends on the situation in which the instrument is to be used and the purpose or objective of the research. If we needed an instrument with a high degree of temporal consistency, or test-retest reliability, then we might not settle for a test-retest correlation less than .80. And yet, there are many acceptable tests with retest correlations below .80, including many medical tests for detecting or diagnosing some illness. Scores on these tests may vary as a function of feelings of anxiety, changes in one's diet, and so on. Besides asking your instructor for guidance, you can develop a sense of the answer in your particular case by reading relevant test reviews by experts in the *Mental Measurements Yearbook* or by perusing the *Directory of Unpublished Experimental Mental Measures* (Goldman et al., 1995, 1996), both mentioned previously (see also Box 6.4).

Box 6.4   **K-R 20 and Cronbach's Alpha**

In your reading, you will find references to other quantitative measures of composite reliability, such as K-R 20 and Cronbach's alpha. **K-R 20,** which takes its name from its originators, G. F. Kuder and M. W. Richardson, is used to estimate overall internal-consistency reliability when the items of a test are scored dichotomously (i.e., scored 1 if marked correctly and 0 if marked otherwise). It has been shown (Novick & Lewis, 1967) to give an estimate of the reliability coefficient for all possible split halves when a special formula (the Rulon formula) is used. **Cronbach's alpha** (invented by Lee J. Cronbach, 1951) is a generalized procedure, not restricted to dichotomously scored items, that is based on the analysis of variance. Cronbach's alpha is also frequently referred to as the **alpha coefficient.** If you have had a course in statistics, you may also recall that another name for the p value is alpha; however, that alpha (which refers to the probability of a Type I error) does not mean the same thing as the alpha coefficient (which refers only to composite reliability). It is beyond the scope of this text to give detailed examples of K-R 20 or Cronbach's alpha, but the same rule applies in both cases: The more homogeneous items there are in the test, the higher is the composite (i.e., the overall) internal-consistency reliability.

To get you started, let us look at the reliabilities of some popular tests discussed in the previous chapter. You will recall that the MMPI (Minnesota Multiphasic Personality Inventory) and the Rorschach inkblot test are both personality measures. As previously noted, the MMPI consists of several hundred statements to which the subject responds by indicating whether or not they apply to her or him; the Rorschach consists of inkblots, and the subject tells what he or she perceives in each blot. A team of psychologists (Parker, Hanson, & Hunsley, 1988) summarized the information reported in articles between 1970 and 1981 concerning the internal consistency and test-retest correlations of these two instruments—the Rorschach and the MMPI—and similar information about another well-known test, the **Wechsler Adult Intelligence Scale (WAIS).** Developed by David Wechsler (a clinical psychologist who had been connected with New York's Bellevue Hospital for many years), the WAIS is the most widely used individually administered intelligence test. It is divided into verbal and performance subtests, the former depending more on school-related abilities than the latter.

Parker et al. found that the average composite reliability was .87 for the overall WAIS, .84 for the MMPI, and .86 for the Rorschach. They also found that the average test-retest correlation was .82 for the overall WAIS, .74 for the MMPI, and .85 for the Rorschach. Internal-consistency correlations are expected to be higher than test-retest correlations, unless the test-retest intervals are very short. These results, then, are consistent with that expectation, although in the case of the Rorschach the difference is hardly noticeable.

More is known about the reliability (and validity) of the WAIS, the MMPI, and the Rorschach than about that of most other psychological tests in current use, including the two attitude tests described in the previous chapter. Let us look first at the test that was built to measure attitudes toward defensive, cooperative, and aggressive war (shown in Figure 5.4 on page 121). The authors of this scale (D. D. Day & Quackenbush, 1942) reported only its composite reliability, which was in the .80 to .87 range for all three referents measured. Let us look next at the socialized-medicine attitude test shown in Figure 5.3 (page 119). Its composite reliability was reported by the author (Mahler, 1953) to be .96. This 20-item test is interesting for another reason having to do with alternate-form reliability, because the test shown in Figure 5.3 actually comprised two comparable 10-item forms. The more the scores on one form are correlated with those on the other, the better is the alternate-form reliability. In this case, the author reported alternate-form reliability in the .81 to .84 range.

Applications to Reliability of Judges

As we first mentioned in Chapter 4, reliability is also a basic consideration in observational studies that use judges or raters. For example, in one popular observational procedure used by developmental psychologists to study attachment behavior in infants and maternal responses, the judges code positive and negative actions in a number of situations. They may do this coding, for example, when the mother and infant are together, when the mother leaves the infant in the presence of a stranger, when the mother returns, when the infant is left by itself, and so forth (Ainsworth, Bell, & Stayton, 1971). Suppose a developmental researcher uses three judges (A, B, and C) to code the maternal behavior of five mothers (a, b, c, d, and e) in one situation on a 7-point scale from "very secure" (1) to "very anxious" (7).

The results are shown in Part A of Table 6.1. After calculating the correlations between pairs of judges (A with B; A with C; and B with C), the researcher obtains

Table 6.1	Ratings and Intercorrelations for Three Judges

A. Judges' ratings

	Judges		
Mothers	A	B	C
a	5	6	7
b	3	6	4
c	3	4	6
d	2	2	3
e	1	4	4

B. Judge-to-judge correlations
$r_{AB} = .645$
$r_{AC} = .800$
$r_{BC} = .582$
$r_{jj} = .676$

the mean of these correlations. The results are given in Part B of Table 6.1, in which the mean correlation is shown as $r_{jj} = .676$ (the subscript jj stands for **judge-to-judge**). This value is an estimate of the reliability of any *single* judge on average (in the same way that r_{ii} was an estimate of the reliability of any single item on average).

We would also like to know the reliability of the group of three judges as a whole, that is, the composite reliability. We can easily find this answer by using the Spearman-Brown formula that we used earlier, and we can then use this same formula to estimate how many additional judges we may need. Using the Spearman-Brown formula, we calculate the composite reliability as

$$R^{SB} = \frac{nr_{jj}}{1 + [(n - 1)r_{jj}]}$$

where R^{SB} = the composite (i.e., overall) reliability of the total set of judges; n = the number of judges; and r_{jj} = the average judge-to-judge reliability. Substituting in the formula gives

$$R^{SB} = \frac{3(.676)}{1 + [(3 - 1).676]} = \frac{2.028}{1 + 1.352} = .862$$

We now know that the reliability of the three judges' ratings as a whole (the composite reliability) is .862 and that the reliability of any single judge is .676 (the average judge-to-judge reliability). We would report both reliabilities and, of course, label each to prevent reader misunderstandings. However, suppose we wanted to know how much the composite reliability would be increased if we used one more judge whose ratings were also correlated approximately .68 with the other judges. We find the answer to our question by substituting in the Spearman-Brown formula, with the number (n) of judges now four instead of three and the average reliability (r_{jj}) rounded to .68:

$$R^{SB} = \frac{4(.68)}{1 + [(4 - 1).68]} = \frac{2.72}{1 + 2.04} = .895$$

This equation predicts that using four instead of three judges will boost the composite reliability from .86 to roughly .90, assuming the judge-to-judge reliability is not reduced by the addition of this fourth judge.

Using a Table of Estimated Values

Table 6.2 is a useful summary table based on the Spearman-Brown formula (Rosenthal & Rosnow, 1991). It shows the composite reliability for values of n ranging from 1 to 20 judges—or 1 to 20 items in a test. When $n = 1$, we see that the composite reliability (R^{SB}) is equivalent to the reliability of a single judge (r_{jj})—or a single test item (r_{ii}). To show you how to use this table, we will start with three questions about judges and then try a fourth question that shifts to test items:

1. Given an obtained or estimated mean reliability, r_{jj}, and a sample of n judges, what is the approximate composite reliability, R^{SB}, of the mean of the judges' ratings? The value of R^{SB} is read from the table at the intersection of the appropriate row (n)

Table 6.2	Estimation of Spearman-Brown Composite Reliability (R^{SB}) Based on Number *(n)* of Judges or Test Items and Mean Interjudge (r_{jj}) or Inter-item (r_{ii}) Reliability

Mean interjudge (r_{jj}) or inter-item (r_{ii}) reliability

n	.05	.10	.15	.20	.25	.30	.35	.40	.45	.50	.55	.60	.65	.70	.75	.80	.85	.90	.95
1	.05	.10	.15	.20	.25	.30	.35	.40	.45	.50	.55	.60	.65	.70	.75	.80	.85	.90	.95
2	.10	.18	.26	.33	.40	.46	.52	.57	.62	.67	.71	.75	.79	.82	.86	.89	.92	.95	.97
3	.14	.25	.35	.43	.50	.56	.62	.67	.71	.75	.79	.82	.85	.88	.90	.92	.94	.96	.98
4	.17	.31	.41	.50	.57	.63	.68	.73	.77	.80	.83	.86	.88	.90	.92	.94	.96	.97	.99
5	.21	.36	.47	.56	.62	.68	.73	.77	.80	.83	.86	.88	.90	.92	.94	.95	.97	.98	.99
6	.24	.40	.51	.60	.67	.72	.76	.80	.83	.86	.88	.90	.92	.93	.95	.96	.97	.98	.99
7	.27	.44	.55	.64	.70	.75	.79	.82	.85	.88	.90	.91	.93	.94	.95	.97	.98	.98	.99
8	.30	.47	.59	.67	.73	.77	.81	.84	.87	.89	.91	.92	.94	.95	.96	.97	.98	.99	.99
9	.32	.50	.61	.69	.75	.79	.83	.86	.88	.90	.92	.93	.94	.95	.96	.97	.98	.99	.99
10	.34	.53	.64	.71	.77	.81	.84	.87	.89	.91	.92	.94	.95	.96	.97	.98	.98	.99	.99
12	.39	.57	.68	.75	.80	.84	.87	.89	.91	.92	.94	.95	.96	.97	.97	.98	.99	.99	1.0
14	.42	.61	.71	.78	.82	.86	.88	.90	.92	.93	.94	.95	.96	.97	.98	.98	.99	.99	1.0
16	.46	.64	.74	.80	.84	.87	.90	.91	.93	.94	.95	.96	.97	.97	.98	.98	.99	.99	1.0
18	.49	.67	.76	.82	.86	.89	.91	.92	.94	.95	.96	.96	.97	.98	.98	.99	.99	.99	1.0
20	.51	.69	.78	.83	.87	.90	.92	.93	.94	.95	.96	.97	.97	.98	.98	.99	.99	.99	1.0

and column (r_{jj}). Suppose we want to work with a variable believed to show a mean reliability of $r_{jj} = .50$ and can afford only four judges. We believe we should go ahead with our study only if the Spearman-Brown composite reliability (R^{SB}) will reach or exceed .75. Shall we go ahead? The answer is yes, because the table shows $R^{SB} = .80$ for an *n* of 4 and an r_{jj} of .50.

2. Given the value of the obtained or desired composite reliability, R^{SB}, and the number of judges actually available, *n*, what will be the approximate value of the required mean reliability, r_{jj}? The table is entered in the row corresponding to the *n* of judges available and is read across until the value of R^{SB} closest to the one desired is reached; the value of r_{jj} is then read as the corresponding column heading. Suppose we will settle for a composite reliability no less than $R^{SB} = .90$ and we have a sample of *n* = 20 judges available. In our selection of variables to be rated by these judges, what should be their minimally acceptable average individual reliability? From this table we see the answer is $r_{jj} = .30$.

3. Given an obtained or estimated mean reliability, r_{jj}, and the obtained or desired composite reliability, R^{SB}, what is the approximate number of judges *(n)* required? The table is entered in the column corresponding to the mean reliability, r_{jj}, and is read down until the value of R^{SB} closest to the one desired is reached; the value of *n* is then read as the corresponding row value. For example, we know our choice of variables to have a mean reliability of .40, and we want to achieve a composite reliability of .85 or higher. How many judges must we allow for in our preparation of a research budget? The answer is *n* = 9 judges.

4. Table 6.2 can be used equally well in estimating the increase in composite reliability of tests when new, homogeneous items are added. In that case, we redefine the n of judges as the n of items, r_{ii} as the average intercorrelation of items (i.e., the item-to-item reliability), and R^{SB} as the overall internal-consistency reliability with n items. In the previous section, we gave the example of a three-item test (i.e., $n = 3$) with an average item-to-item correlation of $r_{ii} = .50$; the researcher wanted to estimate the overall effect of using three, six, or nine items. The table is entered in the column corresponding to this mean reliability, and we then read down the column until we reach the Spearman-Brown value closest to the one desired. Let us say we want to achieve a composite reliability of $R^{SB} = .90$ or higher. How many homogeneous items will we need? When we read across the row, the answer is $n = 9$.

Replication and Reliability

Just as all scientists want to know the dependability of their measuring instruments, they are also interested in the dependability of their research results. Knowing that a set of results is dependable means that it is subject to **replication** (i.e., it can be repeated or duplicated by others). Clearly, the *same* set of results can never be "exactly" repeated by a different worker, because at the very least the subjects would be older. Thus, to avoid the not very helpful conclusion that there can be no exact replication, researchers think of all replications as *relative replications* (e.g., Rosenthal, 1990c; Sidman, 1960). This means that, in the replication attempt, the research procedure is modeled very closely on that in the original study. For the replication attempt to be successful, the pattern of results must not be markedly different in magnitude.

A convenient way to decide whether the results are comparable is to examine the **effect size,** which refers here to the magnitude of the relation between the independent variable *(X)* and the dependent variable *(Y)*. As we will show in a later chapter, the effect size can be directly expressed by the correlation between X and Y. The closer this correlation in the replication study is to that observed in the original study, the more **homogeneity** the set of results is said to have. If the effect sizes are markedly different, the conclusion is that the studies show **heterogeneity.**

For example, suppose we wanted to replicate an experimental finding in which the effect size was originally given as $r_{XY} = .50$. This magnitude of the relation between X (the independent variable) and Y (the dependent variable) is typically labeled as "large" in psychology, following the convention that effect size correlations of .10, .30, and .50 represent small, medium, and large effects, respectively (J. Cohen, 1988). We will refer again to these labels later in this book, but suppose the correlation between the independent and dependent variables in our study is .40. By some easy calculations (given in Appendix C), we compare the effects of .40 and .50 and find they are not significantly different. In other words, the studies comprise a homogeneous set of effect sizes. This tells us that our study (even though our effect is slightly smaller than the original) can be viewed as a successful replication (see also Box 6.5).

Box 6.5	**Comparing and Combining Effect Sizes**

Effect size correlations that scattered around zero would have told us that not much was going on in either study. But both correlations in this case are positive and fairly far from zero, so we know that something reliable was probably going on in both studies. We can also combine the effect sizes and get an estimate of the overall effect size. This procedure is also described in Appendix C on meta-analysis.

Validity

Just as reliability has different facets, so has *validity*. In general, assessing the validity of a test or questionnaire means finding out the degree to which it measures what it is supposed to measure. This assessment is considered the most important criterion in instrument construction and, in test or questionnaire construction, involves accumulating evidence in three categories: (1) content validity, (2) criterion validity, and (3) construct validity.

Content Validity

Content validity means that the test or questionnaire items represent the kinds of material (or content areas) they are supposed to represent, usually a basic consideration in the construction phase of any test or questionnaire. Thus a test or questionnaire with good content validity covers all major aspects of the content areas that are relevant. For example, when the MMPI was being developed, the researchers tried to select a range of statements that would be endorsed in a certain direction by each of several different clinical groups. In this way, they hoped to differentiate among a number of different clinical conditions by including a wide range of items that tapped different content areas. To help them during this initial phase, they called on expert judges to make subjective evaluations of the relevance or appropriateness of each item for assessing different content areas.

Less formal methods are possible in other situations. For instance, a teacher who is making up a final exam and wants it to have content validity may start by asking, "What kinds of material should students be able to master after studying the readings and taking this course?" The teacher would make a list of all the material the exam should sample and then make up questions to represent this material. As students, we have all experienced exams with poor content validity. They are the ones about which we say, "The prof never even mentioned this material, and it was a two-line footnote in the appendix!" (See also Box 6.6.)

<table>
<tr><td>Box 6.6</td><td>Face Validity</td></tr>
</table>

Box 6.6   Face Validity

Another type of validity you may read about is **face validity,** which simply means the extent to which the test seems on the surface (or "face") to be measuring something relevant. It should not be confused with content validity; face validity refers not to what the test actually measures but only to how it looks. In other words, does it "look valid"? If a test does not *appear* to be relevant, then subjects may not take it seriously in a practical situation (Anastasi & Urbina, 1997). Of course, some tests (e.g., the Rorschach and the TAT) purposely do not contain a clue to what they are supposed to be measuring.

Criterion Validity

Criterion validity is the degree to which the test or questionnaire correlates with one or more outcome criteria (a variable with which the instrument should be reasonably correlated). Researchers who were developing a test of college aptitude might use as their criterion the successful completion of the first year of college or maybe the grade point average (GPA) after each year of college. If they were developing a test to measure anxiety, they might use as their criterion the pooled judgments of a group of highly trained clinicians who rate (e.g., on a numerical rating scale) each person to whom the researchers administered the test. In assessing criterion validity, researchers usually try to select the most sensitive and meaningful criterion in the present (also called **concurrent validity**) or future (also called **predictive validity**) and then correlate performance on the test or questionnaire with that criterion.

For example, clinical diagnostic tests are ordinarily assessed for concurrent validity because the criterion of the patient's "real" diagnostic status is in the present with respect to the test being validated. The concurrent validity of shorter forms of longer tests is also typically evaluated, the longer test being used as the criterion (see also Box 6.7). The practical advantage to the researcher of using a criterion in the present is that it is less expensive and less time-consuming than using a criterion that is in the future. It also controls for any possible confounding (or interfering) effect of temporal instability (Anastasi & Urbina, 1997).

Box 6.7   Criteria Evaluated Against Criteria

Frequently, researchers must consider the validity of the criterion itself. Suppose a personality researcher wants to develop a short test of anxiety that will predict the scores on a longer test of anxiety. The longer test serves as the researcher's criterion, and the new short test may be relatively valid with respect to the longer test. But the longer test may be of dubious validity with respect to some other criterion (e.g., clinicians' judgments). In other words, criteria must often be evaluated with respect to other criteria, but there are no firm rules (beyond the use of logic and the consensus of other researchers in that area) about what constitutes an "ultimate" criterion.

Nevertheless, predictive validity also plays an important role in measurement. Tests of college aptitude are normally assessed for predictive validity, inasmuch as the criterion of graduation and GPA are criteria of the future. The aptitude test scores are saved until the future-criterion data become available; the scores are then correlated with them. The resulting correlation coefficient serves as an index of criterion validity. GPA tends to be a fairly reliable criterion, but clinicians' judgments (e.g., about complex behavior) may be a less reliable criterion. Previously we showed how the composite reliability of pooled judgments (r_{jj}) can be increased if more judges are added, and in this way, researchers can also increase the composite reliability of pooled clinical judgments (i.e., by adding similar clinicians to the group whose pooled judgments will serve as their criterion; Rosenthal, 1973, 1982, 1987).

Construct Validity

More sophisticated views of the validation of tests require that researchers be sensitive not only to the correlation between their measures and some appropriate criterion, but also to the correlation between their measures and some "inappropriate" criterion. Suppose a researcher in clinical psychology develops a test of psychological adjustment, which she would like to use in a field experiment. She does some pilot studies to ensure the validity of the test. In one aspect of the pilot work, she has some expert clinicians rate the psychological adjustment of a group of subjects who have just been given the test. She finds that the test scores correlate positively and substantially with the pooled judgment of the expert clinicians, and she correctly interprets this correlation as an attractive outcome of a concurrent validation effort. She has also given the subjects a test of verbal aptitude, and she finds that their scores on this test and on her new test of psychological adjustment also correlate positively and substantially with one another. What should she now conclude?

More specifically, should she conclude that the new test is a reasonably valid measure of psychological adjustment, of verbal aptitude, of both, or of neither? This question is difficult to answer, but she could not claim on the basis of such results to understand the new test very well. It is not intended, after all, to be a measure of verbal aptitude. In short, the new test has good concurrent validity but fails to discriminate: It does not correlate differentially with criteria for different types of observation. This "ability to discriminate" is a vital characteristic of **construct validity,** which in turn is generally considered the most "fundamental and all-inclusive validity concept, insofar as it specifies what the test measures" (Anastasi & Urbina, 1997, p. 114). Content and criterion validity provide valuable information in their own right but now are more basically viewed as improving our understanding of the construct measured by the test.

In a seminal paper, Donald T. Campbell and Donald W. Fiske (1959) sought to formalize the construct validation process. In order to achieve this goal statistically, they proposed two essential kinds of construct validation evidence: (1) the testing for "convergence" across different measures or manipulations of the same trait or behavior (called **convergent validity**) and (2) the testing for "divergence" between measures or manipulations of related but conceptually distinct behaviors or traits (called **discriminant validity**). For example, the finding that the new test of psychological adjustment correlates positively and substantially with expert clinicians' ratings is viewed as convergent validation evidence. However, the finding that the new test also correlates positively and substantially with a test of verbal aptitude (which is conceptually distinct from the construct of psychological adjustment) is quite contrary to the necessary discriminant validation evidence.

Detailed Example: Crowne and Marlowe's Research

To give you a further idea of how some tests are developed and how construct validation is done, we turn to a classic example of such research, performed by personality psychologists Douglas Crowne and David Marlowe in the 1950s. The original purpose of this research was to develop a psychological scale that would measure a source of systematic error in personality test taking, called *socially desirable responding* in the previous chapter. As noted before (see again Box 5.5 on page 115), it means that individuals give answers that make them look good (rather than give the most candid or honest answers). As the research progressed, Crowne and Marlowe realized that the scale they were building might be tapping a more general personality variable, which they termed the **need for social approval** (to reflect the idea that people differ in their need to be thought well of by others). In developing this scale—the **Marlowe-Crowne Social Desirability Scale (MCSD)**—the researchers wanted to measure the degree to which people vary on the need-for-approval dimension independent of their level of psychopathology, and they were also interested in validating the need-for-approval construct.

Crowne and Marlowe began by considering hundreds of personality test items (including a few from the MMPI) that could be answered true or false. To be included, an item had to be one that would reflect socially approved behavior but that would also almost certainly be untrue (i.e., behavior too good to be true). In addition, answers to the items could not have any implications of psychological abnormality or psychopathology. By having a group of psychology graduate students and faculty judge the social desirability of each item, Crowne and Marlowe developed a set of items that would reflect behavior that was too virtuous to be probable, but that would not be influenced primarily by personal maladjustment.

The final form of the MCSD scale (see Box 6.8)—consisting of 33 items chosen by item analysis and ratings by experienced judges (Crowne, 1979; Crowne &

Box 6.8   The Marlowe-Crowne Scale

If you would like to see the final form of the MCSD, you will find it in Robinson et al.'s (1991) *Measures of Personality and Social Psychological Attitudes* (along with commentary by D. L. Paulhus on related measures). It consists of 33 statements; the subject reads each statement and decides whether it is true or false as it pertains to the subject himself or herself. In about half the items, a "true" answer reflects the socially desirable response (i.e., the higher need for approval), and in the remainder, a "false" answer reflects this type of response. An example of the former type of item might be "I have never intensely disliked anyone," whereas the latter type might be "I sometimes feel resentful when I don't get my way."

Marlowe, 1964)—showed a high degree of relationship to those variables with which the scale scores were expected to converge (i.e., convergent validation evidence). For example, high scorers on the final MCSD preferred low-risk behaviors and avoided the evaluations of others. The final form also showed only a low degree of relationship to those variables with which it was expected not to converge but that it was expected to discriminate (i.e., discriminant validation evidence). For example, there were only low to moderate correlations with measures of psychopathology, and there were fewer of these correlations and they were smaller in magnitude than those of an earlier developed scale of social desirability. Also encouraging was an impressive correlation ($r = .88$) between the two testings of a group of subjects who were tested one month apart (i.e., evidence of test-retest reliability).

These were promising beginnings for the MCSD, but it remained to be shown that the concept of need for social approval (and the scale developed to measure it) was meaningful beyond predicting responses on other paper-and-pencil measures. As part of their program of further validating their new scale and the construct that was its basis, the researchers undertook an ingenious series of varied replications relating scores on the MCSD to subjects' behavior in a number of non-paper-and-pencil test situations. They reasoned that "dependence on the approval of others should make it difficult to assert one's independence, and so the approval-motivated person should be susceptible to social influence, compliant, and conforming" (Crowne, 1991, p. 10). A series of relational studies produced results that were generally consistent with this logical expectation.

In the first of these studies, the subjects began by completing various tests, including the MCSD, and then were asked to get down to the serious business of the experiment. This "serious business" required them to (1) pack a dozen spools of thread into a small box, (2) unpack the box, (3) repack the box, (4) unrepack the box, and so on for 25 minutes while the experimenter appeared to be timing the performance and making notes about them. After these dull 25 minutes had elapsed, subjects were asked to rate how "interesting" the task had been, how "instructive," and how "important to science" and how much subjects wanted to participate in similar studies in the future. Those subjects who scored above the mean on social desirability said they found the task more interesting, more instructive, and more important to science and were more eager to participate again in similar studies than those subjects who had scored below the mean. In other words, just as Crowne and Marlowe had predicted, subjects higher in the need for social approval were more compliant and said nicer things to the experimenter about the task that he had set for them.

In still other research, Crowne and Marlowe used a variant of Asch's (1952) conformity procedure (described in Chapter 3). That is, a group of subjects is required to make judgments on specific issues, and all the confederates make the same uniform judgment, one that is quite clearly in error. Conformity is defined as the real subject's "going along with" the majority in his or her own judgment rather than giving the objectively correct response. In one of these experiments, Crowne and Marlowe had the subjects listen to a tape recording of knocks on a table and then report their judgment of the number of knocks. Each subject was led to believe that he or she was the fourth participant. To create this illusion, the experimenter played for the subject the tape-recorded responses of three prior subjects to each series of knocks that was to be judged. The earlier three subjects were the confederates, and they all gave an incorrect response in 12 of 18 trials. It was therefore possible to count the number of times out of 12 that the real subject yielded to the wrong but unanimous majority. The results supported Crowne and Marlowe's hypothesis that the approval-motivated person is conforming: The subjects who had scored higher in the need for social approval went along with the majority judgment more than did the subjects who scored lower in the need for social approval.

Many additional studies were performed by these and other investigators (see, e.g., Allaman, Joyce, & Crandall, 1972; Crowne, 1979; Crowne & Marlowe, 1964; Paulhus, 1991; Weinberger, 1990). As in any well-researched area of behavioral science, some of the follow-up studies produced different results, and an exhaustive literature review (using the search methods described in Chapter 2) will turn up these additional studies. The word *need* in Crowne and Marlowe's *approval need* construct is no longer fashionable (Paulhus, 1991), and researchers have suggested relabeling the construct *evaluative dependence* (Millham & Jacobson, 1978) or simply *approval motivation* (Strickland, 1977). These and other developments are consistent with the course of any successful research program, in which researchers build on, and attempt to improve our understanding of, the earlier seminal work. However, the main point of this example is to pull together some of the ideas that we have discussed in this chapter and to illustrate a systematic approach to construct validity.

Validity in Experimental Design

In the next chapter, we will discuss the logic of a certain class of experimental designs, a process that will implicitly involve thinking about a number of validity-related criteria. In particular, we will focus on certain threats to internal validity in the next chapter. However, other relevant kinds of validity include statistical conclusion validity, construct validity, and external validity, and in subsequent discussions, we will touch on these concepts as well. In concluding this chapter, we now give a flavor of these four types of validity and also remind you about another type that was broached in an earlier discussion: inferential validity. We will see what these concepts generally mean, and we will anticipate their role in the logic of experimental design.

First, **statistical conclusion validity** refers to the accuracy of drawing certain statistical conclusions, such as whether there is a likely relationship between two variables or whether some observed statistical relationship is merely due to chance fluctuations. When we are interested in making a causal inference (i.e., that X causes Y), we first need to show that the presumed cause and the presumed effect actually occur together. We will have much more to say about this in later discussions, but it basically means that we might be interested in the statistical relationship or correlation between X and Y. For example, a "real" relationship may be occurring, but statistical circumstances may not be conducive to detecting it at a given level of significance. That is, our statistical test may not have sufficient "power" to show the relationship or the effect, and we want to know when this has occurred, to try to anticipate and avoid the problem whenever possible, and not to place the full weight of our final conclusion on the significance level (i.e., the p value) alone.

Second, **internal validity** is concerned with ruling out **plausible rival hypotheses,** a term that you previously encountered in Chapter 4. In experimental research, we can think of plausible rival hypotheses as alternative interpretations to the experimenter's hypothesis about whether X causes Y. Suppose a male student and a female student decide to conduct, as a team, an experiment on verbal learning. Their particular interest is the causal effect of stress, in the form of loud noise, on the learning of prose material. In order to divide the work fairly, the students flip a coin to determine which of them will run the subjects in the stress condition and which of them will run the subjects in the no-stress condition. If they find the hypothesized effect, can they confidently ascribe it to the experimental stress?

The answer, of course, is that they cannot, because we have a plausible rival hypothesis to their working hypothesis that the result was due to stress. Our plausible rival hypothesis is "The result is due to experimenter differences" (e.g., personality and gender differences). This rival hypothesis could have been fairly well ruled out in this experiment if each of the students had run half the subjects in the stress condition and half the subjects in the no-stress condition. Such a plan would prevent the confounding (or intermixing) of the effects of stress and the effects of experimenter differences. Preventing such confounding would increase the internal validity of the experiment.

Third, **construct validity,** in the context of experimental design, is concerned with the psychological qualities constituting what has been characterized as the "theoretical scaffolding" that connects X and Y (Cronbach & Meehl, 1955). An example, mentioned in Chapter 2, was Latané and Darley's (1968, 1970) series of experiments in which the construct of "diffusion of responsibility" was used as a theoretical scaffolding to explain why the more witnesses to an emergency *(X)*, the less likely it is that any one of them will offer help *(Y)*. However, constructs, as you have just seen, also play an important role in other research situations, such as Crowne and Marlowe's relational research, the purpose of which was to develop construct validation evidence by examining a range of situations in which particular results could be logically expected on the basis of their construct. It is important to keep in mind that constructs (like theories) can never actually be "verified," however, because we can never complete *every* possible test (Cronbach & Quirk, 1971). For this reason, the term *validity* is perhaps too strong, because a construct cannot be proved; it can only be falsified. Nevertheless repeated failures to falsify a construct provide compelling support for its validity.

Fourth, **external validity,** in the context of causal inference in experimental research, refers to the generalizability of the inferred causal relationship to circumstances beyond those experimentally studied or observed. We might ask, for example, how robust the causal relation between X and Y is in its generalizability across both persons and settings. Later on, we will see that, when subjects are volunteers, it is often necessary to consider the possible interdependence of their volunteer status and the X variable of interest—that is, if the conclusions are to have external validity. Other factors that sometimes threaten the external validity of a set of generalizations are those affecting what were called *experimental realism* (i.e., the psychological impact of the experimental treatment or situation) and *mundane realism* (i.e., the similarity of the treatment or situation to real life) in Chapter 4 (see also Box 6.9).

Box 6.9   Ecological Validity

Another term you may encounter is **ecological validity,** which (like the term *mundane realism*) refers to whether an experimental situation precisely mirrors the outside world. It is true that many real-world phenomena can be studied very well in carefully controlled laboratory situations that mimic (or simulate) the real world (Mook, 1983). But as mentioned in Chapter 4, it is important to be sensitive to the possibility that an experimental simulation may produce results that underestimate or overestimate the magnitude of the real-world effects (e.g., C. A. Anderson & Bushman, 1997).

Finally, we previously mentioned *inferential validity* as a kind of umbrella term to mean that causal inferences made in psychological laboratories about real-life experiences are applicable to the experiences. To clarify the composition of this concept, we can think of internal validity and construct validity as the building blocks of inferential validity; external validity (when it is relevant) is the capstone. Sometimes a researcher's laboratory findings are intended *only* to be theoretically enlightening and are not intended to reach beyond this level of understanding (Mook, 1983). For example, some chemist might be interested in the theoretical nature of some particular compound and not at all interested in its suitability or practicality beyond the laboratory (for the moment, at least). However, when suitability and practicality are of paramount interest, inferential validity is the foremost concern.

Summary of Ideas

1. All measurements are subject to random errors and systematic errors, which may affect reliability and validity.

2. Broadly speaking, *reliability* refers to consistency (e.g., internal-consistency reliability) or stability (test-retest reliability), and *validity* refers to whether the measurements measure what they claim to measure.

3. Test-retest reliability is denoted by the correlation between scores on the same test given to the same subjects on two different occasions, while internal-consistency reliability comprises the item-to-item reliability (r_{ii}) and the composite reliability (as measured, for example, by the Spearman-Brown formula, K-R 20, and Cronbach's alpha).

4. Using the Spearman-Brown "prophecy formula," we can predict an improvement in composite reliability (R^{SB}) as a function of adding homogeneous items to a test.

5. The degree of reliability of widely used tests (e.g., the MMPI, the Rorschach, and the WAIS) provides standards by which to assess what convention specifies as acceptable reliability.

6. The logic of the item-to-item and composite reliability of a test can be applied to estimating the judge-to-judge reliability (r_{jj}) and the composite reliability (R^{SB}) of judges or the optimal number of judges.

7. To say that a replication attempt is successful implies that the research procedure was modeled closely on the original study, that the overall pattern of results was similar, and that the effect sizes (i.e., the correlation between the independent variable, *X,* and the dependent variable, *Y*) of the two studies are homogeneous.

8. Validity in testing usually means accumulating evidence in three categories: (a) content-related validity; (b) criterion-related validity (e.g., predictive, concurrent); and (3) construct validity.

9. In assessing criterion-related validity, researchers must be attuned to the validity of the criterion as well as to other aspects of the situation.

10. Convergent and discriminant validity are essential in construct validity (e.g., Crowne and Marlowe's validation of the construct of "approval need" and the test that would measure it).

11. Four kinds of validity-related evidence in experimental research are (a) statistical conclusion validity, (b) internal validity, (c) construct validity, and (d) external validity.

12. Inferential validity comprises some of these types of validity and is an important concern when we are immediately interested in generalizing to the real-world setting beyond the laboratory.

Key Terms

alpha coefficient   p. 140
alternate-form reliability   p. 137
bias   p. 135
composite reliability   p. 138
concurrent validity   p. 146
construct validity   pp. 147, 151
content validity   p. 145
convergent validity   p. 147
correlation coefficient   p. 136
criterion validity   p. 146
Cronbach's alpha   p. 140
discriminant validity   p. 147
ecological validity   p. 152
effect size   p. 144
error   p. 134
external validity   p. 151
face validity   p. 146
heterogeneity   p. 144
homogeneity   p. 144
inter-item correlation (r_{ii})   p. 138
internal-consistency reliability   p. 137
internal validity   p. 151

judge-to-judge reliability (r_{jj})   p. 142
K-R 20   p. 140
Marlowe-Crowne Social Desirability
  Scale (MCSD)   p. 148
need for social approval   p. 148
Pearson *r* correlation coefficient
  p. 136
plausible rival hypotheses   p. 151
predictive validity   p. 146
random error   p. 135
reliability   p. 135
replication   p. 144
Spearman-Brown "prophecy formula"
  (R^{SB})   p. 138
split-half reliability   p. 137
statistical conclusion validity   p. 150
systematic error   p. 135
test-retest reliability   p. 135
validity   p. 135
Wechsler Adult Intelligence Scale
  (WAIS)   p. 140

Multiple-Choice Questions for Review (answers are found on page 347)

1. Random error is error that (a) isn't worth worrying about; (b) is always in the same direction; (c) has an average of about zero; (d) is also known as *bias*.

2. Broadly speaking, _____ refers to the consistency or stability of measurement. (a) validity; (b) modulation; (c) reliability; (d) invalidity

3. A researcher at Wheelock College administers a test of chronic anxiety. One month later, she administers the same questionnaire and finds that scores on the two administrations of the test correlate highly ($r = .85$). This correlation demonstrates the _____ of the test. (a) internal validity; (b) internal-consistency reliability; (c) external validity; (d) test-retest reliability

4. A researcher at Roosevelt University constructs a five-item measure of attitudes toward national health insurance. The average intercorrelation among the items is $r_{ii} = .40$. Using the Spearman-Brown formula, he determines that $R^{SB} = .77$. This researcher has just calculated the _____ of the attitude scale. (a) internal validity; (b) composite reliability; (c) test-retest reliability; (d) convergent validity

5. In the question above, in which the researcher determined that $R^{SB} = .77$, what is the reliability of the scale as a whole? (a) .77; (b) .5; (c) .40; (d) cannot be determined from the information given

6. One intelligence test has two separate forms. Both measure intelligence, but they contain different questions. A person's score on Form A correlates highly with that person's score on Form B ($r_{AB} = .92$). This correlation demonstrates the _____ reliability of the test. (a) internal-consistency; (b) external-consistency; (c) test-retest; (d) alternate-form

7. In determining whether or not one study replicates the results of another, scientists often examine _____ , which are statistics that reflect the magnitude of the relationship between X and Y. (a) significance levels; (b) alpha coefficients; (c) effect sizes; (d) data on the manipulation checks

8. "A test should correlate with theoretically related external variables; for example, the SAT should correlate with grade point average." This statement defines _____ validity. (a) statistical-conclusion; (b) content; (c) consistency; (d) criterion

9. "A test should not correlate with variables from which it is theoretically distinct." This statement defines _____ validity. (a) convergent; (b) content; (c) discriminant; (d) criterion

10. The generalizability of the results of a study is referred to as the _____ of the study. (a) internal validity; (b) external validity; (c) construct validity; (d) discriminant validity

Discussion Questions for Review (answers are found on page 348)

1. An Emory University student is trying to make her mark in the field of psychology by developing a new scale measuring fear of public speaking. How might she assess her scale's predictive and construct validity?

2. On a quiz, a University of Lethbridge student is asked how we know that the Marlowe-Crowne scale (MCSD) measures need for social approval. What is the answer?

3. A University of Houston student has piloted his observational study using two judges and has found a moderate rater-to-rater reliability ($r = .50$). Because he wants to achieve a higher reliability coefficient, he is distressed by the prospect of having to modify his coding criteria and training procedures. Another student suggests, "Don't bother with all that. Simply add two more judges to improve the reliability." Would you consider the second student's advice sound?

4. A Pennsylvania State University researcher wants to study the effects of the texture of toys on the frequency with which toddlers touch them. She uses the following toys: a brown teddy bear, a smooth blue plastic ball, a green wooden cube, and an orange corduroy-covered rattle. She finds that male toddlers are more likely to touch the ball and the cube than the teddy bear and the rattle, whereas female toddlers are more likely to touch the teddy bear and the rattle than the other two toys. When she reports the results, a member of the audience raises the possibility that male toddlers must therefore prefer hard, less variegated textures to soft, more variegated textures, whereas female toddlers show the reverse preference. What is one rival hypothesis that would also be consistent with the researcher's results? How might the rival hypothesis be ruled out?

5. A Northeastern University researcher wants to build a 20-item test to measure need for power. She assigns several students to assess the internal consistency of her new test based on data recently collected from a large sample. They tell her that the composite reliability equals .50 and that the mean inter-item reliability equals .40. She asks them to check their work. Why?

6. A student at the State University of New York at Binghamton is interested in assessing a new 20-item scale of optimism-pessimism. Describe how he ought to go about assessing the reliability of this scale. The student is also advised by his instructor to measure several different traits using several different methods to demonstrate empirically the convergent and discriminant validity of the new scale. Why does the instructor give this advice?

7. A student at Bridgewater State College weighs an object known to weigh 10 pounds five times. She obtains readings on the scale of 14, 8, 7, 10, and 11 pounds. Describe the systematic error and the random errors characterizing the scale's performance.

7 The Logic of Randomized Experiments

A Basic Framework

Now that you have an understanding of some general methods of data collection, the time is ripe to think about the design of your study. One option (discussed in this chapter) is to design a randomized experiment, if that seems appropriate to your hypothesis or the research question that interests you. The term *experiment* is used in different ways in behavioral science. In the next chapter, we will discuss "*N*-of-1 experiments," which are traditionally performed in an area called the *experimental analysis of behavior.* Such an experiment might involve shaping (i.e., controlling) the responses of a rat that receives reinforcement in the form of a food pellet, or shaping the responses of a person or a group by manipulating relevant situational contingencies. In this chapter, however, we are concerned primarily with a particular category of experiments that are classified as **true experimental designs** (and that in medical experiments are frequently referred to as **randomized trials**).

Previously we said that experimental observations are generally intended to tell us how things are related to other things and how they got to be that way. Another way of saying this is that the purpose of an experiment is to observe

PREVIEW QUESTIONS

▌ What is the difference between a true experimental design and a quasi-experimental design?

▌ What are between-subjects and within-subjects designs?

▌ What is the purpose of random assignment?

▌ What constitutes a "causal" inference?

▌ Why is some degree of uncertainty virtually a constant in causal inference?

▌ What role do necessary and sufficient conditions play in the conceptualization of simple randomized experiments?

▌ What can the Solomon design teach us?

▌ Where do "preexperimental designs" get their name?

▌ How are history, maturation, instrumentation, and selection threats to internal validity?

▌ What do demand characteristics have to do with the "good subject" effect and quasi-control subjects?

▌ What is an experimenter expectancy effect, and how can it be controlled by "blind" designs or detected by an expectancy control design?

and evaluate empirical results that are *causal.* All experiments are characterized by the controlled arrangement or manipulation of some procedures or conditions, also called **treatments.** True experimental designs can be differentiated from other experimental designs by the fact that a true experiment always uses **randomization** (or **random assignment**) in the allocation of the elements or experimental units (also called **sampling units**). Thus the term *true* does not refer to *absolute truth;* it simply means that the design uses a genuinely unbiased method (i.e., random assignment) to allocate the sampling units to the treatment conditions. These sampling units (i.e., the subjects or groups or objects being studied) may be people, schools, countries, agricultural crops, and so forth.

In the next chapter, we will discuss several kinds of research designs that approximate true experimental designs but do not randomly assign the sampling units to the treatment conditions. Such designs are generally classified as **quasi-experimental designs;** *quasi* in this context means "resembling" (or approximating) a true experimental design. In this chapter, we will begin our discussion by noting some methods that can be used to randomly assign sampling units to treatment conditions. Our objective is not to provide an exhaustive list of all the different combinations of true experimental designs (which would be impossible), but to examine the logic (and limits) of experimental research. In particular, we will concentrate on causal inferences in between-subjects designs, although we will also have something to say about within-subjects designs.

The term **between-subjects design** means that the subjects are exposed to one treatment condition each. In randomized drug trials, for example, the subjects may be randomly assigned to a drug treatment condition or a placebo treatment condition. (A **placebo** is a substance without any pharmacological benefit given as a pseudomedicine to a control group.) This basic design is illustrated in Part A of Table 7.1, where we see that 5 subjects receive Treatment A and 5 other subjects receive Treatment B. By contrast, in a **within-subjects design,** the subjects receive two or more treatments in a particular sequence. Suppose that we wanted to observe and measure all subjects' reactions to the new drug *and* to the placebo. In Part B of Table 7.1, we see that all 10 subjects receive A and then B. Because subjects' reactions are measured after each treatment, this is also called a **repeated-measures design** (see also Box 7.1). The subjects are being used more efficiently in Part B, but a problem is that the order in which the treatments are administered may present differences in the successive measurements (discussed in a moment).

Box 7.1   Nested and Crossed Designs

Another statistical name for the basic between-subjects design is **nested design,** because (as Table 7.1 shows) the subjects are "nested" within their own treatment conditions. And another name for the basic within-subjects design of Table 7.1 is **crossed design,** because the subjects can be said to be "crossed" by treatment conditions (i.e., observed under two or more conditions) rather than nested within them.

If you have had a course in chemistry, you know that "doing an experiment" usually means mixing reagents in a test tube in order to cause a certain reaction. If you follow the instructions in the lab manual very carefully (e.g., by using clean test tubes

| Table 7.1 | Examples of Between- and Within-Subjects Designs |

A. Between-subjects design

Treatment A	Treatment B
Subject 1	Subject 2
Subject 3	Subject 4
Subject 5	Subject 6
Subject 7	Subject 8
Subject 9	Subject 10

B. Within-subjects design

Treatment A	Treatment B
Subject 1	Subject 1
Subject 2	Subject 2
Subject 3	Subject 3
Subject 4	Subject 4
Subject 5	Subject 5
Subject 6	Subject 6
Subject 7	Subject 7
Subject 8	Subject 8
Subject 9	Subject 9
Subject 10	Subject 10

and pure reagents, and by measuring, stirring, and heating precisely), your experiment is very likely to produce the predicted causal reaction. However, as we said in Chapter 1 (where we mentioned the Hawthorne effect in Box 1.1), our "test tubes" (i.e., psychology experiments) are frequently contaminated by the fact that the "reagents" (i.e., the research subjects) know perfectly well that they are to play this role in interaction with another human being, the experimenter. Insofar as we can evaluate the bias resulting from uncontrolled aspects of the interaction between the experimenter and the subjects, we should be able to draw more accurate conclusions. We will return to this problem toward the end of this chapter, where we touch on the nature and control of subject-related and experimenter-related artifacts.

Random Assignment of Subjects

For between- and within-subjects experimental designs to qualify as *true experimental designs,* not only some experimental treatment, but also randomization, has to be used. As conceived by the statisticians who invented it, randomization (i.e., random assignment) is meant to serve as a safeguard against the experimenters' subconsciously letting their opinions and preferences influence which sampling units will receive any given treatment (Gigerenzer et al., 1989). Randomization does not guarantee equality in the characteristics of the sampling units assigned to the different treatment conditions, but the idea is to give each unit an equal chance of being assigned to any condition. To guard against unsuspected sources of bias that can be effectively controlled in this way, researchers use a randomized procedure to determine how the sampling units will be allocated to the treatment conditions.

An experimenter may use a variety of procedures to achieve random assignment. For example, imagine a between-subjects design with two treatment conditions and each treatment presented in the form of a booklet or questionnaire. One convenient procedure is to pre-sort the booklets in pairs so that each pair is assigned both treatments. The first subject receives Booklet A or B (decided by a flip of a coin), and the next subject receives the other booklet. For the next two subjects, this random procedure is repeated, so that we end up with an equal number of subjects in each of the treatment conditions. Or, we can arrange the booklets so that, of every 4 or 6 or 8 booklets, half will be A's and half will be B's (also determined by coin flips). If the same experiment were being run on a computer, it would be easier because we could have the machine randomly assign the treatment conditions and tabulate the results.

Suppose that, instead of a booklet or a questionnaire, the subjects in one condition receive a new drug while the subjects in the second condition receive a placebo. An easy way to assign subjects in equal numbers to these two conditions is, first, to write each person's name on a slip of paper and then to "blindly" draw pairs of names. We flip a coin to decide which member of a pair will receive the new drug.

Another standard procedure uses a table of random numbers. Imagine we wanted to assign 40 subjects at random to either an experimental or a control condition based on the following 120 single random digits (taken from a longer table on page 209):

10097	32533	76520	13586	34673
37542	04805	64894	74296	24805
08422	68953	19645	09303	23209
99019	02529	09376	70715	38311
12807	99970	80157	36147	

Suppose we decide to read across and down the first five-digit column (10097, 37542, and 08422) and have any odd numbers (1, 3, 5, 7, 9) designate the subjects assigned to the experimental group and have zero and any even numbers (0, 2, 4, 6, 8) designate those assigned to the control group. We would assign Subject 1 to the experimental condition (1), Subjects 2 and 3 to the control condition (0, 0), Subjects 4 through 8 to the experimental condition (9, 7, 3, 7, 5), Subjects 9 through 15 to the experimental condition (4, 2, 0, 8, 4, 2, 2), and so forth.

Previously we mentioned the problem in within-subjects designs that the *order* in which the treatments are administered may be confounded with the treatment effect. Suppose the treatment conditions are administered to young children who are immediately measured after each treatment (i.e., a repeated-measures design). The children may be nervous when first measured, and they may perform poorly; later on, they may be less nervous, and they may perform better. To deal with the problem of systematic differences between successive treatments (or measurements), we use **counterbalancing,** which means rotating the sequences. That is, some subjects will randomly receive Treatment A before Treatment B, and the others will randomly receive B before A (see also Box 7.2).

Box 7.2 **Latin Square Designs**

A statistical design that has counterbalancing built in is called the **Latin square design.** It is characterized by a square array of letters (representing the treatment conditions) in which each letter appears once and only once in each row and in each column. For example, shown below is a Latin square representing a case in which four treatments (A, B, C, and D) will be administered to all the subjects in a counterbalanced pattern:

	Order of Administration			
	1	2	3	4
Sequence 1	A	B	C	D
Sequence 2	B	C	D	A
Sequence 3	C	D	A	B
Sequence 4	D	A	B	C

The subjects randomly assigned to Sequence 1 receive the treatments in the sequence A, then B, then C, and finally D. In Sequences 2 through 4, the treatments are administered in different sequences, BCDA, CDAB, and DABC, respectively. You will find discussions of Latin square designs in more advanced texts (e.g., Keppel, 1991; Kirk, 1995; Rosenthal & Rosnow, 1991).

Another favorite design is called a **simple factorial design,** because the two or more levels of each independent variable (or "factor") operate in combination with the two or more levels of every other factor. For example, suppose a clinical researcher designed a study using the 2 × 2 layout in Table 7.2 (also called a **two-by-two factorial design**); it represents a between-subjects design in which a computer-simulated "male" or "female" therapist administers a standard form of psychotherapy to male and female college students (who play the role of patient). An easy way to assign "patients" randomly to the four groups would again be to write each subject's name on a slip of paper and to separate the names by sex. We then randomly draw one woman's name at a time and assign the first female subject to Condition A and the second to Condition B. We do the same for the men in order to assign male subjects at random to Conditions C and D, until we have filled our quota of male and female "patients" in the four cells.

Table 7.2	Two-by-Two Factorial Design	
	"Therapist's" Sex	
"Patient's" sex	Female	Male
Female	A	B
Male	C	D

Four Kinds of Causation

We said that the purpose of scientific experiments is to show "what causes what," and before going any further in this chapter, it is important that you understand what scientists themselves generally mean by **causation.** Imagine the flight of a curve ball thrown by a pitcher at a professional baseball game. The batter swings and misses, while you ask yourself, "What caused the ball to break that way?" This is a question also pondered by Isaac Newton—not about baseballs, but about tennis balls. When you think carefully about questions of causation (such as this one), you begin to see that they have more than a single answer. Indeed, more than 2,300 years ago, Aristotle thought carefully about questions of causation (although it was not baseballs or tennis balls that stimulated his interest) and came to realize that they can be answered in four distinct ways.

One answer concerns what is called the **material cause,** which is the substance or substances necessary for the movement or coming into being of the effect. According to the physics of baseball (R. K. Adair, 1990), the roughness on the surface of the ball and the nature of fluid flow constitute the material cause of its unusual movement—and make it hard to hit. A ball with a smooth surface tends to have a smooth flight to the plate, especially if it passes through air at a speed of less than 50 miles an hour. A ball with rough seams that travels at a speed over 50 miles an hour begins to encounter turbulence, particularly when it is thrown in a special way to take advantage of the nature of airflow.

The second answer concerns the **formal cause,** which is the plan or development that gives meaning to the event. In this instance, the idea of throwing a curve ball is formally initiated in the mind of the catcher, who then communicates the plan to the pitcher, who in turn thinks "curve ball" up to the moment the ball is released.

The third answer, termed the **final cause** (also called **teleological,** which means the action is "goal-directed"), refers to the objective or end purpose of the event. In this case, it is the objective of having a ball "break" as it nears the plate, so that the batter will not be able to hit the pitch squarely.

And finally, the fourth answer is the **efficient cause,** or the activating force or event that was responsible for the effect. In the baseball example, the efficient cause is the actual throwing of the ball, which causes it to travel at an optimal velocity and causes its trajectory to deviate from the original horizontal direction of motion.

How may we translate these four "causes" in the case of human behaviors? For human development, for instance, we may say that (1) cellular structure is the material cause (i.e., the "stuff" of development); (2) DNA or genetics is the formal cause (i.e., the biological blueprint); (3) physiological maturation is the final cause (i.e., the end "purpose" or goal); and (4) parenting as an environmental variable is the efficient (i.e., activating or instigating) cause. All four kinds of Aristotelian causation are of interest to different behavioral and social scientists. However, it is the fourth cause, in particular, that experimenting scientists generally have in mind when they theorize that something "produces an effect" (i.e., *causes* something else to occur).

Three Criteria of Efficient Causation

How do scientists actually arrive at the conclusion that something produces an effect or that one thing causes something else to occur, for example, that "repetition enhances belief" or that "frustration causes aggression"? This question has three answers: covariation, temporal precedence, and internal validity.

First, we look for evidence that the independent variable *(X)* and the dependent variable *(Y)* are mutually related (or *covary*). That is to say, we ask whether the presence (and absence) of *X* (the presumed cause) is actually correlated with the presence (and absence) of *Y* (the presumed effect). When we find that *X* and *Y* show a satisfactory correlation, we have evidence of **covariation.** What constitutes "satisfactory correlation"? We alluded to a traditional answer to this question in the previous chapter, where we mentioned the idea of testing a correlation for significance. But we will save this question for Chapter 12, where we return to the idea of effect size (introduced in the previous chapter) and also discuss the mechanics of statistical significance testing and what it tells us (and does not tell us).

Second, we look for evidence that *Y* does not occur until after *X* occurs or is set in motion (called **temporal precedence**). In other words, we ask whether there is clear-cut evidence to support the assumption that the presumed cause actually came before the presumed effect. In relational research, it is frequently hard to find incontrovertible evidence of temporal precedence because we are looking at *X* and *Y* in retrospect (i.e., looking back at them). We will have more to say about this issue in the next chapter, but sometimes it can be argued simply on logical grounds, even retrospectively, that *X* must surely have come before *Y.* Suppose we have found satisfactory evidence of covariation between sex and height and want to underscore which is the independent variable and which is the dependent variable. Common sense leads us to conclude that sex is more likely to determine height than that height is to determine sex, because a person's sex is biologically established at conception.

Third, we look for logical and evidential ways to rule out competing explanations of the relation between *X* and *Y.* In other words, we try to rule out plausible rival hypotheses that may undermine the causal interpretation (i.e., we look for evidence of **internal validity**). To be sure, human beings are not clairvoyant, and therefore there is a human limit on how successful this effort can be. That is, we cannot realistically expect to anticipate all plausible rival hypotheses because we cannot look into the future. Nevertheless some methodologists have compiled lists of conditions that may undermine the four types of validity described earlier (i.e., statistical conclusion validity, internal validity, construct validity, and external validity). We will have more to say about this approach later.

The bottom line, however, is that working even within the limited framework of these three criteria (covariation, temporal precedence, and internal validity), scientists find they must settle for the most compelling evidence *available* of efficient causation, even if that evidence is inconclusive. In other words, **causal inference** is always subject to some degree of uncertainty. This is not surprising, because we know that all methods are limited in some ways, which is why we adopted the philosophy of methodological pluralism. In fact, some degree of uncertainty is virtually a constant in science as it is in everyday life, and it makes clear causal inferences difficult in many situations.

Uncertainty of Causal Inference

As an illustration, imagine we discover an outbreak of strange medical symptoms and want to explain them in causal terms. We might begin by interviewing some or all of those afflicted, with the aim of finding an event they have in common (i.e., a clue to covariation of an event and the strange symptoms). Our interviews suggest that all of them have been taking a new prescription drug whose side effects have not yet been fully established. We now suspect that the drug may be the (efficient) cause of the symptoms, in some persons at least. We could easily confirm our suspicion if we simply arranged to take a sample of subjects and then randomly give half of them the suspected drug. This procedure would allow us to compare the two groups of people to see whether those given the drug are more likely to develop the strange symptoms. However, the ethical cost of such experimental research would be too high, because we would not want to expose people to a drug we had good reason to believe harmful.

As a practical alternative, we can compare persons who have been given the new drug by their physicians with those persons whose physicians have not prescribed the drug. If only those given the drug develop the new symptoms, the drug is more seriously implicated. However, its causal role is still not fully established, because those patients given the new drug may differ in a number of ways from those not given the drug. That is, not the new drug, but an unknown correlate of being given the drug, may be the causal variable.

Another strategy is to correlate the dosage levels with the outcome variable. It is possible that, among those patients given the drug, some have been given large dosages whereas others have been given small dosages. If it turns out that persons on larger dosages suffer more severely from the new symptoms, will this evidence implicate the drug more strongly? Unfortunately the answer is the same one mentioned above: We still cannot be certain about the causal role of the drug because those given larger dosages may have been more ill to begin with. In this case, the illness for which the drug was prescribed, rather than the drug itself, may be the "cause" of the symptoms.

How have we done so far? "Not very well," you might answer. To prove temporal precedence, we need to show that taking the drug preceded the symptoms. Unless our medical records go back far enough, however, we cannot prove that the symptoms did not occur until after the drug had been taken. The covariation proof requires us to show that the drug is related to the symptoms. Even if we can show that taking the drug is correlated with the mysterious symptoms, it might be argued that, in order to be susceptible to the drug, a person already has to be in a given state of distress. According to this argument, it is not the drug, or *not only* the drug, that is related to the symptoms. If the subjects who were in a state of distress are the only ones who have been given the drug, it is possible to explain the observed relationship on the basis of **self-selection;** that is, it can be argued that the subjects have been "self-selected" into the treatment groups. Thus the subjects' state of distress has determined the particular group in which they find themselves.

Despite the difficulty of clear inference in this example, we might still be convinced by strong circumstantial, though inconclusive, evidence. If persons taking the drug are more likely to show the symptoms, if those taking more of the drug show more of the symptoms, and if those taking it over a longer period of time show more of the symptoms, we would be reluctant to say that the drug is not the cause of the symptoms. Even if we were unwilling to say that the drug is *surely* at the root of the symptoms, at least on the basis of the type of evidence outlined, it might well be prudent to act "as though" it were.

Mill's Methods and the Logic of Experimental Control

Had there not been a troublesome question of ethics, a simple randomized design—in which the drug is given to an **experimental group** of subjects and not given to subjects in a **control group**—would have allowed us a more controlled comparison of the rates at which distress occurred. Such control also embodies certain "logical methods" (or propositions) popularized by the 19th-century English philosopher John Stuart Mill, after whom they came to be known as **Mill's methods.** Two of them—agreement and difference—together provide the logical basis of causal inferences in all experiments based on the simple randomized design.

First, the **method of agreement** states, "If X, then Y," X symbolizing the presumed cause and Y the presumed effect. The statement means that, if we find two or more instances in which Y occurs, and if only X is present on each occasion, it follows that X is a **sufficient condition** of Y. Calling X a sufficient condition means that it is *adequate* (i.e., capable or competent enough) to bring about the effect. Stated another way, an effect will be present when this sufficient cause is present. In baseball, we would say that there are several sufficient conditions for getting the batter to first base, such as getting a hit (X_1), being walked by the pitcher (X_2), or being struck by a pitch (X_3).

Second, the **method of difference** states, "If not-X, then not-Y." The statement implies that if the presumed effect *(Y)* does not occur when the presumed cause *(X)* is absent, then X is a **necessary condition** of Y. Calling X a necessary condition means that it is *indispensable;* that is, X is absolutely essential to bring about the effect. Stated another way, the effect will be absent when the necessary cause is absent. To win in baseball (Y), it is *necessary* to score the most runs (X); not scoring any runs (not-X) will therefore result in not winning (not-Y).

To take these ideas one step further, suppose that X represents a new and highly touted tranquilizer, and Y represents a change in measured tension. We give a group of subjects who complain of tension a certain dosage of X, and they show a reduction in measured tension. Can we conclude from this before-and-after observation that the tranquilizer caused the reduction in tension? Not yet, because even if we repeatedly find that giving X is followed by tension reduction, we imply only that X is a sufficient condition of Y. What we seem to need is a control group with which to compare the reaction in the first group. For our control, we use a group of comparable subjects to whom we do not give drug X. If these subjects show no tension reduction, we have implied that X may be a necessary condition of Y.

We can diagram this simple randomized design as follows, and we see that it corresponds precisely to Mill's Methods:

Experimental group	**Control group**
If X, then Y	If not-X, then not-Y

Can we now conclude that taking the drug leads to tension reduction? Yes, but with the stipulation that "taking the drug" implies something more than getting a chemical into the blood stream. "Taking the drug" means among other things (1) having someone give the subject a pill; (2) having someone give the subject the attention that goes with pill giving; (3) having the subject believe that relevant medication has been administered; and (4) having the ingredients of the drug find their way into the blood system of the subject.

Usually, when testing a drug, the researcher is interested only in the subjects' physical reactions to the active ingredients of the medication. The researcher does not care whether the subjects will feel better if they merely *believe* they are being helped, because this fact (i.e., the power of suggestion) has already been established. But if researchers know about the power of suggestion, how are they to separate the effects of the drug's ingredients from the effects of pill giving, of the subjects' expectations of being helped, and of other psychological variables that may also be sufficient conditions of Y? The answer is by the choice of a different (or an additional) control group. So this time, we use not a group given nothing (also called a **zero control group**), but a group given something that differs only in the ingredients whose effects we would like to establish (i.e., a **placebo control group**). The general finding, incidentally, is that placebos are often effective and are sometimes even as effective as the far more expensive drug for which they serve as the control.

In this research, we are using a no-pill control group (i.e., a zero control group) and a group that receives a placebo. Assuming there is often a choice of groups, how can we decide what design to use? If there are two groups, the groups should be as similar as possible except for the effect of interest. If the groups to be compared differ in some factor other than that effect, the influence of this factor is said to be **confounded** (i.e., mixed up or confused) with the effect of interest. In choosing a design, the researcher tries to control for potentially confounding effects while isolating the effect of interest. Let us see how this done.

Teasing Out Effects of Interest

To illustrate, suppose we are interested in studying whether giving children a lesson on the rules of correct spelling will improve their spelling ability. We can design an experiment in which we pretest children on a list of words of equal difficulty by having them spell the words. We then teach half the children at random (i.e., the experimental group) the rules of spelling (the experimental treatment) and do not teach these rules to the other children (i.e., the control group), and afterward we test all of them on the same list of words. However, a problem is that pretesting the experimental group may "sensitize" them to the experimental treatment (called **pretest sensitization**) and distort the outcome. That is, they may perform better or worse on the posttest than if they had not been pretested, as revealed by the **pretest-treatment interaction.**

To begin with, we wanted to know how well these subjects perform with these words before we administer the treatment, but we did not want to "sensitize" the subjects by actually pretesting them. Because random assignment minimizes any biased differences between groups (i.e., by giving each subject an equal opportunity of being assigned to any group), all we need to do is randomly assign some of the subjects to another group that will be pretested but not treated. We can then use the pretest scores from this group to estimate how the unpretested experimental and control groups *would have* done had they also been pretested. We use the untreated groups to address the question of main interest, which was whether giving children a lesson on the rules of correct spelling will improve their spelling ability.

For practical and theoretical reasons, we also wanted to know whether there might be a pretest-treatment interaction in this experimental situation. Once we know this, we can control for that confounding effect in any future investigation. A simple factorial design that can tell us the magnitude and direction of the pretest-treatment interaction is the **Solomon design,** named after Richard L. Solomon (1949), the psychologist who first proposed it.

The Solomon Design

There are many possible factorial designs, but the Solomon design provides an elegant introduction to the logic of teasing out different effects in randomized experiments. Table 7.3 shows the 2 × 2 Solomon design that we would use in this particular case, with the assumption of randomly assigning the subjects to these four groups. Notice that Group I is pretested, receives the experimental treatment, and is then retested. Group II is not pretested but does undergo the same experimental treatment as Group I. Group III is pretested and retested but does not receive the experimental treatment. Group IV gets only the posttest.

Table 7.3	The Solomon Four-Group Design	
	Pretested?	
Experimentally treated?	Yes	No
Yes	Group I	Group II
No	Group III	Group IV

First, we would use Groups I and III (the pretested groups) to estimate the pre-treatment performance in Groups II and IV (the unpretested groups). In other words, without actually pretesting Groups II and IV, we can make a good guess of the mean pretest scores in both groups. This guess will require a leap of faith because we cannot be *absolutely* sure what the mean pretest performance in the unpretested groups would have been. Even if the value of the pretest in Group I is identical to that in Group III, we can only *assume* that the values are close to those that would have been obtained by Groups II and IV. Suppose that, in randomly allocating subjects to these four conditions, we were very careful with some groups and not as careful with others. If the pretest values in Groups I and III differ greatly (because of bias in the assignment of subjects), there is still a possibility that the unknown pretreatment performance in Groups II and IV would have been similar to the mean of Groups I and III (because of the greater attention paid to the random allocation of subjects to these conditions).

Second, on the basis of our estimation of the pretest performance levels in Groups II and IV, we can enrich our comparison of the posttest performance scores in these groups. That is, we can estimate the pre-to-post benefit of the experimental treatment without having contaminated these experimental and control groups by pretesting.

Third, this design can tell us whether there was a pretest-treatment interaction (i.e., any confounding of pretesting and X). One way to find this out is to use a subtraction-difference procedure in which we systematically compare the different posttest means in order to identify the *residual effects* of the interaction (see Box 7.3). For a demonstration of this comparison, we refer to Table 7.4. The rows show the four plausible causal events affecting the outcome measure in each group. We see that the outcome in Group I can be affected by the pretest, the experimental treatment, pretest sensitization (i.e., the pretest-treatment interaction), and any unaccounted-for extraneous effects. The outcome in Group II can be affected by the treatment and any extraneous effects, but by no other conditions because there was no pretest to produce a pretest effect or a pretest-treatment interaction. The outcome in Group III can be affected by the pretest and any extraneous effects, but by no other conditions because there was no treatment to produce a treatment effect or a pretest-treatment interaction. The outcome in Group IV can be affected by extraneous effects, but by no other conditions.

Table 7.4	Teasing Out the Pretest-Treatment Interaction by the Subtraction-Difference Procedure			
		Plausible Effects		
Causal events	Group I	Group II	Group III	Group IV
Pretest	Yes	No	Yes	No
Treatment	Yes	Yes	No	No
Sensitization	Yes	No	No	No
Extraneous effects	Yes	Yes	Yes	Yes

Box 7.3 **Residual Effects**

We will see the term **residual effects** (i.e., leftover effects) again in a later chapter, where we discuss the nature and interpretation of statistical interactions in factorial designs. Interaction effects are thus the leftover effects (i.e., residuals) after other relevant effects are removed, as the teasing out of the pretest-treatment interaction illustrates in this example.

To identify the magnitude and direction of the pretest-treatment interaction, we simply isolate the effect of sensitization in Table 7.4. To do this, we subtract the posttest means of the four groups as follows: (Group I − Group III) − (Group II − Group IV). First, we do subtractions within the parentheses, and then, we subtract what remains in the right side of the equation from what remains in the left side. That is, we first subtract the posttest mean of Group III from the posttest mean of Group I, which will cancel out the pretest and the extraneous effects and leave the treatment and sensitization effects. Next, we subtract the posttest mean of Group IV from the posttest mean of Group II, which will cancel out the extraneous effects and leave the treatment effect. When we subtract what remains in the right side of the equation from what remains in the left side, what is left over is the residual effect of pretest sensitization (i.e., the pretest-treatment interaction effect). Incidentally, Richard Solomon (1949) actually performed a similar experiment and found that taking a pretest made children more resistant to the spelling lesson.

Preexperimental Designs

Some years ago, Donald T. Campbell, Julian C. Stanley, and Thomas D. Cook developed master lists to help experienced researchers check for plausible threats to validity when choosing a basic research design (Campbell & Stanley, 1963; Cook & Campbell, 1976, 1979). Campbell and his associates used symbols to represent the design templates (or models) and speculated on the threats to statistical conclusion validity, internal validity, construct validity, and external validity that are (or are not) controlled in each general case. In the case of the Solomon design's ability to control for pretest sensitization, Campbell et al. conceptualized the interaction of the pretest and X as one of a number of plausible threats to external validity controlled by this design.

Campbell et al. also described two templates, or models, that are so deficient in control as to be labeled **preexperimental designs.** One of these preexperimental designs, called the **one-shot case study,** is symbolized as **X-O,** where X = exposure of a treatment group to an experimental variable or event, and O = an observation or measurement (see also Box 7.4). An illustration would be the introduction of a new educational treatment (X) designed to improve students' concentration and then the use of an achievement test (O) to measure their performance. No allowance is made by this design for a comparison with the reactions of students who have not been subjected to the educational treatment, nor do we know the subjects' pretreatment levels of achievement.

Box 7.4   **Diagramming the Solomon Design**

The four-group Solomon design can also be represented by a symbolic template, in which X = treatment exposure and O = observation or measurement. To show that the sampling units are allocated to separate groups at random, we use the symbol R (for *randomization*), which gives:

Group I	R	O	X	O
Group II	R		X	O
Group III	R	O		O
Group IV	R			O

Notice also that the Solomon design actually consists of two component designs (both simple randomized designs). Groups II and IV comprise what is called a **posttest-only control-group design,** which would be useful if we had no need of a pretreatment measure. Groups I and III comprise what is called a **pre-post control-group design,** which would be useful if we wanted a pretreatment measure and did not have to worry about controlling for pretest sensitization (e.g., Lana, 1969; but see also Entwisle, 1961; Rosnow & Suls, 1970).

A slight improvement on the one-shot case study would be a preexperimental design that at least measured the subjects before and after exposure to the treatment. Called a **one-group pre-post design,** it is symbolized as **O-X-O.** It is still viewed as preexperimental because of the lack of comparison conditions (i.e., beyond the pretreatment measure). We still cannot rule out uncontrolled events between X and O, as well as some other threats to internal validity. There are a number of specific conditions that, Campbell et al. noted, can jeopardize the internal validity of a study. To give you a flavor of some of these conditions, let us look at four: history, maturation, instrumentation, and selection.

History, Maturation, Instrumentation, and Selection

First, the term **history** implies a plausible source of error attributable to an uncontrolled event that occurs between the premeasurement and the postmeasurement and that can bias the postmeasurement. History is a threat to internal validity when the inferred causal relationship is confounded by the irrelevant, uncontrolled event. Suppose a sudden snowstorm results in an unexpected cancellation of classes. Neither preexperimental design would allow us to isolate the effects on motivation of a school closing, or to assess that factor apart from the effects of the new educational treatment designed to improve concentration. The Solomon design, as well as its two component designs (noted in Box 7.4), do allow us to assess this factor in the treated groups apart from the untreated groups.

Second, **maturation** refers to certain intrinsic changes in the research participants, such as their growing older, wiser, stronger, or more experienced between the premeasurement and the postmeasurement. Maturation becomes a threat to internal validity when it is not the variable of interest but the inferred causal relationship is nevertheless confounded by the presence of these changes. Imagine a study in which the posttest is given one year after the pretest. If the students' concentration has improved as a result of their getting older, so that they have become better at the task, neither of the preexperimental designs will tell us whether the gains are due to the students' maturing or to their being subjected to a particular educational treatment. We could, if we used the Solomon design (or either of the component designs in Box 7.4) control for maturation bias by taking immediate and delayed posttreatment measurements.

Third, **instrumentation** refers to the intrinsic changes in the measuring instruments, such as deterioration. Instrumentation would be a threat to internal validity when an effect may be due to unsuspected changes in the instruments over time. In the case of our educational treatment, we might ask whether the effect is caused by instability (i.e., deterioration) of the achievement test or to changes in the students that are caused by the treatment. Or suppose the "instruments" are actually judges who are asked to rate the subjects. Over time, judges may become better raters of student concentration, in which case the confounding is due not to instrument deterioration but to instrument improvement. Instrumentation bias is not a relevant issue in the case of the X-O design because the test is administered only once, but it is both relevant and uncontrolled in the O-X-O design, and relevant and specifically identifiable (i.e., controlled) in the Solomon design and its component designs.

Fourth, **selection** also refers to the subjects, but in this case, the threat to internal validity comes from the selection of the subjects for their assignment to particular treatments. Selection is a threat to internal validity when there are important, unsuspected differences between the subjects in each condition. In the X-O design, there is no way of knowing beforehand anything about the state of the participants because they are observed or measured only after the treatment has been administered. The addition of an observation before the treatment in the O-X-O design results in an improvement over the X-O design; it enables us to ascertain the prior state of the participants. The Solomon design and its two component designs specifically control for selection bias by allocating the subjects randomly.

The Social Psychology of the Experiment

In Chapter 4, the terms *reactive* and *nonreactive* were used to distinguish measurements or observations that do (reactive) from those that do not (nonreactive) affect the behavior being measured or observed. When an engineer carefully takes the dimensions of a large piece of metal, we do not suppose that the act of measurement will have an effect on the metal. Similarly, when a biologist observes the movements of a paramecium, we do not expect the paramecium to change its behavior when the scientist is looking at it through a microscope. However, one may be less sure of the risks of reactive observation when humans or primates are the object of study (see also Box 7.5).

Box 7.5	**Reactive Observations in Animal Research**

The risks of reactive observation are not limited to research with humans and primates. For example, one researcher reported that experienced observers in an animal laboratory could judge which of several experimenters had been handling a rat by the animal's behavior while running a maze or when being picked up (Christie, 1951). Another researcher observed that a dog's heart rate would drop dramatically simply because a certain experimenter was present (Gantt, 1964).

The term used to refer to this problem is **artifact,** which in this context means a finding that results from conditions other than those intended by the experimenter (Blanck, 1993; Rosenthal & Rosnow, 1969; Rosnow & Rosenthal, 1997). However, artifacts are not simply serendipitous findings, but findings resulting from uncontrolled factors that may jeopardize the validity (internal, construct, and external) of the researcher's conclusions about what went on in the study or about the implications of the results. In the remainder of this chapter, we will touch on some of the work in this area (called the **social psychology of the experiment**) and note some ways that subject- and experimenter-related artifacts are handled.

Subject-Related Artifacts

The notion of subject-related artifacts proceeds from the idea that much of the complexity of human activity described by behavioral scientists lies in the nature of the human organism that serves as the model: the research subject. We know, for example, that no two research subjects behave identically, and therefore the "same" careful experiment conducted in one place at one time may yield results very different from those of an experiment conducted in another place at another time. Although it is generally accepted that much of this complexity is due to the complexities of human nature, it is recognized that most subjects know perfectly well that they are research participants and that they are to play out this role in interaction with the experimenter. The role of "research subject" appears to be well understood by most normal adults who find their way into behavioral scientists' subject pools. Thus what one researcher interprets as a causal relationship between X and Y, another researcher may theorize to be the plausible relation between some role variable and Y (J. G. Adair, 1973; Danziger, 1988; Gniech, 1976; Rosenthal & Rosnow, 1969, 1975b; I. Silverman, 1977; Strohmetz & Rosnow, 1994; Suls & Rosnow, 1988).

Pioneering work in the social psychology of the experiment was done by Martin T. Orne, whose interests in subject-related artifacts grew out of his research on hypnosis. Observations in that research led him to theorize that the trance manifestations that subjects exhibit on entering hypnosis are partly determined by their motivation to "act out" the role of a hypnotized person. Both their preconceptions of how a hypnotized person ought to act and the cues communicated by the hypnotist of how the subjects should behave, called **demand characteristics,** were viewed by Orne (1962,

1969, 1970) as plausible determinants of the subjects' expectations concerning how this role was to be enacted. In particular, Orne postulated that typical volunteers for hypnosis have a tendency to act out the role of the **good subject,** that is, the kind of subject who is sensitive to demand characteristics and tries to give experimenters what they seem to want to find (Orne, 1959).

Earlier (in Chapter 5), we spoke of Milton Rosenberg's (1969) view of subjects of behavioral research as being apprehensive about being evaluated, a condition that he called **evaluation apprehension.** Although Rosenberg argued that typical subjects are motivated to "look good" rather than to help the cause of science (Orne's view), he and Orne agreed that typical subjects frequently find meaning in even the most meaningless cues (see, for example, Box 7.6). Orne theorized that most research subjects (especially volunteers for research participation) reason that, no matter how trivial and inane the task outwardly seems, the experimenter must surely have an important scientific purpose that justifies their experimental participation. Feeling that they have a stake in the outcome of the study, the **good subjects** believe that they are making a useful contribution to science by complying with the demand characteristics of the experiment, Orne argued. The puzzle for the researcher is to figure out what demand characteristics may have been inadvertently operating in the experiment.

Box 7.6   **The Good Subject**

The extent to which some research participants will comply with demand characteristics sometimes surprises even the experimenter. At one point in his hypnosis research, Orne (1962) tried to devise a set of dull, meaningless tasks that nonhypnotized persons either would refuse to do or would try for only a short time. One task was to add thousands of rows of two-digit numbers. Five and a half hours after the subjects began, the experimenter gave up. When the subjects were told to tear each worksheet into a minimum of 32 pieces before going on to the next, they *still* persisted.

To help us in this quest, Orne (1962, 1969) proposed that **quasi-control subjects** be used. These are research subjects who are asked to step out of their traditional roles and to serve as "coinvestigators" (that is, rather than as "objects of study" for the experimenter to investigate). Such subjects are usually drawn from the same population as the experimental and control subjects, but the quasi-control subjects are asked to reflect on the context in which the experiment is being conducted. They then free-associate about how they think the situation might influence their behavior if they were in the experimental group. For example, the participation of a few subjects in the experimental group may be terminated at different points during the course of the study. They then become quasi-control subjects, who are carefully interviewed about what they thought to be the demand characteristics of the experiment.

Experimenter Expectancy and Its Control

On the other side of the artifact coin are experimenter-related artifacts, that is, sources of bias (or systematic error) resulting from the uncontrolled intentions or actions of experimenters themselves. There are a number of such sources (Rosenthal, 1966; Rosnow & Rosenthal, 1997), but the one we describe here is particularly intriguing because it occurs when people's expectations unwittingly serve as *self-fulfilling prophecies* (discussed in Chapter 4). That is, someone expects an event to occur, and this expectation then shapes the expecter's behavior in such a way as to make the predicted event more likely to occur. For example, a teacher who believes that certain pupils are especially bright may act more warmly toward them, teach them more material, and spend more time with them. Over time, this behavior may result in greater gains in achievement for those students than would have occurred in the absence of the teacher's positive expectations (see again Box 4.5 on page 94).

When the "prophet" is the experimenter and the research subjects' behavior is at issue, this is called an **experimenter expectancy effect.** In one early study of experimenter expectancy, a dozen student experimenters were each given five rats that were to be taught to run a maze with the aid of visual cues (Rosenthal & Fode, 1963). Half the students were told their rats had been specially bred for maze-brightness, and the remaining students were told their rats had been bred for maze-dullness. Actually, there were no differences in the rats; they had been randomly given the labels of maze-bright and maze-dull. At the end of the experiment, however, there were clear differences. The rats run by experimenters who expected bright behavior did, in fact, perform better than the rats run by experimenters who expected dull behavior.

The study was repeated, this time using a series of learning experiments, each conducted in a Skinner box (Rosenthal & Lawson, 1964). Half the student experimenters were led to believe their rats were "Skinner-box-bright," and half were led to believe their animals were "Skinner-box-dull." Once again, there were not really any differences in the two groups of rats, at least not until the results were analyzed at the end of the study. The allegedly brighter animals really were brighter, and the alleged dullards were really duller. We should emphasize that the experimenters' expectations acted on the actual performance of the animals, not simply on the evaluation of the animals' performance. Neither of these studies showed any evidence that the experimenters were trying to generate false data (i.e., there was no evidence of cheating).

One strategy for dealing with the experimenter expectancy problem is to use **blind experimenters,** that is, experimenters who are unaware of ("blind" to) which subjects are to receive the experimental treatment and which the control treatment. The idea is that, if the experimenters do not know what treatment the subject has received, they are unlikely to communicate expectancies about the nature of that treatment. The necessity of keeping the experimenters blind (i.e., unaware) is well recognized in randomized drug trials. In fact, no drug trial is taken completely seriously unless it has followed elaborate **double-blind procedures** (i.e., procedures in which neither the subjects nor the experimenters know who is in the experimental and who in the control groups). (See also Box 7.7.)

Box 7.7	Blindfolding to Ensure "Blindness"

This principle of ensuring "blindness" may also be applicable to the role of other participants in the research. For example, cognitive psychologists Kathy Hirsh-Pasek and Roberta Michnick Golinkoff (1993) used a novel method to study language comprehension in infants and toddlers, which the researchers called the "preferential looking paradigm." Suppose we want to study noun comprehension in order to find out how early in their lives infants and toddlers are able to distinguish a shoe from a hat. An infant is seated on a blindfolded parent's lap approximately 2½ feet away from a pair of television monitors. By means of a concealed speaker, the word *shoe* is sounded at the same time that one of the monitors shows a shoe and the other monitor shows a hat. A camera records the child's preferential looking behavior over a series of paired-comparison trials that use many different stimuli. Blindfolding eliminates the possibility of the parent's unintentionally signaling the correct responses.

Another approach to the experimenter expectancy problem is to use a simple factorial design that not only assesses whether an expectancy effect is present but also allows a direct comparison of that effect with the phenomenon of theoretical interest. Called an **expectancy control design,** this approach usually takes the form of the 2 × 2 factorial arrangement shown in Table 7.5. Group A represents the condition in which the experimental treatment is administered to subjects by data collectors who expect the occurrence of the experimental effect in this group. Group D represents the condition in which the absence of the experimental treatment is associated with data collectors who expect the nonoccurrence of the experimental effect in this group. But ordinarily we are interested in the experimental effect unconfounded with experimenter expectancy; the addition of the appropriate expectancy control groups will permit us to evaluate the experimental effect separately from the expectancy effect. Subjects in Group B receive the experimental treatment but are contacted by data collectors who do not expect an experimental effect in this group. Subjects in Group C do not receive the experimental treatment but are contacted by data collectors who expect an experimental effect.

You can see that it is an expensive design because it calls for many data collectors who are randomly assigned to the four cells. However, it has been used in a number

Table 7.5	Basic Expectancy Control Design	
	Expectancy Conditions	
Treatment conditions	Experimental treatment	Control treatment
Experimental	Group A	Group B
Control	Group C	Group D

Table 7.6	Expectancy Control Design Used by Burnham (1966) to Study Discrimination Learning in Rats		
	Expectancy Conditions		
Treatment conditions	Lesioning of brain	No lesioning of brain	Row means
Lesioning of brain	46.5	49.0	47.75
No lesioning of brain	48.2	58.3	53.25
Column means	47.35	53.65	

of experimental situations. Illustrative of its use in animal research is a study reported by J. Randolph Burnham (1966), the results of which are shown in Table 7.6. Each of about two dozen student-experimenters ran one rat in a T-maze discrimination task (i.e., a runway with the starting box at the base and the goal at one end of the crossbar). Portions of the brains of approximately half the rats had been surgically removed (*lesioning*). The remaining rats had received only sham surgery, which involved a cut through the skull but no damage to brain tissue (so that it was impossible for the student-experimenters to tell which rats had actually undergone brain lesioning). The purpose of the study was explained to the student-experimenters as an attempt to learn the effects of lesions on discrimination learning. Expectancies were manipulated by the labeling of each rat as "lesioned" or "unlesioned." Some of the really lesioned rats were labeled accurately as lesioned, but some were falsely labeled as unlesioned. Similarly, some of the really unlesioned rats were labeled accurately as unlesioned, but others were falsely labeled as lesioned.

By comparing the means in the row and column margins, we get an idea of the relative effectiveness of the surgical and the expectancy treatments. The higher these scores, the better was the rats' average performance in that row or column. We see that rats that had been surgically lesioned did not perform as well as those that had not been lesioned. We also see that the rats that were *believed* to be lesioned did not perform as well as those that were believed to be unlesioned. The logic of this design is that it enables us to compare the magnitude of the effect of experimenter expectancy with the magnitude of the effect of the actual removal of brain tissue. We see that, in this case, the two effects were similar. Of course, we are not limited to comparing only the differences in row means and column means, and later in this book, we will see how it is possible statistically to compare individual cell means in a factorial design.

Summary of Ideas

1. A "true" experimental design calls for randomization, which is intended to guard against potential sources of bias.
2. Between-subjects and within-subjects designs—which are distinguished, respectively, by whether each sampling unit is observed once or more than once—

include simple randomized and factorial between-subjects designs and Latin square within-subjects designs.

3. Randomization (i.e., random assignment) procedures include coin flipping and using a table of random digits to allocate the sampling units or treatment conditions in an unbiased way.

4. Aristotle described four kinds of causality: material, formal, efficient, and final (or teleological).

5. To help us decide when one thing is the efficient cause of another, we attempt to establish covariation, temporal precedence, and internal validity.

6. In practice, we find that we must frequently settle for the best available evidence even if it is inconclusive.

7. The notion of control embodies Mill's methods of agreement and difference, as basically reflected in simple randomized experimental designs.

8. Using the Solomon design, we can isolate the pretest-treatment interaction effect by using a subtraction-difference procedure.

9. The pre-post control group design and the posttest-only control-group design are components of the Solomon design.

10. Preexperimental designs, such as a one-shot case study or a one-group pre-post study, make no effort to control for threats to internal validity.

11. Campbell and his colleagues developed checklists of threats to validity, including threats to internal validity such as history, maturation, instrumentation, and selection.

12. The *good subject* (a term coined by Orne) is sensitive and accommodating to demand characteristics.

13. The use of quasi controls, in addition to regular control groups, helps us to ferret out demand characteristics.

14. Experimenter expectancy may cause the experimental hypothesis to become a self-fulfilling prophecy.

15. Blind procedures are used to control for expectancy effects, while an expectancy control design allows us to isolate and compare the expectancy effect with the effect of the main independent variable (e.g., Burnham's study of discrimination learning in rats).

Key Terms

artifact p. 171	counterbalancing p. 160
between-subjects design p. 157	covariation p. 162
blind experimenters p. 173	crossed design p. 157
causal inference p. 163	demand characteristics p. 171
causation p. 161	double-blind procedures p. 173
confounded p. 165	efficient cause p. 161
control group p. 164	evaluation apprehension p. 172

Multiple-Choice Questions for Review (answers are found on page 348)

1. Which of the following is considered a defining characteristic of a "true" experimental design? (a) a random sample; (b) randomization; (c) a placebo-control group; (d) all of the above
2. Randomization refers to (a) selecting a sample at random from a larger population; (b) manipulating a random sample of variables within an experiment; (c) ensuring that each subject has an equal chance of being assigned to any condition; (d) randomly determining which experimenter will conduct which experimental condition.
3. Which of the following was a type of cause identified by Aristotle? (a) final; (b) efficient; (c) formal; (d) all of the above
4. To conclude that X causes Y, scientists must be able to rule out plausible rival hypotheses. This is called the criterion of (a) covariation; (b) temporal precedence; (c) internal validity; (d) material causation.
5. Philosopher J. S. Mill stated, "If X, then Y." This is known as Mill's method of (a) agreement; (b) disagreement; (c) difference; (d) covariation.
6. Which of the following is a common threat to internal validity? (a) maturation; (b) covariation; (c) time-series data; (d) none of the above

7. A research design in which there is only one group, and that group is measured only after the treatment, is called (a) the Solomon design; (b) the one-shot case study; (c) the one-group pre-post study; (d) factorial design.

8. A study is conducted in which there is only one group, and that group is measured both before and after the treatment. This design is vulnerable to which of the following threats to internal validity? (a) history; (b) maturation; (c) selection; (d) all of the above

9. Which of the following research designs allows the scientist to examine the possibility of pretest sensitization? (a) the Solomon four-group design; (b) the one-shot case study; (c) the one-group pre-post design; (d) factorial design

10. Cues given off by a researcher that communicate to subjects how they should behave are called (a) artifacts; (b) demand characteristics; (c) experimenter expectancy effects; (d) none of the above.

Discussion Questions for Review (answers on pages 348–49)

1. A Colby student wants to evaluate the effectiveness of a popular method of boosting self-esteem called *I'm-better-than-OK therapy*. In this therapy, clients read pop psychology books, compliment themselves while looking in a mirror, and have group touch-a-lot sessions. What kind of subjects would you recommend be used in the student's control group(s)?

2. A Villanova student believes that positive reinforcement increases self-esteem. To test this hypothesis, she administers a self-esteem scale to 40 other students and correlates the scores with their grade point averages. Can you think of any limitations in this research design?

3. An Auburn student tells his subjects that he is interested in identifying the characteristics associated with good leadership skills. He then administers two measures titled Social Intelligence Survey and Interpersonal Problem-Solving Ability. Do you see any potential problem in this method?

4. A student at the University of New Mexico wants to prove that eating chocolate chip cookies will cure depression. What basic requirements of inference would he have to meet, according to J. S. Mill?

5. An American University student wants to use an expectancy control design to assess a program offering individual tutoring to enhance students' performance on achievement tests. How might she set up this design?

6. A manufacturer of pain relievers wants to market what seems to be a revolutionary new product: a near-cure for the common cold. Researchers in the R & D division select 1,000 persons to participate in a test study. Each participant is observed for six months. For the first three months, baseline data are collected. For the last three months, the participants take a weekly dose of the common-cold cure. Sure enough, 15% of the participants contracted a cold during the first three months, whereas only 5% have done so in the second three months. The investigators rush their findings to the company president, who must decide whether the data are convincing enough for her to put the product on the market. Can you think of any weakness in the research design?

7. On a quiz, University of Arkansas students are asked how the Solomon design allows researchers to rule out the possibility of confounding the pretest and the results of the treatment. What is the answer? The same students are also asked to define the following threats to internal validity: history, maturation, selection, and instrumentation. Do you know the answers?

8. A Howard University medical student designs an experiment to test the effects of a new drug. In consultation with her faculty mentor, she decides to include both a placebo control group and a zero control group. Do you know the difference?

8

The Role of Quasi-Experimental Designs

The Role of Quasi-Experimentation

In the previous chapter, you saw how scientists use randomized treatment conditions to create the equivalence they need to make causal inferences. The basic idea is to use an unbiased procedure (e.g., a table of random digits or the flipping of a coin) to allocate the sampling units (e.g., research subjects) to the treatment conditions so that the groups differ only in respect to the experimental treatment. For practical or ethical reasons, however, randomized experiments are not always possible. Thus, quasi-experimental designs also play an active role in science. As noted, the term *quasi* means "resembling," and the between-subjects and within-subjects designs we now discuss are called **quasi-experimental** because in some ways they resemble "true" experiments. That is, quasi-experiments have the equivalent of treatment conditions, outcome measures, and sampling units, but they do not use randomization to allocate sampling units to treatment conditions.

For example, suppose we wanted to study whether cigarette smoking causes heart disease and lung cancer in human beings. To

PREVIEW QUESTIONS

▮ What are basic forms of quasi-experimental designs, and what circumstances invite their use?

▮ How do nonequivalent-groups designs attempt to compensate for initial differences between groups?

▮ How are necessary and sufficient conditions inferred from circumstantial evidence in such designs?

▮ What is the role of interrupted time-series data in evaluation and other relational research?

▮ What design strategies are used in *N*-of-1 (i.e., single-case) experimental studies, and how do some behavior modification studies use randomization?

▮ How do cross-lagged panel designs attempt to rule out rival causal hypotheses?

▮ What is the danger in using a cross-sectional design to generalize about a longitudinal causal relationship?

perform a randomized experiment, we would use an unbiased procedure to assign nonsmokers to either an experimental condition that requires them to smoke for many years or to a nonsmoking control group. That procedure would be an ethical absurdity, however. Instead, we might do a relational study in which we observed the association of heart attack and lung cancer with smoking. *Association* implies covariation, but it is not the same thing as causation because some hidden confounding factor may induce people to smoke—and may also give them heart attacks and lung cancer (i.e., a "third variable" may be the basis of a rival hypothesis). The best we may be able to do under the circumstances is to try to make sure that the nonsmokers in our study are as similar as possible to the smokers on as many relevant variables as possible (Freedman et al., 1991). We can then compare the results of our quasi-experiment with the results of animal experiments and of other quasi-experimental and survey studies to see whether there is a convergence of evidence.

We will describe the causal reasoning in quasi-experimental designs, which may be like that used by a doctor trying to treat a patient for a dog bite (see Box 8.1) or that used by an epidemiologist trying to uncover the cause of an outbreak of food poisoning by using only the circumstantial evidence that is available. In particular, we will describe three broad categories of designs: (1) nonequivalent-groups designs, (2) time-series designs, and (3) correlational designs. Within the second category, we will focus on a popular strategy in which the sampling units may be limited to a single subject, called an *N*-of-1 design. We will see that *N*-of-1 designs, although they have a special role in behavior modification (e.g., the evaluation of a single subject in clinical research), are not limited to single-case studies. When there are two or more groups in such studies, it may even be possible to assign subjects at random to some treatment conditions, in which case the design will hardly be distinguishable from a true experimental design.

Box 8.1 **Causal Reasoning in the Doctor's Office**

Suppose your hand has been bitten by a dog. You go to a doctor, who prescribes a tetanus shot and an oral antibiotic. You ask the doctor to give the tetanus shot in your bad arm so that you have your good arm to use. But the doctor points out that if she did so and you had a reaction to the tetanus, she would not be able to separate it from the possible continued reaction to the dog bite—which could, in the worst case scenario, also cause the arm, not the hand, to swell. For this reason, she gives the shot in your good arm, so any swelling due to an allergy to the tetanus will not be confounded with a possible reaction to the dog bite. Her causal reasoning will be based on a comparison of her before and after observations.

Nonequivalent-Groups Designs

Nonequivalent-groups designs are between-subjects designs in which the subjects are assigned to experimental and control groups by means other than randomization and are tested before and after the experimental treatment. For example, suppose we wanted to study the effect of some new therapy for treating hyperactive children. If this were a randomized experiment, we would use an unbiased procedure to assign hyperactive children to a treated group or an untreated group. But suppose the circumstances dictate that we *must* use two intact groups: one group of children at School A and one at School B. We can flip a coin to decide which school will be assigned to the experimental group, but unfortunately we cannot use randomization to assign the children *within* each school to the two groups.

The children in the two schools are measured at the beginning and the end of the study according to this diagram:

School 1	NR	O	X	O
School 2	NR	O		O

where X = treatment or intervention, O = observation or measurement, and NR = nonrandomized allocation of subjects to treatment conditions. Our study resembles a randomized experiment in most respects, but because the groups are not equivalent, the design does not control for certain threats to internal validity (e.g., the history of the groups may be different).

How might we increase the likelihood that the two groups will be similar to one another? Previously we alluded to one commonly used procedure, which is to try to match the groups as closely as possible on relevant demographic (and perhaps some other) variables, such as age, sex, and socioeconomic status. However, matching implies the biased dropping of subjects if the groups differ on the variables, so that a certain number of subjects will not be included in the data analysis. The problem, discussed in a later chapter, is that tests of statistical significance (e.g., t, F, and chi-square) are very much affected by the size of the samples to be compared. If the sample size is too small, our statistical test may not have enough "power" to detect a real difference.

In some circumstances, the problem is not that we must work with intact groups, but that there is an objection to depriving some subjects of the benefits of the experimental treatment by assigning them to a zero control group (see also Box 8.2) or perhaps an objection to the risk of exposing some subjects to a treatment that is ineffective or even counterproductive. In fact, some medical researchers who have articulated these concerns have deliberately avoided using true randomized comparisons and instead have used what they call **historical control groups.** This term means that subjects in the control condition(s) are recently examined patients who have the same disorder as those in the experimental condition but who are not chosen to participate in the study. Unfortunately the use of historical controls may result in poorly controlled comparisons, because the experimental and historical control groups may differ in important ways other than whether they have received the medical treatment or not.

This problem was identified by a team of medical researchers (Sacks, Chalmers, & Smith, 1982) based on a meta-analysis of research conducted in several clinical areas (e.g., coronary artery surgery, the treatment of cirrhosis, the use of anticoagulants in

Box 8.2	**Wait-List Controls**

When the concern is that control subjects will be deprived of the benefits of the experimental treatment, rather than settle for a nonequivalent-groups design we might propose a randomized design with a **wait-list control group** (also described in Chapter 4). Those assigned to the experimental condition (Group 1) are given the experimental treatment during the regular period of the experiment, and those assigned to the control condition (Group 2) are given the experimental treatment sometime after the period of the experiment. Depending on the delay before the second group is given the experimental treatment, by measuring the first group after the treatment and again after the second group receives the treatment, we may get valuable information about the long-term effect of the treatment in the first group. This design can be diagrammed as follows:

Group 1	R	O	X	O	O
Group 2	R	O		O	X	O

where R = the randomized allocation of subjects to treatment conditions, and O and X are defined as before.

heart attack cases, and the treatment of certain forms of cancer). In each area, these researchers found that, whether the controls were historical or randomized, the treated patients (i.e., those in the experimental group) responded similarly to the same therapy but the historical controls generally did worse than the randomized controls. The implication is that nonrandomized designs using historical controls may exaggerate the benefits of medical procedures and underestimate their potentially harmful effects. The best protection against this problem, Sacks et al. argued, is to allocate the subjects to experimental and control conditions by some random procedure (i.e., to conduct a true randomized experiment).

Inferring Causation and Moderation

We have noted that inferential risk must be considered in *any* investigation, and we will return to this issue in a later chapter when we discuss statistical significance testing in detail. In quasi-experimental research, we see that the primary risk results from the nonrandom assignment of the sampling units to the treatment conditions. In the previous chapter, we alluded to this problem when we talked about "history" and "selection" as threats to internal validity. In quasi-experimental research, investigators frequently attempt to emulate the causal reasoning of the true experimental approach in order to reach causal inferences that are as sound as possible (i.e., working within the intrinsic limitations of the research; see Cook & Campbell, 1979).

For example, imagine that we want an epidemiological question answered, but that we have only circumstantial evidence. We may still be able to emulate the causal reasoning of the experimental approach by using Mill's methods (see again pages 164–165) to reach highly justified conclusions about the necessary and sufficient conditions of Y. The results in Table 8.1 help to illustrate this approach (Kahane, 1989). They represent a situation in which 12 people ate at the same fast-food restaurant, and we are trying to track down the cause *(X)* of food poisoning *(Y)* in 5 of them (Mimi, Nancy, Michele, John, and Sheila). Although 1 of the 5 (Michele) had a milkshake, we cannot think of any way that a milkshake would have caused food poisoning. Furthermore, Gail and Greg had a milkshake, and they did not get sick. Of the 5 who got sick, 3 (Nancy, Michele, and John) ate a salad, and it is remotely possible that it contained spoiled dressing that no other salads had. Of the 5 who got sick, 4 ate some particularly greasy french fries, which could give anyone an upset stomach, but 2 others (Connie and Richard) also ate fries and did not get sick. The most striking finding in this table is that all 5 who got sick ate a rare hamburger (which no one else ordered), and it is easy to imagine how it might have contained bacteria that were not destroyed in the cooking process.

What should we conclude? If we can safely assume that all 12 people in Table 8.1 would have been found healthy in a pretest, maybe we have a "kind" of nonequivalent-groups design (i.e., poisoned group versus nonpoisoned group). On the surface, the one common factor is the rare hamburger. But the owner tells us that one of the food handlers was feeling ill the day these people were served. He worked for a while but then asked to be excused after he complained of feeling dizzy and nauseous. Is it

Table 8.1	Illustration of Agreement and Difference Methods				
Persons	Ate burger	Ate tuna sandwich	Ate fries	Ate salad	Drank shake	Got food poisoning
Mimi	Yes	No	Yes	No	No	Yes
Gail	No	No	No	Yes	Yes	No
Connie	No	No	Yes	No	No	No
Jerry	No	Yes	No	Yes	No	No
Greg	No	Yes	No	No	Yes	No
Dwight	No	No	No	Yes	No	No
Nancy	Yes	No	Yes	Yes	No	Yes
Richard	No	Yes	Yes	Yes	No	No
Kerry	No	No	No	Yes	No	No
Michele	Yes	No	Yes	Yes	Yes	Yes
John	Yes	No	Yes	Yes	No	Yes
Sheila	Yes	No	No	No	No	Yes

Source: Based on a similar example in *Logic and Philosophy: A Modern Introduction* (6th ed.) by H. Kahane, 1989, Wadsworth. Reprinted with permission of Howard Kahane and Wadsworth Publishing Co.

possible that this food handler was the culprit? Suppose he touched some but not all of the foods eaten that day; maybe he passed on his germs in this way. His possible handling of Mimi's and Sheila's burger, Nancy's salad dressing, and Michele's and John's fries would be another factor common to all the cases. It is possible, in other words, that these particular foods were *sufficient* to bring about poisoning *(Y),* but that this food handler's handling of them *(X?)* was the *necessary* condition.

We think we can safely rule out the food handler because he must have touched many more items than those implicated above. If he were the cause *(X),* then others who ate at the restaurant should have become ill *(Y).* However, this table shows that seven people did not get food poisoning (not-*Y*) even though they ate some of the same things the others ate *(X)*—except for the rare hamburger (the true *X?*). Only the burger was absent in every case in which there was no food poisoning. On the basis of this circumstantial evidence, we now believe that the burger was the necessary and sufficient condition *(X)* that brought about food poisoning *(Y).* This kind of causal reasoning on the basis of circumstantial evidence (in which we examine factors that seem to converge on, or to eliminate, particular causal hypotheses) is typical of that used in many quasi-experimental studies.

Another strategy of inference in relational research (including meta-analytic studies) is based on the search for **moderator variables,** which are factors associated with variations in the magnitude of a given relationship. In this case, the idea is to show that some moderator variable is associated with changes (i.e., alterations) in the magnitude of the given relationship. A host of problems have been investigated in this way (see, e.g., Box 8.3), and although the results cannot be interpreted causally in most cases (H. M. Cooper, 1984, 1989), causal inferences can often be made about the results of relationships that were based on the random allocation of subjects to treatments. Again, the causal reasoning emulates that described above (Rosenthal, 1991).

Box 8.3	**Moderation of Test-Retest Reliability**

An early methodological application was by Robert L. Thorndike (1933), who was interested in how the magnitude of the test-retest correlation was moderated (i.e., altered) by the time interval between the first and second testing. As we would expect, the greater the interval, the lower the correlation tends to be between the same subjects' scores on the pretest and the posttest.

An application by Alice H. Eagly (1978) used the methodology of meta-analysis (see Appendix C). Textbooks had long asserted that women were more conforming and more easily influenced than men. The traditional theoretical interpretation was that this gender difference was due to socialization processes that had taught men to be independent thinkers, a cultural value that was seldom suggested as suitable for women. Reasoning that the historical period in which the results were collected might be a moderator of the correlation between sex and influenceability, Eagly meta-analyzed all the relevant studies. She found that there was a pronounced difference in the correlation between sex and influenceability in studies published before 1970 and in those published during the period of the women's movement in the 1970s. In contrast to the older studies, which found greater influenceability among females than among males, the newer studies found few sex differences in influenceability.

Interrupted Time-Series Designs

A second broad category of quasi-experimental designs is the **interrupted time-series design,** in which the effects of a "treatment" are inferred from a comparison of the outcome measures obtained at different time intervals before and after the treatment (or intervention) is introduced. This data structure is called a *time series* because there is a single data point for each point in time, and it is called an *interrupted time series* because, presumably, there is a clear dividing line at the beginning of the **intervention** (i.e., a line analogous to the start of the experimental treatment). Although some users of this design make and analyze simple tables and charts, others use quite sophisticated statistical procedures that go beyond the scope of this text (see, e.g., Cryer, 1986; Judd & Kenny, 1981).

An early example is the work of social psychologists Leonard Berkowitz and Jacqueline Macaulay (1971), who were interested in whether highly publicized violent crimes are "infectious" (i.e., capable of causing a "contagion of violence" in the population). In the 19th century, a French sociologist (Gabriel de Tarde) argued that a number of violent crimes, having been sensationalized in news reports, had prompted similar crimes. For example, news of the murders by Jack the Ripper in London in 1888 had had this effect, Tarde argued, for within less than a year as many as eight identical crimes had been committed. To test Tarde's ideas, Berkowitz undertook a set of time-series analyses of FBI monthly counts of specific violent crimes in each of 40 cities for the seven years 1960–1966.

In one analysis, Berkowitz and Macaulay wanted to see whether Tarde's hypothesis held up for two sensational crimes during the 1960s in the United States: the assassination of President John F. Kennedy in Dallas on November 22, 1963, and the murder of eight nurses by Richard Speck in Chicago in July 1966. Two pieces of circumstantial evidence that seemed to support the contagion hypothesis were two subsequent murders. A month after the Speck murders, Charles J. Whitman, an engineering student and former marine, killed his wife and mother in their homes and then went on a shooting spree from the top of a tower at the University of Texas, killing 14 and wounding 30 before he was shot to death by a police officer. About three months later, Robert Smith, an 18-year-old high school senior, walked into a Mesa, Arizona, beauty school and killed four women and a child. Afterward, Smith told the police that he had got his idea after reading the news stories of the Speck and Whitman crimes.

In using this approach, Berkowitz and Macaulay had to satisfy four basic requirements of any time-series analysis. First, they had to define the period of observation broadly enough to allow the outcome variable to be examined before, during, and following the intervention (i.e., the heavily publicized violent crime). Second, the same units had to be used throughout the analysis in order to ensure that the observations and time points would be equally spaced. Berkowitz and Macaulay could not, for example, use monthly observations for one year and then quarterly observations for another year because these observations would not be exactly comparable. Third, the time points had to be sensitive to the particular effects of interest (e.g., increases in aggravated assaults). Fourth, the measurements could not fluctuate very much as a result of "instrumentation" changes (i.e., the observations had to be reliable). Berkowitz and Macaulay reasoned that (1) the FBI data would provide an adequate number of data points (i.e., 84 months); (2) the same units could be used throughout (i.e., monthly observations); (3) the crime data would be sensitive to the particular effects that interested them; and (4) the FBI crime data would also satisfy the reliability requirement.

Berkowitz and Macaulay sought to obtain a representative sample of cities by selecting four ranging in size from 260,000 to 1.4 million in each of 10 primary zip-code areas. They then ran various analyses of data from these 40 cities for different categories of crimes (e.g., aggravated assaults, robberies, and homicides). Figure 8.1 shows one of a number of such graphs that were constructed to show any increases or decreases in criminal violence during the observed period in the areas covered by the FBI data. This graph shows a significant increase in aggravated assaults during this 84-month period, with sharp increments after the John F. Kennedy assassination in particular, as well as after the Speck murders.

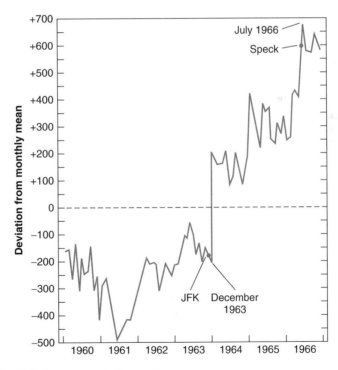

Figure 8.1   **Data for aggravated assaults.**
Source: Reproduced from L. Berkowitz and J. Macaulay, "The Contagion of Criminal Violence," *Sociometry,* 1971, *34,* p. 251. Used by permission of Leonard Berkowitz and the American Sociological Association.

A more recent application of the time-series approach is the work of David P. Phillips, a sociologist at the University of California, San Diego, who has used this method in a number of fascinating field and archival investigations (see also Box 8.4). In one set of studies, Phillips and others investigated the clustering of imitative suicides after televised news stories and televised movies about suicide (e.g., Phillips, Lesyna, & Paight, 1992, for a review). The results showed interesting variations, which were not easy to explain. For example, a New York City study found that suicides by teenagers increased after three televised fictional films about suicide (Gould & Shaffer, 1986), but then a replication by Phillips and Paight (1987) in California and Pennsylvania found no evidence of an increase in teenage suicides after the televised broadcast of the same three films. In another study, however, Phillips and Carstensen (1986) found evidence of what seemed to be an imitative effect of news stories about suicides.

Box 8.4 **When Death Takes a Holiday**

Phillips also studied how mortality rises and dips during certain symbolically meaningful periods in people's lives. In one study, Phillips and King (1988) found that Jewish mortality fell sharply below the expected level just before Passover and rose by an equal amount above the expected level immediately afterward. To replicate this study, Phillips and Smith (1990) next gathered data about Chinese mortality during the Harvest Moon festival and found that mortality among Chinese dipped by 35% in the week before the Festival and peaked by the same amount in the week after. As a result of these time-series studies, Phillips and Smith raised the hypothesis that some people may actually be able to prolong their lives until the arrival of some important, personally meaningful event.

In Vienna, Austria, there was a sharp increase in the number of subway suicides in 1984. Persuaded by the evidence generated by Phillips and others, the Austrian Association for Suicide Prevention, Crisis Intervention and Conflict Resolution argued that there might be a connection between this increase and a sudden heavy emphasis of newspaper stories on subway suicides. The organization drew up media guidelines and persuaded two large-circulation Viennese newspapers to curtail the publicity they gave to subway suicides. This change in policy occurred in June 1987, and Figure 8.2 contains time-series data that show the dramatic reduction in subway suicides and suicide attempts after this policy was enacted (Sonneck, Etzersdorfer, & Nagel-Kuess, 1994). Using the same symbols used earlier, we can diagram this interrupted time-series evaluation as:

$$O\ O\ O\ O\ O\ O\ O\ O\ O\ X\ O\ O\ O\ O\ O$$

where the 0s denote observations of the number (or frequency of occurrence) of subway suicides and suicide attempts per calendar year and the X is the intervention of the media curtailment agreed to by the leading newspapers.

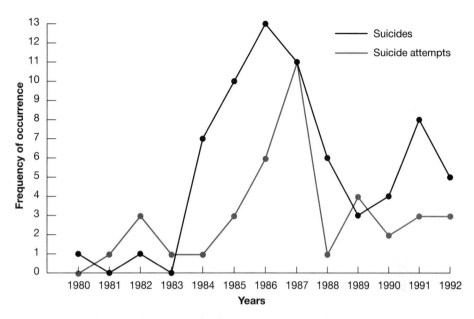

Figure 8.2   **Subway suicides and suicide attempts from 1980 to 1992 in Vienna, Austria.**
Source: Based on data in G. Sonneck, E. Etzersdorfer, and S. Nagel-Kuess, "Imitative Suicide on the Viennese Subway," *Social Science and Medicine,* 1994, *38,* p. 454. Copyright © 1994. Reprinted with permission of Elsevier Science.

Single-Case Experimental Designs

What is frequently seen as a subclass of interrupted time-series designs goes by several different names: **single-case experimental designs, small-*N* experimental designs, and *N*-of-1 experimental designs.** These designs, which are a mainstay of behavior modification research, have the features of an "interrupted time-series case study" but with an additional effort to incorporate the manipulative feature and, occasionally, the between-subjects control feature of true experimental designs. Generally speaking, *N*-of-1 designs have the following characteristics: (1) only one sampling unit is studied, or else only a few units are studied; (2) repeated measures are taken of the unit (i.e., a within-subjects design, as defined in the previous chapter); and (3) random assignment procedures are rarely used. It is, of course, impossible to assign a single subject at random to the various treatment procedures; instead, the occasions (e.g., at intervals of days, weeks, or months) may be assigned at random to the various treatment procedures, and the results are then compared.

Although the sampling unit in *N*-of-1 designs is frequently a single subject (human or animal), it may also be a group, such as an assembly line, a class of students, one shift in a manufacturing plant, or even a set of hungry pigeons (see Box 8.5). In one case, for example, the unit was the offensive backfield on a football team of 9- 10-year-olds, the purpose of the study being to test a schedule of feedback to improve their execution of plays (Komaki & Barnett, 1977). In another case, the unit was a community, and the objective was to encourage drivers to use child safety seats by rewarding them with coupons they could exchange for a seat and training in its use (Lavelle, Hovell, West, & Wahlgren, 1992).

Box 8.5   Superstition in the Pigeon and the Financial Market

In a fascinating single-case study by B. F. Skinner (1948a), the unit was eight hungry pigeons. The birds were housed in cages in which there was a food hopper (containing grain) that swung into and away from the cage at regular intervals. A timing mechanism automatically moved the hopper into the cage so that all the pigeon had to do was reach into the hopper and eat. But six of the birds developed "superstitious" movements, in that whatever they had been doing in the moment when they were first rewarded with food became imprinted. One pigeon made counterclockwise motions about the cage before taking the grain; another performed a tossing motion of the head; and others persisted in making pendulum-type motions of the head and body or brushing movements toward the floor. Some behavioral economists theorize that this behavior is similar to what goes on in financial markets, where people make causal connections between two occurrences when, in fact, there is no causal link (Fuerbringer, 1997).

Single-case experimental designs are widely used in educational, clinical, and counseling settings to evaluate the effects of operant conditioning interventions (Hersen & Barlow, 1976; Kazdin, 1992; Kazdin & Tuma, 1982). In operant conditioning (described in Chapter 2), one way to strengthen behavior is to use positive reinforcement (i.e., to reward the behavior), and one way to weaken behavior is to use extinction (i.e., no longer reinforcing the response). Such designs use as a **behavioral baseline** observations of the subject's behavior before the experimental treatment (or intervention) has been applied. That is, the assessment of behavior prior to the treatment or intervention serves as a kind of "pretest" with which information about the level of behavior after the treatment can be compared. In this way, the unit serves as its own control in a simple within-subjects design.

To illustrate, R. Vance Hall, Diane Lund, and Dolores Jackson (1968) used a single-case design to track the effects of interventions used in the classroom to shape the behavior of a child named Robbie. The results of this study are shown in Figure 8.3. During the baseline period (a class spelling period), the psychologists recorded Robbie's study behavior, which varied from a low of about 15% of the time to a high of slightly over 40%, and an average of about 25%. The rest of the time, they observed, Robbie's behavior was disruptive: He snapped rubber bands, played with toys in his pocket, slowly drank his milk and played with the milk carton, and laughed with those around him. Almost 55% of his teacher's attention was absorbed by this disruptive behavior.

The psychologists believed that the teacher's attention was actually maintaining Robbie's disruptive behavior. To modify his behavior, they decided to use a twofold intervention: (1) ignoring the nonstudy and disruptive behavior (extinction) and

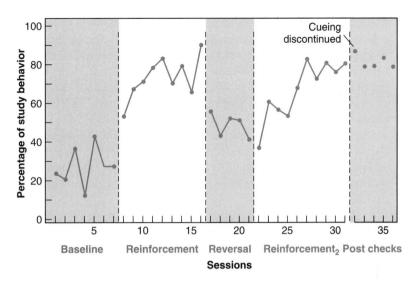

Figure 8.3 **Robbie's study behavior record.**
Source: Reproduced from R. V. Hall, D. Lund, and D. Jackson, "Effects of Teacher Attention on Study Behavior," *Journal of Applied Behavior Analysis,* 1968, *1,* 1–12. Used by courtesy of R. Vance Hall and the *Journal of Applied Behavior Analysis.*

(2) attending to the study behavior (positive reinforcement). Whenever Robbie engaged in 1 minute of continuous study, the observer would quietly signal the teacher and she would come over and compliment him, saying such things as "Good work, Robbie." The second part of Figure 8.3 shows Robbie's increased study behavior during the nine sessions of this stage. Then, to verify the effect of the teacher's attention, the consequences were reversed. The teacher ignored Robbie, remaining with the group. His study behavior decreased to about 50% over these five sessions. When reinforcement was restored, Robbie's study behavior increased to and leveled off at about 75%. A checkup over the following weeks, when the teacher continued to praise his study behavior, showed that Robbie continued to study. Robbie's spelling performance also improved, with a jump from fewer than 5 words correct out of 10 to 9 correct out of 10 (although this improvement might also be attributed to certain uncontrolled sources of internal invalidity)

Alternative Single-Case Designs

Instead of using Xs and Os, a different notation system is used to represent the different designs that are used in *N*-of-1 experiments. The basic model is called an **A-B-A design,** which evolved out of an even simpler prototype, the **A-B design** (which is the simplest of all single-case designs). In the A phase, no treatment (or intervention) is in effect, and in the B phase, a treatment (or intervention) is operating. The first A in the A-B-A and A-B designs is, therefore, the baseline period. Once the researcher observes steady, continuous behavior in the baseline phase, then the treatment (B) is introduced. In other words, the researcher is observing and recording the behavior repeatedly within all phases of the design: the A phase *and* the B phase. In an A-B design, the dependent variable is measured repeatedly throughout the baseline and intervention phases of the study. In the A-B-A design, the treatment is withdrawn at the end of the B phase and the behavior is measured; that is, there are repeated measures before the treatment, during the treatment, and then with the treatment withdrawn.

A number of other single-case designs are used in clinical intervention assessment. In the **A-B-BC-B design,** for example, B and C are two different therapeutic interventions The symbols tell us that the individual's behavior is measured or observed (1) before the introduction of either intervention; (2) during Intervention B; (3) during the combination of Intervention B and Intervention C; and (4) during B alone. The purpose of this design is to evaluate the effect of B both in combination with C and apart from C.

Still another basic variant is the **A-B-A-B design.** Here the strategy again ends in a treatment phase of B, but this model provides two occasions (B to A and then A to B) for demonstrating the positive effects of the intervention (Hersen & Barlow, 1976). Returning to the illustrative study in Figure 8.3, we can see that it is a simple variant on this design, that is, an **A-B-A-B-A design.** Robbie's behavior was observed (1) before the reinforcement intervention; (2) during the intervention; (3) after removal of the invention; (4) during its restoration; and (5) after the desired behavior had been shaped by the prior intervention. The advantage of this design is that it allows us to compare Robbie's behavior during different phases, although, as noted, it does not control for threats to internal validity (such as the instrumentation problem). Although the interpretation of single-case results typically depends on visual inspection, there are also standard statistical techniques for evaluating the effects (see, e.g., Kazdin, 1976; Kratochwill & Levin, 1992).

We mentioned that researchers occasionally use other variants of behavior modification designs that are hard to distinguish from true experimental designs. An example is a study done by researchers at the University of Notre Dame (Anderson, Crowell, Hantula, & Siroky, 1988), in which the unit consisted of workers in a student-managed bar. The bar was a haunt of many students and faculty members, but the state board of health threatened to close it after citing health problems (e.g., a pervasive accumulation of grease, and garbage areas strewn with debris). The researchers agreed to try to modify the behavior of the students who worked at the bar, and they used a variant of the A-B-C design, in which the B phase consisted of exposing the workers to a task clarification treatment, and the C phase was a feedback period.

What makes this design resemble a true experiment is that the researchers allocated the workers to three groups at random in an effort to control for the delay of feedback. The A phase was the baseline period, in which the workers' usual behavior was recorded. During the B phase, all the workers were instructed in how to work less messily, and a set of criteria was posted for all to see (e.g., put refrigerated items in the refrigerator, pick up garbage in the men's bathroom, clean bar utensils, and wipe off all games). A week later, each worker in Group 1 was given feedback, which continued for two more weeks. The feedback treatment in Group 2 did not begin until one week after it had been initiated in Group 1, and the feedback in Group 3 was initiated a week after this. Thus it was possible for the researchers to compare the effects of immediate and delayed feedback in this combination of a between-groups (i.e., delay of feedback) and within-groups (i.e., A-B-C) design. The result of the behavior modification effort was that sanitary conditions in the bar improved markedly, so much, in fact, that it was not closed—to the gratification of the students and the researchers alike.

Correlational Designs

The largest general class of quasi-experimental designs is called **correlational,** which in this case is actually a catchall term for odds and ends of quasi-experimental studies. Some of these studies have characteristics of the other two categories but do not fall neatly into either one of them. In fact, the term *correlational* is not really a helpful description, because we know that correlations are also part of what one looks for in true experiments (i.e., the covariation of X and Y). We will describe some hybrid designs and studies that are generally lumped together in this category, beginning with a correlational design that was used by Robert W. Weisberg (1994), a cognitive psychologist who was interested in an old theory asserting that madness fosters creativity.

One way we might test this theory in a quasi-experimental correlational fashion would be to compile lists of all the musical compositions by a number of great and ordinary composers; we would then have expert critics rate the quality of each composition. We should find a relationship between the fame of the composer and the number of quality works by that composer. We would next do a search of biographical and autobiographical archives (e.g., books and letters) in order to find further data about any episodes of "madness" (which we conceptualize as a moderator variable) affecting the creativity of these composers. Specifically, we hypothesize that the great composers were most creative when they were quite mad. We can also hypothesize that, when they were not mad, the quality and quantity of their work should be no different than that of ordinary composers.

Weisberg did not conduct this particular study. Instead, he did a correlational case study of one noted composer. He chose for his case the musical compositions of the German composer Robert Schumann (1810–1856), who suffered from manic-depression (called *bipolar disorder*) and eventually committed suicide. Weisberg compiled an exhaustive list of Schumann's musical compositions, noted those regarded by experts as works of genius, and also documented the specific years in which Schumann suffered from depression or hypomania (i.e., a mild form of mania, characterized by elation and quickness of thought). Weisberg found no support for the general prediction that madness fostered brilliance in Schumann's work; that is, the quality of his work seemed unaffected. However, as Table 8.2 shows, the specific state of Schumann's mental health seemed to be linked with the *quantity* of musical compositions that he produced. That is, he had a tendency to produce more compositions when he was in a hypomanic than when he was in a depressive state. (We will see these data again in a later chapter.)

Weisberg's study is clearly correlational, but it also has features of an interrupted time-series design, where Schumann's career was interrupted periodically by bouts of depression and hypomania. In the designs we turn to next, each can be more clearly identified as a particular subtype of correlational design: the cross-lagged panel design and the longitudinal design using cohorts.

Table 8.2	Robert Schumann's Bouts of Depression and Hypomania and His Compositional Productivity		
Periods of Depression		Periods of Hypomania	
Year	Number of compositions	Year	Number of compositions
1830	1	1829	1
1831	1	1832	4
1839	4	1840	25
1842	3	1843	2
1844	0	1849	28
1847	5	1851	16
1848	5		

Source: Reproduced from R. W. Weisberg, "Genius and Madness? A Quasi-Experimental Test of the Hypothesis That Manic-Depression Increases Creativity," *Psychological Science,* 1994, *5,* 361–367.

Cross-Lagged Panel Designs

A **cross-lagged panel design** is called *cross-lagged* because, while it is basically another variant of a correlational design, some data points are treated as temporally "lagged" (or delayed) values of the outcome variable. It is called a *panel design* because, in social survey terms, a **panel study** is another name for a **longitudinal study** (i.e., a study that examines the change in a person or a group of people over an extended period of time), and the roots of this design are in longitudinal investigations in sociological survey research (see also Box 8.6).

Box 8.6	**Historical Note**

When the cross-lagged panel design was invented in the 1940s, longitudinal measurements of the same two variables, A and B, were assumed to provide information about any causal relationships among the variables (Lazarsfeld, 1978). In other words, even though nonexperimental, the cross-lagged panel design was originally intended to be a method for choosing among competing causal hypotheses (cf. Campbell & Stanley, 1963; Lazarsfeld, 1978; Pelz & Andrew, 1964; Rozelle & Campbell, 1969). While seldom used today, the cross-lagged design is still a convenient way of fostering an understanding of the problems associated with causal inferences based on relational data.

You will recall that the correlation coefficient is a measure of the mutual relationship between two variables or measurements; we gave as an example the Pearson *r*. It will be recalled that *r*s can range from -1.0 (a perfect negative relationship) through

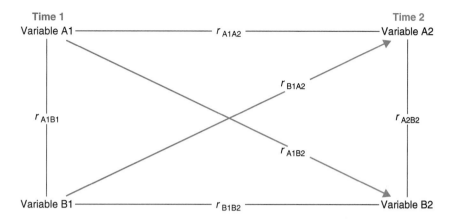

Figure 8.4   Design for cross-lagged and other correlations between Variables A and B.
Source: Reproduced from R. Rosenthal and R. L. Rosnow, *Essentials of Behavioral Research: Methods and Data Analysis,* 2nd ed., McGraw-Hill, 1991, p. 99. Reprinted with permission of McGraw-Hill, Inc.

0 (no relationship) to $+1.0$ (a perfect positive relationship). As illustrated in Figure 8.4, A and B represent two variables, each of which has been measured individually at two successive time periods. Three sets of paired correlations are also represented: test-retest, synchronous, and cross-lagged correlations.

First, the two **test-retest correlations** (r_{A1A2} and r_{B1B2})—which indicate the reliability of A and B over time—refer to the relationship, respectively, between A1 and A2 and between B1 and B2. Second, the two **synchronous correlations** (r_{A1B1} and r_{A2B2})—which, when compared, indicate the reliability of the association between A and B over time—refer to the relationship, respectively, between A1 and B1 and between A2 and B2. Third, the two **cross-lagged correlations** (r_{A1B2} and r_{B1A2})—which show the relationships between two sets of data points, where one is treated as a lagged value of the outcome variable—in this case refer to the association, respectively, between A1 and B2 and between B1 and A2.

The causal question concerns whether A is a more likely cause of B than B is of A, or whether A causes B to a greater extent than B causes A. The basic logic used to arrive at the answer is that, given equally reliable test-retest correlations and synchronous correlations equal in magnitude, comparing the cross-lagged correlations should enable us to conclude which is the more likely causal direction, or which variable shows the preponderance of causal influence. Presumably, we would conclude that A is a more likely (or more important) cause of B than B is of A if r_{A1B2} is appreciably higher than r_{B1A2}. On the other hand, we would conclude that B is a more likely (or more important) cause of A than A is of B if r_{B1A2} is appreciably higher than r_{A1B2}. Let us use a real-life example to show how this design is used, and also to reveal the hidden problem of **confounded hypotheses** (i.e., competing confounded pairs of hypotheses).

Figure 8.5 is taken from a study by Louise H. Kidder, Robert L. Kidder, and Paul Snyderman (1976). These investigators used archival data in the *FBI Uniform Crime Reports* for 1968–1969; the variables noted are the number of police (A) and the number of burglaries (B) in 724 U.S. cities during each year. Looking first at the

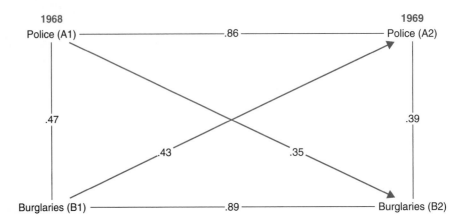

Figure 8.5 **Correlation of number of police and number of burglaries per capita measured in 1968 and 1969 in 724 cities.**
Source: Adapted from Kidder, Kidder, and Snyderman, 1976, by permission of L. H. Kidder.

test-retest correlations (.86 and .89), we see that both the number of police and the number of burglaries were reliable during this two-year period. That is, cities with a lot of police in 1968 had a lot of police in 1969, and also cities with a lot of burglaries in 1968 continued to have a lot of burglaries in 1969. The synchronous correlations of .47 and .39 between the number of police and the number of burglaries for 1968 and 1969, respectively, were substantial in magnitude.

At first glance, our intuition says that burglaries may cause an increase in the number of police. The problem of confounded hypotheses is that it might just as well be hypothesized that police increase burglaries, because the more police there are available, the more opportunities there are to keep thorough records of all the burglaries reported. That is, when there are not many police, some reported burglaries may go unrecorded. The cross-lagged correlations do not allow us to rule out either competing hypothesis and, in fact, provide some support for both (.43 and .35). If you think carefully, you are sure to come up with other rival hypotheses. There are statistical ways of trying to rule out rival causal hypotheses in cross-lagged designs, but they are not without problems (Kenny, 1979; Rozelle & Campbell, 1969). As a consequence, such designs—which were used in the past with some frequency—are now treated with "skeptical advocacy" (Cook & Campbell, 1979, p. 309).

Longitudinal Designs Using Cohorts

Suppose we wanted to study the *life course* of some variable of interest. One possibility is to estimate maturational effects by using a **cross-sectional design,** that is, a design that takes a slice of time and, in this case, examines several age groups during one period. An example would be a cross-sectional survey performed in 1999 to study the maturational effects of the variable of interest in cohorts (see also Box 8.7) born in 1959, 1969, 1979, and 1989. The purpose of the survey is to develop a growth curve of the effects of interest in people who are 10, 20, 30, and 40 years old. This approach would be a lot easier than, for example, examining people's responses or behavior over an extended period of time (i.e., a longitudinal study).

Box 8.7   Cohorts and Generation Gaps

In ancient times, a **cohort** referred to a company of soldiers in the Roman Legion. In behavioral and social science, the term means any group sharing a given trait, usually age. Thus a group of people born around the same time and having had similar life experiences constitutes a cohort or generation. As shown in Table 8.3, a generation is usually defined as 20 years, so a "generation gap" implies a 20-year differential between cohorts.

The problem with our cross-sectional design is that those who are 40 in 1999 may have had different life experiences at age 10 (in 1969), from those who are 10 years old in 1999. That is, it is likely that children who are born and grow up in one period have life events quite different from those of children who are born and grow up in another period. Some of these experiences (e.g., schooling, repeated exposure to TV, growing up with the Internet) may, in turn, systematically affect the normal development of the two groups. The problem in research is that a possible confounding of cohort and maturation would be hidden in a design that failed to look at several cohorts longitudinally. Insofar as such experiences are associated with the variable of interest, we might be led to spurious conclusions about maturational effects if we relied solely on a cross-sectional design to find them.

Table 8.3 illustrates how the relationship between maturation (age) and another variable may be misinterpreted because of a reliance on the results of cross-sectional studies instead of on the results of longitudinal studies of cohorts. This table shows the results of a study done in the Netherlands by Jacques A. Hagenaars and Niki P. Cobben (1978), in which data were compiled on the percentages of women with no religious affiliation, by age and time period. The results are shown for seven different cohorts (or generations) of women in the Netherlands. The values in the vertical rectangle beneath Period 4 provide the basic data for a cross-sectional analysis, and the values in the parallelogram for Cohort 4 provide the basic data for a longitudinal analysis. Notice that the trends are opposite in these two sets of values and therefore lead to completely opposite conclusions.

A graph showing this difference appears in Figure 8.6; it allows us to compare the cross-sectional data for Period 4 (1969) with the longitudinal data for Cohort 4 in Table 8.3. The cross-sectional curve would mislead us to the conclusion that, with the passing of years and the approach of the end of life, religious observance increased (i.e., the percentage of nonaffiliation decreased) in these women. By contrast, the cohort curve tells us that the opposite is true: Religious observance actually decreased (i.e., the percentage of nonaffiliation increased) in these women as they became older.

Researchers who like to use longitudinal designs—including animal researchers (e.g., Fairbanks, 1993)—also attempt, whenever possible, to examine several cohorts cross-sectionally and longitudinally. In this way they learn about cohort changes as

Table 8.3	Percentages of Women in the Netherlands with No Religious Affiliation According to Age and Time Period			
	Period 1 (1909)	Period 2 (1929)	Period 3 (1949)	Period 4 (1969)
Age 20–30	Cohort 4 4.8%	Cohort 5 13.9%	Cohort 6 17.4%	Cohort 7 23.9%
Age 40–50	Cohort 3 3.1%	Cohort 4 11.9%	Cohort 5 17.2%	Cohort 6 22.0%
Age 60–70	Cohort 2 1.9%	Cohort 3 6.7%	Cohort 4 11.9%	Cohort 5 19.4%
Age 80–	Cohort 1 1.2%	Cohort 2 3.8%	Cohort 3 6.6%	Cohort 4 12.2%

Note: An example of a cross-sectional design is shown by the vertical analysis (Period 4), and an example of a longitudinal design is shown by the diagonal analysis (Cohort 4).

Source: Reproduced from "Age, Cohort and Period: A General Model for the Analysis of Social Change" by J. A. Hagenaars and N. P. Cobben, 1978, *Netherlands Journal of Sociology, 14,* pp. 58–91. Used by permission of J. A. Hagenaars and Elsevier Science Publishers.

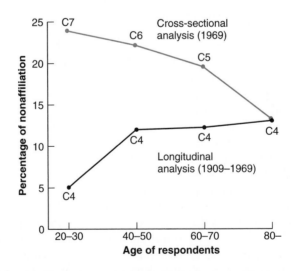

Figure 8.6 **Percentages of nonaffiliation with church of women in the Netherlands, as shown by a cross-sectional design in 1969 and a longitudinal design from 1909 to 1969.** Cohorts are symbolized as C7 (Cohort 7), C6 (Cohort 6), and so forth.

Source: Reproduced from J. A. Hagenaars and N. P. Cobben, "Age, Cohort and Period: A General Model for the Analysis of Social Change," *Netherlands Journal of Sociology,* 1978, *14,* pp. 58–91. Used by permission of J. A. Hagenaars and Elsevier Science Publishers.

well as age group changes as a function of period. Other informative uses of longitudinal designs are possible, although each is limited in some predictable ways (for discussion, see Rosenthal & Rosnow, 1991, pp. 105–109). Thus, as stated earlier, it is a good idea to use several different strategies that allow convergence on the phenomenon of interest. Each strategy will be limited in some way, but the objective is to use procedures whose strengths and weaknesses will compensate for one another.

Summary of Ideas

1. Quasi-experiments resemble true experimental designs in some respects, but do not use a randomization procedure.
2. Three general classes of quasi-experimental designs are (a) nonequivalent-groups designs; (b) interrupted time-series designs; and (c) correlational designs.
3. In nonequivalent-groups designs, matching may be used to create comparability of the subjects found in the treatment conditions.
4. The use of historical controls in quasi-experimental studies has generally overestimated the benefits, and underestimated the dangers, of certain medical treatments.
5. Recommending the use of wait-list controls can sometimes overcome objections to randomized experiments with zero controls.
6. Inferring causation in quasi-experimental research often emulates the causal reasoning used in true experiments (e.g., the epidemiological study of a case of food poisoning).
7. Moderator variables are factors that alter the magnitude of a given relationship (e.g., Eagly's meta-analytic study of how the period of history moderated the relationship between gender and influenceability, and Thorndike's study of how test-retest reliability is moderated by the time interval involved).
8. Interrupted time-series designs compare the effects of an intervention with the situation before and after it occurred (e.g., Berkowitz and Macaulay's study of homicide rates, Phillips's work on the delay of death and on imitative suicide, and the latter's implications for the Vienna subway system).
9. Single-case experimental designs, a subclass of time-series designs, come in many different forms (e.g., A-B-BC-B and A-B-A-B); the unit of study may be an N of 1 (e.g., the study of Robbie) or a few subjects (e.g., Skinner's study of superstition in pigeons) or several groups of subjects with one of the treatments randomized (e.g., the behavior modification study of workers at a University of Notre Dame student bar).
10. So-called correlational quasi-experimental designs include any designs that do not easily fit into the other two categories (e.g., Weisberg's study of Robert Schumann's hypomania and musical productivity).
11. In the cross-lagged panel approach, some data points are treated as temporally delayed values, and the cross-lagged correlations are analyzed along with test-retest and synchronous correlations for the direction of causation (e.g., Kidder et al.'s study of the number of police and the number of burglaries).

12. In studies in which age is the independent variable, a cross-sectional analysis may lead to spurious conclusions (e.g., the study of women's religiosity in the Netherlands).

13. To achieve optimal understanding, it is best to use multiple methods, each of which has its own but different limitations.

Key Terms

A-B design   p. 191
A-B-A design   p. 191
A-B-A-B design   p. 192
A-B-A-B-A design (the Robbie study)   p. 192
A-B-BC-B design   p. 192
behavioral baseline   p. 190
cohort   p. 197
confounded hypotheses (in panel designs)   p. 195
correlational design   p. 193
cross-lagged correlations   p. 195
cross-lagged panel design   p. 194
cross-sectional design   p. 196
historical control group   p. 182

interrupted time-series design   p. 186
intervention   p. 186
longitudinal study   p. 194
moderator variable   p. 185
N-of-1 experimental design   p. 189
nonequivalent-groups design   p. 181
panel study   p. 194
quasi-experimental design   p. 180
single-case experimental design   p. 189
small-N experimental design   p. 189
synchronous correlations (in panel designs)   p. 195
test-retest correlations (in panel designs)   p. 195
wait-list control group   p. 183

Multiple-Choice Questions for Review (answers are found on page 349)

1. Which of the following is definitely not characteristic of quasi-experimental designs? (a) experimental group; (b) randomization; (c) control group; (d) repeated measurement

2. A researcher at North Carolina State University develops a new treatment program for alcoholism. He allows participants to choose whether they want to be in the experimental group or in the control group. This is an example of a (a) correlational design; (b) nonequivalent-groups design; (c) time-series design; (d) cohort design.

3. In the case directly above, which threat to internal validity is this study least able to rule out? (a) selection; (b) history; (c) maturation; (d) instrumentation

4. One type of research design involves measuring a single variable on many separate occasions, and assessing the impact of interventions on this variable. This type of design is called a (a) correlational design; (b) cohort design; (c) cross-sectional design; (d) time-series design.

5. A behavioral therapist at Northeastern University is working with autistic children. He decides first to observe their baseline levels of disruptive behavior and then to observe their behavior several times after administering his intervention. He then removes his intervention to determine whether their disruptive behavior will return to baseline levels. This type of design is called an (a) A-B design; (b) A-B-C design; (c) A-B-A design; (d) A-B-A-C design.

6. A study examining changes in individuals over an extended period of time is called a (a) longitudinal study; (b) quasi-longitudinal study; (c) nonequivalent-groups design; (d) time-series study.

7. A researcher at the University of Montana conducts a study on the relationship between watching TV (Variable A) and violent behavior (Variable B). She measures both variables at two points in time. She calculates the correlation between watching TV at Time 1 and watching TV at Time 2. This is an example of a(n) _____ correlation. (a) internal validity; (b) test-retest; (c) synchronous; (d) cross-lagged

8. The same researcher calculates the correlation between watching TV at Time 2 and violent behavior at Time 2. This is an example of a(n) _____ correlation. (a) internal consistency; (b) test-retest; (c) synchronous; (d) cross-lagged

9. In the study above, this researcher also calculates the correlation between watching TV at Time 2 and violent behavior at Time 1. This is an example of a(n) _____ correlation. (a) internal validity; (b) test-retest; (c) synchronous; (d) cross-lagged

10. The researcher finds that $r_{A1B2} = .30$ and $r_{B1A2} = .02$. These results suggest that (a) it is more likely that watching TV causes violent behavior; (b) it is more likely that violent behavior causes TV watching; (c) there is no causal relationship between watching TV and violent behavior; (d) watching TV and violent behavior have reciprocal causal effects.

Discussion Questions for Review (answers are found on page 350)

1. A University of Toledo student wants to assess the possible causal relationship between therapist approval, expressed in tone of voice, and degree of patient progress. Using a sample of 45 therapist-patient dyads, he measures these variables at the beginning and end of treatment. Based on the results shown below, what do you think he will conclude?

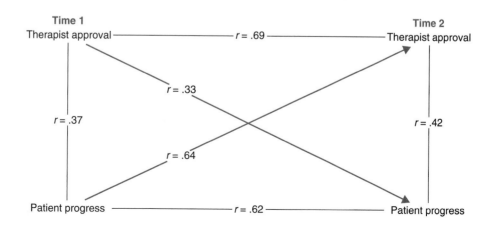

2. Using a cross-sectional design, an Oklahoma University student found a lower degree of androgyny in women aged 40–45 than in women aged 20–25. What confounding variable prevents him from concluding that androgyny decreases with age? Can you think of a better way to do the study?

3. A University of Nevada student wants to evaluate the effects of an educational intervention that is purported to motivate elementary-school children to do their homework. She had hoped to perform an experiment in which she would randomly assign large numbers of children in Reno either to the intervention treatment or to a large control group. However, she ran into complications and found that she would not be able to use randomization. Can you think of some other way that she might evaluate the effects of the intervention without the use of randomization? What are the limitations of this way?

4. A Catholic University student wants to do a time-series analysis of the effects of assassination attempts on U.S. presidents but cannot decide on the dependent variable. What dependent variable would you advise her to track, and how would you suggest she locate the kind of data she needs for such a study?

9 Survey Designs and Subject Recruitment

Selecting the Research Participants

In the two preceding chapters, we examined the logic of some designs used in relational and experimental research, and in this chapter, we turn our attention to the selection of subjects. In particular, we will focus our attention on prototypical designs used in survey research. This discussion will serve as a springboard for issues of importance in the recruitment of subjects for experimental research as well. Because most experimenters in behavioral science are interested in learning about human nature in general, they typically use **opportunity samples** (i.e., samples made up of the first units that are available). By contrast, most survey researchers are interested in generalizing their results to a specified larger pool of individuals. The name for the larger pool is the **population,** and the name for the fraction is the **sample.** For example, pollsters use survey designs to map out some specified population's opinions on a wide variety of issues, such as their fears of crime or their choice of political candidates (see also Box 9.1).

PREVIEW QUESTIONS

- What is the purpose of random selection, and how does it differ from random assignment?
- What is meant by the avoidance of bias and instability in survey designs?
- What is simple random sampling, and how is it done?
- What advantages does stratified random sampling have over simple random sampling?
- What is the role of stratification in area probability sampling?
- What are the characteristics of unbiased sampling plans in survey research?
- What is nonresponse bias, and how is it minimized?
- How is nonresponse bias related to volunteer subject bias in experimental research?
- How is the direction of volunteer bias estimated, and what recruitment methods minimize this bias?
- What is the final step before implementing any study?

Box 9.1   Applications of Survey Designs

Similar methods are used in epidemiological research, forensic research, economic research, and many other areas. For example, when health officials wanted to find out about trends in cases of tuberculosis contracted on the job, they used descriptive surveys of hospitals to make a count of reported employees with TB (Kilborn, 1994). As the federal courts became inundated with mass torts involving asbestos cases (averaging 1,140 per month in 1990, or one third of the federal criminal caseload), one solution was to sample asbestos cases from the total filed within a court's jurisdiction. The assessed damages in randomly sampled cases from each of five disease categories were then applied to each larger pool (Saks & Blanck, 1992).

Instead of questioning every member of the population (which is usually impossible), survey researchers focus on a segment presumed to be typical of the larger pool. How can these researchers be certain that the segment is **representative** (or typical) of the larger pool? For example, how can researchers be sure that fears of crime in the sample duplicate percentages in segments of the specified population or (as mentioned in Box 9.1) know for sure that reported TB cases in sampled hospitals are representative of trends in all similar hospitals? Although they cannot be 100% sure, they can make a leap of faith by relying on a blueprint (called the **sampling plan**) for selecting the sample by using a method of probability sampling. This term means that randomness enters into the selection process (also called **random selection**) at some stage, so that the laws of mathematical probability apply.

The term **probability** refers to the mathematical chance of an event's occurring, such as the likelihood of getting heads when you flip a coin once (1 chance in 2), or getting a 2 when you throw a die once (1 chance in 6), or knowing what a 20-to-1 shot at the racetrack is (see Box 9.2). The point is that, although survey studies can take many different forms, all use sampling plans in which some method of probability sampling determines the random selection of subjects. Such plans enable the researcher to assume reasonably—but with no guarantee of being correct—that the sample is representative of its population. What is the difference between random assignment (discussed in Chapter 7) and random selection? As explained earlier, random assignment is the unbiased allocation of the sampling units to treatment conditions; it controls the differences in the groups to be compared so that differences will not bias the results of the experiment. As explained in this chapter, random selection increases the sampling units' representativeness of the specified larger pool of units from which they are drawn.

We will begin by describing some basic concepts in survey sampling and will then turn to the logic and implementation of probability sampling plans. However, even in the most carefully conducted survey study, not everyone who is asked to participate will accept. If respondents are different from the nonrespondents, we cannot easily generalize

---

Box 9.2   ## What Are Racetrack Odds?

A "20-to-1 shot" means that, in the eyes of the odds setters, this particular long shot will win about once in every 21 races, given the conditions under which the horse is currently running. Why should a horse ever beat other horses that are faster? Because of the relative uncertainty in the actions that determine the outcome of a horse race. The lead horse may stumble, the jockey on the second horse may fall off, and so forth. Unlikely? Yes—but that is why the track management is willing to pay 20-to-1 odds. This example gives us two ideas about probability: (1) it expresses uncertainty, and (2) it deals with chance. We will have more to say about probability in later chapters.

---

from the former to the specified population as a whole. We will discuss how survey researchers confront this problem of subject-selection bias and will then examine how experimenters cope with a similar problem. Finally, we will underscore the importance of pilot-testing the research materials before implementing the full-scale study.

Basic Concepts in Survey Samples

Survey research is done not only by private organizations (the Gallup Organization and Louis Harris & Associates, among others), but by individual researchers working alone or with ties to private organizations (e.g., the Research Triangle Institute in North Carolina), and in the United States at three university-based institutes that do face-to-face interviewing in national probability surveys (i.e., the University of Chicago's National Opinion Research Center, the University of Michigan's Institute for Social Research, and Temple University's Institute for Survey Research). Although this research can take many different forms, all valid survey research is characterized by sampling plans in which every element, or sampling unit, in the population has a known nonzero probability of being selected. Two important statistical requirements of a probability sampling plan are (1) that the sample values be unbiased and (2) that there be stability in the samples.

To be **unbiased,** the values produced by the sample must, on average, coincide with the "true" values of the population—although we can never actually be sure that this requirement has been met in a given study (i.e., unless we know the characteristics of the population). **Stability,** on the other hand, means that there is not much variability (or spread) in the sample values; stability can be directly measured by statistical procedures described in the next chapter. Figure 9.1 helps us to see these two technical requirements more clearly. In the design, the O denotes a particular sampling unit, the X represents the true population mean, and the horizontal line indicates the underlying continuum on which the relevant values are determined.

Suppose we were trying to estimate the number of widgets that teams of assembly-line workers make in a given period. In the diagram, O = a work team's output,

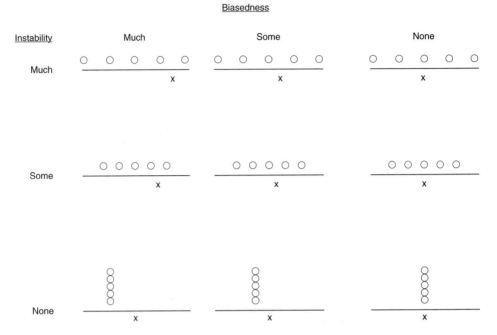

Figure 9.1 **Illustrations of bias and instability in sampling.**
The O circles represent sampling units located on some dimension, and *X* represents the population mean.

Source: From *Essentials of Behavioral Research: Methods and Data Analysis* (2nd ed., p. 208), by R. Rosenthal and R. L. Rosnow, 1991, New York: McGraw-Hill. Reprinted with permission of McGraw-Hill, Inc.

X = the value we are trying to estimate, and the continuum ranges from a low to a high number. The distance between the true population value and the midpoint of the sampling units indicates the amount of **bias** (or systematic error). The spread (variability) among the sampling units indicates their degree of instability. We see that the amount of instability is constant within each row, going from a high amount of instability (or spread) in row 1 to no instability in row 3. The amount of bias is constant in each column, going from a high bias in column 1 to zero bias in column 3. Thus, in the three cases in column 3, the sample values are balanced around the population mean, but with much instability in row 1, some in row 2, and none in row 3. In the three cases in row 3, there is no instability, but there is much bias in column 1, some in column 2, and none in column 3. The hypothetical case at the intersection of row 3 and column 3 represents the best of all situations, although it is unlikely that we will ever find such complete agreement.

Generally speaking, the more homogeneous (alike) the members of the population are, the fewer of them need to be sampled (see also Box 9.3). If all widget makers were exactly alike (i.e., the case in row 3, column 3), *any* sampling unit would provide complete information about the population as a whole. The more heterogeneous (dissimilar) the different teams are, the more sampling units are needed to ensure that we will sample the full range of dissimilarity.

Box 9.3	The Wine Taster

In the manufacture of red wine, grapes are crushed and the residue is put into huge vats in which fermentation occurs. The wine is then drawn off into barrels, where fermentation continues, and the product is periodically sampled by the wine taster. The wine taster needs to draw only a small sample in order to evaluate the quality of the wine in the barrel. It is the same in survey research: The more homogeneous the population, the smaller the sample that needs to be drawn.

In connection with our never knowing "for sure" whether there is bias in the results, it is sometimes said that election forecasting allows us to know for sure because we can compare the predicted results with the actual results. For example, Gallup Survey records in U.S. presidential elections show discrepancies that are remarkably small. In the 1996 election, the final election poll conducted by the Gallup Organization for *USA Today* and CNN, using 1,448 "likely voters" who were sampled on November 3–4, 1996, predicted that Bill Clinton would win 48%, Robert Dole 40%, and Ross Perot 6% of the vote. The prediction that Clinton would top Dole by 8% was right on the mark, and the specific vote predictions were close to the actual election result of 49% for Clinton, 41% for Dole, and 8% for Perot (Kagay, 1996). Polls that are conducted very close to the election are bound to be better predictors than early polls, but there is no guarantee that voters will not change their minds between the poll and the election. In fact, in the 1996 election, many early polls reported a landslide 15% lead by Clinton, which may have made some Clinton supporters complacent and therefore less likely to vote.

Simple Random Sampling

We said earlier that there is only *one sure* way to find out whether a sample is biased, and that is to examine every member of the population and the sample *at the same time* the sampling is conducted. If the pattern of replies in the sample exactly matches the pattern of replies in the population, we know for certain that there is no sampling bias in the survey sample. Such a procedure, of course, makes no sense, practically speaking. That is, we would have no need of a sample if we knew the responses of everyone in the population. Instead, we use a selection process involving probability sampling, of which the basic prototype is called **simple random sampling.**

The *simple* tells us that the sample is selected from an undivided population, and *random* means that the sample is to be chosen by a process that will give each sampling unit in the population the same chance of being selected (see also Box 9.4). In order for this to occur, the selection of one unit must have no influence on the selection of other units. In the case of simple random sampling, a further requirement is that we have knowledge of the existence of all the units in the population. The idea is to draw units (e.g., names) one at a time until we have as large a sample as we require. The actual method of subject selection might consist of throwing dice, using a table of random digits, or even spinning a roulette wheel or drawing capsules from an urn. In connection with telephone interviewing (discussed in Chapter 5), **random digit dialing** is used to include people with unlisted numbers; the researcher selects the first three digits according to the geographic area of interest and then uses a computer program to select the last four digits.

Box 9.4   **Randomness and Aimlessness**

Do not confuse randomness with **aimlessness,** or "hit-or-miss" sampling, which, in fact, can seldom be called random. You can prove this to yourself by asking a friend to write down "at random" several hundred one-digit numbers from 0 to 9. Afterward, tabulate the 0s, 1s, 2s, and so on. If the numbers were truly random, there would be few obvious sequences, and each digit would occur approximately 10% of the time. You will find, however, that the results are inconsistent with the hypothesis of randomness. You will see obvious sequences, and some digits will occur with high frequency, whereas others will appear hardly at all (Wallis & Roberts, 1956).

Procedures such as drawing capsules from an urn provide the least complex approach, but they are not without potential problems. A famous example of the hazards of "inadequate randomization" occurred in 1970. The previous year, while the war in Vietnam was in progress, the U.S. Congress had passed a bill allowing the use of a random lottery to select conscripts for the armed forces. To give each individual an equal chance of being selected or not selected, the planners decided to pick birthdays out of an urn. The 365 days of the year were written on slips of paper and placed inside tiny cylindrical capsules. Once all the capsules were inside the urn, it was shaken for several hours, and then the capsules were removed, one by one. However, the results were biased in spite of the precautions taken to ensure a random sample: The birth dates in December tended to be drawn first, those in November next, then those in October, and so on. The reason was that the January capsules were put in the urn first, the February capsules next, and so forth, and layers were formed with the December capsules on top. Even shaking the urn for several hours did not ensure a thorough mixing of the capsules (Broome, 1984; Kolata, 1986).

The use of a table of random digits, such as Table 9.1, helps us to avoid such pitfalls. The 2,250 digits in this list came from a million random digits that were generated by an electronic roulette wheel programmed to produce a random frequency pulse every tiny fraction of a second (Rand Corporation, 1955). As a check on the hypothesis of randomness, the computer also counted the frequency of 0s, 1s, 2s, and so on in the final results. A probability method that is impartial would produce an approximately equal number of 0s, 1s, 2s, and so on in the overall table of a million random digits. This equality is exactly what was observed.

Table 9.1   2,250 Random Digits

Rows	1–5	6–10	11–15	16–20	21–25	26–30	31–35	36–40	41–45	46–50
1	10097	32533	76520	13586	34673	54876	80959	09117	39292	74945
2	37542	04805	64894	74296	24805	24037	20636	10402	00822	91665
3	08422	68953	19645	09303	23209	02560	15953	34764	35080	33605
4	99019	02529	09376	70715	38311	31165	88676	74397	04436	27659
5	12807	99970	80157	36147	64032	36653	98951	16877	12171	76833
6	66065	74717	34072	76850	36697	36170	65813	39885	11199	29170
7	31060	10805	45571	82406	35303	42614	86799	07439	23403	09732
8	85269	77602	02051	65692	68665	74818	73053	85247	18623	88579
9	63573	32135	05325	47048	90553	57548	28468	28709	83491	25624
10	73796	45753	03529	64778	35808	34282	60935	20344	35273	88435
11	98520	17767	14905	68607	22109	40558	60970	93433	50500	73998
12	11805	05431	39808	27732	50725	68248	29405	24201	52775	67851
13	83452	99634	06288	98083	13746	70078	18475	40610	68711	77817
14	88685	40200	86507	58401	36766	67951	90364	76493	29609	11062
15	99594	67348	87517	64969	91826	08928	93785	61368	23478	34113
16	65481	17674	17468	50950	58047	76974	73039	57186	40218	16544
17	80124	35635	17727	08015	45318	22374	21115	78253	14385	53763
18	74350	99817	77402	77214	43236	00210	45521	64237	96286	02655
19	69916	26803	66252	29148	36936	87203	76621	13990	94400	56418
20	09893	20505	14225	68514	46427	56788	96297	78822	54382	14598
21	91499	14523	68479	27686	46162	83554	94750	89923	37089	20048
22	80336	94598	26940	36858	70297	34135	53140	33340	42050	82341
23	44104	81949	85157	47954	32979	26575	57600	40881	22222	06413
24	12550	73742	11100	02040	12860	74697	96644	89439	28707	25815
25	63606	49329	16505	34484	40219	52563	43651	77082	07207	31790
26	61196	90446	26457	47774	51924	33729	65394	59593	42582	60527
27	15474	45266	95270	79953	59367	83848	82396	10118	33211	59466
28	94557	28573	67897	54387	54622	44431	91190	42592	92927	45973
29	42481	16213	97344	08721	16868	48767	03071	12059	25701	46670
30	23523	78317	73208	89837	68935	91416	26252	29663	05522	82562
31	04493	52494	75246	33824	45862	51025	61962	79335	65337	12472
32	00549	97654	64051	88159	96119	63896	54692	82391	23287	29529
33	35963	15307	26898	09354	33351	35462	77974	50024	90103	39333
34	59808	08391	45427	26842	83609	49700	13021	24892	78565	20106
35	46058	85236	01390	92286	77281	44077	93910	83647	70617	42941
36	32179	00597	87379	25241	05567	07007	86743	17157	85394	11838
37	69234	61406	20117	45204	15956	60000	18743	92423	97118	96338
38	19565	41430	01758	75379	40419	21585	66674	36806	84962	85207
39	45155	14938	19476	07246	43667	94543	59047	90033	20826	69541
40	94864	31994	36168	10851	34888	81553	01540	35456	05014	51176
41	98086	24826	45240	28404	44999	08896	39094	73407	35441	31880
42	33185	16232	41941	50949	89435	48581	88695	41994	37548	73043
43	80951	00406	96382	70774	20151	23387	25016	25298	94624	61171
44	79752	49140	71961	28296	69861	02591	74852	20539	00387	59579
45	18633	32537	98145	06571	31010	24674	05455	61427	77938	91936

Source: From *A Million Random Digits with 100,000 Normal Deviates,* 1955, New York: Free Press. Reprinted by permission of the Rand Corporation.

In Chapter 7, we showed how to use such a table to allocate subjects to experimental and control conditions (i.e., random assignment). To see how you might use such a table if you were doing a survey (i.e., a random selection), imagine you want to conduct a public opinion poll, and you decide to interview 10 men and 10 women individually after choosing them at random from a list of 96 men and a list of 99 women. You begin by numbering the population of men consecutively from 01 to 96 and the population of women from 01 to 99. You are now ready to use the random digits in Table 9.1. To do so, you put your finger blindly on a starting position. You can start anywhere in the table and then move your finger in any direction, as long as you do not pick a set of numbers because they "look right" to you or avoid a set of numbers because they "do not look right" to you. Suppose you put your finger on the first five-digit number in row 5, column 1. Beginning with this number, 12807, you will read across the line two digits at a time, selecting the men numbered 12, 80, 79, 99, and so on, until you have randomly chosen the 10 male subjects. You do the same thing, beginning at another blindly chosen point, to select the 10 female subjects. If you had fewer than 10 persons on each list, you would need to read only one digit at a time; if you had between 100 and 999 persons on your list, you would need to read three digits at a time, and so forth.

Random Sampling Options

Suppose you choose the same two-digit number more than once, or suppose you choose a two-digit number not represented by any name in the population. In either case, you go on to the next two-digit number in the row (that is, unless you are sampling with replacement, as discussed next). What if your population is so small that you are forced to skip many numbers in the table because they are larger than the largest number of people in your population? For example, what if there are 450 members in the population and you want to select 50 members at random? Because the population is numbered from 001 to 450, you will have to skip approximately one half the three-digit numbers in the section of the table you have chosen. As a simple solution (also acceptable in terms of randomness), you may mentally subtract 500 from any number in the range from 501 to 999. This additional option will result in fewer unusable selections.

Another option in some situations is whether to sample with or without replacement (see also Box 9.5). **Sampling with replacement** means that the selected names are placed in the selection pool again and may be reselected on subsequent draws. Thus, every element in the population continues to have the same probability of being chosen every time a number is read. In **sampling without replacement,** a previously selected name cannot be reselected and must be disregarded on any later draw. The population shrinks each time you remove a name, but all names remaining still have the same likelihood of being drawn on the next occasion. Either option is technically acceptable, although most survey researchers prefer to do sampling without replacement (because they do not want to use the same sampling units twice or more).

Box 9.5	**Sampling With or Without Replacement**

To do random sampling with replacement, we would have to be selecting items one at a time. For example, suppose the sampling units are days of the year sealed in tiny capsules in an urn stirred so completely that there are no layers or nonrandom clusters. We simply select a capsule, read it, and put it back, which means that the same capsule may be selected more than once. For random sampling without replacement, we do not need to select items one at a time. For example, if we scooped a handful of capsules, recorded each, and then discarded them all and called it quits, this would be sampling without replacement. The wine taster (Box 9.3) who draws and then spits out a small sample of wine in the barrel is also doing simple random sampling without replacement. We wouldn't have it any other way!

Stratification in Sampling

Simple random sampling is frequently used either when the population is known to be homogeneous or when its precise composition is unknown. When we know something about its exact composition, then we may be able to use a more efficient method of sampling, where we sample from the different substrates of the population. Professional polling organizations frequently use this approach to probability sampling, that is, randomly selecting sampling units (e.g., persons or households) from several subpopulations (termed **strata** or **clusters**) into which the population is divided. For example, if we know the population is 60% female and 40% male (i.e., a ratio of 3 to 2), and that gender is related to the variable in which we are interested, we can improve our sampling procedure by selecting subsamples proportionate in size to this 3:2 ratio of females to males.

Called **stratified random sampling,** this is a very efficient way of probability sampling; that is, a separate sample is randomly selected from each homogeneous stratum (or "layer") of the population. The stratum means are then statistically weighted to form a combined estimate for the entire population. In a survey of political opinions, for example, it might be useful to stratify the population according to party affiliation, gender, socioeconomic status, and other meaningful categories related to voting behavior. This method ensures that one will have enough men, women, Democrats, Republicans, and so on to draw descriptive or relational inferences about each respective subgroup. We will have more to say about this method of sampling in a moment.

Area Probability Sampling

A popular variant of this sampling strategy is called **area probability sampling,** because the population is divided into geographic areas (i.e., population clusters or strata). This method is applicable to any population divisible into meaningful geographic areas related to the variables of interest. For example, depending on the variables of interest, meaningful geographic areas might be people living in urban neighborhoods, Inuits in igloos, or nomads in tents. The assumption is that, within each of the areas, the sampling units will have the same probability of being chosen. The sampling procedure can be more complicated than those described above, but the method is cost-effective because the research design can be used repeatedly with only minor modifications (e.g., Fowler, 1993). Suppose a polling organization needed an area probability sample of 300 out of 6,000 estimated housing units in a city, and a good list of all the dwellings in the entire city does not exist (and would be too costly to prepare). Using a city map, the pollsters can instead obtain a sample of dwellings by selecting small clusters of blocks.

To do this in the simplest case, they divide the entire map of the city into blocks and then select 1 of, say, every 20 blocks for the sample. If they define the sample as the housing units located within the boundaries of the sample blocks, the probability of selection for *any* unit is the selection of its block—which is set at $1/20$ to correspond to the desired sampling rate of $300/6,000$ (Kish, 1965). In other cases, researchers categorize the blocks by taking into account their size or some other factor of interest and then treat this factor as a stratum to sample in a specific way. Although the procedure gets more complicated as the area gets bigger, the key requirements are to ensure (1) that all areas will have some chance of selection and (2) that units within the areas will be chosen impartially (Fowler, 1993). To use the same plan over and over, all that must be altered are the randomly selected units within each area.

Lessons Learned by George Gallup

The late George Gallup, the pioneering survey researcher who founded the Gallup Survey, once noted some of the methodological lessons learned by survey researchers going back to 1936 (Gallup, 1976). That year, Franklin D. Roosevelt (the Democratic presidential candidate) was running against Governor Alfred Landon of Kansas (the Republican candidate). Most people thought Roosevelt would win easily, but a pseudoscientific poll conducted by a current events magazine, the *Literary Digest,* predicted that Landon would win an overwhelming victory. What gave the prediction credence was that the *Digest* had successfully predicted the winner in every presidential election since 1916. Moreover, this time, they announced they had based their prediction on a sample of 2.4 million respondents!

They got these 2.4 million by drawing a sample of 10 million people from sources like telephone directories, automobile registration lists, and club membership lists; they then mailed straw vote ballots to each name. The lists had actually been compiled for solicitation purposes, and advertising was included with the straw vote ballot (D. Katz & Cantril, 1937). One problem was that few people in 1936 had a telephone (only one in four households), owned a car, or belonged to a club, so that the final list was biased in favor of wealthy Republican households. Another problem was that there was a large number of nonrespondents, and subsequent analyses suggest that had they responded, the results might have been very different because of the factor of self-selection bias (Squire, 1988); we will return to this problem later.

As it turned out, the election voting was split pretty much along economic lines, the more affluent voting for Landon and the less affluent voting for Roosevelt. The *Digest* predicted that Landon would win by 57% to Roosevelt's 43%, but the election results were Roosevelt 62% and Landon 38% (Freedman et al., 1991). Interestingly, the *Digest* could actually have used the information that the sample was top-heavy in upper-income Republicans to correct its estimate, but it deliberately ignored this information. Instead, the *Digest* proudly proclaimed that the "figures had been neither weighted, adjusted, nor interpreted." After making the largest error ever made by political pollsters in a presidential election, the *Digest* (which had been in financial trouble before the election) declared bankruptcy.

George Gallup was just getting started in those days. Using his own polling method, he was able to predict that Roosevelt would win (although he was off by 6 percentage points)—as well as to predict what the *Literary Digest* results would be! Gallup's method, called **quota sampling,** was an early precursor of current methods; it assigned a quota of people to be questioned and let the questioner build up a sample that was roughly representative of the population. Now, of course, we use random selection procedures instead of leaving the selection of units to the judgment of the questioner (see also Box 9.6). However, the important lesson that Gallup and other pollsters learned from the *Digest*'s debacle was that large numbers do not, in and of themselves, increase the representativeness of a sample.

Box 9.6	**Bias in Quota Sampling**

In early political polling, in the 1930s, the interviewer would be given ranges of variables and told to identify by sight people who seemed to fit this quota. For example, an interviewer might be told to talk to so many people of ages 21–35, 36–55, and 56 or over. We do not know how much of this interviewing took place on busy street corners and at trolley stops rather than in house-to-house canvassing, but bias might be introduced simply as a consequence of the interviewed individuals' being more accessible than others (Rossi et al., 1983).

In the congressional election of 1942, the pollsters encountered a new problem. They had not reckoned with voter turnout, which was at an all-time low because citizens were changing their places of residence to work in war factories or to enter the military. Gallup's polls correctly predicted that the Democrats would retain control of the House of Representatives, but the margin of victory turned out to be much smaller than either he or any other pollsters had predicted. The important lesson learned this time was to give far more attention to the factor of voter turnout in making predictions.

In the 1948 presidential election, Harry S Truman, by luring Democratic defectors back into the fold during the last two weeks before Election Day, turned the tide against his Republican opponent, Thomas E. Dewey. However, many public opinion polls predicted that *Dewey* would win. This time, Gallup and other pollsters learned that political polling should be done as close to Election Day as possible.

After 1948, the Gallup Survey (and other respected polls) adopted area probability sampling, in which election districts are randomly selected throughout the nation, and then randomly chosen households within these districts are contacted by interviewers. Using this procedure and the lessons learned from the mistakes made in previous polls quickly brought about further improvements. By 1956, the Gallup Survey, based on a little over 8,000 respondents, was able to predict with a margin of error of only 1.7% that Dwight D. Eisenhower would be reelected president. The term **margin of error** means that, based on the laws of mathematical probability, it was predicted that the anticipated percentages would fall within an interval bound by plus and minus 1.7 percentage points. Prudent poll watchers now expect a margin of error of no more than 2 or 3 percentage points in national elections, if the random sampling is properly implemented.

Point and Interval Estimates

Whatever technique is used, survey researchers are usually interested in making point estimates and interval estimates of the population values in question. **Point estimates** are designed to tell researchers about some particular characteristic of the population. For example, in a survey of a college population, we might want to make a point estimate of the number of seniors who plan to continue their education after graduating. Other examples noted earlier were the number of widgets made by assembly-line workers and the number of cases of tuberculosis contracted on the job. **Interval estimates** tell survey researchers how much the point estimates are likely to be in error (e.g., because of variability in the composition of the population).

Imagine a simple random survey of 100 college students out of a population of 2,500 graduating seniors at a large state university. Each student is asked, "Do you plan to continue your education after you graduate from college, by going on to graduate school, business school, medical school, dental school, or law school?" In answer to the researchers' question, 25 of them reply yes. In order to make a point estimate, the researchers generalize from this sample value to the population of graduating seniors. They multiply the sample proportion replying yes (.25) by the total number of students in the population (2,500). The result tells them that approximately 625 seniors at this university hope to continue their education.

How "approximate" is this estimate? The interval estimate gives the answer to this question; that is, it tells us the probability that the estimated population value is correct within plus-or-minus some specified interval. Let us say that, using certain statistical procedures, the researchers compute as "95 chances in 100" the probability that an interval of "25% plus-or-minus 9%" contains the true proportion of graduating seniors who plan to continue their education. The point estimate of 625, with its associated interval estimate, enables the researchers to feel fairly confident that the population value falls within the range of 400 to 850 graduating seniors (Cochran, 1963, pp. 57–58).

In this case, the researchers randomly selected individual sampling units, using the population of graduating seniors as a single heterogeneous cluster. In most cases of survey research, however, sampling several strata or clusters is more efficient if the population can be conveniently separated into homogeneous strata. The following example illustrates these advantages and shows what is meant by an unbiased sampling plan in the case of simple random sampling and stratified random sampling.

Benefits of Stratification

Suppose we want to use a random sampling plan to estimate the average hourly production of widgets by teams of assembly-line workers. To keep this example simple, we will imagine that the entire population consists of four teams and that the mean number of widgets produced per hour is

Team A	11.5
Team B	12.5
Team C	13.0
Team D	19.0
	14.0 (true population value)

Adding the average hourly production rates $(11.5 + 12.5 + 13.0 + 19.0 = 56.0)$ and dividing by four $(56.0/4 = 14.0)$ tells us that the true population value is 14.0. But for this example, we ask, "How accurate an estimate of the true population value would we obtain by simple random sampling or stratified random sampling?" Finding the answer to this question will reveal what an **unbiased sampling plan** means.

We must initially decide on the size of the sample we wish to use to estimate the population value. To keep it simple, we will define the sample size as any two teams selected at random. For example, were we to randomly select Team A and Team B, we would get a point estimate of 12.0, computed as $(11.5 + 12.5)/2 = 12.0$. How good is this estimate? The answer, called the **error of estimate,** is defined in this case as the closeness of 12.0 to the true population value of 14.0. We figure this answer out by subtracting the population value from the sample mean, or $12.0 - 14.0 = -2.0$. In other words, this particular sample underestimated the true population by 2.0 (the negative difference means it is an underestimate, whereas a positive difference would indicate an overestimate). Table 9.2 lists all possible combinations

| **Table 9.2** | Results for All Possible Simple Random Samples of Size Two |

Sample	Sample values	Estimate of population value	Error of estimate
Team A, Team B	11.5, 12.5	12.00	−2.00
Team A, Team C	11.5, 13.0	12.25	−1.75
Team A, Team D	11.5, 19.0	15.25	+1.25
Team B, Team C	12.5, 13.0	12.75	−1.25
Team B, Team D	12.5, 19.0	15.75	+1.75
Team C, Team D	13.0, 19.0	16.00	+2.00
Total		84.00	0.00
Mean		14.00	0.00

of two-member samples, the estimates derived from them, and the error of estimate for each sample. The average of the errors of estimate (when we take account of their signs) gives the *bias* of the general sampling plan. Not surprisingly, we see (at the bottom of the last column) that the general sampling plan produces an unbiased estimate—even though there is error associated with individual sample values.

In stratified random sampling (to which we now turn), we begin by dividing the population into a number of parts. We then randomly sample independently in each part. To get started, notice that the last column in Table 9.2 shows that every simple random sample containing Team D overestimates the population value, and that every random sample without this team underestimates it. If we had reason to suspect this fact before the sampling, we could make use of this information to form strata so that a heterogeneous population is divided into two parts, each of which is fairly homogeneous (Snedecor & Cochran, 1989). One stratum will consist of Teams A, B, and C, and the second stratum will consist of Team D alone, as Table 9.3 shows. This table helps us to see clearly why this general sampling plan is called *unbiased* and also to see the advantages of stratification in probability sampling.

Starting with the first row, notice under "Weighted sample values" that Team A's score is $11.5 \times 3 = 34.5$, whereas Team D's score is not weighted (19.0). The reason we weight Team A's score by multiplying it by 3 is that it is one of three members of Stratum 1. By the same reasoning, we did not weight Team D's score because it is the sole occupant of Stratum 2. To compute the scores under "Estimate of population value," we add Team A's weighted score to Team D's unweighted score and then divide by the total number of members, or $(34.5 + 19.0)/4 = 13.375$. The "Error of estimate" is obtained by subtracting the true population mean from this result, or $13.375 - 14.0 = -0.625$ (which indicates that the Team A + Team D sample underestimates the true population value by a small amount). This table shows the results of all possible stratified random samples of size two. Again, we find (not unexpectedly) that the general sampling plan is unbiased in that the average of the errors of estimate (bottom of last column) is zero.

By comparing the results in Tables 9.2 and 9.3, you will see in quantitative terms the advantages of separating selections from strata of the population. The most extreme errors in Table 9.2 range from -2.00 to $+2.00$, a difference of 4.00. By contrast, the most extreme errors in Table 9.3 range from -0.625 to $+0.500$, a difference of 1.125. Notice that fewer samples are possible of size two in Table 9.3 than

Table 9.3	Results for All Possible Stratified Random Samples of Size Two			
Sample	Stratum 1	Stratum 2	Weighted sample values	Estimate of population value	Error of estimate
1	Team A	Team D	34.5, 19.0	13.375	−0.625
2	Team B	Team D	37.5, 19.0	14.125	+0.125
3	Team C	Team D	39.0, 19.0	14.500	+0.500
Total				42.000	0.000
Mean				14.000	0.000

in Table 9.2. In summary, the error of an individual sample is greater in simple random sampling of a heterogeneous population than in stratified random sampling of that same population divided into homogeneous strata—in this case, by a magnitude of $4.00/1.125 = 3.56$, or more than three times the size. And the potential for error is also greater in simple random sampling than in stratified random sampling. Some forethought—and reliable information, of course—is needed about possible mean differences when one is dividing the population into homogeneous strata; these can pay off handsomely in the utility of stratification.

Estimating the Bias Due to Nonresponse

A growing problem in the use of polling methods is that, as surveys proliferate, random samples become harder to obtain because more and more people shut the door or hang up the phone on the pollsters (see also Box 9.7). As a consequence of many individuals' reluctance to be polled, statisticians and survey researchers have devoted considerable effort to studying the possible effects on accuracy of **nonresponse bias** (i.e., an error due to nonparticipation or nonresponse). Not only might this result in a smaller **effective sample size** (i.e., the size of the sample that the researcher ends up with) than the researcher planned on for statistical reasons (discussed in a later chapter), but the accuracy of estimates of population values may be seriously jeopardized when the researcher fails to collect data from a high percentage of those randomly selected to be in the sample.

Box 9.7   Types of Nonresponse

There are several types of nonresponse. One type is when people are not at home, such as when both parents work. Another type is the person who is unable or unwilling to answer questions by the pollster. A third type is the person who is simply too busy to answer. For example, several years ago, an association of survey researchers reported that 38% of consumers had turned down their interviewers. A typical answer by one person who turned down a telephone request to interview her about where she shops was "It was 7 o'clock, I was putting the kids to bed, and it was zoo time around here, which is when these people call" (Rothenberg,1990, p. A1).

Table 9.4 illustrates in quantitative terms the basic idea of nonresponse bias, and it also illustrates one way in which people who conduct large public opinion polls using mailed questionnaires attempt to reduce this bias by sending out questionnaires more than once. The data in this table are based on three waves of questionnaires that were mailed out to peach growers in North Carolina (Finkner, 1950). One variable in this study was the number of peach trees owned, and data were available for the entire population of growers for just this variable. As a consequence, it is possible to quantify the amount of the bias due to nonresponse remaining after the first, second, and third mailings (Cochran, 1963, 1977).

Table 9.4   Example of Bias Due to Nonresponse in Survey Research

| | \multicolumn{5}{c}{Response to three mailings} |
Basic data	First wave	Second wave	Third wave	Nonre-spondents	Total population
1. Number of respondents	300	543	434	1,839	3,116
2. Percentage of population	10	17	14	59	100
3. Mean trees per respondent	456	382	340	290	329
Cumulative data					
4. Mean trees per respondent (Y_1)	456	408	385		
5. Mean trees per nonrespondent (Y_2)	315	300	290		
6. Difference $(Y_1 - Y_2)$	141	108	95		
7. Percentage of nonrespondents (P)	90	73	59		
8. Bias $= (P) \times (Y_1 - Y_2)$	127	79	56		

Source: From *The Volunteer Subject* (p. 4), by R. Rosenthal and R. L. Rosnow, 1975, New York: Wiley. Copyright © by authors. Based on data from Finkner (1950) and Cochran (1963). Reprinted by permission.

The first three rows provide basic data in the form of (1) the number of respondents to each wave of questionnaires and the number of nonrespondents; (2) the percentage of the total population of growers (3,116) represented by each wave of respondents and nonrespondents; and (3) the mean number of trees owned by the respondents in each wave. To calculate the effective sample size after each mailing, we cumulate the number of respondents to that point. Thus the effective sample size is 300 after the first mailing; 300 + 543 = 843 after two mailings; and 843 + 434 = 1,277 after three mailings. To convert the values in row 1 into the percentages in row 2, we divide the row 1 values by the total population size and then multiply by 100 to convert the proportion into a percentage. For example, dividing the number of respondents to the first mailing by the total population value gives us 300/3116 = .096, which, when rounded to .10 and multiplied by 100, tells us that 10% of the growers responded to the first mailing.

The remaining five rows of data are based on the cumulative number of respondents after the first, second, and third mailings. For each wave, five items of information are provided: (4) the mean number of peach trees owned by the respondents up to that point in the survey; (5) the mean number of trees owned by those not yet responding; (6) the difference between these two values; (7) the percentage of the population not yet responding; and (8) the magnitude of the bias (defined in terms of peach trees owned) up to that point in the survey. This last row shows that with each successive wave of respondents there was a decrease in the magnitude of the bias—a fairly typical result in such cases. The implication is that increasing the effort to recruit the nonrespondents should lessen the bias of the point estimates.

Furthermore, knowing the magnitude and direction of the nonresponse bias can help us adjust our estimate of the generalizability of the results. To do this, we need information about the nonrespondents as well as the respondents on some variable that is related to what we are interested in. The problem for many researchers is that they do not have this information at their finger tips. In other words, they can compute the proportion of population participants (P) and the statistic of interest (the point estimate) for these respondents (Y_1), but they may be unable to compute the statistic of interest (the corresponding point estimate) for those who did not respond (Y_2). With the information we do have, we may be in a position to suspect bias but may be unable to give an accurate estimate of its magnitude. We will come back to this problem again (in our discussion of volunteer bias), but one way to minimize nonresponse bias is to try to increase the rate of response.

Increasing the Rate of Response

In the case of mail surveys, more nonrespondents may be drawn into the subject sample by one or more follow-up mailings or reminders. Experts who do mail surveys often advise telephoning the nonrespondents if the response rate is still not satisfactory. Professional pollsters attempt to increase the initial rate of participation by using various kinds of incentives and attention-getting techniques, such as using special delivery as opposed to ordinary mail, using hand-stamped rather than postage-permit envelopes, and sometimes including a courtesy gift (e.g., a 50-cent piece or a Susan B. Anthony dollar) at the time of the request for participation (Linsky, 1975). In Chapter 5, we discussed the development of questionnaires; to increase response rates, it is important that the instructions be clear, that the items be easy to read and the layout attractive, and that the task of answering the questions not be burdensome (Fowler, 1993; Tryfos, 1996).

Techniques of increasing subject participation in telephone surveys, were also alluded to in Chapter 5. For example, response rates may be increased by an informative advance letter that emphasizes the purpose and importance of the study, by the pilot testing of probing questions to ensure that the persons contacted will not feel intimidated by them or by the uses to which the data will be put, and by the training of interviewers and the screening out of bad ones. One or more follow-up telephone calls on evenings and weekends may also improve the response rate (Fowler, 1993; Tryfos, 1996).

Characteristics of Volunteer Subjects

So far, we have focused on the prototypical survey study. We turn now to a problem that is similar to nonresponse bias, but that may occur in experimental and quasi-experimental studies in which the subjects are individually recruited. Most experimenters, for example, do not concern themselves with the particulars of a probability sampling plan when recruiting research subjects. One reason for this lack of concern (noted earlier) is that it is often impossible to work within the confines of such a plan. Can you imagine, for example, trying to persuade a randomly selected sample of adults to agree to be assigned to a smoking treatment for many years?

A second reason for experimenters' lack of concern is that, even when random subject selection is feasible, many believe that "people are people" in terms of the psychological mechanisms they are studying. That is, the belief is that, as long as subjects are randomly assigned to treatments, it should make little difference whether the subjects in the experimental and control groups are volunteer subjects (i.e., a self-selected sample) or a random sample of some specified population as a whole. In some cases, as we will show, the use of volunteers may lead to biased conclusions—even when the volunteers are randomly assigned to the experimental and control conditions (see also Box 9.8). Fortunately, we are now able to estimate the direction of this bias in many instances (Rosenthal & Rosnow, 1975b; Rosnow & Rosenthal, 1997).

Box 9.8   The Ubiquitous Volunteer

When scientists recruit volunteers for randomized trials involving risk (e.g., an experiment testing the effects of different diets on cholesterol), it is possible that those already at high risk are the most likely to volunteer. However, "volunteer bias" is not limited to experimental studies. Suppose a cable television company randomly selected subscribers to be interviewed in a telephone survey. The dissatisfied subscribers might be more likely to go to the trouble to voice their grievances (Tryfos, 1996). The question is how to generalize from these volunteers to the target population.

In particular, we have come to know a great deal about the personal characteristics of the typical volunteers for behavioral and social research, and, in turn, about the typical nonvolunteers. You may be asking yourself how a researcher can identify the characteristics of nonvolunteers (i.e., people who refuse to participate in research). One technique used by researchers who want to compare the characteristics and reactions of volunteers and nonvolunteers is to recruit research subjects from a population for which information is already available on all the potential recruits (e.g., biographical data and psychological test results). Requests for research volunteers are then made some time later—sometimes years later—and those who volunteer are compared with those who do not volunteer on all the items of information in which the investigator is interested. For instance, most colleges administer psychological tests and questionnaires to all incoming students during an orientation period. The results, if they are obtainable by researchers, can be used not only to compare those who volunteer with those who do not volunteer for a psychological experiment later that same year, but also to compare the respondents with the nonrespondents to an alumni-organization questionnaire sent out years later.

To explain **volunteer bias** (and to explain how it is controlled), we must first know the characteristics of typical volunteers and nonvolunteers. Table 9.5 contains a summary list of nine characteristics of volunteers for research participation; they are ranked in the descending order of their approximate accuracy based on the available data (Rosenthal & Rosnow, 1975b). However, the nature of these relationships is context-dependent to a large degree, for example:

Table 9.5	Characteristics of Typical Volunteers for Research Participation

1. Better educated
2. Higher social-class status
3. Higher IQ scores
4. Higher need for social approval
5. More sociable
6. More arousal-seeking
7. More unconventional
8. More often women
9. Less authoritarian

1. Volunteer subjects tend to be better educated than nonvolunteers, especially in studies in which personal contact between investigator and respondent is not required.
2. Volunteers are characteristically higher in social-class status than nonvolunteers, but only defined by the respondents' own status rather than by parental status.
3. People who volunteer for somewhat less typical types of research (e.g., hypnosis, sensory isolation, sex research, and small-group and personality research) typically score higher on IQ tests than nonvolunteers do.
4. Volunteers tend to be higher than nonvolunteers in need for social approval (i.e., the variable studied by Marlowe and Crowne, discussed in Chapter 6).
5. Volunteers are typically more sociable than nonvolunteers, according to their responses on personality tests.
6. Volunteers tend to be more arousal-seeking than nonvolunteers, especially when the volunteering is for studies of stress, sensory isolation, and hypnosis.
7. Volunteers tend to be more unconventional than nonvolunteers, especially when the volunteering is for studies of sexual behavior.
8. Women are more likely to volunteer for research in general, but they are less likely than men to volunteer for physically and emotionally stressful research (e.g., electric shock, high temperature, sensory deprivation, and interviews about sexual behavior).
9. Volunteers tend to be less authoritarian than nonvolunteers (a characteristic implying that volunteers are typically less rigid thinkers and are likely to put a high value on individual freedom).

Implications for Research Conclusions

Knowing that research volunteers are likely to be brighter (Conclusion 3), higher in approval need (Conclusion 4), less authoritarian (Conclusion 9), and so on than nonvolunteers allows us to predict the direction of volunteer bias in many situations. For example, imagine that an educational researcher wants to assess experimentally the validity of a new teaching procedure that is purported to make young children less rigid in their thinking. The researcher asks parents or teachers to volunteer their children or pupils as participants in the investigation because, realistically, it is impossible to draw a random sample for participation. The researcher expects that the children who are volunteered will—like adults who volunteer themselves—be low in authoritarianism (Characteristic 9). Because people who are low in authoritarianism are also likely to be less rigid thinkers, the researcher suspects that using these volunteered children will lead to a more conservative assessment of the new teaching procedure than if it were possible to use a randomly selected subject sample. The reason is that the experimental group will already be unusually low on the dependent variable (rigidity of thinking). Knowing this, however, the researcher can have greater confidence in the existence of the causal relationship to which the visible evidence in this study points, because that relationship is likely to be even greater in the specified general population.

We can also imagine the opposite type of inferential error in another situation. Suppose a marketing researcher wants to find out how persuasive an advertisement is before recommending its use in a heavily funded television campaign. The researcher finds it most convenient to pilot-test the advertisement on volunteer subjects, who are assigned at random to an experimental group that sees the advertisement or a control group that sees something else that will fill the same amount of time. The researcher knows that volunteer subjects tend to be relatively high in approval need (Characteristic 4), and also (from working in the area and knowing the background literature) that people who are high in approval need are likely to be more influenced than those who are low in approval need (Buckhout,1965). Putting these facts together, the researcher feels it prudent not to make too strong a claim about the causal relationship evidence in this pilot study. Because the volunteers may have overreacted to the treatment in the experimental group, the predicted effect of the new advertisement on the general population may be exaggerated by the pilot study results.

Knowing that biased conclusions are likely in a given experimental or nonexperimental situation, researchers try to avoid this problem when possible. For example, the use of volunteer subjects may lead to biased conclusions in the standardization of a new test. As noted in earlier discussions, uniform procedures are established for administering and scoring standardized tests, so that every competent tester is likely to obtain the same "unbiased" results. Many standardized tests are accompanied by **norms,** or tables of values representing the typical performance of a given group. The norms provide a standard of comparison so that we can see how much any person's score deviates from the average of a large group of representative individuals.

For example, if you are planning to apply to law school, you may want to know how much your score on the Law School Admission Test (LSAT) deviates from the scores of other highly qualified college students with similar career plans. In the next chapter, we will explain how to interpret a "standard score," but what is more relevant here is that a crucial assumption of researchers in developing norms for new tests is that the resulting values are representative of the target population. For example, the developers of the LSAT have such information on everyone in the target group because everyone in the group must take this test. However, suppose that a researcher uses volunteer subjects to standardize a brand new intelligence test but wants to use the test and the resulting norms in a population consisting of typical volunteers *and* nonvolunteers. Based on Characteristic 3, our best guess is that the researcher's estimates of population norms will be inflated values, because volunteers can be expected to score higher on intelligence tests than nonvolunteers in the same population.

Increasing Participation and Ethical Accountability

Previously we summarized some of the techniques used to stimulate participation by typical nonrespondents in survey research. Researchers in other areas can use a number of incentives to stimulate participation by typical nonvolunteers (Rosenthal & Rosnow, 1975b; Rosnow & Rosenthal, 1997). Increasing such participation should, in turn, lessen the likelihood of subject selection bias by drawing a more representative subject sample.

One effective recruitment technique is to explain to the potential subjects *why* they will find the research interesting and worthwhile. This approach is based on the research finding that persons more interested in the research are more likely to participate. A second technique is to explain the research in a way that is nonthreatening, so that potential participants are not put off by unwarranted fears of unfavorable evaluation. The basis of this approach is another set of research findings that persons who expect to be unfavorably evaluated by the investigator are less likely, and those who expect to be favorably evaluated are more likely, to volunteer. Some other empirically based techniques for stimulating research participation are emphasizing the scientific importance of the research, offering small courtesy gifts to potential participants simply for taking the time to consider participating, and avoiding unnecessary procedures that may be perceived as psychologically or biologically stressful.

A hasty reading of these techniques may give the impression that they are designed only to increase rates of participation. However, there is another, more subtle, benefit. When we tell our prospective subjects as much as possible about the significance of the research, avoid doing unnecessary psychological or biologically stressful research, and so on, it follows that more care and thought probably went into our planning in order to ensure that the study will stand up to the scrutiny of critical evaluations. In effect, we are treating the participants as if they are another "granting agency"—which in fact they are, granting us their time and cooperation. Thus another benefit of these techniques is that they provide incentives to us to be ethically responsible and humane when we decide what kind of research to do and how to do it (Blanck et al., 1992; Rosenthal, 1994b; Rosnow, 1997).

Pilot Testing as a Final Step

Whatever your research project, whether it involves a survey, an experiment, a quasi experiment, or some combination of these, the final step before implementing the study is to pilot-test the materials. For example, suppose we want to study a sensitive topic and fear that people will be reluctant to tell the truth (e.g., Lee, 1993). We might pilot-test two or three versions of the questionnaire or interview schedule. If we are concerned about nonresponse bias, we might pilot-test different recruitment procedures. Interestingly, even when conducting the actual survey, researchers use embedded randomized experiments on subsets of the sample (e.g., Fienberg & Tanur, 1989; Schuman & Presser, 1996; Tanur, 1994). As the old saying goes, an ounce of prevention is worth a pound of cure. The purpose of pilot testing (and embedded experiments in survey studies) is to prevent the production of incurably flawed data.

Summary of Ideas

1. Probability sampling plans ensure that the selection process will use a random procedure.

2. To be absolutely sure that a sample is representative, we would need to know the particular population characteristics that we are studying, in which case there would be no reason to study the sample.

3. A *biased* sample overestimates or underestimates the true population value; an *unstable* sample is characterized by sampling units that vary greatly from one another.

4. Inadequate randomization occurs when a probability sampling plan is not implemented properly (e.g., the first draft lottery during the war in Vietnam). One way to avoid this problem is to use a table of random digits to select the sampling units.

5. Two options in simple random sampling are (a) sampling with replacement and (b) sampling without replacement (e.g., the wine taster).

6. Area probability sampling is a variant of stratified random sampling in which the strata are geographic clusters.

7. Point estimates are designed to tell us about a particular characteristic of the target population, whereas interval estimates describe how much the point estimates are likely to be in error.

8. As the widget example illustrated, both the error of estimate of an individual sample and the likelihood of making that error tend to be greater in simple random samples than in stratified random samples.

9. In survey research that uses a probability sampling plan, bias due to nonresponse is likely to diminish with each successive wave of respondents (e.g., in the survey of peach growers). Other ways to reduce nonresponse bias in survey research include (a) using reminders and follow-up communications; (b) personalizing the contact; and (c) offering an incentive to respond.

10. As Gallup and other political pollsters have learned from experience, it is best to take the final survey close to election time and to give attention to the factor of voter turnout.

11. On practical, ethical, and theoretical grounds (e.g., the premise that "people are people"), behavioral experimenters tend to pay little attention to whether their subjects constitute a random sample of a specified target population.

12. Knowing the relationship between the characteristics of volunteer subjects and the variable of theoretical interest, we can sometimes predict the direction of volunteer bias in experimental and nonexperimental studies.

13. Procedures for stimulating subject participation (e.g., telling subjects as much as possible about the significance of the research and avoiding psychologically or biologically stressful manipulations) also provide incentives to researchers to act ethically and humanely.

Key Terms

aimlessness   p. 208
area probability sampling   p. 211
bias   p. 206
clusters   p. 211
effective sample size   p. 217
error of estimate   p. 215
interval estimates   p. 214
margin of error   p. 214
nonresponse bias   p. 217
norms   p. 222
opportunity samples   p. 203
point estimates   p. 214
population   p. 203
probability   p. 204
quota sampling   p. 213

random digit dialing   p. 208
random selection   p. 204
representative   p. 204
sample   p. 203
sampling plan   p. 204
sampling without replacement   p. 210
sampling with replacement   p. 210
simple random sampling   p.207
stability   p. 205
strata   p. 211
stratified random sampling   p. 211
unbiased   p. 205
unbiased sampling plan   p. 215
volunteer bias   p. 220

Multiple-Choice Questions for Review (answers are found on page 350)

1. Which of the following is most commonly used in public opinion polling? (a) random selection; (b) random assignment; (c) random processing; (d) opportunity sampling

2. A _____ is the total group of participants in which one is interested; a _____ is a segment of the total group which will be studied more closely. (a) universe of subjects; population; (b) population; sample; (c) sample; population; (d) sample; microsample

3. The true population mean is 4. A sample is chosen with the following values: 2, 3, 4, 5, 6. This sample is (a) unbiased; (b) biased; (c) random; (d) nonrandom.

4. The true population mean is 4. Sample A has the following values: 3, 4, 4, 5. Sample B has the following values: 0, 4, 4, 8. Compared to Sample B, Sample A is more (a) unbiased; (b) biased; (c) stable; (d) random.

5. A sampling plan is created in which each member of the population has an equal probability of being selected. This is called a(n) _____ plan. (a) quota sampling; (b) simple random sampling; (c) stratified random sampling; (d) area probability sampling

6. A public opinion pollster divides the population into subpopulations of males and females, and of Democrats and Republicans. She then takes a random sample from each of these subpopulations. This approach is called (a) area probability

sampling; (b) stratified random sampling; (c) simple random sampling; (d) quota sampling.

7. A researcher concludes that 1,000 students at a particular college plan to go to graduate school. This is an example of a(n) (a) reliable measure; (b) interval estimate; (c) point estimate; (d) judge's rating.

8. The same researcher states that it is 95% likely that between 900 and 1,100 students at the college plan to go to graduate school. This is an example of a(n) (a) observation measure; (b) interval estimate; (c) point estimate; (d) judge's rating.

9. In some circumstances, subjects who agree to participate are significantly different from subjects who refuse to participate. This problem is sometimes called (a) lack of randomization; (b) sampling without replacement; (c) instability in sampling; (d) nonresponse bias.

10. Compared to nonvolunteers, those who volunteer to participate in psychological research tend to be (a) less authoritarian; (b) higher in arousal-seeking; (c) more sociable; (d) all of the above.

Discussion Questions for Review (answers are found on pages 350–51)

1. Do you know the answer to the following question asked of a University of Vermont student? Given a true population mean of 12 and the following subjects' scores, (a) which group is measured with greatest stability, and (b) which group is the most biased?

Group 1	Group 2	Group 3
10	10	9
11	12	12
12	14	15
13	16	18

2. Fed up with studying for midterms, four Smith College students—Susan, Valerie, Ellen, and Jane—decide to throw darts at Susan's encyclopedia, which contains one volume for each letter of the alphabet. Because the word *midterm* begins with the letter *M*, the *M* volume is chosen as the target. Each person gets three darts. Susan hits the *M* volume every time; Valerie hits the *N* volume every time; Ellen hits the *L* volume, the *M* volume, and the *N* volume once each; and Jane hits the *M* volume, the *N* volume, and the *O* volume once each. Assuming that each volume of the encyclopedia is the same size, interpret the performance of each person in terms of bias and instability.

3. A Virginia Polytechnic Institute student is interested in the relationship between IQ and sociability. He designs a questionnaire to study this relationship and sends it out to hundreds of people. Twenty percent of the people complete and return the questionnaire. What is a possible source of bias in the results this student will obtain? How would you improve on his design?

4. A University of Kansas student is asked by his instructor to think up experimental cases in which the difference between volunteer subjects and nonvolunteers might

lead the researcher (a) to overestimate the effectiveness of the experimental treatment and (b) to underestimate the effectiveness of the experimental treatment. Can you help the student? Can you also think of how these situations might be remedied?

5. A University of Michigan student wants to sample the opinions of all graduating seniors on various issues. However, because the graduating class is so large, she decides it would be best to sample a representative group rather than try to contact every one of the graduating seniors. Describe the steps she should take to develop a representative sampling plan, as well as some further steps she might take to deal with the problem of nonresponse bias.

6. An Eastern College student wants to conduct an interview study using married adults who frequent the King of Prussia shopping mall. Because she is worried about volunteer bias, she would like to make every reasonable effort to obtain as representative a sample as she possibly can. What can she do to induce people to participate in her study?

10 Summarizing the Data

PREVIEW QUESTIONS

■ How are frequency distributions used to summarize data?

■ How do stem-and-leaf plots work?

■ When are means, medians, and modes used?

■ What are the effects of outliers on measures of location?

■ Which range should be reported?

■ What is the difference between variance and standard deviation?

■ What are descriptive and inferential measures?

■ What is the role of the standard normal distribution?

■ Why are z scores called *standard scores,* and how are they used?

Statistical Procedures

In Chapter 1, we noted that the scientific method, like all methods of explanation, is characterized by a distinctive language particular to the area it represents. So far, we have discussed a number of aspects of this rhetoric (e.g., the use of technical definitions and the nature of hypotheses and theories), and we turn now to statistical methods that are also a part of many research reports. The purpose of the remaining chapters is to help you develop an intuitive understanding of the proper use (and limitations) of these methods. Some will be particularly useful as you analyze your own results and prepare to write a final report (see also Appendix A), but you will find these methods useful even beyond your research. For example, once you understand the logic of using graphs, descriptive and inferential measures, z scores, probabilities, correlations, and so on, you will be in a better position to evaluate claims made on the basis of such methods.

If you are working with a computer and learning to use a statistics package, you will find that the quantitative methods to be described in the remaining chapters are among the most common statistical tools. When you understand the logic of these methods, you will have a better intuitive sense of what your computer churns out.

However, these methods are simple enough so that all you need to work out the examples explained here is a pocket calculator that can compute the standard deviation and variance of a sample (S, S^2) and a population (σ, σ^2). If your budget permits, you will find statistical calculators that compute correlations and t tests quite directly; some also give precise p values (so you won't have to root around for a table of values) and can be programmed with your favorite formulas (e.g., for computing effect sizes, as described in later chapters).

In this chapter, we review some older and newer procedures to help us summarize and evaluate tendencies of the data. We will begin by showing some ways of graphing data to reveal underlying patterns, with particular emphasis on the use of stem-and-leaf displays. We then review basic summary measures that are used to indicate the central or typical value (e.g., mean, median, or mode) and the spread of scores around that value (e.g., range, standard deviation, or variance). A valuable piece of information is that population data often take the form of a symmetrical, bell-shaped curve, and we can also convert scores from distributions of widely differing types to a common metric (by z-scoring them) in order to compare scores based on distributions with widely varying means and standard deviations. In the following chapters, we will show how these concepts provide the basic ingredients of more advanced data-analytic procedures.

Visualizing Data

It is often said that a good picture is worth a thousand words, which may be particularly true in reporting research data. If we want to emphasize the overall pattern of the data, we may find it useful to create a **frequency distribution.** Such a "picture" shows the number of times each score or other unit of observation occurs in a set of scores. A frequency distribution can take the form of a chart (e.g., a histogram or a frequency polygon) or a table, such as Table 10.1.

Table 10.1	Palatability Evaluation by 50 Tasters of Two Food Products	
Score	Control product	New product
−3	1	0
−2	3	1
−1	8	2
0	17	11
+1	15	16
+2	5	13
+3	1	7

Source: From *Statistics: Guide to the Unknown* by Tanur et al. Copyright© 1972 Holden Day. Reprinted by permission of Brooks/Cole Publishing Company, Pacific Grove, CA, a division of International Thomson Publishing Inc.

This table shows part of the results of an evaluation of a new food product by Elizabeth Street and Mavis B. Carroll (1989). This aspect involved a palatability evaluation, in which Street and Carroll had 50 people taste and evaluate a new food product and a competitive food product (i.e., a control) already on the market. Instead of using a rating scale with words such as *terrible, very poor, poor, average, good, very good,* and *excellent,* the subjects were given a variation of the pictorial scale in Figure 10.1. In the scoring of the results, each of the faces was assigned a number (or score) in the sequence −3, −2, −1, 0, +1, +2, +3, with −3 implying the least agreeable and +3 being most agreeable. Table 10.1 shows the number (i.e., frequency) of tasters who chose each option in the face scale. For example, in the top row of Table 10.1, we see that only one person rated the control product −3 (least agreeable), whereas no one gave the new product this "terrible" rating.

Figure 10.2 recasts the results as two **histograms** (i.e., bar charts) showing the number (frequency) of tasters who chose each option. Notice that the implicit scale values appear on the horizontal axis (called the *x* **axis**) and the number of tasters appears on the vertical axis (called the *y* **axis**). Another name for the horizontal (*x*) axis, is the **abscissa;** another name for the vertical (*y*) axis, is the **ordinate.** (To keep these names straight, remember that the "abscissa sits," or rests, on the bottom.) Comparing the two histograms allows us to see that the new food product was rated, in general, as more agreeable than the control product.

Another conventional way of graphing the frequency of scores is called a **frequency polygon,** as shown in Figure 10.3 (often referred to as a *frequency distribution* and as a **line graph**). You may recall seeing other examples of frequency polygons in Chapter 8, such as Figure 8.1 (page 187) and Figure 8.2 (page 189). How do you know whether to use a histogram or a frequency polygon in a given situation? The rule of thumb is to use a frequency polygon (line chart) when the rise and fall of the line reflects a continuous variation in the data being graphed, and to use a histogram (bar chart) when the data are noncontinuous. In other words, the properties of the visual pattern should be compatible with the properties of the data reflected in the graph; this rule is also called the **principle of compatibility** (Kosslyn, 1994).

PLEASE CHECK THE BOX UNDER THE PICTURE WHICH EXPRESSES HOW YOU
FEEL TOWARD THE PRODUCT YOU HAVE JUST TASTED.

Figure 10.1 Pictorial taste-test scale (the scores −3 to +3 were assigned the figures from left to right) used in a palatability evaluation study.

Source: From *Statistics: Guide to the Unknown* by Tanur et al. Copyright © 1972 Holden Day. Reprinted by permission of Brooks/Cole Publishing Company, Pacific Grove, CA, a division of International Thomson Publishing Inc.

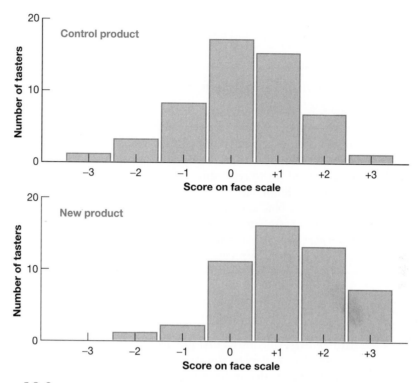

Figure 10.2   A pair of histograms that display the results in Table 10.1.

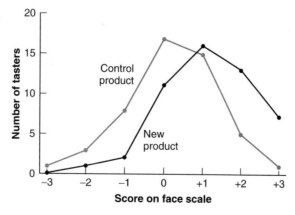

Figure 10.3   Frequency polygons that display the results in Table 10.1.

In the present case, the scores on the face scale (Figure 10.1) imply a continuum from least to most agreeable, and so this line chart is satisfactory (see also Box 10.1).

Box 10.1   The Stroop Phenomenon

In his text *Elements of Graph Design* (1994) Harvard psychologist Stephen M. Kosslyn noted what can happen when the principle of compatibility is violated. For example, suppose we use a color graph to show the performance of two teams, the Blue Team and the Red Team, and use blue ink to represent the Red Team and red ink to represent the Blue Team. This choice will create confusion because people will have a tendency to perceive the red line as reflecting the Red Team and the blue line as reflecting the Blue Team. This phenomenon, in which the mind attempts to bring coherence to quite different inputs, is called the *Stroop phenomenon* (after its discoverer, John Ridley Stroop, in 1935). As Kosslyn cautioned, "A graph is no place for the Stroop phenomenon" (p. 8).

Stem-and-Leaf Displays

No hard-and-fast rule insists that graphs always resemble these figures. For example, the **stem-and-leaf display,** invented by the noted statistician John W. Tukey, provides a flexible and effective technique for making sense of a batch of data. It is a hybrid between a table and a graph because it preserves the original numbers and yet manages to give an economic visual summary of them. It also does not involve any elaborate statistical theory; instead, it relies on the creative imagination of the researcher who uses it to test a particular hypothesis or to do exploratory data analysis (Chambers, Cleveland, Kleiner, & Tukey, 1983; Emerson & Hoaglin, 1983; Tukey, 1977).

Suppose we ask 15 students to rate a rap group, famous for its social statements and wry political observations, on a scale from 0 ("the most shallow") to 100 ("the most profound"), and we get the following results: 66, 87, 47, 74, 56, 51, 37, 70, 82, 66, 41, 52, 62, 79, 69. Figure 10.4 shows a stem-and-leaf display of these ratings. The stems are the first digits of these two-digit numbers, and the leaves are the second digits. For example, there were two scores concentrated in the 80s (82 and 87),

Stems	Leaves
8	2 7
7	0 4 9
6	2 6 6 9
5	1 2 6
4	1 7
3	7

Figure 10.4   **A stem-and-leaf display of students' ratings of a rap group.**

Depression	Stems	Hypomania
	2	5 8
	1	6
5 5 4 3 1 1 0	0	1 2 4

Figure 10.5   **Back-to-back stem-and-leaf displays of Schumann's number of compositions during his bouts of depression and hypomania (Weisberg, 1994).**

three scores in the 70s (70, 74, and 79), four scores in the 60s (62, 66, 66, and 69), and so forth. The stem-and-leaf display allows us to see the batch as a whole and to notice (1) how symmetrical it is; (2) how spread out the scores are; (3) whether any scores are outside the batch, (4) whether there are small and large concentrations of scores; (5) and whether there are any gaps (Emerson & Hoaglin, 1983).

As another illustration, in Chapter 8 we discussed a correlational study of the composer Robert Schumann's productivity and his bouts of depression and hypomania (Weisberg, 1994). Returning to Table 8.2 (page 194), we see the annual rates of musical compositions when he was feeling depressed or hypomanic. Another way of representing these data is shown in Figure 10.5, which plots the rates in adjoining stem-and-leaf displays. Called a **back-to-back stem-and-leaf display,** it lets us see at a glance that the rates are spread out more for hypomania than for depression, and that the rates during bouts of depression are concentrated in a single stem.

Percentiles and the Median

So far, the charts we have looked at were used to summarize *all* the data, but researchers also find it useful to summarize part of the batch. For example, there is often a practical value in knowing the point in the distribution below and above which a certain percentage of sampling units falls, called the *percentile:* 25% of the scores fall below the 25th percentile, 75% of the scores fall below the 75th percentile, and so on. In practice, quantitative summaries of data displayed in stem-and-leaf displays often include a listing of the scores falling at the 25th, 50th, and 75th percentiles.

In most cases, it is highly useful to know the location of the typical score and the spread of scores around that location. We will return to measures of spread in a moment, but one common measure of typical location is the 50th percentile, also called the **median** (symbolized as *Mdn*). It is one of several useful measures of **central tendency,** which means that such measures tell us the location of central or typical values. In the case of the median, the typical score is defined as the midmost score (i.e., the score below which 50 percent of all the scores fall, and above which 50 percent of all the scores fall).

For example, when the total number of scores (symbolized as *N*) is an odd number, the median is simply the midmost score. Thus, in the series 2, 3, 3, 4, 4, 5, 6, 7, 7, 8, 8, the *Mdn* = 5 because it is midmost, leaving five scores below it (2, 3, 3, 4, 4) and five scores above it (6, 7, 7, 8, 8). When the number of scores is an even number (so that there are two midmost scores), the median is computed as half the distance between the two midmost numbers. In the series 2, 3, 3, 4, 4, 7, the $Mdn = 3.5$, halfway between the 3 and the 4 at the center of the set of scores (see also Box 10.2).

Box 10.2   Ties and Medians

Ties create a small problem when one is computing medians. The series 3, 4, 4, 4, 5, 6, 7 has one score below 4 and three above. What shall we regard as the median? A useful procedure is to imagine such a series as perfectly ranked, so that a series 1, 2, 3, 3, 3 is seen as made up of a 1, a 2, a "small" 3, a "larger" 3, and a "still larger" 3. The assumption here is that more precise measurement procedures would have allowed us to break the ties. In the series 1, 2, 3, 3, 3, we regard the "small 3" as the median, because there are two scores below this particular 3 and two above it. In reporting this result, however, the researcher would simply state "$Mdn = 3$."

An easy way to locate the median (the 50th percentile) is to multiply $N + 1$ (where N is again the total number of scores in the ordered set) by .50. As reported in the stem-and-leaf display in Figure 10.5, Schumann's annual rate of musical compositions was 0, 1, 1, 3, 4, 5, 5 when he was depressed. The median is given by $.50(N + 1)$, or. $50(7 + 1) = $ 4th score in this set of seven ordered scores, or $Mdn = 3$ compositions. His annual rate of compositions was 1, 2, 4, 16, 25, 28 when he was hypomanic. The median rate is given by $.50(6 + 1) = $ 3.5th score in this set; that is, the median is halfway between the number 4 and the number 16, or $Mdn = 10$.

We can also use this procedure to locate other percentiles. The 75th percentile is $.75(N + 1)$, and the 25th percentile is $.25(N + 1)$. In the 0, 1, 1, 3, 4, 5, 5 set, the 75th percentile is $.75(8) = $ 6th score, or 5 compositions. The 25th percentile in this set is $.25(8) = $ 2nd score, that is, 1 lone composition. In the 1, 2, 4, 16, 25, 28 set, the 75th percentile is $.75(7) = $ 5.25th score (i.e., 25% of the distance between the 5th and 6th scores), which gives 25.75 compositions. For these same six scores, the 25th percentile is $.25(7) = $ 1.75th score (i.e., 75% of the distance between the 1st and 2nd scores), which is 1.75 compositions.

Applying What We Have Learned

Previously, we mentioned that the stem-and-leaf can be used not only to do hypothesis testing (also called **confirmatory data analysis**), but to do **exploratory data analysis** as well. Exploratory data analysis is detective work because we are looking for clues, and to do it properly, we must look in the right places (Tukey, 1977). Thus we would not stop with a visual display of the overall batch of data but would also

Stems	Leaves
.4	0 1 2
.3	0 0 1 2 6 6 7 7 7 8
.2	4
.1	0 2 4 6 9
.0	3

Figure 10.6   **A stem-and-leaf display of the proportion of no-shows in 20 studies (Rosenthal & Rosnow, 1975b).**

look for patterns in parts of the batch. Let us see how to do this using only the stem-and-leaf display and the calculation of percentiles.

In the previous chapter, we referred to research on volunteer characteristics. As part of that research, a number of investigators were interested in what kind of volunteers become **no-shows** (i.e., volunteers who fail to show up for their scheduled research appointments). Suppose we want to know how many volunteer subjects we need to ensure that at least 40 will show up. Some years ago, a literature review (Rosenthal & Rosnow, 1975b) turned up 20 studies that had reported the proportion of no-shows. Those proportions are listed in the stem-and-leaf display in Figure 10.6. In other words, the proportion of no-shows (reading from top to bottom) was .42 in one study, .41 in another study, .40 in another study, .38 in another study, and so forth. To continue our detective work, we will compute the 25th, 50th (*Mdn*), and 75th percentiles on these data.

Reading now from the lowest to the highest score in Figure 10.6, the sequence of values is as follows:

(1)	.03	(6)	.19	(11)	.32	(16)	.37
(2)	.10	(7)	.24	(12)	.36	(17)	.38
(3)	.12	(8)	.30	(13)	.36	(18)	.40
(4)	.14	(9)	.30	(14)	.37	(19)	.41
(5)	.16	(10)	.31	(15)	.37	(20)	.42

and the location of the median is the $.50(20 + 1) = 10.5$th score. That is, the median is halfway between the 10th score (.31) and the 11th score (.32), or *Mdn* = .32 (i.e., .315 rounded to the nearest even value).

The location of the 25th percentile score is given by $.25(N + 1)$, and therefore $.25(21) = 5.25$th score (i.e., 25% of the distance between the 5th and 6th scores), which gives us .17. The location of the 75th percentile score is $.75(N + 1)$, which we calculate as $.75(21) = 15.75$th score, 75% of the distance between the 15th and 16th scores. In this case, the 15th and 16th scores are both .37, so 75% of the distance between them is zero, and therefore the 75th percentile = .37.

To summarize this stem-and-leaf display in certain key values of the distribution, we can report the following:

Maximum value	.42
75th percentile	.37
Mdn (50th percentile)	.32
25th percentile.	.17
Minimum value	.03

What have we learned? The distance between the 25th and 75th percentiles, called the **interquartile range,** tells us that 50% of the studies that are midmost have values between .17 and .37. From the fact that the median no-show rate is .32, a practical recommendation emerges: If we are counting on 40 volunteer participants to show up for our research, we should probably schedule about 60 (i.e., one third of 60 = 20, and 60 − 20 = 40), or one-half more research subjects than we absolutely need. Incidentally, recent findings by Aditya (1996) indicate that the median no-show rate has remained relatively unchanged (still about one third), so this recommendation seems reliable.

The Mode and the Mean

Besides the median, another informative measure of central tendency is the **mode.** It is the score, or category of scores, that occurs with the greatest frequency. In the series 3, 4, 4, 4, 5, 5, 6, 6, 7, the mode = 4. The series 3, 4, 4, 4, 5, 5, 6, 7, 7, 7 has two modal scores (at values 4 and 7) and is thus described as **bimodal.** For the stem-and-leaf display in Figure 10.6, we refer to the modal *category* as the ".30s" (stem of .3 and leaves of 0, 0, 1, 2, 6, 6, 7, 7, 7, 8).

A third measure of central tendency is the ordinary mean, or **arithmetic mean,** called the **mean** for short, and symbolized as *M*. It is the arithmetic average of the scores. That is, it is the sum of the scores (ΣX) divided by the total number *(N)* of scores. The formula for the mean is

$$M = \frac{\Sigma X'}{N}$$

where Σ (the uppercase Greek letter sigma) tells us to "sum" the *X* scores. In the series 1, 2, 3, 3, 3, the sum of the scores is 12, the number of scores is 5, and therefore *M* = 12/5 = 2.4. For the stem-and-leaf values in Figure 10.6, the mean is calculated as the sum of the reported proportions (5.65) divided by 20, which gives

---

Box 10.3 **A Shortcut Calculation**

In Table 10.1, how would you calculate the mean of the scores for each of the two food products? You could add up the 50 scores (i.e., −3 to +3 ratings) in each group and divide by 50, which gives *M* = .22 for the control product and *M* = 1.18 for the new product. A shortcut procedure for averaging these scores is to multiply each score by its frequency, sum the results, and divide by *N*.

$M = .28$ (i.e., .2825 rounded to .28) as the mean proportion of no-shows (see also Box 10.3).

Dealing with Outliers

Distributions of scores may also be described as *symmetrical* or *asymmetrical,* which means that there is (symmetrical) or is not (asymmetrical) correspondence in arrangement on the opposite sides of the middle plane (see Figure 10.7). When the mean of the distribution is much larger than the median, the stretched out tail points conspicuously toward the positive end (called a **positively skewed distribution**). When the mean is smaller than the median, the stretched-out tail points toward the negative end (called a **negatively skewed distribution**). In a symmetrical (or **nonskewed**) distribution, the mean, median, and mode all have the same value.

Scores that lie far outside the normal range are called **outliers.** When a distribution of scores is strongly asymmetrical because of outliers, researchers frequently prefer a **trimmed mean** to an ordinary mean. The reason for using trimmed means is that ordinary means are the most sensitive to extreme values. Trimming implies giving the series a "light haircut" by cutting off not just the one or more outliers from one side, but the same percentage of the scores from *both* ends of the series.

Consider this strongly asymmetrical series: −20, 2, 3, 6, 7, 9, 9, 10, 10, 10. The −20 is an outlier that clearly disrupts the homogeneity of the series. To expunge outliers fairly, we trim an equal number of scores from each end. In this case, trimming one score from each end leaves 2, 3, 6, 7, 9, 9, 10, 10. What if we had *not* given the series a haircut? Would leaving the outlier in have distorted the average by very much? It depends on how the "average" is defined in a given situation. The trimmed mean = 7.0 and the untrimmed mean = 4.6, so the answer is yes in the case of the ordinary mean (*M*). The median is unaffected by trimming, so for these scores *Mdn* = 8 with or without trimming. The mode, which may be affected by trimming, is 10 for the scores before trimming but is bimodal at 9 and 10 after trimming (see also Box 10.4).

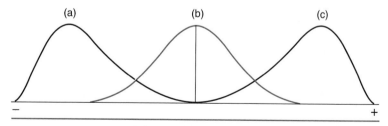

Figure 10.7 Illustrations of symmetry and asymmetry.
Only distribution (b) is symmetrical, in that both sides of the middle line are identical. When the pointed end is toward the right (or positive direction) as represented by (a), the distribution is positively skewed. When the pointed end is toward the left (or negative direction) as illustrated by (c), the distribution is negatively skewed.

Box 10.4	Misleading Interpretations and Wild Scores

Medians and trimmed means protect us in certain cases from possibly misleading interpretations based on very unusual scores. For example, if we listed the family income for 10 families and found 9 of them with 0 income and 1 with a $10 million income, the mean income of $1 million would be highly unrepresentative compared to the trimmed mean, the median, or (in this case) even the mode. Medians and trimmed means also protect us somewhat against the intrusion of certain scores recorded erroneously (also called **wild scores**). Imagine the series 4, 5, 5, 6, 6, 6, 7, 7, 8, of which the mean, median, mode, and trimmed mean are all 6. However, suppose we erred and entered the data as 4, 5, 5, 6, 6, 6, 7, 7, 80. Our new (erroneous) mean would now be 14, but our median or trimmed mean would remain unaffected.

The Crude and Extended Range

Besides knowing the central tendency (or "typical value") of a set of scores, researchers also usually want to know how "spread out" the scores are. That is, they want to know how far the scores deviate from the value of the central tendency measure. Just as there are different measures of central tendency, there are also several different measures of **spread, dispersion, or variability.** For example, we previously mentioned the *interquartile range* (i.e., the distance between the 25th and 75th percentiles), which tells us the variability characteristic of the middle 50% of the scores. Other measures of spread include the range (crude and extended), the variance, and the standard deviation.

We will start with the ordinary **range** (or **crude range**), which is simply the difference between the highest and lowest scores. If you are administering a scale, you will want to report the potential range as well as the observed (or obtained) range. If the potential range is very narrow, it may be impossible to detect any appreciable differences among the subjects; that is, there is a flaw in the design. On the other hand, it does not follow that simply having a very wide potential range will automatically result in a substantial observed range. The range is interpreted within the context of the study's purpose or objective and the nature of the instruments used.

For example, if you used a scale consisting of 20 five-point items, each item scored from 1 to 5, the potential range is from 20 to 100. You would report the crude range (CR) as being the highest score (H) minus the lowest score (L), or $CR = H - L = 80$ points. Using the same method, you would also report the crude range for the observed scores.

A further distinction is made between the crude range and **extended range** (also called the **corrected range**). In the series 2, 3, 4, 4, 6, 7, 9, the crude range is the highest score minus the lowest score, or $CR = 9 - 2 = 7$. The extended range (ER) is a refinement that recognizes that, in more precise measurements, a score of 9 may fall somewhere between 8.5 and 9.5 and that a score of 2 may fall somewhere between 1.5 and 2.5. To adjust for this possibility, we view the extended range as running from a high of 9.5 to a low of 1.5. The extended range (or corrected range) is then $9.5 - 1.5 = 8$. The extended range thus adds a half unit at the top of the distribution and a half unit at the bottom of the distribution, or a total of one full unit, and it can be computed as $ER = (H - L) + 1$ (see also Box 10.5).

Box 10.5   **Which Range Should You Report?**

For most practical purposes, you can report either the crude range (CR) or the extended range (ER). However, when measurement is not very precise and when the crude range is small, you will convey a more accurate picture of the actual range when you report the extended range. Suppose you use a 3-point rating scale in your research and all the judges' ratings are at the midpoint value (i.e., 2 on your scale of 1 to 3). The $CR = 2 - 2 = 0$, and the $ER = (2 - 2) + 1 = 1$ (because some of your judges might theoretically have rated nearly as high as 2.5 and some nearly as low as 1.5 had those ratings been possible). To decide which range to report, you can consult the ratio of the CR divided by the ER. This $CR/ER = 0$ in the extreme example just given, and $CR/ER = .90$ if the crude range is 9 and the extended range is 10. With CR/ER as high as .90, it seems reasonable to report either the CR or the ER. With CR/ER much lower, it may be more informative to report only the ER.

The crude range and the extended range tell us about the extreme scores in a set of scores, while the next two measures of spread—the variance and the standard deviation—use information from all the scores.

The Variance and the Standard Deviation

The **variance** of a set of scores tells us the deviation from the mean of the scores, but instead of using deviation values directly, it squares the deviations and averages them. In other words, it is the mean of the squared deviations of the scores (X) from their mean (M). The variance of a set of scores is also commonly referred to as the **mean square** (i.e., the mean of the squared deviations), and you will see this term again in our discussion of the F test (which is used in the statistical procedure known as *analysis of variance*). The symbol used to denote the variance of a population is σ^2 (read as "sigma-squared"), and the formula used to calculate the population variance is

$$\sigma^2 = \frac{\Sigma(X - M)^2}{N}$$

where the numerator tells us to sum the squared deviations of the individual scores from the mean of the set of scores, and the denominator tells us to divide that sum by the total number of scores.

The **standard deviation** is by far the most widely used and reported of all measures of spread around the average. Symbolized as σ, the standard deviation of a population is simply the square root of the population variance. That is,

$$\sigma = \sqrt{\sigma^2}$$

or calculated from the original data as

$$\sigma = \sqrt{\frac{\Sigma(X - M)^2}{N}}$$

Thus another name for the standard deviation is the **root mean square,** which is shorthand for the square root of the mean of the squared deviations, as the formula above shows.

If you do not have a calculator that allows you to compute the standard deviation and the variance directly from "raw" (i.e., obtained) scores (and are not using a computer with a statistics package), it is still easy to compute these values with the calculator you use to balance your checkbook. Table 10.2 shows the summary data we need to calculate the variance and standard deviation of the set of raw scores in the first column. We compute the population variance and standard deviation in five easy steps:

Step 1 (in the first column) is to add up the six raw scores ($\Sigma X = 30$), and then to find their mean by dividing the sum by the number of scores ($M = 30/6 = 5$).

Step 2 (in the second column) is to subtract the mean from each raw score. As a check on our arithmetic, we will find that these deviation scores sum to zero, that is, $\Sigma(X - M) = 0$.

Step 3 (in the last column) is to square the deviation scores in column 2, and then to add up the squared deviations, which gives $\Sigma(X - M)^2 = 24$.

Step 4 is to compute the population variance (σ^2) by substituting the value gotten in Step 3 in the numerator, and the number of scores in the denominator, which gives us

$$\sigma^2 = \frac{\Sigma(X - M)^2}{N} = \frac{24}{6} = 4$$

Table 10.2	Summary Data for Computing the Variance and the Standard Deviation	
Raw scores	$X - M$	$(X - M)^2$
2	-3	9
4	-1	1
4	-1	1
5	0	0
7	2	4
8	3	9
$\Sigma X = 30$	$\Sigma(X - M) = 0$	$\Sigma(X - M)^2 = 24$
$M = 5$		

Step 5 is to find the standard deviation, either by obtaining the square root of the value in Step 4, that is,

$$\sigma = \sqrt{\sigma^2} = \sqrt{4} = 2$$

or by direct substitution in the formula noted earlier, that is,

$$\sigma = \sqrt{\frac{\Sigma(X - M)^2}{N}} = \sqrt{\frac{24}{6}} = \sqrt{4} = 2$$

Descriptive and Inferential Formulas

Another distinction is that made between descriptive and inferential measures. Suppose we are interested in the variability of the batting averages of a favorite baseball team. We collect the scores of *all* the players and then compute the standard deviation using the formula described above. In this case, the equation used for measuring variability is characterized as a **descriptive measure,** because it describes a *complete population* of scores or events—with Greek letters used to symbolize the particular measure (e.g., σ or σ^2).

Researchers are also interested in generalizing from a sample of known scores or events to a population of unknown scores or events, which may be finite or infinite. Suppose we are interested in knowing the variability of all major-league baseball players' batting averages. We collect a sample of scores and then make inferences about the variability of scores in the population from which they were drawn. (See also Box 10.6.) The equation we now use to measure variability will be characterized as an **inferential measure**—with roman letters now used to symbolize the particular measure (e.g., S or S^2).

Box 10.6   Finite and Infinite

In the baseball example, we are dealing with both a finite sample and a finite population. **Finite** means that all the units or events can, at least in theory, be completely counted. **Infinite,** on the other hand, means boundless or without limits. Suppose, based on samples of sand that have been randomly collected, we want to make a generalization about the variability of all the sand at Atlantic City. Here, we are attempting to make an inference from a finite sample to a population of unknown "events" that is regarded as infinite (because of ecological changes and so on).

Except for the denominator and the symbol (Greek or roman), the descriptive and inferential formulas for computing variances (σ^2 and S^2)—and, therefore, standard deviations (σ and S)—are identical. In the descriptive formulas for variances and standard deviations, the numerator is divided by N (as previously shown). In the inferential formulas, the numerator is instead divided by $N - 1$ (because it can be shown statistically that, with repeated sampling, this procedure gives the most accurate inferences). Thus, if our aim is to estimate the σ^2 of a population, we use the statistic S^2 (referred to as the **unbiased estimator of the population value of σ^2**), using the following formula:

$$S^2 = \frac{\Sigma(X - M)^2}{N - 1}$$

And if we want to estimate the σ of a population, we use the statistic S and the following formula:

$$S = \sqrt{S^2} = \sqrt{\frac{\Sigma(X - M)^2}{N - 1}}$$

For example, if we wanted to generalize from the raw scores in the first column of Table 10.2 to the target population from which the scores were obtained, we would compute

$$S^2 = \frac{\Sigma(X - M)^2}{N - 1} = \frac{24}{5} = 4.8$$

and

$$S = \sqrt{S^2} = \sqrt{4.8} = 2.19$$

The Normal Distribution

When scores on a variety of types of measures (e.g., intelligence test scores, physical performance measures, or scores on an attitude scale) are collected by means of a representative sampling procedure, the distribution of these scores will form a curve that has a distinct bell-like shape (as shown in Figure 10.8). This curve is called a **normal distribution** because of the large number of different kinds of measurements that are assumed to be ordinarily (i.e., "normally") distributed in this manner.

The normal distribution is particularly useful in providing a mathematical description of populations because it can be completely described from our knowledge of just the mean and the standard deviation. For example, we can say that roughly two thirds of the area of the normal distribution is within one standard deviation of the mean, and so on. More specifically (as represented in Figure 10.8), 68.3% of

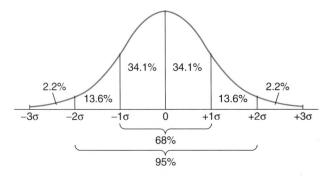

Figure 10.8 **The normal distribution divided up into standard deviation units.**

normally distributed scores will fall between -1σ and $+1\sigma$, 95.4% will fall between -2σ and $+2\sigma$, and 99.7% will fall between -3σ and $+3\sigma$. Even though over 99% of the scores fall between -3σ and $+3\sigma$, notice that the tails of the normal curve never do touch down on the horizontal continuum, or abscissa (instead, they stretch into infinity).

One reason the normal distribution is so useful is that, by some simple arithmetic, we can translate raw scores obtained by different measures into standard deviation units. Not only does this process make the different scores comparable, but we can usually specify what proportion of normally distributed scores in the population can be found in any region of the curve. Because so many measurements are distributed normally, the statistics derived from this bell-shaped curve are also very important in the testing of hypotheses. We will return to this topic in Chapter 12, but let us see how we might translate a raw score into a standard deviation unit, or standard score.

Standard Scores

A normal curve with a mean set equal to 0 and standard deviation set equal to 1 is called a **standard normal curve.** Any individual raw score can be statistically translated (referred to as **transformation**) into a **standard score** corresponding to a location on the abscissa of a standard normal curve. A standard score (also called a **z score**) expresses, in standard deviation units, the raw score's distance from the mean of the normative group. We make such a transformation by subtracting the mean of the group (M) from the individual raw score (X) and then dividing this difference by the standard deviation (σ) of the normative group, that is,

$$z \text{ score} = \frac{X - M}{\sigma}$$

For example, scores on the Scholastic Assessment Test (SAT) have a normative group mean of 500 and a standard deviation of 100. Suppose we want to transform an individual raw score of 625 into a z score with a distribution mean of 0 and standard deviation of 1. We simply calculate as follows:

$$z = \frac{X - M}{\sigma} = \frac{625 - 500}{100} = 1.25$$

and find that the raw score of 625 corresponds to a z score of 1.25, which tells us how far above the mean (in terms of the standard deviation of the distribution) this score is. To transform the z score back to the original raw score, we multiply the z score by σ and add it to M, which gives us

$$X = (z \text{ score})(\sigma) + M = (1.25)(100) + 500 = 625$$

In Table B.1 in Appendix B (see page 408), we find a listing of z scores (standardized normal deviates). The z column (with rows ranging from .0 to 4.0) lists z values to one decimal place. The remaining columns (.00 to .09) carry z to two decimal places. The body of the table shows the proportion of the area of the normal distribution that includes and is to the right of (i.e., above) the value of any particular z

on the abscissa. We can use this information to estimate the proportion of normally distributed scores in the population that are higher (or lower) than the raw score of 625 (corresponding to a z score of 1.25) on the SAT.

Given $z = 1.25$, we simply locate the intersection that corresponds to 1.2 (row 13) and .05 (column 6). That value is .1056, which estimates the proportion of SAT scores including and higher than an obtained score of 625 in the normative group of students taking the SAT. Multiplying .1056 by 100 transforms the proportion into a percentage, which informs us that 10.56% of those tested will ordinarily score as high as 625 or higher. Subtracting this percentage from 100 estimates how many ordinarily score lower than 625 (i.e., $100 - 10.56 = 89.44\%$ score lower).

Comparing Standard Scores

Note that the title of Table B.1 refers to "one-tailed" p values. We will have more to say about "one-tailed" (or "one-sided") significance levels in other chapters, but basically the term means that we are concentrating on one part of the normal distribution. In the case of a positive z score, we are focusing on the part from the midpoint (0) to the end of the right tail. If the z were a negative score, we would be concentrating on the part from the midpoint to the end of the left tail. In summary, then, a positive z score is above the mean, a negative z score is below the mean, and a zero z score is at the mean.

It is not necessary for scores on different tests to be normally distributed for us to transform them into z scores and then to compare them in terms of this common metric. For example, by calculating z scores for height and weight, we can tell whether a person is taller than he or she is heavy, relative to others in the normative distribution of height and weight. However, only if they are distributed approximately normally can we tell from a z score how many scored above or below a given z score. We can do so for SAT scores because they are approximately normally distributed.

As an illustration of the utility of z scores, imagine that an instructor has two measures of course grades on five male and five female students, as shown in Table 10.3. One set of scores (X_1) is based on an essay exam of 50 points with $M = 21.2$ and $\sigma = 11.69$, and another (X_2) is based on a multiple-choice exam of 100 points with $M = 68.8$ and $\sigma = 17.47$. The instructor transforms the raw scores into standard scores, with the results shown in the z_1 and z_2 columns. For example, Student 1 received a raw score of 42 on Exam 1, which the instructor converts to a z score by computing $(42 - 21.2)/11.69 = 1.78$. Student 1's score on Exam 1 is thus almost two standard deviations above the mean, but Student 2's score on the same exam is approximately one standard deviation *below* the mean.

The z scores take this information into account, allowing the instructor to make easy comparisons within and across students. Here, the instructor counted the two exams equally to get the average score (in the last column), but it is easy enough to weight them. Suppose she had wanted to count the second exam twice as much as the first exam; she would double the Exam 2 z scores before averaging the two exams and divide by 3 instead of 2. Notice also that the standard deviation (SD) at the bottom of the last column is not 1.0; the reason is that the averages of two or more z scores

Table 10.3   Raw Scores (X) and Standard Scores (z) on Two Exams

Student ID and gender	Exam 1 X_1 score	Exam 1 z_1 score	Exam 2 X_2 score	Exam 2 z_2 score	Average of z_1 and z_2 scores
1 (M)	42	+1.78	90	+1.21	+1.50
2 (M)	9	−1.04	40	−1.65	−1.34
3 (F)	28	+0.58	92	+1.33	+0.96
4 (M)	11	−0.87	50	−1.08	−0.98
5 (M)	8	−1.13	49	−1.13	−1.13
6 (F)	15	−0.53	63	−0.33	−0.43
7 (M)	14	−0.62	68	−0.05	−0.34
8 (F)	25	+0.33	75	+0.35	+0.34
9 (F)	40	+1.61	89	+1.16	+1.38
10 (F)	20	−0.10	72	+0.18	+0.04
Sum (Σ)	212	0	688	0	0
Mean (M)	21.2	0	68.8	0	0
SD (σ)	11.69	1.0	17.47	1.0	0.98

are not themselves distributed as z scores with $\sigma = 1.0$. If we wanted the averages of these z scores to be distributed as z, we would first have to z-score these averages.

Summary of Ideas

1. In a frequency distribution, a set of scores is arranged according to incidence of occurrence either in a table or in a figure such as a histogram or a frequency polygon.
2. In a stem-and-leaf display, the original data are preserved with any desired precision so that we can visually detect the symmetry, spread, and concentration of the batch as well as any outliers.
3. A percentile locates a score in a distribution by defining the point below which a given proportion (or percentage) of the cases falls.
4. The median (*Mdn*, or 50th percentile) is the midmost score of a distribution.
5. A stem-and-leaf display used to analyze a reported proportion of no-shows revealed that it is a good idea to schedule half again as many subjects as are needed.
6. The mode is the score (or the batch of scores in a stem-and-leaf display) occurring with the greatest frequency.
7. The mean (*M*) is the arithmetic average of a set of scores.
8. Trimmed means are useful when distributions are strongly asymmetrical.
9. Medians and trimmed means often protect us against the intrusion of wild scores.

10. The range is the distance between the highest and the lowest scores, sometimes corrected (extended) to increase precision.

11. The variance (or mean square) is the average squared distance from the mean of all the scores.

12. The standard deviation (or root mean square) is the square root of the variance.

13. Descriptive measures (e.g., σ and σ^2) are used to calculate population values, and inferential measures (S and S^2) are used to estimate population values based on a sample of values.

14. The normal distribution is a bell-shaped curve that is completely described by the mean and the standard deviation.

15. We calculate standard scores (z scores) by transforming raw scores to standard deviation units.

16. Standard scores permit the comparison (and averaging) of scores from different distributions of widely differing means and standard deviations.

Key Terms

Multiple-Choice Questions for Review (answers are found on page 351)

1. A graph in which the horizontal axis contains the score values, and in which the vertical axis reflects the frequency of a given score, is called a (a) stem-and-leaf display; (b) cascade plot; (c) data summary graph; (d) frequency distribution.

2. Participants in a study at Iona College are asked to take a test of anxiety. Forty percent of the subjects receive scores lower than 12 on this test. For this sample, the value 12 is considered the (a) mean; (b) 40th percentile; (c) 60th percentile; (d) median.

3. Which of the following is considered a measure of central tendency? (a) mean; (b) 50th percentile; (c) mode; (d) all of the above

4. In a data set consisting of 0, 0, 0, 2, 2, 8, what is the mode? (a) 0; (b) 1; (c) 2; (d) 8

5. In the data shown above, what is the M? (a) 0; (b) 1; (c) 2; (d) 8

6. In the same data set, what is the Mdn? (a) 0; (b) 1; (c) 2; (d) 8

7. Consider the following set of data points: 0, 1, 2, 3, 4. What is the crude range of these scores? (a) 2.5; (b) 0; (c) 4; (d) 5

8. Formulas that are used to calculate information about a population are called ———— . (a) popular; (b) descriptive; (c) inferential; (d) none of the above

9. A standard normal distribution has a mean of ———— and a standard deviation of ———— . (a) 0; 1; (b) 1; 0; (c) 1; 1; (d) cannot be determined from this information

10. A DePaul researcher administers an attitude scale to a group of I/O students. The average score is 2, and the standard deviation is 2. Suppose that you receive a score of 0. What is your z score? (a) 2, (b) −2; (c) 0; (d) −1.

Discussion Questions for Review (answers are found on page 352)

1. A University of Oregon student conducted a study on anxiety in 11 business executives. Their scores on a standardized test of anxiety were 32, 16, 29, 41, 33, 37, 27, 30, 22, 38, and 33. Can you reconstruct the student's stem-and-leaf plot for these scores? What is the median of these scores, and what are the extended range and the interquartile range?

2. A Fordham student is interested in studying ways of cutting down noise pollution in Manhattan. Her first step is to buy a machine that will measure the loudness of various sounds. In order to decide which machine to buy, she tests four brands against a standard tone of 85 decibels for five trials each, with the results shown below. Assuming that all the machines have the same price, which should be her first choice?

	Machine A	Machine B	Machine C	Machine D
	76	84	83	85
	82	87	89	81
	78	83	91	93
	84	85	77	89
	80	86	105	77
M	80	85	89	85
S	3.16	1.58	10.49	6.32

Oops—the manufacturer has run out of her first-choice brand. Which machine would you recommend as her second choice, and why?

3. A Haverford student recorded the following scores: 22, 14, 16, 24, 13, 26, 17, 98, 11, 9, and 21. What measure of central tendency would you advise him to calculate? Why?

4. A Florida State student was looking at her grades for the midterm and the final exam. On the midterm she got a score of 58 and the class mean was 52 with a standard deviation of 12. On the final she got a score of 110; the class mean was 100 with a standard deviation of 30. On which test did she do better?

5. A Brandeis student calls home to tell his family that he just received a score of 2 on a new IQ test. As they wonder why they are spending so much money on his tuition, he reassures them that 2 is his z score. What percentage of the population did he score above?

6. A University of Missouri professor has three sections with three graduate assistants—Tom, Dick, and Harry—each of whom has six students. The time has come to grade papers. In order to ensure uniform grading standards across the sections, the professor instructs the assistants to give an average score of 8.0 (equivalent to B−) on a scale of 1 to 12 (where 1 represents a grade of F, and 12 represents a grade of A). The assistants submit the following sets of grades:

Tom	Dick	Harry
12	8	7
6	8	7
5	10	8
5	7	5
8	8	6
12	7	9

The professor calls in Harry and says, "You have not followed my instructions. Your scores are biased toward having your section do better than it is supposed to." Calculate the means of each section, and then argue the truth or falsity of the professor's accusation. The professor next calls in Tom and Dick and says, "Although both of your sections have a mean grade of 8.0, Tom's scores look more spread out." Calculate and then compare the variance of the scores in the sections to decide whether the professor is right. Which is a better grade (relative to one's own section), a 5 in Tom's section or a 7 in Dick's section?

7. Compute the σ, σ^2, S, and S^2 on the no-show data in the stem-and-leaf display shown in Figure 10.6 (page 235).

11 Examining Relationships

The Correlation Coefficient

We have seen that researchers view variables not in isolation, but as being systematically and meaningfully associated with or related to other variables. In this chapter, we examine how correlational procedures are used to measure the strength of association between two variables (X and Y). In particular, we describe correlation coefficients that reflect the degree to which mutual relations between X and Y resemble a straight line (also called **linearity**). The **Pearson r** is the correlation coefficient of choice in such situations, with values of 1.0 (positive *or* negative) indicating a perfect linear relation (see also Box 11.1). A positive r means that an increase in X is associated with an increase in Y, whereas a negative r means that an increase is X is associated with a *decrease* in Y.

Causation implies correlation (or covariation), but finding that X and Y are correlated does not necessarily imply causation. In Chapter 7, we mentioned that, although covariation is essential evidence for making causal inferences, other requirements of evidence include temporal precedence and internal validity. Another important consideration is whether another variable that is correlated with both X and Y could be the cause of both—called the **third-variable problem.** For

PREVIEW QUESTIONS

- What are continuous and discrete variables, and when are discrete variables dichotomous?
- What is the "third-variable problem"?
- Why is the Pearson r measure called the *product-moment correlation?*
- When would you use a rank-order correlation?
- Why is the Spearman rho classified as a product-moment r?
- What is the purpose of the point-biserial r?
- How is dummy coding used to quantify dichotomous variables?
- How is the phi coefficient related to the Pearson r?
- What do these different names tell us about characteristics of the data?

Box 11.1 **Galton, Pearson, and *r***

In an earlier chapter we mentioned Francis Galton's work. One of his many research projects concerned the relationship between traits of fathers and their adult sons. Galton, who was very intuitive about both research methods and statistics, invented a way of measuring the strength of association between the two variables. Inspired by his mentor's statistical thinking, Karl Pearson (1857–1936) perfected Galton's idea into the more general method of correlation that has come to be known as the Pearson *r* (Stigler, 1986).

example, it is well known that there is a high positive correlation between the size of children's feet and their spelling ability. Should we therefore use foot stretchers to increase children's spelling scores? The answer, of course, is no, because it is not the length of the children's feet that is the causal variable but the fact that children with bigger feet are usually older, and older children spell better (Paulos, 1991). In other words, a third variable (age) can account for the correlation between *X* and *Y*.

We will begin by examining what different values of *r* look like. Then we proceed through the steps in computing the correlation coefficient when the raw data have different characteristics (previewed in Table 11.1), such as when the values of *X* and *Y* are continuous or dichotomous. A **continuous variable** means that we can always imagine another value falling between any two adjacent scores, whereas a **dichotomous variable** is divided into two discrete parts (more generally referred to as a **discrete variable,** i.e., a variable with two or more distinct or separate parts). For example, a psychophysicist who studies the discrimination of pitch (i.e., the highness or lowness of a tone) may want to correlate changes in the frequency of sound waves with the differing ability of subjects to discriminate the changes. Both variables are said to be continuous, in that we can imagine a score of 1.5 between 1 and 2, or 1.55 between 1.5 and 1.6. Alternatively, suppose the psychophysicist wants to correlate the subjects' gender with their abilities to discriminate pitch. Pitch discrimination is a

Table 11.1 Basic Forms of Product-Moment Correlations

Common name	Characteristics of the data
Pearson *r*	Two continuous variables, such as the correlation of scores on the Scholastic Assessment Test (SAT) with grade point average (GPA) after four years of college
Spearman rho (r_s)	Two ranked variables, such as the correlation of the ranking of the top 25 college basketball teams by sports writers (Associated Press ranking) with the ranking of the same teams by college coaches (*USA Today* ranking)
Point-biserial (r_{pb})	One continuous and one dichotomous variable, such as the correlation of subjects' gender with their performance on the SAT-Verbal
Phi coefficient (ϕ)	Two dichotomous variables, such as the correlation of subjects' gender with their yes-no responses to a specific question

continuous variable, but gender is a discrete variable that is dichotomous (i.e., divided into two separate parts). We can frequently create dichotomies by splitting variables at the median point (the split is called a *median split;* we will return to this idea when we discuss the binomial effect-size display in the next chapter).

Visualizing the Correlation Coefficient

In addition to the graphics described in the preceding chapter, another informative visual display is called a **scatter plot** (or **scatter diagram**). It takes its name from the fact that it looks like a cloud of scattered dots. Each dot represents the intersection of a line extended from a point on the X axis (the horizontal axis, or abscissa) and a line extended from a point on the Y axis (the vertical axis, or ordinate). To illustrate, Table 11.2 repeats the data we used in the previous chapter to explain z scores, and we will continue to discuss these data in this chapter. For now, we will concentrate on the raw scores (i.e., the X_1 and X_2 scores) of these 10 students on the two exams. Figure 11.1 displays these scores in the form of a scatter plot.

By way of comparison, Figure 11.2 shows additional scatter plots (each containing 50 dots) that represent different values of the correlation coefficient, including zero and near-perfect rs. However, remember that even a perfect r is not necessarily indicative of a cause-and-effect relation, because there might be a third variable (i.e., the true cause) that correlates perfectly with both X and Y (see also Box 11.2). Notice in Figure 11.2 that the higher the correlation is, the more tightly clustered along a straight line are the dots. Observe also that the cloud of dots slopes up for positive correlations and slopes down for negative correlations, whereas the linearity becomes clearer as the correlation becomes higher. From these diagrams, what would you guess is the size of the Pearson r represented by the data in Figure 11.1?

Table 11.2   Raw and Standardized Data for Pearson r Correlation Coefficient

Student ID and gender	Exam 1		Exam 2		Product of z_1 and z_2 scores
	X_1 score	z_1 score	X_2 score	z_2 score	
1 (M)	42	+1.78	90	+1.21	+2.15
2 (M)	9	−1.04	40	−1.65	+1.72
3 (F)	28	+0.58	92	+1.33	+0.77
4 (M)	11	−0.87	50	−1.08	+0.94
5 (M)	8	−1.13	49	−1.13	+1.28
6 (F)	15	−0.53	63	−0.33	+0.17
7 (M)	14	−0.62	68	−0.05	+0.03
8 (F)	25	+0.33	75	+0.35	+0.12
9 (F)	40	+1.61	89	+1.16	+1.87
10 (F)	20	−0.10	72	+0.18	−0.02
Sum (Σ)	212	0	688	0	+9.03
Mean (M)	21.2	0	68.8	0	.90
SD (σ)	11.69	1.0	17.47	1.0	

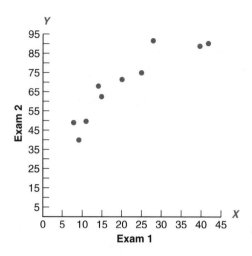

Figure 11.1   Scatter plot of raw scores in Table 11.2

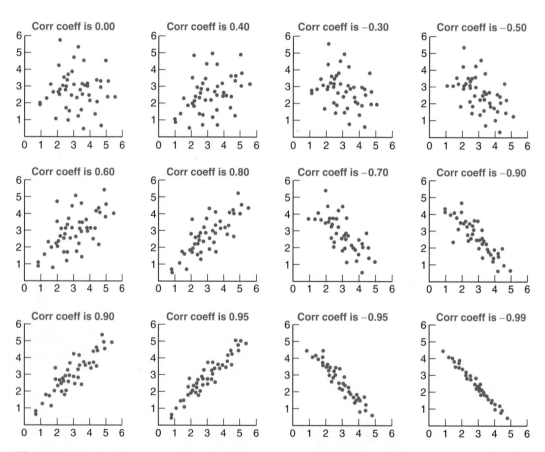

Figure 11.2   Scatter plots representing different values of the correlation coefficient.

Source: From *Statistics* (2nd ed., pp. 119, 121), by D. Freedman, R. Pisani, R. Purves, and A. Adhikari, 1991, New York: W. W. Norton. Reproduced by permission of the first author and the publisher.

Box 11.2 **The Third-Variable Problem**

John Paulos, a mathematician who has drawn attention to mathematical illiteracy (he calls it "innumeracy"), has mentioned other fascinating examples of the third-variable problem (Paulos, 1990). One concerns the positive correlation between milk consumption and the incidence of cancer in various societies. Paulos explains this correlation by the fact that people in relatively wealthy societies live longer, and increased longevity increases the likelihood of getting cancer. Thus any health practice (such as milk drinking) that increases longevity will probably correlate positively with cancer incidence. Another example is the small negative correlation observed between death rates and divorce rates (i.e., more divorce, less death) in various regions of the country. The third variable proposed by Paulos to explain this relation is the age distribution of the various regions, because older married couples are less likely to divorce and more likely to die than younger couples.

Calculating the Pearson r

There are many useful formulas for computing the Pearson r correlation coefficient. But the following formula (which defines the Pearson r conceptually) can be used quite generally, and we will use it later to show you that all the correlations discussed in this chapter (defined in Table 11.1) are Pearson rs in one form or another:

$$r_{xy} = \frac{\Sigma z_x z_y}{N}$$

This formula signifies that the linear correlation between two variables (X and Y) is equal to the sum of the products of the z scores of X and Y divided by the number (N) of pairs of X and Y scores (see also Box 11.3).

Box 11.3 **Linearity and Nonlinearity**

Linearity means that the mutual relation between two variables resembles a straight line, whereas **nonlinearity** can take many different forms (e.g., U-shaped, J-shaped, and wave-shaped curves). Suppose you were studying the relationship between age and the latency of some response, and you found that latency decreased up to a certain age and then gradually increased. If you plotted the results by means of a frequency polygon, your curve showing this nonlinear relation would resemble a U with age plotted on the abscissa (X axis) and latency of response (from low to high) on the ordinate (Y axis). Other examples of nonlinear relations include curves for learning, extinction, dark adaptation, and response rate as a function of the amount of reinforcement (e.g., Grant, 1956; Malmo, 1959).

The Pearson r correlation is also called the **product-moment correlation** because the zs (in the numerator of the formula) are distances from the mean (also called *moments*) that we multiply by each other to form "products." To use this formula, we would begin by transforming the raw scores to z scores following the procedure described in the previous chapter. That is, we would calculate the mean and the standard deviation of each column of raw scores and substitute in the $(X - M)/\sigma$ formula. In Table 11.2 we see such z scores corresponding to the students' raw scores on Exam 1 and Exam 2. Notice that, for Student 5, the z score for Exam 1 is identical to the z score for Exam 2, even though the raw scores are very different. The reason, of course, is that the z scores for Exam 1 were computed by the use of the mean and the standard deviation of Exam 1 (21.2 and 11.69, respectively), whereas the z scores for Exam 2 were computed by the use of the mean and the standard deviation of that exam (68.8 and 17.47, respectively). Instead of averaging the z scores (as we did in the previous chapter for a very different purpose), the last column in Table 11.2 gives the products of the z scores and their mean, showing that the Pearson $r = .90$ (see also Box 11.4).

Box 11.4 | **Shortcut for Computing Pearson r**

If you are working with a statistics package and a computer, or if you have a statistical calculator that computes rs directly, it is a snap to calculate the Pearson r. But if all you have is a simple pocket calculator, there is an easier way to calculate the Pearson r than by the conceptual formula. All you need do is cumulate scores and squares of scores and then use the following formula, which is based on raw scores alone:

$$r_{xy} = \frac{N\Sigma XY - (\Sigma X)(\Sigma Y)}{\sqrt{[N\Sigma X^2 - (\Sigma X)^2][N\Sigma Y^2 - (\Sigma Y)^2]}}$$

where N = the number of X and Y pairs of scores, and Σ directs us to sum a set of values. This formula may look difficult, but it is not hard to use. All we need are the sums of the scores and of the squared scores. To illustrate, Table 11.3 shows the basic data required to compute r from the raw scores in Table 11.2. Substituting these numbers in the formula above gives

$$r_{xy} = \frac{10(16,430) - (212)(688)}{\sqrt{[10(5,860) - (212)^2][10(50,388) - (688)^2]}}$$

$$= \frac{164,300 - 145,856}{\sqrt{(58,600 - 44,944)(503,880 - 473,344)}}$$

$$= \frac{18,444}{\sqrt{(13,656)(30,536)}} = \frac{18,444}{\sqrt{416,999,616}} = \frac{18,444}{20,420.57} = .90$$

When using this formula, don't forget to take the square root of the denominator!

Table 11.3	Basic Data for Computing Pearson r (see Box 11.4)				
	Exam 1		Exam 2		
Student	X	X^2	Y	Y^2	XY
1	42	1,764	90	8,100	3,780
2	9	81	40	1,600	360
3	28	784	92	8,464	2,576
4	11	121	50	2,500	550
5	8	64	49	2,401	392
6	15	225	63	3,969	945
7	14	196	68	4,624	952
8	25	625	75	5,625	1,875
9	40	1,600	89	7,921	3,560
10	20	400	72	5,184	1,440
Sum (Σ)	212	5,860	688	50,388	16,430

Spearman Rank Correlation

Suppose that our data are ranks rather than scores on a rating scale. When the data are in this form, the correlation coefficient is called the **Spearman rho (r_s),** but this, as you will see, is nothing more than the product-moment r calculated on numbers that happen to be ranks. Because ranked numbers are more predictable (in the sense that knowing only the number of pairs of scores tells us both the mean and the standard deviation of the scores that have been ranked), we can work with the formula below for scores that have been ranked:

$$r_s = 1 - \frac{6\Sigma D^2}{N^3 - N}$$

where 6 is a constant value, and N = the number of pairs of scores or ranks. The only new element is D, the difference between the ranks assigned to the two variables being correlated.

To illustrate the use of this formula, we turn to Table 11.4, which shows a portion of the data collected by Paul Slovic (1987) in his investigation of the perception of risk. He was interested in comparing the judgments people make when they are asked to characterize and evaluate hazardous activities and technologies. This table shows the overall rankings made by 15 national experts on risk assessment and 40 members of the League of Women Voters (LWV). We see, for example, that the experts ranked motor vehicles as most hazardous (Rank 1) and skiing as least hazardous (Rank 30), whereas the LWV members ranked nuclear power as most hazardous (Rank 1) and vaccinations as least hazardous (Rank 30). Notice that the sums of the ranks are equal for the two variables (465). The column headed D lists the differences between the ranks. For example, the difference in ranking of nuclear power is

Table 11.4	Ordering of Perceived Risk for 30 Activities and Technologies			
Activity or technology	Leage of Women Voters	Experts	D	D²
Nuclear power	1	20	−19	361
Motor vehicles	2	1	1	1
Handguns	3	4	−1	1
Smoking	4	2	2	4
Motorcycles	5	6	−1	1
Alcoholic beverages	6	3	3	9
General (private) aviation	7	12	−5	25
Police work	8	17	−9	81
Pesticides	9	8	1	1
Surgery	10	5	5	25
Fire fighting	11	18	−7	49
Large construction	12	13	−1	1
Hunting	13	23	−10	100
Spray cans	14	26	−12	144
Mountain climbing	15	29	−14	196
Bicycles	16	15	1	1
Commercial aviation	17	16	1	1
Electric power (nonnuclear)	18	9	9	81
Swimming	19	10	9	81
Contraceptives	20	11	9	81
Skiing	21	30	−9	81
X-rays	22	7	15	225
High school and college football	23	27	−4	16
Railroads	24	19	5	25
Food preservatives	25	14	11	121
Food coloring	26	21	5	25
Power mowers	27	28	−1	1
Prescription antibiotics	28	24	4	16
Home appliances	29	22	7	49
Vaccinations	30	25	5	25
Sum (Σ)	465	465	0	1,828

Source: From "Perception of Risk," by P. Slovic, 1987, *Science, 236,* p. 281. Copyright © 1987 by American Association for the Advancement of Science. Reprinted with permission of Paul Slovic and the American Association for the Advancement of Science.

computed as $D = 1 - 20 = -19$. The sum of the D scores is always 0. The column headed D^2 shows such differences squared, so that $(-19)^2 = 361$.

The sum of the squared differences (indicated as 1,828 at the bottom of the column headed D^2) is now substituted in the Spearman rho formula:

$$r_s = 1 - \frac{6(1,828)}{(30)^3 - 30} = .59$$

In interpreting rank correlations, we may use the *D* scores and the ranks to identify similarities and differences in the results. A positive difference tells us that the LWV members perceived the activity or technology as less risky than did the experts, whereas a negative difference indicates the opposite conclusion. For example, we see that these two groups of raters disagreed little about the high risks associated with motor vehicles, handguns, and motorcycles (*D*s of +1 or −1). There was little

| Table 11.5 | Ranked and Standardized Data for Spearman rho Correlation | | | | |

Activity or Technology	League of Women Voters		Experts		Product of z scores
	Rank	z score	Rank	z score	
Nuclear power	1	−1.68	20	+0.52	−0.87
Motor vehicles	2	−1.56	1	−1.68	+2.62
Handguns	3	−1.44	4	−1.33	+1.92
Smoking	4	−1.33	2	−1.56	+2.07
Motorcycles	5	−1.21	6	−1.10	+1.33
Alcoholic beverages	6	−1.10	3	−1.44	+1.58
General aviation	7	−0.98	12	−0.40	+0.39
Police work	8	−0.87	17	+0.17	−0.15
Pesticides	9	−0.75	8	−0.87	+0.65
Surgery	10	−0.64	5	−1.21	+0.77
Fire fighting	11	−0.52	18	+0.29	−0.15
Large construction	12	−0.40	13	−0.29	+0.12
Hunting	13	−0.29	23	+0.87	−0.25
Spray cans	14	−0.17	26	+1.21	−0.21
Mountain climbing	15	−0.06	29	+1.56	−0.09
Bicycles	16	+0.06	15	−0.06	0.00
Commercial aviation	17	+0.17	16	+0.06	+0.01
Electric power	18	+0.29	9	−0.75	−0.22
Swimming	19	+0.40	10	−0.64	−0.26
Contraceptives	20	+0.52	11	−0.52	−0.27
Skiing	21	+0.64	30	+1.68	+1.08
X-rays	22	+0.75	7	−0.98	−0.74
High school and college football	23	+0.87	27	+1.33	+1.16
Railroads	24	+0.98	19	+0.40	+0.39
Food preservatives	25	+1.10	14	−0.17	−0.19
Food coloring	26	+1.21	21	+0.64	+0.77
Power mowers	27	+1.33	28	+1.44	+1.92
Prescription antibiotics	28	+1.44	24	+0.98	+1.41
Home appliances	29	+1.56	22	+0.75	+1.17
Vaccinations	30	+1.68	25	+1.10	+1.85
Sum (Σ)	465	0	465	0	17.82
Mean (M)	15.50	0	15.50	0	.59
SD (σ)	8.655	1.00	8.655	1.00	—

disagreement about the much lower risk associated with power mowers ($D = -1$), but there was strong disagreement about nuclear power ($D = -19$), X-rays ($D = 15$), and mountain climbing ($D = -14$).

To show why we characterized the Spearman rho as a Pearson r calculated on numbers that happen to be ranks, we turn to Table 11.5 on page 257. The columns containing z scores show the standard scores of the ranks. For example, to find the z score corresponding to the LWV's ranking of nuclear power, we computed

$$z = \frac{X - M}{\sigma} = \frac{1 - 15.50}{8.655} = -1.68$$

The last column shows the products of the z-scored ranks, with the sum and mean indicated at the bottom. Recalling that the mean of the products is the Pearson r, we see that it is identical to the value we obtained using the Spearman rho formula, that is,

$$r_s = \frac{\Sigma z_x z_y}{N} = \frac{17.82}{30} = .59$$

Suppose we are working with raw scores that are continuous but we want to recast them as ranks and compute a Spearman rho (see also Box 11.5). Table 11.6

Box 11.5   **Using Rankings for Quick Estimates**

Why use rankings when continuous data are available? In almost all cases, it is preferable to stay with the continuous data and use the Pearson r, but suppose you wanted a quick estimate of the correlation between the six pairs of scores shown below:

	Raw score for X	Raw score for Y	Rank of X	Rank of Y
Pair 1	73.8	801.76	2	1
Pair 2	186.2	732.90	1	2
Pair 3	44.4	539.57	3	3
Pair 4	38.6	206.11	4	5
Pair 5	37.5	210.56	5	4
Pair 6	21.8	159.33	6	6

Clearly it would be tedious to calculate the Pearson r by hand from the raw scores in the first two columns. Transforming the scores into ranks and then calculating the Spearman rho on the basis of the values in the last two columns is much easier, although by sacrificing the continuity of the raw scores, we are also missing the fine distinctions. In some situations, however, we may prefer to use rank ordering, such as when judges have no measuring instrument and must resort to rank ordering or when the raw scores include extreme outliers that may lead to misleading correlations (ranked scores never have extreme outliers).

Table 11.6	Raw Data from Table 11.2 Ranked for Spearman Rho Correlation					
	Exam 1		**Exam 2**			
Student	X_1 score	Rank	X_2 score	Rank	D	D^2
1	42	1	90	2	-1	1
2	9	9	40	10	-1	1
3	28	3	92	1	2	4
4	11	8	50	8	0	0
5	8	10	49	9	1	1
6	15	6	63	7	-1	1
7	14	7	68	6	1	1
8	25	4	75	4	0	0
9	40	2	89	3	-1	1
10	20	5	72	5	0	0
Sum (Σ)	212	55[a]	688	55[a]	0[b]	10

[a]Note that the sum of the ranks is equal for the two variables.
[b]Note that the sum of D is always 0.

shows how this is done from our continuing example. The students are ranked from 1 (highest raw score) to 10 (lowest raw score), and again the D score is the difference between these rankings. The sum of the squared differences (indicated as 10 at the bottom of the column headed D^2) is substituted in the numerator of the Spearman rho formula:

$$r_s = 1 - \frac{6\Sigma D^2}{N^3 - N}$$

$$= 1 - \frac{6(10)}{(10)^3 - 10} = .94$$

Point-Biserial Correlation

Another special case of the product-moment r is the **point-biserial correlation** (r_{pb}). In this case one variable is continuous, and the other variable is dichotomous with arbitrarily applied values such as 0 and 1 or -1 and $+1$. The quantification of the two levels of a dichotomous variable is called **dummy coding** when 0 and 1 are used. Dummy coding is a tremendously useful procedure, for it allows us to quantify dichotomous variables. For example, suppose the dichotomous variable is the treatment condition to which the subjects have been assigned in a study consisting of an experimental and a control group. To dummy-code this variable, we simply record 1 for experimental and 0 for control. Other examples of dichotomous variables that can be easily recast into 0s and 1s are gender (female vs. male), survival rate (live vs. die), and success rate (succeed vs. fail).

Going back to our continuing example in Table 11.2, suppose we want to compare males with females on Exam 1. The scores on that exam were as follows:

Males	Females
42	28
9	15
11	25
8	40
14	20

Although we have two groups of scores, the arrangement does not look like the typical one for a correlation coefficient—where we would expect to see *pairs* of scores (e.g., X_1 and X_2 scores, or X and Y scores). The data arrangement rewritten into a form that "looks more correlational" is shown in Table 11.7.

The first column of data repeats the identification (ID) and gender information, and the next two columns show again the raw and standardized scores for Exam 1. Under "Student's gender," the first column shows the dummy-coded scores for gender, with the female students coded 1 and the male students coded 0. The next column shows the z-score results of standardizing the dummy-coded values. For example, to get the z score for Student 1's gender, we computed

$$z = \frac{X - M}{\sigma} = \frac{0 - 0.5}{0.5} = -1$$

where X = the dummy score of 0 for Student 1, M = the mean of the column of dummy scores ($M = 5/10 = 0.5$), and σ = the standard deviation (SD) shown at the bottom of that column (0.5).

Table 11.7 Raw, Dummy-Coded, and Standardized Data for Point-Biserial Correlation

Student ID and gender	Exam 1 Raw score	Exam 1 z score	Student's gender Dummy code	Student's gender z score	Product of z scores
1 (M)	42	+1.78	0	−1	−1.78
2 (M)	9	−1.04	0	−1	+1.04
3 (F)	28	+0.58	1	+1	+0.58
4 (M)	11	−0.87	0	−1	+0.87
5 (M)	8	−1.13	0	−1	+1.13
6 (F)	15	−0.53	1	+1	−0.53
7 (M)	14	−0.62	0	−1	+0.62
8 (F)	25	+0.33	1	+1	+0.33
9 (F)	40	+1.61	1	+1	+1.61
10 (F)	20	−0.10	1	+1	−0.10
Sum (Σ)	212	0	5	0	+3.77
Mean (M)	21.2	0	0.5	0	.38
SD (σ)	11.69	1.0	0.5	1.0	

Notice that, as always, the z scores sum to zero; another sum would signal either a computational or a recording mistake. Observe also that the standard deviation scores within the column of z scores are -1 for a dummy code of 0 and a $+1$ for a dummy code of 1, a situation always found when the number of 0 scores equals the number of 1 scores. And finally, the sum of the products of the z scores (shown at the bottom of the last column of data) is $+3.77$. When we divide this result by the number of students ($N = 10$), we find the point-biserial correlation, that is,

$$r_{pb} = \frac{\Sigma z_x z_y}{N} = \frac{3.77}{10} = .38$$

which tells us that this group of students showed a moderate relation between gender and scores on Exam 1.

Phi Coefficient

Not infrequently, both of the variables to be correlated are dichotomous. In Chapter 8, we noted a hypothetical case in which people who ate a burger became sick. Going back to Table 8.1 (page 184), suppose we are interested in quantifying the relation between these two variables. In such a situation, we have another special case of the product-moment r called the **phi coefficient** (symbolized by ϕ, the lowercase Greek letter phi). In this instance, both variables are dichotomous (with arbitrarily applied numerical values such as 0 and 1 or -1 and $+1$).

We can find the value of the phi coefficient in several different ways; two of them are shown here. The conceptual procedure, represented in Table 11.8, illustrates why

Table 11.8 Dummy-Coded and Standardized Data for Phi Coefficient

Persons	Ate a burger? Y = 1; N = 0	z score	Got food poisoning? Y = 1; N = 0	z score	Product of z scores
Mimi	1	+1.183	1	+1.183	1.400
Gail	0	−0.846	0	−0.846	0.716
Connie	0	−0.846	0	−0.846	0.716
Jerry	0	−0.846	0	−0.846	0.716
Greg	0	−0.846	0	−0.846	0.716
Dwight	0	−0.846	0	−0.846	0.716
Nancy	1	+1.183	1	+1.183	1.400
Richard	0	−0.846	0	−0.846	0.716
Kerry	0	−0.846	0	−0.846	0.716
Michele	1	+1.183	1	+1.183	1.400
John	1	+1.183	1	+1.183	1.400
Sheila	1	+1.183	1	+1.183	1.400
Sum (Σ)	5	0.00	5	0.00	12.012
Mean (M)	.417	0.00	.417	0.00	1.00
SD (σ)	.493	1.000	.493	1.000	.337

we say that ϕ is another special case of the product-moment r. Under the "Ate burger?" heading, the first column shows the dummy scores of Yes = 1 and No = 0. The next column shows standardized scores corresponding to the dummy-coded values. So, for example, we computed the z score corresponding to Mimi's 1 as

$$z = \frac{X - M}{\sigma} = \frac{1 - .417}{.493} = +1.183$$

Similarly, under the "Got food poisoning?" heading, the dummy coding is again Yes = 1 and No = 0, followed by the corresponding z scores.

The last column in this table shows the mean of the product of the z scores as 1.00, which is the phi coefficient, that is,

$$\phi = \frac{\Sigma z_x z_y}{N} = \frac{12.012}{12} = 1.00$$

In other words, we have treated phi (ϕ) no differently from any product-moment r calculated on the basis of z scores.

There is an easier way to compute ϕ by using an alternative formula that takes advantage of the fact that the data can be represented in a 2 × 2 table of frequencies (or **counts**), also called a **contingency table.** You will see this 2 × 2 format in Table 11.9, which shows that all five people who ate the burgers then got food poisoning and that the seven people who did not eat them remained well. Notice that the cells are labeled A, B, C, and D. Using this code, we would calculate

$$\phi = \frac{BC - AD}{\sqrt{(A + B)(C + D)(A + C)(B + D)}}$$

$$= \frac{(7)(5) - (0)(0)}{\sqrt{(7)(5)(5)(7)}} = \frac{35 - 0}{\sqrt{1,225}} = \frac{35}{35} = 1.0$$

and (not unexpectedly) obtain the same result as with the conceptual formula for the Pearson r.

Table 11.9 2 × 2 Contingency Table Coded for Computation of Phi Coefficient

Ate a burger?	Got food poisoning? Yes	No	Totals
No	A 0	B 7	(A + B) = 7
Yes	C 5	D 0	(C + D) = 5
Totals	(A + C) = 5	(B + D) = 7	

A Final Note

We will have more to say about the point-biserial correlation (r_{pb}) and the phi coefficient (ϕ) in the following chapters, in which we return to the idea that the correlation coefficient can be a very valuable index of effect size. It is becoming increasingly important in empirical research that scientists routinely report the effect size, and (as we show in the following chapters) the r_{pb} and ϕ are easily computed and interpreted as one type of indication of the "practical importance" of the size of the effect. This does not mean that small correlations indicate that an effect size is of little or no practical importance, but knowing the size of the effect gives us another piece of information that can help us decide whether, and to what extent, the effect size is meaningful in a practical or personal way.

Summary of Ideas

1. The Pearson r is a standard index of linear relationship, with values from -1.0 to $+1.0$.

2. The third-variable problem is that another variable that is correlated with both X and Y may be the cause of both (e.g., children's foot size and spelling ability).

3. Scatter plots let us visualize the clustering and slope of dots that represent the relationship between X and Y.

4. The Pearson r, defined as $(\Sigma z_x z_y)/N$, is called the product-moment correlation because zs (i.e., standardized distances from the mean) are also known as *moments*.

5. The Spearman rho (r_s) is the Pearson r calculated on scores that happen to be in ranked form (e.g., the data on perceptions of risk).

6. Calculating r on the unranked scores typically results in a different value for the correlation than calculating r_s on the ranks, and therefore any correlation must be interpreted in the context of the data.

7. The point-biserial correlation (r_{pb}) is the Pearson r where one of the variables is continuous and the other is dichotomous (e.g., exam score and students' gender).

8. Dummy-coding the dichotomous variable (e.g., female vs. male, live vs. die, or succeed vs. fail) allows us to calculate r_{pb} by the Pearson r formula.

9. In dummy-coded data, 0 converts to a negative z and 1 converts to a positive z; the particular value of z is computed as $(X - M)/\sigma$.

10. The phi coefficient (ϕ) is the Pearson r where both variables are dichotomous (e.g., "Ate burger?" and "Got food poisoning?").

11. To calculate the correlation between two dichotomous variables, we can (a) dummy-code both variables (e.g., Yes = 1 and No = 0) and then use the corresponding z scores to compute the Pearson r or (b) compute ϕ directly from the 2×2 contingency table.

Key Terms

Multiple-Choice Questions for Review (answers are found on page 352)

1. A correlation coefficient reflects the degree of _____ relationship between two variables. (a) linear; (b) curvilinear; (c) any kind of; (d) positive
2. Correlation coefficients range from _____ (a) 0 to 1; (b) −1 to 0; (c) 1 to 10; (d) −1 to +1.
3. A variable (such as gender) with two possible values is called a _____ variable. (a) continuous; (b) dichotomous; (c) binomial; (d) linear
4. A graph is created in which the X variable is plotted along one axis and the Y variable is plotted along the other axis. Each data point is then represented as a dot in this graph. This kind of graph is called a (a) partial plot; (b) multivariate plot; (c) scatter plot; (d) median-split plot.
5. Another name for the Pearson r is the (a) Spearman rank correlation; (b) product-moment correlation; (c) phi coefficient; (d) point-biserial correlation.
6. Consider the following set of data:

	X	z_x	Y	z_y	$z_x z_y$
	8	1.34	16	1.34	1.80
	6	0.45	12	0.45	0.20
	4	−0.45	8	−0.45	0.20
	2	−1.34	4	−1.34	1.80
Sum (Σ)	20	0.00	40	0.00	4.00

What is the correlation between X and Y? (a) 0.1; (b) −0.1; (c) 1.0; (d) −1.0.
7. A distance from a mean is called an _____ ; the result of two numbers that are multiplied together is called a _____ . (a) deviation; sum; (b) deviation; divisor; (c) error; multiplicative index; (d) moment; product
8. A correlation between two variables that are ranked is most specifically called a _____ . (a) point-biserial correlation; (b) phi coefficient; (c) Pearson r; (d) Spearman rho
9. A student at Holy Family College wants to determine whether gender (male or female) is related to one's position on abortion (measured as "pro-choice" or "pro-life"). To test this hypothesis, this student is most likely to use a (a) Spearman rho; (b) phi coefficient; (c) point-biserial correlation; (d) none of the above.

10. A student at the London School of Economics wants to determine whether political party affiliation (Labor or Conservative) is related to intelligence (measured by an IQ test that yields a series of continuous scores). To test this hypothesis, the student is most likely to use a (a) Spearman rho; (b) phi coefficient; (c) point-biserial correlation; (d) none of the above.

Discussion Questions for Review (answers are found on pages 353–55)

1. A St. Bonaventure researcher administers tests of IQ and reading ability to four high school students. In addition, their grade point averages (GPAs) are obtained from school records, with the following results:

	IQ	Reading	GPA
Student 1	105	13	2.6
Student 2	113	17	3.4
Student 3	87	10	2.0
Student 4	125	19	3.8

The correlation between IQ and reading ability is $r = .98$. Without doing any direct calculation, the researcher says he knows the correlation between reading and GPA. Do you know this correlation? What about the correlation between IQ and GPA—without any direct calculation?

2. Twenty subjects take part in a University of Minnesota study on the relationship between socioeconomic status (SES: coded as rich = 1, poor = 0) and shyness (coded as shy = 1, not shy = 0). Given the results shown below, what is the correlation between these two variables? What specific type of Pearson correlation is this?

	SES	Shyness		SES	Shyness
Subject 1	0	1	Subject 11	0	0
Subject 2	0	1	Subject 12	1	1
Subject 3	0	0	Subject 13	0	0
Subject 4	0	1	Subject 14	1	0
Subject 5	1	1	Subject 15	0	1
Subject 6	0	0	Subject 16	1	0
Subject 7	1	1	Subject 17	1	0
Subject 8	1	0	Subject 18	1	1
Subject 9	0	1	Subject 19	0	1
Subject 10	1	0	Subject 20	1	0

3. A student at the University of Waterloo had two judges rate infants' fussiness, with the following results:

	Rater 1	Rater 2
Infant 1	60	30
Infant 2	40	50
Infant 3	30	60
Infant 4	50	40

The interjudge agreement, in terms of *r*s, was not what the student had hoped for: $r = -1.0$. So he got himself two more raters, whose ratings were as follows:

	Rater 3	Rater 4
Infant 1	60	130
Infant 2	40	150
Infant 3	30	160
Infant 4	50	140

What is the agreement, in terms of *r*, between Raters 3 and 4?

4. A Georgia State student has a job managing a 200-seat summer-stock theater that is filled to capacity on Saturday nights. To study the effect of staff courtesy on audience enjoyment, she asks the ticket taker to smile at randomly selected patrons. After the show, each member of the audience rates his or her enjoyment of the performance on a 7-point scale. Can you identify the independent and dependent variables and then figure out a way to calculate the correlation between them?

5. A student at California State University at Chico administered two tests to five subjects with the following results:

	Test A	Test B
Subject 1	1	4
Subject 2	2	3
Subject 3	3	2
Subject 4	4	1
Subject 5	5	100

Show a scatter plot of the relationship between the scores on Test A and Test B. Is there anything troubling about this plot? Can you adjust this problem by using a different version of a Pearson *r*? Show a scatter plot of the revised or transformed scores on Tests A and B. What is the correlation between the tests if you use (a) the original scores and (b) the revised or transformed scores?

6. Two students from Foothill College compared their obtained scatter plots. Which plot is associated with the higher correlation? How can you tell just from inspecting the scatter plots? What are the actual *r*s associated with each plot?

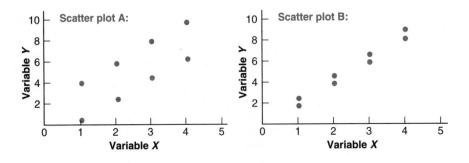

12 Statistical Significance and Practical Importance

Use of Statistics and Probabilities

Besides describing data (Chapter 10) and looking for mutual relations between variables (Chapter 11), scientists frequently make comparisons among research groups. For example, in Chapter 10, we described a study in which the subjects rated the palatability of a new food product and a comparison food product already on the market. The new food was rated more favorably on the average than was the comparison product. Because these researchers wanted to know whether the difference between the two means might be due to chance, they performed a simple test of significance. Finding the **probability (p value)** associated with the observed difference to be quite small, they concluded that the difference was "real" and not a result of chance (Street & Carroll, 1989). We will describe the usual reasoning behind this traditional procedure, called **null hypothesis significance testing (NHST).**

In recent years, there has also been a gradual realization (and reluctant acceptance) of the fact that NHST is limited in certain ways. One limitation is that the ability to detect an obtained relationship at the desired p level depends on both the size of the sample (N) and the size of the relation

PREVIEW QUESTIONS

▌ What is the traditional rationale behind null hypothesis significance testing (NHST)?

▌ What is the difference between Type I and Type II errors?

▌ How might NHST be misleading as an indicator of "practical importance"?

▌ What, then, does the p value actually tell us?

▌ What does all this have to do with the *power* of the statistical test?

▌ Why is it useful to know the effect size correlation?

▌ What is the purpose of the binomial effect-size display (BESD)?

▌ How might the coefficient of determination underestimate the effect size?

▌ What is the confidence interval around the effect size, and how is it computed?

between the independent variable (X) and the dependent variable (Y). It is easier to detect a larger than a smaller relationship, and it is easier to detect a relationship of any given magnitude at the desired p level when we are working with a larger sample size than with a smaller sample size. Therefore it is important to understand that "nonsignificance" is not the same thing as "no effect," because it is possible to have a genuine effect even though the statistical test lacks sufficient "power" to detect it at the desired p level. We show how to estimate the number of subjects you will need to ensure adequate power, and this analysis (called a **power analysis**) is also frequently done again after the study is completed as a check on the "effective power" of the study.

In other words, it is important that you focus your attention not just on the p value, but on other vital aspects of the results, such as the size of the relation between X and Y (also called the **effect size**). Scientists define an effect size in many ways (e.g., R. Rosenthal, 1994a; Tatsuoka, 1993), but in this book we emphasize the **effect size correlation,** symbolized here as r_{effect} (see also Box 12.1). We also show how to compute an interval estimate of the upper and lower bounds of the r_{effect}— called a **confidence interval.** For example, suppose the study is a randomized trial with a drug condition (experimental group) and a placebo condition (control group), and we define the effect size correlation as a point-biserial correlation (i.e., r_{pb}). That is, the r_{effect} is defined as the relation between certain dummy-coded scores (e.g., 1 = drug and 0 = placebo) and the observed scores on some continuous dependent variable. We then compute the confidence interval and report, for example, that "the probability is 95 chances in 100 that the interval between r_{effect} =.20 and .40 contains the size of the effect of the new drug"—called a *95% confidence interval.*

Box 12.1   The Effect Size Correlation

We use *effect size correlation* (r_{effect}) as an umbrella term that covers the use of specific rs, such as phi (ϕ) and the point-biserial (r_{pb}) correlation, to represent the relation between scores on the dependent variable (Y) and the individual subject's membership in a specified condition or group (e.g., experimental or control group). In your literature search, you may note some other ways of indicating the effect size correlation (e.g., Rosnow & Rosenthal, 1996a), but in this book we use the symbol r_{effect} because it is easy to remember and should help you avoid confusion with other applications of r.

This chapter also serves as a prelude to our discussion in the following chapters of the applications of these ideas. That is, in this chapter, we explain the reasoning behind the use of statistics and probabilities in NHST, as well as the nature of p values and effect sizes, and in the remainder of the book, we concentrate on the computation and interpretation of three popular statistical tests—the t test, the F test, and the chi-square (χ^2) test—and their corresponding effect-size correlations. In describing this logic, we outline a two- or three-step process in which the aim of the scientist is to gain some degree of information about the research results (Nelson, Rosenthal, & Rosnow, 1986). We review the reasoning and mechanics involved in each step, while keeping in mind the need to examine not just the "statistical significance" of the results, but their "practical importance" as well.

Briefly, in one of the steps, some degree of information is gleaned when the **null hypothesis** (i.e., a supposition implying no real difference between the means, or a correlation of zero between variables) can be rejected. Particular attention is paid to a specified level of probability that serves as the basis of this rejection (i.e., the *p* value, also symbolized as **alpha** to refer to the probability that is set in advance). In another step, which may precede or follow the step already described, the scientist gains further information from the size of the effect, which, interpreted in the context of the study's measurements and objective, implies the "practical importance" of the observed result. In a third step—taken if the null hypothesis has not been rejected, but the magnitude of the effect seems promising—the scientist examines the actual power of the statistical test to see whether there was a realistic chance of rejecting the null hypothesis at the specified alpha. However, as noted above, it is also important to consider the power of the statistical test even before implementing the study, because power improves with increases in the number of sampling units.

The Null Hypothesis in Significance Testing

To help you understand intuitively what the null hypothesis and related concepts mean, we will borrow an analogy suggested by Howard Wainer (1972). Imagine you are walking along the Atlantic City boardwalk or the Las Vegas strip when a shady character approaches and whispers he has a quarter that he is willing to sell you for *only* five dollars. What makes the coin worth so much more than its face value? The answer, he tells you, is that this is a quarter with extraordinary properties. When properly used, this quarter can win you fame and fortune because it does not come up heads and tails with equal regularity. Instead, one outcome is more likely than the other. A smart person can, when flipping the coin, bet on the outcome and win a fortune, he says. "It might sound like a cock-and-bull story," he says, "but flip the coin and see for yourself."

If the coin is not what the street entrepreneur says it is, getting a head or a tail is the result purely of chance. Thinking empirically, you decide to test whether the probability of heads does or does not equal the probability of tails. You flip the coin once and heads appears. You flip the coin again, and again it comes up heads. Suppose you flip the coin nine times and each time it comes up heads. Would you believe him at this point? If your answer is yes, then would you believe him if, in nine tosses, the coin came up heads eight times and tails once? This is the essential problem in significance testing. You can be as stringent as you like in setting a rejection criterion, but you *may* eventually pay for this decision by rejecting what you perhaps should not (see also Box 12.2).

> **Box 12.2 Paradigms in Transition**
>
> If you would like to know more about how the classical idea of probability evolved, you will find an excellent historical account in a book by cognitive psychologist Gerd Gigerenzer and others called *The Empire of Chance* (1989). The book describes how the concept of probability altered biology, physics, and psychology and, in turn, has changed our conceptualization of social reality. Unlike a machine that runs with clockwork precision and is precisely predictable, social behavior is viewed as variable and chancy. In other words, there has been a "paradigm shift" in both our conceptualization of behavior and the multiple methods needed to explicate it (Rosnow, 1981).

The ideas involved in significance testing evolved out of the arguments of different statisticians. Let us state these ideas more precisely. When you decide to test whether the probability of heads "does or does not" equal the probability of tails, two hypotheses are implied. One is that the quarter is unbiased (i.e., the probability of heads *does* equal the probability of tails), and the second is that the coin is biased (i.e., the probability of heads *does not* equal the probability of tails). Think of the "experiment" of tossing a coin as a way of trying to determine which of these hypotheses you cannot logically reject. In statistical terms, we call the first hypothesis the **null hypothesis** (symbolized as H_0) and the second the **alternate hypothesis** (symbolized as H_1). That is,

> H_0 *(null hypothesis):* The probability of heads equals the probability of tails in the long run (i.e., the coin is not biased).
>
> H_1 *(alternate hypothesis):* The probability of heads is not equal to the probability of tails in the long run (i.e., the coin is biased).

Notice that the two hypotheses are **mutually exclusive;** that is, when one is true, the other must be false. Experimenters who do NHST are usually interested in testing the specific H_0 (i.e., no difference) against a general H_1 (i.e., some difference). Given the typical experimental design, the null hypothesis would imply no difference in performance between the experimental and the control groups. Experimenters try to reject H_0 and yet be reasonably sure that they will not be wrong in doing so. We will return to the coin example in a moment, but first, we need to revisit the concept of probability (which was briefly introduced in Chapter 9) and explain the difference between Type I and Type II errors.

Probability Revisited

If we were to ask someone what **probability** means, the reply might be something like "It means things that sometimes happen and sometimes do not." This is not a bad description, because the probability that one particular event will occur is the proportion of times that the event would occur if all the possible events were repeated indefinitely (see also Box 12.3). When you throw a die, for example, there are six possibilities, and (unless a die is loaded) the probability of any particular outcome is therefore 1/6, or .167. Thus you can recognize another important characteristic of probabilities (see again Box 9.2 on page 205). If all the outcomes are **independent** (i.e., one outcome is not influenced by any other), the sum of all the probabilities associated with a particular event is equal to 1. This characteristic means that one of the six sides *must* appear on any roll of the die.

Box 12.3   **Will It Rain Tomorrow?**

We frequently hear weather reports that include a statement like "There is a 70% probability of rain tomorrow." Does this mean that it is going to rain for 70% of the day? No, it means that, when examined over the long run, 70% of all the days that follow weather characteristics like today's have been rainy. In other words, probabilities are long-term measures that deal with uncertain events. As noted, the probability that one particular event, out of many possible events, will occur is the proportion of times out of all outcomes that the event would occur.

Instead of throwing a die, suppose we had two fair coins and flipped them simultaneously. There are four possible combinations of heads (H) and tails (T): HH, HT, TH, and TT. In determining probabilities, the general rule is to count the total number of possible outcomes and then to count the number of outcomes that yield the event you are interested in. The probability of that event is the ratio of the number you are looking for (the favorable event) to the total number of outcomes. For example, the probability of two heads (out of the four possible events) can occur in only one way (HH) and is therefore 1 divided by 4, or .25. The probability of one head (out of these four possible events) can occur in two ways (HT or TH) and is therefore 2 divided by 4, or .5.

Type I and Type II Errors

To see what all this has to do with Type I and Type II errors, imagine a law-school admissions officer whose job it is to decide between two alternatives. One alternative is that the prospective student will be able to do the work required in the school and will succeed if admitted, and the other alternative is that the student will not be able to do the required work and will flunk out. For the sake of this illustration, think of the first alternative as the "null hypothesis" (i.e., the candidate will succeed because she is no less qualified than the accepted students) and the second alternative as the "alternate hypothesis" (i.e., the candidate will not succeed because she is less qualified than the accepted students). The dilemma the admissions officer faces is that a risk of error is associated with either alternative. If the officer rejects a student and the student could have done well, the officer commits what would be classified as a Type I error; that is, the null hypothesis is true. If, on the other hand, the officer accepts a student and the student flunks out, the officer has committed a Type II error; that is, the null hypothesis is false.

In the framework of NHST, a **Type I error** means that one has mistakenly rejected the null hypothesis (H_0) when it is, in fact, true and should not have been rejected. A **Type II error** means that one has mistakenly failed to reject the null hypothesis when it is, in fact, false and should have been rejected. The risk (or probability) of making a Type I error is called by three different names: **alpha** (symbolized as α), the **significance level**, and the p **value**. The risk (or probability) of making a Type II error is known by one name: **beta** (symbolized as β). To make the most informed decision, the scientist would, of course, like to know what each risk is in a given case, so that he or she can balance those risks in some way.

However, we are jumping ahead. Let us return with this newfound knowledge to the analogy of the street entrepreneur with the coin for sale. Suppose you decide that you do not want to be wrong more than 1 time out of 20—called the **5% significance level** (see also Box 12.4). You flip the coin 9 times and get 8 heads and 1 tail. To make an informed decision, you need to know about the chances of obtaining this result or a result even more extreme. That is, you need to know the probability of obtaining this result (or a more extreme result) if the null hypothesis is true, and so you think, "If this probability is less than $1/20$ (i.e., $p < .05$, where $<$ is read as "less than"), I will reject the null hypothesis and buy the coin; if not (i.e., $p > .05$, where $>$ is read as "greater than"), I will not buy the coin." Because it can be shown that the probability of 8 or 9 heads in 9 tosses is less than 1 out of 20 (p is approximately .02, or 1 out of 50), you decide to reject the null hypothesis and buy the coin.

Box 12.4 ## The 5% Solution

The ultimate day-to-day decision about what is a reasonable risk is a personal one. But as you do your literature search, you will notice that many researchers use the .05 level of probability as a kind of "critical demarcation point" for deciding whether or not to reject the null hypothesis. The conventional wisdom behind this procedure goes something like this: The logic begins, more or less, with the proposition that one does not want to accept an alternate hypothesis that stands a fairly good chance of being false (i.e., one ought to avoid Type I errors). The logic goes on to state that one either accepts an alternate hypothesis as probably true (not false) or rejects it, concluding that the null is too likely for one to regard *it* as rejectable. The .05 alpha is seen by many scientists as a good "fail-safe" standard because it is convenient (most statistical tables show 5% values) and stringent enough to safeguard against accepting a statistically nonsignificant result (i.e., the null hypothesis is true) as significant (Rosnow & Rosenthal, 1989b).

In other words, assuming you have no pangs of conscience about accepting a crooked coin, you are doing so for two reasons: (1) because the resultant probability leads you to reject the null hypothesis of a fair coin, with 50% heads, at your chosen significance level of 5%, and (2) because you think that the alternate hypothesis (i.e., the coin is biased) is tenable and that the data (i.e., 8 heads and 1 tail, or 89% heads instead of 50%) support this hypothesis.

Risks of Gullibility and Blindness

This analogy is a simplified one, not an exact representation of what goes on in NHST. One reason the coin example falls short is that it is not a relational event; that is, there is only one variable: the result of the coin toss. The scientist who does NHST, however, usually wants to estimate the probability of claiming that two variables (X and Y) are related when, in fact, they are unrelated. The Type I error can thus be seen as claiming a relationship that truly does not exist; it is the likelihood of this particular risk that initially most interests scientists who rely on NHST. In other words, the question that such scientists want answered is "What is the probability of a Type I error?"

Although the scientist is not indifferent to the probability of making a Type II error (i.e., failing to claim a relation that truly does exist), those scientists who do NHST have traditionally attached greater psychological importance to the risk of making a Type I error than to the risk of making a Type II error (see also Box 12.5). The reason the scientist attaches greater weight to alpha (the risk of making a Type I error) than to beta (the risk of making a Type II error) is explained in Table 12.1. The risk of making a Type I error is synonymous with an inferential mistake involving **gullibility,** whereas the risk of making a Type II error is synonymous with an inferential mistake involving **blindness to a relationship.** Traditionally, scientists have been taught to believe that it is worse to risk being gullible than to risk being blind to a relationship, and some philosophers have characterized this choice as the "healthy skepticism" of the scientific outlook (Axinn, 1966; Kaplan, 1964).

Box 12.5   **Innocent or Guilty?**

Imagine that a man is being tried for a brutal murder, and suppose that, if he is convicted, execution is the likely penalty. As a member of the jury, you have to vote on whether he is innocent or guilty of the charges against him. If you vote "guilty" and in fact he is not guilty, you may be sending an innocent man to be executed. If you vote "innocent" and in fact he is not innocent, you could be turning a brutal murderer loose in the community. In the United States, it is generally accepted that convicting an innocent person is a more serious risk than finding a guilty person innocent. The lesson? Just as most scientists who do NHST do not weight Type I and Type II errors equally, in everyday life we also give greater weight to some decision risks than to others.

Table 12.1	Illustration of Definitions of Type I and Type II Errors	
	True state	
Your decision	The coin is unbiased	The coin is biased
The coin is biased (i.e., it won't come up heads and tails equally)	Type I error (gullibility risk)	No error of inference
The coin is unbiased (i.e., it is an ordinary coin)	No error of inference	Type II error (blindness risk)

Table 12.2	Implications of the Decision to Reject or Not to Reject the Null Hypothesis (H_0)	
	True state	
Scientist's decision	H_0 is true	H_0 is false
To reject H_0	Type I error	No error of inference
Not to reject H_0	No error of inference	Type II error

In Table 12.2, we see these ideas translated into the tactical language of NHST. For researchers, the null hypothesis is the assumption that no relation between two variables is present in the population from which a sample was drawn, or that there is no difference in the responses to the treatments. The researcher considers the possibility of making a Type I error whenever a true null hypothesis is tested. As this table shows, Type I errors occur when the researcher mistakenly rejects the null hypothesis by claiming a relationship that does not exist. Type II errors occur when the researcher mistakenly accepts the null hypothesis by failing to claim a relationship that does exist.

Finding the Significance of r

Especially when the p value is low enough to justify rejecting the null hypothesis, the scientist increases her or his information about the results by knowing the effect size and its practical importance. Thus, if you are going to do NHST, you need to know how to determine the p value. Table 12.3, which contains a portion of a longer table in Appendix B (see Table B.5 on p. 417), shows the p levels associated with different values of r. The first column lists $N - 2$ (where N is the total number of sampling units), while the other columns indicate p levels (i.e., Type I error risks). Notice that both one-tailed and two-tailed p levels are given and that the two-tailed ps are twice

Table 12.3	Significance Levels of r				
			Probability level (p)		
	.05	.025	.01	.005	one-tail
$N-2$	.10	.05	.02	.01	two-tail
1	.988	.997	.9995	.9999	
2	.900	.950	.980	.990	
3	.805	.878	.934	.959	
4	.729	.811	.882	.917	
5	.669	.754	.833	.874	
10	.497	.576	.658	.708	
20	.360	.423	.492	.537	
30	.296	.349	.409	.449	
40	.257	.304	.358	.393	
50	.231	.273	.322	.354	
100	.164	.195	.230	.254	
200	.116	.138	.164	.181	
300	.095	.113	.134	.148	
500	.074	.088	.104	.115	
1,000	.052	.062	.073	.081	

Note: For a more complete table, see Appendix B, Table B.5.

the size of the one-tailed. The term **two-tailed p value** implies that the alternate hypothesis (H_1) did *not* specifically predict in which side (or tail) of the probability distribution the significance would be detected. **One-tailed p values** (obtained by halving the two-tailed p values) imply that the alternate hypothesis requires the significance to be in one tail rather than in the other tail.

As an illustration of how to read Table 12.3 (and Table B.5), suppose you conducted a questionnaire study to test whether people's level of self-esteem (as measured by a standardized personality inventory) is correlated with the extent to which they engage in gossiping (measured by peer ratings). However, you are unsure of the direction this relation will take because (based on your literature review) you feel that a positive *or* a negative correlation is possible (Jaeger, Skleder, & Rosnow, in press). That is, some writers have portrayed the typical gossip as a social isolate, the least popular member of a group, and as characterized by feelings of little self-worth, social anxiety, and a need for esteem from others, who gossips in order to become the center of attention and to obtain status or esteem from others. By contrast, others have characterized the typical gossip as sensitive, curious, social, and involved, a person who gossips out of a need to control or manipulate those he or she perceives to be subordinates. Because you are unable to predict whether the correlation will be positive or negative, you will do a two-tailed (rather than a one-tailed) test of significance.

Continuing with this example, suppose that, in a total N of 52 subjects, you find that the correlation between self-esteem and the tendency to gossip is $r = .33$. The positive r is consistent with the notion that high gossipers are higher in self-esteem. However, suppose you also want to test $r = .33$ for statistical significance to find out whether a correlation of this magnitude may have occurred by chance. For your alpha, let us say you pick the conventional 5% significance level as a helpful (but not critical) demarcation point. Looking at the intersection of $N - 2 = 50$ and the column labeled .05 two-tail in Table 12.3, you can see that r needs to be at least .273 to be beyond the level of risk you have picked in order to reject the null hypothesis. As this table shows, the obtained p is somewhere between .02 and .01 two-tailed. That is, $r = .33$ is larger than the listed value for $p = .02$ two-tailed ($r = .322$) and smaller than the listed value for $p = .01$ two-tailed ($r = .354$).

In reporting p values, you have several options. One alternative, which is typically used, is to state only that "$p < .05$ two-tail" (that is, the two-tailed probability of mistakenly rejecting the null hypothesis is less than 1 chance in 20). The problem with this option is that it is imprecise. For example, were the researcher to report that "$p > .05$," we would have no idea whether the obtained p was .06 (which is not very different from .05) or .50 (which is no better than pure chance). A second alternative—if you want to use this table a little more precisely—is to state that "$.01 <$ two-tailed $p < .02$" (that is, the two-tailed probability of mistakenly rejecting the null hypothesis is "more than 1 chance in 100" but "less than 1 chance in 50"). A third alternative, recommended by many statisticians, is to state the exact p value, which may be easy enough to do if you are using a computer or an expensive statistics calculator to do your data analyses.

Notice in Table 12.3 that a correlation can be significant at $p = .05$, no matter whether it is a very large correlation or a very small correlation. What counts most, it seems, is whether the "$N - 2$" is sufficiently large to allow us to detect the particular magnitude of r at the desired level of significance. For example, we see that even an r as small as .062 would be significant at $p = .05$ two-tail with $N = 1,002$, whereas an r nine times larger would not be significant at the same level with $N = 12$. Yet surely an effect size correlation of .558 should not be ignored merely because it is not *statistically* significant (i.e., at $p = .05$ two-tail and $N - 2 = 10$). This implies an important limitation of NHST, and it reminds us not to confuse statistical significance with the size of the effect or its practical importance.

Binomial Effect-Size Display (BESD)

In the following chapters, we will present simple formulas for computing r_{effect} when using particular statistical tests. For now, we will examine how to transform the r_{effect} into a convenient display that frequently reveals its practical importance—called the **BESD,** short for **binomial effect-size display** (Rosenthal & Rubin, 1982b). The BESD is described as a *display* because it converts the "success rates" in the experimental and control groups into a 2×2 table, and it is called *binomial* (which means "two terms") because two variables are presented as dichotomous. To show how the BESD works, we will use the data in a widely publicized biomedical study, in which the independent variable was whether or not the subjects were given an aspirin every other day and the dependent variable was whether or not they experienced a heart attack.

The study reported that heart attack risk is cut in half by aspirin (Steering Committee of the Physicians' Health Study Research Group, 1988). Presumably, the way that aspirin works to reduce mortality from heart attack, or myocardial infarction (MI), is by promoting circulation even when fatty deposits have collected along the walls of the coronary arteries. That is, aspirin makes the transport of blood easier as the arteries get narrower. The finding that heart attack risk is "cut in half" was based on a five-year study of 22,071 male physicians, approximately half of whom (11,037) received an ordinary aspirin tablet (325 mg) every other day, while the remainder (11,034) were given a placebo. Part of the results are shown in Table 12.4 (see also Box 12.6).

Box 12.6 **Finding the Effect Size Yourself**

You can frequently find sufficient details about biomedical experiments in newspaper stories to allow you to reconstruct a 2 × 2 table, and then compute a simple statistic (e.g., the chi-square, as described in a later chapter) and figure out the effect size and the BESD. In this way, you can see for yourself how large or small an effect was obtained, and you need not depend on the reporter's statement that the results were "significant."

Table 12.4 Aspirin's Effect on Heart Attack

A. Myocardial infarction (MI) in aspirin and placebo conditions

Condition	No heart attack	Heart attack	Total
Aspirin	10,933	104	11,037
Placebo	10,845	189	11,034
Total	21,778	293	22,071

B. Binomial effect-size display of $r_{effect} = .034$

Condition	MI absent	MI present	Total
Aspirin	51.7[a]	48.3[b]	100
Placebo	48.3[b]	51.7[a]	100
Total	100	100	200

[a]Computed from $100(.500 + r/2)$
[b]Computed from $100(.500 - r/2)$

Source: Based on results reported in "Preliminary Report: Findings from the Aspirin Component of the Ongoing Physicians' Health Study," by Steering Committee of the Physicians' Health Study Research Group, 1988, *New England Journal of Medicine, 318*, pp. 262–264.

The top part of this table shows the number of participants in each condition who did or did not have a heart attack. A chi-square (χ^2) test of the statistical significance of these results—using a procedure described in a later chapter—yielded a p value that was considerably smaller than the conventional .05 significance level. It was "p is approximately .0000006," which tells us conclusively that the result of NHST was very unlikely to be a fluke or a lucky coincidence. But when we calculate the effect size as a standard phi (ϕ) coefficient, using the procedure described in the previous chapter, the result is only $r_{effect} = .034$. We say "only" because effect size correlations of .1 or less are typically considered small in behavioral science. But before we dismiss this "small" effect as inconsequential, let us also see what it means in terms of practical importance.

We said that the scientists reported that heart attack risk is cut in half, and let us see how they arrived at this conclusion. In the placebo condition, 189 out of 11,034 subjects had a heart attack, which is 1.7% (i.e., 189/11,034 multiplied by 100). In the aspirin condition, 104 out of 11,037 subjects had a heart attack, which is 0.9% (i.e., 104/11,037 multiplied by 100). Dividing 0.9 by 1.7 tells us that the risk of having a heart attack was cut approximately in half. However, despite this good news, we also see that the percentages are quite small, indicating that relatively few people were actually in jeopardy of having a heart attack (1.3% of the 22,071 subjects). The question is how to display the importance of the results for the population as a whole, and yet not exaggerate their implications.

No measure can capture the full picture, but the purpose of the BESD (which is used in conjunction with other measures) is to translate the effect size correlation into a population in which both the independent variable and the dependent variable are viewed as dichotomous and each is split in half. In this way, we can compare different BESDs because they are all predicated on the same equalization assumptions. In this case, we would assume that half the population had heart attacks and half did not (i.e., the dichotomous dependent variable), and that half got aspirin and half did not (i.e., the dichotomous independent variable). In other situations, the BESD might define the dependent variable as success and failure, improved and not improved, and so forth.

Part B of Table 12.4 provides us with a BESD that corresponds to $r_{effect} = .034$ calculated from the results in Part A, and we see that it resembles a 2 × 2 contingency table of the kind from which we calculated ϕ at the end of Chapter 11. However, whereas the rows and columns of ordinary contingency tables may sum to any number, notice that each row and column of the BESD table adds up to 100. Equalizing the row and column marginal values (or **margins** for short) makes the values in the A, B, C, D cells easier to interpret and compare as proportions or percentages. This BESD tells us that approximately 3.4% of persons (in a population split into halves) who would probably have experienced a myocardial infarction (i.e., given these particular conditions) did not experience one if they followed the regimen as prescribed in the aspirin treatment condition. In other words, the BESD preserves the effect size but lets us see that it is equivalent to reducing the heart attack rate from 51.7% to 48.3% in a population in which half the people are given aspirin and half are not, and half have heart attacks and half do not (see also Box 12.7).

Box 12.7   BESD on Continuous Data

In the aspirin example, both the independent variable (aspirin versus placebo) and the dependent variable (no heart attack or heart attack) were already dichotomous. But it is also possible to use the BESD when the dependent variable is continuous rather than discrete. For example, in the next chapter, we show how r_{pb} can be easily computed from a t test, and the BESD constructed by adding and subtracting half of r_{pb} to and from .50 (and multiplying by 100 to change the cell proportions to percentages). We simply redefine the dependent variable in terms of dichotomous outcomes.

One great convenience of the BESD is how easily we can go from the 2×2 display to an r_{effect} (simply by taking the difference between the percentages of the experimental group and the control group, then dividing by 100) and how easily we go from an r_{effect} to the display (by calculating the experimental success rate as .50 plus one half of r and then multiplying by 100, and by calculating the control group success rate as .50 minus one half of r and then multiplying by 100). In the case where $r_{effect} = .034$, the experimental success rate is $.50 + .017 = .517$, multiplied by 100 to change .517 to 51.7%. In the placebo group, we calculate $.50 - .017 = .483$ and then multiply by 100 to change the proportion to 48.3%.

Please Don't Square the Effect Size!

In your literature search, you may have noticed that some researchers, when reporting the effect size, refer to a squared correlation coefficient. This value (r^2) is also called the **coefficient of determination**, or **proportion of variation explained**. However, the terms *determination* and *explained* are used in a technical sense and, despite the names, do not mean that r^2 explains the causal relation between X and Y. They mean only that r^2 represents the fraction or proportion of the variability shared by X and Y. For example, a positive or negative Pearson r of 1.0—in which case r^2 also equals 1.0—implies that the variation in the Y scores is perfectly associated with the variation in the X scores (and vice versa).

While the coefficient of determination is useful in a number of situations, unfortunately it can seriously underestimate the practical importance of the results. For example, if we go back to the aspirin study, squaring $r_{effect} = .034$ suggests there was *no* effect (i.e., $r^2 = .00$)! But when we think of $r_{effect} = .034$ as reflecting a 3.4% decrease in heart attacks (which was the interpretation given in Table 12.4), the effect size takes on practical importance—especially if you can count yourself or a loved one among that percentage (Rosenthal, 1990a, 1990b). Thus, although squaring the effect size r is recommended in a number of influential books (e.g., American Psychological Association, 1994), Table 12.5 shows the extent to which it may underestimate the practical importance of an observed effect.

Column 1 shows the result of squaring the rs in column 2 (e.g., $.10 \times .10 = .01$), and columns 3 and 4 show the percentage increases in success rates as they

Table 12.5 Increases in Success Rates Corresponding to Values of r^2 and r_{effect}

Coefficient of determination (r^2)	Effect size (r_{effect})	Success rate increased From (%)	Success rate increased To (%)	Differences in success rates
.01	.10	45	55	10% (or .10)
.04	.20	40	60	20% (or .20)
.09	.30	35	65	30% (or .30)
.16	.40	30	70	40% (or .40)
.25	.50	25	75	50% (or .50)
.36	.60	20	80	60% (or .60)
.49	.70	15	85	70% (or .70)
.64	.80	10	90	80% (or .80)
.81	.90	5	95	90% (or .90)
1.00	1.00	0	100	100% (or 1.00)

would be revealed by a BESD corresponding to the values in column 2. The final column shows the difference between the values in columns 3 and 4 as a percentage and (in parenthesis) a proportion. The proportions change the percentages back into the values in column 2, thus showing that the difference in success rates (e.g., survival rate, cure rate, improvement rate, or selection rate) is exactly equal to r_{effect}. In other words, the effect size correlation itself (r_{effect}) tells us the practical importance of a given experimental outcome—although we must also consider the nature of the variables and the dependent measures to decide how to frame the implications of the results.

Statistical Power Analysis

If the null hypothesis has not been rejected in a given study, the scientist analyzes the **effective power** (i.e., actual power) of the statistical test used in the NHST procedure. The reason is that the **power of a test** has to do with the sensitivity of the significance test in providing an adequate opportunity to reject the null hypothesis if it warrants rejection (e.g., J. Cohen, 1988, 1990; Keppel, 1991; Kirk, 1995; Kraemer & Thiemann, 1987). Thus the purpose of the power analysis is to learn whether there was a reasonable chance of rejecting the null hypothesis and whether the power should be increased in any future study to increase the sensitivity of the significance test.

To illustrate, suppose that young researcher Smith conducts an experiment (with $N = 80$) on productivity and finds that Managerial Style A is better than B (the old standard), with p less than .05 and $r_{effect} = .22$. That is, Smith's results are statistically significant at the conventional 5% alpha. Old researcher Jones, the creator of Style B is skeptical and asks his graduate students to try to replicate Smith's results (with $N = 20$). The graduate students, to Jones's perverse delight, report a failure to replicate Smith's results. Their obtained two-tailed p value, they gleefully tell Jones, is *greater* than .30. However, before savoring his victory, Jones tells his graduate students to calculate the effect size of their result. They return with glum faces to report that their effect size is *identical* ($r_{effect} = .22$) to Smith's.

In other words, Jones's students have found exactly what Smith found, even though the *p* values of the two studies are not very close. The problem, as we will now show, is that the students were working with a level of statistical power that was too low to obtain the *p* value reported by Smith. Because of the smaller sample size of 20, it turns out that their power to reject the null hypothesis at .05 two-tailed is about .15, whereas Smith's power of about .50 (using an *N* of 80) is more than three times as great.

You will recall that beta (β) is the probability of a Type II error (i.e., the probability of failing to claim a relationship that does exist). **Power** is simply $1 - \beta$, or the probability of not making a Type II error. In the language of statistics, *power* refers to the probability of rejecting the null hypothesis when it is false and needs rejecting. For any given statistical test of a null hypothesis (e.g., *t*, *F*, or χ^2), the power of the statistical test is determined by three factors: (1) the level of the risk of drawing a spuriously positive conclusion (i.e., the *p* level); (2) the size of the study (i.e., the sample size); and (3) the effect size. These three factors are so related that, when any two of them are known, the third can be determined. Thus, if you know the values for Factors 1 and 3, you should be able to figure out how big a sample you will need to achieve your desired level of significance.

Table 12.6 provides a compact way of figuring out the total number of subjects needed to detect various effects at the .05 (two-tailed) significance level. Suppose you decide to work with power = .8 or better, because this happens to be a recommended level (J. Cohen, 1988). Let us also say you anticipate finding a "small" effect (i.e., $r_{effect} = .10$) based on your review of the research literature. Given this magnitude of

Table 12.6	Rounded Sample Sizes (Total *N*) Required to Detect Effects at .05 Two-Tailed						
	Effect size correlation (r_{effect})						
Power	.10	.20	.30	.40	.50	.60	.70
.15	85	25	10	10	10	10	10
.20	125	35	15	10	10	10	10
.30	200	55	25	15	10	10	10
.40	300	75	35	20	15	10	10
.50	400	100	40	25	15	10	10
.60	500	125	55	30	20	15	10
.70	600	155	65	40	25	15	10
.80	800	195	85	45	30	20	15
.90	1,000	260	115	60	40	25	15

Source: From *Statistical Power Analysis for the Behavioral Sciences* (2nd ed., pp. 92–93), by J. Cohen, 1988 Hillsdale, NJ: Lawrence Erlbaum Associates, Inc. Reprinted by permission of Jacob Cohen and Lawrence Erlbaum Associates, Inc.

effect (.10) and power (.8), you will need approximately 800 subjects to reject the null hypothesis at .05 two-tailed. This is a lot of subjects! Had you chosen to work in an area with typically larger effects, your recruitment of subjects would have been made much easier. With an effect size $r = .30$ and power $= .8$, you would need approximately 85 subjects. With $r_{effect} = .50$, you would need a total N of only 30 subjects (see also Box 12.8).

Box 12.8   **Good News, Bad News, Good News!**

You will be happy to know that most reported experimental effects in behavioral science are quite a bit larger than $r_{effect} = .10$. They frequently tend to be in the .30 to .50 range, which means that, with power of .80, you would need a total N of 30 ($r_{effect} = .50$) to 85 ($r_{effect} = .30$) subjects. The bad news is that, as noted in Chapter 10, a proportion of volunteer subjects tend not to show up, and you therefore may need to multiply your estimated N by 1.5 to compensate for the possibility that a third of the volunteers may be no-shows. However, the good news is that, in addition to increasing the total N, you may use other techniques to increase power, and in the next chapter, you will find more information to help you conduct your research with greater statistical power.

Constructing a Confidence Interval

In our previous discussion of survey designs (Chapter 9), we referred to the "margin of error," which is usually reported by pollsters (e.g., political pollsters now expect a margin of error of no more than 2 or 3 percentage points in national elections). The margin of error, it will be recalled, is the interval estimate made by the pollster; another name for this interval is the **confidence interval.** Pollsters usually work with a 95% confidence interval; that is, they set upper and lower limits within which they expect the predicted value to fall 95% of the time (i.e., over repeated sampling under the same conditions). The use of confidence intervals in reporting effect sizes is also growing in popularity, and we will show how a confidence interval for r_{effect} is computed and interpreted.

The confidence level is defined as $(1 - \alpha)100$. Thus, if you choose to work with two-tailed $p = .05$ (which is the customary alpha in behavioral and social science), you are working with 95% confidence, that is, $(1 - .05)100 = 95\%$. To find the 95% confidence interval for any effect size r, you would proceed in four steps:

Step 1 is to consult Table B.6 in Appendix B (page 418), which is used to transform the r_{effect} to what is called a Fisher z_r (which is a log-based transformation of r). This transformation changes the finite scale of rs (which range from -1.0 to $+1.0$) into a normal distribution without limits. To distinguish the Fisher z_r from the standard score z noted in previous chapters, we use the subscript "r" to remind you that this particular z is related to r.

Step 2 is to substitute the value of N in your study (i.e., the total sample size in your study) in the following equation:

$$\left(\frac{1}{\sqrt{N-3}}\right)1.96$$

where 1.96 is the standard score z for $p = .05$ two-tailed, and the other value defines the "standard error" of Fisher z_r. You will find discussions of the standard error in statistics texts, but in general, it refers to the standard deviation of a given statistic. (In the next chapter, where we describe the formula for the t test as resembling a "signal-to-noise" ratio, you can think of the standard error as the more technical definition of noise in the denominator of the t formula.)

Step 3 is to find the limits of the 95% confidence interval by subtracting (to create the lower limit) the result in Step 2 from, and adding it (to create the upper limit) to, the Fisher z_r transformed effect size in Step 1.

Step 4 is to consult Table B.7 in Appendix B (page 419) to transform these lower and upper z_r values back to r_{effect} values to define the 95% confidence interval around the effect.

To illustrate, suppose we find that $r_{effect} = .33$ based on a total sample size of $N = 80$, and we want to compute the 95% confidence interval. The first step is to look in Table B.6 at the intersection of the row labeled .3 and the column labeled .03, where we find that Fisher $z_r = .343$. The second step is to substitute $N = 80$ in the formula, that is,

$$\left(\frac{1}{\sqrt{N-3}}\right)1.96 = \left(\frac{1}{\sqrt{77}}\right)1.96 = 0.2234$$

The third step is to subtract the result in Step 2 from the result in Step 1 to find the lower limit of z_r (i.e., $.343 - .2234 = .1196$, rounded to .12), and to add the result in Step 2 to the result in Step 1 to find the upper limit of z_r (i.e., $.343 + .2234 = .5664$, rounded to .57). The final step is to transform both results of Step 3 into effect size rs, which we do by consulting Table B.7. For $z_r = .12$, we see at the intersection of the row labeled .1 and the column labeled .02 that .119, rounded to .12, is the lower limit of our r_{effect} of .33. For $z_r = .57$, we see at the intersection of the row labeled .5 and the column labeled .07 that .515, rounded to .52, is the upper limit of our r_{effect} of .33. We can now say, with 95% confidence, that the effect size is between .12 and .52.

To see how the confidence interval is affected by smaller and larger Ns, suppose that the N is 20 instead of 80. Substituting in the formula in Step 2 gives

$$\left(\frac{1}{\sqrt{17}}\right)1.96 = .4754$$

which, when we carry out the remaining calculations, results in a 95% confidence interval from $-.13$ to .67. A negative effect-size r means that the pattern of the observed effect is opposite that predicted, so in this case, the confidence interval is so wide that it includes unexpected as well as expected directional patterns.

What if we increase the sample to 320? Substituting in the formula in Step 2 gives us

$$\left(\frac{1}{\sqrt{317}}\right)1.96 = .1101$$

which, when we follow through with the remaining steps, yields a 95% confidence interval from .23 to .42. Thus we see that working with a smaller N widens the confidence interval, and that working with a larger N shrinks the confidence interval. Since we would prefer a narrow rather than a wide confidence interval, the lesson is to work with the largest N possible (see also Box 12.9).

Box 12.9 **90% and 99% Confidence Intervals**

You need not restrict yourself to a 95% confidence interval if you prefer working with some other interval. The table below shows values of alpha (i.e., p levels), confidence intervals, and the corresponding standard score z for $p = .10, .05,$ and .01 two-tail:

Alpha (α)	.10	.05	.01
Confidence interval (%)	90	95	99
2-tailed z	1.64	1.96	2.58

For example, if you wanted a 90% confidence interval, you would substitute 1.64 for 1.96 in the formula in Step 2, and if you wanted a 99% confidence interval, you would instead substitute 2.58. Increasing the confidence interval from 95% to 99% will, in turn, widen the confidence interval, and vice versa. (If you ask yourself how wide an interval you would need to be 100% sure about some risky event, you will see intuitively why increasing the confidence level results in a wider confidence interval.)

Summary of Ideas

1. Three procedures discussed in this chapter that use statistics and probabilities are (a) null hypothesis significance testing (NHST); (b) effect size estimation (and the corresponding BESD and confidence interval), and (c) power analysis.

2. The probability of a particular outcome is the number of favorable events divided by the total number of possible events.

3. The null hypothesis (H_0) and the alternate hypothesis (H_1) are mutually exclusive: When one is true, the other must be false.

4. A Type I error is a mistake in rejecting H_0 when it is true, whereas a Type II error is a mistake in failing to reject H_0 when it is false.

5. The probability of a Type I error is called alpha (α), the significance level, and the *p* value; the probability of a Type II error is called beta (β).

6. The .05 significance level is commonly used by behavioral researchers as a basis for deciding whether or not to reject the null hypothesis.

7. Traditionally scientists have believed that it is worse to make a Type I error (i.e., an error of gullibility) than to make a Type II error (i.e., an error of blindness to a relationship).

8. When doing NHST, scientists try to see whether they can reject the null hypothesis and yet be reasonably sure that they will not be wrong in doing so.

9. Failure to reject the null hypothesis does not automatically imply "no effect," and therefore statistical significance should not be confused with the practical importance of the obtained effect.

10. The binomial effect-size display (BESD), which is one way of emphasizing the practical importance of an obtained effect, shows the difference in success rates (e.g., survival rate, cure rate, improvement rate, or selection rate) between the experimental and the control condition based on the magnitude of the effect size correlation (r_{effect}).

11. Using r^2 (the coefficient of determination) as an effect size index is misleading under almost all circumstances, because it underestimates the practical importance of the observed effect when r_{effect} is not 0 or 1.

12. Power, defined as $1 - \beta$, refers to the probability of not making a Type II error.

13. Given a particular effect size, we can determine how big a sample we need to achieve any desired level of significance, with a known probability of success (i.e., power).

14. The confidence level is defined as $1 - \alpha$, and we create a confidence interval around an r_{effect} by using Fisher z_r transformations to locate upper and lower limits.

15. The smaller the N or the higher the desired confidence (e.g., 99% instead of 95%), the wider is the confidence interval.

Key Terms

Multiple-Choice Questions for Review (answers are found on page 355)

1. "There will be no difference between the experimental group and the control group." This statement is an example of a(n) (a) alternate hypothesis; (b) experimental hypothesis; (c) directional hypothesis; (d) null hypothesis.

2. "There will be a difference between the experimental group and the control group." This statement is an example of (a) H_0; (b) H_1; (c) H_2; (d) H_3.

3. Rejecting the null hypothesis when it is true is called a (a) Type 0 error; (b) Type I error; (c) Type II error; (d) Type III error.

4. Failing to reject H_0 when it is false is called a (a) Type 0 error; (b) Type I error; (c) Type II error; (d) Type III error.

5. A Type II error can be thought of as an error of (a) imprecision; (b) deafness; (c) gullibility; (d) blindness.

6. Scientists usually consider a _____ error to be more serious than a _____ error. (a) Type I; Type II; (b) null hypothesis; alternate hypothesis; (c) alternate hypothesis; null hypothesis; (d) Type II; Type I

7. A student at Lincoln University conducts a study with 52 subjects and finds the correlation between authoritarianism and prejudice to be $r = .25$. According to Table 12.3, what is the two-tailed significance level associated with this correlation? (a) .10; (b) .05; (c) .01; (d) .001

8. Squaring a correlation coefficient yields a statistic known as the (a) coefficient of determination; (b) binomial effect-size display; (c) proportion of variability unexplained; (d) none of the above.

9. A student at Central Arkansas wants to conduct a study with power of .60 and, based on previous research, expects to get an effect size r of .20. According to Table 12.6, how many subjects should she obtain in order to reject the null hypothesis at the .05 level two-tailed? (a) 10; (b) 20; (c) 60; (d) 125

10. A student at the University of Alaska is planning a study. He expects to find a correlation of .30 but unfortunately can obtain only 25 subjects. According to Table 12.6, what will the power of his study be? (a) .20; (b) .25; (c) .30; (d) .40

Discussion Questions for Review (answers are found on pages 355–56)

1. A Notre Dame student manipulated the presence or absence of a confederate in a wheelchair on subjects' willingness to sign a petition urging more handicapped parking spaces for public and private buildings. The effect size of the result was $r_{effect} = .40$. Can you create and interpret a BESD for this effect size?

2. A Gallaudet student was asked by her professor to define the Type II error in the context of the aspirin study (Table 12.4) and to tell how it is related to the power of a test. Do you know the answer? Do you know what factors determine the power of a test of significance?

3. A panicking friend asks a University of Texas student for help with a project she is doing at Southern Methodist University on sex differences in scores on a new test of assertiveness. Her study will involve a randomly sampled group of males and a randomly sampled group of females. She tells the Texas student that effect sizes in this area of research have tended to be approximately $r_{effect} = .20$. She wants to present her findings at the Southeastern Psychological Association meeting in New Orleans but worries that the study will not be accepted for presentation unless the group difference reaches a significance level (alpha) of $p = .05$ two-tailed. She also tells her Texas friend that the power level she is seeking for her study is .7. Given all this information, how many subjects should the friend advise her to run in each condition?

4. A St. Lawrence student does a study and gets $p = .05$. Exactly what does this p value tell him? What doesn't it tell him that is also important to know?

5. The first three students to complete their course research projects at Minot State College displayed their BESDs to the other students, to inspire them. All three students had developed new methods of teaching vocabulary. What was r_{effect} associated with each of the following BESDs?

Student A:

Method	Above average	Below average
New	75	25
Old	25	75

Student B:

Method	Above average	Below average
New	55	45
Old	45	55

Student C:

Method	Above average	Below average
New	35	65
Old	65	35

6. The Gallaudet student in Question 2 is also asked by her professor to create a 95% confidence interval for the effect size correlation of .034 in the aspirin study. Do you know how to do it?

13 The *t* Test

Comparing Two Means

We have examined the logic of using statistics and probabilities to test hypotheses, and with this chapter we begin our discussion of the three most popular statistical tests: the *t* test (described in this chapter), the *F* test (Chapter 14), and the chi-square (χ^2) test (Chapter 15). The choice of a statistical test depends on the research question and the design of the study. If we are interested in comparing the means of two groups (e.g., experimental and control groups), we will find the **t test** (also called **Student's *t***) a convenient and powerful method (see also Box 13.1). It allows us to test the likelihood that the population means represented by the two groups are equal (i.e., the null hypothesis), by setting up a **signal-to-noise ratio.** In this ratio, the "signal" is represented by the difference between the two means and the "noise" is represented by the variability of the scores within the samples. The larger the signal is in relation to the noise, the more likely the null hypothesis is to be rejected.

However, as you learned in the previous chapter, we would not want to place the weight of our decision about the *practical importance* of an obtained effect on the *p* value,

PREVIEW QUESTIONS

▌ How does the concept of a signal-to-noise ratio apply to *t* tests?

▌ How is a two-sample *t* computed for a comparison of independent groups?

▌ What do degrees of freedom (*df*) have to do with *p* values?

▌ How is the effect size of *t* computed?

▌ How can you apply what you previously learned about confidence intervals and BESDs?

▌ Why is *t* also conceptualized as the product of the effect size and the size of the study?

▌ What are the implications of this conceptual relationship for optimizing *t*?

▌ How is a one-sample *t* computed on groups that are not independent?

▌ How is a BESD created and interpreted for the paired *t*?

Box 13.1 **Student's *t***

The *t* test is called **Student's *t*** in honor of William Sealy Gosset, its inventor. Gosset worked for Guinness, the famous Irish brewery, which for security reasons prohibited the publication of research done by its staff. Gosset was able to persuade the company to relax this rule for the statistical methods he had developed, but it agreed only on condition that he use a pen name. The one he chose was Student.

because p is an indicator only of statistical significance. We also want to know the magnitude of the effect of the independent variable (X) on the dependent variable (Y). In this chapter, we will show that it is easy to calculate the effect size correlation (r_{effect}) from just our knowledge of the value of the t test and its associated "degrees of freedom" (defined in a moment). Given this information, we can easily calculate the 95% confidence interval (or any other level of confidence) by following the steps described in the previous chapter. We can recast r_{effect} into a BESD in order to reveal the practical importance of the observed effect.

We begin our discussion of the t test by explaining how signal-to-noise ratios operate. We will later use this discussion and another conceptual relationship (i.e., significance test = effect size × study size) as our point of departure for showing how you can optimize the detection of a real difference between means. We will describe two general forms of the t test, one for use with independent groups (i.e., an independent, or two-sample, t test) and the other for use with groups that are not independent (i.e., a paired, or one-sample, t test). We will also apply what you learned in the previous chapter to create both BESDs and confidence intervals.

Signal-to-Noise Ratios

As an illustration of how t tests can be thought of as **signal-to-noise ratios,** suppose a researcher is conducting an experiment on the effect of vitamins on the academic performance of children from families below the poverty level. In Chapter 7, we described the statistical plan as a simple randomized design; that is, the sampling units are randomly assigned to the treatments. The researcher has randomly assigned the children to an experimental group (which has received vitamins at regular intervals) or to a control group (which has received a placebo). The alternate hypothesis (H_1), stated in terms of the experimenter's working hypothesis, is that vitamins will have a positive effect on the children's academic performance. The null hypothesis (H_0) is that vitamins will have no effect on the children's academic performance. Table 13.1 and Figure 13.1 show two alternative outcomes of this experiment and help to illustrate the signal-to-noise idea.

We see that the means of the vitamin groups are identical ($M = 15$), as are the means of the control groups ($M = 10$). The only difference between Results A and

Table 13.1	Simple Randomized Design with Alternative Results A and B			
	Results A		Results B	
	Vitamins	Control	Vitamins	Control
	13	8	9	4
	15	10	15	10
	17	12	21	16
Mean (M)	15	10	15	10

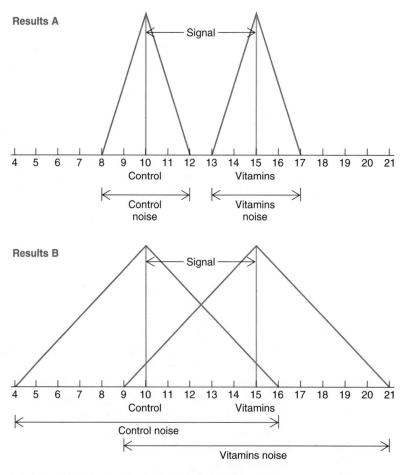

Figure 13.1 **Graphical display of the data in Table 13.1.**
Note that Results A have no overlapping data but that Results B overlap from the scores of 9 to 16.

Results B is that one set of results (B) is more variable. That is, the scores of B are less tightly bunched than the scores of A. When we compare the mean differences *between* the groups ($15 - 10 = 5$), it seems that we should also take into consideration the amount of variability *within* the groups. That is, the 5 points of difference between the groups look larger to us when seen against the backdrop of the small within-group variation of A than when seen against the backdrop of the larger within-group variation of B.

This is the way the t test works. It is a test of statistical significance that examines the difference between two means (the **signal**) against the background of the within-group variability (the **noise**). The larger the difference between the means, or the smaller the within-group variability for any given size of study, the greater will be the signal-to-noise ratio, that is, the magnitude of t (see also Box 13.2). Because large ts are associated with differences between means that are more statistically significant, researchers generally prefer larger ts. That is, larger ts have a lower level of probability (p value or alpha), which in turn allows researchers to reject the null hypothesis that there is no difference between means.

Box 13.2 **Shouting to Make Yourself Heard!**

Suppose you are trying to conduct an intimate conversation in a noisy restaurant. You have to shout to make your words (i.e., the signal) understood over the background din (i.e., the noise). However, if there is not much noise, you can whisper and have your communication easily picked up. By analogy, t tests are more sensitive to differences between groups (i.e., the signal) when the variability within groups (the din) does not overwhelm the magnitude of a real difference.

Comparing Independent Samples

In the example we have been considering, the two groups are presumed to be **independent** of one another; that is, the results in one group are not influenced by the results in the other group. Had this been a repeated-measures design, the two scores on each sampling unit would not be independent. We will examine this second situation in a moment, but several formulas can be used to calculate t when we want to compare independent samples. A general purpose one is

$$t = \frac{M_1 - M_2}{\sqrt{\left(\dfrac{1}{n_1} + \dfrac{1}{n_2}\right)S^2}}$$

in which M_1 and M_2 are the means of the two groups; n_1 and n_2 are the number of sampling units (e.g., subjects) in each of the two groups; and S^2 is what was called in Chapter 9 the *unbiased estimator of the population variance*.

In this case, the S^2 is defined as the "pooled estimate" of the population variance (i.e., a single estimate of the variance associated with both populations from which the two groups were drawn), computed as

$$S^2 = \frac{\Sigma(X_1 - M_1)^2 + \Sigma(X_2 - M_2)^2}{n_1 + n_2 - 2}$$

where X_1 and X_2 are individual raw scores, and the other symbols are as defined above.

Table 13.2 provides the basic data we need to compute t for the two sets of results in Table 13.1. For each group, we compute the sum of the squares of the deviations of the scores from their mean, and we then enter this information in the formula for S^2. With Results A we find

$$S^2 = \frac{8.0 + 8.0}{3 + 3 - 2} = 4.0$$

so

$$t = \frac{15 - 10}{\sqrt{\left(\dfrac{1}{3} + \dfrac{1}{3}\right)4.0}} = \frac{5}{1.63} = 3.06$$

Table 13.2   Basic Data for Calculating t for Results A and B in Table 13.1

Results A

	Vitamin group			Control group		
	X_1	$X_1 - M_1$	$(X_1 - M_1)^2$	X_2	$X_2 - M_2$	$(X_2 - M_2)^2$
	13	−2.0	4.0	8	−2.0	4.0
	15	0.0	0.0	10	0.0	0.0
	17	+2.0	4.0	12	+2.0	4.0
Sum (Σ)	45	0	8.0	30	0	8.0
Mean (M)	15	—	—	10	—	—

Results B

	Vitamin group			Control group		
	X_1	$X_1 - M_1$	$(X_1 - M_1)^2$	X_2	$X_2 - M_2$	$(X_2 - M_2)^2$
	9	−6.0	36.0	4	−6.0	36.0
	15	0.0	0.0	10	0.0	0.0
	21	+6.0	36.0	16	+6.0	36.0
Sum (Σ)	45	0	72.0	30	0	72.0
Mean (M)	15	—	—	10	—	—

Performing these same calculations on Results B gives

$$S^2 = \frac{72.0 + 72.0}{3 + 3 - 2} = \frac{144.0}{4} = 36.0$$

and

$$t = \frac{15 - 10}{\sqrt{\left(\frac{1}{3} + \frac{1}{3}\right)36.0}} = \frac{5}{4.90} = 1.02$$

Not surprisingly, *t* is larger for Results A than for Results B. We expected this effect because of the difference in variability (i.e., the difference in noise levels) between A and B. In null hypothesis significance testing (NHST), the next step is to look up the *p* values in a suitable table. Because larger *t*s are rarer events, we expect to find a smaller *p* associated with Results A than with Results B. Before we show how to look up the *p* values, some background information will be useful.

Using the *t* Table to Find *p*

Although it is convenient to think of *t* as a single test of statistical significance, it may also be thought of as a family of curves. The reason is that there is a different curve (each resembling the standard normal distribution) for every possible value of what are called the **degrees of freedom** (symbolized as **df**) of the *t* test. In the case we have been considering, the degrees of freedom are defined as $n_1 + n_2 - 2$ (see also Box 13.3). One of the great contributions by the inventor of the *t* test, William Gosset (Box 13.1), was to figure out the curve for each number of degrees of freedom. However, instead of having to make our way through scores of different curves, we can use a table that summarizes the most pertinent information from these curves for selected *p* values. Such information is contained in Table 13.3, which gives the areas found in one or both tails of selected *t* curves. That is, for one-tailed *p* values, this table gives the areas found in the right-hand tail, whereas for two-tailed *p*s, it gives the areas found in both tails.

Box 13.3   **Degrees of Freedom**

The origin of degrees of freedom (*df*) has to do in a way with the standard deviation, which in turn depends on the deviations from the mean (i.e., the $X - M$ values). Suppose we have five raw (*X*) scores: 1, 3, 5, 7, 9, with $\Sigma X = 25$ and $M = 5$. The sum of the deviations from the mean has to be zero. That is, $\Sigma(X - M) = 0$ because $(1 - 5) + (3 - 5) + (5 - 5) + (7 - 5) + (9 - 5)$ equals zero. Knowing this, if we were given all but one value, we could easily find the missing value. In other words, one deviation in the group is not free to vary, so 1 *df* is eliminated. Thus, with a batch of five scores, we have 4 *df* remaining. In the case of a *t* test on two independent samples, we lose 1 *df* for each group, so that $df = n_1 + n_2 - 2$.

Table 13.3	*t* Values Required for Significance at Various *p* Levels				
			Probability level (*p*)		
	.10	.05	.025	.005	one-tail
df	.20	.10	.05	.01	two-tail
1	3.08	6.31	12.71	63.66	
2	1.89	2.92	4.30	9.92	
3	1.64	2.35	3.18	5.84	
4	1.53	2.13	2.78	4.60	
5	1.48	2.02	2.57	4.03	
6	1.44	1.94	2.45	3.71	
8	1.40	1.86	2.31	3.36	
10	1.37	1.81	2.23	3.17	
15	1.34	1.75	2.13	2.95	
20	1.32	1.72	2.09	2.84	
25	1.32	1.71	2.06	2.79	
30	1.31	1.70	2.04	2.75	
40	1.30	1.68	2.02	2.70	
60	1.30	1.67	2.00	2.66	
80	1.29	1.66	1.99	2.64	
100	1.29	1.66	1.98	2.63	
1,000	1.28	1.65	1.96	2.58	
∞	1.28	1.64	1.96	2.58	

Note: For a more complete table, see Appendix B, Table B.2.

Studying Table 13.3 teaches us that, for any level of *p*, the *t* value required to reach that level is smaller and smaller as the degrees of freedom (*df*) increase. In addition, for any *df*, a higher *t* value is required to reach more extreme (smaller) *p* values. One way to think about *t* is that, if the null hypothesis is true (i.e., if the means in the population do not differ), the most likely value of *t* is zero. However, even if the population mean difference were truly zero, we would often find nonzero *t* values by sheer chance alone. For example, suppose the direction of the effect is predicted, in which case we may use the one-tailed *p* values. With *df* = 8, we would obtain a *t* value of 1.40 or greater (favoring the predicted outcome) about 10% of the time (i.e., one-tailed *p* = .10), or of 1.86 or greater about 5% of the time (one-tailed *p* = .05), or of 3.36 or greater about 0.5% of the time (one-tailed *p* = .005).

We are now ready to look up our two *t*s, and we will assume that the direction of the effect was predicted. For this step, we will use the more comprehensive listing found in Table B.2 (see pp. 409–410). The rows show the degrees of freedom, which will be 4 for both sets of results because we eliminate 1 *df* in each group (i.e., *df* = 3 + 3 − 2 = 4). We put a finger on the row labeled 4 *df* and read across the columns until we find a value that is the same as or larger than the obtained value of *t*. We see that our *t* of 3.06 is larger than the value listed for $p = .025$ one-tail (2.776) but smaller than the value listed for $p = .01$ one-tail (3.747). Thus the one-tailed *p* of $t = 3.06$ is less than .025 (i.e., $p < .025$ one-tail) but greater than .01 (i.e., $p > .01$ one-tail). We next see that our *t* of 1.02 is larger than the value listed for $p = .25$ one-tail (.741) but smaller than the value listed for $p = .10$ one-tail (1.533). In other words, the one-tailed *p* for $t = 1.02$ with 4 *df* is $< .25$ but $> .10$ (see also Box 13.4).

Box 13.4	**The Increasing Stability of *t* Values**

Notice also in Table B.2 (and Table 13.3) that the values of *t* in each column become more stable as the degrees of freedom increase. The reason is that the *t* distribution gradually approximates the standard normal distribution as the size of the samples is increased. At 30 *df*, the *t* distribution is fairly close to that of the standard normal distribution, and with $df = \infty$ (infinity), the *t* distribution gives values identical to those for the standard normal distribution. This information may come in handy if you decide to do a meta-analysis (described in Appendix C), because the implication is that you can look up the *p* values of *z*s in the $df = \infty$ row of Table B.2.

We must decide for ourselves whether we will regard any given *t* as an event rare enough to make us doubt that the null hypothesis is true. Of course, we cannot simply decide, for example, that "$p < .20$ is a reasonable risk" and then expect that instructors, reviewers, or editors will necessarily accept that decision. If we follow the NHST convention, which dictates that the .05 significance level be used as a critical demarcation point, we will conclude that Results A are "statistically significant" and that Results B are "not statistically significant at the 5% alpha." However, more informative ways of evaluating the "significance" of the results were discussed in the previous chapter, and let us now see how you might compute effect sizes, confidence intervals, and BESDs when using *t* tests.

Measuring the Effect Size

First, in the previous chapter, we developed the argument that, in defining the results of research, the *p* value alone fails to tell the whole story. We wanted to know the effect size so that we could get an idea of the practical significance of the results (using the BESD) and make plans to do a follow-up study with increased power if necessary. You will recall that the power of a statistical test is determined by (1) the level of the risk of drawing a spuriously favorable conclusion (i.e., the *p* level); (2) the size of the study (i.e., the sample size); and (3) the effect size. Thus, if we know the *p* value we are trying to "reach" and the effect size likely to be found in nature, we can easily figure out how big a sample we need to achieve any desired level of statistical power (see again Table 12.6 on p. 281).

We also showed that the effect size tells us something very different from the p value. A result that is statistically significant is not necessarily practically significant as judged by the size of the effect or its application in a given situation. Thus highly significant p values should not be interpreted as automatically reflecting substantial effects. A case in point is that much research on medications results in very small effects, even though many such medications are often advertised as providing relief in a "significant" percentage of cases (Paulos, 1990). On the other hand, if we do not have enough power, small effects of some practical importance may be ignored because of their failure to reach statistical significance (i.e., a Type II error). If the effect size is theoretically interesting, the researcher should continue the investigation with a larger sample before deciding that nothing happened (i.e., that the null hypothesis is true).

The procedure for computing the effect size, r_{effect}, from a t test is simple enough to be performed on any pocket calculator. As you take notes for your literature review, you can also use this procedure to compute the effect sizes of reported ts as a prelude to synthesizing them (described in Appendix C on meta-analysis). To reiterate, we will be emphasizing the product-moment r as an index of the effect size, because it can be interpreted by the BESD procedure described in the previous chapter (see also Box 13.5). Also noted previously was the fact that you will find other indices of effect size in published reports, and if you are interested in converting them to r_{effect}, you will find formulas for doing so elsewhere (e.g., Rosenthal & Rosnow, 1991).

Box 13.5 **Defining r_{effect} as the Point-Biserial**

In the case of the independent (or two-sample) t test on a continuous dependent variable, the effect size correlation is the point-biserial (r_{pb}) correlation described in Chapter 11. To illustrate this, you dummy-code the particular group or condition (e.g., 1 = experimental and 0 = control) and then, after standardizing these scores and the scores on the dependent variable, correlate them with one another. This will give you the same answer as using the formula

$$r_{effect} = \sqrt{\frac{t^2}{t^2 + df}}$$

In the case of the paired (or one-sample) t test, the statistical meaning of the effect size r is more subtle, but we can still easily calculate r_{effect} by the simple formula shown above.

When the significance test is a t test, the corresponding effect size r can be calculated quite simply as

$$r_{effect} = \sqrt{\frac{t^2}{t^2 + df}}$$

In the case of Results A in Table 13.2, with $t = 3.06$ and $df = n_1 + n_2 - 2 = 4$, we find

$$r_{effect} = \sqrt{\frac{(3.06)^2}{(3.06)^2 + 4}} = .84$$

which indicates a "jumbo-sized" effect. In the case of Results B, with $t = 1.02$ and the same df, we find

$$r_{effect} = \sqrt{\frac{(1.02)^2}{(1.02)^2 + 4}} = .45$$

which indicates a substantial effect in spite of the failure of the test to achieve significance at the conventional 5% level.

The Confidence Interval and the BESD

We can now create a confidence interval around these effects by following the four easy steps in the previous chapter. To review, with 95% confidence and $r_{effect} = .84$, the first step is to use Table B.6 (page 418) to find the corresponding Fisher z_r, which is 1.221. In Step 2, we substitute $N = 6$ in the formula

$$\left(\frac{1}{\sqrt{N-3}}\right)1.96 = \left(\frac{1}{\sqrt{3}}\right)1.96 = 1.1316$$

where 1.96 represents the 95% confidence level, although we can (as described in the previous chapter) choose another confidence level if we wish. In Step 3, we subtract the value obtained in Step 2 from 1.221 to find the lower limit of z_r (0.0894, rounded to .09) and add 1.1316 to 1.221 to find the upper limit of z_r (2.3526, rounded to 2.35). In the final step, we use Table B.7 (p. 419) to transform these lower and upper z_r values back into rs and, on the basis of this transformation, conclude that we can be 95% confident that the effect size r in the population is between .09 and .98. As you also learned in the previous chapter, had we worked with a much larger N or a less stringent confidence level (e.g., 90% rather than 95%), the interval would not have been this wide.

Applying what you learned previously about BESDs, you can now create such displays for the lower and upper limits surrounding the BESD for the obtained effect size. Table 13.4 shows these BESDs for the results we have seen, and it gives us a clearer sense of the possible practical importance of the effect in question (because it is now encapsulated within the boundaries of the confidence interval). We see that the effect of taking vitamins is important at either extreme of the 95% confidence interval.

Optimizing the t Test

The t test, like any significance test (e.g., F and χ^2), can be mathematically shown to consist of two components, one having to do with the effect size and the other with the **size of the study** (i.e., the number of sampling units). The way these two components come together is expressed by the following conceptual equation:

Table 13.4	BESDs for Results A in Table 13.2

Lower limit BESD (95% confidence)

	Improved	Not improved
Vitamins	54.5	45.5
Control	45.5	54.5

Obtained-effect BESD

	Improved	Not improved
Vitamins	92	8
Control	8	92

Upper limit BESD (95% confidence)

	Improved	Not improved
Vitamins	99	1
Control	1	99

Significance test = (Size of effect) (Size of study)

which tells us that t is the product of the effect size and the study size. That is, the larger the effect or the more subjects used, the greater will be the size of the t. This equation helps us to plan specific ways of optimizing (or maximizing) the t test in a given situation (i.e., ways of strengthening the power of the t test).

For example, here is another formula in which t is mathematically broken down into an effect size and a study size component:

$$t = \left(\frac{M_1 - M_2}{S} \right) \left(\sqrt{\frac{n_1 n_2}{n_1 + n_2}} \right)$$

but where the effect size is now defined as $(M_1 - M_2)/S$. This different way of defining the effect size—called **Hedges's g**—views it not as a Pearson r, but in z-score-like terms. It is a useful way of denoting and interpreting the effect size, and you will find detailed discussions of it elsewhere (e.g., Hedges & Olkin, 1985). However, our reason for noting the equation above is not to explicate this measure of effect size, but instead to suggest how you can optimize t in three ways: (1) by driving the means further apart; (2) by decreasing the variability within groups; and (3) by increasing the effective size of the study.

First, we might try to optimize t by using a stronger treatment to drive the means of the experimental and control groups further apart. For example, if our working hypothesis is that longer treatment sessions are more beneficial than shorter treatment sessions, we are more apt to find a significant difference if we compare the control group with an experimental group that has been treated for 45 minutes than if we compare it with a group treated for just 15 minutes. This tactic should increase the $M_1 - M_2$ in the numerator of the effect size component.

Second, by decreasing the variability of response within groups, we decrease the *S* in the denominator of the effect size component and thereby strengthen the power of *t*. This is what happened in Results A, in which the variability of response within groups was substantially less than that in Results B. Two ways of decreasing the variability of response are (1) standardizing the research procedures in order to make them more uniform and (2) recruiting subject samples that are fairly homogeneous in those characteristics that are substantially correlated with the dependent variable.

Third, as implied in the previous chapter, we also strengthen the power of *t* by increasing the size-of-study component. That is, we simply increase the total *N* (i.e., the total number of subjects). Another way to increase this component is to make the sample size as nearly equal as possible in the two groups (i.e., have $n_1 = n_2$). The reason is that *t* tests thrive more when sample sizes are not very different for any given total *N* (Rosenthal & Rosnow, 1991, pp. 304–305).

Comparing Related Samples

So far, we have used *t* to compare the means of two *independent* groups. That is, we regarded the scores in one group as having no inherent relationship to the scores in the other group. However, suppose we measure the *same* subjects more than once (e.g., before and after they are exposed to a learning experience) and want to compare the means of these two measures. Now the two groups of scores are no longer independent because of the repeated-measures design, or within-subjects design. A perhaps less obvious example of samples that are not independent would occur if the two groups consisted of children who were related by birth, and one member were assigned to Group 1 and the other to Group 2. The common family membership has introduced a degree of prior relatedness between the scores in Group 1 and those in Group 2.

When samples that are not independent are compared by the independent *t* test, the resulting value is biased (it is *usually* too small, but also sometimes too large). To avoid this problem, we instead use a **paired-*t*** (or one-sample) formula (also called a **correlated *t*** or **matched *t***) for samples that are not independent. To illustrate this approach, we refer to the basic data in Table 13.5, which shows a hypothetical study in which girls were predicted to be more sociable than boys. The scores are ratings by a judge on a 9-point scale of sociability. What makes this study appropriate for a paired *t* is that these were six *pairs* of girls and boys, each pair from a different family. When we examine the judge's ratings over these pairs, we find that a child's sociability score is to some degree predictable from family membership. For instance, the column of means shows that the Smith and Jones children were judged (on the average) to be less sociable than the Kern and Brown children.

In *t* tests for matched (or correlated) data, we perform our calculations on the difference score (*D*) for each pair of lined-up scores. We use the following formula:

$$t = \frac{M_D}{\sqrt{\left(\frac{1}{N}\right)S_D{}^2}}$$

Table 13.5   Basic Data for Paired-*t* Test

Family	Group 1 X_1 (girls)	Group 2 X_2 (boys)	Mean (M_X)	D	$D - M_D$	$(D - M_D)^2$
Smith	4	3	3.5	1	−1	1
Ross	6	4	5.0	2	0	0
Kern	8	5	6.5	3	1	1
Jones	4	3	3.5	1	−1	1
Hill	6	4	5.0	2	0	0
Brown	8	5	6.5	3	1	1
Sum (Σ)	36	24	30.0	12	0	4
Mean (M)	6	4	5.0	2.0		

Note: The value of M_D is shown as 2.0 at the bottom of the column of differences (D) between Groups I and II (i.e., $D = X_1 - X_2$), and the value of $\Sigma(D - M_D)^2$ is shown as 4 at the bottom of the last column.

in which M_D is the mean of the $D = X_1 - X_2$ scores; N is the number of D scores (i.e., the number of lined-up pairs); and S_D^2 gives us the unbiased estimate of the population value of σ_D^2, with S_D^2 defined by

$$S_D^2 = \frac{\Sigma(D - M_D)^2}{N - 1}$$

and *df* now defined as $N - 1$, where N is the number of paired scores. Thus the paired, or one-sample, *t* operates by subtracting the values of one of the correlated samples from the corresponding values of the other correlated sample, thereby creating a new *single* sample of difference scores.

Substituting the data in Table 13.5, we find

$$S_D^2 = \frac{4}{6 - 1} = .80$$

and

$$t = \frac{2.0}{\sqrt{\left(\frac{1}{6}\right).80}} = \frac{2.0}{.365} = 5.48$$

We can now look up *p* as a one-tailed value (because we predicted that girls would score higher than boys), also compute the effect size and its confidence interval, and finally display the effect size as a BESD. First, for the *p* value, we turn to Table B.2 (p. 409), but we now read across the row labeled 5 *df* (because the degrees of freedom for a single sample are defined as $N - 1$, or $6 - 1 = 5$). Our *t* of 5.48 is larger than 4.773 but smaller than 5.893, so one-tailed $p < .0025$ but $> .001$ (see also Box 13.6). When we calculate the effect size, we find

$$r_{\text{effect}} = \sqrt{\frac{t^2}{t^2 + df}} = \sqrt{\frac{(5.48)^2}{(5.48)^2 + 5}} = .926$$

which leads us to conclude that we have another "jumbo-sized" effect in addition to a statistically significant one.

Box 13.6   ## How Many Decimal Places?

When you use a calculator to compute statistics, it is a good idea not to scrimp on the number of decimal places in the intermediate calculations because rounding errors can produce inaccurate results. Suppose you were a NASA engineer trying to figure out how much fuel it would take a manned rocket to reach Mars. By rounding off the calculations, you might send the astronauts on an impossible mission. However, what if you are puzzling over how many decimals to report in p values? As noted in the previous chapter, many statisticians report the actual descriptive level of significance because it carries more information than the phrases "significant difference" or "no significant difference at the 5% level" (e.g., Mosteller, Fienberg, & Rourke, 1983; Snedecor & Cochran, 1989). There is something absurd, they would argue, about regarding as a "real" effect one that is supported by $p = .05$ and as a "zero" effect one that is supported by $p = .06$. Instead of listing a string of zeros, you can use **scientific notation** as a more compact way to show a very small p value. That is, instead of reporting $p = .00000025$, you report 2.5×10^{-7}, where -7 (i.e., the exponent of 10) tells us to count 7 places to the left of the decimal in 2.5 and make that the decimal place.

Table 13.6 shows what this imaginary effect will look like as a BESD with equal totals in the margins. The cell values should not be mistaken for the actual frequencies that would be obtained in a random sample; instead, they should be seen as standardized values because of the uniform totals that we imposed on the margins for ease

Table 13.6   Binomial Effect-Size Display of Results in Table 13.5

	Sociability		
Gender	More sociable	Less sociable	Total
Girls	96.3	3.7	100
Boys	3.7	96.3	100
Total	100	100	200

of interpretation. Using the procedure described previously, we can calculate the 95% confidence interval of the effect, which we now find to be between rs of .46 and .99.

Summary of Ideas

1. The t test operates like a signal-to-noise ratio used to compare two means relative to the variability of scores within each group.
2. When we look up a one- or two-tailed p, we need to know the degrees of freedom (df) as well as the value of t.
3. Using a one-tailed p implies that we predicted in which side of the t distribution the p value would be situated.
4. In an independent, or two-sample, t test, the df are defined as $n_1 + n_2 - 2$ because, in each group, one deviation from the mean is not free to vary.
5. Once we have created a confidence interval for the obtained r_{effect}, we can create BESDs to represent the lower and upper limits.
6. Like any significance test, the t test is made up of two components: the size of the effect and the size of the study.
7. We can optimize the power of the independent t by (a) drawing the means further apart; (b) decreasing the variability within groups; and (c) increasing the effective size of the study.
8. We used a paired t to compare the means of two groups that are not independent, in which case $df = N - 1$, where N is the total number of paired scores.
9. The effect size of t can be computed as

$$r_{effect} = \sqrt{\frac{t^2}{t^2 + df}}$$

and the result then displayed in a BESD.

Key Terms

correlated t p. 299
degrees of freedom (df)   p. 293
Hedges's g p. 298
independent t p. 291
matched t p. 299
noise   p. 291
paired t p. 299

scientific notation   p. 301
signal   p. 291
signal-to-noise ratio   p. 289
size of the study   p. 297
Student's t p. 288
t test   p. 288

Multiple-Choice Questions for Review (answers are found on page 356)

1. In a t test, the difference between the two means can be thought of as the (a) significance level; (b) noise; (c) signal; (d) none of the above.
2. In a t test, the variability of scores within samples can be thought of as the (a) significance level; (b) noise; (c) signal; (d) none of the above.

3. A researcher at Santa Fe Community College conducts a study with 5 subjects in the experimental group and 6 subjects in the control group. She then calculates a *t* test. How many degrees of freedom will be associated with this test? (a) 4; (b) 5; (c) 6; (d) 9

4. A researcher conducts a *t* test for independent samples. There is a total of 8 subjects, and *t* = 5. What is the appropriate one-tailed *p* value? (a) <.05; (b) <.0025; (c) <.005; (d) <.001

5. A very small *p* value (e.g., .001) automatically means that you have a (a) large effect; (b) medium effect; (c) small effect; (d) cannot be determined from this information.

6. A researcher at Williams College conducts a study with an experimental group and a control group. There are 4 subjects in each group. He calculates that *t* = 3. The effect size is the square root of (a) 9/15; (b) 3/13; (c) 3/4; (d) 3/7.

7. Fill in the blanks in the following conceptual equation: Significance test = _____ × _____ . (a) *t*; *r*; (b) *t*; size of study; (c) effect size; size of study; (d) *r*; effect size.

8. Which of the following can be used in maximizing *t*? (a) decreasing the difference between the means; (b) calculating *r* instead of *t*; (c) decreasing the variability within groups; (d) all of the above

9. Scores on two variables might be nonindependent because they were obtained (a) from the same subjects; (b) by means of a within-subjects design; (c) from brother-sister pairs from the same family; (d) all of the above.

10. A study is conducted in which scores are obtained from 4 subjects on two separate occasions. In other words, there are 8 total observations from 4 subjects. The data are analyzed by means of a paired-*t* test. How many degrees of freedom will there be? (a) 3; (b) 4; (c) 7; (d) 8

Discussion Questions for Review (answers are found on pages 356–58)

1. A Kent State researcher hypothesizes that marijuana use decreases short-term memory. He brings five subjects to his laboratory. Each subject is given a test of short-term memory. Each subject is then given marijuana and administered another test of short-term memory. The results are given below (high scores indicate good memory):

	Test 1	Test 2
Subject 1	5	2
Subject 2	7	5
Subject 3	4	5
Subject 4	8	3
Subject 5	8	4

Can you set up the formula and insert the numbers that would be used to test the hypothesis that the scores on Test 2 are significantly lower than the scores on Test 1? What would be the degrees of freedom? If you found a significant difference and a large effect size, should you conclude that marijuana causes a decrease in short-term memory? Why or why not?

2. A Loyola student conducted a study comparing the creativity scores of four biology and four history majors. The results were

Biology	History
4	7
6	3
3	5
3	6

Can you set up the formula that would be used to compute a t test? What would be the degrees of freedom? How would you compute and interpret the effect size?

3. An experimenter at the University of California at San Diego studied sex differences in nonverbal sensitivity. Her results showed that the women were significantly better at decoding nonverbal cues than were the men, with $t = 2.34$, $df = 62$, $p < .05$, and $r_{effect} = .28$. Pretend that the experimenter added an additional 60 subjects, randomly selected from the same population as the original sample. When the analysis is recalculated with the extra subjects, should the new t be larger, smaller, or about the same size? Should the p value be larger, smaller, or about the same size? Should r_{effect} be larger, smaller, or about the same size? Should the 95% confidence interval be wider, narrower, or about the same size?

4. A Santa Fe College student has developed a brief training program that increases sensitivity to nonverbal cues. He plans to compare it to a brief training program that increases sensitivity to people in general. He plans on randomly assigning 10 subjects to each treatment, the subjects having been found through newspaper ads. He describes his plan to his professor, who suggests he think hard about trying to obtain a larger t than he is likely to get in the planned study. What might the student do to get a larger t?

14 The *F* Test

F and *t*

The *t* test is useful whenever there are two groups to be compared, but some randomized designs contain more than two groups. A general test of significance frequently used for such designs is the *F* test, a statistic based on the **analysis of variance (ANOVA).** The *F* test may also be used whenever a *t* test is useful, so that *F* is an "all-purpose" significance test for comparing two or more groups. In this chapter, we illustrate the use of ANOVA in one-way and two-way designs. In a **one-way design,** two or more groups make up a single dimension (e.g., a design consisting of a medication group, a placebo group, and a zero control group). In a **two-way design** (also called a **two-way factorial**), each entry in the table is associated with a row variable and a column variable (see, for example, Table 7.2, p. 161).

In fact, the *F* and *t* tests are related statistically; the value of $F = t^2$ when there are only two groups to be compared. Because the effect size of *t* is computed as

$$r_{\text{effect}} = \sqrt{\frac{t^2}{t^2 + df}}$$

305

it follows that whenever there are only two groups to be compared, the effect size of F can be computed as

$$r_{\text{effect}} = \sqrt{\frac{F}{F + df}}$$

where df refers to the degrees of freedom "within conditions," obtained by determining the df within each group (or condition) and then adding. If there are more than two groups, we do not compute the effect size for that dimension because the result will be uninterpretable. One possibility, discussed here, is to compute planned t tests on paired comparisons and then to compute and interpret the effect sizes of the ts as we did in Chapter 13.

That F is based on the analysis of variance implies that we are analyzing variances (also called **mean squares** in Chapter 10) instead of analyzing means (see Box 14.1). For example, in two-way designs in which the sampling units are exposed to one treatment condition each, the analysis of variance allows us to apportion the variability of the rows, columns, and so forth, and to test (using F) how large each variance is relative to the variance within conditions (also called the **mean square for error**). We begin by describing the basic ideas involved in computing and interpreting one-way ANOVAs and then discuss factorial designs in which there are two levels of each of two independent variables operating simultaneously. In the course of your literature search, you may find designs with additional sources of variation (e.g., three-way or four-way designs). The logic is basically the same as that for the two-way design, but we do not go further than the two-way ANOVA in illustrating calculations. We conclude with an example of an ANOVA table for a repeated-measures design in the context of a two-way layout.

Box 14.1   ## Comparing Spreads

In Chapter 10, we described the variance (S^2 or σ^2) as a measure of the spread of scores around the mean. The strategy of ANOVA in between-group comparisons is to compare the spread of scores *between* the conditions (S^2_{between}) with the spread of scores *within* the conditions (S^2_{within}). That is, the ANOVA can be used to create a ratio of

$$F = \frac{S^2_{\text{between}}}{S^2_{\text{within}}}$$

where we can think of S^2_{between} as the "signal" and S^2_{within} as the "noise."

The Logic of ANOVA

In the previous chapter, we began with a hypothetical case to illustrate the signal-to-noise idea. If we look at another example, we will see that the logic is essentially the same for analysis of variance. In this illustration, we will imagine that an experimenter interested in the effects of nutrition on the academic performance of children decides to use a four-group instead of a two-group randomized design. One group of randomly

Table 14.1	Fully Randomized Design with Alternative Results A and B

Results A

	Group 1 Zero	Group 2 Milk	Group 3 Vitamins	Group 4 Hot lunch
	8	10	13	17
	10	12	15	19
	12	14	17	21
Mean (*M*)	10	12	15	19

Results B

	Group 1 Zero	Group 2 Milk	Group 3 Vitamins	Group 4 Hot lunch
	4	6	9	13
	10	12	15	19
	16	18	21	25
Mean (*M*)	10	12	15	19

assigned children gets a hot lunch daily, another group gets free milk, a third group gets a vitamin supplement, and the fourth group gets nothing extra. Once again, imagine two different sets of results of this experiment, as represented by A and B in Table 14.1.

In examining these results, what conclusions would we be willing to draw on the basis of A compared to B? We note that the outcome in the group receiving no special nutritional bonus (Group 1) has an average of 10 units of academic performance, whereas the average performance of the group receiving milk is 12 (Group 2), of that receiving vitamins (Group 3) is 15, and of that receiving hot lunches (Group 4) is 19. By applying the logic about within-group variance described in the previous chapter, we find ourselves feeling more impressed by Results A than by Results B. In Results A, the subjects have never varied in their performance by more than 2 points from the average score of their group. The few points of difference between the mean scores of the four groups look larger when seen against the backdrop of the small within-group variation of Results A, whereas they look smaller when examined against the backdrop of the large within-group variation of Results B.

The analysis of variance provides researchers with a more formal comparison of the variation between the average results per condition and the average variation within the different conditions. In this kind of analysis, as we see next, a ratio (the **F ratio**, or **F test**) is formed (note again Box 14.1). You will recall that the *t* has a value of 0 when the null hypothesis (H_0) is true. The *F* ratio has a value close to 1.0 when the variation between conditions is not different from the variation within conditions (i.e., when H_0 is true); we will explain why this is so later. The larger the *F* ratio becomes, the greater is the dispersion of group means relative to the dispersion of scores within groups. In other words, as with the *t*, researchers generally prefer larger *F*s because they are associated with smaller *p*s (see also Box 14.2).

Box 14.2 **Fisher's Ideas of Significance and Nonsignificance**

The *F* test is named after its inventor, Ronald A. Fisher (1890–1962), who also invented the null hypothesis. Another essential idea of Fisher's was that there is no sharp dividing line between a "significant" and a "nonsignificant" difference, but that the strength of the NHST evidence for or against the null hypothesis may be viewed as a fairly continuous function of the magnitude of *p*. In his seminal text, *The Design of Experiments* (1960, 1971), Fisher stated that

> convenient as it is to note that a hypothesis is contradicted at some familiar level of significance such as 5% or 2% or 1% we do not . . . ever need to lose sight of the exact strength which the evidence has in fact reached, or to ignore the fact that with further trial it might come to be stronger or weaker. (p. 25)

Fisher did not specifically advise researchers how to appraise "the exact strength" of the evidence, but the use of statistical power analysis (Chapter 12), effect size estimation (Chapters 13–15), confidence intervals (Chapter 12), and meta-analytic procedures (Appendix C) enables us to do this with relative ease.

Dividing Up the Variance

The calculation of *F* tests is only one purpose of the analysis of variance. A more general purpose is to divide up the variance of all the observations into a number of separate sources of estimation and significance testing. In this illustration of comparing the means of four groups, the total variation among the 12 scores is broken into two sources: (1) systematic variation between groups or conditions (i.e., the signal) and (2) error variation within groups or conditions (i.e., the noise).

It will be useful here to look again at the basic idea of variance:

$$S^2 = \frac{\Sigma(X - M)^2}{N - 1}$$

where S^2 is the unbiased estimate of the population value of σ^2, and σ^2 differs from S^2 only in that the denominator $N - 1$ is replaced by N. As noted in Chapter 10, the quantity S^2 is also called a *mean square* (abbreviated as **MS**) because when the sum of the squares—that is, $\Sigma(X - M)^2$—is divided by $N - 1$ (or *df*), the result is the squared deviation per *df*, representing a kind of average.

In the analysis of variance, we are especially interested in the numerators of our various S^2 values (e.g., for between conditions and for within conditions). This interest has to do with the additive property of the numerators, or the **sum of squares** (abbreviated as **SS**) of deviations about the mean. These *SS* values add up to the total sum of squares in the following way:

Total *SS* = between-conditions *SS* + within-conditions *SS*

In one-way designs, the analysis of variance requires the calculation of the between-conditions *SS* and the within-conditions *SS*. If you are doing these calculations using a pocket calculator, compute the total *SS* as a check on your arithmetic. If you are using a computer, running the program on the data in this chapter will allow you to see what the results in your printout actually tell you. Before we start crunching numbers, let us pause for a moment and look at the formulas for each of these three sums of squares.

First, the total *SS* is defined as the sum of squares of deviations of all the measurements from the grand mean. What goes into the total *SS* is given by the following formula:

$$\text{Total } SS = \Sigma(X - M_G)^2$$

where X is each observation and M_G is the grand mean (i.e., the mean of the condition means).

Second, the between-conditions *SS* is defined as the sum of squares of deviations of the condition means from the grand mean. This between-conditions value is computed by the following formula:

$$\text{Between } SS = \Sigma\left[n_k(M_k - M_G)^2\right]$$

where n_k is the number of observations in the kth condition (and k is *any* particular condition), M_k is the mean of the kth condition, and M_G is again the grand mean.

And finally, the within-conditions *SS* is defined as the sum of squares of deviations of the measurements from their condition means, as given by the following formula:

$$\text{Within } SS = \Sigma(X - M_k)^2$$

where X is each observation and M_k is again the mean of the condition to which X belongs.

Computing the One-Way ANOVA

We will now use these formulas to analyze the scores of Results A in Table 14.1. Table 14.2 provides the basic data for this analysis, with the addition of two new symbols: M_k for the group or the condition mean and M_G for the grand mean.

Table 14.2	Data for ANOVA Based on Results A in Table 14.1		
	Group 1 Zero	Group 2 Milk	Group 3 Vitamins	Group 4 Hot lunch
	8	10	13	17
	10	12	15	19
	12	14	17	21
M_k	10	12	15	19

$$M_G = \frac{10 + 12 + 15 + 19}{4} = 14$$

First, we compute the total SS. The formula instructs us to subtract the grand mean from each individual score and then add up the squared deviations:

$$
\begin{aligned}
\text{Total } SS = {} & (8 - 14)^2 + (10 - 14)^2 + (12 - 14)^2 \\
& + (10 - 14)^2 + (12 - 14)^2 + (14 - 14)^2 \\
& + (13 - 14)^2 + (15 - 14)^2 + (17 - 14)^2 \\
& + (17 - 14)^2 + (19 - 14)^2 + (21 - 14)^2 \\
= {} & 170
\end{aligned}
$$

Next, we compute the between-conditions SS. The formula instructs us to subtract the grand mean from each condition mean and then add up the weighted squared deviations:

$$
\begin{aligned}
\text{Between } SS = {} & 3(10 - 14)^2 \\
& + 3(12 - 14)^2 \\
& + 3(15 - 14)^2 \\
& + 3(19 - 14)^2 \\
= {} & 138
\end{aligned}
$$

And finally, we compute the within-conditions SS. The formula instructs us to subtract the appropriate condition mean from each individual score and then add up the squared deviations:

$$
\begin{aligned}
\text{Within } SS = {} & (8 - 10)^2 + (10 - 10)^2 + (12 - 10)^2 \\
= {} & (10 - 12)^2 + (12 - 12)^2 + (14 - 12)^2 \\
= {} & (13 - 15)^2 + (15 - 15)^2 + (17 - 15)^2 \\
= {} & (17 - 19)^2 + (19 - 19)^2 + (21 - 19)^2 \\
= {} & 32
\end{aligned}
$$

As a check on our arithmetic, we add the sum of squares between conditions to the sum of squares within conditions to make sure their total equals the total sum of squares, that is,

$$
\begin{aligned}
\text{Total } SS &= \text{between } SS + \text{within } SS \\
170 &= \quad\ 138 \quad + \quad 32
\end{aligned}
$$

The ANOVA Summary Table

The results of one-way ANOVAs may be displayed in the form shown in Table 14.3. The rows label the source of variation, in this case the variation between and within conditions. Listed in the SS column are sum-of-squares values for each source of variation. The degrees of freedom (df) are listed in the next column. Because there were four conditions (symbolized as $k = 4$), three of those means were free to vary once the mean of the means (M_G) was determined. We define the degrees of freedom between conditions as

$$
df \text{ between} = k - 1
$$

which gives us $4 - 1 = 3$ df between.

Table 14.3	Summary ANOVA Table				
Source	SS	df	MS	F	p
Between conditions	138	3	46	11.50	.003
Within conditions	32	8	4		

Note: The effect size correlation, r_{effect}, is not reported here because it is not interpretable when the numerator $df > 1$. That is, we compute the effect size of *F* only when the between-conditions variable is based on a single df (e.g., the situation we find when two means are being compared).

We obtain the degrees of freedom within conditions by determining the df within each condition (defined as $n - 1$) and then adding. The reason we have $n - 1$ degrees of freedom within each condition is that all but one score is free to vary within each condition, and so we eliminate 1 df within each condition. Thus the df within conditions are found by

$$df \text{ within} = N - k$$

where *N* is the total number of measurements or sampling units and *k* is the number of conditions, giving us $12 - 4 = 8$ df within.

The total df (not shown in Table 14.3) are defined as the total number of measurements minus 1, that is,

$$df \text{ total} = N - 1$$

which gives us $12 - 1 = 11$ df total. After we have computed the df between and within conditions, we can check our calculations by adding these df to see whether they agree with the df total. In the present case, we have

$$df \text{ total} = df \text{ between} + df \text{ within}$$
$$11 = 3 + 8$$

The *MS* column shows the mean squares, which we obtain by dividing the sums of squares by the corresponding df. We divide 138 by 3 to get 46, and we divide 32 by 8 to get 4. Thus the *MS* values can be seen as the amounts of the total variation (measured in *SS*) attributable to each df. The larger the *MS* for the between-condition source of variance (the signal) relative to the within-condition source of variance (the noise), the less likely becomes the null hypothesis of no difference between the conditions. If the null hypothesis were true, the variation per df should be roughly the same for the df between groups and the df within groups. The *F* in the next column provides this information. We compute it by dividing the mean square between conditions by the mean square within conditions; the result is a signal-to-noise ratio of $F = 46/4 = 11.5$.

To review, *F* is called the *F* ratio to reflect the fact that it is a ratio of two mean squares (i.e., two variances, as noted in Box 14.1). The denominator mean square (i.e., the mean square for error) serves as a kind of base rate for noise level, or typical variation. The numerator (i.e., the signal) is a reflection of both the size of the effect and the size of the study. That is, a numerator *MS* may be large relative to a denominator *MS* because (1) the effect is large; (2) the *n* per condition is large; or (3) both are large. As a consequence, large *F*s should not be automatically interpreted as reflecting large effects. In the case of *F* with numerator $df > 1$, the idea of interpreting the effect size is academic, because we report the effect size only for *F*s with numerator $df = 1$ (see also Box 14.3).

Box 14.3   **Focused and Omnibus *F* Tests**

F tests with 1 *df* in the numerator are characterized as **focused tests,** because they address a very specific hypothesis, for example, that Condition 1 is different from Condition 2. All *t* tests are also characterized as focused tests, because they concentrate on a specific comparison, for example, that two groups differ from each other or that one group differs from zero or some other specified value. *F* tests with numerator $df > 1$ are called **omnibus tests** because of their inherently diffuse nature; that is, they can tell us only whether there is *any* significant difference between the $k = 3$ or more groups or conditions. The rule of thumb is to compute r_{effect} only for focused tests (e.g., *F* tests with numerator $df = 1$ and any *t* test) and not for omnibus tests (e.g., *F* tests with numerator $df > 1$).

Using the *F* Table to Find *p*

The final value in Table 14.3 is the probability that an *F* of this size or larger, with this number of degrees of freedom, might occur if the null hypothesis of no difference among the means were true. In the previous chapter, we noted that there is a different distribution of *t* values for every possible value of the degrees of freedom. The situation for *F* is similar but more complicated, because for every *F* ratio there are *two* relevant *df* values to take into account: the *df* between conditions and the *df* within conditions. For every combination of *df* between and *df* within, there is a different curve. As is the case for *t*, small values of *F* are likely when the null hypothesis of no difference between conditions is true, but large values are unlikely and are used as evidence to suggest that the null hypothesis is probably false.

Another important difference between *t* and *F* curves was alluded to earlier, when we said that the expected value of *t* is zero when the null hypothesis is true but that the expected value of *F* is approximately 1 when the null is true. The symmetrical bell shape of *t* curves means that they are centered at 0, with negative values running to negative infinity and positive values running to positive infinity. However, *F* curves are positively skewed, with values beginning at zero and ranging upward to positive infinity. In other words, *F* is intrinsically one-tailed as a test of significance. When the null hypothesis is true, the expected value of *F* is $df/(df - 2)$, where these *df* are for within conditions. For most values of *df*, then, the expected value of *F* when the null hypothesis is true is a little more than 1.0, as noted in Table 14.4.

Table 14.4 enables us to locate the *p* value of a given *F*, while a more comprehensive table can be found in Appendix B (see pp. 411–15). In Table 14.4, notice

Table 14.4   *F* Values Required for Significance at the .05 (Upper Entry) and .01 Levels

Degrees of freedom within conditions (denominator)	Degrees of freedom between conditions (numerator)						Expected value of *F* when H_0 true
	1	2	3	4	6	∞	
1	161	200	216	225	234	254	—
	4052	4999	5403	5625	5859	6366	
2	18.5	19.0	19.2	19.3	19.3	19.5	—
	98.5	99.0	99.2	99.3	99.3	99.5	
3	10.1	9.55	9.28	9.12	8.94	8.53	3.00
	34.1	30.8	29.5	28.7	27.9	26.1	
4	7.71	6.94	6.59	6.39	6.16	5.63	2.00
	21.2	18.0	16.7	16.0	15.2	13.5	
5	6.61	5.79	5.41	5.19	4.95	4.36	1.67
	16.3	13.3	12.1	11.4	10.7	9.02	
6	5.99	5.14	4.76	4.53	4.28	3.67	1.50
	13.7	10.9	9.78	9.15	8.47	6.88	
8	5.32	4.46	4.07	3.84	3.58	2.93	1.33
	11.3	8.65	7.59	7.01	6.37	4.86	
10	4.96	4.10	3.71	3.48	3.22	2.54	1.25
	10.0	7.56	6.55	5.99	5.39	3.91	
15	4.54	3.68	3.29	3.06	2.79	2.07	1.15
	8.68	6.36	5.42	4.89	4.32	2.87	
20	4.35	3.49	3.10	2.87	2.60	1.84	1.11
	8.10	5.85	4.94	4.43	3.87	2.42	
25	4.24	3.38	2.99	2.76	2.49	1.71	1.09
	7.77	5.57	4.68	4.18	3.63	2.17	
30	4.17	3.32	2.92	2.69	2.42	1.62	1.07
	7.56	5.39	4.51	4.02	3.47	2.01	
40	4.08	3.23	2.84	2.61	2.34	1.51	1.05
	7.31	5.18	4.31	3.83	3.29	1.80	
∞	3.84	2.99	2.60	2.37	2.09	1.00	1.00
	6.64	4.60	3.78	3.32	2.80	1.00	

Note: For a more complete table see Appendix B, Table B.3.

that the critical values of *F* required to reach the .05 and .01 levels decrease as the *df* within increase for any given *df* between. Similarly, the critical values of *F* decrease as the *df* between increase for any given *df* within—except for the special cases of *df* within = 1 or 2. For *df* within = 1, there is a substantial increase in the *F*s required to reach the .05 and .01 levels as the *df* between increase from 1 to infinity. For *df* within = 2, only a very small increase in the *F*s is required to reach the .05 and .01

levels as the df between increase from 1 to infinity. In practice, however, there are very few studies with large df between and only 1 or 2 df within.

To look up our F of 11.50 in Table 14.4, we put a finger on the intersection of 3 df between conditions and 8 df within conditions. The two values are 4.07 (the F value required for significance at $p = .05$) and 7.59 (the F value required for significance at $p = .01$). Because our obtained F is larger than 7.59, we know that the corresponding p must be less than .01. As implied by the extended table on pages 411–15, the actual p is approximately .003. Performing the same calculations on Results B in Table 14.1, we would find F to be 1.28 (again with 3 and 8 degrees of freedom). Looking up this value in Table B.3, we find it to be too small to be significant at even the .20 level: The actual p is approximately .35.

What do the more precise p values tell us? The p value of .003 for Results A indicates that we would obtain an F of 11.50 or larger (for numerator $df = 3$ and denominator $df = 8$) only 3 in 1,000 times if we repeatedly conducted this study under the same conditions and if there really were no differences between the four groups (i.e., if the null hypothesis were true). The p value of .35 for Results B informs us that we would obtain an F of 1.28 with 3 and 8 df once every 3 times if we conducted the study under *these* conditions over and over, and if the null hypothesis were true. In reporting the p level, there is no need to state that it is one-tailed, because this fact is implicit in F (see also Box 14.4).

Box 14.4   ## Using t to Boost Power

The F tests we have looked at so far are all omnibus tests, and we cannot take the square root of an omnibus F and get t. But taking the square root of a focused F (i.e., F with numerator $df = 1$) gives us t, and we can then compute and interpret the effect size in the usual way. An interesting characteristic of F distributions is that the p values, although naturally one-tailed, translate into two-tailed p values in t curves. Suppose we had a focused F and found $p = .06$ in the predicted direction. If we report t instead of F, we have the option of reporting "$p = .03$ one-tail" (because we predicted the direction) or "$p = .06$ two-tail" (if we choose a more conservative p), but we do not have this option with F. There is, of course, not much difference between $p = .06$ and $p = .03$, except that they fall on either side of the conventional $p = .05$. But the essential point is that we have another way of boosting the statistical power if t rather than F is used when appropriate.

After the F, t Revisited

Now we know that, for the data in Table 14.2, the group means are not likely to be this far apart if the null hypothesis is true. But knowing that the four groups of our study differ does not tell us whether milk helps in and of itself and whether vitamins help in and of themselves. To address these questions, we need to compare (1) the results in Group 2 with the results in Group 1 (the zero control) and (2) the results in

Group 3 with the zero control. These comparisons are called **tests of simple effects,** and an easy way to do them is by *t* tests. Using the formula for comparing independent means given in the previous chapter, we continue to define S^2 as the pooled value (as described in the previous chapter), although we can find this value simply from our ANOVA because it is the denominator of our *F* ratio.

To illustrate the test of simple effects using the results in Table 14.2, we substitute the values of Groups 1 and 3 in our general formula:

$$t = \frac{M_3 - M_1}{\sqrt{\left(\frac{1}{n_3} + \frac{1}{n_1}\right)S^2}} = \frac{15 - 10}{\sqrt{\left(\frac{1}{3} + \frac{1}{3}\right)4}} = \frac{5}{\sqrt{2.67}} = 3.06$$

where M_3 is the mean of Group 3; M_1 is the mean of Group 1; n_3 and n_1 are the sample sizes of these groups; and S^2 is the value of the within-conditions *MS* shown in Table 14.3. When we test this *t* for significance, we base our *df* not on $n_3 + n_1 - 2$ (as we did previously), but on *df* equal to the within-conditions *SS* (i.e., 8 *df*) because we are using a pooled estimate of S^2. Referring to Table B.2 (see pp. 409–10), we find the significance of $t = 3.06$ to be less than $p = .01$ but more than $p = .005$ one-tail. The actual one-tailed *p* is approximately .008 (and the two-tailed $p = .016$, or .008 × 2).

Had we planned from the beginning to compute a specific *t* test, we could do so whether our overall *F* was significant or not. That is, we do not have to engage in a kind of "Simon says" game in which we seek "permission" from the *p* value associated with an omnibus test before we examine the effect of interest. However, if we are going to be exploring for large differences that we have not specifically predicted, our *t*-test results are going to be much more interpretable if our overall *F* is significant. The reason is that if we use a lot of *t* tests to go on a "fishing expedition" for significant differences, some of them will turn out to be significant by chance. One procedure that researchers sometimes use to try to avoid an excess of findings of significant *t*s when there are lots of possible *t*s, or the *t* tests were unplanned, is to use a more conservative level of significance, such as .01 instead of .05, or even .005 or .001 (all listed in Table B.2).

However, we recommend not placing the full weight of your decision on the significance value alone, but also paying attention to the effect size and its corresponding confidence interval and BESD. To calculate the effect size correlation on our *t* we use the same formula as before, but we define the degrees of freedom from the groups being compared, that is,

$$r_{\text{effect}} = \sqrt{\frac{t^2}{t^2 + df}} = \sqrt{\frac{(3.06)^2}{(3.06)^2 + 4}} = .84$$

where *df* is based on the fact that there were 3 subjects in Group 3 and 3 subjects in Group 1, and therefore $n_3 + n_1 - 2 = 4$. The confidence interval would be computed as before. In terms of the BESD, this r_{effect} of .84 amounts to a difference in success rates of 8% to 92% between nonusers and users of vitamins, respectively (i.e., if half the population used vitamins and half the population showed improved performance).

Two-Way Designs

R. A. Fisher, the British statistician who invented the F test, noticed that it is sometimes possible to rearrange a one-way design to form a two-way design of much greater power to reject the null hypothesis. We turn now to an analysis of the simplest two-way design, one in which there are two levels of each factor (i.e., a 2 × 2 factorial). An example is essential, and we study again the hypothetical effects of nutrition on academic performance. However, we slightly change the question we asked earlier about the differences among our four nutritional conditions. Instead we will ask several questions simultaneously:

1. What is the effect on academic performance of daily milk?
2. What is the effect on academic performance of daily vitamins?
3. What is the effect on academic performance of both milk and vitamins (i.e., the hot lunch includes both milk and vitamins)?
4. Is the effect of vitamins different when milk is also given from when milk is not given?
5. Is the effect of milk different when vitamins are also given from when vitamins are not given?

We can answer all these questions by using a two-way design of the kind shown in Table 14.5. We have used the same scores as those in Table 14.2, so that later we can give you a further insight into the two-way factorial by allowing you to compare its summary ANOVA with the one-way ANOVA computed previously. Table 14.6 shows the group means of the sets of scores in Table 14.5, and Table 14.6 also illustrates how factorial designs allow us to answer more questions than one-way designs. In this case, for example, we can learn whether the effect of one of our factors is much the same for each of the two or more conditions of the other factor. As noted earlier, another name for the difference between group means is **simple effects.** Here, a comparison of the differences between the simple effects tells us that there is a two-unit effect $(12 - 10 = 2)$ of milk when no vitamins are given, and that there is a four-unit effect $(19 - 15 = 4)$ of milk when vitamins are given. Similarly, there is a five-unit effect $(15 - 10 = 5)$ of vitamins when no milk is given and a seven-unit effect $(19 - 12 = 7)$ of vitamins when milk is given.

Not only do factorial designs allow us to answer more questions than one-way designs, but having subjects serve double duty increases the power to reject the null

Table 14.5 Raw Scores of Two-Way Design

Vitamin treatment	Milk treatment Present	Milk treatment Absent	Row means
Present	17, 19, 21	13, 15, 17	17
Absent	10, 12, 14	8, 10, 12	11
Column means	15.5	12.5	14

Table 14.6   Means and Effects of Results in Table 14.5

Vitamin treatment	Milk treatment Present	Milk treatment Absent	Row means	Row effects
Present	19	15	17	+3.0
Absent	12	10	11	−3.0
Column means	15.5	12.5	14 (grand mean)	
Column effects	+1.5	−1.5		

hypotheses regarding overall effects if the null hypotheses are false. That is, more of the subjects available for the study are able to contribute to the major comparisons (milk versus no milk; vitamins versus no vitamins). In this case, half of all the subjects of the experiment are in the milk conditions instead of the quarter of all subjects that would be in the milk condition in a one-way design. Thus half of the subjects can be compared to the remaining half of the subjects who received no milk, so that all the subjects of the experiment shed light on the question of the effect of milk. The overall effect (also called a **main effect**) of milk is assessed by a comparison of the milk and no-milk column means (15.5 and 12.5, respectively). At the same time that all subjects are providing information on the milk comparison, they are also providing information on the effect of vitamins. The main effect of vitamins is assessed by a comparison of the vitamin and no-vitamin marginal values in the rows (means of 17 and 11, respectively).

As described next, another advantage of factorial designs is that they allow us to examine **interaction effects**. As we show, the interaction, although it represents the combination of the independent variables, is (in a statistical sense) made up of "left-over effects," called **residuals**. Because an ANOVA interaction represents the combination of variables, it is designated as "rows × columns" (stated as "rows by columns") or "vitamins × milk" (stated as "vitamins by milk") to imply this combination (see also Box 14.5). Once you fully understand these ideas, you will have a better sense of when you have actually hypothesized an "interaction" (in the

Box 14.5   Cell Means and Residuals

In the past, the idea of residual effects has been a source of confusion even to many researchers, who, when interpreting an interaction, have not examined the residual effects but have confused them with the cell (or condition) means. It is possible, as we illustrated in our discussion of the Solomon design (in Chapter 7), to use a "subtraction-difference procedure" in which we subtract the condition means from one another in order to make the most parsimonious statement about the "pretest × treatment interaction." But as we show next, it is also generally true that, if we are looking at the cell means, we are not looking at *only* the interaction (Rosnow & Rosenthal, 1989a, 1991, 1995, 1996b).

statistical sense of ANOVA) and when all you have hypothesized is a main effect or a comparison of simple effects (Rosnow & Rosenthal, 1989a, 1991, 1995). You will also have a clear sense of how to interpret *all* your results if you are computing a two-way (or three-way, etc.) ANOVA.

Effects and the Factorial ANOVA

Previously we noted that a general purpose of the analysis of variance is to divide up the variance of all the observations into a number of separate sources of estimation and significance testing. To understand how a two-way ANOVA does its job, we think of the group means (as well as each individual score) as comprising a number of separate statistical elements. In a 2×2 design, the group means (and measurements) can be broken into (1) the grand mean; (2) the row effects; (3) the column effects; (4) the interaction effects; and (5) error. We will begin by describing how the first four elements (grand mean, row effect, column effect, and interaction effect) are conceptualized in terms of an **additive model** (i.e., a model in which the components sum to the group means).

As noted previously, the **grand mean** (M_G) is the mean of all group means, or $(19 + 15 + 12 + 10)/4 = 14$. As shown in Table 14.6, the **row effect** for each row is the mean of that row minus the grand mean, or

$$\text{Row effect} = M_r - M_G$$

Thus the row effects are computed as $17 - 14 = +3.0$ for vitamins-present and $11 - 14 = -3.0$ for vitamins-absent. The **column effect** of each column is the mean of that column (M_c) minus the grand mean, or

$$\text{Column effect} = M_c - M_G$$

which gives us $15.5 - 14 = +1.5$ for milk-present and $12.5 - 14 = -1.5$ for milk-absent. Each set of effects sums to zero when totaled over all conditions, a result that is characteristic of all row, column, and interaction effects.

Not visible in Table 14.6 are the interaction effects (i.e., the residuals, or leftover effects). These effects are what remain after the grand mean, the row effect, and the column effect are subtracted from the group mean. In other words,

Interaction effect = group mean − grand mean − row effect − column effect

so for these data, the interaction effects for the vitamins-plus-milk group (VM), the vitamins-only group (V), the milk-only group (M), and zero control (O) are computed as follows:

	Group mean	−	Grand mean	−	Row effect	−	Column effect	=	Interaction effect
VM	19	−	14	−	3.0	−	1.5	=	0.5
V	15	−	14	−	3.0	−	(−1.5)	=	(−0.5)
M	12	−	14	−	(−3.0)	−	1.5	=	(−0.5)
O	10	−	14	−	(−3.0)	−	(−1.5)	=	0.5
Sum	56	−	56	−	0.0	−	0.0	=	0.0

What can we learn about the results of our experiment by studying the above table of effects? The grand mean tells us the general "level" of our measurements and is usually not of great intrinsic interest. The +3 and −3 row effects show us that the groups receiving vitamins (VM and V) did better than those not receiving vitamins (M and O). The +1.5 and −1.5 column effects show us that the groups receiving milk (VM and M) did better than those not receiving milk (V and O). The column of +0.5 and −0.5 interaction effects shows us that the group receiving *both* vitamins and milk (VM) and the group receiving *neither* vitamins nor milk (O) did better than the groups receiving *either* vitamins (V) or milk (M). But although it is slightly better from the viewpoint of the interaction effect alone to receive neither treatment, this statistical advantage in the interaction effect (i.e., 0.5) is more than offset by the statistical disadvantage in the row effect (i.e., −3.0) and the column effect (i.e., −1.5) to be receiving neither treatment (see also Box 14.6).

Box 14.6   **The Additive Model**

We said that the idea of ANOVA is based on an **additive model;** that is, components sum to the group means. You can see this more clearly when you total all four conditions of the two-way table:

	Group mean	=	Grand mean	+	Row effect	+	Column effect	+	Interaction effect
VM	19	=	14	+	3.0	+	1.5	+	0.5
V	15	=	14	+	3.0	+	(−1.5)	+	(−0.5)
M	12	=	14	+	(−3.0)	+	1.5	+	(−0.5)
O	10	=	14	+	(−3.0)	+	(−1.5)	+	0.5
Sum	56	=	56	+	0.0	+	0.0	+	0.0

The conceptual advantage of the additive structure is that it provides a baseline that allows us to compare row, column, and interaction effects with one another; the statistical advantage is that it makes *F* tests possible.

The Concept of Error

That the mean of each group in a two-way design can be broken into the grand mean, the row effect, the column effect, and the interaction does not quite tell the whole story—because **error** is omitted. That is, it is not taken into account that the various scores found in each group may be rewritten as a deviation from the mean of that condition. The term *error* takes its name from the idea that the magnitude of these deviations reflects how poorly we have done in predicting individual scores from a knowledge of condition or group membership. A particular score shows a large error if it falls far from the mean of its group but only a small error if it falls close to the mean of its group.

We can now write error as

$$\text{Error} = \text{score} - \text{group mean}$$

and therefore

$$\text{Score} = \text{group mean} + \text{error}$$

but

$$\text{Group mean} = \text{grand mean} + \text{row effect} + \text{column effect} + \text{interaction effect}$$

so

$$\text{Score} = \text{grand mean} + \text{row effect} + \text{column effect} + \text{interaction effect} + \text{error}$$

Computing the Two-Way ANOVA

Earlier, when we analyzed the results of the present study as a one-way analysis, we computed the total sum of squares as

$$\text{Total } SS = \Sigma(X - M_G)^2 = 170$$

where X is each observation or measurement, and M_G is the mean of all the condition means. We computed the within-conditions SS as

$$\text{Within } SS = \Sigma(X - M_k)^2$$

where M_k is the mean of the group or condition to which each observation or measurement (X) belongs. For our two-way ANOVA, we may use the same (above) formulas, but we also need to compute the sums of the squares of the rows, the columns, and the interaction.

The sum of squares of the rows is defined as

$$\text{Row } SS = \Sigma[nc(M_r - M_G)^2]$$

where n is the number of observations in each condition; c is the number of columns contributing to the computation of M_r (the mean of the rth row); and M_G is again the grand mean. The sum of squares of the columns is defined as

$$\text{Column } SS = \Sigma[nr(M_c - M_G)^2]$$

where n is the number of observations in each condition; r is the number of rows contributing to the computation of M_c (the mean of the cth column); and M_G is the grand mean. And finally, the interaction sum of squares is defined as

$$\text{Interaction } SS = \text{total } SS - (\text{row } SS + \text{column } SS + \text{within } SS)$$

With our newfound knowledge about the effects, at the same time that we compute the formulas above we can take apart the individual scores to help us understand better the various terms of the analysis of variance. The ANOVA summary is presented in Table 14.7, and Table 14.8 reminds us where the SS values came from. The only new values in Table 14.8 are those for error, which for each subject is computed as the individual's raw score minus the group mean. Thus, for the VM subject in

Table 14.7 Summary Table for Two-Way ANOVA

Source	SS	df	MS	F	p	r_{effect}
Vitamins (rows)	108	1	108	27.0	.0008	.88
Milk (columns)	27	1	27	6.75	.03	.68
Interaction	3	1	3	0.75	.41	.29
Within error	32	8	4	—	—	—

Note: Although the listing of effect sizes for *F*s with numerator *df* = 1 is not yet standard, it is a practice we strongly recommend.

Table 14.8 Table of Effects for Computing ANOVA

Group	Score	=	Grand mean	+	Row effect	+	Column effect	+	Interaction effect	+	Error
VM	17	=	14	+	3.0	+	1.5	+	0.5	+	(−2)
VM	19	=	14	+	3.0	+	1.5	+	0.5	+	0
VM	21	=	14	+	3.0	+	1.5	+	0.5	+	2
V	13	=	14	+	3.0	+	(−1.5)	+	(−0.5)	+	(−2)
V	15	=	14	+	3.0	+	(−1.5)	+	(−0.5)	+	0
V	17	=	14	+	3.0	+	(−1.5)	+	(−0.5)	+	2
M	10	=	14	+	(−3.0)	+	1.5	+	(−0.5)	+	(−2)
M	12	=	14	+	(−3.0)	+	1.5	+	(−0.5)	+	0
M	14	=	14	+	(−3.0)	+	1.5	+	(−0.5)	+	2
O	8	=	14	+	(−3.0)	+	(−1.5)	+	0.5	+	(−2)
O	10	=	14	+	(−3.0)	+	(−1.5)	+	0.5	+	0
O	12	=	14	+	(−3.0)	+	(−1.5)	+	0.5	+	2
ΣX	168	=	168	+	0	+	0	+	0	+	0
ΣX^2	2,522	=	2,352	+	108	+	27	+	3	+	32

Table 14.5 who scored 17, we subtract 19 (the mean of this group) to get the error score of −2 in Table 14.8. Beneath each column in Table 14.8 are shown the sums of the listed values (ΣX) and the sums of squares of the listed values (ΣX^2).

In the formula above, the total *SS* is defined as the sum of the squared deviations between every single score and the grand mean, that is, $(17 - 14)^2 + (19 - 14)^2 + \ldots + (12 - 14)^2 = 170$. Alternatively, we see in Table 14.8 that subtracting the sum of the squared grand means (shown as 2,352) from the sum of the squared scores (shown as 2,522) gives us the same value (i.e., total *SS* = 2,522 − 2,352 = 170). Looking again at Table 14.3, we are reminded that, in the one-way analysis of variance, this total *SS* is allocated to two sources of variance: a between-conditions and a within-conditions source. In the move from a one-way to a two-way ANOVA, the within-conditions source of variance (i.e., the source attributable to error) remains unchanged (i.e., "Within error" or "Within conditions" *SS* = 32 in Tables

14.3, 14.7, and 14.8). The between-conditions source of variance in the one-way ANOVA (shown in Table 14.3 as 138) is broken down into three components in our two-way ANOVA: a row effect SS, a column effect SS, and an interaction effect SS.

Table 14.8 shows the origin of these values in the individual measurements, and let us also compute them using our formulas. First, we obtain the row effect sum of squares from

$$\text{Row } SS = \Sigma[nc(M_r - M_G)^2]$$
$$= [(3)(2)(17 - 14)^2] + [(3)(2)(11 - 14)^2]$$
$$= 108$$

giving us the value shown in the bottom row of Table 14.8.

Next, we obtain the column effect sum of squares from

$$\text{Column } SS = \Sigma[nr(M_c - M_G)^2]$$
$$= [(3)(2)(15.5 - 14)^2] + [(3)(2)(12.5 - 14)^2]$$
$$= 27$$

again giving the value in Table 14.8.

Finally, we obtain the sum of squares of the interaction from

$$\text{Interaction } SS = \text{total } SS - (\text{row } SS + \text{column } SS + \text{within } SS)$$

which gives us

$$\text{Interaction } SS = 170 - (108 + 27 + 32) = 3$$

and as anticipated, it is the value shown in Table 14.8.

The logic of computing the degrees of freedom of the two-way ANOVA is the same as that in the one-way analysis, but we must apportion the between-conditions df to the row main effect, the column main effect, and the interaction. The degrees of freedom for rows in Table 14.7 are

$$df \text{ rows} = r - 1$$

where r is the number of rows (i.e., $2 - 1 = 1\ df$). The degrees of freedom for columns are

$$df \text{ columns} = c - 1$$

where c is the number of columns (i.e., $2 - 1 = 1$). The degrees of freedom for the interaction are

$$df \text{ interaction} = (r - 1)(c - 1)$$

which gives us $(2 - 1)(2 - 1) = 1\ df$.

The degrees of freedom for the "Within error" are the same as those in Table 14.3, defined as

$$df \text{ within} = N - k$$

where N is the total number of observations or measurements and k is the number of groups or conditions (i.e., $12 - 4 = 8$). In other words, this is the number of subjects in each group or condition minus 1 totaled over all groups, or $(3 - 1) + (3 - 1) + (3 - 1) + (3 - 1) = 8$ *df* within conditions. As a check on the degrees of freedom, we compute the *df* of the total *SS* as $N - 1$ (i.e., $12 - 1 = 11$) and find this result to be identical to the sum of the *df* in Table 14.7 (i.e., $1 + 1 + 1 + 8 = 11$).

As before, we obtain the mean square (*MS*) values in Table 14.7 by dividing the sums of squares by the corresponding *df*. For example, we divide 108 by 1 to get 108, and we divide 32 by 8 to get 4 (i.e., the amount of the total variation, measured in *SS*, attributable to each *df*). We compute the *F* ratios by dividing the mean squares for rows, columns, and interaction (the signals) by the mean square within conditions (the noise). Thus we divide 108 by 4 to get 27.0, and we divide 27 by 4 to get 6.75, and we divide 3 by 4 to get 0.75. Because the effect sizes of *F* ratios with 1 *df* in the numerator are readily interpretable, we calculate the effect size of each of these *F* values by

$$r_{\text{effect}} = \sqrt{\frac{F}{F + df \text{ within}}}$$

We can interpret the results as we would any effect-size correlation, including using the confidence interval and the BESD described in Chapter 12.

Table 14.7 shows precise values of *p*. The *F* of 6.75 for the effect of milk could have occurred by chance approximately 3 times in 100, and the *F* of 27.0 for the effect of vitamins could have occurred by chance far less often, if the null hypothesis were true. By contrast, the *F* for interaction was so small that it could easily have arisen by chance. However, if the interaction were of interest, we would analyze it as before (i.e., as a comparison between the residuals of the diagonal cells). What we learn from these effect sizes is that both milk and vitamins have a beneficial effect, and that more of the effect is attributable to vitamins than to milk. We can also compute tests of simple effects by using the *t* procedure described previously.

Repeated-Measures ANOVA Designs

In earlier discussions, we referred to **repeated-measures designs,** so called because the sampling units are measured on the dependent variable more than once. Table 14.9 illustrates such a design, in which one factor is the repeated-measures factor of treatments, and the second factor is subjects. Because there is only a single score for each subject entered for each condition, there can be no estimate of within-cell variability. Previously each subject was observed only once, but here we see that each subject was observed once a month for a total of four times. The analysis of variance computed on these scores is summarized at the bottom of Table 14.9. The *F* test was computed as a ratio of the mean square for treatments (46) divided by the mean square for treatments × subjects (4), with degrees of freedom defined as 3 and 6.

The statistical analysis of repeated-measures designs involves intricacies that go beyond the scope of this text, but you will find detailed discussions and illustrations in advanced texts (e.g., , Keppel, 1991; Kirk, 1995; Rosenthal & Rosnow, 1991). In analyzing designs of the repeated-measures kind (including mixed designs, in which some variables involve repeated measures), we must be especially sensitive to the

Table 14.9 Repeated Measures Design and ANOVA

Design and raw scores

	January Condition 1 (Zero)	February Condition 2 (Milk)	March Condition 3 (Vitamins)	April Condition 4 (Hot lunch)
Subject 1	8	12	15	21
Subject 2	10	14	17	19
Subject 3	12	10	13	17

Summary ANOVA

Source	SS	df	MS	F	p
Treatments	138	3	46	11.50	.007
Subjects	8	2	4		
Treatments × subjects	24	6	4		

error terms to be inserted in the denominators of *F* ratios. The same caution applies to the specification of the appropriate degrees of freedom. However, the interpretation of such designs uses a logic similar to that used to interpret all factorial ANOVAs.

Summary of Ideas

1. The limitation of the two-sample *t* is that it can be used only when there are two means to be compared; the advantage of *F* is that it can be used for any number of groups (i.e., two or more groups).
2. The *F* test used in a between-conditions ANOVA is a ratio of the spread of mean scores around the grand mean (the signal) to the spread of scores within each condition (the noise).
3. For the special case of the comparison of two groups, $F = t^2$, and in that particular case, we can calculate the effect size for *F* as

$$r_{effect} = \sqrt{\frac{F}{F + df \text{ within}}}$$

4. *F* tests with numerator $df = 1$ and all *t* tests are characterized as *focused tests*, whereas *F* tests with numerator $df > 1$ are called *omnibus tests*.
5. When computing *t* tests on simple effects after the omnibus *F*, we define S^2 in the *t* formula as the *MS* within (i.e., the pooled error term) in the ANOVA summary table.
6. When computing effect size *r*s on simple effects after the omnibus *F*, we define *df* in the r_{effect} formula by the *n*s of the groups being compared.
7. In factorial designs, two or more levels of each factor (independent variable) are administered in combination with two or more levels of every other factor.

8. Such designs use sampling units more efficiently and address more questions than do ordinary one-way ANOVAs.

9. The error of individual scores (i.e., the deviation of each score from the mean of the group) represents the extent to which the score can be predicted from a knowledge of group membership.

10. The summary table for the factorial ANOVA differs from the summary table for the one-way ANOVA in reflecting the subdivision of the between-conditions *SS* into main and interaction *SS*.

11. The additive model is based on the idea that each group mean is the sum of the grand mean, the row effect, the column effect, and the interaction effect.

12. The conceptual advantage of the additive model is that it provides a baseline that allows us to compare these effects with one another.

13. Interaction effects are the effects left over (residuals) after the grand mean and the row and column effects are removed from the group means.

14. In repeated-measures designs, the observations or measurements are repeated on the same units, and when analyzing such designs, we need to be especially attentive to the error term used in the *F* ratio.

Key Terms

additive model   p. 319
analysis of variance (ANOVA)   p. 305
column effects   p. 318
error   p. 319
focused tests   p. 312
F ratio   p. 307
F test   p. 307
grand mean (M_G)   p. 318
interaction effects   p. 317
main effect   p. 317
mean square (S^2, or *MS*)   p. 306

mean square for error   p. 306
omnibus tests   p. 312
one-way design   p. 305
repeated-measures designs   p. 323
residuals   p. 317
row effects   p. 318
simple effects   p. 316
sum of squares   p. 308
tests of simple effects   p. 315
two-way design   p. 305
two-way factorial   p. 305

Multiple-Choice Questions for Review (answers are found on page 358)

1. When comparing only two groups, $F =$ _____ . (a) *t*; (b) 2*t*; (c) t^2; (d) *t*/2

2. A "one-dimensional ANOVA" has only one _____ variable. (a) dependent; (b) independent; (c) control; (d) demographic

3. S^2 is also called _____ . (a) sum of squares; (b) σ^2; (c) *F* ratio; (d) mean square

4. Total *SS* = _____ *SS* + _____ *SS*. (a) experimental; control; (b) dependent; independent; (c) between; within; (d) all of the above

5. In a two-way factorial, the between *SS* = _____ . (a) main effects *SS*; (b) main effects *SS* + interaction *SS*; (c) main effects *SS* + interaction *SS* + error *SS*; (d) none of the above

6. A student at the University of Tennessee conducts an experiment with three groups. Each group contains four subjects. How many between-conditions degrees of freedom will there be? (a) 2; (b) 3; (c) 4; (d) 11

7. In the study above, what are the total degrees of freedom? (a) 2; (b) 3; (c) 4; (d) 11

8. A student at Southern Illinois University conducts a study with two groups and five subjects in each group. She calculates that $F = 5$. Using Table 14.4, find the appropriate p value. (a) $p > .05$; (b) $p < .05$; (c) $p < .01$; (d) cannot be determined

9. A student at the University of Arizona conducts an experiment with four groups. He calculates an F test to examine the overall differences between the groups. He then computes t tests to compare each group to all of the others. These t tests are said to be tests of (a) within-subjects effects; (b) main effects; (c) repeated-measures effects; (d) simple effects.

10. Both F with numerator $df = 1$ and any t test are (a) focused tests; (b) unfocused tests; (c) omnibus tests; (d) diffuse tests.

Discussion Questions for Review (answers are found on pages 358–59)

1. From a population of 50 male professional runners, an Ohio State researcher randomly assigns 10 to each of five groups. Each group receives a different brand of running shoe. The brands are coded A, B, C, D, E. Each member of a group receives a new pair of the top-of-the-line shoe made by the shoe company and then rates the shoe for comfort. Below are the mean comfort ratings (on a scale from 1 to 20) given to the different brands:

Brand	Rating
A	19
B	13
C	17
D	9
E	10

Suppose the researcher performs an analysis of variance, and the within-shoe-brands mean square is 94, whereas the mean square for between-shoe-brands is 188. What is the value of the F testing the significance of the difference among the shoe brands? What are the associated degrees of freedom?

2. A University of Pittsburgh researcher has the following two sets of data, each of which contains three independent groups. The 12 subjects in each set were randomly assigned to the groups; 4 subjects were assigned to each group. The numbers are scores on some dependent measure.

Set A

	Group 1	Group 2	Group 3
	2	5	11
	3	5	10
	2	4	9
	1	6	10
Mean	2	5	10

Set B

	Group 1	Group 2	Group 3
	9	11	23
	−6	−10	10
	4	0	−2
	1	19	9
Mean	2	5	10

Which set of data is likely to yield a larger *F* ratio in an analysis of variance? How can you be sure?

3. A University of Colorado student obtains the following set of means in a study that measures the benefits of vacations in rural versus urban areas for subjects who live in rural or urban areas. Higher numbers indicate greater benefits. Figure out the row effects, the column effects, and the interaction residuals, and then decide how they should be interpreted.

	Urban subjects	Rural subjects
Urban vacations	5	3
Rural vacations	11	1

4. A University of Maine student obtains the data shown in Table 14.2 and computes the ANOVA shown in Table 14.3. His primary interest, however, is in whether the hot lunch group performed significantly better than did the average of the remaining three groups. How would you advise him to address his question?

15

Chi-Square

The Utility of Chi-Square

To review, in our discussion of the correlation coefficient (Chapter 11), we said that it could be viewed quite directly as a measure of the degree of relation between two variables. As noted in Chapter 12, when the number of pairs of scores on which r is computed is small, a very large r may not differ significantly from chance. In that case, although there is a strong relation between the two variables, relations that strong occur quite often by chance even if the true correlation is zero. For that reason, we would like to know for any r not only its size but also the probability of its having occurred by chance (e.g., its confidence interval).

Whereas r tells us immediately how "big" a relation there is between variables, but not how unlikely it is to have occurred by chance, t and F tell us immediately (with the help of some tables) how unlikely it is that a given relation has occurred by chance, but not how "big" the relation is. However, by taking a simple additional step, described in Chapters 13 and 14, we can compute the size of the relation that a large t or F (based on two conditions) has convinced us is unlikely to have occurred by chance. Thus r gives us the size of the relation and permits us a further assessment of statistical significance, whereas t and F give us statistical significance and permit us a further assessment of the size of the relation.

The statistic we discuss in this final chapter is the **chi-square**, symbolized as χ^2 and pronounced "ki (rhymes with eye) square." Invented in 1900 by Karl Pearson

PREVIEW QUESTIONS

▪ What is the purpose of chi-square, and how is it related conceptually to t and F?

▪ How do I calculate chi-square on a table of counts?

▪ How are the p value and the effect size found?

▪ What are the expected values of χ^2, t, and F when H_0 is true?

▪ What is the relation between chi-square and the phi coefficient?

▪ What are some options in the interpretation of large tables of counts?

▪ How are the margins standardized by successive iterations?

(who also invented the product-moment r), it is a statistic that, like t and F, tells us how unlikely it is that the relation investigated has occurred by chance, and like t and F, it does not tell us immediately about the strength of the relation between the variables (see also Box 15.1). Just as in the case of t and F, any given value of χ^2 is associated with a stronger degree of relation when it is based on a smaller number of sampling units. In other words, a relation must be quite strong to result in a large χ^2 (or t or F) with only a small number of subjects.

Box 15.1   Fisher as Detective

In the 19th century, Gregor Mendel, the legendary Austrian botanist, performed experiments that became the basis of the modern science of genetics. Working with garden peas, he showed that their characteristics could be predicted from the characteristics of their "parents." In a famous piece of scientific detective work, Ronald A. Fisher (the inventor of the F test and the null hypothesis) later used the chi-square to ask whether Mendel's data may have been manipulated so that they would seem to be more in line with his theory. Fisher used the chi-square as a "goodness-of-fit" test of Mendel's reported findings compared with statistically expected values, and he found Mendel's data *too perfect* to be plausible. Fisher concluded that Mendel had been deceived by a research assistant, who knew what Mendel wanted to find and who manipulated the data *too* well.

We compute χ^2 for tables of frequencies, or counts; χ^2 can be thought of as a comparison of counts. That is, it does its job of testing the relation between two variables by assessing the discrepancy between a theoretically **expected frequency** (f_e) and an obtained or **observed frequency** (f_o). In other words, it differs from the other significance tests we have examined in that it can be used for dependent variables that are not scored or scaled. In all the earlier examples of t and F, subjects' responses were recorded as scores in such a way that some could be regarded as so many units greater or less than other scores. Because chi-square is a comparison of counts, it allows us to deal with categories of response that are not so easily ordered, scaled, or scored.

Computing 2 × 2 Chi-Squares

Imagine that we want to study the food preferences of members of two campus organizations, which call themselves the Junk Food Junkies (JFJ) and the Green Earthies (GE). We give each subject a choice of one of two foods, a juicy grilled hamburger with onions, pickles, relish, and barbecue sauce on a sesame seed bun (called a Big Jack) or a grilled soyburger with lettuce and tomato on whole wheat bread. Table 15.1 provides the basic data for computing a simple chi-square, a 2 × 2 table. Membership in the organizations is thought of as the independent variable; each member of the two samples of subjects falls into one and only one of the four possible cells. In Section A, the "observed frequencies" are the number of people in that column

Table 15.1   Basic Data for 2 × 2 Chi-Square

A. Observed frequencies (f_o)

Food choice	JFJ	GE	Row sums
Big Jack	24	13	37
Soyburger	12	30	42
Column sums	36	43	79

B. Expected frequencies (f_e)

Food choice	JFJ	GE	Row sums
Big Jack	16.861	20.139	37.000
Soyburger	19.139	22.861	42.000
Column sums	36.000	43.000	79.000

C. $(f_o - f_e)^2 / f_e$ values

Food choice	JFJ	GE	Row sums
Big Jack	3.023	2.531	5.554
Soyburger	2.663	2.229	4.892
Column sums	5.686	4.760	10.446

(organization) who chose the alternative listed in that row. Of the members of the Junk Food Junkies, 24 chose a Big Jack, and 12 chose the soyburger, and of the members of the Green Earthies, 13 chose a Big Jack, and 30 chose the soyburger.

The following general formula summarizes the steps we will take in analyzing those observed frequencies:

$$\chi^2 = \sum \frac{(f_o - f_e)^2}{f_e}$$

where f_o is the observed frequency in each cell, and f_e is the expected frequency in that cell. This formula instructs us to sum the squared differences between the observed frequencies (f_o) and the expected frequencies (f_e) after first dividing each squared difference by the expected frequency. If the null hypothesis of no relation between the rows and columns were true, we would expect the f_o and f_e scores to be similar in magnitude. In other words, observed frequencies that are substantially larger and smaller than the expected frequencies are needed to throw doubt on the null hypothesis, because the value of chi-square will be small when the difference $f_o - f_e$ is small (see also Box 15.2).

To use this formula, we must first determine for each of our observed frequencies the number of "expected" entries, that is, the number expected if the null hypothesis

Box 15.2   **A Special Formula for 1 $df \chi^2$**

The following is a useful formula for computing chi-square directly from the observed frequencies (f_o) in a 2 × 2 table:

$$\chi^2 = \frac{N(BC - AD)^2}{(A + B)(C + D)(A + C)(B + D)}$$

where the letters refer to particular cells and marginal values in the 2 × 2 table of counts:

A	B	(A + B)
C	D	(C + D)
(A + C)	(B + D)	(N = A + B + C + D)

For the data in Table 15.1, then, we find

$$\chi^2 = \frac{79[(13 \times 12) - (24 \times 30)]^2}{(37)(42)(36)(43)} = \frac{79(318,096)}{2,405,592} = 10.446$$

of no relation between the independent and dependent variable were true. To compute this expected frequency (f_e) for each cell, we multiply the column total by the row total where that row and that column intersect in that cell. We then divide this quantity by the grand total of entries. That is,

$$f_e = \frac{(\text{Column total})(\text{Row total})}{\text{Grand total}}$$

For example, the upper-left cell in Section A of Table 15.1 is at the intersection of the JFJ column and the Big Jack row. The appropriate totals multiplied together and divided by the grand total are (36 × 37)/79 = 16.861. Section B gives all the expected frequencies computed in this way. These values, row by row, are

$$(36 \times 37)/79 = 16.861$$
$$(43 \times 37)/79 = 20.139$$
$$(36 \times 42)/79 = 19.139$$
$$(43 \times 42)/79 = 22.861$$

As a check on our arithmetic, notice that the row totals, the column totals, and the grand total of all the values in Section B are equal to the corresponding totals of the values in Section A. Substituting in the formula for chi-square, we now add up the $(f_o - f_e)^2/f_e$ values (i.e., for each cell, the square of the difference between the observed and expected frequency divided by the expected frequency), which gives us

$$\chi^2 = \sum \frac{(f_o - f_e)^2}{f_e}$$

$$= \frac{(24 - 16.861)^2}{16.861} + \frac{(13 - 20.139)^2}{20.139} + \frac{(12 - 19.139)^2}{19.139} + \frac{(30 - 22.861)^2}{22.861}$$

$$= 10.446$$

The $(f_o - f_e)^2/f_e$ values for each cell also appear in Section C of Table 15.1, which underscores the idea that the total of all these values is the chi-square.

Finding the p Value, Effect Size, and Confidence Interval

As is true of t and F, there is a different chi-square curve for every value of the degrees of freedom. The degrees of freedom (df) of chi-square are defined as

$$df = (\text{rows} - 1)(\text{columns} - 1)$$

or the number of rows minus 1 times the number of columns minus 1. The larger the χ^2, the less likely are the observed frequencies to differ from the expected frequencies only by chance. Table 15.2 gives a sample listing of χ^2 values with 1 to 5 df for $p = .10, .05,$ and $.01$. A more comprehensive listing can be found in Table B.4 (see page 416). Notice that a chi-square must be larger than the degrees of freedom to throw doubt on the null hypothesis.

In this example, the 1 df chi-square of 10.446 is larger than the largest value shown for $df = 1$ (6.64 for $p = .01$); the actual p is approximately .001. Thus a chi-square value this large or larger would occur 1 time in 1,000 repeated samplings if the null hypothesis were true. That is, there is about 1 chance in 1,000 that a chi-square this large would occur if there really were no relation between organizational membership and food preference (see also Box 15.3).

We now compute the effect size, and it should be obvious that we will do so by using the **phi coefficient** (ϕ) introduced in Chapter 11. In computing phi, we use the following general formula:

$$\phi = \frac{BC - AD}{\sqrt{(A + B)(C + D)(A + C)(B + D)}}$$

Table 15.2	Chi-Square Values for Significance at .10, .05, and .01		
df	p = .10	p = .05	p = .01
1	2.71	3.84	6.64
2	4.60	5.99	9.21
3	6.25	7.82	11.34
4	7.78	9.49	13.28
5	9.24	11.07	15.09

Box 15.3 Chi-Square and the Null Hypothesis

Reminiscent of F, all chi-square curves begin at zero and range upward to infinity. You will recall that the expected value of t is zero when the null hypothesis is true, and the expected value of F is $df/(df - 2)$ where df are for the denominator mean square. For chi-square distributions, the expected value (when the null hypothesis of no relation is true) is equal to the df defining that chi-square distribution (i.e., rows $- 1 \times$ columns $- 1$). Thus, for chi-squares based on 2×2, 2×3, and 2×4 tables, the average value of the χ^2 obtained if the null hypothesis were true would be 1, 2, and 3, respectively. The maximum possible value of χ^2 is the total N.

---

where the letters refer to particular cells and marginal values in the 2×2 table of counts, as noted in Box 15.2.

Substituting the data in Section A ("observed frequencies") of Table 15.1, we find

$$\phi = \frac{(13 \times 12) - (24 \times 30)}{\sqrt{(37)(42)(36)(43)}} = \frac{-564}{1551} = .36$$

which indicates what is conventionally called a *medium-sized* effect in behavioral science. Although we see that the numerator of this phi is negative because of the particular arrangement of the cell counts, we also see that Junk Food Junkiness (scored 1 or 0) is positively correlated with Big Jackness (scored 1 or 0). We can now translate this effect into a binomial effect-size display (BESD) with uniform row and column totals.

And finally, we compute a 95% confidence interval around the observed effect by using the procedure described in Chapter 12. To review, we first consult Table B.6 (p. 418) to convert our $r_{\text{effect}} = .36$ into Fisher $z_r = .377$. Step 2 substitutes the value of $N = 79$ in the formula

$$\left(\frac{1}{\sqrt{N-3}}\right)1.96 = \left(\frac{1}{\sqrt{76}}\right)1.96 = .2248$$

In Step 3, we subtract and add this value to the value in Step 1 to find the lower and upper limits of the Fisher z_r values. The lower limit is $.377 - .2248 = .1522$ (rounded to .15), and the upper limit is $.377 + .2248 = .6018$ (rounded to .60). In the final step, we convert these scores back into the metric of the effect size correlation by using Table B.7 (p. 419). We have 95% confidence that the r_{effect} is between .15 and .54. Had the total sample size been larger, or had we decided to work with 90% confidence, the interval would be narrower.

Phi and Chi-Square

If the sample size (N) is not too small ($N > 20$), and if the smallest expected frequency is not too small (e.g., less than 3 or so), we can test the significance of phi coefficients by chi-square tests, because

$$\chi^2 = (\phi^2)(N)$$

Having satisfied these assumptions in our present data set, we substitute in this formula and find

$$\chi^2 = (.3636^2)(79) = 10.444$$

which, not surprisingly, is the same value of chi-square we obtained before (within rounding error).

Notice also that the formula above serves as another example of the conceptual relation described in Chapter 13, that is,

Significance test = (Size of effect)(Size of study)

which reminds us that χ^2 (like t and F) is the product of the effect size and the study size. Hence, the larger the effect or the more subjects used, the greater will be the size of the χ^2. This equation underscores the importance of doing a power analysis, and it implies that, as in the case of t and F, a relation must be quite strong (i.e., the effect must be large) to result in a large chi-square with only a small number of subjects.

More often, we will compute the χ^2 first and then calculate the r_{effect}, and as in the case of other statistical tests, we report the effect size only when working with 1-df chi-squares. To find the value of the effect size correlation from any 1-df chi-square value, we substitute in the following formula:

$$\phi = \sqrt{\frac{\chi^2}{N}}$$

Box 15.4   **Small, Medium, and Large**

Earlier we mentioned that behavioral scientists typically characterize effect size correlations of .10, .30, and .50 as small, medium, and large, respectively (J. Cohen, 1988). Also noted was that effect sizes of .30 to .50 are common in behavioral science, but effects of a much smaller magnitude are typical in biomedical research. In Chapter 12, we described a major biomedical experiment that found that heart attack risk was cut in half by aspirin (Steering Committee of the Physicians' Health Study Research Group, 1988), and the r_{effect} was noted as .034 (see Table 12.4 on p. 277). Using the procedure described in this chapter, you can calculate this result for yourself and thus see how easy it sometimes is to identify the obtained effect size even when you are working with the minimal raw ingredients found in newspaper reports of scientific findings.

and this value serves as our index of r_{effect} of any 1-df chi-square and can be interpreted by means of the BESD. In our continuing example, substituting in the above formula gives us

$$r_{effect} = \sqrt{\frac{\chi^2}{N}} = \sqrt{\frac{10.446}{79}} = .36$$

which, of course, is the same value that we calculated previously (see also Box 15.4).

Larger Tables of Counts

When there are many cells in a chi-square table (i.e., a table of counts, or frequencies), a statistically significant chi-square may be more difficult to interpret than in a 2 × 2 table. Table 15.3 illustrates this situation in a 2 × 4 table, constructed by the addition of two new groups to Table 15.1. One new group (designated as PC) consists of 35 members of the Psychology Club, and the other new group consists of 11 members of the Mathematics Club (MC). The working hypothesis is that psychology and mathematics students are more like Junk Food Junkies than like Green Earthies in choosing grilled beef over grilled soy.

Table 15.4 shows in Section A the expected frequencies computed from the obtained counts in Table 15.3. For example, in Table 15.3 we see that 21 of the 35 members of the Psychology Club chose grilled beef. To obtain the expected frequency shown as 18.480 in Table 15.4, we multiply the appropriate row total (shown as 66 in Table 15.3) by the appropriate column total (35) and then divide the product by the total number of observations (125); the result is (66 × 35)/125 = 18.480. Notice that the row and column sums in Section A of Table 15.4 are identical to the corresponding values in Table 15.3.

The calculation of the 3-df chi-square is accomplished by the general procedure and formula given earlier:

$$\chi^2 = \sum \frac{(f_o - f_e)^2}{f_e}$$

and the entries in Section B of Table 15.4 show the $(f_o - f_e)^2/f_e$ results used in this procedure. The value of this chi-square, then, is the grand total of these cell data, or 14.046. The p value of this chi-square (with 3 df) is approximately .003.

Table 15.3	Obtained Frequencies (f_o) for 2 × 4 Chi-Square				
Food choice	PC	MC	JFJ	GE	Row sums
Big Jack	21	8	24	13	66
Soyburger	14	3	12	30	59
Column sums	35	11	36	43	125

Table 15.4 Expected Frequencies (f_e) and ($f_o - f_e)^2/f_e$ Values

A. Expected frequencies (f_e)

Food choice	PC	MC	JFJ	GE	Row sums
Big Jack	18.480	5.808	19.008	22.704	66
Soyburger	16.520	5.192	16.992	20.296	59
Column sums	35	11	36	43	125

B. ($f_o - f_e)^2/f_e$ values

Food choice	PC	MC	JFJ	GE	Row sums
Big Jack	0.344	0.827	1.311	4.148	6.630
Soyburger	0.384	0.925	1.467	4.640	7.416
Column sums	0.728	1.752	2.778	8.788	14.046 (grand total)

The larger the value of chi-square, the less likely are the observed frequencies to differ only by chance from the expected frequencies, and this chi-square is interestingly large. However, all it tells us is that *somewhere* in the data the observed frequencies depart noticeably from the expected values. In a way, it reminds us of the case of analysis of variance with $df > 1$ in the numerator of F. That is, a significant omnibus F tells us that there is some difference but not where that difference may be found (see also Box 15.5). To help us interpret chi-square tables with $df > 1$, let us review some of the options available.

Interpreting Large Tables

One procedure when chi-square $df > 1$ is to inspect closely the ($f_o - f_e)^2/f_e$ results, because these results show which of the cells contributed most to the overall large chi-square. A large cell entry in such a table indicates that the cell in question is "surprising" to us given the magnitude of the row and column totals that are affected by that cell. That is, the cell is "unexpected" in terms of chance or likelihood—not necessarily in terms of our research hypothesis, however. In Table 15.4, the largest values

---

Box 15.5 **Focused and Omnibus Chi-Squares**

Previously we defined F with numerator $df = 1$ and any t test as focused tests, and we defined F with numerator $df > 1$ as an omnibus test. We said that omnibus tests are diffuse tests, and that therefore we cannot compute a meaningful r_{effect} in conjunction with such tests. Similarly, any χ^2 with $df > 1$ is defined as an **omnibus chi-square**, while χ^2 with $df = 1$ is defined as a **focused chi-square.** The rule of thumb regarding the interpretability of the effect size r remains the same, in that we report r_{effect} only for a focused (i.e., 1 df) chi-square.

in Section B suggest that Green Earthies reacted in a less likely way than would be expected by chance on the basis of the choices of the other three groups.

A second option for dealing with larger tables of counts is to subdivide them into smaller (e.g., 2 × 2) tables. In this procedure, called **partitioning of tables,** we compute additional chi-squares based on portions of the overall table. Either a prior theory or hypothesis or the nature of the obtained results can guide our judgment about which additional chi-squares to compute. The number and size of the subtables are guided by certain statistical rules, and the calculations also call for certain statistical adjustments. Students who would like to know more about partitioning chi-square tables will find a detailed discussion in our advanced textbook (Rosenthal & Rosnow, 1991).

For a third option, called **standardizing the margins** (Mosteller, 1968), all that you will need is a pocket calculator and a little patience. This option will enable you to take the size of the row and column totals (or "margins") into account by setting all the row totals equal to each other and all the column totals equal to each other. This process is, however, different from a BESD, which sets the row and column margins equal to 100. To show you how standardizing the margins is accomplished, we illustrate this method with our continuing example.

Taking the Margins Into Account

One of the special problems of trying to understand the results in large tables of counts is that our eye is likely to be fooled by the absolute magnitude of the frequencies displayed (i.e., the f_o data). Suppose we were to ask of the data in Table 15.3 which group of subjects is most overrepresented in the Big Jack category. Our eye notes that Psychology Club members (PC) and Junk Food Junkies (JFJ) have the greatest frequency of occurrence in that category, and we might erroneously conclude that one of these groups is most overrepresented in the Big Jack category. Our conclusion would be in error because we looked only at the interior of the table and not, at the same time, at the sums in the row and column margins.

A look at these margins suggests that the PC and JFJ groups *should* have larger obtained frequencies in the Big Jack category than the Mathematics Club members (MC) because the PC and JFJ groups have more members than the MC group. In addition, there are slightly more subjects in general in the Big Jack category than in the soyburger category. Taking all these margins into account simultaneously would show us that it is actually the MC subjects who are most overrepresented in the Big Jack category.

In large tables, however, "taking the margins into account" becomes a very difficult matter without the use of systematic aids to eye and mind. Standardizing the margins allows us to "correct" for the unequal column and row margins and thus provides us with a systematic procedure for taking the unequal margins into account. Table 15.5 illustrates the steps taken to correct for the unequal column and row margins in Table 15.3.

The results in Section A illustrate the first step, which is to divide each obtained frequency (in Table 15.3) by its column sum. For example, to obtain the "corrected"

Table 15.5   Steps in Standardizing the Margins

A. Results "corrected" for unequal column margins in Table 15.3

Food choice	PC	MC	JFJ	GE	Row sums
Big Jack	.600	.727	.667	.302	2.296
Soyburger	.400	.273	.333	.698	1.704
Column sums	1.000	1.000	1.000	1.000	4.000

B. Results "corrected" for unequal row margins in A (above)

Food choice	PC	MC	JFJ	GE	Row sums
Big Jack	.261	.317	.291	.132	1.001
Soyburger	.235	.160	.195	.410	1.000
Column sums	.496	.477	.486	.542	2.001

C. Final "corrected" results

Food choice	PC	MC	JFJ	GE	Row sums
Big Jack	.517	.657	.589	.238	2.001
Soyburger	.483	.343	.411	.762	1.999
Column sums	1.000	1.000	1.000	1.000	4.000

D. Results in C (above) shown as deviations from an expected value of .500

Food choice	PC	MC	JFJ	GE	Row sums
Big Jack	+.017	+.157	+.089	−.262	+.001
Soyburger	−.017	−.157	−.089	+.262	−.001
Column sums	.000	.000	.000	.000	.000

values for 21 and 14 in Table 15.3, we divide each by 35; to find the "corrected" values for 8 and 3 in Table 15.3, we divide each by 11; and so on. These calculations yield the results in Section A of Table 15.5, in which we see that the column margins have been equalized but that the row margins remain very unequal. To "correct" for the latter, we now divide each of the new values in Section A by its row margin. To obtain the "corrected" values for .600, .727, .667, and .302, we divide each by 2.296. To obtain the "corrected" values for .400, .273, .333, and .698, we divide each by 1.704. The results appear in Section B of Table 15.5.

Section B has equalized the row margins, at least within rounding error, but now the column margins are no longer equal. By now, we know what to do about that: Simply divide each entry of Section B by its new column margin. That process will equalize the column margins but *may* make our new row margins unequal. We repeat this procedure until further repetitions (also called **iterations**) no longer affect the margins. For our present data, the final results obtained by successive iterations are shown in Section C of Table 15.5, which shows margins equalized within rounding error and allows us to interpret the table entries without worrying about the confusing effects of variations in margins. It shows that, in the Big Jack category, the Mathematics Club (MC) is overrepresented most, and that, in the soyburger category, the Green Earthies (GE) are overrepresented most.

There is one final step we can take to throw the results into still bolder relief: We can show the cell entries as deviations from the values we would expect if there were no differences whatever among the groups in their representation in the Big Jack and soyburger categories. If there were no such differences, and given the margins of Section C, all the values in the table would be .500. In forming our final table, we subtract this expected value of .500 from each entry in Section C; the results are shown in Section D.

The interpretation of the final table is fairly direct. Besides the big difference between the Green Earthies, who are overrepresented very heavily in the soyburger category, and all the other groups, which are more modestly overrepresented in the Big Jack category, there are other differences that help us to interpret our earlier results. For example, even though some of the sample sizes are too small to be very stable, we can also raise some tentative questions about differences among the three groups overrepresented in the Big Jack category. The Mathematics Club is substantially more overrepresented in the Big Jack category than is the Psychology Club, which is virtually not overrepresented at all. The Junk Food Junkies fall almost exactly midway between the PC and MC groups in their degree of overrepresentation in the Big Jack category.

Because of the small sample sizes in this study, the differences among these three groups (PC, MC, and JFJ) are not significant statistically, but with larger sample sizes, they might be. In any case, the purpose of the procedure of standardizing the margins is to highlight the differences among groups, whether these achieve statistical significance or not.

A Journey Begun

The *beginning* in the title of this book is intended to have a double meaning, as it not only describes the level of the text but also conveys the idea of a journey. For some students, the journey embarked on at the start of this course is now complete, whereas for others it is still just beginning. In either case, it should be recognized that, particularly in some of their statistical aspects, the design of experiments and the comparison of research conditions constitute a very specialized and highly developed field. The purpose of these last six chapters was to further your understanding of the logic and meaning of the statistical procedures and concepts associated with the application of the scientific method, an understanding that may have been initiated in a basic statistics course.

A thorough knowledge of the characteristics of both the data obtained and the statistics used is assumed by professional researchers in all fields to be an essential aspect of good scientific practice. Whether the conclusion of this chapter represents the start or the end of your journey in behavioral research, you should now have a deeper understanding of the applicability and limitations of the scientific method in many fields. Many of the procedures you have learned about in these final chapters can be addressed to questions you have about the scientific results you read about in newspapers and magazines (or hear about in chat groups on the World Wide Web) and to many everyday questions that can be framed in ways that allow you to reach beyond others' conclusions and, using empirical reasoning, decide for yourself what is true.

Summary of Ideas

1. Chi-square (χ^2) is used to test the degree of agreement between the data actually obtained (or "observed") and the data expected under a particular hypothesis (e.g., the null hypothesis).

2. The expected value of chi-square when the null hypothesis is true is equal to the degrees of freedom defining the particular chi-square distribution.

3. The effect size r for 2×2 chi-squares (i.e., focused chi-squares) is phi (ϕ), which is computed directly from chi-square by

$$r_{\text{effect}} = \phi = \sqrt{\frac{\chi^2}{N}}$$

4. We compute the confidence interval and use the BESD to interpret the effect size as described in previous chapters.

5. If the sample size is not too small, and if the variables are split not more than 3 to 1, we test the significance of the effect size r by $\chi^2 = (\phi^2)(N)$, which reflects the conceptual relationship that significance test = size of effect × size of study.

6. As in the case of t and F, a relationship must be quite strong to result in a large chi-square with only a small number of sampling units.

7. Effect size correlations of .10, .30, and .50 are conventionally referred to as small, medium, and large, respectively, while "jumbo" effects are substantially larger than .50.

8. One option in interpreting larger tables of counts is to examine the $(f_o - f_e)^2/f_e$ results, because they show which of the cells in the table of counts contributed most to the overall chi-square.

9. A second option is to partition the larger table of counts into smaller (e.g., 2×2) chi-square tables.

10. A third option is to standardize the margins (totals) by making all row margins equal and by, at the same time, making all column margins equal.

Key Terms

chi-square (χ^2)   p. 328
expected frequency (f_e)   p. 329
focused chi-square   p. 336
iterations   p. 339
observed frequency (f_o)   p. 329

omnibus chi-square   p. 336
partitioning of tables   p. 337
phi coefficient (ϕ)   p. 332
standardizing the margins   p. 337

Multiple-Choice Questions for Review (answers are found on page 359)

1. Chi-square differs from significance tests such as t and F in that it is specifically designed for use when (a) there are multiple dependent variables; (b) there are multiple independent variables; (c) the dependent variables are not ordered, scored, or scaled beyond two levels; (d) none of the above.

2. Chi-squares are calculated by examining the differences between _____ and _____ frequencies. (a) expected; obtained; (b) theoretical; operational; (c) between; within; (d) none of the above

3. In the following 2 × 2 table, what is the expected frequency in the upper-left cell? (a) 1; (b) 4; (c) 19; (d) 25

	Democrats	Republicans
Males	4	1
Females	1	19

4. A student at Kutztown University examines a 2 × 2 table of counts and calculates chi-square to be 6. Using Table 15.2, find the appropriate p value. (a) < .10; (b) < .05; (c) < .01; (d) cannot be determined from this information

5. The same student examines a 4 × 2 table of counts and calculates chi-square to be 6. Using Table 15.2, find the appropriate p value. (a) > .10; (b) < .10; (c) < .05; (d) cannot be determined from this information

6. The effect size measure typically associated with chi-square is _____ . (a) ϕ; (b) f_e; (c) f_o; (d) z_r

7. $\chi^2 = $ _____ × _____ . (a) ϕ^2; N; (b) row total; column total; (c) rows − 1; columns − 1; (d) none of the above

8. Chi-square tables are also called tables of _____ . (a) means; (b) ANOVAs; (c) counts; (d) unequaled margins

9. A study is conducted which yields a 3 × 4 chi-square table. The overall chi-square is found to be significant. To interpret the results more fully, the researcher decides to examine a table of $(f_o - f_e)^2/f_e$ scores. In this table, the cells with _____ numbers indicate "unexpected" results. (a) small; (b) positive; (c) no; (d) large

10. A study is conducted which yields a 3 × 4 chi-square table. To interpret the results more fully, the researcher uses a procedure setting the row and column totals equal to each other. This procedure is called (a) partitioning; (b) examining a table of $(f_o - f_e)^2/f_e$ scores; (c) standardizing the margins; (d) binary analysis.

Discussion Questions for Review (answers are found on pages 360–61)

1. A clinical psychologist at the University of Alabama examines the relation of three types of psychopathology to socioeconomic status (SES) in 100 subjects. Her table of counts is

SES	Schizophrenic	Neurotic	Depressed
High	5	5	20
Medium	5	15	20
Low	10	10	10

How should she test the hypothesis that this table of counts is significantly different from what would be expected by chance if there were no relation between these variables? How many degrees of freedom will her statistic have?

2. A Brigham Young student obtained the following data, where the numbers are frequencies (counts). How should she plan to standardize the margins?

Annual carrot consumption	Visual acuity		
	High	Average	Low
11–20 lb	9	3	1
1–10 lb	5	8	2
0 lb	1	8	7

3. A researcher at Rochester Institute of Technology asks 10 engineering students from the freshman, sophomore, junior, and senior classes whether they plan to attend graduate school. The results are

	Frosh	Sophs	Juniors	Seniors
Want advanced degree	7	6	3	1
Want out of school	3	4	7	9

How many degrees of freedom would the chi-square for this table have? How should the researcher calculate the expected frequencies? What is the nature of the relation between year in college and wanting an advanced degree?

4. Three students at the College of New Jersey each conduct the same study with the following results:

	x^2(1 df)	N	p
Student 1	2.00	20	.16
Student 2	3.00	30	.08
Student 3	4.00	40	.05

Student 3 claims a significant relationship between the two levels of her independent variable (0, 1) and the two levels of her dependent variable (0, 1). Students 1 and 2 chide her, saying that they have not found a significant effect and that her results are therefore undependable and unreplicable. How should Student 3 reply?

Answers to Review Questions

Chapter 1

Multiple-Choice Questions

1. a	**6.** d
2. c	**7.** c
3. d	**8.** c
4. b	**9.** d
5. a	**10.** d

Discussion Questions

1. First, the method of tenacity would be if you believed something because it is an idea that has been around for a long time (e.g., Elvis is alive). Second, the method of authority would be if you believed something told to you by an expert in the field (e.g., cutting back on fatty foods because the doctor told you to do so). Third, the a priori method would be if you used pure reason as a basis of belief (e.g., reasoning that $12 \times 100 = 120 \times 10 = 1 \times 1200$). Fourth, the scientific method would be if you used empirical reasoning as a basis of belief (e.g., believing the earth is round because you have circled the globe by foot, boat, and vehicle and not fallen off).

2. Empirical reasoning is considered the "most fundamental" characteristic of the scientific method. Three characteristics in addition to this one are the rhetoric of science, the use of imagery, and the aesthetics of good theories, models, methods, and so on.

3. This is relational research because the relation of two sets of observations (TV diary entries and playground aggression) is examined. It is not experimental because neither of the variables is manipulated by the investigator.

4. This is experimental research because the investigator has manipulated the type of movie shown.

5. This is descriptive research because the data are collected on student shyness, but these scores are not examined for their relation to any other variable.

6. For his descriptive research, he might collect data on the creativity scores of other students. For his relational research, he might examine the relationship between creativity scores and SAT scores. For his experimental research, he might experimentally manipulate the type of music being played in the background while the students' creativity is being measured to see whether Mozart makes students more creative than does hard rock.

7. No, it certainly *is* possible to study the concept of prayer, and Galton conducted a relational study of prayer and longevity. An experimental study might employ prayer for a randomly chosen half of 20 people who are ill and no prayer for the remaining people to see whether prayer causes faster recovery.

8. The nine orienting attitudes are (a) enthusiasm for the process of research; (b) being open-minded so as not to miss a promising lead, and to learn from your mistakes and from others' criticisms; (c) using good sense rather than doing something only because it is convenient to do so; (d) taking the role of the research participant and of the research consumer; (e) being inventive and also being principled; (f) having confidence in your own good judgment after applying your mind to the facts; (g) learning to communicate clearly; (h) being consistent and careful about details; and (i) being honest in every aspect of the research.

Chapter 2

Multiple-Choice Questions

1. c	**6.** b
2. c	**7.** a
3. c	**8.** d
4. d	**9.** b
5. d	**10.** c

Discussion Questions

1. His independent variable was operationalized by scores on the self-esteem scale; his dependent variable was operationalized by self-reported GPA. Because this is a relational study rather than an experimental study, he would not be justified in drawing the causal inference that either variable led to or affected the other.

2. An operational definition might be "score earned on Hans Eysenck's test." A theoretical definition might be "the degree of social ease and smoothness shown in a group setting."

3. Science is defined by its procedures rather than by the status of a person who labels a particular belief system a "science." One study of the accuracy of astrological forecasts might ask a panel of "expert" astrologers to prepare a brief description of the personality of persons born under each of the 12 signs of the zodiac. A large number of students would then be asked to rate each of these 12 descriptions on the extent to which each of the descriptions applied to them. As long as the students knew nothing about astrology, evidence for the accuracy of astrology would be obtained if the students rated the personality descriptions of their signs as more characteristic of them than the average of the other 11 descriptions. These students' roommates or friends could also rate the students, assuming the roommates or friends also knew nothing about astrology.

4. A causal hypothesis might be that revenge is more likely to occur when people feel they have been harmed intentionally by another. To evaluate the acceptability of

this hypothesis, we would examine the correspondence with reality of this hypothesis, its coherence and parsimony, and its falsifiability. On these grounds, it seems we are ready to proceed to the stage of operationalizing our independent and dependent variables.

5. The doctor did not take the boy's cultural background or context into account. We might study the boy by administering standard medical, neurological, and psychological evaluations; by giving him a wide choice of cultural artifacts (toys, tools, foods, pictures, videos, etc.) to observe, use, and explore; and by accompanying him to settings (e.g., parks, lakes, and forests) more like those in which he had grown up in order to observe his behavior in a habitat more natural to him.

Chapter 3

Multiple-Choice Questions

1. d   6. a
2. d   7. c
3. d   8. d
4. a   9. a
5. b   10. d

Discussion Questions

1. Some possible costs include time, energy, income lost by spending time on the questionnaire items, possible embarrassment at "being studied" in an unsavory location or occupation, and the danger of discovery of subjects' criminal behavior because someone in law enforcement obtains the questionnaire and can link it to the respondents.

2. Observing the thefts might be quite upsetting to the real customers, who may be put at risk of, say, anxiety reactions or heart attacks. The confederate "robbers" may also be put at risk of being attacked by a customer trying to foil the robbery. We need to ask whether what we might be able to learn from this research is really worth the risk to the real customers and the confederate "robbers."

3. The student has failed to debrief the subjects, so they may leave feeling that they were really insensitive to others. He should, of course, debrief them.

4. They mean that the costs and benefits are in such balance that it is very difficult to reach a decision on whether to go ahead with the research. For removal of the study from the diagonal of indecision, the costs of the study should be decreased, the benefits should be increased, or both.

5. That the subject understands what the research will require from her or him, that the subject may leave at any time, and that he or she will remain anonymous.

6. The Rushton study also raised no questions of deception or invasion of privacy. However, the issue of fair-mindedness *was* raised. Were some of the organization's workers going to be "treated specially," or would they get to ride the "gravy train" in the eyes of other workers?

Chapter 4

Multiple-Choice Questions

1. b	**6.** b
2. c	**7.** a
3. d	**8.** b
4. d	**9.** d
5. c	**10.** d

Discussion Questions

1. To learn the "effects" of legislation on some outcome behavior (e.g., drunk driving) by comparing the changes in behavior in states (or counties) changing their laws with the change in behavior in states not changing their laws. To predict legislators' votes from an analysis of their past votes or the style of communication revealed in their earlier speeches. To predict future intelligence, personality, and psychopathology from archived early childhood drawings.

2. The student could correlate the frequency of reported fights, stampedes, and riots with the aggressiveness of various sports as defined by the average number of injuries per player sustained in each sport.

3. To examine the hypothesis that comic strips featuring children are designed for a younger readership, the mean word length in comic strips featuring children is compared to the mean word length in comic strips not featuring children. The student should check the reliability of two judges' (a) classifying the strips as featuring or not featuring children and (b) counting the word lengths and computing their average. We may also want to sample the comic strips over a period of several weeks or months.

4. The most important advice is that he should be clear about what he wants to learn from this research. Beyond that, he should consider the general questions suggested by Goodenough and described on pages 86–88.

5. A descriptive study may reveal a high rate of wheezing, coughing, illness, and death among those exposed to cigarette smoke. A relational study may show that those who are exposed to greater amounts of cigarette smoke suffer from higher rates of illness and death. An experimental study may show that animals experimentally exposed to higher dosages of cigarette smoke have higher rates of illness and death than do animals exposed to lower dosages.

6. That the teachers' ratings of their students' intellectual ability were nothing more than the teachers' accurate diagnosing of IQ. It would take an experimental manipulation of teachers' expectations to demonstrate that they played a causal role.

Chapter 5

Multiple-Choice Questions

1. a	**6.** b
2. b	**7.** d
3. c	**8.** c
4. a	**9.** b
5. a	**10.** b

Discussion Questions

1. Define the aspects of attitudes about abortion you want to have covered by your measure, and be sure the items are easily understood. Decide how many response categories you want to use in your numerical and segmented graphic scales.

2. Leniency bias, acquiescent response set, central tendency bias, and halo effect (or logical error in rating), respectively. The section on "rating errors" gives suggestions on how to control for each of these rating errors.

3. Most of the chapter contributes to an answer to this question, but you might begin with the answer to Review Question 1 above.

4. Have a large number of judges sort a large number of items into 11 piles numbered 1 to 11 in order of item favorableness. The median rating of favorableness of each item is computed, and items are selected for the final scale on the basis of (a) the judges' agreement on each item's degree of favorableness and (b) the items' being spread fairly evenly throughout the range of attitudes from 1 to 11.

5. The major difference is that the Likert 5-point (or 7-point or 9-point) rating scale is used only if it correlates highly enough with the total score.

6. Select a sample of bipolar cue words that represent the evaluative, potency, and activity dimensions of the so-called semantic space created by these three dimensions.

7. Instead of supposing what the ideal candidate might be like, it may be better to ask respondents about characteristics of candidates that would elicit the respondents' votes.

8. One wording might be: Describe in detail a situation in which you felt pleased and proud to be an employee of the company. What led up to the situation, and what was its outcome? The same question might well be asked again, this time with "unhappy and ashamed" substituted for "pleased and proud."

9. It has been shown to lead to more accurate data.

Chapter 6

Multiple-Choice Questions

1. c	**6.** d
2. c	**7.** c
3. d	**8.** d
4. b	**9.** c
5. a	**10.** b

Discussion Questions

1. By showing that her scale correlates substantially with future symptoms of fear when subjects are asked to speak in public (convergent validity). In addition, the new scale should not correlate substantially with such less relevant variables as height, spatial relations abilities, and political party preference.
2. Because it correlates highly with behaviors defined as reflecting high need for social approval, but not as highly with behaviors not reflecting high need for approval.
3. Yes, because a total of four judges will yield a composite reliability of .80 when the typical judge-to-judge reliability is .50 (see Table 6.2).
4. Perhaps female toddlers prefer more complex shapes than do male toddlers. A new study might add four new stimuli: a smooth, hard teddy bear and rattle, and a soft, fuzzy ball and cube. If the plausible rival hypothesis were correct, female toddlers would prefer the new smooth, hard teddy bear and rattle to the new fuzzy ball and cube. Considering all eight stimuli, then, female toddlers would prefer the four complexly shaped stimuli compared to male toddlers, who would prefer the four simply shaped stimuli if the rival hypothesis is accurate.
5. Because Table 6.2 shows that, for 20 items, a mean inter-item reliability of .40 is associated with composite reliability of .93, not .50.
6. The test-retest reliability can be computed by administering the test twice to the same subjects (for example, four weeks apart) and computing the correlation between the two administrations. The composite reliability can be computed by correlating all the items with each other and then applying the Spearman-Brown formula to the mean inter-item correlation (or using Table 6.2) to get the overall internal-consistency reliability. The reason for administering the several different measures was that the student could show convergent validity with the measures with which his new scale should correlate substantially and discriminant validity with the measures with which his new scale should not correlate substantially.
7. There is no systematic error because the average reading is accurate (10 pounds). The random errors are +4, −2, −3, 0, and +1 on the five readings, or errors of +40%, −20%, −30%, 0%, and 10%, respectively, a not very precise performance.

Chapter 7

Multiple-Choice Questions

1. b	6. a
2. c	7. b
3. d	8. d
4. c	9. a
5. a	10. b

Discussion Questions

1. A placebo control group might be used to which clients would be randomly assigned. This placebo control group would receive a pseudo method of boosting self-esteem, for example, reading material believed to be irrelevant to self-esteem,

watching irrelevant movies, and the like. The clients assigned to this placebo control group should believe that their "treatment" will have beneficial effects to the same degree as do the clients assigned to the "real" treatment.

2. Because the positive reinforcement (grades) was not experimentally manipulated, there is no basis for our concluding that it "caused" the self-esteem scores even if there is a positive correlation between self-esteem and GPA. Self-esteem may as well "cause" grades, or some other variable may "cause" both grades and self-esteem.

3. Telling subjects the hypothesis and the names of the measuring instruments is likely to result in strong demand characteristics.

4. According to Mill's methods of agreement and of difference, the student would have to show that eating chocolate chip cookies is followed by a reduction in depression (method of agreement) and that not eating chocolate chip cookies is not followed by a reduction in depression (method of difference).

5. The basic plan could be implemented by use of the following four conditions, analogous to those shown in Tables 7.5 and 7.6:

| Actual | Expectancy | |
treatment	Experimental	Control
Tutoring	A	B
Control	C	D

6. As in all one-group pre-post studies, history, maturation, and instrumentation all threaten the internal validity of the research.

7. By using the subtraction difference procedure in order to compare the difference between the experimental and control groups obtained when pretests were and were not used. The four threats to internal validity were described as part of Campbell's analysis in this chapter.

8. A placebo control group offers a treatment-like condition that serves to control for subjects' beliefs or expectations about the efficacy of any treatments that might be administered. A zero control group is characterized by the absence of any intervention, "real" or "pseudo" (placebo).

Chapter 8

Multiple-Choice Questions

1. b	6. a
2. b	7. b
3. a	8. c
4. d	9. d
5. c	10. a

Discussion Questions

1. Since (a) the test-retest correlations are similar to each other, (b) the synchronous correlations are similar to each other, and (c) the cross-lagged correlations differ appreciably from each other (.64 versus .33), it might be reasonable for him to conclude a preponderance of causal influence of the patient progress variable over the therapist approval variable.

2. The cohort of women is confounded with their age, so we cannot tell whether age or cohort differences or both are reflected in the obtained differences. For example, it may be that the women aged 40–45 have been showing an *increasing* degree of androgyny as they developed from age 20–25 to age 40–45. A longitudinal design of the type shown in Table 8.3 would be a better way to do this study.

3. She might try to match the children finding their way into each of the two conditions on as many relevant variables as possible and then perform her data analysis only on the subset of children for whom there are very close matches. Because of the large proportion of children for whom there may be no good matches, and who would therefore be omitted from the design, the generalizability of the study may be decreased substantially. In addition, the lack of randomization may seriously limit the internal validity of the study.

4. Some dependent variables that may reflect presidential assassination attempts are stock market figures, mental-health-facility-usage data, gun-control legislation activity, the number of people announcing for elective positions, views of the United States reflected in the foreign press, and changes in party affiliation. Reference librarians can help her find the government and other documents that carry the needed information. These documents would also be a rich source of ideas for other dependent variables for which data are available.

Chapter 9

Multiple-Choice Questions

1. a	6. b
2. b	7. c
3. a	8. b
4. c	9. d
5. b	10. d

Discussion Questions

1. Group 1 is measured with the greatest stability; its subjects' scores range only from 10 to 13, while Groups 2 and 3 range from 10 to 16 and from 9 to 18, respectively. The means of Groups 1, 2, and 3 are 11.5, 13.0, and 13.5, respectively; therefore the mean of Group 3 is the most biased.

2. Susan showed no bias with respect to the target volume (her average hit was *M*, the target volume) and no instability (she hit the same volume each time). Valerie

showed a one-volume-away bias, hitting N on average, instead of volume M; she showed no instability, hitting the same volume each time. Ellen showed no bias (her average volume hit was M, the target volume, but she showed a three-volume instability, hitting three adjacent volumes). Jane showed a one-volume-away bias, hitting volume N on average instead of volume M; she showed a three-volume instability, hitting three adjacent volumes. We can summarize the results as follows:

	Bias	No bias
Some instability	Jane	Ellen
No instability	Valerie	Susan

3. Since volunteers or respondents tend to be more intelligent and more sociable than the general population, the correlation between IQ and sociability found in this self-selected sample may be quite different from the correlation we would find in the general population. One way to improve on the design might be to use follow-up questionnaires to increase the representativeness of our sample. Another way to improve on the design might be to try to locate data archives that include data from almost all of a given target population, for example, a college sample, all of whom were tested at the time of admission or orientation.

4. In a study of the effects of a placebo on self-reported happiness, volunteers might show a larger placebo effect (i.e., the difference between the placebo and no-treatment condition) than nonvolunteers because volunteers are more likely to want to please the experimenter. In a study of the effects of a treatment designed to increase sociability, volunteers might show a smaller treatment effect than non-volunteers because volunteers might already score so much higher on sociability that it might be hard to show further changes. Any procedures reducing volunteer bias would help reduce these potential problems.

5. She might draw a random sample of graduating seniors and contact them several times to reduce nonresponse bias. If she knew what characteristics were likely to be highly correlated with questionnaire responses, she might do her random se-lection within the various strata formed by her subdividing the sample into rela-tively more homogeneous subgroups.

6. She can try to make her appeal for volunteers as interesting, nonthreatening, and rewarding as possible.

Chapter 10

Multiple-Choice Questions

1. d	6. b
2. b	7. c
3. d	8. b
4. a	9. a
5. c	10. d

Discussion Questions

1. The stem-and-leaf plot is

Stem	Leaf
4	1
3	0 2 3 3 7 8
2	2 7 9
1	6

The median score can be found from $.5(N + 1) = .5(12) = 6$. Because the sixth score is 32, that is our median. The extended range is the crude range $(41 - 16)$ plus 1 unit, or $25 + 1 = 26$. The interquartile range is from the $.25(N + 1)$th to the $.75(N + 1)$th score, or from 27 to 37.

2. Her first choice is Machine B because it shows no bias and the least instability or variability. Her second choice might be Machine D because it shows no bias or Machine A because, although it shows a 5-decibel bias, it measures volume more consistently. As long as she remembers to correct for the 5-decibel bias, she might be well advised to get Machine A.

3. Because of the outlier score of 98, he should prefer the median or a trimmed mean to the ordinary mean. In this example, the mean of the 11 untrimmed scores is 24.6, whereas the median is only 17 and the trimmed mean (trimming by 1 on each end) is 18.2.

4. She did better on the midterm—z score $= (58 - 52)/12 = .50$—than on the final—z score $= (110 - 100)/30 = .33$.

5. He scored above 97.7% of the normative population.

6. The professor is correct in thinking Harry's grading to be biased. However, the professor is wrong about the direction of the bias. Harry's average grade is a C+ (7) instead of a B− (8). The professor *is* correct in thinking Tom's grades to be more spread out than Dick's grades. The three standard deviations are 3.00, 1.00, and 1.29 for Tom, Dick, and Harry, respectively. Students earning 5s in Tom's section performed the same as those earning 7s in Dick's section; in both cases, $z = -1.00$.

7. The answers are $\sigma = .115$, $\sigma^2 = .013$, $S = .118$, and $S^2 = .014$.

Chapter 11

Multiple-Choice Questions

1. a	**6.** c
2. d	**7.** d
3. b	**8.** d
4. c	**9.** b
5. b	**10.** c

Discussion Questions

1. The correlation between reading ability and GPA is 1.00 because the z scores for reading and for GPA are identical. Careful inspection of the original reading and GPA scores shows that the GPA scores are always one fifth the size of the reading scores. If a variable (X) is multiplied by any constant (c), it yields a new variable (cX) that is correlated 1.00 with the original variable (X). The reason is that the old scores are multiplied by c, the old mean is multiplied by c, and the old σ is multiplied by c. Thus

$$\text{old } z = \frac{X - M}{\sigma}$$

and in turn,

$$\text{new } z = \frac{cX - cM}{c\sigma} = \frac{X - M}{\sigma}$$

Since reading ability and GPA have the same z scores, GPA z scores can be substituted for reading z scores, and GPA will be correlated .98 with IQ just as reading is correlated .98 with IQ. You can check this out by computing z scores for all three variables (IQ, reading, and GPA) and computing the correlations among these three variables.

2. The correlation is $-.20$, computed by ϕ, the two-dichotomous-variables version of the Pearson r. It can be computed by the z-score method or by the 2×2 contingency table method; that is,

$$\phi = \frac{\Sigma z_x z_y}{N}$$

or

$$\phi = \frac{BC - AD}{\sqrt{(A + B)(C + D)(A + C)(B + D)}}$$

3. The correlation between Raters 3 and 4 is also -1.00. We can compute that directly, or we can notice that Rater 3 rates identically to Rater 1 and that Rater 4 rates identically to Rater 2, except for adding a constant of 100 points to each of Rater 2's ratings. Adding a constant (c) to each score also adds the constant to the mean, so adding a constant to the raw scores does not change the z scores because

$$\text{old } z = \frac{X - M}{\sigma}$$

and

$$\text{new } z = \frac{(X + c) - (M + c)}{\sigma} = \frac{X - M}{\sigma}$$

4. The independent variable is smiling (scored 1) or frowning (scored 0). The dependent variable is the rating of enjoyment. For the 200 patrons, we correlate the scores on the treatment variable (1 or 0) with the scores on the 7-point enjoyment scale.

5.

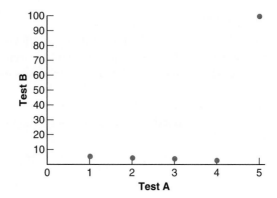

The score of 100 on Test B appears to be an outlier. We can solve the outlier problem by using rank instead of scores, as shown below:

Test A		Test B	
Score	Rank	Score	Rank
1	5	4	2
2	4	3	3
3	3	2	4
4	2	1	5
5	1	100	1

Our scatter plot based on ranks is

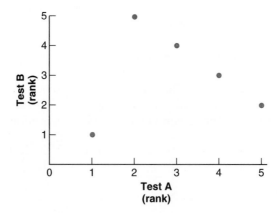

The correlation between Test A and Test B is .69 if we use the original scores; it is .00 if we use the ranks. A discrepancy that large is unusual and needs to be evaluated further before we can confidently say we "know" the correlation between Test A and Test B.

6. Scatter plot B is associated with the higher correlation because its points are more tightly clustered around the straight-line relationship between variables X and Y. The correlation between variables X and Y is .83 for scatter plot A and .98 for scatter plot B.

Chapter 12

Multiple-Choice Questions

1. d	6. a
2. b	7. b
3. b	8. a
4. c	9. d
5. d	10. c

Discussion Questions

1. The BESD is shown below, and the interpretation would be that the effect size amounts to a 40% difference between rates of petition signing in the wheelchair-present and in the wheelchair-absent condition. The percentages in the BESD are not the raw percentages (rates) in the actual data but are "standardized" so that the values in the margins are equalized (i.e., we assume that half the population was in each condition, and that half the population was in each outcome group).

Condition	Signing petition	Not signing petition	Total
Wheelchair present	70	30	100
Wheelchair absent	30	70	100
Total	100	100	200

2. A Type II error would have occurred if it had been concluded that there was a correlation of zero between taking aspirin and having a heart attack when that correlation was not really zero. The power of a test is the probability that results will be found significant at a given p value; power is defined as $1 - \text{beta}$ (β), where β = the probability of making a Type II error. The power of a test of significance depends on the alpha (α) we set, the actual size of the effect being investigated, and the size of the sample.

3. In Table 12.6, the intersection of the column headed ".20" and the row labeled ".70" shows the required total N to be 155. Therefore, she should run about half that number in each condition.

4. It tells him that only 5% of the time would he obtain a result that significant, or more significant, if the null hypothesis (H_0) were really true. It does not tell him about the size of the effect being studied.

5. Since r is simply the difference between the proportions successful in the treatment and the control conditions, the three rs are:

Student A's results $.75 - .25 = .50$
Student B's results $.55 - .45 = .10$
Student C's results $.35 - .65 = -.30$

Notice that the result for Student C reflects a negative r; the new method is *worse* than the old.

6. Step 1 is to use Table B.6 (on page 418) to get the Fisher z_r that corresponds to $r_{effect} = .034$, and we find $z_r = .034$ (i.e., no different from r in this particular case). Step 2 is to substitute the N of 22,071 in the formula

$$\left(\frac{1}{\sqrt{N-3}}\right)1.96$$

which gives us .0132. Step 3 is to subtract this value from .034 to get the lower limit of z_r (.02 rounded), and to add the value to .034 to get the upper limit of z_r (.05). Step 4 is to use Table B.7 (on page 419) to transform lower and upper limits of z_r to r_{effect}. We can say that, with 95% confidence, the effect size r of the aspirin study is between .02 and .05.

Chapter 13

Multiple-Choice Questions

1. c   6. a
2. b   7. c
3. d   8. c
4. b   9. d
5. d   10. a

Discussion Questions

1. The difference or change scores (D) for the five subjects are $-3, -2, +1, -5, -4$. The paired t can be computed from

$$t = \frac{M_D}{\sqrt{\left(\frac{1}{N}\right)S_D{}^2}} = \frac{[(-3) + (-2) + (+1) + (-5) + (-4)]/5}{\sqrt{\left(\frac{1}{5}\right)5.30}} = 2.53$$

obtaining $S_D{}^2$ from

$$S_D{}^2 = \frac{\Sigma(D - M_D)^2}{N-1} =$$

$$\frac{[(-3) - (-2.6)]^2 + [(-2) - (-2.6)]^2 + [(+1) - (-2.6)]^2 + [(-5) - (-2.6)]^2 + [(-4) - (-2.6)]^2}{5 - 1}$$

$$= 5.30$$

The df are $N - 1 = 5 - 1 = 4$. Had we found a significant and large change in memory test scores, we would not be able to conclude that the change was due to marijuana use. There was no control group to rule out plausible rival hypotheses. Had we been able to compute the significance level and effect size, we would have used Table B.2 (on page 409) and found our t with 4 df to be significant at $p < .05$ one-tailed (but not quite significant at $p = .025$ one-tailed). The effect size r would have been computed from

$$r = \sqrt{\frac{t^2}{t^2 + df}} = \sqrt{\frac{(2.53)^2}{(2.53)^2 + 4}} = .78$$

2. We would compute t from

$$t = \frac{M_1 - M_2}{\sqrt{\left(\frac{1}{n_1} + \frac{1}{n_2}\right)S^2}} = \frac{4.00 - 5.25}{\sqrt{\left(\frac{1}{4} + \frac{1}{4}\right)2.46}} = 1.13$$

The df would be $n_1 + n_2 - 2 = 6$, and the effect size could be computed from

$$r = \sqrt{\frac{t^2}{t^2 + df}} = \sqrt{\frac{(1.13)^2}{(1.13)^2 + 6}} = .42$$

a very substantial effect size though t is not significant ($p = .30$ two-tail).

3. From the prose equation:

Significance test = size of effect × size of study,

we can see that increasing the size of the study would increase the magnitude of the significance test, and the result would be a smaller (more significant) p value. However, the effect size would not be systematically affected by the addition of more subjects of the same type. To illustrate, we assume the following original ingredients of t:

$$t = \frac{2.585 - 2.000}{\sqrt{\left(\frac{1}{32} + \frac{1}{32}\right)1.00}} = 2.34, \, p = .023, \, r_{effect} = .28$$

We then add 60 subjects (30 to each group), yielding

$$t = \frac{2.585 - 2.000}{\sqrt{\left(\frac{1}{62} + \frac{1}{62}\right)1.00}} = 3.26, \, p = .0014, \, r_{effect} = .28$$

Therefore, with nothing changing but n_1 and n_2, we see that t increases, p decreases, and the effect size r remains unchanged. The 95% confidence interval will shrink with the additional subjects, as illustrated in the previous chapter.

4. The student might try three approaches. First, he might try to drive the means further apart by using a control group that is not as similar to the treatment

group. Second, he might use subjects who are more homogeneous than the subjects who answer newspaper ads. Third, he might use larger sample sizes for each condition.

Chapter 14

Multiple-Choice Questions

1. c	**6.** a
2. b	**7.** d
3. d	**8.** a
4. c	**9.** d
5. b	**10.** a

Discussion Questions

1. An appropriate table of variance for this study is:

Source	SS	df	MS	F	p
Between brands	752	4	188	2.0	.11
Within brands	4,230	45	94		

We find F from MS between/MS within, and we find df from $k - 1$ for numerator df and $N - k$ for denominator df. We do not report r_{effect} because this is an omnibus F test (i.e., one with numerator $df > 1$).

2. Set A would yield a larger F because its within-condition variability is much smaller than that of Set B. Since the means of Sets A and B are equal, the MS between for Sets A and B are equal; therefore the results with the smaller MS within will yield the larger F.

3. The following table shows the means, row effects, and column effects (as in Table 14.6):

	Type of subjects			
Type of vacation	Urban (US)	Rural (RS)	Row means	Row effects
Urban (UV)	5	3	4	−1
Rural (RV)	11	1	6	+1
Column means	8	2	5 (grand mean)	
Column effects	+3	−3		

The interaction effects for each of the four conditions are computed from:

	Group mean	−	Grand mean	−	Row effect	−	Column effect	=	Interaction effect
UV,US	5	−	5	−	(-1)	−	3	=	(-2)
UV,RS	3	−	5	−	(-1)	−	(-3)	=	2
RV,US	11	−	5	−	1	−	3	=	2
RV,RS	1	−	5	−	1	−	(-3)	=	(-2)
Sum	20	−	20	−	0.0	−	0.0	=	0.0

If we disregard matters of statistical significance, these results show that the type of subjects made the largest difference, the type of vacation made the smallest difference, and the interaction made an intermediate amount of difference. The urban subjects benefited more than the rural subjects, the rural vacations were associated with greater benefits than were the urban vacations, and the interaction showed greater benefits for those vacationing in the setting in which they did *not* reside.

4. A t test following the F would address the question appropriately. The two means to be compared would be the hot lunch mean and the mean of the means of the remaining three groups, that is, $(10 + 12 + 15)/3 = 12.33$. The two required sample sizes, n_1 and n_2, would be the n for the hot lunch (i.e., 3) and the n for the children in the remaining three groups (i.e., $3 + 3 + 3 = 9$). As in the case of most t tests computed after the ANOVA, the S^2 used in computing t is the S^2 obtained from the ANOVA, the MS within. Thus

$$t = \frac{19 - 12.33}{\sqrt{\left(\frac{1}{3} + \frac{1}{9}\right)4}} = 5.00, \, p = .0005, \text{ with } 8 \, df$$

Whenever we compute t, or F with 1 df in the numerator, we want to know the effect size. So we compute the effect size correlation from

$$r_{effect} = \sqrt{\frac{t^2}{t^2 + df}} = \sqrt{\frac{(5.0)^2}{(5.0)^2 + 8}} = .87$$

which is a jumbo-sized effect.

Chapter 15

Multiple-Choice Questions

1. c   6. a
2. a   7. a
3. a   8. c
4. b   9. d
5. a   10. c

Discussion Questions

1. She would compute a χ^2 for which the *df* would be

$$(\text{rows} - 1)(\text{columns} - 1) = (3 - 1)(3 - 1) = 4$$

2. Following the procedures in Table 15.5, we arrive at the approximate solution:

Annual carrot consumption	Visual acuity			
	High	Average	Low	Sum
11–20 lb	.64	.20	.14	.98
1–10 lb	.31	.45	.23	.99
0 lb	.05	.34	.62	1.01
Sum	1.00	.99	.99	2.98

We can display these results as deviations from an expected value of .33 (i.e., the total of 3.00 divided by 9 cells = 3/9 = .33), yielding the following:

Annual carrot consumption	Visual acuity			
	High	Average	Low	Sum
11–20 lb	.31	−.13	−.19	−.01
1–10 lb	−.02	.12	−.10	.00
0 lb	−.28	.01	.29	.02
Sum	+.01	.00	.00	.01

These results show very clearly that high-visual-acuity subjects are relatively over-represented among high carrot consumers, whereas low-visual-acuity subjects are relatively overrepresented among low carrot consumers. As a corollary, we find high-visual-acuity subjects underrepresented among low carrot consumers, whereas low-visual-acuity subjects are relatively underrepresented among high carrot consumers. Unless this was a randomized experiment, we should be cautious about inferring causality. While it is possible that eating more carrots leads to better visual acuity, it may also be that better visual acuity leads to finding more carrots in the darker regions of the refrigerator.

3. The *df* for this χ^2 are obtained from $(\text{rows} - 1)(\text{columns} - 1) = (2 - 1)(4 - 1) = 3$. The expected frequencies are obtained from

$$f_e = \frac{(\text{Row total})(\text{Column total})}{\text{Grand total}}$$

which, for these data, results in

	Frosh	Sophs	Juniors	Seniors
Want degree	4.25	4.25	4.25	4.25
Want out	5.75	5.75	5.75	5.75

With each advancing year, a greater proportion of students want out, a result shown clearly in the final results, in deviation form, of standardizing the margins:

	Frosh	Sophs	Juniors	Seniors
Want degree	.26	.20	−.10	−.36
Want out	−.26	−.20	.10	.36

Once again, we must be careful in our interpretation of the results. Because this is a cross-sectional study, we cannot distinguish differences in year at college from cohort differences (discussed in Chapter 8).

4. Student 3 should ask that all three students compute the effect size correlation that is associated with their results, using the following formula:

$$r_{effect} = \phi = \sqrt{\frac{\chi^2}{N}}$$

When the three students compute their rs, they all find exactly the same effect size ($r_{effect} = .316$). Student 3 shows thereby that the three studies agree with one another remarkably well.

Writing Up the Research

The Research Report

For scientists in all fields, the research process is not complete until the results have been reported in a written document. Indeed, it is often said that scientists are measured by the quality of their publications (R. A. Day, 1983). The purpose of reporting the what, why, and how of the study is to enable others to replicate the investigation or to assess for themselves what the researchers believe they have learned. Instructors of research methods courses do not expect that many of their undergraduate students will actually submit their research findings for publication, as the rejection rate of our top journals in psychology is 80%–90%. But instructors do measure the achievement of their students in part by the logic, clarity, and precision of their written reports. Some instructors prefer that their students go through the exercise of writing up their research findings in the style of a journal article.

In this appendix, we give a thumbnail sketch of the basic steps in writing up your research results. If you follow the steps described here, you will find that the reporting process will help you clarify your thoughts as it leads you to find good reasons for what you want to say. Your instructor will tell you whether your submitted paper should adhere to the undergraduate paper format represented in Exhibit A.2 (pp. 374–391) or to the journal submission format represented in Exhibit A.3 (pp. 392–406). Exhibit A.2 is based on Rosnow and Rosnow's (1998) simplified guide to writing term papers and undergraduate research reports, and you will find further pointers in that book. Exhibit A.3 is based on the *Publication Manual of the American Psychological Association* (APA, 1994), which is the standard reference used by many journals in the behavioral and social sciences.

Getting Organized

The most difficult step for many students is simply getting started on writing the report, but getting started early ensures that your task will not be rushed and that you will have ample time to revise your work before the due date. One reason that students have trouble getting going is that they are unclear about the assignment. Thus, before you do anything else, make sure you know what is expected. You can talk with other students to get their impressions, but that approach may stress you out even more. The best person for you to consult is the instructor or grader, to make sure that you are on the right track.

Besides knowing the form of the final report, here are some questions to keep in mind as you get organized:

- When is the final report due?
- How will it be graded?
- Will there be an opportunity to obtain feedback as the project progresses?
- Is there a specified length for the final report?
- Are intermediate drafts or outlines required, and when are they due?
- Are other sample reports available to provide a further idea of what is expected?

Questions about due dates are very important because missing deadlines—just like unexcused absences on a job—is a sure way to elicit disapproval. If you are someone who has a hard time meeting deadlines, remember that instructors have heard all the excuses. Try keeping a pocket calendar and checking it every morning and evening to see what your responsibilities are for the next several days. If that approach fails, try posting scheduled dates and appointments over your mirror or desk—anywhere you routinely look.

To help you keep on schedule, you can jot down both self-imposed and assigned dates, such as:

- Completion of proposal for research
- Completion of data collection
- Completion of data analysis
- Completion of first draft of research report
- Completion of revised draft(s) of research report
- Due date for submission of final report

Writing a Research Proposal

Many instructors require one or more preliminary research proposals, in which you sketch your ideas and give a justification of what you propose. You may be asked to tell how you arrived at your ideas and why you believe the topic is interesting and important. The purpose of these questions is (1) to help you crystallize your ideas; (2) to encourage you to focus on a topic you find intrinsically interesting; and (3) to make sure that these are *your* ideas. We will have more to say about the last point, but it is essential that the work be your own even when it builds on previous research by others. A series of preliminary papers will allow the instructor to monitor how your project is developing and how you respond to suggestions and constructive criticisms.

What should a research proposal look like? Instructors may differ in terms of what they require, but Exhibit A.1 proceeds on the assumption that the student has been asked (1) to state the objective of the research; (2) to provide a justification for the hypothesis or research question; (3) to sketch the method and instruments proposed; (4) to state in general terms how the data will be analyzed; and (5) to defend the ethicalness of the research. The proposal in this exhibit shows a set of specific ideas that include a tentative plan for proceeding (although your instructor may ask for additional details). Having put his or her ideas down on paper, the student now awaits feedback concerning modifications and improvements and also the instructor's final approval to proceed with the research.

Rind   1

Research Proposal for (Course No.)
Submitted by Bruce Rind
(Date Submitted)

Working Title

Biasing Effects of Drug Testing Results

Objective

The purpose of this study will be to examine whether harsher bail judgments are likely to result when judges are told that the defendant tested positive for drug usage than when no testing information is made available. My hypothesis, based on a preliminary examination of the relevant literature in forensic psychology and attribution research, is that such an effect will emerge.

Proposed Method

I propose to use a simple randomized design in which the research participants will be assigned to one of two conditions. The subject sample will consist of approximately 30 students in an undergraduate class. I have been given permission by the instructor to ask these students to participate. I have developed a "crime scenario" that the subjects will read; it describes a man seen running from a burglarized house.

Exhibit A.1   **Sample research proposal.**

Rind   2

In the experimental condition, the scenario will state that the suspect tested positive for drugs while in custody:

A man was arrested as a suspected burglar. He fit the description of a man seen running from the burglarized house. While in custody, the man submitted to a blood test, and it was determined that he had very recently used drugs.

In the control condition, neutral information (i.e., the suspect ate and phoned someone) will be presented in lieu of the information about having tested positive for drugs:

A man was arrested as a suspected burglar. He fit the description of a man seen running from the burglarized house. The man spent enough time in custody so that he received two meals and made three phone calls.

The dependent measure will be the subjects' responses to the following question:

If you were the bail judge, what would you set the bail to be? Choose a dollar amount from $0 to $50,000.

I am specifying a range in order to give the subjects a common metric, and I chose this range because it seemed realistic and sufficiently wide to allow differences to result between the experimental and control groups. At the beginning of the questionnaire, I will also ask for some

Exhibit A.1 *(continued)*

Rind   3

general demographic data (e.g., age, sex, year in college, GPA) but will not ask for the respondent's name.

<u>Proposed Data Analysis</u>

I anticipate analyzing the results using an independent t and also interpreting the effect size (r).

<u>Ethical Considerations</u>

Although I have the instructor's permission to run my study in this class, I will emphasize at the outset that any student who does not wish to participate may decline to respond. The responses will be anonymous to reduce the likelihood of social desirability bias. The study does not involve deception. At the end of the study, I will debrief the students and answer any questions.

Exhibit A.1   *(continued)*

Avoiding Plagiarism

Before we go any further, let us return to the point about your work's being original. The cornerstone of science is that it progresses by building on previous work, and it is important that you try to do the same in your research. In Chapter 2, we described the process of doing a literature search and the importance of taking accurate and complete notes, including the full reference and page numbers of any quoted material (see Figure A.1). We also illustrated how to use quoted and paraphrased material so as not to fall into the trap of accidental plagiarism. We will not reiterate what we said earlier, but we want to add one additional caution. Although it does not happen frequently, a student who has larcenous intent, or who is just plain lazy, may fall victim to the temptation to lift material either from the Internet or other published or unpublished sources. The instructor, or a graduate assistant, who is grading the papers usually has a "sixth sense" that zeros in on any suspected plagiarism. The penalty in the course will be failure, and your college may have rules that exact an even stronger punishment.

Cooke, Gerald (1980). An introduction to basic issues and concepts in forensic psychology. In Gerald Cooke (Ed.), The Role of the Forensic Psychologist (pp. 5–15). Springfield, Illinois: Charles C. Thomas Publisher.

This book defines forensic psychology as a content area in the interface of law and psychology. Cooke writes: "The law is a reflection of societal standards. As these standards change, so does the law. Similarly, the concepts having to do with the relationship between an individual's mental condition and his status under the law are fluid and everchanging ones. For example, the degree to which mental status mitigates responsibility and the specific manner in which the law treats those who are deemed to have diminished responsibility has changed frequently and is related to changing attitudes over the relative weight to be given to the rights of the individual and the rights of society at large." (page 5)

Figure A.1 **An example of how to take library notes.**

Title Page

We turn now to the structure and form of your final report, beginning with the title page. If you have been instructed to use the simplified format of an undergraduate research paper, as represented in Exhibit A.2, notice that the title page contains a **page header** in the upper right corner, and in the center of the page is the student's name, the course number, the name of the instructor, and the date when the report was submitted. The purpose of the page header is to make it easier for the instructor to keep the pages of your paper together, should the paper clip or staple become unattached. In journal submissions, the purpose of the page header is to allow the editor or printer to pull together pages that may become accidentally separated during the production process.

If you have been instructed to use the technical format of a journal submission, illustrated in Exhibit A.3, observe that, besides the page header and some identifying information about the author (and his or her institution), there is something called the **running head.** It refers to the abbreviated title that is printed at the top of the odd-numbered pages of many published articles. If you must include a running head, the APA rule is that it should be typed flush left below the page header and in all uppercase letters. The running head is limited to 50 characters, including punctuation and spaces between words.

If you want to sharpen your writing skills, we recommend that you consult Strunk and White's *Elements of Style* (1979). One of Professor Strunk's famous dictums is "Omit needless words. Omit needless words. Omit needless words." If you were submitting an article for publication, this rule would apply to all aspects of your article; journal space is limited, and editors often insist that authors pare their manuscripts to the essentials. In your case, where space is not at a premium, your instructor will presumably be more lenient as he or she does *not* want you to leave out any relevant details. Thus Bruce's title (although the subtitle is too wordy to include in a journal article) adequately summarizes the main idea of his research. Incidentally, if you started with a working title, do not hesitate to change or polish the final title if it no longer aptly describes the project.

Abstract

Although the **abstract** (or summary) is page 2 of your report, it is usually a good idea to write it *after* you have completed the rest of your paper. The reason is that it is a distillation of the important points covered in the body of your report. It tells the reader what your research is about in one succinct paragraph. In the sample report, Bruce gives a synopsis of the background of his research, his hypothesis, the way he tested it, and the results. The abstract in Exhibit A.3 is slightly shorter than that in Exhibit A.2, reflecting the APA rule that abstracts of reports of research submitted for publication are limited to 960 characters and spaces, or approximately 120 words.

Here are some further questions to guide you as you prepare your abstract:

- What was the problem under investigation or the objective of the study?
- What was the principal method used (a laboratory experiment, a survey questionnaire, judges as raters, etc.)?
- Who were the research participants (i.e., their pertinent characteristics)?
- What were the major results?
- What are the primary conclusions and implications that appear in the discussion section?

Introduction

The introduction should emphasize linking ideas to past research and should lead into your hypotheses. Basically it describes the point of the research and also provides a framework for your later description of the method used. The idea of writing a strong introduction is to get the reader to think, "Yes, of course, that's what the student *had* to do to test this hypothesis." Bruce begins by describing a debate he saw on television, enabling the reader to view the research in a practical light that is both compelling and significant. He also defines the area of his project—forensic psychology—and develops his hypothesis in such a way that the method section (which follows) will seem a natural consequence of the introduction.

Here are some questions to help you plan the introduction:

- What got me thinking about this study?
- How did I come up with my working hypothesis, and what did I expect to find?
- What terms do I need to define for the reader who may be unfamiliar with this area?
- Do I need to define any terms for special reasons, because they are used differently in different contexts or because I use them in a new way?

- How does the study build on, or derive from, other studies?
- Is each of my hypotheses clearly explained and justified in terms of its logical basis?

If you did not outline your introduction before you drafted it, a useful trick is to outline the introduction *after* it is written. Outlining it at the end will expose any lapses in logic that need to be corrected. You can practice by outlining Bruce's introduction and asking yourself how it might be improved. If you compare Exhibits A.2 and A.3, you will notice that the APA format (Exhibit A.3) leaves out the word *introduction* and instead repeats the title of the manuscript. The APA style assumes that the opening section is the introduction, whereas the term paper (Exhibit A.2) uses the word *introduction* as a reminder to the student of what this section should contain.

Method

In the method section, you will describe the procedures used and give a detailed account of the pertinent characteristics of the subject sample. Bruce describes where his subjects came from ("an introductory statistics class"), the number that participated in the experimental and control conditions, and the fact than men and women participated who were not volunteers but part of an intact class. Some authors report more detailed demographic data, and you can ask your instructor for further guidance if you are unsure what to report. For example, in your method section you may tell the subjects' ages (average and range), their racial and gender designations, and so on, insofar as any of these characteristics are essential to the generality of the results.

Included in this section is a brief description of the tests and measurements you used. In his materials section, Bruce describes the two forms of his questionnaire. Finally, the procedure for administering the treatments or questionnaires is described. Bruce's procedure is one paragraph long, but other projects may call for more detailed presentations. He describes how the two forms of his questionnaire were distributed so that both he and the subjects were blind to which treatment any individual had received. Bruce ends up noting that he debriefed the subjects.

Results

Beginning with the main results, you will describe your data in this section. Try to strike a balance between being discursive and being overly precise. You might, as Bruce does, present the results in a table (or a figure, e.g., a stem-and-leaf; see Chapter 10). It is important to label your table or figure, both with a caption ("Mean, Variance, and Number of Subjects") and with row headings ("Mean," "S," "n") and column headings ("Experimental group," "Control group"). Except for many single-case studies (see Chapter 8), you are not expected to list individual scores in this section.

Bruce's results section gets right down to business, as he tells us how he analyzed the results in order to test his hypothesis. He reports the significance test ("t = 2.08, df = 29, p = .023 one-tail") and then shows that he consulted an advanced textbook to do a more sophisticated analysis. When he recomputed his results after adjusting for heterogeneity, they were no longer statistically significant. He reports the effect size in anticipation of his discussion section. He does not go into the implications of his data, which go in the discussion section.

A trick to help you pull the results together before you start writing is to set down a list of your statistical findings. Divide the list into coherent sets of results, and then decide the sequence in which you will discuss the sets according to their order of importance or relevance to your study's objective. Experienced authors try to anticipate questions the reader may have, such as questions about ambiguous results that call for clarification or further analysis.

Here are some questions to help you structure this section:

▪ What were the different results, and what is their order of importance or relevance?

▪ How can I describe what I found in a careful, detailed way that will make complete sense to someone who is not informed on this topic?

▪ Have I omitted any necessary details or included superfluous information?

▪ In reporting my statistical results, am I being sufficiently precise?

Discussion

In the discussion section, you will synthesize and interpret the various parts of your report to form a cohesive unit from the facts that you have gathered. Without being overly repetitive, Bruce begins by reminding us of the background that he developed in the introduction. That is, he recapitulates his original hypothesis, thereby underscoring the logical continuity of his presentation. Had he found any unexpected results, this would be the place to note how serendipity (discussed in Chapter 2) entered into his investigation.

Bruce also writes "defensively" in that he plays his own devil's advocate. He reminds the reader that "The results, although in the hypothesized direction, were not statistically significant after the appropriate adjustment was made for heterogeneity of variance." In the APA version (Exhibit A.3), he also notes the alpha level used in this decision (as the APA *Publication Manual* asks for this information). However, he does not dwell on the significance level alone but notes that the effect size ($r = .20$) was "theoretically interesting and suggested that follow-up studies are warranted." Incidentally, the APA manual (1994, p. 18) does not recommend r as an effect size index but lists r^2 (i.e., the coefficient of determination) and various other measures. As squaring r can seriously underestimate the practical importance of an effect, we suggest that you not take the APA manual's advice and instead simply report and interpret r_{effect} (using the BESD, as discussed in Chapter 12). Bruce also points out potential implications and future directions of his research, thus communicating that he has thought deeply about this area.

Questions to consider as you begin to structure this section include:

▪ What was the major purpose of this study, and were there any secondary objectives?

- How do my results relate to that purpose and those objectives?
- Were there any unexpected findings of interest, and how can I describe them to show their relevance to this project and to possible follow-up research?
- How valid and generalizable are my findings, and what are their limitations?
- What can I say about the wider implications of the results?

References

The title page and abstract are on separate pages, but the other sections follow one another without any page breaks (introduction, method, results, discussion). The reference section begins on a separate page, and you can now see why it was important to make complete and accurate notes. This section is an alphabetized listing of all the sources of information on which you drew, and your notes (e.g., using an index card for each reference) or a running list of sorted references in a file on your computer will now provide the final list.

However, list only those references that you have actually discussed or cited. This is not a bibliography (i.e., a comprehensive listing of everything on the subject), but a compilation of the material that you have used and discussed. Both versions of Bruce's paper (Exhibits A.2 and A.3) give us examples of the style recommended by the American Psychological Association (1994) in referencing books, journal reports, magazine articles, and chapters in edited volumes. If you run into a problem—and if the instructor is a stickler for having you use the APA style—consult the fourth edition of the *Publication Manual of the American Psychological Association*. Otherwise, just use common sense and Bruce's reference section as a general model.

Appendix

The term paper version of Bruce's paper in Exhibit A.2 has an appendix as a final section. However, your instructor may require that you incorporate an appendix into your paper and also use the APA style, in which case you can use the sample appendix in Exhibit A.2 as a model. The purpose of the appendix is to display the raw material and calculations of your study. Here is also where you will display any questionnaires or tests that you constructed but did not fully present in the main body of your report.

Observe in Exhibit A.2 that Bruce's report contains an "Appendix A" (displaying the questionnaires he developed) and an "Appendix B" (showing his raw data and the t test and effect size, r, he computed). If the student has made a mistake in the data analysis, the grader can easily examine his or her results to trace how far back the error occurred. As a result, the grader will not penalize the student for making what might seem a mistake in interpretation or understanding when it is a less serious typographical error or a recording mistake.

Writing and Revising

Now that you know what is expected, it is time to begin writing a first draft. A good place to start is to compose a "self-motivator" statement that you can refer to as a way of focusing your thoughts. Such a statement can be posted over your word processor to serve as a guidepost to keep you from wandering off on a tangent. Bruce's self-motivator might be "My report will focus on what I know about whether disclosing the results of drug tests influences bail judgments in criminal proceedings."

If you are someone who has trouble getting started, one trick is to begin not at the beginning but with the section you feel will be easiest to write. Once the ideas begin to flow, you can tackle the introductory section. This approach will also bolster flagging spirits, because you can reread the sections you have already written when you begin to feel a loss of energy or determination. Try not to fall into the trap of escaping by napping or watching television. If you recognize these counterproductive moves for what they are, you should be able to avoid them.

Here are some helpful hints to make the writing go more smoothly:

- Find a quiet, well-lighted place in which to write, and do your writing in two-hour stretches.
- Double-space your first draft so you can get an idea of how long the final (double-spaced) paper will be.
- Double spacing will also give you room for legible revisions if you like to revise your work in the printed version (which we each like to do) rather than on a computer screen.
- Number your pages even if you are writing on a note pad.
- Pace your work so that you can complete the first draft and let it rest for at least 24 hours.

Layout and Printing

After you have revised your paper and are satisfied with the final version, it is time to "package" it for the instructor. The final report must not contain any typographical errors or spelling mistakes. To help you catch misspellings, use a spell check if you are processing the paper on a computer. But do not stop here, because there may be technical words that the spell check missed. It may also not catch typos such as a capital "I" when you meant to type "in," but using a grammar check should catch this kind of mistake (as long as the grammar check doesn't drive you to distraction by querying every phrase and line you write). Put the printed paper aside for a day or two, and then look at it again with a fresh eye. This is called *proofreading* or *proofing*, and it is a final step before you submit your paper.

It is a good idea to proof the paper more than once because gremlins in a program can sometimes introduce weird changes. Also, you will be surprised how elusive some typos can be; you can stare at them and still not see them immediately. Ask yourself:

- Are there omissions?
- Are there misspellings?
- Are the numbers correct?
- Are the hyphenations correct?

▌ Are all the references cited in the body of the paper listed in the reference section, and vice versa?

Make sure the print is dark enough to be easily read, as you do not want to frustrate the grader (frustration can lead to aggression!) by submitting a paper with typescript so light or blurry that it taxes the eyes. Use 8½ × 11-inch white paper. The APA manual requires that there be at least 1-inch margins on all four sides of the page, that no typed line exceed 6½ inches, and that there be no more than 27 lines of text on the page. Double-space the printout, and print on one side of the paper only, numbering the pages consecutively as illustrated in the appropriate exhibit. Also, words or symbols to be italicized are underlined; do not use the italic typeface on the word processor to create italics (unless your instructor says it is OK).

Assuming you are using a word processor, be sure to back up your work routinely. You never know when somebody may playfully touch a couple of keys and erase all your hard work. It is also a good idea to print a hard copy of each day's labors, so you have a double guarantee that you will not lose your work. When the clean, corrected final draft is completed, make an extra copy—just in case. The original is for the instructor, and the duplicate copy ensures that a spare copy will be readily available if a problem arises.

If you do not have access to a letter-quality printer (laserjet, inkjet, or an old-fashioned daisy wheel), use the strikeover mode rather than the first-draft mode to print your final copy. Notice that both versions of Bruce's paper leave the right margin "ragged" (i.e., uneven), which is also a requirement of the APA manual. In fact, most people seem to find a page with a ragged right margin more readable in typed papers (but not in books or journal articles) than one with a "justified" (i.e., even) right margin. If this were an article for submission to a journal, although your manuscript would have a ragged right margin, the printed version would appear justified.

Give your report a final look, checking to see that all the pages are there and in order, and then turn it in on schedule. Having adhered to these guidelines, you should feel the satisfaction of a job well done.

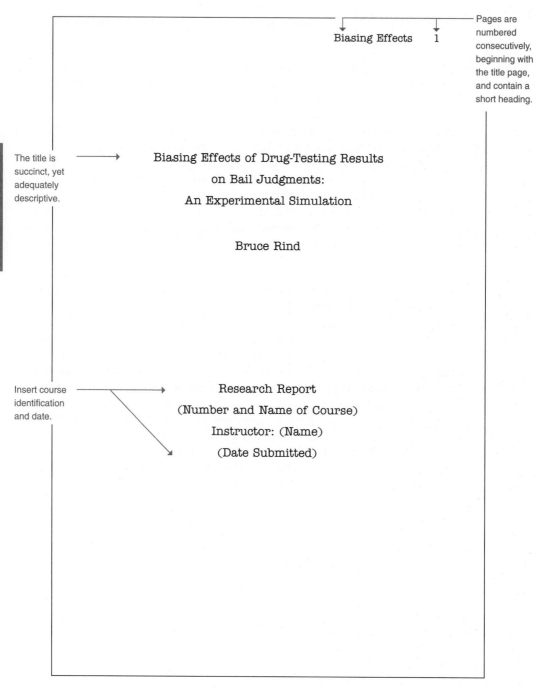

Biasing Effects   1   Pages are numbered consecutively, beginning with the title page, and contain a short heading.

The title is succinct, yet adequately descriptive.

Biasing Effects of Drug-Testing Results
on Bail Judgments:
An Experimental Simulation

Bruce Rind

Insert course identification and date.

Research Report
(Number and Name of Course)
Instructor: (Name)
(Date Submitted)

Exhibit A.2 **Format of an undergraduate research report submitted as a term paper (based on Rosnow and Rosnow's** *Writing Papers in Psychology: A Student Guide***), 4th ed.**

Biasing Effects   2 ←—Abstract begins on a new page.

Abstract

Abstract is not → indented.

Why was the → research important and worth doing?

This experimental simulation was addressed to a recent legal debate concerning the institution of mandatory drug testing of all suspects upon arrest. The crime control side has held that this testing will have no biasing effects in legal proceedings, whereas the due process side has argued that drug information will have prejudicial effects. Drawing on correspondent inference theory (Jones & Davis, 1965) and the general function of inferring traits (Baron & Byrne, 1987), I hypothesized that harsher bail judgments are likely to result when judges are informed that the defendant has tested positive for drug usage than when no testing information is made available. The results were in the hypothesized direction but were not statistically significant after an adjustment for heterogeneity of variance was made. The wider implications of this field of research are discussed.

What was the ←— purpose of the study?

←— What were the results?

What else appears in the → discussion?

Exhibit A.2   *(continued)*

The title of this section ("Introduction") is a reminder of its purpose.

The opening paragraph sets the stage in an inviting way.

Double-space between all lines of text.

Abbreviation for *id est* ("that is").

The Introduction begins on a new page.

Introduction

In the summer of 1988, the ABC television program <u>Nightline</u> featured a debate between a representative from the American Civil Liberties Union (ACLU) and a spokesperson for a national group of prosecutors. The focus of the debate was whether mandatory drug testing should be performed on all persons arrested. The prosecutors' representative proposed that the institution of mandatory drug testing would be one more weapon for law enforcement officials in fighting the drug war by identifying drug offenders who would otherwise escape detection. The ACLU representative argued that the institution of this program would result in serious threats to individual rights regarding the bail issue. He contended that positive results would unfairly bias the bail judge's decision on how much bail to impose. Drug-positive suspects, the ACLU representative contended, would tend to receive higher bail judgments, which would be a violation of the rights of suspects when there is no necessary connection between drug usage and the particular crime that was committed. The prosecutor responded that the drug information would have no effect on a bail judge's decision.

Forensic psychology (i.e., the application of psychological principles and methods to the legal

Abbreviations are first spelled out.

Although the left margin is even, the right margin is left ragged.

Exhibit A.2   *(continued)*

Biasing Effects 4

process) has been successful in providing insight
into a number of legal issues. For example, Loftus,
Miller, and Burns (1978) demonstrated the
distorting effects of misleading questions on the
memories of eyewitnesses. Subjects were shown a
sequence of 30 slides depicting successive stages of
an automobile-pedestrian accident. In one of the
slides, half the subjects saw a stop sign, while the
other half saw a yield sign. Subjects were later
asked a question that made reference to the sign
they had actually seen or to a sign they had not
seen. When they were subsequently asked what
sign they had seen, subjects exposed to the
misleading question tended to misremember the
sign.

In fact, many studies have demonstrated that
eyewitness testimony is often inaccurate. For
example, Buckhout (1974) staged an "assault" on
a professor which was witnessed by 141 students.
When these students were asked seven weeks later
to identify the assailant from a group of six
photographs, 60% chose an innocent person. Wells,
Lindsay, and Ferguson (1979) staged hundreds of
eyewitnessed thefts and found that not only did the
eyewitnesses have difficulty in correctly identifying
the culprits, but other subjects who judged the
accuracy of these eyewitnesses were also incapable
of distinguishing between accurate and inaccurate
accounts.

Exhibit A.2 *(continued)*

Biasing Effects   5

How does the study build on, or derive from, previous work?

Abbreviation for *exempli gratia* ("for example").

Citations in the text are by authors' surnames and dates.

Aside from the forensic aspects of eyewitness testimony, other facets of the legal process have also been investigated, such as defendant attractiveness (e.g., Efran, 1974), the judge's instructions to the jury (e.g., Sue, Smith, & Caldwell, 1973), juror characteristics (e.g., Saks & Hastie, 1978), and group decisions among jurors (e.g., Kalven & Zeisel, 1966). These investigations, among others, have demonstrated the utility of applying psychological principles and methods to legal situations in order to understand them better. In the light of this background, the present investigation addressed the issue raised in the Nightline debate between the ACLU representative and the prosecutors' spokesperson. That is, will drug information tend to prejudice a bail judge's decision regarding the amount of bail to set?

The main task of the bail judge is to set bail at a certain level so as to make it likely that the defendant will appear for trial. In making this decision, the bail judge is perhaps apt to consider factors suggestive of the defendant's traits (i.e., lasting characteristics) so as to predict the likelihood that the defendant will skip bail or show up for the trial. Attribution theory is the area of psychology concerned with factors such as inferring the traits of others (e.g., Jones & Davis, 1965; Kelley, 1972) and using this trait

Works by different authors are listed in alphabetical order by first author's surname.

Exhibit A.2   *(continued)*

information to make decisions or judgments regarding these other individuals (Baron & Byrne, 1987).

Jones and Davis (1965) proposed a framework describing how individuals (i.e., observers) go about inferring the traits of others (i.e., actors). According to the theory of correspondent inferences, observers focus mainly on certain types of observed behavior to infer traits because they believe that only certain behaviors are indicative of traits. The primary questions observers will ask themselves, according to Jones and Davis, are: (a) Was the behavior freely chosen? (b) Did the behavior produce uncommon effects? And (c) was the behavior low in social desirability? The third question is particularly relevant to the topic of this research report. Because drug usage is held by our society to be low in social desirability, it follows from correspondent inference theory that observers will be likely to focus on this socially undesirable behavior in judging the actor's traits. Once observers have inferred traits, they tend to use this information to predict the actor's future behavior and to assess and guide their own actions, decisions, and judgments regarding the actor (Baron & Byrne, 1987). Thus I hypothesized that positive results from a drug test will result in harsher bail judgments than when no such information is made available.

The introduction leads into the hypotheses, or the questions that guided the research.

Connecting points are lettered for clarity.

What was the hypothesis?

Exhibit A.2 *(continued)*

Appendix A

Biasing Effects   7

First level headings are centered. → Method ← The major sections of the text follow each other without a break.

Second level headings are flush left and underlined.

What was the subject pool?

Participants

Temple University undergraduate students in an introductory statistics class served as subjects in this study. The sample of 31 subjects consisted of both men and women, and the materials were administered during the class meeting with the permission of the instructor and the consent of the students.

Materials

Second level heading.

Two forms of a crime scenario were developed. Both forms stated that a man was arrested as a suspected burglar because he fit the description of a man seen running from a burglarized house. In the experimental condition the scenario stated that the suspect tested positive for drugs while in custody. In the control condition, the scenario continued with neutral information (i.e., the suspect received two meals and made three phone calls while in custody). Following both versions of the crime scenario was the dependent measure, requesting the subjects to play the role of the bail judge and to set a bail amount between \$0 and \$50,000.

Second level heading.

Subgroups are denoted by underlined lower-case n.

Design and Procedure

Subjects were randomly assigned to the control ($n = 16$) or experimental ($n = 15$) condition. The

Exhibit A.2   *(continued)*

Appendix A

Biasing Effects   8

experimental and control handout sheets were mixed together and passed out at the same time. Subjects were told to fill out certain preliminary information on their sheets and then to read the scenario and make their judgment. When the subjects were finished, they were debriefed.

Results

Another major section of the text, which follows without a break.

The overall findings are given in Table 1, which shows that the mean judgment of the subjects exposed to the drug information was higher than the mean judgment of the subjects exposed to the neutral information. Computing a t test on these data yielded a significant result ($t = 2.08$, $df = 29$, $p = .023$ one-tail). However, Table 1 also raises the possibility that the variabilities were different in the two conditions. I tested that possibility by dividing the larger of the two variances (277,058,355.31) by the smaller of the two variances (30,798,060.16) and referring the quotient to an F table. The result was highly significant: $F(14, 15) = 9.0$, $p < .001$, which indicated that the homogeneity of variance required by the t test had been violated (Rosenthal & Rosnow, 1991).

Statistical test, degrees of freedom, and significance.

Letters used as statistical symbols are underlined: t, F, N, n, p, and so forth.

Degrees of freedom are 14 and 15.

Exhibit A.2   *(continued)*

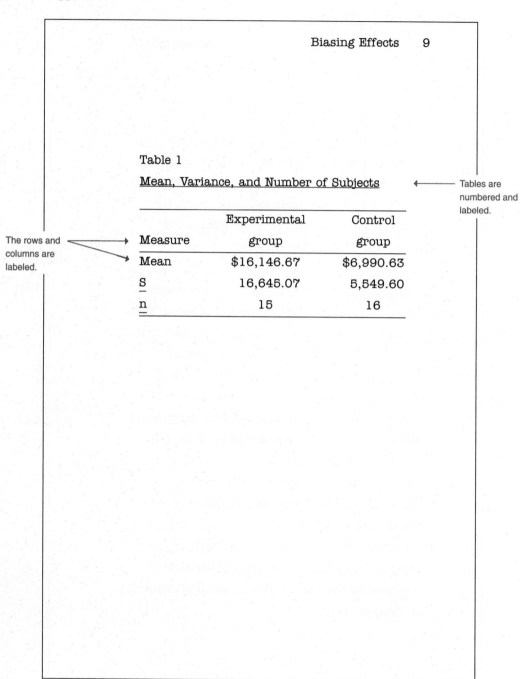

Biasing Effects   9

Table 1

Mean, Variance, and Number of Subjects ←——— Tables are numbered and labeled.

Measure	Experimental group	Control group
Mean	$16,146.67	$6,990.63
S	16,645.07	5,549.60
n	15	16

The rows and columns are labeled.

Exhibit A.2 *(continued)*

Biasing Effects   10

In an alternative analysis, the raw scores were transformed by means of a log transformation. Computing a $\underline{t}$ test on these values yielded a nonsignificant result: $\underline{t} = 1.09$, effect size $\underline{r} = .20$. Other methods of analysis were still possible, although a more prudent alternative would be to view the effect size as theoretically interesting but in need of replication with a larger sample. If the results are replicated in follow-up studies, it will also then be possible to employ a meta-analysis in order to increase statistical power and obtain a more reliable estimate of the effect size.

The effect size is reported.

Discussion

This research was an attempt to use the principles and methods of experimental forensic psychology to clarify certain aspects of the legal system. Specifically, this study addressed the contention of the representative from the ACLU that even drug information unrelated to the crime under consideration will tend to bias bail judgments. One fundamental purpose of our criminal justice system is, of course, to be just and unbiased in all of its aspects. The results, although in the hypothesized direction, were not statistically significant after the appropriate adjustment was made for heterogeneity of variance. Nevertheless, the effect size was theoretically interesting and suggested that follow-up studies are warranted.

The discussion continues on the same page.

The opening discussion reminds the reader of the study's purpose.

Appendix A

Exhibit A.2 *(continued)*

Appendix A

The discussion should pull together the various parts of the paper.

If future studies provide stronger support for the ACLU representative's contention, it may be possible to argue on empirical grounds that the goal of being just and unbiased would be jeopardized with the institution of mandatory drug testing upon arrest. It would then follow that this biasing effect could be circumvented if the bail judge were not given access to the results of the drug testing. Such follow-up findings would, in turn, fit in with correspondent inference theory (Jones & Davis, 1965), because knowledge about socially undesirable behavior (i.e., having taken drugs recently) could be said to lead subjects to infer certain traits of the suspect. This chain of logic is interesting to contemplate, but it is premature at this stage in the research.

The limitations and wider significance of the study are noted.

I believe the criminal justice system can benefit from forensic research such as that performed in this study. At the moment, however, the courts' procedures are mostly based on tradition and precedent and do not take into strong consideration the results of scientific investigations. For example, jurors who are willing to follow the law that the death penalty should sometimes be imposed are referred to as <u>death-qualified jurors</u>. Psychological research has demonstrated that death-qualified jurors are more likely to convict (Ellsworth, 1985). However, in a split decision in 1986, the U.S. Supreme Court overturned a lower court ruling

Any special terms are defined.

Exhibit A.2   *(continued)*

Biasing Effects   12

that such jurors are indeed a biased sample.
Another example concerns the research finding
that the confidence of eyewitnesses is unrelated to
their accuracy unless witnessing conditions are
very favorable (Wells & Murray, 1984). However,
the U.S. Supreme Court declared in 1972 that
among the factors that jurors can use in
determining the accuracy of eyewitnesses is the
level of certainty demonstrated by the witnesses.
The results of scientific investigations of the
various aspects of the legal system point to the
need for the courts to acknowledge and incorporate
these and future results so as to build a justice
system that is truly just.

The importance of the study is underscored.

Using a sample of college students, the present
investigation studied the biasing effect of drug
results. Even if these results were statistically
significant, they still might not be generalizable to
actual bail judges. Therefore, future research
should address this potential problem of external
validity. Future research should also directly
assess subjects' inferences of corresponding traits
from socially undesirable behavior. In this study,
these inferences were hypothesized to occur based
on the subjects' bail judgments. It is interesting to
note that, while the subjects seemingly judged the
suspect more harshly based on the drug
information in the burglary scenario, there is no
necessary connection between drug usage and

Future research is suggested.

Exhibit A.2 *(continued)*

burglary. However, the subjects may have been drawing on a stereotype to assume that the association was likely because the media often report property crimes that are motivated by the need to get money to purchase drugs. Thus it would be valuable to use other crime scenarios that are not so stereotypically associated with drugs to determine whether the biasing effect is more general.

Exhibit A.2 *(continued)*

Appendix A

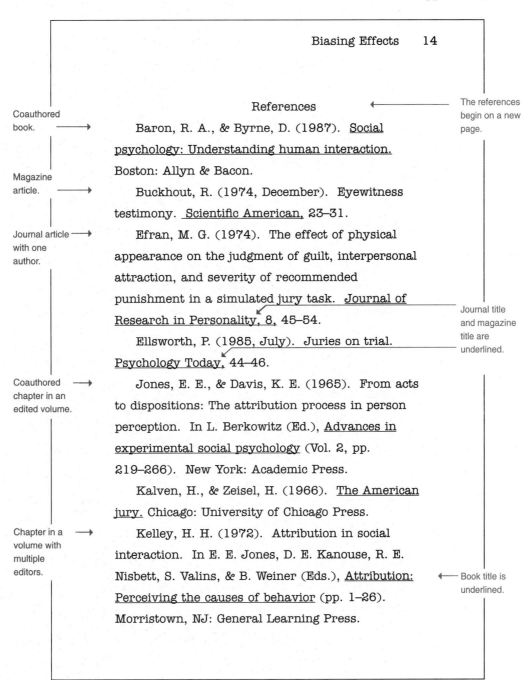

Biasing Effects   14

Coauthored book.

Magazine article.

Journal article with one author.

Coauthored chapter in an edited volume.

Chapter in a volume with multiple editors.

References

The references begin on a new page.

Baron, R. A., & Byrne, D. (1987). Social psychology: Understanding human interaction. Boston: Allyn & Bacon.

Buckhout, R. (1974, December). Eyewitness testimony. Scientific American, 23–31.

Efran, M. G. (1974). The effect of physical appearance on the judgment of guilt, interpersonal attraction, and severity of recommended punishment in a simulated jury task. Journal of Research in Personality, 8, 45–54.

Ellsworth, P. (1985, July). Juries on trial. Psychology Today, 44–46.

Journal title and magazine title are underlined.

Jones, E. E., & Davis, K. E. (1965). From acts to dispositions: The attribution process in person perception. In L. Berkowitz (Ed.), Advances in experimental social psychology (Vol. 2, pp. 219–266). New York: Academic Press.

Kalven, H., & Zeisel, H. (1966). The American jury. Chicago: University of Chicago Press.

Kelley, H. H. (1972). Attribution in social interaction. In E. E. Jones, D. E. Kanouse, R. E. Nisbett, S. Valins, & B. Weiner (Eds.), Attribution: Perceiving the causes of behavior (pp. 1–26). Morristown, NJ: General Learning Press.

Book title is underlined.

Exhibit A.2 *(continued)*

Biasing Effects   15

Journal article with multiple authors. →

Loftus, E. F., Miller, D. G., & Burns, H. J. (1978). Semantic integration of verbal information into a visual memory. Journal of Experimental Psychology: Human Learning and Memory, 4, 19–31.

Rosenthal, R., & Rosnow, R. L. (1991). Essentials of behavioral research: Methods and data analysis (2nd ed.). New York: McGraw-Hill.

Book in second edition. →

Saks, M. J., & Hastie, R. (1978). Social psychology in the court. New York: Van Nostrand Reinhold.

Sue, S., Smith, R. E., & Caldwell, C. (1973). Effects of inadmissible evidence on the decisions of simulated jurors: A moral dilemma. Journal of Applied Social Psychology, 3, 345–353.

Wells, G. L., Lindsay, R. C. L., & Ferguson, T. (1979). Accuracy, confidence, and juror perceptions in eyewitness identification. Journal of Applied Psychology, 64, 440–448.

Coauthored chapter in a coedited volume. →

Wells, G. L., & Murray, D. M. (1984). Eyewitness confidence. In G. L. Wells & E. F. Loftus (Eds.), Eyewitness testimony: Psychological perspectives (pp. 15–170). New York: Cambridge University Press.

Volume number is underlined.

Exhibit A.2   *(continued)*

Biasing Effects   16

Appendix A: Research Materials

The appendix begins on a new page.

The experimental group's questionnaire (Form A) was as follows:

Please answer the following questions in the spaces provided below:

_____ age

_____ sex

_____ year in college

_____ grade point average (GPA)

_____ major

Questionnaires or tests that you constructed for this project appear in the appendix.

Now please read the following paragraph carefully, and then answer the question that follows it:

A man was arrested as a suspected burglar. He fit the description of a man seen running from the burglarized house. While in custody the man submitted to a blood test, and it was determined that he had very recently used drugs.

If you were the bail judge, what bail would you set? Choose a dollar amount from $0 to $50,000:

_____ amount of bail

Exhibit A.2   *(continued)*

Biasing Effects   17

The control group's questionnaire (Form B) was as follows:

Please answer the following questions in the spaces provided below:

_____ age

_____ sex

_____ year in college

_____ grade point average (GPA)

_____ major

Now please read the following paragraph carefully, and then answer the question that follows it:

A man was arrested as a suspected burglar. He fit the description of a man seen running from the burglarized house. The man spent enough time in custody so that he received two meals and made three phone calls.

If you were the bail judge, what bail would you set? Choose a dollar amount from $0 to $50,000:

_____ amount of bail

Exhibit A.2 *(continued)*

Biasing Effects   18

A second
Appendix
begins on a ⟶   Appendix B: Statistical Calculations
new page
and is
labeled.

Drug Test

Raw scores	Log data
10,000	4.00
12,500	4.10
2,000	3.30
50,000	4.70
20,000	4.30
200	2.30
500	2.70
30,000	4.48
2,000	3.30
10,000	4.00
5,000	3.70
10,000	4.00
50,000	4.70
30,000	4.48
10,000	4.00

Neutral information

Raw scores	Log data
10,000	4.00
4,000	3.60
5,000	3.70
350	2.54
5,000	3.70
15,000	4.18
500	2.70
5,000	3.70
500	2.70
1,500	3.18
10,000	4.00
10,000	4.00
20,000	4.30
5,000	3.70
10,000	4.00
10,000	4.00

This appendix
contains the
raw data and
computations
of the study.

These data
do not have
to be typed.

$\bar{X} = 16{,}146.67$ (Drug Raw) 3.871 (Drug Log) $6{,}990.63$ (Neutral Raw) 3.625 (Neutral Log)

$S = 16{,}645.07$ (Drug Raw) 0.7041 (Drug Log) $5{,}549.60$ (Neutral Raw) 0.5524 (Neutral Log)

$$t_{raw\ scores} = \frac{16{,}146.67 - 6{,}990.63}{\sqrt{\frac{3.9\times10^9 + 4.6\times10^8}{15+16-2}\left(\frac{1}{15}+\frac{1}{16}\right)}}$$

$$t_{log\ data} = \frac{3.871 - 3.625}{\sqrt{\frac{6.941 + 4.577}{15+16-2}\left(\frac{1}{15}+\frac{1}{16}\right)}}$$

$t_{29} = 2.08$ $r = \sqrt{\frac{2.08^2}{29 + 2.08^2}} = .36$ $t_{29} = 1.09$ $r = \sqrt{\frac{1.09^2}{29 + 1.09^2}} = .20$

Exhibit A.2   *(continued)*

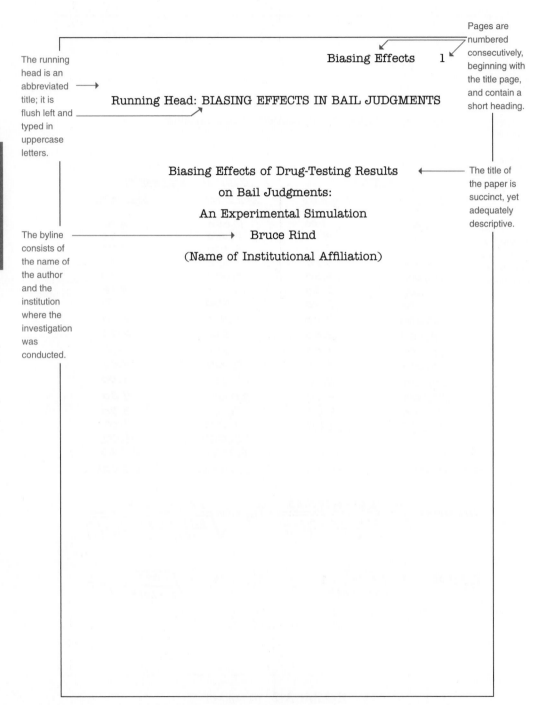

Pages are numbered consecutively, beginning with the title page, and contain a short heading.

The running head is an abbreviated title; it is flush left and typed in uppercase letters.

Biasing Effects   1

Running Head: BIASING EFFECTS IN BAIL JUDGMENTS

Biasing Effects of Drug-Testing Results
on Bail Judgments:
An Experimental Simulation
Bruce Rind
(Name of Institutional Affiliation)

The title of the paper is succinct, yet adequately descriptive.

The byline consists of the name of the author and the institution where the investigation was conducted.

Exhibit A.3 **Format of a manuscript submitted for publication as described in the *Publication Manual of the American Psychological Association* (1994).**

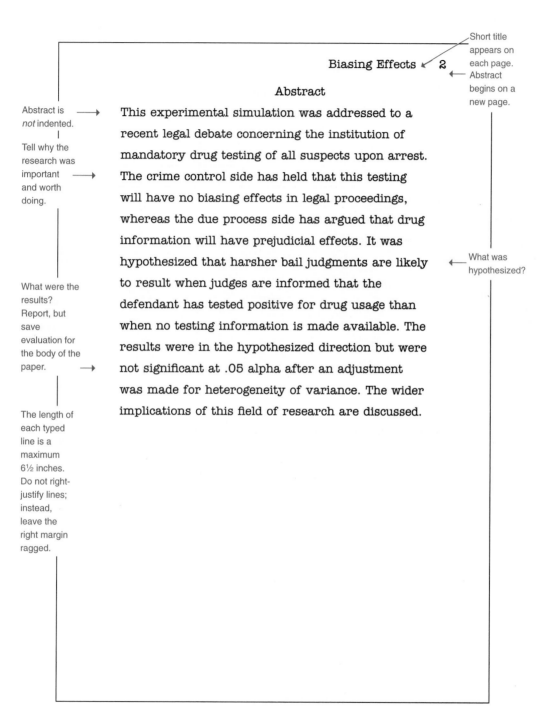

Short title appears on each page.

Abstract begins on a new page.

Biasing Effects   2

Abstract

Abstract is *not* indented.

Tell why the research was important and worth doing.

This experimental simulation was addressed to a recent legal debate concerning the institution of mandatory drug testing of all suspects upon arrest. The crime control side has held that this testing will have no biasing effects in legal proceedings, whereas the due process side has argued that drug information will have prejudicial effects. It was hypothesized that harsher bail judgments are likely to result when judges are informed that the defendant has tested positive for drug usage than when no testing information is made available. The results were in the hypothesized direction but were not significant at .05 alpha after an adjustment was made for heterogeneity of variance. The wider implications of this field of research are discussed.

What was hypothesized?

What were the results? Report, but save evaluation for the body of the paper.

The length of each typed line is a maximum 6½ inches. Do not right-justify lines; instead, leave the right margin ragged.

Appendix A

Exhibit A.3 *(continued)*

Appendix A

Biasing Effects   3   ← The text begins on page 3.

Text begins with the full title repeated. →   Biasing Effects of Drug-Testing Results on Bail Judgments:

An Experimental Simulation

Indent each paragraph 5 to 7 spaces. →   In the summer of 1988, the ABC television program Nightline featured a debate between a representative from the American Civil Liberties Union (ACLU) and a spokesperson for a national group of prosecutors. The focus of the debate was whether mandatory drug testing should be performed on all persons arrested. The prosecutors' representative proposed that the institution of mandatory drug testing would be one more weapon for law enforcement officials in fighting the drug war by identifying drug offenders who would otherwise escape detection. The ACLU representative argued that the institution of this program would result in serious threats to individual rights regarding the bail issue. He contended that positive results would unfairly bias the bail judge's decision on how much bail to impose. Drug-positive suspects, the ACLU representative contended, would tend to receive higher bail judgments, which would be a violation of the rights of suspects when there is no necessary connection between drug usage and the particular crime that was committed. The prosecutor responded that the drug information would have no effect on a bail judge's decision.

The opening paragraph sets the stage in an inviting way.

Double-space between all lines of text.

Abbreviations are first spelled out.

Although left margins are even, right margins are left ragged.

Exhibit A.3   *(continued)*

Biasing Effects   4

Abbreviation for *id est* ("that is").

Forensic psychology (i.e., the application of psychological principles and methods to the legal process) has been successful in providing insight into a number of legal issues. For example, Loftus, Miller, and Burns (1978) demonstrated the distorting effects of misleading questions on the memories of eyewitnesses. Subjects were shown a sequence of 30 slides depicting successive stages of an automobile-pedestrian accident. In one of the slides, half the subjects saw a stop sign, while the other half saw a yield sign. Subjects were later asked a question that made reference to the sign they had actually seen or to a sign they had not seen. When they were subsequently asked what sign they had seen, subjects exposed to the misleading question tended to misremember the sign.

In fact, many studies have demonstrated that eyewitness testimony is often inaccurate. For example, Buckhout (1974) staged an "assault" on a professor which was witnessed by 141 students. When these students were asked seven weeks later to identify the assailant from a group of six photographs, 60% chose an innocent person. Wells, Lindsay, and Ferguson (1979) staged hundreds of eyewitnessed thefts and found that not only did the eyewitnesses have difficulty in correctly identifying

Citations buttress the introduction.

Summaries of studies are succinct, but precise.

Type no more than 27 lines of text on an 8½ x 11-inch page with 1-inch margins

Exhibit A.3 *(continued)*

Biasing Effects   5

the culprits, but other subjects who judged the accuracy
of these eyewitnesses were also incapable
of distinguishing between accurate and inaccurate
accounts.

Aside from the forensic aspects of eyewitness
testimony, other facets of the legal process have
also been investigated, such as defendant
attractiveness (e.g., Efran, 1974), the judge's
instructions to the jury (e.g., Sue, Smith, &
Caldwell, 1973), juror characteristics (e.g., Saks &
Hastie, 1978), and group decisions among jurors
(e.g., Kalven & Zeisel, 1966). These investigations,
among others, have demonstrated the utility of
applying psychological principles and methods to
legal situations in order to understand them better.
In the light of this background, the present
investigation addressed the issue raised in the
Nightline debate between the ACLU representative
and the prosecutors' spokesperson. That is, will
drug information tend to prejudice a bail judge's
decision regarding the amount of bail to set?

The main task of the bail judge is to set bail at a
certain level so as to make it likely that the
defendant will appear for trial. In making this
decision, the bail judge is perhaps apt to consider
factors suggestive of the defendant's traits (i.e.,
lasting characteristics) so as to predict the
likelihood that the defendant will skip bail or show
up for the trial. Attribution theory is the area of

Abbreviation for *exempli gratia* ("for example").

Ampersand (&) is used instead of *and* for citations in parentheses.

Abbreviation was defined previously.

Exhibit A.3 *(continued)*

Biasing Effects 6

psychology concerned with factors such as inferring the traits of others (e.g., Jones & Davis, 1965; Kelley, 1972) and using this trait information to make decisions or judgments regarding these other individuals (Baron & Byrne, 1987).

Works by different authors are listed in alphabetical order by first author's surname.

Jones and Davis (1965) proposed a framework describing how individuals (i.e., observers) go about inferring the traits of others (i.e., actors). According to the theory of correspondent inferences, observers focus mainly on certain types of observed behavior to infer traits because they believe that only certain behaviors are indicative of traits. The primary questions observers will ask themselves, according to Jones and Davis, are: (a) Was the behavior freely chosen? (b) Did the behavior produce uncommon effects? And (c) was the behavior low in social desirability? The third question is particularly relevant to the topic of this research report. Because drug usage is held by our society to be low in social desirability, it follows from correspondent inference theory that observers will be likely to focus on this socially undesirable behavior in judging the actor's traits. Once observers have inferred traits, they tend to use this information to predict the actor's future behavior and to assess and guide their own actions, decisions, and judgments regarding the actor (Baron & Byrne, 1987).

Connecting points are lettered for clarity.

Exhibit A.3 *(continued)*

Appendix A

Biasing Effects　　7

What was → the hypothesis?

Thus I hypothesized that positive results from a drug test will result in harsher bail judgments than when no such information is made available.

First-level headings are centered.

Method ←

The major sections of the text follow each other without a break.

Participants

Second-level headings are flush left and underlined.

Temple University undergraduate students in an introductory statistics class served as subjects in this study. The sample of 31 subjects consisted of both men and women, and the materials were administered during the class meeting with the permission of the instructor and the consent of the students.

Materials

Two forms of a crime scenario were developed. Both forms stated that a man was arrested as a suspected burglar because he fit the description of a man seen running from a burglarized house. In the experimental condition, the scenario stated that the suspect tested positive for drugs while in custody. In the control condition, the scenario continued with neutral information (i.e., the suspect received two meals and made three phone calls while in custody). Following both versions of the crime scenario was the dependent measure, requesting the subjects to play the role of the bail judge and to set a bail amount between $0 and $50,000.

Exhibit A.3　*(continued)*

Biasing Effects   8

Second-level → headings.

Design and Procedure

Subjects were randomly assigned to the control ($\underline{n}$ = 16) or the experimental ($\underline{n}$ = 15) condition. The experimental and control handout sheets were mixed together and passed out at the same time. Subjects were told to fill out certain preliminary information on their sheets and then to read the scenario and make their judgment. When the subjects were finished, they were debriefed.

Subgroups are denoted by lowercase $\underline{n}$.

Results

Another major section of the text, which follows without a break.

The overall findings are given in Table 1, which shows that the mean judgment of the subjects exposed to the drug information was higher than the mean judgment of the subjects exposed to the neutral information. Computing a $\underline{t}$ test on these data yielded a significant result ($\underline{t}$ = 2.08, $\underline{df}$ = 29, $\underline{p}$ = .023 one-tail). However, Table 1 also raises the possibility that the variabilities were different in the two conditions. That possibility was tested by dividing the larger of the two variances by the smaller of the two variances and referring the quotient to an $\underline{F}$ table. The result was highly significant: $\underline{F}$(14, 15) = 9.0, $\underline{p}$ < .001, which indicated that the homogeneity of variance required by the $\underline{t}$ test had been violated (Rosenthal & Rosnow, 1991). In an alternative analysis, the raw scores were transformed by means of a log

Statistical test, degrees of freedom, and significance.

Letters used as statistical symbols are underlined: $\underline{t}$, $\underline{F}$, $\underline{N}$, $\underline{n}$, $\underline{p}$, and so forth.

Degrees of freedom are 14 and 15.

Exhibit A.3 *(continued)*

Appendix A

Biasing Effects   9

transformation. Computing a t test on these values
yielded a nonsignificant result: $t = 1.09$, effect size
$r = .20$. Other methods of analysis were still possible,
although a more prudent alternative would be to
view the effect size as theoretically interesting but in
need of replication with a larger sample. If the results are replicated in follow-up studies, it will also
then be possible to employ a meta-analysis in order
to increase statistical power and obtain a more reliable estimate of the effect size.

The effect
size is
reported to
two decimal
places.

Discussion

The
discussion
continues
without a
break in the
text, except
for the
heading.

This research was an attempt to use the
principles and methods of experimental forensic
psychology to clarify certain aspects of the legal
system. Specifically, this study addressed the
contention of the representative from the ACLU
that even drug information unrelated to the crime
under consideration will tend to bias bail
judgments. One fundamental purpose of our
criminal justice system is, of course, to be just and
unbiased in all of its aspects. The results, although
in the hypothesized direction, were not statistically
significant after the appropriate adjustment was
made for heterogeneity of variance. Nevertheless,
the effect size was theoretically interesting and
suggested that follow-up studies are warranted.

The opening
of the
discussion
reminds the
reader of the
study's
purpose.

The
discussion
should pull
together the
various parts
of the paper.

Future
implications
are
projected.

If future studies provide stronger support for
the ACLU representative's contention, it may be

Exhibit A.3   *(continued)*

Biasing Effects   10

possible to argue on empirical grounds that the
goal of being just and unbiased would be
jeopardized with the institution of mandatory drug
testing upon arrest. It would then follow that this
biasing effect could be circumvented if the bail
judge were not given access to the results of the
drug testing. Such follow-up findings would, in

The
limitations
and wider
significance
of the study
are noted.

turn, fit in with correspondent inference theory
(Jones & Davis, 1965), because knowledge about
socially undesirable behavior (i.e., having taken
drugs recently) could be said to lead subjects to
infer certain traits of the suspect. This chain of
logic is interesting to contemplate, but it is
premature at this stage in the research.

   I believe the criminal justice system can benefit
from forensic research such as that performed in

Remind the ⟶
reader of the
importance
of the study.

this study. At the moment, however, the courts'
procedures are mostly based on tradition and
precedent and do not take into strong consideration
the results of scientific investigations. For example,
jurors who are willing to follow the law that the
death penalty should sometimes be imposed are

Any special ⟶
terms are
defined.

referred to as death-qualified jurors. Psychological
research has demonstrated that death-qualified
jurors are more likely to convict (Ellsworth, 1985).
However, in a split decision in 1986, the U.S.
Supreme Court overturned a lower court ruling
that such jurors are indeed a biased sample.
Another example concerns the research finding

Exhibit A.3   (continued)

Appendix A

that the confidence of eyewitnesses is unrelated to their accuracy unless witnessing conditions are very favorable (Wells & Murray, 1984). However, the U.S. Supreme Court declared in 1972 that among the factors that jurors can use in determining the accuracy of eyewitnesses is the level of certainty demonstrated by the witnesses. The results of scientific investigations of the various aspects of the legal system point to the need for the courts to acknowledge and incorporate these and future results so as to build a justice system that is truly just.

Using a sample of college students, the present investigation studied the biasing effect of drug results. Even if these results were statistically significant, they still might not be generalizable to actual bail judges. Therefore, future research should address this potential problem of external validity. Future research should also directly assess subjects' inferences of corresponding traits from socially undesirable behavior. In this study, these inferences were hypothesized to occur based on the subjects' bail judgments. It is interesting to note that, while the subjects seemingly judged the suspect more harshly based on the drug information in the burglary scenario, there is no necessary connection between drug usage and burglary. However, the subjects may have been drawing on a stereotype to assume that the

Future research is suggested. →

Exhibit A.3   *(continued)*

Biasing Effects   12

association was likely because the media often report property crimes that are motivated by the need to get money to purchase drugs. Thus it would be valuable to use other crime scenarios that are not so stereotypically associated with drugs to determine whether the biasing effect is more general.

Exhibit A.3   *(continued)*

Appendix A

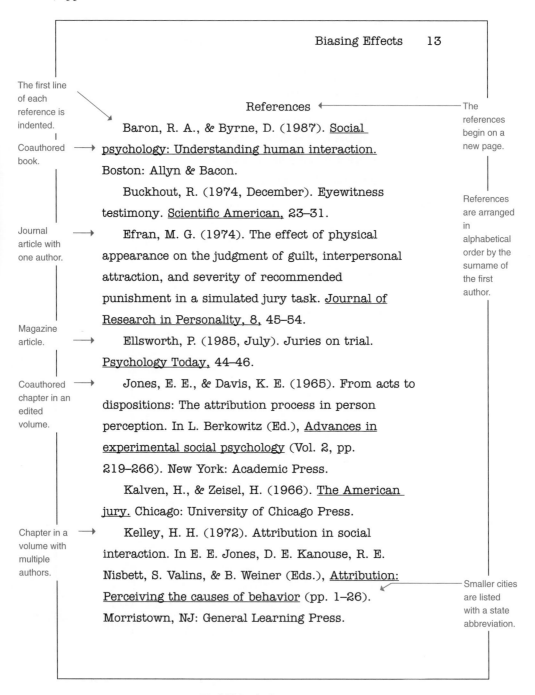

Biasing Effects   13

The first line of each reference is indented.

Coauthored book. →

Journal article with one author. →

Magazine article. →

Coauthored chapter in an edited volume. →

Chapter in a volume with multiple authors. →

References ←   The references begin on a new page.

Baron, R. A., & Byrne, D. (1987). Social psychology: Understanding human interaction. Boston: Allyn & Bacon.

Buckhout, R. (1974, December). Eyewitness testimony. Scientific American, 23–31.

Efran, M. G. (1974). The effect of physical appearance on the judgment of guilt, interpersonal attraction, and severity of recommended punishment in a simulated jury task. Journal of Research in Personality, 8, 45–54.

Ellsworth, P. (1985, July). Juries on trial. Psychology Today, 44–46.

Jones, E. E., & Davis, K. E. (1965). From acts to dispositions: The attribution process in person perception. In L. Berkowitz (Ed.), Advances in experimental social psychology (Vol. 2, pp. 219–266). New York: Academic Press.

Kalven, H., & Zeisel, H. (1966). The American jury. Chicago: University of Chicago Press.

Kelley, H. H. (1972). Attribution in social interaction. In E. E. Jones, D. E. Kanouse, R. E. Nisbett, S. Valins, & B. Weiner (Eds.), Attribution: Perceiving the causes of behavior (pp. 1–26). Morristown, NJ: General Learning Press.

References are arranged in alphabetical order by the surname of the first author.

Smaller cities are listed with a state abbreviation.

Exhibit A.3   (continued)

Biasing Effects   14

Journal article with multiple authors. → Loftus, E. F., Miller, D. G., & Burns, H. J. (1978). Semantic integration of verbal information into a visual memory. <u>Journal of Experimental Psychology: Human Learning and Memory, 4,</u> 19–31.

Book in second edition. → Rosenthal, R., & Rosnow, R. L. (1991). <u>Essentials of behavioral research: Methods and data analysis</u> (2nd ed.). New York: McGraw-Hill.

Major cities are listed without a state abbreviation.

← Underline title of book

Saks, M. J., & Hastie, R. (1978). <u>Social psychology in the court.</u> New York: Van Nostrand Reinhold.

Sue, S., Smith, R. E., & Caldwell, C. (1973). Effects of inadmissible evidence on the decisions of simulated jurors: A moral dilemma. <u>Journal of Applied Social Psychology, 3,</u> 345–353.

Wells, G. L., Lindsay, R. C. L., & Ferguson, T. (1979). Accuracy, confidence, and juror perceptions in eyewitness identification. <u>Journal of Applied Psychology, 64,</u> 440–448.

← Underline name of journal and the volume number, including punctuation.

Coauthored chapter in a coedited volume. → Wells, G. L., & Murray, D. M. (1984). Eyewitness confidence. In G. L. Wells & E. F. Loftus (Eds.), <u>Eyewitness testimony: Psychological perspectives</u> (pp. 15–170). New York: Cambridge University Press.

Exhibit A.3   *(continued)*

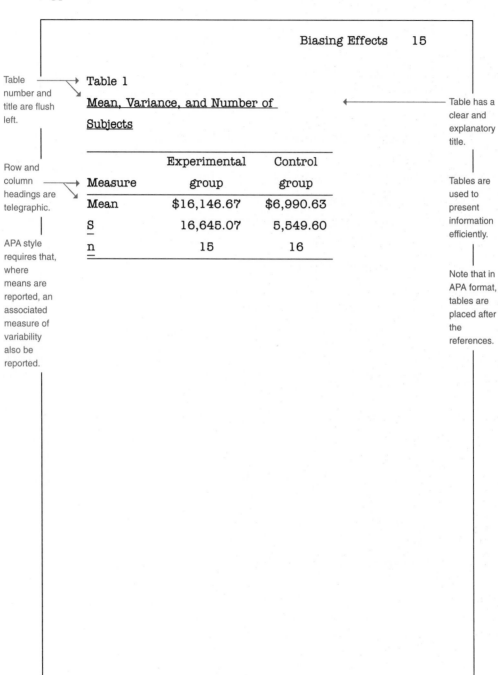

Statistical Tables

Table B.1 z Values and Their Associated One-Tailed p Values

Second digit of z

z	.00	.01	.02	.03	.04	.05	.06	.07	.08	.09
.0	.5000	.4960	.4920	.4880	.4840	.4801	.4761	.4721	.4681	.4641
.1	.4602	.4562	.4522	.4483	.4443	.4404	.4364	.4325	.4286	.4247
.2	.4207	.4168	.4129	.4090	.4052	.4013	.3974	.3936	.3897	.3859
.3	.3821	.3783	.3745	.3707	.3669	.3632	.3594	.3557	.3520	.3483
.4	.3446	.3409	.3372	.3336	.3300	.3264	.3228	.3192	.3156	.3121
.5	.3085	.3050	.3015	.2981	.2946	.2912	.2877	.2843	.2810	.2776
.6	.2743	.2709	.2676	.2643	.2611	.2578	.2546	.2514	.2483	.2451
.7	.2420	.2389	.2358	.2327	.2296	.2266	.2236	.2206	.2177	.2148
.8	.2119	.2090	.2061	.2033	.2005	.1977	.1949	.1922	.1894	.1867
.9	.1841	.1814	.1788	.1762	.1736	.1711	.1685	.1660	.1635	.1611
1.0	.1587	.1562	.1539	.1515	.1492	.1469	.1446	.1423	.1401	.1379
1.1	.1357	.1335	.1314	.1292	.1271	.1251	.1230	.1210	.1190	.1170
1.2	.1151	.1131	.1112	.1093	.1075	.1056	.1038	.1020	.1003	.0985
1.3	.0968	.0951	.0934	.0918	.0901	.0885	.0869	.0853	.0838	.0823
1.4	.0808	.0793	.0778	.0764	.0749	.0735	.0721	.0708	.0694	.0681
1.5	.0668	.0655	.0643	.0630	.0618	.0606	.0594	.0582	.0571	.0559
1.6	.0548	.0537	.0526	.0516	.0505	.0495	.0485	.0475	.0465	.0455
1.7	.0446	.0436	.0427	.0418	.0409	.0401	.0392	.0384	.0375	.0367
1.8	.0359	.0351	.0344	.0336	.0329	.0322	.0314	.0307	.0301	.0294
1.9	.0287	.0281	.0274	.0268	.0262	.0256	.0250	.0244	.0239	.0233
2.0	.0228	.0222	.0217	.0212	.0207	.0202	.0197	.0192	.0188	.0183
2.1	.0179	.0174	.0170	.0166	.0162	.0158	.0154	.0150	.0146	.0143
2.2	.0139	.0136	.0132	.0129	.0125	.0122	.0119	.0116	.0113	.0110
2.3	.0107	.0104	.0102	.0099	.0096	.0094	.0091	.0089	.0087	.0084
2.4	.0082	.0080	.0078	.0075	.0073	.0071	.0069	.0068	.0066	.0064
2.5	.0062	.0060	.0059	.0057	.0055	.0054	.0052	.0051	.0049	.0048
2.6	.0047	.0045	.0044	.0043	.0041	.0040	.0039	.0038	.0037	.0036
2.7	.0035	.0034	.0033	.0032	.0031	.0030	.0029	.0028	.0027	.0026
2.8	.0026	.0025	.0024	.0023	.0023	.0022	.0021	.0021	.0020	.0019
2.9	.0019	.0018	.0018	.0017	.0016	.0016	.0015	.0015	.0014	.0014
3.0	.0013	.0013	.0013	.0012	.0012	.0011	.0011	.0011	.0010	.0010
3.1	.0010	.0009	.0009	.0009	.0008	.0008	.0008	.0008	.0007	.0007
3.2	.0007									
3.3	.0005									
3.4	.0003									
3.5	.00023									
3.6	.00016									
3.7	.00011									
3.8	.00007									
3.9	.00005									
4.0	.00003									

Source: From *Nonparametric Statistics* (p. 247), by S. Siegel, 1956, New York: McGraw-Hill. Reprinted by permission of McGraw-Hill, Inc.

Table B.2 t Values and Their Associated One-Tailed and Two-Tailed p Values

p	.50	.20	.10	.05	.02	.01	.005	.002	two-tail
df	.25	.10	.05	.025	.01	.005	.0025	.001	one-tail
1	1.000	3.078	6.314	12.706	31.821	63.657	127.321	318.309	
2	.816	1.886	2.920	4.303	6.965	9.925	14.089	22.327	
3	.765	1.638	2.353	3.182	4.541	5.841	7.453	10.214	
4	.741	1.533	2.132	2.776	3.747	4.604	5.598	7.173	
5	.727	1.476	2.015	2.571	3.365	4.032	4.773	5.893	
6	.718	1.440	1.943	2.447	3.143	3.707	4.317	5.208	
7	.711	1.415	1.895	2.365	2.998	3.499	4.029	4.785	
8	.706	1.397	1.860	2.306	2.896	3.355	3.833	4.501	
9	.703	1.383	1.833	2.262	2.821	3.250	3.690	4.297	
10	.700	1.372	1.812	2.228	2.764	3.169	3.581	4.144	
11	.697	1.363	1.796	2.201	2.718	3.106	3.497	4.025	
12	.695	1.356	1.782	2.179	2.681	3.055	3.428	3.930	
13	.694	1.350	1.771	2.160	2.650	3.012	3.372	3.852	
14	.692	1.345	1.761	2.145	2.624	2.977	3.326	3.787	
15	.691	1.341	1.753	2.131	2.602	2.947	3.286	3.733	
16	.690	1.337	1.746	2.120	2.583	2.921	3.252	3.686	
17	.689	1.333	1.740	2.110	2.567	2.898	3.223	3.646	
18	.688	1.330	1.734	2.101	2.552	2.878	3.197	3.610	
19	.688	1.328	1.729	2.093	2.539	2.861	3.174	3.579	
20	.687	1.325	1.725	2.086	2.528	2.845	3.153	3.552	
21	.686	1.323	1.721	2.080	2.518	2.831	3.135	3.527	
22	.686	1.321	1.717	2.074	2.508	2.819	3.119	3.505	
23	.685	1.319	1.714	2.069	2.500	2.807	3.104	3.485	
24	.685	1.318	1.711	2.064	2.492	2.797	3.090	3.467	
25	.684	1.316	1.708	2.060	2.485	2.787	3.078	3.450	
26	.684	1.315	1.706	2.056	2.479	2.779	3.067	3.435	
27	.684	1.314	1.703	2.052	2.473	2.771	3.057	3.421	
28	.683	1.313	1.701	2.048	2.467	2.763	3.047	3.408	
29	.683	1.311	1.699	2.045	2.462	2.756	3.038	3.396	
30	.683	1.310	1.697	2.042	2.457	2.750	3.030	3.385	
35	.682	1.306	1.690	2.030	2.438	2.724	2.996	3.340	
40	.681	1.303	1.684	2.021	2.423	2.704	2.971	3.307	
45	.680	1.301	1.679	2.014	2.412	2.690	2.952	3.281	
50	.679	1.299	1.676	2.009	2.403	2.678	2.937	3.261	
55	.679	1.297	1.673	2.004	2.396	2.668	2.925	3.245	
60	.679	1.296	1.671	2.000	2.390	2.660	2.915	3.232	
70	.678	1.294	1.667	1.994	2.381	2.648	2.899	3.211	
80	.678	1.292	1.664	1.990	2.374	2.639	2.887	3.195	
90	.677	1.291	1.662	1.987	2.368	2.632	2.878	3.183	
100	.677	1.290	1.660	1.984	2.364	2.626	2.871	3.174	
200	.676	1.286	1.652	1.972	2.345	2.601	2.838	3.131	
500	.675	1.283	1.648	1.965	2.334	2.586	2.820	3.107	
1,000	.675	1.282	1.646	1.962	2.330	2.581	2.813	3.098	
2,000	.675	1.282	1.645	1.961	2.328	2.578	2.810	3.094	
10,000	.675	1.282	1.645	1.960	2.327	2.576	2.808	3.091	
∞	.674	1.282	1.645	1.960	2.326	2.576	2.807	3.090	

Appendix B

Table B.2   *t* Values and Their Associated One-Tailed and Two-Tailed *p* Values (*continued*)

p → *df* ↓	.001 / .0005	.0005 / .00025	.0002 / .0001	.0001 / .00005	.00005 / .000025	.00002 / .00001
1	636.619	1,273.239	3,183.099	6,366.198	12,732.395	31,830.989
2	31.598	44.705	70.700	99.992	141.416	223.603
3	12.924	16.326	22.204	28.000	35.298	47.928
4	8.610	10.306	13.034	15.544	18.522	23.332
5	6.869	7.976	9.678	11.178	12.893	15.547
6	5.959	6.788	8.025	9.082	10.261	12.032
7	5.408	6.082	7.063	7.885	8.782	10.103
8	5.041	5.618	6.442	7.120	7.851	8.907
9	4.781	5.291	6.010	6.594	7.215	8.102
10	4.587	5.049	5.694	6.211	6.757	7.527
11	4.437	4.863	5.453	5.921	6.412	7.098
12	4.318	4.716	5.263	5.694	6.143	6.756
13	4.221	4.597	5.111	5.513	5.928	6.501
14	4.140	4.499	4.985	5.363	5.753	6.287
15	4.073	4.417	4.880	5.239	5.607	6.109
16	4.015	4.346	4.791	5.134	5.484	5.960
17	3.965	4.286	4.714	5.044	5.379	5.832
18	3.922	4.233	4.648	4.966	5.288	5.722
19	3.883	4.187	4.590	4.897	5.209	5.627
20	3.850	4.146	4.539	4.837	5.139	5.543
21	3.819	4.110	4.493	4.784	5.077	5.469
22	3.792	4.077	4.452	4.736	5.022	5.402
23	3.768	4.048	4.415	4.693	4.972	5.343
24	3.745	4.021	4.382	4.654	4.927	5.290
25	3.725	3.997	4.352	4.619	4.887	5.241
26	3.707	3.974	4.324	4.587	4.850	5.197
27	3.690	3.954	4.299	4.558	4.816	5.157
28	3.674	3.935	4.275	4.530	4.784	5.120
29	3.659	3.918	4.254	4.506	4.756	5.086
30	3.646	3.902	4.234	4.482	4.729	5.054
35	3.591	3.836	4.153	4.389	4.622	4.927
40	3.551	3.788	4.094	4.321	4.544	4.835
45	3.520	3.752	4.049	4.269	4.485	4.766
50	3.496	3.723	4.014	4.228	4.438	4.711
55	3.476	3.700	3.986	4.196	4.401	4.667
60	3.460	3.681	3.926	4.169	4.370	4.631
70	3.435	3.651	3.962	4.127	4.323	4.576
80	3.416	3.629	3.899	4.096	4.288	4.535
90	3.402	3.612	3.878	4.072	4.261	4.503
100	3.390	3.598	3.862	4.053	4.240	4.478
200	3.340	3.539	3.789	3.970	4.146	4.369
500	3.310	3.504	3.747	3.922	4.091	4.306
1,000	3.300	3.492	3.733	3.906	4.073	4.285
2,000	3.295	3.486	3.726	3.898	4.064	4.275
10,000	3.292	3.482	3.720	3.892	4.058	4.267
∞	3.291	3.481	3.719	3.891	4.056	4.265

(The two-tail *p* values are .001, .0005, .0002, .0001, .00005, .00002; the corresponding one-tail *p* values are .0005, .00025, .0001, .00005, .000025, .00001.)

Source: From "Extended Tables of the Percentage Points of Student's *t*-Distribution," by E. T. Federighi, 1959, *Journal of the American Statistical Association, 54*, pp. 683–688. Reprinted by permission of the American Statistical Association.

Table B.3 — F Values and Their Associated p Values

df_2	p	1	2	3	4	5	6	8	12	24	∞
1	.001	405284	500000	540379	562500	576405	585937	598144	610667	623497	636619
	.005	16211	20000	21615	22500	23056	23437	23925	24426	24940	25465
	.01	4052	4999	5403	5625	5764	5859	5981	6106	6234	6366
	.025	647.79	799.50	864.16	899.58	921.85	937.11	956.66	976.71	997.25	1018.30
	.05	161.45	199.50	215.71	224.58	230.16	233.99	238.88	243.91	249.05	254.32
	.10	39.86	49.50	53.59	55.83	57.24	58.20	59.44	60.70	62.00	63.33
	.20	9.47	12.00	13.06	13.73	14.01	14.26	14.59	14.90	15.24	15.58
2	.001	998.5	999.0	999.2	999.2	999.3	999.3	999.4	999.4	999.5	999.5
	.005	198.50	199.00	199.17	199.25	199.30	199.33	199.37	199.42	199.46	199.51
	.01	98.49	99.00	99.17	99.25	99.30	99.33	99.36	99.42	99.46	99.50
	.025	38.51	39.00	39.17	39.25	39.30	39.33	39.37	39.42	39.46	39.50
	.05	18.51	19.00	19.16	19.25	19.30	19.33	19.37	19.41	19.45	19.50
	.10	8.53	9.00	9.16	9.24	9.29	9.33	9.37	9.41	9.45	9.49
	.20	3.56	4.00	4.16	4.24	4.28	4.32	4.36	4.40	4.44	4.48
3	.001	167.5	148.5	141.1	137.1	134.6	132.8	130.6	128.3	125.9	123.5
	.005	55.55	49.80	47.47	46.20	45.39	44.84	44.13	43.39	42.62	41.83
	.01	34.12	30.81	29.46	28.71	28.24	27.91	27.49	27.05	26.60	26.12
	.025	17.44	16.04	15.44	15.10	14.89	14.74	14.54	14.34	14.12	13.90
	.05	10.13	9.55	9.28	9.12	9.01	8.94	8.84	8.74	8.64	8.53
	.10	5.54	5.46	5.39	5.34	5.31	5.28	5.25	5.22	5.18	5.13
	.20	2.68	2.89	2.94	2.96	2.97	2.97	2.98	2.98	2.98	2.98
4	.001	74.14	61.25	56.18	53.44	51.71	50.53	49.00	47.41	45.77	44.05
	.005	31.33	26.28	24.26	23.16	22.46	21.98	21.35	20.71	20.03	19.33
	.01	21.20	18.00	16.69	15.98	15.52	15.21	14.80	14.37	13.93	13.46
	.025	12.22	10.65	9.98	9.60	9.36	9.20	8.98	8.75	8.51	8.26
	.05	7.71	6.94	6.59	6.39	6.26	6.16	6.04	5.91	5.77	5.63
	.10	4.54	4.32	4.19	4.11	4.05	4.01	3.95	3.90	3.83	3.76
	.20	2.35	2.47	2.48	2.48	2.48	2.47	2.47	2.46	2.44	2.43
5	.001	47.04	36.61	33.20	31.09	29.75	28.84	27.64	26.42	25.14	23.78
	.005	22.79	18.31	16.53	15.56	14.94	14.51	13.96	13.38	12.78	12.14
	.01	16.26	13.27	12.06	11.39	10.97	10.67	10.29	9.89	9.47	9.02
	.025	10.01	8.43	7.76	7.39	7.15	6.98	6.76	6.52	6.28	6.02
	.05	6.61	5.79	5.41	5.19	5.05	4.95	4.82	4.68	4.53	4.36
	.10	4.06	3.78	3.62	3.52	3.45	3.40	3.34	3.27	3.19	3.10
	.20	2.18	2.26	2.25	2.24	2.23	2.22	2.20	2.18	2.16	2.13
6	.001	35.51	27.00	23.70	21.90	20.81	20.03	19.03	17.99	16.89	15.75
	.005	18.64	14.54	12.92	12.03	11.46	11.07	10.57	10.03	9.47	8.88
	.01	13.74	10.92	9.78	9.15	8.75	8.47	8.10	7.72	7.31	6.88
	.025	8.81	7.26	6.60	6.23	5.99	5.82	5.60	5.37	5.12	4.85
	.05	5.99	5.14	4.76	4.53	4.39	4.28	4.15	4.00	3.84	3.67
	.10	3.78	3.46	3.29	3.18	3.11	3.05	2.98	2.90	2.82	2.72
	.20	2.07	2.13	2.11	2.09	2.08	2.06	2.04	2.02	1.99	1.95
7	.001	29.22	21.69	18.77	17.19	16.21	15.52	14.63	13.71	12.73	11.69
	.005	16.24	12.40	10.88	10.05	9.52	9.16	8.68	8.18	7.65	7.08
	.01	12.25	9.55	8.45	7.85	7.46	7.19	6.84	6.47	6.07	5.65
	.025	8.07	6.54	5.89	5.52	5.29	5.12	4.90	4.67	4.42	4.14
	.05	5.59	4.74	4.35	4.12	3.97	3.87	3.73	3.57	3.41	3.23
	.10	3.59	3.26	3.07	2.96	2.88	2.83	2.75	2.67	2.58	2.47
	.20	2.00	2.04	2.02	1.99	1.97	1.96	1.93	1.91	1.87	1.83

Appendix B

Table B.3   *F* Values and Their Associated *p* Values (*continued*)

df_2	p	1	2	3	4	5	6	8	12	24	∞
8	.001	25.42	18.49	15.83	14.39	13.49	12.86	12.04	11.19	10.30	9.34
	.005	14.69	11.04	9.60	8.81	8.30	7.95	7.50	7.01	6.50	5.95
	.01	11.26	8.65	7.59	7.01	6.63	6.37	6.03	5.67	5.28	4.86
	.025	7.57	6.06	5.42	5.05	4.82	4.65	4.43	4.20	3.95	3.67
	.05	5.32	4.46	4.07	3.84	3.69	3.58	3.44	3.28	3.12	2.93
	.10	3.46	3.11	2.92	2.81	2.73	2.67	2.59	2.50	2.40	2.29
	.20	1.95	1.98	1.95	1.92	1.90	1.88	1.86	1.83	1.79	1.74
9	.001	22.86	16.39	13.90	12.56	11.71	11.13	10.37	9.57	8.72	7.81
	.005	13.61	10.11	8.72	7.96	7.47	7.13	6.69	6.23	5.73	5.19
	.01	10.56	8.02	6.99	6.42	6.06	5.80	5.47	5.11	4.73	4.31
	.025	7.21	5.71	5.08	4.72	4.48	4.32	4.10	3.87	3.61	3.33
	.05	5.12	4.26	3.86	3.63	3.48	3.37	3.23	3.07	2.90	2.71
	.10	3.36	3.01	2.81	2.69	2.61	2.55	2.47	2.38	2.28	2.16
	.20	1.91	1.94	1.90	1.87	1.85	1.83	1.80	1.76	1.73	1.67
10	.001	21.04	14.91	12.55	11.28	10.48	9.92	9.20	8.45	7.64	6.76
	.005	12.83	9.43	8.08	7.34	6.87	6.54	6.12	5.66	5.17	4.64
	.01	10.04	7.56	6.55	5.99	5.64	5.39	5.06	4.71	4.33	3.91
	.025	6.94	5.46	4.83	4.47	4.24	4.07	3.85	3.62	3.37	3.08
	.05	4.96	4.10	3.71	3.48	3.33	3.22	3.07	2.91	2.74	2.54
	.10	3.28	2.92	2.73	2.61	2.52	2.46	2.38	2.28	2.18	2.06
	.20	1.88	1.90	1.86	1.83	1.80	1.78	1.75	1.72	1.67	1.62
11	.001	19.69	13.81	11.56	10.35	9.58	9.05	8.35	7.63	6.85	6.00
	.005	12.23	8.91	7.60	6.88	6.42	6.10	5.68	5.24	4.76	4.23
	.01	9.65	7.20	6.22	5.67	5.32	5.07	4.74	4.40	4.02	3.60
	.025	6.72	5.26	4.63	4.28	4.04	3.88	3.66	3.43	3.17	2.88
	.05	4.84	3.98	3.59	3.36	3.20	3.09	2.95	2.79	2.61	2.40
	.10	3.23	2.86	2.66	2.54	2.45	2.39	2.30	2.21	2.10	1.97
	.20	1.86	1.87	1.83	1.80	1.77	1.75	1.72	1.68	1.63	1.57
12	.001	18.64	12.97	10.80	9.63	8.89	8.38	7.71	7.00	6.25	5.42
	.005	11.75	8.51	7.23	6.52	6.07	5.76	5.35	4.91	4.43	3.90
	.01	9.33	6.93	5.95	5.41	5.06	4.82	4.50	4.16	3.78	3.36
	.025	6.55	5.10	4.47	4.12	3.89	3.73	3.51	3.28	3.02	2.72
	.05	4.75	3.88	3.49	3.26	3.11	3.00	2.85	2.69	2.50	2.30
	.10	3.18	2.81	2.61	2.48	2.39	2.33	2.24	2.15	2.04	1.90
	.20	1.84	1.85	1.80	1.77	1.74	1.72	1.69	1.65	1.60	1.54
13	.001	17.81	12.31	10.21	9.07	8.35	7.86	7.21	6.52	5.78	4.97
	.005	11.37	8.19	6.93	6.23	5.79	5.48	5.08	4.64	4.17	3.65
	.01	9.07	6.70	5.74	5.20	4.86	4.62	4.30	3.96	3.59	3.16
	.025	6.41	4.97	4.35	4.00	3.77	3.60	3.39	3.15	2.89	2.60
	.05	4.67	3.80	3.41	3.18	3.02	2.92	2.77	2.60	2.42	2.21
	.10	3.14	2.76	2.56	2.43	2.35	2.28	2.20	2.10	1.98	1.85
	.20	1.82	1.83	1.78	1.75	1.72	1.69	1.66	1.62	1.57	1.51
14	.001	17.14	11.78	9.73	8.62	7.92	7.43	6.80	6.13	5.41	4.60
	.005	11.06	7.92	6.68	6.00	5.56	5.26	4.86	4.43	3.96	3.44
	.01	8.86	6.51	5.56	5.03	4.69	4.46	4.14	3.80	3.43	3.00
	.025	6.30	4.86	4.24	3.89	3.66	3.50	3.29	3.05	2.79	2.49
	.05	4.60	3.74	3.34	3.11	2.96	2.85	2.70	2.53	2.35	2.13
	.10	3.10	2.73	2.52	2.39	2.31	2.24	2.15	2.05	1.94	1.80
	.20	1.81	1.81	1.76	1.73	1.70	1.67	1.64	1.60	1.55	1.48

Table B.3 F Values and Their Associated p Values (continued)

df_2	p	1	2	3	4	5	6	8	12	24	∞
15	.001	16.59	11.34	9.34	8.25	7.57	7.09	6.47	5.81	5.10	4.31
	.005	10.80	7.70	6.48	5.80	5.37	5.07	4.67	4.25	3.79	3.26
	.01	8.68	6.36	5.42	4.89	4.56	4.32	4.00	3.67	3.29	2.87
	.025	6.20	4.77	4.15	3.80	3.58	3.41	3.20	2.96	2.70	2.40
	.05	4.54	3.68	3.29	3.06	2.90	2.79	2.64	2.48	2.29	2.07
	.10	3.07	2.70	2.49	2.36	2.27	2.21	2.12	2.02	1.90	1.76
	.20	1.80	1.79	1.75	1.71	1.68	1.66	1.62	1.58	1.53	1.46
16	.001	16.12	10.97	9.00	7.94	7.27	6.81	6.19	5.55	4.85	4.06
	.005	10.58	7.51	6.30	5.64	5.21	4.91	4.52	4.10	3.64	3.11
	.01	8.53	6.23	5.29	4.77	4.44	4.20	3.89	3.55	3.18	2.75
	.025	6.12	4.69	4.08	3.73	3.50	3.34	3.12	2.89	2.63	2.32
	.05	4.49	3.63	3.24	3.01	2.85	2.74	2.59	2.42	2.24	2.01
	.10	3.05	2.67	2.46	2.33	2.24	2.18	2.09	1.99	1.87	1.72
	.20	1.79	1.78	1.74	1.70	1.67	1.64	1.61	1.56	1.51	1.43
17	.001	15.72	10.66	8.73	7.68	7.02	6.56	5.96	5.32	4.63	3.85
	.005	10.38	7.35	6.16	5.50	5.07	4.78	4.39	3.97	3.51	2.98
	.01	8.40	6.11	5.18	4.67	4.34	4.10	3.79	3.45	3.08	2.65
	.025	6.04	4.62	4.01	3.66	3.44	3.28	3.06	2.82	2.56	2.25
	.05	4.45	3.59	3.20	2.96	2.81	2.70	2.55	2.38	2.19	1.96
	.10	3.03	2.64	2.44	2.31	2.22	2.15	2.06	1.96	1.84	1.69
	.20	1.78	1.77	1.72	1.68	1.65	1.63	1.59	1.55	1.49	1.42
18	.001	15.38	10.39	8.49	7.46	6.81	6.35	5.76	5.13	4.45	3.67
	.005	10.22	7.21	6.03	5.37	4.96	4.66	4.28	3.86	3.40	2.87
	.01	8.28	6.01	5.09	4.58	4.25	4.01	3.71	3.37	3.00	2.57
	.025	5.98	4.56	3.95	3.61	3.38	3.22	3.01	2.77	2.50	2.19
	.05	4.41	3.55	3.16	2.93	2.77	2.66	2.51	2.34	2.15	1.92
	.10	3.01	2.62	2.42	2.29	2.20	2.13	2.04	1.93	1.81	1.66
	.20	1.77	1.76	1.71	1.67	1.64	1.62	1.58	1.53	1.48	1.40
19	.001	15.08	10.16	8.28	7.26	6.61	6.18	5.59	4.97	4.29	3.52
	.005	10.07	7.09	5.92	5.27	4.85	4.56	4.18	3.76	3.31	2.78
	.01	8.18	5.93	5.01	4.50	4.17	3.94	3.63	3.30	2.92	2.49
	.025	5.92	4.51	3.90	3.56	3.33	3.17	2.96	2.72	2.45	2.13
	.05	4.38	3.52	3.13	2.90	2.74	2.63	2.48	2.31	2.11	1.88
	.10	2.99	2.61	2.40	2.27	2.18	2.11	2.02	1.91	1.79	1.63
	.20	1.76	1.75	1.70	1.66	1.63	1.61	1.57	1.52	1.46	1.39
20	.001	14.82	9.95	8.10	7.10	6.46	6.02	5.44	4.82	4.15	3.38
	.005	9.94	6.99	5.82	5.17	4.76	4.47	4.09	3.68	3.22	2.69
	.01	8.10	5.85	4.94	4.43	4.10	3.87	3.56	3.23	2.86	2.42
	.025	5.87	4.46	3.86	3.51	3.29	3.13	2.91	2.68	2.41	2.09
	.05	4.35	3.49	3.10	2.87	2.71	2.60	2.45	2.28	2.08	1.84
	.10	2.97	2.59	2.38	2.25	2.16	2.09	2.00	1.89	1.77	1.61
	.20	1.76	1.75	1.70	1.65	1.62	1.60	1.56	1.51	1.45	1.37
21	.001	14.59	9.77	7.94	6.95	6.32	5.88	5.31	4.70	4.03	3.26
	.005	9.83	6.89	5.73	5.09	4.68	4.39	4.01	3.60	3.15	2.61
	.01	8.02	5.78	4.87	4.37	4.04	3.81	3.51	3.17	2.80	2.36
	.025	5.83	4.42	3.82	3.48	3.25	3.09	2.87	2.64	2.37	2.04
	.05	4.32	3.47	3.07	2.84	2.68	2.57	2.42	2.25	2.05	1.81
	.10	2.96	2.57	2.36	2.23	2.14	2.08	1.98	1.88	1.75	1.59
	.20	1.75	1.74	1.69	1.65	1.61	1.59	1.55	1.50	1.44	1.36

Table B.3 F Values and Their Associated p Values *(continued)*

df_2	p	1	2	3	4	5	6	8	12	24	∞
22	.001	14.38	9.61	7.80	6.81	6.19	5.76	5.19	4.58	3.92	3.15
	.005	9.73	6.81	5.65	5.02	4.61	4.32	3.94	3.54	3.08	2.55
	.01	7.94	5.72	4.82	4.31	3.99	3.76	3.45	3.12	2.75	2.31
	.025	5.79	4.38	3.78	3.44	3.22	3.05	2.84	2.60	2.33	2.00
	.05	4.30	3.44	3.05	2.82	2.66	2.55	2.40	2.23	2.03	1.78
	.10	2.95	2.56	2.35	2.22	2.13	2.06	1.97	1.86	1.73	1.57
	.20	1.75	1.73	1.68	1.64	1.61	1.58	1.54	1.49	1.43	1.35
23	.001	14.19	9.47	7.67	6.69	6.08	5.65	5.09	4.48	3.82	3.05
	.005	9.63	6.73	5.58	4.95	4.54	4.26	3.88	3.47	3.02	2.48
	.01	7.88	5.66	4.76	4.26	3.94	3.71	3.41	3.07	2.70	2.26
	.025	5.75	4.35	3.75	3.41	3.18	3.02	2.81	2.57	2.30	1.97
	.05	4.28	3.42	3.03	2.80	2.64	2.53	2.38	2.20	2.00	1.76
	.10	2.94	2.55	2.34	2.21	2.11	2.05	1.95	1.84	1.72	1.55
	.20	1.74	1.73	1.68	1.63	1.60	1.57	1.53	1.49	1.42	1.34
24	.001	14.03	9.34	7.55	6.59	5.98	5.55	4.99	4.39	3.74	2.97
	.005	9.55	6.66	5.52	4.89	4.49	4.20	3.83	3.42	2.97	2.43
	.01	7.82	5.61	4.72	4.22	3.90	3.67	3.36	3.03	2.66	2.21
	.025	5.72	4.32	3.72	3.38	3.15	2.99	2.78	2.54	2.27	1.94
	.05	4.26	3.40	3.01	2.78	2.62	2.51	2.36	2.18	1.98	1.73
	.10	2.93	2.54	2.33	2.19	2.10	2.04	1.94	1.83	1.70	1.53
	.20	1.74	1.72	1.67	1.63	1.59	1.57	1.53	1.48	1.42	1.33
25	.001	13.88	9.22	7.45	6.49	5.88	5.46	4.91	4.31	3.66	2.89
	.005	9.48	6.60	5.46	4.84	4.43	4.15	3.78	3.37	2.92	2.38
	.01	7.77	5.57	4.68	4.18	3.86	3.63	3.32	2.99	2.62	2.17
	.025	5.69	4.29	3.69	3.35	3.13	2.97	2.75	2.51	2.24	1.91
	.05	4.24	3.38	2.99	2.76	2.60	2.49	2.34	2.16	1.96	1.71
	.10	2.92	2.53	2.32	2.18	2.09	2.02	1.93	1.82	1.69	1.52
	.20	1.73	1.72	1.66	1.62	1.59	1.56	1.52	1.47	1.41	1.32
26	.001	13.74	9.12	7.36	6.41	5.80	5.38	4.83	4.24	3.59	2.82
	.005	9.41	6.54	5.41	4.79	4.38	4.10	3.73	3.33	2.87	2.33
	.01	7.72	5.53	4.64	4.14	3.82	3.59	3.29	2.96	2.58	2.13
	.025	5.66	4.27	3.67	3.33	3.10	2.94	2.73	2.49	2.22	1.88
	.05	4.22	3.37	2.98	2.74	2.59	2.47	2.32	2.15	1.95	1.69
	.10	2.91	2.52	2.31	2.17	2.08	2.01	1.92	1.81	1.68	1.50
	.20	1.73	1.71	1.66	1.62	1.58	1.56	1.52	1.47	1.40	1.31
27	.001	13.61	9.02	7.27	6.33	5.73	5.31	4.76	4.17	3.52	2.75
	.005	9.34	6.49	5.36	4.74	4.34	4.06	3.69	3.28	2.83	2.29
	.01	7.68	5.49	4.60	4.11	3.78	3.56	3.26	2.93	2.55	2.10
	.025	5.63	4.24	3.65	3.31	3.08	2.92	2.71	2.47	2.19	1.85
	.05	4.21	3.35	2.96	2.73	2.57	2.46	2.30	2.13	1.93	1.67
	.10	2.90	2.51	2.30	2.17	2.07	2.00	1.91	1.80	1.67	1.49
	.20	1.73	1.71	1.66	1.61	1.58	1.55	1.51	1.46	1.40	1.30
28	.001	13.50	8.93	7.19	6.25	5.66	5.24	4.69	4.11	3.46	2.70
	.005	9.28	6.44	5.32	4.70	4.30	4.02	3.65	3.25	2.79	2.25
	.01	7.64	5.45	4.57	4.07	3.75	3.53	3.23	2.90	2.52	2.06
	.025	5.61	4.22	3.63	3.29	3.06	2.90	2.69	2.45	2.17	1.83
	.05	4.20	3.34	2.95	2.71	2.56	2.44	2.29	2.12	1.91	1.65
	.10	2.89	2.50	2.29	2.16	2.06	2.00	1.90	1.79	1.66	1.48
	.20	1.72	1.71	1.65	1.61	1.57	1.55	1.51	1.46	1.39	1.30

Table B.3   F Values and Their Associated p Values *(continued)*

df_2	df_1 p	1	2	3	4	5	6	8	12	24	∞
29	.001	13.39	8.85	7.12	6.19	5.59	5.18	4.64	4.05	3.41	2.64
	.005	9.23	6.40	5.28	4.66	4.26	3.98	3.61	3.21	2.76	2.21
	.01	7.60	5.42	4.54	4.04	3.73	3.50	3.20	2.87	2.49	2.03
	.025	5.59	4.20	3.61	3.27	3.04	2.88	2.67	2.43	2.15	1.81
	.05	4.18	3.33	2.93	2.70	2.54	2.43	2.28	2.10	1.90	1.64
	.10	2.89	2.50	2.28	2.15	2.06	1.99	1.89	1.78	1.65	1.47
	.20	1.72	1.70	1.65	1.60	1.57	1.54	1.50	1.45	1.39	1.29
30	.001	13.29	8.77	7.05	6.12	5.53	5.12	4.58	4.00	3.36	2.59
	.005	9.18	6.35	5.24	4.62	4.23	3.95	3.58	3.18	2.73	2.18
	.01	7.56	5.39	4.51	4.02	3.70	3.47	3.17	2.84	2.47	2.01
	.025	5.57	4.18	3.59	3.25	3.03	2.87	2.65	2.41	2.14	1.79
	.05	4.17	3.32	2.92	2.69	2.53	2.42	2.27	2.09	1.89	1.62
	.10	2.88	2.49	2.28	2.14	2.05	1.98	1.88	1.77	1.64	1.46
	.20	1.72	1.70	1.64	1.60	1.57	1.54	1.50	1.45	1.38	1.28
40	.001	12.61	8.25	6.60	5.70	5.13	4.73	4.21	3.64	3.01	2.23
	.005	8.83	6.07	4.98	4.37	3.99	3.71	3.35	2.95	2.50	1.93
	.01	7.31	5.18	4.31	3.83	3.51	3.29	2.99	2.66	2.29	1.80
	.025	5.42	4.05	3.46	3.13	2.90	2.74	2.53	2.29	2.01	1.64
	.05	4.08	3.23	2.84	2.61	2.45	2.34	2.18	2.00	1.79	1.51
	.10	2.84	2.44	2.23	2.09	2.00	1.93	1.83	1.71	1.57	1.38
	.20	1.70	1.68	1.62	1.57	1.54	1.51	1.47	1.41	1.34	1.24
60	.001	11.97	7.76	6.17	5.31	4.76	4.37	3.87	3.31	2.69	1.90
	.005	8.49	5.80	4.73	4.14	3.76	3.49	3.13	2.74	2.29	1.69
	.01	7.08	4.98	4.13	3.65	3.34	3.12	2.82	2.50	2.12	1.60
	.025	5.29	3.93	3.34	3.01	2.79	2.63	2.41	2.17	1.88	1.48
	.05	4.00	3.15	2.76	2.52	2.37	2.25	2.10	1.92	1.70	1.39
	.10	2.79	2.39	2.18	2.04	1.95	1.87	1.77	1.66	1.51	1.29
	.20	1.68	1.65	1.59	1.55	1.51	1.48	1.44	1.38	1.31	1.18
120	.001	11.38	7.31	5.79	4.95	4.42	4.04	3.55	3.02	2.40	1.56
	.005	8.18	5.54	4.50	3.92	3.55	3.28	2.93	2.54	2.09	1.43
	.01	6.85	4.79	3.95	3.48	3.17	2.96	2.66	2.34	1.95	1.38
	.025	5.15	3.80	3.23	2.89	2.67	2.52	2.30	2.05	1.76	1.31
	.05	3.92	3.07	2.68	2.45	2.29	2.17	2.02	1.83	1.61	1.25
	.10	2.75	2.35	2.13	1.99	1.90	1.82	1.72	1.60	1.45	1.19
	.20	1.66	1.63	1.57	1.52	1.48	1.45	1.41	1.35	1.27	1.12
∞	.001	10.83	6.91	5.42	4.62	4.10	3.74	3.27	2.74	2.13	1.00
	.005	7.88	5.30	4.28	3.72	3.35	3.09	2.74	2.36	1.90	1.00
	.01	6.64	4.60	3.78	3.32	3.02	2.80	2.51	2.18	1.79	1.00
	.025	5.02	3.69	3.12	2.79	2.57	2.41	2.19	1.94	1.64	1.00
	.05	3.84	2.99	2.60	2.37	2.21	2.09	1.94	1.75	1.52	1.00
	.10	2.71	2.30	2.08	1.94	1.85	1.77	1.67	1.55	1.38	1.00
	.20	1.64	1.61	1.55	1.50	1.46	1.43	1.38	1.32	1.23	1.00

Source: Reproduced from Table V of R. A. Fisher and F. Yates, *Statistical Tables for Biological, Agricultural and Medical Research* (6th ed.), 1974, published by Longman Group UK Ltd., London (previously published by Oliver and Boyd Ltd., Edinburgh) and by permission of the authors and publishers. The 0.5% and 2.5% points are reproduced from "Tables of Percentage Points of the Inverted Beta *(F)* Distribution," *Biometrika,* Vol. 33 (April 1943), pp. 73–88, by permission of the Biometrika Trustees, Imperial College of Science, Technology, and Medicine, London, England.

Appendix B

Table B.4 χ^2 Values and Their Associated p Values

Probability

df	.99	.98	.95	.90	.80	.70	.50	.30	.20	.10	.05	.02	.01	.001
1	.0³157	.0³628	.00393	.0158	.0642	.148	.455	1.074	1.642	2.706	3.841	5.412	6.635	10.827
2	.0201	.0404	.103	.211	.446	.713	1.386	2.408	3.219	4.605	5.991	7.824	9.210	13.815
3	.115	.185	.352	.584	1.005	1.424	2.366	3.665	4.642	6.251	7.815	9.837	11.345	16.268
4	.297	.429	.711	1.064	1.649	2.195	3.357	4.878	5.989	7.779	9.488	11.668	13.277	18.465
5	.554	.752	1.145	1.610	2.343	3.000	4.351	6.064	7.289	9.236	11.070	13.388	15.086	20.517
6	.872	1.134	1.635	2.204	3.070	3.828	5.348	7.231	8.558	10.645	12.592	15.033	16.812	22.457
7	1.239	1.564	2.167	2.833	3.822	4.671	6.346	8.383	9.803	12.017	14.067	16.622	18.475	24.322
8	1.646	2.032	2.733	3.490	4.594	5.527	7.344	9.524	11.030	13.362	15.507	18.168	20.090	26.125
9	2.088	2.532	3.325	4.168	5.380	6.393	8.343	10.656	12.242	14.684	16.919	19.679	21.666	27.877
10	2.558	3.059	3.940	4.865	6.179	7.267	9.342	11.781	13.442	15.987	18.307	21.161	23.209	29.588
11	3.053	3.609	4.575	5.578	6.989	8.148	10.341	12.899	14.631	17.275	19.675	22.618	24.725	31.264
12	3.571	4.178	5.226	6.304	7.807	9.034	11.340	14.011	15.812	18.549	21.026	24.054	26.217	32.909
13	4.107	4.765	5.892	7.042	8.634	9.926	12.340	15.119	16.985	19.812	22.362	25.472	27.688	34.528
14	4.660	5.368	6.571	7.790	9.467	10.821	13.339	16.222	18.151	21.064	23.685	26.873	29.141	36.123
15	5.229	5.985	7.261	8.547	10.307	11.721	14.339	17.322	19.311	22.307	24.996	28.529	30.578	37.697
16	5.812	6.614	7.962	9.312	11.152	12.624	15.338	18.418	20.465	23.542	26.296	29.633	32.000	39.252
17	6.408	7.255	8.672	10.085	12.002	13.531	16.338	19.511	21.615	24.769	27.587	30.995	33.409	40.790
18	7.015	7.906	9.390	10.865	12.857	14.440	17.338	20.601	22.760	25.989	28.869	32.346	34.805	42.312
19	7.633	8.567	10.117	11.651	13.716	15.352	18.338	21.689	23.900	27.204	30.144	33.687	36.191	43.820
20	8.260	9.237	10.851	12.443	14.578	16.266	19.337	22.775	25.038	28.412	31.410	35.020	37.566	45.315
21	8.897	9.915	11.591	13.240	15.445	17.182	20.337	23.858	26.171	29.615	32.671	36.343	38.932	46.797
22	9.542	10.600	12.338	14.041	16.314	18.101	21.337	24.939	27.301	30.813	33.924	37.659	40.289	48.268
23	10.196	11.293	13.091	14.848	17.187	19.021	22.337	26.018	28.429	32.007	35.172	38.968	41.638	49.728
24	10.856	11.992	13.848	15.659	18.062	19.943	23.337	27.096	29.553	33.196	36.415	40.270	42.980	51.179
25	11.524	12.697	14.611	16.473	18.940	20.867	24.337	28.172	30.675	34.382	37.652	41.566	44.314	52.620
26	12.198	13.409	15.379	17.292	19.820	21.792	25.336	29.246	31.795	35.563	38.885	42.856	45.642	54.052
27	12.879	14.125	16.151	18.114	20.703	22.719	26.336	30.319	32.912	36.741	40.113	44.140	46.963	55.476
28	13.565	14.847	16.928	18.939	21.588	23.647	27.336	31.391	34.027	37.916	41.337	45.419	48.278	56.893
29	14.256	15.574	17.708	19.768	22.475	24.577	28.336	32.461	35.139	39.087	42.557	46.693	49.588	58.302
30	14.953	16.306	18.493	20.599	23.364	25.508	29.336	33.530	36.250	40.256	43.773	47.962	50.892	59.703

Source: Reproduced from Table III of R. A. Fisher, *Statistical Methods for Research Workers*, (14th ed.), 1973, copyright by Oxford University Press, England. Used by permission of Oxford University Press (originally published by Oliver and Boyd, Ltd.).

Table B.5 r Values and Their Associated p Values

$(N-2)$	Probability level				
	.10	.05	.02	.01	.001
1	.988	.997	.9995	.9999	1.000
2	.900	.950	.980	.990	.999
3	.805	.878	.934	.959	.991
4	.729	.811	.882	.917	.974
5	.669	.754	.833	.874	.951
6	.622	.707	.789	.834	.925
7	.582	.666	.750	.798	.898
8	.549	.632	.716	.765	.872
9	.522	.602	.685	.735	.847
10	.497	.576	.658	.708	.823
11	.476	.553	.634	.684	.801
12	.458	.532	.612	.661	.780
13	.441	.514	.592	.641	.760
14	.426	.497	.574	.623	.742
15	.412	.482	.558	.606	.725
16	.400	.468	.542	.590	.708
17	.389	.456	.528	.575	.693
18	.378	.444	.516	.561	.679
19	.369	.433	.503	.549	.665
20	.360	.423	.492	.537	.652
22	.344	.404	.472	.515	.629
24	.330	.388	.453	.496	.607
25	.323	.381	.445	.487	.597
30	.296	.349	.409	.449	.554
35	.275	.325	.381	.418	.519
40	.257	.304	.358	.393	.490
45	.243	.288	.338	.372	.465
50	.231	.273	.322	.354	.443
55	.220	.261	.307	.338	.424
60	.211	.250	.295	.325	.408
65	.203	.240	.284	.312	.393
70	.195	.232	.274	.302	.380
75	.189	.224	.264	.292	.368
80	.183	.217	.256	.283	.357
85	.178	.211	.249	.275	.347
90	.173	.205	.242	.267	.338
95	.168	.200	.236	.260	.329
100	.164	.195	.230	.254	.321
125	.147	.174	.206	.228	.288
150	.134	.159	.189	.208	.264
175	.124	.148	.174	.194	.248
200	.116	.138	.164	.181	.235
300	.095	.113	.134	.148	.188
500	.074	.088	.104	.115	.148
1,000	.052	.062	.073	.081	.104
2,000	.037	.044	.052	.058	.074

Note: All p values are two-tailed in this table.

Source: From *Some Extensions of Student's t and Pearson's r Central Distributions,* by A. L. Sockloff and J. N. Edney, May 1972, Temple University Technical Report 72–5, Measurement and Research Center. Reprinted with the permission of Alan Sockloff.

Appendix B

Table B.6   Transformations of r to Fisher z_r

Second digit of r

r	.00	.01	.02	.03	.04	.05	.06	.07	.08	.09
.0	.000	.010	.020	.030	.040	.050	.060	.070	.080	.090
.1	.100	.110	.121	.131	.141	.151	.161	.172	.182	.192
.2	.203	.213	.224	.234	.245	.255	.266	.277	.288	.299
.3	.310	.321	.332	.343	.354	.365	.377	.388	.400	.412
.4	.424	.436	.448	.460	.472	.485	.497	.510	.523	.536
.5	.549	.563	.576	.590	.604	.618	.633	.648	.662	.678
.6	.693	.709	.725	.741	.758	.775	.793	.811	.829	.848
.7	.867	.887	.908	.929	.950	.973	.996	1.020	1.045	1.071
.8	1.099	1.127	1.157	1.188	1.221	1.256	1.293	1.333	1.376	1.422

Third digit of r

r	.000	.001	.002	.003	.004	.005	.006	.007	.008	.009
.90	1.472	1.478	1.483	1.488	1.494	1.499	1.505	1.510	1.516	1.522
.91	1.528	1.533	1.539	1.545	1.551	1.557	1.564	1.570	1.576	1.583
.92	1.589	1.596	1.602	1.609	1.616	1.623	1.630	1.637	1.644	1.651
.93	1.658	1.666	1.673	1.681	1.689	1.697	1.705	1.713	1.721	1.730
.94	1.738	1.747	1.756	1.764	1.774	1.783	1.792	1.802	1.812	1.822
.95	1.832	1.842	1.853	1.863	1.874	1.886	1.897	1.909	1.921	1.933
.96	1.946	1.959	1.972	1.986	2.000	2.014	2.029	2.044	2.060	2.076
.97	2.092	2.109	2.127	2.146	2.165	2.185	2.205	2.227	2.249	2.273
.98	2.298	2.323	2.351	2.380	2.410	2.443	2.477	2.515	2.555	2.599
.99	2.646	2.700	2.759	2.826	2.903	2.994	3.106	3.250	3.453	3.800

Source: Reprinted by permission from *Statistical Methods,* Eighth Edition by Snedecor and Cochran © 1989 by Iowa State University Press, Ames, IA 50010.

Table B.7   Transformations of Fisher z_r to r

z_r	.00	.01	.02	.03	.04	.05	.06	.07	.08	.09
.0	.000	.010	.020	.030	.040	.050	.060	.070	.080	.090
.1	.100	.110	.119	.129	.139	.149	.159	.168	.178	.187
.2	.197	.207	.216	.226	.236	.245	.254	.264	.273	.282
.3	.291	.300	.310	.319	.327	.336	.345	.354	.363	.371
.4	.380	.389	.397	.405	.414	.422	.430	.438	.446	.454
.5	.462	.470	.478	.485	.493	.500	.508	.515	.523	.530
.6	.537	.544	.551	.558	.565	.572	.578	.585	.592	.598
.7	.604	.611	.617	.623	.629	.635	.641	.647	.653	.658
.8	.664	.670	.675	.680	.686	.691	.696	.701	.706	.711
.9	.716	.721	.726	.731	.735	.740	.744	.749	.753	.757
1.0	.762	.766	.770	.774	.778	.782	.786	.790	.793	.797
1.1	.800	.804	.808	.811	.814	.818	.821	.824	.828	.831
1.2	.834	.837	.840	.843	.846	.848	.851	.854	.856	.859
1.3	.862	.864	.867	.869	.872	.874	.876	.879	.881	.883
1.4	.885	.888	.890	.892	.894	.896	.898	.900	.902	.903
1.5	.905	.907	.909	.910	.912	.914	.915	.917	.919	.920
1.6	.922	.923	.925	.926	.928	.929	.930	.932	.933	.934
1.7	.935	.937	.938	.939	.940	.941	.942	.944	.945	.946
1.8	.947	.948	.949	.950	.951	.952	.953	.954	.954	.955
1.9	.956	.957	.958	.959	.960	.960	.961	.962	.963	.963
2.0	.964	.965	.965	.966	.967	.967	.968	.969	.969	.970
2.1	.970	.971	.972	.972	.973	.973	.974	.974	.975	.975
2.2	.976	.976	.977	.977	.978	.978	.978	.979	.979	.980
2.3	.980	.980	.981	.981	.982	.982	.982	.983	.983	.983
2.4	.984	.984	.984	.985	.985	.985	.986	.986	.986	.986
2.5	.987	.987	.987	.987	.988	.988	.988	.988	.989	.989
2.6	.989	.989	.989	.990	.990	.990	.990	.990	.991	.991
2.7	.991	.991	.991	.992	.992	.992	.992	.992	.992	.992
2.8	.993	.993	.993	.993	.993	.993	.993	.994	.994	.994
2.9	.994	.994	.994	.994	.994	.995	.995	.995	.995	.995

Source: Reprinted by permission from *Statistical Methods, Eighth Edition* by Snedecor and Cochran © 1989 by Iowa State University Press, Ames, IA 50010.

Appendix B

APPENDIX C

Introduction to Meta-Analysis

Utility of Meta-Analysis

Meta-analysis, a term coined by Gene V Glass (1976), is the use of quantitative and graphical methods to sum up a body of similar studies. It is a rapidly growing field which has spawned insights in behavioral and social science, medicine, policymaking, and other areas. Although many different procedures are available, meta-analysts in behavioral science frequently report the same general kind of information (Rosenthal, 1995). The first step in a meta-analysis is to define the problem of interest specifically enough to be addressed by an accessible cluster of relevant studies. The next step is to collate the studies and to develop categories of information for judges to code (e.g., independent and dependent variables, summary statistics about the central tendencies and spread of the data, effect sizes and confidence intervals, and so forth).

Once all the information is organized and coded, quantitative and graphical procedures are used to compare and combine the results. For example, we can use stem-and-leaf displays to get an overall impression (illustrated in Figure 10.6 in Chapter 10), and we can use statistical methods to see the degree to which different studies constitute a homogeneous cluster. Especially if we find they are heterogeneous, we may want to divide them into conceptually meaningful subgroups and explore for moderator variables that may have altered the size of the effects in different subgroups. Other procedures combine the conceptually related results into a meaningful mosaic revealing patterns in the data. Studies with seemingly contradictory results sound a clarion call for a meta-analytic examination to help explain the differences with the help of moderator variables.

The purpose of this appendix is to give you a flavor of some procedures used to compare and combine p values and effect size rs, although we limit this discussion to the meta-analysis of two independent studies. We also give an example of the detective-like probing of reported data for an unreported effect size, when all we have in hand are certain meager raw ingredients in the published report. And finally, we describe the "file drawer problem" and how it is handled. If you would like to learn more about meta-analysis, you will find Morton Hunt's *How Science Takes Stock* (1997) to be an engaging introduction to this field, and you will find comprehensive reviews in Harris M. Cooper and Larry V. Hedges's *Handbook of Research Synthesis* (1994) and in a number of basic and advanced texts (e.g, Cook et al., 1994; H. M. Cooper, 1989; Glass, McGaw, & Smith, 1981; Hedges & Olkin, 1985; Hunter & Schmidt, 1990; Light & Pillemer, 1984; Mullen & Rosenthal, 1985; Rosenthal, 1991; Rosenthal & Rosnow, 1991).

Importance of Effect Sizes

Throughout the second half of this book, we have emphasized the importance of using the effect size as one indicator of the "practical importance" of the results. For example, in a classic meta-analysis, Mary Lee Smith and Gene V Glass (1977) used meta-analysis to answer the question of whether psychotherapy really works. They synthesized the results of nearly 400 controlled evaluations of psychotherapy and counseling, coding and systematically analyzing each study for the kind of experimental and control conditions and the results obtained. They were able to show that, on the average, the typical psychotherapy client was better off than 75% of the untreated "control" individuals.

In their meta-analysis, Smith and Glass concentrated on the analysis of "average" effect sizes (but not the simple arithmetic average, as we will show in a moment) rather than merely on p values. The reason why meta-analysts are usually more interested in effect sizes than in p values is illustrated in Table C.1 (Rosenthal, 1990c). Set A shows two results with the p values rejecting the null (i.e., both $ps = .05$) and with a difference in effect sizes of .30 in units of r (i.e., $.50 - .20 = .30$). That both studies were able to reject the null and at exactly the same p level is a function of sample size, whereas the difference in effect sizes implies the degree of failure to replicate. Set B shows two studies with different p values, one significant at $p < .05$ and the other not significant; the two effect sizes, on the other hand, are in excellent agreement.

The meta-analyst would say, accordingly, that Set B shows more successful replication than does Set A. Set C shows two studies differing markedly in both level of significance and magnitude (and direction) of effect size. Observe that one of the effects is reported as a negative r, which in the language of meta-analysis tells us that this result was not in the same direction as the other result. Set C, then, is a not very subtle example of a clear failure to replicate. That the combined probabilities of all three sets are identical to one another (combined $p = .0028$) teaches that the pooled significance level is uninformative in differentiating successful from unsuccessful sets of replication studies.

Another way of looking at the effect size results is illustrated in Figure C.1, which shows the **replication plane** generated by crossing the effect size r of the first study with the results of the second study. All perfect replications (i.e., those in which the

Table C.1	Comparison of Three Sets of Replications					
	Set A		Set B		Set C	
	Study 1	Study 2	Study 1	Study 2	Study 1	Study 2
N	96	15	98	27	12	32
p (two-tail)	.05	.05	.01	.18	.000001	.33
r_{effect}	.20	.50	.26	.26	.72	−.18
Combined p (one-tail)		.0028		.0028		.0028

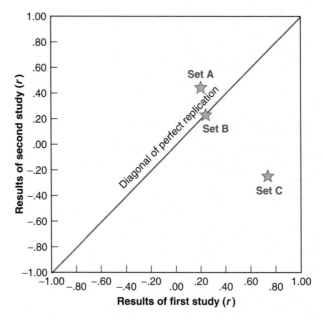

Figure C.1 The replication plane.

Source: Adapted from Rosenthal, 1990c.

effect sizes in the two studies are identical) fall on a diagonal rising from the lower left corner $(-1.0, -1.0)$ to the upper right corner $(+1.0, +1.0)$. The results of the studies in Set B from Table C.1 are shown to fall exactly on the diagonal of perfect replication $(+.26, +.26)$. The results of Set A fall somewhat above the line representing perfect replication. In sum, the figure shows that, although Set B reflects more successful replication than Set A, Set A is also located fairly close to the line and is therefore a "fairly successful" replication set as well. The results of Set C, however, fall rather far from the diagonal of perfect replication.

Comparing Two Effect Sizes

So far, we have examined the results of separate but similar studies, and we now describe how the meta-analyst might use statistical techniques in this process. Before synthesizing the effect sizes of separate studies, the meta-analyst usually finds it instructive to compare the results to learn the degree of their actual similarity. One common approach is to define the effect size rs as heterogeneous if they are significantly different from one another, and as homogeneous if they are not significantly different from one another. In using this approach, we must be careful not to fall into the trap of equating significance values with effect sizes, however. This analysis can be done in four steps.

First, we give the rs the same sign if both studies show effects in the same direction, but different signs if the results are in the opposite direction. Second, we find for each r the Fisher z_r, which (as you learned in Chapter 12) is the log transformation of

r found in Table B.6 (p. 418). Third, we substitute in the following to find the standard normal deviate (z) corresponding to the difference between **Fisher z_rs**:

$$z \text{ of difference} = \frac{z_{r_1} - z_{r_2}}{\sqrt{\dfrac{1}{N_1 - 3} + \dfrac{1}{N_2 - 3}}}$$

where z_{r_1} and z_{r_2} are the log transformations found in Step 2 for the effect size rs of Studies 1 and 2, respectively, and N_1 and N_2 are the total sample sizes of Studies 1 and 2, respectively. The final step is to look up the result in Table B.1 (p. 408), which gives the associated p value of the z of difference. Let us try some examples.

Example 1. Suppose you have used 100 subjects to try to replicate an experiment that reported a large effect ($r_{\text{effect}} = .50$) based on only 10 subjects. You find a smaller sized effect ($r_{\text{effect}} = .31$), but it is in the opposite direction of the one previously reported. You code your effect as negative, to reflect the fact that it is in the opposite direction, and then consult Table B.6 (p. 418) to find the Fisher z_r corresponding to each r_{effect}. For $r = .50$, you find $z_r = .549$ at the intersection of the ".5" row and ".00" column. For $r = -.31$, you find $z_r = .321$ at the ".3" row and ".01" column intersection, and code the result as $-.321$ because your empirical finding was in the "wrong" direction.

Next, from the previous formula, you compute

$$z = \frac{z_{r_1} - z_{r_2}}{\sqrt{\dfrac{1}{N_1 - 3} + \dfrac{1}{N_2 - 3}}} = \frac{(.549) - (-.321)}{\sqrt{\dfrac{1}{7} + \dfrac{1}{97}}} = \frac{.870}{.391} = 2.22$$

as the z of the difference between the two effect sizes. Finally, looking up the p value associated with a z of 2.22 in Table B.1 (p. 408), you find $p = .0132$ one-tail, which you can round to .01 one-tail or .03 two-tail (i.e., $.0132 \times 2 = .03$ rounded). The p value is small enough to convince you that your result differs from the original one, and because the difference between the r values is so large as well as significant statistically, you wisely decide they should not be combined without careful thought and comment. In describing the results of both studies considered together, you would report the differences between them and try to think of an explanation for their differences.

Example 2. Alternatively, suppose your result is in the same direction as the original one and of a similar magnitude, and you have used the same number of subjects. This time, imagine that the original effect size was $r_{\text{effect}} = .45$ ($N = 120$) and your effect size is $r_{\text{effect}} = .40$ ($N = 120$). Following the same procedure as in Example 1, you find in Table B.6 the z_r values corresponding to these effect size rs to be .485 and .424, respectively.

From the preceding formula you compute

$$z = \frac{z_{r_1} - z_{r_2}}{\sqrt{\dfrac{1}{N_1 - 3} + \dfrac{1}{N_2 - 3}}} = \frac{.485 - .424}{\sqrt{\dfrac{1}{117} + \dfrac{1}{117}}} = \frac{.061}{.131} = .47$$

Appendix C

as your obtained z of the difference. In Table B.1, you find the p associated with $z =$ .47 to be .3192 one-tail. Here, then, is an example of two studies that do not disagree significantly in their estimates of the size of the relation between X and Y, and are quite similar in magnitude. They can now be routinely combined by means of a simple meta-analytic technique, as shown next.

Combining Two Effect Sizes

Given two effect size rs that are combinable on statistical and/or logical grounds, we can find out the typical (or average) effect size by using the following formula

$$\text{Mean } z_r = \frac{z_{r_1} + z_{r_2}}{2}$$

and afterward transforming the resulting Fisher z_r into the metric of an effect size correlation. In this formula the denominator is the number of z_r scores in the numerator; the resulting value is an average Fisher z_r (also symbolized as $\bar{z}_r$, where the bar over the z denotes that it is a mean value). Example 3 shows how this number crunching proceeds.

Example 3. In Example 2, one $r_{\text{effect}} = .45$ and the other $r_{\text{effect}} = .40$ (both coded as positive to show that both results were in the predicted direction. You found the Fisher z_r scores corresponding to the effect size rs to be .485 and .424, respectively. From the formula above you compute

$$\bar{z}_r = \frac{z_{r_1} + z_{r_2}}{2} = \frac{.485 + .424}{2} = .45$$

as the average Fisher z_r. Finally, looking in Table B.7 (p. 419), you find that a Fisher z_r of .45 is associated with an r of .422, which is the r_{effect} estimate of the two studies combined.

Comparing Two Significance Levels

Meta-analysts are typically more interested in effect sizes than in p values, but they sometimes find it useful to compare significance levels. To make such a comparison, the meta-analyst first obtains an accurate p value—accurate, say, to two digits (not counting zeros before the first nonzero value), such as $p = .43$ or .024 or .0012. That is, if t with 30 $df = 3.03$, we code p as .0025, not as $p < .05$. Extended tables of the t distribution may be helpful here (such as Table B.2 on p. 409), but more helpful still is to use a computer or to have a calculator that spits out accurate ps at the touch of a couple of buttons.

For each p, the meta-analyst finds z (not the Fisher z_r, but the standard normal deviate z). The table of zs in Appendix B (Table B.1) will be helpful if the meta-analyst does not have a calculator that gives accurate values of p. Both ps should also be one-tailed, and we give the corresponding zs the same sign if both studies showed effects in the same direction, but different signs if the results are in the opposite direction. The difference between the two zs when divided by the square root of 2 yields a new z. This new z corresponds to the p value of the difference between the two zs if the null hypothesis were true (i.e., if the two zs did not really differ).

Recapping, we solve for the difference between two zs by using the following formula to compute the z of the difference:

$$z \text{ of difference} = \frac{z_1 - z_2}{\sqrt{2}}$$

and we enter this newly calculated z in a table of standard normal deviates to find the p value associated with a z of the size obtained or larger.

Example 4. Suppose that Studies A and B yield results in opposite directions, and neither is "significant." One p is .075 one-tail, and the other p is .109 one-tail, but in the opposite tail. The zs corresponding to these ps are found in Table B.1 to be $+1.44$ and -1.23 (note the opposite signs, which indicate results in opposite directions). Then, for our formula, we have

$$z = \frac{z_1 - z_2}{\sqrt{2}} = \frac{(1.44) - (-1.23)}{\sqrt{2}} = \frac{2.67}{1.41} = 1.89$$

as the z of the difference between the two p values or their corresponding zs. The p associated with a z of 1.89 is .0294 one-tail (rounded to .03). The two p values may thus be seen to differ significantly (or nearly so, if we used the two-tailed p of .0294 $\times$ 2 = .0588).

Example 5. Alternatively, suppose that Studies A and B yield results in the same direction. However, although the p values appear to be very similar, one result is called "significant" by the author of A because $p = .05$, and the other is called "not significant" by the author of B because $p = .07$. The zs corresponding to these ps are 1.64 and 1.47. From our formula we have

$$z = \frac{z_1 - z_2}{\sqrt{2}} = \frac{1.64 - 1.47}{\sqrt{2}} = \frac{.17}{1.41} = .12$$

as our obtained z of the difference between a p value of .05 and one of .07. The p associated with $z = .12$ is .4522 one-tail and thus shows clearly (as noted in Chapter 10) just how trivial the conventional line of demarcation between "significant" and "nonsignificant" results sometimes is.

Combining Two Significance Levels

It is an easy matter to combine the p values and get an overall estimate of the probability that the two ps might have been obtained if the null hypothesis of no relation between X and Y were true. To perform these calculations, we modify the numerator of the formula for comparing p values that we just described. We obtain accurate p values for each of the two studies and then find the z corresponding to each of these

p values. Also, as before, both ps must be given in one-tailed form, and the corresponding zs will have the same sign if both studies show effects in the same direction and will have different signs if the results are in the opposite direction.

The only change in the previous formula is to add the z values instead of subtracting them:

$$\text{Combined } z = \frac{z_1 + z_2}{\sqrt{2}}$$

That is, the sum of the two zs when divided by the square root of the number of zs combined yields a new z. This new z corresponds to the p value of the two studies combined if the null hypothesis of no relation between X and Y were true.

Example 6. As an illustration, suppose Studies A and B yield homogeneous results in the same direction but neither is statistically significant. One p is .121, and the other is .084; their zs are 1.17 and 1.38, respectively. From the preceding formula we have

$$z = \frac{z_1 + z_2}{\sqrt{2}} = \frac{1.17 + 1.38}{\sqrt{2}} = \frac{2.55}{1.41} = 1.81$$

as our combined z. The p associated with this z is .035 one-tail (or .07 two-tail).

Detective-Like Probing of Reported Data

For our illustrations of meta-analytic comparisons and combinations of rs and ps, we have focused on the case of only two results to be compared or combined. However, meta-analysts generally work with scores of results to be coded, compared, and combined. The procedures used are quite similar in spirit to the procedures described above, and you will find descriptions in the texts cited at the beginning of this appendix. Those texts also contain tips on how to estimate effect sizes when the published reports provide only limited details. To give you a flavor of how this detective-like probing is done, let us say we were interested in knowing the effect size r but all that is provided is that $N = 36$ and $p = .005$ in a 2×2 chi-square. Nevertheless, we can estimate the corresponding phi (ϕ) coefficient (i.e., r_{effect}) because of the relationship of χ^2 to z.

When χ^2 is based on 1 df, the square root of the χ^2 is equal to z; that is,

$$\sqrt{\chi^2} = z$$

In Chapter 15, you learned that, if $N > 20$ and the smallest expected frequency is greater than 3 or so, we can test the significance of phi coefficients by

$$\chi^2 = (\phi^2)(N)$$

So it follows that

$$\sqrt{\chi^2} = z = (\phi)(\sqrt{N})$$

and thus

$$\phi = \frac{z}{\sqrt{N}}$$

Given this relationship, we find the z associated with the reported $p = .005$ for the 2×2 chi-square (i.e., $1\ df\ \chi^2$) to be 2.58 in Table B.1 (p. 408). We then substitute $z = 2.58$ and $N = 36$ in the above formula and find

$$r_{\text{effect}} = \frac{z}{\sqrt{N}} = \frac{2.58}{\sqrt{36}} = .43$$

which is our approximation of the obtained effect, given the meager ingredients we had to work with.

The File Drawer Problem

Because many journal editors are reluctant to accept "nonsignificant" results, researchers' file drawers may contain unpublished studies that failed to yield significant results (Bakan, 1967; Sterling, 1959). If there were a substantial number of such studies in the file drawers, the meta-analyst's evaluation of the overall significance level might be unduly optimistic. One solution to this **file drawer problem** is to calculate the number of studies averaging null results that would be required to nudge the significance level for *all* studies (i.e., retrieved and unretrieved combined) to the

Number of studies summarized	Original average significance level		
	.05	.01	.001
1	1	2	4
2	4	8	15
3	9	18	32
4	16	32	57
5	25	50	89
6	36	72	128
7	49	98	173
8	64	128	226
9	81	162	286
10	100	200	353
15	225	450	795
20	400	800	1,412
25	625	1,250	2,206
30	900	1,800	3,177
40	1,600	3,200	5,648
50	2,500	5,000	8,824

Table C.2   Tolerances for Future Null Results

Note: Entries in this table are the total number of old and new studies required to bring an original average p of .05, .01, or .001 down to an overall $p > .05$ (i.e., just barely to "nonsignificance").

"wrong" side of $p = .05$ (Rosenthal, 1979, 1983, 1991). If the overall significance level computed on the basis of the retrieved studies can be brought down to the wrong side of p (i.e., $p > .05$) by the addition of just a few more null results, then the original estimate of p is clearly *not robust* (i.e., not resistant to the file drawer threat).

Table C.2 illustrates the results of such calculations. It shows a table of "tolerance" values in which the rows represent the number of retrieved (i.e., meta-analyzed) studies and the columns represent three different levels of the average statistical significance of the retrieved studies. The intersection of any row and column shows the sum of old and new studies required to bring the p for all studies (i.e., retrieved *and* unretrieved) down to the level of being barely "nonsignificant" at $p > .05$. Suppose we meta-analyzed eight studies and found the average (not the combined, but the mean) p value to be .05. The 64 that is shown tells us that it will take an additional 56 unretrieved studies averaging null results to bring the original average $p = .05$ based on eight studies (i.e., $64 - 8 = 56$) down to an overall $p > .05$.

As a general rule of thumb, it has been suggested that we regard as robust any combined results for which the tolerance level reaches $5(k) + 10$, where k is the number of studies retrieved (Rosenthal, 1991). In our example of eight studies retrieved, this means that we will be satisfied that the original conclusion that $p \leq .05$ is robust if we feel that there are fewer than an additional $5(8) + 10 = 50$ studies with null results squirreled away in file drawers. Because Table C.2 shows a tolerance for an additional 56 studies, we decide that the original conclusion is robust.

Glossary

Note: Indicated in parentheses is the primary chapter(s) or appendix where each term is discussed.

A-B design Simplest *N*-of-1 design, in which the dependent variable is measured throughout the pretreatment or baseline period (the A phase) and the treatment period (the B phase). (8)

A-B-A design *N*-of-1 design in which there are repeated measures before the treatment (the A phase), during the treatment (the B phase), and then with the treatment withdrawn (the final A phase). (8)

A-B-A-B design *N*-of-1 design in which there are two types of occasions (B to A and A to B) for demonstrating the effects of the treatment variable. (8)

A-B-A-B-A design *N*-of-1 design in which there are repeated measures before, during, and after treatment (the B phase). (8)

A-B-BC-B design *N*-of-1 design in which there are repeated measures before the introduction of the treatments (the A phase), then during Treatment B, during the combination of Treatments B and C, and, finally, during Treatment B alone; the purpose of the design is to tease out the effect of B both in combination with C and apart from C. (8)

Abscissa See *x axis*.

Abstract Brief, comprehensive summary of the content of a paper. (Appendix A)

Acceptability stage Stage 3 of discovery, in which a working hypothesis is fashioned according to the criteria of correspondence with reality, a combination of coherence and parsimony, and falsifiability. (2)

Accidental plagiarism Unwittingly falling into plagiarism. (2)

Accounting for conflicting results One of several possible scenarios for coming up with an acceptable idea. (2)

Acquiescent response set The tendency of individuals to go along with any request or attitudinal statement. (5)

Active deception (deception by commission) Actively misleading subjects, such as giving them false information about the purpose of the research, or by having them unwittingly interact with confederates. (3)

Additive model The components sum to the group means in ANOVA. (14)

Ad hoc hypothesis A conjecture or speculation developed on the spot to explain a result. (1)

Aesthetics The idea that intellectual beauty is one criterion of accepted truths. (1)

Aimlessness Hit-or-miss sampling. (9)

Alpha (α) Probability of a Type I error. (12)

Alpha coefficient See *Cronbach's alpha*.

Alternate-form reliability The correlation between two forms of a test with different items that are measuring the same attribute. (6)

Alternate hypothesis (H_1) The experimental hypothesis. (12)

Analysis of variance (ANOVA) Subdivision of the total variance of a set of scores into its components. (14)

ANOVA See *Analysis of variance*.

Anything-goes view of science Feyerabend's view that doing research involves a "let's try it and see" attitude, where anything that works is permissible. (4)

APA manual *Publication Manual of the American Psychological Association*. (Appendix A)

A priori method The use of individual powers of pure reason and logic as a basis of explanation (Charles Peirce). (1)

Archive   A relatively permanent repository of data or material. (4)

Area probability sampling   A type of survey sampling in which the subclasses are geographic areas. (9)

Arithmetic mean (*M*)   Arithmetic average. (10)

Artifact   A specific threat to validity, or a confounded aspect of the scientist's observations. (7)

Attitude   A predisposition (or "posture of the mind") that is presumed to lead a person to behave one way and not another. (1)

Autonomy   The person's "independence"; in the context of research ethics, also refers to a prospective subject's right as well as ability to "choose" whether to participate in the study or to continue in the study. (3)

Back-to-back stem-and-leaf display   The back-to-back plots of distributions in which the original data are preserved with any desired precision. (10)

Back-translation   See *Translation and back-translation.*

Behavior   What someone does or how someone acts. (1)

Behavioral baseline   A comparison base, operationally defined as the continuous and continuing, performance of a single individual in small-*N* research. (8)

Behavioral diaries   Data collection method in which the research participant keeps a record of events at the time they occur. (5)

Behavioral science   An umbrella term that encompasses scientific disciplines in which empirical inquiry is used to study motivation, cognition, and behavior. (1)

Belmont Report   The name given to a study developed by a national commission in 1974 to protect the rights and welfare of participants in biomedical and behavioral research. (3)

Beneficence   The "doing of good," which is one of the guidelines of the discussed ethical principles. (3)

BESD   See *Binomial effect-size display.*

Beta (β)   Probability of a Type II error. (12)

Between-subjects designs   Statistical designs in which the sampling units (e.g., the research participants) are exposed to one treatment each. (7)

Bias   Net systematic error. (6)

Big Five factors   The collective name for five broad domains of individual personality: (a) neuroticism, (b) extraversion, (c) openness to experience, (d) agreeableness, and (e) conscientiousness. (5)

Bimodal   A distribution showing two modes. (10)

Binomial effect-size display (BESD)   Procedure for the display of the practical importance of an effect size correlation (r_{effect}) of any magnitude. (12)

Bipolar scale   Rating scale in which the ends of the scale are extreme opposites. (5)

Blind experimenters   Experimenters who are unaware of which subjects receive the experimental and control treatments. (7)

Blindness to a relationship   See *Type II error.*

Causal inference   The act or process of inferring that *X* causes *Y*. (7)

Causation   The relation of cause to effect. (7)

Ceiling effect   Situation in which the amount of change that can be produced is limited by the upper boundary of the measure. (5)

Central tendency   Location of the bulk of a distribution; measured by means, medians, modes, and trimmed means. (10)

Central tendency bias   A type of response set in which the respondent is reluctant to give extreme ratings and instead rates in the direction of the mean of the total group. (5)

Certificate of confidentiality   A formal agreement between the investigator and the government agency sponsoring the research that requires the investigator to keep the data confidential. (3)

Checklists   Method of counting the frequency of occurrence. (4)

Chi-square (χ^2)   A statistic used to test the degree of agreement between the data actually obtained and those expected under a particular hypothesis (e.g., the null hypothesis). (15)

Closed (structured, fixed-choice, or precoded) measures   See *Structured items.*

Clusters   See *Strata.*

Coefficient of determination (r^2)   Proportion of variance shared by two variables. (12)

Coherence   The extent to which things (e.g., components of a theory) "stick together" logically. (2)

Cohort   A collection of individuals who were born in the same general period. (8)

Column effects   Column means minus grand mean. (14)

Composite reliability   The aggregate reliability of two or more items or judges' ratings. (6)

Concealed measurement   The use of hidden measurements, such as a hidden recording device to eavesdrop on conversations. (4)

Conceptual definitions   See *Theoretical definitions.*

Concurrent validity   The extent to which test results are correlated with some criterion in the present. (6)

Confidence interval   The upper and lower bounds of a statistic (e.g., the r_{effect}), with confidence defined as $1 - \alpha$. (12)

Confidentiality   Protection of subjects' disclosures against unwarranted access. (3)

Confirmatory data analysis   Analysis of data for the purpose of testing hypotheses. (10)

Confounded hypotheses (in panel designs)   The inability to separate the effect attributed to one hypothesis from the effect attributed to another hypothesis in cross-lagged panel designs. (8)

Connotative meaning   Subjective or representational meaning, that is, one's own subjective associations. (5)

Construct   Abstract variable, formulated from ideas or images, that serves as an explanatory concept. (2)

Construct validity   A type of test or research validity that addresses the psychological qualities contributing to the relation between X and Y. (6)

Content analysis   A method of categorizing communication content based on frequency of occurrence. (4)

Content validity   A type of test validity that addresses whether the test adequately samples the relevant material. (6)

Contingency table   A table of frequencies (counts) coded by row and column variables. (11)

Continuous variable   A variable for which we can imagine another value falling between any two adjacent scores. (11)

Contrived observation   Unobtrusive observation of the effects of some variable that has been introduced into a situation. (4)

Control group   A condition with which the effects of the experimental or test condition are compared. (1, 7)

Convergent validity   Validity supported by a substantial correlation of conceptually similar measures. (6)

Corrected range   See *Extended range.*

Correlated *t*   See *Paired t.*

Correlational design   A class of quasi-experimental designs. (8)

Correlation coefficient   An index of the degree of association between two variables, typically Pearson *r* or related product-moment correlation. (6, 11)

Correspondence with reality   The extent to which a hypothesis agrees with accepted truths based on reliable empirical findings. (2)

Cost-benefit analysis   An evaluation of the ethical and/or methodological pros and cons of studies. (3)

Counterbalancing   A procedure in which some subjects receive Treatment A before Treatment B, and the others receive B before A. (7)

Counts   Frequencies. (11)

Covariation   The principle that, in order to demonstrate causation, what is labeled as the "cause" should be shown to be positively correlated with what is labeled as the "effect." (7)

Criterion validity   The extent to which a measure correlates with one or more criterion variables. (6)

Critical incident technique   Open-ended method that instructs the respondent to describe an observable action the purpose of which is fairly clear to the respondent and the consequences of which are sufficiently definite to leave little doubt about its effects. (5)

Cronbach's alpha   A measure of internal-consistency reliability, proposed by L. J. Cronbach. (6)

Cross-lagged correlations   Correlations of the degree of association between two sets of variables, of which one is treated as a lagged value of the outcome variable. (8)

Cross-lagged panel design   A relational research design using cross-lagged correlations, cross-sectional correlations repeated over time, and test-retest correlations. (8)

Cross-sectional design   Research that takes a slice of time and compares subjects on one or more variables simultaneously. (8)

Crude range   Highest score minus lowest score. (10)

Cue words Guiding labels that define particular points or categories of response. (5)

Dayyan's decree The principle that there may be more than one right answer, and that sometimes two researchers disagree and yet are both right. (2)

Debriefing Disclosing to subjects the nature of the research in which they have participated. (3)

Deception by commission See *Active deception.*

Deception by omission See *Passive deception.*

Decision-plane model A two-dimensional schema of the costs and benefits of doing research. (3)

Degrees of freedom (*df*) The number of observations minus the number of restrictions limiting the observations' freedom to vary. (13)

Demand characteristics The mixture of various hints and cues that govern the subject's perception of his or her role and of the experimenter's hypothesis. (7)

Denotative meaning The dictionary definition or assigned meaning. (5)

Dependent variable A variable the changes in which are viewed as dependent on changes in one or more other (independent) variables. (2)

Descriptive measures Measures such as σ and σ^2 that are used to calculate population values. (10)

Descriptive research An empirical investigation in which the objective is to map out a situation or set of events. (1)

df See *Degrees of freedom.*

Dichotomous variable A variable that is divided into two classes. (11)

Discovery A term in the philosophy of science referring to the origin, creation, or invention of ideas for scientific justification. (2)

Discrete variable A variable taking on two or more distinct values. (11)

Discriminant validity Validity supported by a lack of correlation between conceptually unrelated measures. (6)

Double-blind procedures Procedures in which neither the experimenters nor the subjects know who has been assigned to the experimental and control groups. (7)

Double deception A deception embedded in what the subject thinks is the official debriefing. (3)

Drunkard's search See *Principle of the drunkard's search.*

Dummy coding Giving arbitrary numerical values (often 0 and 1) to the two levels of a dichotomous variable. (11)

Ecological validity The extent to which a laboratory simulation reflects the outside world it is intended to represent. (6)

Effective power The actual power (i.e., $1 - \beta$) of the statistical test used. (12)

Effective sample size The net equivalent sample size that the researcher ends up with. (9)

Effect size The magnitude of an experimental effect (i.e., the size of the relation between X and Y. (6, 12)

Effect size correlation (r_{effect}) The magnitude of an experimental effect defined on the basis of the correlation between X and Y. (12)

Efficient cause The propelling or instigating condition (i.e., the X that sets in motion or alters Y). (7)

Empirical Controlled observation and measurement. (1)

Empirical reasoning A use of logic that is aided by controlled observation and measurement. (1)

Error Fluctuation in measurements; also deviation of a score from the mean of the group or condition. (6, 9, 14)

Error of estimate Closeness of estimate to actual value. (9)

Ethical guidelines A set of principles (such as those discussed here) that help researchers decide what aspects of a study might pose an ethical problem. (3)

Ethics The system of moral values by which behavior is judged. (3)

Ethnographic research The use of a relatively standardized methodology to study how people in a cultural setting make sense of things (i.e., sense making). (4)

Ethnomethodology An ethnographic approach pioneered by Harold Garfinkel.

Evaluation apprehension The experience of feeling anxious about being negatively evaluated, or at least not being positively evaluated. (5, 7)

Evaluation, potency, and activity Three primary dimensions of connotative meaning, which are typically measured by a semantic differential. (5)

Evaluation research   Research designed to evaluate the efficacy or value of a procedure or intervention used in a real-world setting. (4)

Expectancy bias   The idea that the scientist's hypothesis can, in and of itself, affect the likelihood of its confirmation. (2)

Expectancy control design   An experimental design in which the expectancy variable operates separately from the independent variable of interest. (7)

Expected frequency (f_e)   Counts expected under specified row and column conditions if certain hypotheses (e.g., the null hypothesis) are true. (15)

Expedited review   The evaluation of proposed research without undue delay. (3)

Experimental group   A group or condition in which the subjects undergo a manipulation or an intervention. (7)

Experimental hypothesis   See *Working hypothesis*.

Experimental realism   The extent to which the subject is drawn into or is affected by the experimental treatment. (4)

Experimental research   An empirical investigation in which the objective is causal explanation. (1)

Experimenter expectancy effect   Experimenter-related artifact that results when the hypothesis held by the experimenter leads unintentionally to behavior toward the subjects that, in turn, increases the likelihood that the hypothesis will be confirmed (also called a *self-fulfilling prophecy*). (7)

Exploratory data analysis   A detective-like searching for clues, leads, and insights in the data. (10)

Extended range (corrected range)   Crude range plus one unit. (10)

External validity   The degree of generalizability. (6)

Face-to-face interview   An interview in which the interviewer and the respondent directly interact with one another face to face. (5)

Face validity   The extent to which a test seems on its surface to be measuring what it purports to measure. (6)

Fair-mindedness   Impartiality. (3)

False-negative reports   Failure to report information. (5)

Falsifiability (refutability)   The principle (advanced by Karl Popper) that a theoretical assertion is scientific only if it is stated in such a way that it can, if incorrect, be refuted by empirical tests. (2)

Field experiments   Experimental research that is done in a naturalistic setting. (4)

File drawer problem   The concern that a substantial number of studies with nonsignificant results are tucked away in file drawers. (Appendix C)

Final (teleological) cause   The end goal toward which a person or thing tends naturally to strive (Aristotle). (7)

Finite   All the units or events can, at least in theory, be completely counted. (10)

Fisher z_r   The log transformation of r, as shown in Table B.6. (Appendix C)

Fixed-choice measures   See *Structured items*.

Floor effect   Situation in which the amount of change that can be produced is limited by the lower boundary of the measure. (5)

Focused chi-square χ^2 with 1 df. (15)

Focused tests   Any t test, 1-$df\chi^2$, or F with numerator $df = 1$. (14)

Forced-choice scales   Measures that use an item format requiring the respondent to select a single item (or a specified number of items) from a presented set of choices, even when the respondent finds none or more than one of the choices acceptable. (5)

Formal cause   The implicit form or meaning of something (Aristotle). (7)

F ratio   Ratio of mean squares that are distributed as F when the null hypothesis is true, where F is a test of significance used to judge the tenability of the null hypothesis of no relation between two or more variables (or of no difference between two or more variabilities). (14)

F test   See *F ratio*.

Free association method   A method in which the subject tells whatever passes through his or her mind. (2)

Frequency distribution   A chart that shows the number of times each score or other unit of observation occurs in a set of scores. (10)

Frequency polygon   A line-graph distribution of frequencies of occurrence. (10)

Fugitive literature   Hard-to-find material, including unpublished manuscripts, technical reports, and presentations at meetings and conferences. (2)

Generative Theories that allow us to generate new hypotheses and observations. (2)

Good subjects Research participants who seek to provide responses that will validate the experimenter's hypothesis. (7)

Grand mean (M_G) The mean of means, or the mean of all observations. (14)

Graphic scales Rating scales in the form of a straight line with cue words attached. (5)

Gullibility See *Type I error.*

Halo effect A response set in which the bias results from the judge's overextending a favorable impression of someone, based on some central trait, to the person's other characteristics. (5)

Hawthorne effect The effect on research participants of merely being studied. (1)

Hedges's g An index of effect size in z-score-like terms. (13)

Heterogeneity Dissimilarity among the elements of a set. (6)

Histogram A bar chart. (10)

Historical control group Comparison groups in which the subjects are recently examined patients with the same disorder as those subjects in the experimental group. (8)

History A plausible threat to internal validity when an event or incident that takes place between the premeasurement and the postmeasurement contaminates the results of research not using randomization. (7)

Homogeneity Similarity among the elements of a set. (6)

Hypothesis A research idea that serves as a premise or supposition that organizes facts and guides observations. (2)

Improving on older ideas One of several possible scenarios for coming up with an innovative discovery. (2)

Independent One outcome is not influenced by any other. (12)

Independent variable A variable on which the dependent variable depends; in experiments, a variable that the experimenter manipulates to determine whether there are effects on another variable, the dependent variable. (2)

Inferential measures Measures such as S and S^2 that are used to estimate population values based on a sample of values. (10)

Inferential validity The implication is that causal inferences made in a laboratory setting are applicable to the real-life experiences they are meant to represent. (1)

Infinite Boundless, or without limits. (10)

Informed consent The procedure in which prospective subjects, who have been told what they will be getting into, give their formal consent to participate in the research. (3)

Initial thinking stage The first stage in the development of a scientific hypothesis; this stage often involves introspection and intuition. (2)

Institutional review board (IRB) A group set up to make cost-benefit analyses of proposed studies. (3)

Instrumentation A plausible threat to internal validity that occurs when changes in the measuring instrument (e.g., deterioration of the instrument) bias the results of research not using randomization. (7)

Intensive case study An analysis that is characterized by meticulous records and sharp discriminations rather than by the usual casual discriminations and inferences that are associated with our daily encounters with "cases." (2)

Interaction effects (residuals) In factorial designs, condition means minus grand mean, row effects, and column effects. (14)

Interaction of independent variables The combinatory effect of two or more independent variables. (2)

Intercoder reliability The extent to which raters or judges who do coding of data are in agreement. (4)

Interdisciplinary Combining methods and theory from different fields (disciplines) in order to develop a more complete and integrated picture. (1)

Inter-item correlation (r_{ii}) The relation of responses to one item with the responses to another item. (6)

Internal-consistency reliability Reliability based on the intercorrelation among components of a test, such as subtests or all the individual test items. (6)

Internal validity The degree of validity of statements made about whether X causes Y. (6, 7)

Interpreter biases Systematic errors that result when the researcher's interpretation of the observational records is slanted. (4)

Interquartile range The difference between the 75th and 25th percentile. (10)

Interrupted time-series design Research in which the effects of a treatment are inferred from a comparison of the outcome measures obtained at different time intervals before and after the treatment is introduced. (8)

Interval estimates The extent to which point estimates are likely to be in error. (9)

Intervention An experimental treatment. (8)

Interview schedule A script that contains the questions the interviewer will ask. (5)

Item analysis A procedure used for selecting items (e.g., for a Likert attitude scale). (5)

Iterations Repetitions. (15)

Judges Coders, raters, decoders, or others who assist in describing and categorizing ongoing events or existing records of events. (4)

Judge-to-judge reliability (r_{jj}) The relation of one judge's responses with those of another judge. (6)

Justification A term in the philosophy of science referring to the defense or confirmation of hypotheses. (2, 4)

K-R 20 A measure of internal-consistency reliability, developed by Kuder and Richardson. (6)

Latin square design A repeated-measures design with built-in counterbalancing. (7)

Lazy writing Papers saturated with quoted material that, with a little more effort, could be paraphrased. (2)

Leading questions Questions that can constrain responses and produce biased answers. (5)

Leftover effects See *Residual effects.*

Leniency bias A type of rating error in which the ratings are consistently more positive than they should be. (5)

Lie (L) Scale A set of items in the MMPI that were designed to identify respondents who are deliberately trying to appear socially desirable. (5)

Likert scales Attitude scales constructed by the method of summated ratings, developed by Rensis Likert. (5)

Linearity The mutual relation between two variables that resembles a straight line. (11)

Line graph See *Frequency polygon.*

Logical error in rating A type of response set in which the judge gives similar ratings for variables or traits that are only intuitively related. (5)

Longitudinal study Research in which the same subjects are studied over a period of time. (8)

Machine-readable reference databases Another name for computer-based sources of abstracts and reference material, such as PsycLIT. (2)

Main effect The effect of an independent variable apart from its interaction with other independent variables. (14)

Margin of error Interval within which an anticipated value is expected to occur. (9)

Margins Row and column marginal values. (12)

Marlowe-Crowne Social Desirability Scale (MCSD) A standardized test that measures social desirability responding and need for social approval. (6)

Matched t See *Paired t.*

Material cause The substance out of which something is made (Aristotle). (7)

Maturation A plausible threat to internal validity that occurs when results not using randomization are contaminated by the participants' having, for instance, grown older, wiser, stronger, or more experienced between the pretest and the posttest. (7)

Mean The arithmetical average of a set of scores. (10)

Mean square (S^2), or *MS* Variance. (14)

Mean square for error Variance used as the denominator of F ratios. (14)

Median (*Mdn*) The midmost score of a distribution. (10)

Mental imagery Thinking in which images have a hand, which is presumed to be an aspect of theoretical reasoning. (1)

Meta-analysis The use of quantitative and graphical methods to summarize a group of similar studies. (Appendix C)

Metaphor A word or phrase applied to a concept or phenomenon it does not literally denote. (2)

Method of agreement If X, then Y—which implies that X is a sufficient condition of Y (J. S. Mill). (7)

Method of authority The acceptance of an idea as valid because it is stated by someone in a position of power or authority (Charles Peirce). (1)

Method of difference   If not-X, then not-Y—which implies that X is a necessary condition of Y (J. S. Mill). (7)

Method of equal-appearing intervals   An attitude-scaling technique, developed by L. L. Thurstone, in which values are obtained for items on the assumption that the underlying intervals are equidistant; also called a *Thurstone scale*. (5)

Method of self-report   The procedure of having research participants describe their own behavior or state of mind (e.g., used in interviews, questionnaires, and behavioral diaries). (5)

Method of tenacity   Clinging stubbornly to an idea because it seems obvious or is "common sense" (Charles Peirce). (1)

Methodological pluralism   The use of multiple methods of controlled observation in science. (1)

Methodological triangulation   The approach of "zeroing in" on a pattern by using multiple but imperfect perspectives. (4)

Milgram experiments   A set of experiments performed by Stanley Milgram in which he investigated the willingness of subjects to give "electric shocks" to another subject, who was actually a confederate. (3)

Mill's methods   Logical methods (or propositions) popularized by the 19th-century English philosopher J. S. Mill, exemplified by the method of agreement and the method of difference. (7)

Minimal risk   Studies in which the likelihood and extent of harm to subjects is no greater than that typically experienced in everyday life; such studies are generally eligible for an expedited review. (3)

Minnesota Multiphasic Personality Inventory (MMPI)   A structured personality test containing hundreds of statements that reflect general health, sexual attitudes, religious attitudes, emotional state, and so on. (5)

MMPI   See *Minnesota Multiphasic Personality Inventory*.

Mode   The score occurring with the greatest frequency. (10)

Moderator variable   A condition that alters the relation between X and Y. (8, Appendix C)

Mundane realism   A condition in which the various dimensions of the experiment are very similar to those in the real world. (4)

Mutually exclusive   Describing the condition: If A is true, then not-A is false. (12)

N   The total number of scores in a study, whereas the number of scores in one condition or subgroup is denoted as n. (10)

Naturalistic observation   Research that looks at behavior in its usual natural environment. (4)

Necessary condition   A requisite or essential condition. (7, 8)

Need for social approval   The desire to be positively evaluated, or approved of. (6)

Negatively skewed distribution   An asymmetrical distribution in which the pointed end is toward the left (i.e., the negative tail). (10)

Nested design   Another name for the basic between-subjects design because the subjects are "nested" within their own treatment conditions. (7)

N-of-1 experimental design   Another name for single-case experimental designs. (8)

Noise   The variability within the samples. (13)

Nonequivalent-groups design   Nonrandomized research in which the responses of a treatment group and a control group are compared on measures collected at the beginning and end of the research. (8)

Nonlinearity   A relation between two variables that does not resemble a straight line (e.g., U-shaped, J-shaped, and wave-shaped curves). (11)

Nonmaleficence   Not doing harm, which is one of the guidelines of the discussed ethical principles. (3)

Nonreactive observation   Any observation that does not affect what is being observed. (4)

Nonresponse bias   Error that is due to nonresponse or nonparticipation. (9)

Nonskewed distribution   A symmetrical distribution. (10)

Normal distribution   Bell-shaped curve that is completely described by its mean and standard deviation. (10)

Norms   Tables of values representing the typical performance of a given group. (9)

No-shows   Subjects who fail to show up for their scheduled appointments. (10)

Null hypothesis (H_0)   The hypothesis that there is no relation between two or more variables. (12)

Null hypothesis significance testing (NHST) The use of statistics and probabilities to evaluate the null hypothesis. (12)

Numerical scales Rating scales in which the respondent works with a sequence of defined numbers. (5)

Observed frequency (f_o) Counts obtained in specific rows and columns. (15)

Occam's razor The principle that explanations should be as parsimonious as possible (William of Occam). (2)

Omnibus chi-square χ^2 with $df > 1$. (15)

Omnibus tests F with numerator $df > 1$, or χ^2 with $df > 1$. (14)

One-group pre-post design (O-X-O) A pre-experimental design in which the reactions of only one group of subjects are measured before and after exposure to the treatment. (7)

One-shot case study (X-O) A preexperimental design in which the reactions of only one group of subjects are measured after the event or treatment has occurred. (7)

One-tailed p value The p value associated with a result supporting a prediction of a specific direction of a research result, e.g., $M_A > M_B$ or the sign of r is positive. (12)

One-way design A statistical design in which two or more groups comprise a single dimension. (14)

Open-ended measures Questions or items that offer the respondent an opportunity to express feelings, motives, or behaviors spontaneously. (5)

Operational definitions The meaning of a variable in terms of the operations used to measure it or the experimental methods involved in its determination. (2)

Opportunity sample A sample using the first units that are available. (9)

Ordinate See *y axis.*

Outliers Scores lying far outside the normal range. (10)

Page header Two or three words from the title that are typed in the upper-right corner of the manuscript. (Appendix A)

Paired-t (correlated t or matched t) The t test computed on nonindependent samples. (13)

Panel study Another name for a longitudinal study. (8)

Paradoxical incident An occurrence characterized by seemingly self-contradictory aspects. (2)

Parsimony The degree to which the propositions of a theory are "sparing" or "frugal"; see also *Occam's razor.* (2)

Partial concealment Observation in which the researcher conceals only who or what is being observed. (4)

Participant-observer research Studies in which a group or a community is studied from within by a researcher who records behavior as it occurs. (4)

Partitioning of tables Subdividing larger chi-square tables into smaller tables (e.g., into 2×2 tables). (15)

Passive deception (deception by omission) The withholding of certain information from the subjects, such as not informing them of the meaning of their responses when they are given a projective test or not telling them the full details of the study. (3)

Payoff potential Subjective assessment of the likelihood that the idea will be corroborated. (2)

Pearson r correlation coefficient Standard index of linear relationship. (6, 11)

Phi coefficient (ϕ) Pearson r where both variables are dichotomous. (11, 15)

Physical traces Material evidence of behavior. (4)

Pilot testing The evaluation of some aspect of the research before the study is implemented. (5)

Placebo A substance without any pharmacological benefit given as a pseudomedicine to a control group. (3, 7)

Placebo control group A control group that receives a placebo. (7)

Plagiarism Representing someone else's work as one's own. (2)

Plausibility stage That phase in the development of a research hypothesis in which the scientist evaluates the plausibility of an initial lead or idea. (2)

Plausible rival hypotheses Propositions, or sets of propositions, that provide a reasonable alternative to the working hypothesis. (6)

Point estimates Estimates of particular characteristics of the population (e.g, the number of times an event occurs). (9)

Point-biserial correlation (r_{pb}) Pearson r where one of the variables is continuous and the other is dichotomous. (11)

Population The universe of elements from which sample elements are drawn, or the universe of elements to which we want to generalize. (9)

Positively skewed distribution An asymmetrical distribution in which the pointed end is toward the right (i.e., the positive tail). (10)

Posttest-only control-group design An after-only experimental design containing an experimental and a control group. (7)

Power (1 − β) In significance testing, the probability of not making a Type II error. (12)

Power analysis Estimation of the effective power of a statistical test, or of the sample size needed to detect an obtained effect given a specified level of power. (12)

Power of a test The probability, when using a particular test statistic (e.g., t, F, χ^2), of not making a Type II error. (12)

Predictive validity The extent to which a test can predict future outcomes. (6)

Preexperimental designs Research designs in which there is such a total absence of control that they are of minimal value in establishing causality. (7)

Pre-post control-group design Before-after experimental design. (7)

Pretest The measurement made before an experimental manipulation or intervention. (5)

Pretest sensitization The confounding of pretesting and X, the independent variable of interest. (7)

Pretest-treatment interaction The statistical evaluation of pretest sensitization. (7)

Principle of compatibility The principle that the properties of the visual pattern should be compatible with the properties of the data reflected in the graph. (10)

Principle of the drunkard's search The gathering of data in a convenient place but not a relevant one. (1)

Probability The mathematical chance of an event's occurring. (9, 12)

Product-moment correlation Standard index of linear relationship, or Pearson r. (11)

Projective test A psychological measure that operates on the principle that the subject will project some unconscious aspect of his or her life experience and emotions onto ambiguous stimuli in the spontaneous responses that come to mind (e.g, the Rorschach test and the Thematic Apperception Test). (5)

Proportion of variation explained See *Coefficient of determination.*

Pseudoscience Bogus claims masquerading as scientific facts. (1)

Psychophysics The study of the relationship between physical stimuli and our experience of them. (1)

PsycLIT A computerized database of abstracts compiled and distributed by the American Psychological Association. (2)

***p* value** Probability value or level obtained in a test of significance. (12)

Qualitative methods An observation method in which the raw data exist in a nonnumeric form (e.g., reports of conversations). (4)

Quantitative methods Observation methods in which the raw data exist in a numerical form (e.g., observers' or judges' ratings). (4)

Quasi-control subjects Participants who reflect on the context in which an experiment is conducted and speculate on ways in which the context may influence their own and research subjects' behavior. (7)

Quasi-experimental design Research that resembles an experimental design (in that there are treatments, outcome measures, and experimental units), but in which there is no random assignment to create the comparisons from which treatment-caused changes can be inferred. (7, 8)

Quota sampling A procedure that assigns a quota of people to be interviewed and lets the questioner build up a sample that is roughly representative of the population. (9)

r^2 See *Coefficient of determination.*

Random assignment See *Randomization.*

Random digit dialing The researcher selects the first three digits of telephone numbers and then uses a computer program to select the last digits at random. (9)

Random error The effects of uncontrolled variables that cannot be specifically identified; such effects are, theoretically speaking, self-canceling in that the average of the errors will probably equal zero in the long run. (6)

Randomization (random assignment) Random allocation of sampling units to treatment conditions. (7)

Randomized trials Another name for medical experiments that use true experimental designs. (7)

Random selection A sample chosen by chance procedures and with known probabilities of selection. (9)

Range Distance between the highest and lowest scores. (10)

Rating errors (response biases) Systematic errors in responses on rating scales. (5)

Rating scales The common name for a variety of measuring instruments on which the observer or judge gives a numerical value (either explicitly or implicitly) to certain judgments or assessments. (5)

Reactive observation An observation that affects what is being observed or measured. (4)

Refutability See *Falsifiability*.

Relational research An empirical investigation in which the objective is to identify relations among variables. (1)

Reliability The extent to which observations or measures are consistent or stable. (6)

Repeated-measures design Statistical design in which the sampling units generate two or more measurements. (7, 14)

Replicate To repeat or duplicate a scientific observation. (1)

Replication The duplication of a scientific observation, usually an experimental result. (6)

Replication plane A plane generated by crossing the effect size of a study with that of its attempted replication. (Appendix C)

Representative Typical, such as when the segment is representative (or typical) of the larger pool. (9)

Residual (leftover) effects Effects left over when appropriate components are subtracted from scores or means. (7, 14)

Residuals See *Interaction effects*.

Response biases See *Rating errors*.

Retest reliability See *Test-retest reliability*.

Rhetoric of science The language of a given field, which encompasses the proper use of technical definitions, hypotheses and theories, and so forth. (1)

Rival hypotheses Competing hypotheses. (4)

Root mean square See *Standard deviation*.

Rorschach test A projective test that consists of a set of inkblots on pieces of cardboard. (5)

Row effects Row means minus grand mean. (14)

Running head An abbreviated title at the top of published articles. (Appendix A)

Rushton study A field experiment, conducted in a mining company, which raised the ethical issue of fair-mindedness. (3)

Sample A subset of the population. (9)

Sampling plan A design, scheme of action, or procedure that specifies how the participants are to be selected in a survey study. (9)

Sampling units The elements that make up the sample (e.g., people, schools, or cities). (7)

Sampling without replacement A type of random sampling in which a previously selected name cannot be chosen again and must be disregarded in any later draw. (9)

Sampling with replacement A type of random sampling in which the selected names are placed in the selection pool again and may be reselected in subsequent draws. (9)

Scatter diagram See *Scatter* plot.

Scatter plot (scatter diagram) A visual display of the correlation between two variables that looks like a cloud of scattered dots. (11)

Scientific method An outlook (rather than a single method) emphasizing the use of empirical reasoning. (1)

Scientific notation A compact way of reporting numbers with many decimal places. (13)

Secondary observation An observation that is twice removed from the source. (4)

Segmented graphic scale A rating scale in the form of a line that is broken into segments. (5)

Selection A plausible threat to the internal validity of research not using randomization when the kinds of research subjects selected for one treatment group are different from those selected for another group. (7)

Self-report See *Method of self-report*.

Self-selection The subject chooses for himself or herself whether to enter a treatment condition. (7)

Semantic differential method A type of rating procedure in which connotative (or subjective) meaning is judged in terms of several dimensions, usually evaluation, potency, and activity. (5)

Sense making The use of ethnographic methodology to explore how people "make sense" of things. (4)

Serendipity A lucky or accidental discovery. (1, 2)

Signal Information. (13)

Signal-to-noise ratio A ratio of information to lack of information, for example, the ratio of the variability between samples (the signal) to the variability within the samples (the noise). (13)

Significance level (e.g., 5% significance level) The probability of a Type I error. (12)

Simple effects Differences between group or condition means. (14)

Simple factorial design A statistical design in which the two or more levels of each independent variable (or factor) operate in combination with the two or more levels of every other factor. (7)

Simple observation Unobtrusive observation of events without trying to affect them. (4)

Simple random sampling A sampling plan in which the participants are selected individually on the basis of a randomized procedure (e.g, a table of random digits). (9)

Single-case experimental designs Repeated-measures designs in which $N = 1$ subject, or one group. (8)

Size of the study The number of sampling units. (13)

Small-N experimental design Repeated-measures designs in which the treatment effect is evaluated within the same subject or a small number of subjects. (8)

Social constructionism K. J. Gergen's thesis that *no* social situations have intrinsic meaning, but all have meaning imposed on them. (4)

Socially desirable responding The tendency to respond in ways that seem to elicit a favorable evaluation. (5)

Social psychology of the experiment The study of the ways in which subject-related and experimenter-related artifacts operate. (7)

Solomon design A four-group experimental design developed by R. L. Solomon as a means of assessing pretest sensitization effects without contamination by pretesting. (7)

Spearman-Brown "prophecy formula" (R^{SB}) A traditional equation that measures the overall internal-consistency reliability of a test from a knowledge of the reliability of its components. (6)

Spearman rho (r_s) Pearson r computed on scores in ranked form. (11)

Split-half reliability Splitting a test in half and correlating the scores on the halves with one another. (6)

Spread Dispersion or variability. (10)

Stability The extent to which a set of measurements does not vary. (9)

Standard deviation (root mean square) An index of the variability of a set of data around the mean value in a distribution. (10)

Standardized measures Measures of judgment and attitude that require that certain rules be followed in the development, administration, and scoring of the measuring instrument. (5)

Standardizing the margins Setting all row totals equal to each other and all column totals equal to each other. (15)

Standard normal curve Normal curve with mean $= 0$ and $\sigma = 1$. (10)

Standard score (z score) Score converted to a standard deviation unit. (10)

Statistical conclusion validity The relative accuracy of drawing statistical conclusions. (6)

Stem-and-leaf display The plot of a distribution in which the original data are preserved with any desired precision. (10)

Strata (clusters) Subpopulations (or layers) in survey sampling. (9)

Stratified random sampling Probability sampling plan in which a separate sample is randomly selected within each homogeneous stratum (or layer) of the population. (9)

Structured items Response items with fixed options. (5)

Student's t The pen name used by the inventor of the t test, William Sealy Gosset, was "Student." (13)

Sufficient condition A condition that is adequate to bring about some effect or result. (7)

Summated ratings method A method of attitude scaling, developed by Rensis Likert, that uses item analysis to select the best items. (5)

Sum of squares (SS) The sum of the squared deviations from the mean in a set of scores. (14)

Synchronous correlations (in panel designs) Correlations that indicate the degree of relationship of variables at a moment in time. (8)

Systematic error The effect of uncontrolled variables that often can be specifically identified; such effects are, theoretically speaking, not self-canceling (in contrast to the self-canceling nature of random errors). (6)

Systematic observation Observation that is guided or influenced by preexisting questions or hypotheses. (4)

Tally sheets Method of counting frequency of occurrence. (4)

Teleological cause See *Final cause*.

Telephone interview An interview that is conducted by phone rather than face to face. (5)

Temporal precedence The principle that what is labeled as the "cause" must be shown to have occurred before the "effect." (7)

Test-retest correlations (in panel designs) Correlations of temporal stability in cross-lagged panel designs. (8)

Test-retest reliability The degree of consistency of a test or measurement, or of the characteristic it is designed to measure, from one administration to another; also called *retest reliability*. (6)

Tests of simple effects Statistical tests of differences between group or condition means. (14)

Thematic Apperception Test (TAT) A projective test that consists of a set of pictures, usually of people in various life contexts. (5)

Theoretical (conceptual) definitions The meaning of a variable in abstract or conceptual terms. (2)

Theoretical ecumenism The use of more than one relevant theoretical perspective, in order to foster a holistic picture. (1)

Theory A set of proposed explanatory statements connected by logical arguments and by explicit and implicit assumptions. (2)

Third-variable problem A condition in which a variable correlated with X and Y is the cause of both. (11)

Three Rs of humane animal experimentation The argument that scientists should (1) *reduce* the number of animals used in research; (2) *refine* the experiments so that there is less suffering; and (3) *replace* animals with other procedures whenever possible. (3)

Thurstone scale See *Method of equal-appearing intervals*.

Transformation Conversion of data to another mathematical form. (10)

Translation and back-translation Method used in cross-cultural research in which the researcher has one bilingual person translate the questionnaire items from the source to the target language and then has another bilingual person independently translate the items back into the source language. The researcher then compares the original with the twice-translated version to see whether anything important was lost in the translation. (4)

Treatments The procedures or conditions of an experiment. (7)

Trimmed mean The mean of a distribution from which a specified highest and lowest percentage of scores has been dropped. (10)

True experimental designs Research designs characterized by the random assignment of treatment conditions to sampling units. (7)

t test A test of significance used to judge the tenability of the null hypothesis of no relation between two variables. (13)

Two-by-two factorial design A statistical design with two rows and two columns. (7)

Two-tailed p value The p value associated with a result supporting a prediction of a nonspecific direction of a research result; e.g., either $M_A > M_B$ or $M_B > M_A$ or the sign of r is either positive or negative. (12)

Two-way design (or two-way factorial) A statistical design in which each entry in the table is associated with a row variable and a column variable. (14)

Two-way factorial See *Two-way design*.

Type I error (gullibility) The error of rejecting the null hypothesis when it is true. (12)

Type II error (blindness to a relationship) The error of failing to reject the null hypothesis when it is false. (12)

Unbiased Describing a case in which the values produced by the sample coincide with the "true" values of the population. (9)

Unbiased estimator of the population value of σ^2 A specific statistic usually written as S^2. (10)

Unbiased sampling plan Survey design in which the values produced by the samples coincide with the "true" values in the population. (9)

Unobtrusive observation Measurements or observation used to study behavior when the subjects are unaware of being measured or observed. (4)

Unstructured measures   See *Open-ended measures*.

Validity   The degree to which what was observed or measured is the same as what was purported to be observed or measured. (6)

Variability.   See *Spread*.

Variables   Attributes of sampling units that can take on two or more values. (2)

Variance (mean square)   The mean of the squared deviations of scores from their means. (10)

Volunteer bias   Systematic error resulting when participants who volunteer respond differently from how individuals in the general population would respond. (9)

Wait-list control group   The use of a control group in which the subjects wait to be given the experimental treatment until after it has been administered to the experimental group. (4, 8)

Wechsler Adult Intelligence Scale (WAIS)   The most widely used of the individual intelligence tests; divided into verbal and performance scores. (6)

Wild scores   Extreme scores that result from computational or recording mistakes. (10)

Within-subjects design   Statistical design in which the sampling units (e.g., the research participants) generate two or more measurements. (7)

Working hypothesis   A testable supposition; also called an *experimental hypothesis* in experimental research. (2)

***x* axis (abscissa)**   The horizontal axis of a distribution. (10)

***y* axis (ordinate)**   The vertical axis of a distribution. (10)

Yea-sayers   Respondents who answer questions consistently in the affirmative. (5)

Zero control group   A group that receives no treatment of any kind. (7)

$\bar{z}_r$ The average Fisher z_r. (Appendix C)

***z* score**   See *Standard score*.

References

Abelson, R. P. (1995). *Statistics as principled argument.* Hillsdale, NJ: Erlbaum.

Adair, J. G. (1973). *The human subject: The social psychology of the psychological experiment.* Boston: Little, Brown.

Adair, J. G. (1984). The Hawthorne effect: A reconsideration of the methodological artifact. *Journal of Applied Psychology, 69,* 334–345.

Adair, R. K. (1990). *The physics of baseball.* New York: Harper & Row.

Aditya, R. N. (1996). *The not-so-good subject: Extent and correlates of pseudovolunteering in research.* Unpublished M.A. thesis, Temple University Department of Psychology, Philadelphia.

Aiken, L. R., Jr. (1963). Personality correlates of attitude toward mathematics. *Journal of Educational Research, 56,* 576–580.

Ainsworth, M. D. S., Bell, S. M., & Stayton, D. J. (1971). Individual differences in strange situation behavior of one-year-olds. In H. R. Schaffer (Ed.), *The origins of human social relations.* London: Academic Press.

Allaman, J. D., Joyce, C. S., & Crandall, V. C. (1972). The antecedents of social desirability response tendencies of children and young adults. *Child Development, 43,* 1135–1160.

Allport, G. W., & Postman, L. (1947). *The psychology of rumor.* New York: Holt, Rinehart & Winston.

American Association for the Advancement of Science. (1988). *Project on scientific fraud and misconduct.* Washington, DC: Author.

American Psychological Association. (1973). *Ethical principles in the conduct of research with human participants.* Washington, DC: Author.

American Psychological Association. (1982). *Ethical principles in the conduct of research with human participants.* Washington, DC: Author.

American Psychological Association. (1993). *Journals in psychology.* Washington, DC: Author.

American Psychological Association. (1994). *Publication manual of the American Psychological Association* (4th ed.). Washington, DC: Author.

American Psychological Association. (1997). *Guidelines for researchers studying human behavior* (draft report). Washington, DC: Author.

Anastasi, A., & Urbina, S. (1997). *Psychological testing* (7th ed.). Upper Saddle River, NJ: Prentice Hall.

Anderson, C. A., & Bushman, B. J. (1997). External validity of "trivial" experiments: The case of laboratory aggression. *Review of General Psychology, 1,* 19–41.

Anderson, D. C., Crowell, C. R., Hantula, D. A., & Siroky, L. M. (1988). Task clarification and individual performance posting for improving cleaning in a student-managed university bar. *Journal of Organizational Behavior Management, 9,* 73–90.

Arellano-Galdames, F. J. (1972). *Some ethical problems in research on human subjects.* Unpublished doctoral dissertation, University of New Mexico, Albuquerque.

Arendt, H. (1963). *Eichmann in Jerusalem: A report on the banality of evil.* New York: Viking Press.

Aronson, E., & Carlsmith, J. M. (1968). Experimentation in social psychology. In G. Lindzey & E. Aronson (Eds.), *The handbook of social psychology* (2nd ed., Vol. 2, pp. 1–79). Reading, MA: Addison-Wesley.

Asch, S. E. (1952). Effects of group pressure upon the modification and distortion of judgments. In G. E. Swanson, T. M. Newcomb, & E. L. Hartley (Eds.), *Readings in social psychology* (Rev. ed., pp. 393–401). New York: Holt, Rinehart & Winston.

Atwell, J. E. (1981). Human rights in human subjects research. In A. J. Kimmel (Ed.), *Ethics of human subject research* (pp. 81–90). San Francisco: Jossey-Bass.

Axinn, S. (1966). Fallacy of the single risk. *Philosophy of Science, 33,* 154–162.

Babad, E. (1993). Pygmalion—25 years after interpersonal expectations in the classroom. In P. D. Blanck (Ed.), *Interpersonal expectations: Theory, research, and applications* (pp. 125–153). New York: Cambridge University Press.

Baenninger, R. (1974). Some consequences of aggressive behavior: A selective review of the literature on other animals. *Aggressive Behavior, 1,* 17–37.

Baenninger, R. (1987). Some comparative aspects of yawning in *Betta splendens, Homo sapiens,*

Panthera leo, and *Papio sphynx. Journal of Comparative Psychology, 110,* 349–354.

Baenninger, R., Binkley, S., & Baenninger, M. (1996). Field studies of yawning and activity in humans. *Physiology and Behavior, 59,* 421–425.

Baenninger, R. Estes, R. D., & Baldwin, S. (1977). Anti-predator behavior of baboons and impalas toward a cheetah. *Journal of East African Wildlife, 15,* 327–329.

Bailey, P., & Bremer, F. (1921). Experimental diabetes insipidus. *Archives of Internal Medicine, 28,* 773–803.

Bakan, D. (1967). *On method: Toward a reconstruction of psychological investigation.* San Francisco: Jossey-Bass.

Barker, P. (1996). *Psychotherapeutic metaphors: A guide to theory and practice.* New York: Brunner/Mazel.

Barrass, R. (1978). *Scientists must write.* London: Chapman & Hall.

Bauer, M. I., & Johnson-Laird, P. N. (1993). How diagrams can improve reasoning. *Psychological Science, 4,* 372–378.

Baughman, E. E., & Dahlstrom, W. G. (1968). *Negro and white children: A psychological study in the rural South.* New York: Academic Press.

Baumrind, D. (1964). Some thoughts on ethics of research: After reading Milgram's "Behavioral Study of Obedience." *American Psychologist, 19,* 421–423.

Beck, S. J., Beck, A., Levitt, E., & Molish, H. (1961). *Rorschach's test: Vol. 1. Basic processes.* New York: Grune & Stratton.

Bem, D. J. (1965). An experimental analysis of self-persuasion. *Journal of Experimental Social Psychology, 1,* 199–218.

Bem, D. J. (1972). Self-perception theory. In L. Berkowitz (Ed.), *Advances in experimental social psychology* (Vol. 6, pp. 1–62). New York: Academic Press.

Berelson, B. (1952). *Content analysis in communication research.* Glencoe, IL: Free Press.

Berelson, B. (1954). Content analysis. In G. Lindzey (Ed.), *Handbook of social psychology* (Vol. 1, pp. 488–522). Reading, MA: Addison-Wesley.

Bergum, B. O., & Lehr, D. J. (1963). Effects of authoritarianism on vigilance performance. *Journal of Applied Psychology, 47,* 75–77.

Berkowitz, L., & Macaulay, J. (1971). The contagion of criminal violence. *Sociometry, 34,* 238–260.

Bernard, H. B., & Killworth, P. D. (1970). Informant accuracy in social network data, Part 2. *Human Communication Research, 4,* 3–18.

Bernard, H. B., & Killworth, P. D. (1980). Informant accuracy in social network data: 4. A comparison of clique-level structure in behavioral and cognitive network data. *Social Networks, 2,* 191–218.

Bernard, H. R. (1994). *Research methods in anthropology: Qualitative and quantitative approaches.* Thousand Oaks, CA: Sage.

Bersoff, D. N. (Ed.). (1995). *Ethical conflicts in psychology.* Washington, DC: American Psychological Association.

Billow, R. M. (1977). Metaphor: A review of the psychological literature. *Psychological Bulletin, 84,* 81–92.

Biocca, F., & Levy, M. R. (Eds.). (1995). *Communication in the age of virtual reality.* Hillsdale, NJ: Erlbaum.

Blanck, P. D. (Ed.). (1993). *Interpersonal expectations: Theory, research, and applications.* New York: Cambridge University Press.

Blanck, P. D., Bellack, A. S., Rosnow, R. L., Rotheram-Borus, M. J., & Schooler, N. R. (1992). Scientific rewards and conflicts of ethical choices in human subjects research. *American Psychologist, 47,* 959–965.

Blumberg, M., & Pringle, C. D. (1983). How control groups can cause loss of control in action research: The case of Rushton coal mine. *Journal of Applied Behavioral Science, 19,* 409–425.

Bolton, R. N. (1993). Pretesting questionnaires: Content analyses of respondents' concurrent verbal protocols. *Marketing Science, 12,* 280–303.

Boorstein, D. J. (1985). *The discoverers.* New York: Vintage.

Bradburn, N. M. (1982). Question-wording effects in surveys. In R. Hogarth (Ed.), *New directions for methodology of social and behavioral science: Question framing and response contingency* (No. 11, pp. 65–76). San Francisco: Jossey-Bass.

Bradburn, N. M. (1983). Response effects. In P. H. Rossi, J. D. Wright, & A. B. Anderson (Eds.), *Handbook of survey research* (pp. 289–328). New York: Academic Press.

Bramel, D., & Friend, R. (1981). Hawthorne, the myth of the docile worker, and class bias in psychology. *American Psychologist, 36,* 867–878.

Braun, H. I., & Wainer, H. (1989). Making essay test scores fairer with statistics. In J. M. Tanur, F.

Mosteller, W. H. Kruskal, E. L. Lehmann, R. F. Link, R. S. Pieters, & G. S. Rising (Eds.), *Statistics: A guide to the unknown* (3rd ed., pp. 178–187). Pacific Grove, CA: Wadsworth & Brooks/Cole.

Brehm, S. S., & Kassin, S. M. (1996). *Social psychology*. Boston: Houghton Mifflin.

Bridgstock, M. (1982). A sociological approach to fraud in science. *Australian and New Zealand Journal of Sociology, 18,* 364–383.

Brooks-Gunn, J., & Rotheram-Borus, M. J. (1994). Rights to privacy in research: Adolescents versus parents. *Ethics and Behavior, 4,* 109–121.

Broome, J. (1984). Selecting people randomly. *Ethics, 95,* 38–55.

Brown, R. (1965). *Social psychology*. New York: Free Press.

Brown, W. (1910). Some experimental results in the correlation of mental abilities. *British Journal of Psychology, 3,* 296–322.

Buckhout, R. (1965). Need for approval and attitude change. *Journal of Psychology, 60,* 123–128.

Burnham, J. R. (1966). *Experimenter bias and lesion labeling*. Unpublished manuscript, Purdue University, West Lafayette, IN.

Byrne, D. (1961). Interpersonal attraction and attitude similarity. *Journal of Abnormal and Social Psychology, 62,* 713–715.

Byrne, D. (1971). *The attraction paradigm*. New York: Academic Press.

Byrne, D., Clore, G. L., & Smeaton, G. (1986). The attraction hypothesis: Do similar attitudes affect anything? *Journal of Personality and Social Psychology, 51,* 1167–1170.

Cacioppo, J. T., Gardner, W. L., & Berntson, G. G. (1997). Beyond bipolar conceptualizations and measures: The case of attitudes and evaluative space. *Personality and Social Psychology Review, 1,* 3–25.

Campbell, D. T. (1950). The indirect assessment of attitudes. *Psychological Bulletin, 47,* 15–38.

Campbell, D. T. (1974). Evolutionary epistemology. In P. A. Schilpp (Ed.), *The philosophy of Karl Popper* (pp. 413–463). La Salle, IL: Open Court.

Campbell, D. T., & Fiske, D. W. (1959). Convergent and discriminant validation by the multitrait-multimethod matrix. *Psychological Bulletin, 56,* 81–105.

Campbell, D. T., & Stanley, J. C. (1963). *Experimental and quasi-experimental designs for research*. Chicago: Rand McNally.

Cannell, C. F., Miller, P. V., & Oksenberg, L. (1981). Research on interviewing technique. In S. Leinhardt (Ed.), *Sociological methodology*. San Francisco: Jossey-Bass.

Cantor, N., & Kihlstrom, J. F. (1989). *Personality and social intelligence*. Englewood Cliffs, NJ: Prentice Hall.

Carr, K., & England, R. (Eds.). (1995). *Simulated and virtual realities: Elements of perception*. London: Taylor & Francis.

Ceci, S. J. (1990). *On intelligence . . . more or less: A bio-ecological treatise on intellectual development*. Englewood Cliffs, NJ: Prentice Hall.

Ceci, S. J. (1996). *On intelligence: A bio-ecological treatise on intellectual development* (Expanded ed.). Cambridge: Harvard University Press.

Ceci, S. J., & Bruck, M. (1993). Suggestibility of the child witness: A historical review and synthesis. *Psychological Bulletin, 113,* 403–439.

Ceci, S. J., & Bruck, M. (1995). *Jeopardy in the courtroom: A scientific study of children's testimony*. Washington, DC: American Psychological Association.

Ceci, S. J., Leichtman, M., & White, T. (1995). Interviewing preschoolers: Remembrance of things planted. In D. P. Peters (Ed.), *The child witness: Cognitive, social, and legal issues*. Netherlands: Kluwer.

Ceci, S. J., Peters, D., & Plotkin, J. (1985). Human subjects review, personal values, and the regulation of social science research. *American Psychologist, 40,* 994–1002.

Chambers, J. M., Cleveland, W. S., Kleiner, B., & Tukey, P. A. (1983). *Graphical methods for data analysis*. Pacific Grove, CA: Wadsworth.

Chandrasekhar, S. (1987). *Truth and beauty: Aesthetics and motivations in science*. Chicago: University of Chicago Press.

Christie, R. (1951). Experimental naiveté and experiential naiveté. *Psychological Bulletin, 48,* 327–339.

Clark, R. W. (1971). *Einstein: The life and times*. New York: World.

Cochran, W. G. (1963). *Sampling techniques* (2nd ed.). New York: Wiley.

Cochran, W. G. (1977). *Sampling techniques* (3rd ed.). New York: Wiley.

Cohen, J. (1965). Some statistical issues in psychological research. In B. B. Wolman (Ed.), *Handbook of clinical psychology* (pp. 95–121). New York: McGraw-Hill.

Cohen, J. (1988). *Statistical power analysis for the behavioral sciences* (2nd ed.). Hillsdale, NJ: Erlbaum.

Cohen, J. (1990). Things I have learned (so far). *American Psychologist, 45,* 1304–1312.

Cohen, J. (1994). The earth is round ($p < .05$). *American Psychologist, 49,* 997–1003.

Cohen, M. R. (1959). *Reason and nature: An essay on the meaning of scientific method.* New York: Dover. (Original work published 1931).

Conant, J. B. (1957). Introduction. In J. B. Conant & L. K. Nash (Eds.), *Harvard case studies in experimental science* (Vol. 1, pp. vii–xvi). Cambridge: Harvard University Press.

Conrath, D. W. (1973). Communications environment and its relationship to organizational structure. *Management Science, 20,* 586–603.

Conrath, D. W., Higgins, C. A., & McClean, R. J. (1983). A comparison of the reliability of questionnaire versus diary data. *Social Networks, 5,* 315–322.

Converse, J. M., & Presser, S. (1986). *Survey questions: Handcrafting the standardized questionnaire.* Beverly Hills, CA: Sage.

Cook, T. D., & Campbell, D. T. (1976). The design and conduct of quasi-experiments and true experiments in field settings. In M. D. Dunnette (Ed.), *Handbook of industrial and organizational psychology* (pp. 223–326). Chicago: Rand McNally.

Cook, T. D., & Campbell, D. T. (1979). *Quasi-experimentation: Design and analysis issues for field settings.* Chicago: Rand McNally.

Cook, T. D., Cooper, H., Cordray, D. S., Hartmann, H., Hedges, L. V., Light, R. J., Louis, T. A., & Mosteller, F. (1994). *Meta-analysis for explanation: A casebook.* New York: Russell Sage Foundation.

Cooper, H. M. (1984). *The integrative research review: A social science approach.* Beverly Hills, CA: Sage.

Cooper, H. M. (1985). Literature searching strategies of integrative research reviewers. *American Psychologist, 40,* 1267–1269.

Cooper, H. M. (1989). *Integrating research: A guide to literature reviews* (2nd ed.). Newbury Park, CA: Sage.

Cooper, H. M., & Hedges, L. V. (Eds.). (1994). *The handbook of research synthesis.* New York: Russell Sage.

Cooper, M. (1997, February 4). For greedy fugitives, it's "go directly to jail." *New York Times,* p. B3.

Corsini, R. J. (Ed.). (1984). *Encyclopedia of psychology* (Vols. 1–4). New York: Wiley.

Crabb, P. B., & Bielawski, D. (1994). The social representation of maternal culture and gender in children's books. *Sex Roles, 30,* 69–79.

Crabtree, B. F., & Miller, W. L. (Eds.). (1992). *Doing qualitative research: Multiple strategies.* Thousand Oaks, CA: Sage.

Crancer, J., Dille, J., Delay, J., Wallace, J., & Haybin, M. (1969). Comparison of the effects of marijuana and alcohol on simulated driving performance. *Science, 164,* 851–854.

Crano, W. D. (1981). Triangulation and cross-cultural research. In M. B. Brewer & B. E. Collins (Eds.), *Scientific inquiry and the social sciences* (pp. 317–344). San Francisco: Jossey-Bass.

Cronbach, L. J. (1951). Coefficient alpha and the internal structure of tests. *Psychometrika, 16,* 297–334.

Cronbach, L. J. (1960). *Essentials of psychological testing* (2nd ed.). New York: Harper.

Cronbach, L. J., & Meehl, P. E. (1955). Construct validity in psychological tests. *Psychological Bulletin, 52,* 281–302.

Cronbach, L. J., & Quirk, T. J. (1971). Test validity. In L. C. Deighton (Ed.), *Encyclopedia of education* (Vol. 9, pp. 165–175). New York: Macmillan and Free Press.

Crowne, D. P. (1979). *The experimental study of personality.* Hillsdale, NJ: Erlbaum.

Crowne, D. P. (1991). From response style to motive. *Current Contents: Social and Behavioral Sciences, 23*(30), 10.

Crowne, D. P., & Marlowe, D. (1964). *The approval motive: Studies in evaluative dependence.* New York: Wiley.

Cryer, J. D. (1986). *Time series analysis.* Boston: PWS-Kent.

Csikszentmihalyi, M., & Larson, R. (1984). *Being adolescent: Conflict and growth in the teenage years.* New York: Basic Books.

Danziger, K. (1988). A question of identity: Who participated in psychological experiments? In J. Morawski (Ed.), *The rise of experimentation in American psychology* (pp. 35–52). New York: Oxford University Press.

Darley, J. M., & Latané, B. (1968). Bystander intervention in emergencies. *Journal of Personality and Social Psychology, 8,* 377–383.

Davis, J. D., Gallagher, R. L., & Ladove, R. (1967). Food intake controlled by blood factors. *Science, 156,* 1247–1248.

Day, D. D., & Quackenbush, O. E. (1942). Attitudes toward defensive, cooperative, and aggressive wars. *Journal of Social Psychology, 16,* 11–20.

Day, R. A. (1983). *How to write and publish a scientific paper* (2nd ed.). Philadelphia: ISI Press.

Denzin, N. K., & Lincoln, Y. S. (Eds.). (1994). *Handbook of qualitative research.* Thousand Oaks, CA: Sage.

DePaulo, B. M., & Kashy, D. A. (1998). Everyday lies in close and casual relationships. *Journal of Personality and Social Psychology, 74,* 63-79.

DePaulo, B. M., Kashy, D. A., Kirkendol, S. E., Wyer, M. M., & Epstein, J. A. (1996). Lying in everyday life. *Journal of Personality and Social Psychology, 70,* 979–995.

De Vos, G. A., & Boyer, L. B. (1989). *Symbolic analysis cross-culturally: The Rorschach test.* Berkeley: University of California Press.

DiFonzo, N., Bordia, P., & Rosnow, R. L. (1994). Reining in rumors. *Organizational Dynamics, 23,* 47–62.

Dohrenwend, B. S., & Richardson, S. A. (1963). Directiveness and nondirectiveness in research interviewing: A reformulation of the problem. *Psychological Bulletin, 60,* 475–485.

Dorn, L. D., Susman, E. J., & Fletcher, J. C. (1995). Informed consent in children and adolescents: Age, maturation and psychological state. *Journal of Adolescent Health, 16,* 185–190.

Downs, C. W., Smeyak, G. P., & Martin, E. (1980). *Professional interviewing.* New York: Harper & Row.

Eagly, A. H. (1978). Sex differences in influenceability. *Psychological Bulletin, 85,* 86–116.

Eagly, A. H., & Chaiken, S. (1993). *The psychology of attitudes.* Fort Worth, TX: Harcourt Brace Jovanovich.

Ebbinghaus, H. (1885). *Über das Gedächtnis: Untersuchungen zur experimentellen Psychologie.* Leipzig, Germany: Duncker & Humblot.

Elgie, D. M., Hollander, E. P., & Rice, R. W. (1988). Appointed and elected leader responses to favorableness of feedback and level of task activity from followers. *Journal of Applied Social Psychology, 18,* 1361–1370.

Emerson, J. D., & Hoaglin, D. C. (1983). Stem-and-leaf displays. In D. C. Hoaglin, F. Mosteller, & J. W. Tukey (Eds.), *Understanding robust and exploratory data analysis* (pp. 7–32). New York: Wiley.

Emerson, R. M., Fretz, R. I., & Shaw, L. L. (1995). *Writing ethnographic fieldnotes.* Chicago: University of Chicago Press.

Entwisle, D. R. (1961). Interactive effects of pretesting. *Educational and Psychological Measurement, 21,* 607–620.

Ericsson, K. A., & Simon, H. A. (Eds.). (1993). *Protocol analysis: Verbal reports as data* (Rev. ed.). Cambridge, MA: MIT Press.

Esposito, J. L., Agard, E., & Rosnow, R. L. (1984). Can confidentiality of data pay off? *Personality and Individual Differences, 5,* 477–480.

Evans, I. H. (Ed.). (1993). *The Wordsworth dictionary of phrase and fable.* London: Wordsworth Editions.

Exner, J. E. (1993). *The Rorschach: A comprehensive system* (3rd ed., Vol. 1). New York: Wiley.

Fairbanks, L. A. (1993). What is a good mother? Adaptive variation in maternal behavior of primates. *Current Directions in Psychological Science, 2,* 179–183.

Federighi, E. T. (1959). Extended tables of the percentage points of Student's *t* distribution. *Journal of the American Statistical Association, 54,* 683–688.

Ferster, C. B., & Skinner, B. F. (1957). *Schedules of reinforcement.* New York: Appleton-Century-Crofts.

Festinger, L. (1954). A theory of social comparison processes. *Human Relations, 7,* 117–140.

Festinger, L. (1957). *A theory of cognitive dissonance.* Evanston, IL: Row Peterson.

Festinger, L., Gerard, H., Hymovitch, B., Kelley, H., & Raven, B. H. (1952). The influence process in the presence of extreme deviates. *Human Relations, 5,* 327–346.

Feyerabend, P. (1988). *Against method* (Rev. ed.). London: Verso.

Feynman, R. P. (1988). *"What do I care what other people think?" Further adventures of a curious character.* New York: Bantam Books.

Fienberg, S. E., & Tanur, J. M. (1989). Combining cognitive and statistical approaches to survey design. *Science, 243,* 1017–1022.

Finkner, A. L. (1950). Methods of sampling for estimating commercial peach production in North

Carolina. *North Carolina Agricultural Experiment Station Technical Bulletin, 91* (whole).

Fischer, K. W., Pipp, S. L., & Bullock, D. (1984). Detecting developmental discontinuities. In R. N. Emde & R. J. Harmon (Eds.), *Continuities and discontinuities in development* (pp. 95–121). New York: Plenum.

Fisher, R. A. (1960). *The design of experiments* (7th ed.). Edinburgh, Scotland: Oliver & Boyd.

Fisher, R. A. (1971). *The design of experiments* (8th ed.). New York: Hafner.

Fisher, R. A., & Yates, F. (1974). *Statistical tables for biological, agricultural, and medical research* (6th ed.). London: Longman.

Fisher, R. J. (1993). Social desirability bias and the validity of indirect questioning. *Journal of Consumer Research, 20,* 303–315.

Flanagan, J. C. (1954). The critical incident technique. *Psychological Bulletin, 51,* 327–358.

Fletcher, G. (1995). *The scientific credibility of folk psychology.* Mahwah, NJ: Erlbaum.

Forrest, D. W. (1974). *Francis Galton: the life and work of a Victorian genius.* New York: Taplinger.

Fossey, D. (1981). Imperiled giants of the forest. *National Geographic, 159,* 501–604.

Fossey, D. (1983). *Gorillas in the mist.* Boston: Houghton Mifflin.

Fowler, F. J., Jr. (1993). *Survey research methods* (2nd ed.). Newbury Park, CA: Sage.

Franke, R. H., & Kaul, J. D. (1978). The Hawthorne experiments: First statistical interpretation. *American Sociological Review, 43,* 623–643.

Freedman, D., Pisani, R., Purves, R., & Adhikari, A. (1991). *Statistics* (2nd ed.). New York: Norton.

Fuerbringer, J. (1997, March 30). Why both bulls and bears can act so bird-brained: Quirky behavior is becoming a realm of economics. *New York Times,* Section 3, pp. 1, 6.

Gallup, G. (1976, May 21). *Lessons learned in 40 years of polling.* Paper presented before National Council on Public Polls.

Galton, F. (1869). *Hereditary genius.* London: Macmillan.

Gantt, W. H. (1964). Autonomic conditioning. In J. Wolpe, A. Salter, & L. J. Reyna (Eds.), *The conditioning therapies* (pp. 115–126). New York: Holt, Rinehart & Winston.

Gardner, H. (1985). *Frames of mind: The theory of multiple intelligences.* New York: Basic Books.

Gardner, H. (1986). *The mind's new science: A history of the cognitive revolution.* New York: Basic Books.

Gardner, H. (Ed.). (1993). *Multiple intelligences: The theory in practice.* New York: Basic Books.

Gardner, M. (1957). *Fads and fallacies in the name of science.* New York: Dover.

Garfield, E. (1989a). Art and science: 1. The art-science connection. *Current Contents, 21*(8), 3–10.

Garfield, E. (1989b). Art and science: 2. Science for art's sake. *Current Contents, 21*(9), 3–8.

Gazzaniga, M. S., & LeDoux, J. E. (1978). *The integrated mind.* New York: Plenum Press.

Gentner, D., & Markman, A. B. (1997). Structure mapping in analogy and similarity. *American Psychologist, 52,* 45–56

Gephart, R. P., Jr. (1993). The textual approach: Risk and blame in disaster sense-making. *Academy of Management Journal, 36,* 1465–1514.

Gergen, K. J. (1985). The social constructionist movement in modern psychology. *American Psychologist, 40,* 266–275.

Gibson, E. J. & Walk, R. D. (1960, April). The visual cliff. *Scientific American, 202*(4), 64–71.

Gigerenzer, G. (1991). From tools to theories: A heuristic of discovery in cognitive psychology. *Psychological Review, 98,* 254–267.

Gigerenzer, G., Swijtink, Z., Porter, T., Daston, L., Beatty, J., & Krüger, L. (1989). *The empire of chance: How probability changed science and everyday life.* New York: Cambridge University Press.

Gilgun, J. F., Daly, K., & Handel, G. (Eds.). (1992). *Qualitative methods in family research.* Thousand Oaks, CA: Sage.

Gillespie, R. (1988). The Hawthorne experiments and the politics of experimentation. In J. Morawski (Ed.), *The rise of experimentation in American psychology* (pp. 114–137). New York: Oxford University Press.

Gilovich, T. (1991). *How we know what isn't so: The fallibility of human reason in everyday life.* New York: Free Press.

Glass, G. V. (1976) Primary, secondary, and meta-analysis of research. *Educational Researcher, 5,* 3–8.

Glass, G. V, McGaw, B., & Smith, M. L. (1981). *Meta-analysis in social research.* Beverly Hills, CA: Sage.

Gniech, G. (1976). *Störeffekte in psychologischen Experimenten.* Stuttgart: Kohlhammer.

Goldberg, L. R. (1993). The structure of phenotypic personality traits. *American Psychologist, 48,* 26–34.

Goldman, B. A., & Mitchell, D. F. (1995). *Directory of unpublished experimental mental measures* (Vol. 6). Washington, DC: American Psychological Association.

Goldman, B. A., Osborne, W. L., & Mitchell, D. F. (Eds.). (1996a). *Directory of unpublished experimental mental measures* (Vols. 4–5). Washington, DC: American Psychological Association.

Goldman, B. A., Saunders, J. L., & Busch, J. C. (Eds.). (1996b). *Directory of unpublished experimental mental measures* (Vols. 1–3). Washington, DC: American Psychological Association.

Gombrich, E. H. (1963). *Meditations on a hobby horse.* London: Phaidon.

Goodenough, W. H. (1980). Ethnographic field techniques. In H. C. Triandis & J. W. Berry (Eds.), *Handbook of cross-cultural psychology: Methodology* (Vol. 2, pp. 29–55). Boston: Allyn & Bacon.

Gould, M. S., & Shaffer, D. (1986). The impact of suicide in television movies: Evidence of imitation. *New England Journal of Medicine, 315,* 690–694.

Grant, D. A. (1956). Analysis-of-variance curves in the analysis and comparison of curves. *Psychological Bulletin, 53,* 141–154.

Greco, M., Baenninger, R., & Govern, J. (1993). On the context of yawning: When, where, and why? *Psychological Record, 43,* 175–183.

Gross, A. E., & Fleming, I. (1982). Twenty years of deception in social psychology. *Personality and Social Psychology Bulletin, 8,* 402–408.

Gross, A. G. (1990). *The rhetoric of science.* Cambridge: Harvard University Press.

Gubrium, J. F., & Sankar, A. (Eds.). (1993). *Qualitative methods in aging research.* Thousand Oaks, CA: Sage.

Guilford, J. P. (1954). *Psychometric methods* (2nd ed.). New York: McGraw-Hill.

Guilford, J. P. (1967). *The nature of intelligence.* New York: McGraw-Hill.

Hagenaars, J. A., & Cobben, N. P. (1978). Age, cohort and period: A general model for the analysis of social change. *Netherlands Journal of Sociology, 14,* 58–91.

Hall, J. A. (1984). *Instructor's manual to accompany Rosenthal/Rosnow: Essentials of behavioral research.* New York: McGraw-Hill.

Hall, R. V., Lund, D., & Jackson, D. (1968). Effects of teacher attention on study behavior. *Journal of Applied Behavior Analysis, 1,* 1–12.

Harré, R., & Lamb, R. (Eds.). (1983). *Encyclopedic dictionary of psychology.* Cambridge, MA: MIT Press.

Harris, B. (1988). Key words: A history of debriefing in social psychology. In J. Morawski (Ed.), *The rise of experimentation in American psychology* (pp. 188–212). New Haven, CT: Yale University Press.

Harrower, M., & Bowers, D. (1987). *The inside story: Self-evaluations reflecting basic Rorschach types.* Hillsdale, NJ: Erlbaum.

Härtel, C. E. J. (1993). Rating format research revisited: Format effectiveness and acceptability depend on rater characteristics. *Journal of Applied Psychology, 78,* 212–217.

Hartmann, G. W. (1936). A field experiment on the comparative effectiveness of "emotional" and "rational" political leaflets in determining election results. *Journal of Abnormal and Social Psychology, 31,* 99–114.

Haviland, J. B. (1977). Gossip as competition in Zinacantan. *Journal of Communication, 27,* 186–191.

Haywood, H. C. (1976). The ethics of doing research . . . and of not doing it. *American Journal of Mental Deficiency, 81,* 311–317.

Hedges, L. V., & Olkin, I. (1985). *Statistical methods for meta-analysis.* New York: Academic Press.

Heise, G. A., & Miller, G. A. (1951). Problem solving by small groups using various communication nets. *Journal of Abnormal and Social Psychology, 46,* 327–331.

Hersen, M., & Barlow, D. H. (1976). *Single-case experimental designs: Strategies for studying behavior change.* Oxford: Pergamon Press.

Higbee, K. L., & Wells, M. G. (1972). Some research trends in social psychology during the 1960s. *American Psychologist, 27,* 963–966.

Hirsh-Pasek, K., & Golinkoff, R. M. (1993). Skeletal supports for grammatical learning: What infants bring to the language learning task. In C. Rovee-Collier & L. P. Lipsitt (Eds.), *Advances in infancy research* (Vol. 8, pp. 299–315). Norwood, NJ: Ablex.

Hogan, R., Hogan, J., & Roberts, B. W. (1996). Personality measurement and employment decisions. *American Psychologist, 51,* 469–477.

Hollander, E. P. (1992). The essential independence of leadership and followership. *Current Directions in Psychological Science, 1,* 71–74.

Holsti, O. R. (1969). *Content analysis for the social sciences and humanities.* Reading, MA: Addison-Wesley.

Holyoak, K. J., & Thagard, P. (1997). The analogical mind. *American Psychologist, 52,* 35–44.

Hoover, K., & Donovan, T. (1995). *The elements of social scientific thinking* (6th ed.). New York: St. Martin's Press.

House, R. J., & Aditya, R. (1997). The social scientific study of leadership: *Quo vadis? Journal of Management, 23,* 409–473

Houts, A. C., Cook, T. D., & Shadish, W., Jr. (1986). The person-situation debate: A critical multiplist perspective. *Journal of Personality, 54,* 52–105.

Hult, C. A. (1996). Researching and writing in the social sciences. Boston: Allyn & Bacon.

Hunt, M. (1997). *How science takes stock: The story of meta-analysis.* New York: Russell Sage Foundation.

Hunter, J. E., & Schmidt, F. L. (1990). *Methods of meta-analysis: Correcting error and bias in research findings.* Newbury Park, CA: Sage.

Huttenlocher, J., & Newcombe, N. (1984). The child's representation of information about location. In C. Sophian (Ed.), *Origins of cognitive skills* (pp. 81–111). Hillsdale, NJ: Erlbaum.

Huttenlocher, J., Newcombe, N., & Sandberg, E. H. (1994). The coding of spatial location in young children. *Cognitive Psychology, 27,* 115–147.

Imber, S. D., Glanz, L. M., Elkin, I., Sotsky, S. M., Boyer, J. L., & Leber, W. R. (1986). Ethical issues in psychotherapy research: Problems in a collaborative clinical trials study. *American Psychologist, 41,* 137–146.

Jaeger, M. E., Rosnow, R. L. (1988). Contextualism and its implications for psychological inquiry. *British Journal of Psychology, 79,* 63–75.

Jaeger, M. E., Skleder, A. A., & Rosnow, R. L. (in press). Who's up on the low down: Gossip in interpersonal relations. In B. H. Spitzberg & W. Cupach (Eds.), *The dark side of close relationships.* Hillsdale, NJ: Erlbaum.

Jammer, M. (1966). *The conceptual development of quantum mechanics.* New York: McGraw-Hill.

Johnson-Laird, P. N. (1983). *Mental models: Towards a cognitive science of language, inference, and consciousness.* Cambridge: Harvard University Press.

Johnson-Laird, P. N., & Byrne, R. M. J. (1991). *Deduction.* Hillsdale, NJ: Erlbaum.

Jones, E. E., & Gerard, H. B. (1967). *Foundations of social psychology.* New York: Wiley.

Jones, J. H. (1993). *Bad blood: The Tuskegee syphilis experiment* (Rev. ed.). New York: Free Press.

Jones, M. B., & Fennell, R. S., III (1965). Runway performance in two strains of rats. *Quarterly Journal of the Florida Academy of Sciences, 28,* 289–296.

Judd, C. M., & Kenny, D. A. (1981). *Estimating the effects of social interventions.* Cambridge: Cambridge University Press.

Judd, C. M., Smith, E. R., & Kidder, L. H. (1991). *Research methods in social relations* (6th ed.). New York: Holt, Rinehart & Winston.

Jung, C. G. (1910). Ein Beitrag zur Psychologie des Gerüchtes. *Zentralblatt für Psychoanalyse, 1,* 81–90.

Jung, C. G. (1959). A visionary rumor. *Journal of Analytical Psychology, 4,* 5–19.

Jung, J. (1969). Current practices and problems in the use of college students for psychological research. *Canadian Psychologist, 10,* 280–290.

Kagay, M. R. (1996, December 15, 1996). Experts say refinements are needed in the polls. *New York Times,* p. 34.

Kahane, H. (1989). *Logic and philosophy: A modern introduction* (6th ed.). Belmont, CA: Wadsworth.

Kaplan, A. (1964). *The conduct of inquiry: Methodology for behavioral science.* Scranton, PA: Chandler.

Kashy, D. A., & DePaulo, B. M. (1996). Who lies? *Journal of Personality and Social Psychology, 70,* 1037–1051.

Katz, D., & Cantril, H. (1937). Public opinion polls. *Sociometry, 1,* 155–179.

Katz, J. (1972). *Experimentation with human beings.* New York: Sage.

Kazdin, A. E. (1976). Statistical techniques for single-case experimental designs. In M. Hersen & D. H. Barlow (Eds.), *Single-case experimental designs: Strategies for studying behavior change* (pp. 265–316). Oxford, England: Pergamon Press.

Kazdin, A. E. (1980). *Research design in clinical psychology.* New York: Harper & Row.

Kazdin, A. E. (1992). *Research design in clinical psychology* (2nd ed.). Boston: Allyn & Bacon.

Kazdin, A. E., & Tuma, A. H. (Eds.). (1982). *Single-case research designs.* San Francisco: Jossey-Bass.

Kelly, D., Julian, T., & Hollander, E. P. (1992, April 4). *Further effects of good and bad leadership as revealed by critical incidents and rating scales.* Paper presented at Eastern Psychological Association meeting, Boston.

Kelman, H. C. (1968). *A time to speak: On human values and social research.* San Francisco: Jossey-Bass.

Kendall, P. C., Flannery-Schroeder, E., Panichelli-Mindel, S. M., Southam-Gerow, M., Henin, A., & Warman, M. (1997). Therapy for anxiety-disordered youth: A second randomized clinical trial. *Journal of Consulting and Clinical Psychology, 65,* 366–380.

Kendall, P. C., Howard, B. C., & Hays, R. C. (1989). Self-referent speech and psychopathology: The balance of positive and negative thinking. *Cognitive Therapy and Research, 13,* 583–598.

Kenny, D. A. (1979). *Correlation and causality.* New York: Wiley.

Keppel, G. (1991). *Design and analysis: A researcher's handbook* (3rd ed.). Englewood Cliffs, NJ: Prentice Hall.

Kerner, O., et al. (1968). *Report of the National Advisory Commission on Civil Disorders.* New York: Bantam.

Kidder, L. H. (1972). On becoming hypnotized: How skeptics become convinced: A case of attitude change? *Journal of Abnormal Psychology, 80,* 317–322.

Kidder, L. H., Kidder, R. L., & Snyderman, P. (1976). *A cross-lagged correlational analysis of the causal relationship between police employment and crime rates.* Paper presented at the meeting of the American Psychological Association, Washington.

Kilborn, P. T. (1994, January 23). Alarming trend among workers: Surveys find clusters of TB cases. *New York Times,* pp. A1, A16.

Kimble, G. A. (1989). Psychology from the standpoint of a generalist. *American Psychologist, 44,* 491–499.

Kimmel, A. J. (Ed.). (1981). *Ethics of human subjects research.* San Francisco: Jossey-Bass.

Kimmel, A. J. (1988). *Ethics and values in applied social research.* Beverly Hills, CA: Sage.

Kimmel, A. J. (1991). Predictable biases in the ethical decision making of American psychologists. *American Psychologist, 46,* 786–788.

Kimmel, A. J. (1996). *Ethical issues in behavioral research: A survey.* Cambridge, MA: Blackwell.

Kirk, R. E. (1995). *Experimental design: Procedures for the behavioral sciences* (3rd ed.). Pacific Grove, CA: Brooks/Cole.

Kish, L. (1965). *Survey sampling.* New York: Wiley.

Kleinmuntz, B. (1982). *Personality and psychological assessment.* New York: St. Martin's Press.

Klopfer, B., & Kelley, D. M. (1942). *The Rorschach technique.* New York: World Book.

Knapp, R. H. (1944). A psychology of rumor. *Public Opinion Quarterly, 8,* 22–37.

Koch, S. (1959). General introduction to the series. In S. Koch (Ed.), *Psychology: A study of a science* (Vol. 1, pp. 1–18). New York: McGraw-Hill.

Kolata, G. B. (1986). What does it mean to be random? *Science, 231,* 1068–1070.

Kolodner, J. L. (1997). Educational implications of analogy: A view from case-based reasoning. *American Psychologist, 52,* 57–66.

Komaki, J., & Barnett, F. T. (1977). A behavioral approach to coaching football: Improving the play execution of the offensive backfield on a youth football team. *Journal of Applied Behavior Analysis, 10,* 657–664.

Kordig, C. R. (1978). Discovery and justification. *Philosophy of Science, 45,* 110–117.

Koshland, D. E., Jr. (1988). Science, journalism, and whistle-blowing. *Science, 240,* 585.

Kosslyn, S. M. (1994). *Elements of graph design.* New York: W. H. Freeman.

Kraemer, H. C., & Thiemann, S. (1987). *How many subjects? Statistical power analysis in research.* Newbury Park, CA: Sage.

Kratochwill, T. R., & Levin, J. R. (Eds.). (1992). *Single-case research design and analysis: New directions for psychology and education.* Hillsdale, NJ: Erlbaum.

Kraus, S. J. (1991). Attitudes and the prediction of behavior: A meta-analysis of the empirical literature. *Personality and Social Psychology Bulletin, 21,* 58–75.

Kraus, S. J. (1993). *Instructor's manual with tests for "Beginning behavioral research."* New York: Macmillan.

Krippendorff, K. (1980). *Content analysis: An introduction to its methodology.* Beverly Hills, CA: Sage.

Labaw, P. (1980). *Advanced questionnaire design.* Cambridge, MA: ABT Books.

La Greca, A. M. (Ed.). (1990). *Through the eyes of the child: Obtaining self-reports from children and adolescents.* Boston: Allyn & Bacon.

Lana, R. E. (1959). Pretest-treatment interaction effects in attitudinal studies. *Psychological Bulletin, 56,* 293–300.

Lana, R. E. (1969). Pretest sensitization. In R. Rosenthal & R. L. Rosnow (Eds.), *Artifact in behavioral research* (pp. 119–141). New York: Academic Press.

Lana, R. E. (1991). *Assumptions of social psychology: A reexamination.* Hillsdale, NJ: Erlbaum.

Lana, R. E., & Rosnow, R. L. (1972). *Introduction to contemporary psychology.* New York: Holt, Rinehart & Winston.

Latané, B., & Darley, J. M. (1968). Group inhibition of bystander intervention in emergencies. *Journal of Personality and Social Psychology, 10,* 215–221.

Latané, B., & Darley, J. M. (1970). *The unresponsive bystander: Why doesn't he help?* New York: Appleton-Century-Crofts.

Lavelle, J. M., Hovell, M. F., West, M. P., & Wahlgren, D. R. (1992). Promoting law enforcement for child protection: A community analysis. *Journal of Applied Behavior Analysis, 25,* 885–892.

Lavrakas, P. J. (1987). *Telephone survey methods: Sampling, selection, and supervision.* Beverly Hills, CA: Sage.

Lazarsfeld, P. F. (1978). Some episodes in the history of panel analysis. In D. B. Kandel (Ed.), *Longitudinal research for drug abuse* (pp. 249–265). New York: Hemisphere Press.

Leary, D. E. (Ed.). (1990). *Metaphors in the history of psychology.* Cambridge: Cambridge University Press.

Lee, R. M. (1993). *Doing research on sensitive topics.* London: Sage.

Leong, F. T. L., & Pfaltzgraff, R. E. (1996). Finding a research topic. In F. T. L. Leong & J. T. Austin (Eds.), *The psychology research handbook* (pp. 3–16). Thousand Oaks, CA: Sage.

Levi, P. (1984). *The periodic table.* New York: Schocken Books.

Lewin, T. (1994, January 7). Prize in an unusual lottery: A scarce experimental drug. *New York Times,* pp. A1, A17.

Lewis, M. J. (1996). Alcohol reinforcement and neuropharmacological therapeutics. *Alcohol and Alcoholism, 31,* Suppl. 1, pp. 17–25.

Ley, R. (1990). *A whisper of espionage.* Garden City, NJ: Avery.

Ley, R. (1993). Breathing retraining in the treatment of hyperventilation complaints and panic disorder: A reply to Garssen, DeRuiter, and Van Dyck. *Clinical Psychology Review, 13,* 393–408.

Li, H., Rosenthal, R., & Rubin, D. B. (1996). Reliability of measurement in psychology: From Spearman-Brown to maximal reliability. *Psychological Methods, 1,* 98–107.

Light, R. J., & Pillemer, D. B. (1984). *Summing up: The science of reviewing research.* Cambridge: Harvard University Press.

Likert, R. A. (1932). A technique for the measurement of attitudes. *Archives of Psychology, 140,* 1–55.

Lindquist, E. F. (1953). *Design and analysis of experiments in psychology and education.* Boston: Houghton Mifflin.

Linsky, A. S. (1975). Stimulating responses to mailed questionnaires: A review. *Public Opinion Quarterly, 39,* 83–101.

Liss, M. B. (1994). Child abuse: Is there a mandate for researchers to report? *Ethics and Behavior, 4,* 133–146.

London, P. (1970). The rescuers: Motivational hypotheses about Christians who saved Jews from the Nazis. In. J. Macaulay & L. Berkowitz (Eds.), *Altruism and behavior* (pp. 241–250). New York: Academic Press.

Maher, B. (1978). A reader's, writer's, and reviewer's guide to assessing research reports in clinical psychology. *Journal of Consulting and Clinical Psychology, 46,* 835–934.

Mahler, I. (1953). Attitude toward socialized medicine. *Journal of Social Psychology, 38,* 273–282.

Malmo, R. B. (1959). Activation: A neuropsychological dimension. *Psychological Review, 66,* 367–386.

Mann, T. (1994). Informed consent for psychological research: Do subjects comprehend consent forms and understand their legal rights? *Psychological Science, 5,* 140–143.

Marks, G., & Miller, N. (1987). Ten years of research on the false-consensus effect: An empirical and theoretical review. *Psychological Bulletin, 102,* 72–90.

Martin, P., & Bateson, P. (1993). *Measuring behaviour: An introductory guide* (2nd ed.). Cambridge: Cambridge University Press.

Maurer, T. J., Palmer, J. K., & Ashe, D. K. (1993). Diaries, checklists, evaluations, and contrast effects in measurement of behavior. *Journal of Applied Psychology, 78,* 226–231.

McClelland, D. C., Atkinson, J. W., Clark, R. A., & Lowell, E. L. (1953). *The achievement motive.* New York: Appleton-Century-Crofts.

McCrae, R. R., & Costa, P. T., Jr. (1997). Personality trait structure as a human universal. *American Psychologist, 52,* 509–516.

McGuire, W. J. (1964). Inducing resistance to persuasion: Some contemporary approaches. In L. Berkowitz (Ed.), *Advances in experimental social psychology.* (Vol 1, pp. 191–229). New York: Academic Press.

McGuire, W. J. (1969). Suspiciousness of experimenter's intent. In R. Rosenthal & R. L. Rosnow (Eds.), *Artifact in behavioral research* (pp. 13–57). New York: Academic Press.

McGuire, W. J. (1973). The yin and yang of progress in social psychology: Seven koan. *Journal of Personality and Social Psychology, 26,* 446–456.

McKillip, J., Duppong, K., & Tinsley, L. J. (1997). Three views of *Beginning Behavioral Research. Contemporary Psychology, 42,* 835–837.

McNemar, Q. (1946). Opinion-attitude methodology. *Psychological Bulletin, 43,* 289–374.

Medawar, P. B. (1969). *Induction and intuition in scientific thought* (Jayne Lectures for 1968). Philadelphia: American Philosophical Society.

Melton, G. B., Levine, R. J., Koocher, G. P., Rosenthal, R., & Thompson, W. C. (1988). Community consultation in socially sensitive research: Lessons from clinical trials of treatments for AIDS. *American Psychologist, 43,* 573–581.

Menges, R. J. (1973). Openness and honesty versus coercion and deception in psychological research. *American Psychologist, 28,* 1030–1034.

Merriam, S. B. (1991). *Case study research in education.* San Francisco: Jossey-Bass.

Merritt, C. B., & Fowler, R. G. (1948). The pecuniary honesty of the public at large. *Journal of Abnormal and Social Psychology, 43,* 90–93.

Merton, R. K. (1948). The self-fulfilling prophecy. *Antioch Review, 8,* 193–210.

Merton, R. K. (1993). *On the shoulders of giants: A Shandean postscript.* Chicago: University of Chicago Press.

Meyrowitz, J. (1985). *No sense of place: The impact of electronic media on social behavior.* New York: Oxford University Press.

Milgram, S. (1963). Behavioral study of obedience. *Journal of Abnormal and Social Psychology, 67,* 371–378.

Milgram, S. (1974). *Obedience to authority: An experimental view.* New York: Harper & Row.

Milgram, S. (1977). *The individual in a social world: Essays and experiments.* Reading, MA: Addison-Wesley.

Milgram, S., Mann, L., & Harter, S. (1965). The lost-letter technique: A tool of social research. *Public Opinion Quarterly, 29,* 437–438.

Miller, A. I. (1986). *Imagery in scientific thought: Creating 20th century physics.* Cambridge, MA: MIT Press.

Miller, A. I. (1996). *Insights of genius: imagery and creativity in science and art.* New York: Springer-Verlag.

Miller, G. A., & Newman, E. B. (1958). Tests of a statistical explanation of the rank-frequency relation for words in written English. *American Journal of Psychology, 71,* 209–258.

Miller, N., & Pollock, V. E. (1994). Meta-analytic synthesis for theory development. In H. Cooper & L. V. Hedges (Eds.), *The handbook of research synthesis* (pp. 457–484). New York: Sage.

Miller, P. V., & Cannell, C. F. (1982). A study of experimental techniques for telephone interviewing. *Public Opinion Quarterly, 46,* 250–269.

Millham, J., & Jacobson, L. I. (1978). The need for approval. In H. London & J. E. Exner (Eds.), *Dimensions of personality* (pp. 365–390). New York: Wiley.

Mook, D. G. (1983). In defense of external invalidity. *American Psychologist, 38,* 379–387.

Morse, J. M. (Ed.). (1993). *Critical issues in qualitative research methods.* Thousand Oaks, CA: Sage.

Mosteller, F. (1968). Association and estimation in contingency tables. *Journal of the American Statistical Association, 63,* 1–28.

Mosteller, F., Fienberg, S. E., & Rourke, R. E. K. (1983). *Beginning statistics with data analysis.* Reading, MA: Addison-Wesley.

Mullen, B., & Rosenthal, R. (1985). *BASIC meta-analysis: Procedures and programs.* Hillsdale, NJ: Erlbaum.

Murphy, K. R., Jako, R. A., & Anhalt, R. L. (1993). Nature and consequences of halo effect: A critical analysis. *Journal of Applied Psychology, 78,* 218–225.

National Commission for the Protection of Human Subjects of Biomedical and Behavioral Research. (1979). *The Belmont report: Ethical principles and guidelines for the protection of human subjects of research*. Washington, DC: U.S. Government Printing Office.

Nelson, N., Rosenthal, R., & Rosnow, R. L. (1986). Interpretation of significance levels and effect sizes by psychological researchers. *American Psychologist, 41,* 1299–1301.

Newcombe, N., & Huttenlocher, J. (1992). Children's early ability to solve perspective-taking problems. *Developmental Psychology, 28,* 635–643.

Nisbet, R. (1976). *Sociology as an art form.* London: Oxford University Press.

Nisbett, R. E., & Wilson, T. D. (1977). Telling more than we can know: Verbal reports on mental processes. *Psychological Review, 84,* 231–259.

Nouri, H., Blau, G., & Shahid, A. (1995). The effect of socially desirable responding (SDR) on the relation between budgetary participation and self-reported job performance. *Advances in Management Accounting, 4,* 163–177.

Novick, M. R., & Lewis, C. (1967). Coefficient alpha and the reliability of composite measurements. *Psychometrika, 32,* 1–13.

Oleson, K. C., & Arkin, R. A. (1996). Reviewing and evaluating a research article. In F. T. L. Leong & J. T. Austin (Eds.), *The psychology research handbook* (pp. 40–55). Thousand Oaks, CA: Sage.

Ones, D. S., Viswesvaran, C., & Reiss, A. D. (1996). Role of social desirability in personality testing for personnel selection: The red herring. *Journal of Applied Psychology, 81,* 660–679.

Orne, M. T. (1959). The nature of hypnosis: Artifact and essence. *Journal of Abnormal and Social Psychology, 58,* 277–299.

Orne, M. T. (1962). On the social psychology of the psychological experiment: With particular reference to demand characteristics and their implications. *American Psychologist, 17,* 776–783.

Orne, M. T. (1969). Demand characteristics and the concept of quasi-controls. In R. Rosenthal & R. L. Rosnow (Eds.), *Artifact in behavioral research* (pp. 143–179). New York: Academic Press.

Orne, M. T. (1970). Hypnosis, motivation, and the ecological validity of the psychological experiment. In W. J. Arnold & M. M. Page (Eds.), *Nebraska Symposium on Motivation* (pp. 187–265). Lincoln: University of Nebraska Press.

Osgood, C. E., Suci, G. L., & Tannenbaum, P. H. (1957). *The measurement of meaning.* Urbana: University of Illinois Press.

Overton, W. F. (1991a). Historical and contemporary perspectives on developmental theory and research strategies. In R. Downs, L. Liben, & D. Palermo (Eds.), *Visions of aesthetics, the environment, and development: The legacy of Joachim Wohlwill* (pp. 263–311). Hillsdale, NJ: Erlbaum.

Overton, W. F. (1991b). The structure of developmental theory. In H. W. Reese (Ed.), *Advances in child development and behavior* (Vol. 23, pp. 1–37). New York: Academic Press.

Pareek, U., & Rao, T. V. (1980). Cross-cultural surveys and interviewing. In H. C. Triandis & J. W. Berry (Eds.), *Handbook of cross-cultural psychology: Methodology* (Vol. 2, pp. 127–179).

Park, C. L., & Folkman, S. (1997). Meaning in the context of stress and coping. *Review of General Psychology, 1,* 115–144.

Parker, K. C. H., Hanson, R. K., & Hunsley, J. (1988). MMPI, Rorschach, and WAIS: A meta-analytic comparison of reliability, stability, and validity. *Psychological Bulletin, 103,* 367–373.

Parloff, D. N. (Ed.). (1995). *Ethical conflicts in psychology.* Washington, DC: American Psychological Association.

Parsons, H. M. (1974). What happened at Hawthorne? *Science, 183,* 922–932.

Paulhus, D. L. (1991). Measurement and control of response bias. In J. P. Robinson, P. R. Shaver, & L. S. Wrightsman (Eds.), *Measures of personality and social psychological attitudes* (pp. 17–59). San Diego, CA: Academic Press.

Paulos, J. A. (1990). *Innumeracy: Mathematical illiteracy and its consequences.* New York: Vintage Books.

Paulos, J. A. (1991, April 24). Math moron myths. *New York Times OP-ED,* p. 25.

Peirce, C. S. (1966). *Charles S. Peirce: Selected writings (Values in a universe of chance).* P. P. Weiner, (Ed.). New York: Dover.

Pelz, D. C., & Andrew, F. M. (1964). Detecting causal priorities in panel study data. *American Sociological Review, 29,* 836–848.

Pera, M., & Shea, W. R. (Eds.). (1991). *Persuading science: The art of scientific rhetoric.* Canton, MA: Science History Publications.

Pessin, J. (1933). The comparative effects of social and mechanical stimulation on memorizing. *American Journal of Psychology, 45,* 263–270.

Peterson, C., & Ulrey, L. M. (1994). Can explanatory style be scored from TAT protocols? *Personality and Social Psychology Bulletin, 20,* 102–106.

Phillips, D. P., & Carstensen, M. S. (1986). Clustering of teenage suicides after television news stories about suicide. *New England Journal of Medicine, 315,* 685–689.

Phillips, D. P., & King, E. W. (1988). Death takes a holiday: Mortality surrounding major social occasions. *Lancet, 2,* 728–732.

Phillips, D. P., Lesyna, K., & Paight, D. J. (1992). Suicide and the media. In R. W. Maris, A. L. Berman, J. T. Maltsberger, & R. I. Yufit (Eds.), *Assessment and prediction of suicide* (pp. 499–519). New York: Guilford Press.

Phillips, D. P., & Paight, B. A. (1987). The impact of televised movies about suicide: A replicative study. *New England Journal of Medicine, 317,* 809–811.

Phillips, D. P., & Smith, D. G. (1990). Postponement of death until symbolically meaningful occasions. *Journal of the American Medical Association, 263,* 1947–1951.

Pierce, C. A., & Aguinis, H. (1997). Using virtual reality technology in organizational behavior research. *Journal of Organizational Behavior, 18,* 407-410.

Platt, J. (1992). Cases of cases . . . of cases. In C. C. Ragin & H. S. Becker (Eds.), *What is a case? Exploring the foundations of social inquiry* (pp. 21–52). Cambridge: Cambridge University Press.

Polanyi, M. (1966). *The tacit dimension.* New York: Doubleday Anchor.

Popper, K. R. (1934). *Logik der Forschung.* Vienna: Springer-Verlag.

Popper, K. R. (1961). *The logic of scientific inquiry.* New York: Basic Books.

Popper, K. R. (1963). *Conjectures and refutations.* London: Routledge.

Postman, L., Bruner, J. S., & McGinnies, E. (1948). Personal values as selective factors in perception. *Journal of Abnormal and Social Psychology, 43,* 142–154.

Ragin, C. C. (1992). Introduction: Cases of "What is a case?" In C. C. Ragin & H. S. Becker (Eds.), *What is a case? Exploring the foundations of social inquiry* (pp. 1–17). Cambridge: Cambridge University Press.

Ragin, C. C., & Becker, H. S. (Eds.). (1992). *What is a case? Exploring the foundations of social inquiry.* Cambridge: Cambridge University Press.

Ramachandran, V. S. (Ed.). (1994). *Encyclopedia of human behavior* (Vols. 1–4). Orlando, FL: Academic Press.

Rand Corporation. (1955). *A million random digits with 100,000 normal deviates.* New York: Free Press.

Randhawa, B. S., & Coffman, W. E. (Eds.). (1978). *Visual learning, thinking, and communication.* New York: Academic Press.

Raudenbush, S. W. (1984). Magnitude of teacher expectancy effects on pupil IQ as a function of the credibility of expectancy induction: A synthesis of findings from 18 experiments. *Journal of Educational Psychology, 76,* 85–97.

Reed, J. G., & Baxter, P. M. (1994). Using reference databases. In H. Cooper & L. V. Hedges (Eds.), *The handbook of research synthesis* (pp. 57–70). New York: Russell Sage Foundation.

Reed, S. K. (1988). *Cognition: Theory and applications* (2nd ed.). Pacific Grove, CA: Brooks/Cole.

Regis, E. (1987). *Who got Einstein's office? Eccentricities and genius at the Institute for Advanced Study.* Reading, MA: Addison-Wesley.

Reichenbach, H. (1938). *Experience and prediction.* Chicago: University of Illinois Press.

Riessman, C. K. (Ed.). (1993). *Qualitative studies in social work research.* Thousand Oaks, CA: Sage.

Rind, B., & Bordia, P. (1996). Effect on restaurant tipping of male and female servers drawing a happy, smiling face on the backs of customers' checks. *Journal of Applied Social Psychology, 26,* 218–225.

Roberts, R. M. (1989). *Serendipity: Accidental discoveries in science.* New York: Wiley.

Robin, H. (1993). *The scientific image: From cave to computer.* New York: W. H. Freeman.

Robinson, J. P., Shaver, P. R., & Wrightsman, L. S. (Eds.). (1991). *Measures of personality and social psychological attitudes.* San Diego, CA: Academic Press.

Roethlisberger, F. J., & Dickson, W. J. (1939). *Management and the worker.* Cambridge: Harvard University Press.

Rosenbaum, M. (1986a). Comments on a proposed two-stage theory of relationship: First repulsion; then attraction. *Journal of Personality and Social Psychology, 51,* 1171–1172.

Rosenbaum, M. (1986b). The repulsion hypothesis: On the nondevelopment of relationship. *Journal of Personality and Social Psychology, 51,* 1156–1166.

Rosenberg, M. J. (1969). The conditions and consequences of evaluation apprehension. In R. Rosenthal & R. L. Rosnow (Eds.), *Artifact in behavioral research* (pp. 279–349). New York: Academic Press.

Rosengren, K. E. (Ed.). (1981). *Advances in content analysis.* Beverly Hills, CA: Sage.

Rosenthal, M. (1971). Where rumor raged. *Trans-Action, 8*(4), 34–43.

Rosenthal, M. C. (1985). Bibliographic retrieval for the social and behavioral scientist. *Research in Higher Education, 22,* 315–333.

Rosenthal, M. C. (1994). The fugitive literature. In H. Cooper & L. V. Hedges (Eds.), *The handbook of research synthesis* (pp. 85–94). New York: Russell Sage Foundation.

Rosenthal, R. (1966). *Experimenter effects in behavioral research.* New York: Appleton-Century-Crofts.

Rosenthal, R. (1973). Estimating effective reliability in studies that employ judges' ratings. *Journal of Clinical Psychology, 29,* 342–345.

Rosenthal, R. (1976). *Experimenter effects in behavioral research* (enlarged ed.). New York: Irvington.

Rosenthal, R. (1979). The "file drawer problem" and tolerance for null results. *Psychological Bulletin, 86,* 638–641.

Rosenthal, R. (1982). Conducting judgment studies. In K. R. Scherer & P. Ekman (Eds.), *Handbook of methods in nonverbal behavior research* (pp. 287–361). New York: Cambridge University Press.

Rosenthal, R. (1983). Meta-analysis: Toward a more cumulative social science. In L. Bickman (Ed.), *Applied social psychology annual* (Vol. 4, pp. 65–93). Beverly Hills, CA: Sage.

Rosenthal, R. (1985). From unconscious experimenter bias to teacher expectancy effects. In J. B. Dusek (Ed.), *Teacher expectancies* (pp. 37–65). Hillsdale, NJ: Erlbaum.

Rosenthal, R. (1987). *Judgment studies: Design, analysis, and meta-analysis.* Cambridge: Cambridge University Press.

Rosenthal, R. (1990a). Evaluation of procedures and results. In K. W. Wachter & M. L. Straf (Eds.), *The future of meta-analysis* (pp. 123–133). New York: Russell Sage Foundation.

Rosenthal, R. (1990b). How are we doing in soft psychology? *American Psychologist, 45,* 775–777.

Rosenthal, R. (1990c). Replication in behavioral research. *Journal of Social Behavior and Personality, 5,* 1–30.

Rosenthal, R. (1991). *Meta-analytic procedures for social research* (Rev. ed.). Newbury Park, CA: Sage.

Rosenthal, R. (1993). Interpersonal expectations: Some antecedents and some consequences. In P. D. Blanck (Ed.), *Interpersonal expectations: Theory, research, and applications* (pp. 3–24). Cambridge: Cambridge University Press.

Rosenthal, R. (1994a). Parametric measures of effect size. In H. Cooper & L. V. Hedges (Eds.), *The handbook of research synthesis* (pp. 231–244). New York: Russell Sage Foundation.

Rosenthal, R. (1994b). Science and ethics in conducting, analyzing, and reporting psychological research. *Psychological Science, 5,* 127–134.

Rosenthal, R. (1995). Writing meta-analytic reviews. *Psychological Bulletin, 118,* 183–192.

Rosenthal, R., & Fode, K. L. (1963). The effect of experimenter bias on the performance of the albino rat. *Behavioral Science, 8,* 183–189.

Rosenthal, R., Hall, J. A., DiMatteo, M. R., Rogers, P. L., & Archer, D. (1979). *Sensitivity to nonverbal communication: The PONS test.* Baltimore: Johns Hopkins University Press.

Rosenthal, R., & Jacobson, L. (1968). *Pygmalion in the classroom: Teacher expectation and pupils' intellectual development.* New York: Holt, Rinehart & Winston.

Rosenthal, R., & Lawson, R. (1964). A longitudinal study of experimenter bias on the operant learning of laboratory rats. *Journal of Psychiatric Research, 2,* 61–72.

Rosenthal, R., & Rosnow, R. L. (Eds.). (1969). *Artifact in behavioral research.* New York: Academic Press.

Rosenthal, R., & Rosnow, R. L. (1975a). *Primer of methods for the behavioral sciences.* New York: Wiley.

Rosenthal, R., & Rosnow, R. L. (1975b). *The volunteer subject.* New York: Wiley.

Rosenthal, R., & Rosnow, R. L. (1984). Applying Hamlet's question to the ethical conduct of research: A conceptual addendum. *American Psychologist, 39,* 561–563.

Rosenthal, R., & Rosnow, R. L. (1991). *Essentials of behavioral research: Methods and data analysis* (2nd ed.). New York: McGraw-Hill.

Rosenthal, R., & Rubin, D. B. (1978). Interpersonal expectancy effects: The first 345 studies. *Behavioral and Brain Sciences, 3,* 377–386.

Rosenthal, R., & Rubin, D. B. (1979a). Comparing significance levels of independent studies. *Psychological Bulletin, 86,* 1165–1168.

Rosenthal, R., & Rubin, D. B. (1979b). A note on percent variance explained as a measure of the importance of effects. *Journal of Applied Social Psychology, 9,* 395–396.

Rosenthal, R., & Rubin, D. B. (1982a). Comparing effect sizes of independent studies. *Psychological Bulletin, 92,* 500–504.

Rosenthal, R., & Rubin, D. B. (1982b). A simple general purpose display of magnitude of experimental effect. *Journal of Educational Psychology, 74,* 166–169.

Rosnow, R. L. (1980). Psychology of rumor. *Psychological Bulletin, 87,* 578–591.

Rosnow, R. L. (1981). *Paradigms in transition: The methodology of social inquiry.* New York: Oxford University Press.

Rosnow, R. L. (1983). Von Osten's horse, Hamlet's question, and the mechanistic view of causality: Implications for a post-crisis social psychology. *Journal of Mind and Behavior, 4,* 319–338.

Rosnow, R. L. (1986). Shotter, Vico and fallibilistic indeterminacy. *British Journal of Social Psychology, 25,* 215–216.

Rosnow, R. L. (1988). Rumor as communication: A contextualist approach. *Journal of Communication, 38*(1), 12–28.

Rosnow, R. L. (1989, May). Die macht des Gerüchts. *Psychologie Heute,* pp. 20–24.

Rosnow, R. L. (1990a). The researcher's worst friend. In P. Chance & T. G. Harris (Eds.), *The best of Psychology Today* (pp. 260–264). New York: McGraw-Hill.

Rosnow, R. L. (1990b). Teaching research ethics through role-play and discussion. *Teaching of Psychology, 17,* 179–181.

Rosnow, R. L. (1991). Inside rumor: A personal journey. *American Psychologist, 46,* 484–496.

Rosnow, R. L. (1993). The volunteer problem revisited. In P. D. Blanck (Ed.), *Interpersonal expectations: Theory, research, applications* (pp. 418–436). New York: Cambridge University Press.

Rosnow, R. L. (1997). Hedgehogs, foxes, and the evolving social contract in psychological science: Ethical challenges and methodological opportunities. *Psychological Methods 2,* 345–356.

Rosnow, R. L., & Aiken, L. S. (1973). Mediation of artifacts in behavioral research. *Journal of Experimental Social Psychology, 9,* 181–201.

Rosnow, R. L., Esposito, J. L., & Gibney, L. (1987). Factors influencing rumor spreading: Replication and extension. *Language and Communication, 7,* 1–14.

Rosnow, R. L., & Fine, G. A. (1974, August). Inside rumors. *Human Behavior,* pp. 64–68.

Rosnow, R. L., & Fine, G. A. (1976). *Rumor and gossip: The social psychology of hearsay.* New York: Elsevier.

Rosnow, R. L. & Georgoudi, M. (Eds.) (1986). *Contextualism and understanding in behavioral science.* New York: Praeger.

Rosnow, R. L., Goodstadt, B. E., Suls, J. M., & Gitter, A. G. (1973). More on the social psychology of the experiment: When compliance turns to self-defense. *Journal of Personality and Social Psychology, 27,* 337–343.

Rosnow, R. L., & Rosenthal, R. (1970). Volunteer effects in behavioral research. In K. H. Craik, B. Kleinmuntz, R. L. Rosnow, R. Rosenthal, J. A. Cheyne, & R. H. Walters, *New directions in psychology* (No. 4, pp. 211–277). New York: Holt, Rinehart & Winston.

Rosnow, R. L., & Rosenthal, R. (1976). The volunteer subject revisited. *Australian Journal of Psychology, 28,* 97–108.

Rosnow, R. L., & Rosenthal, R. (1988). Focused tests of significance and effect size estimation in counseling psychology. *Journal of Counseling Psychology, 35,* 203–208.

Rosnow, R. L., & Rosenthal, R. (1989a). Definition and interpretation of interaction effects. *Psychological Bulletin, 105,* 143–146.

Rosnow, R. L., & Rosenthal, R. (1989b). Statistical procedures and the justification of knowledge in psychological science. *American Psychologist, 44,* 1276–1284.

Rosnow, R. L., & Rosenthal, R. (1991). If you are looking at the cell means, you're not looking at *only* the interaction (unless all main effects are zero). *Psychological Bulletin, 110,* 574–576.

Rosnow, R. L., & Rosenthal, R. (1995). "Some things you learn aren't so": Cohen's paradox, Asch's paradigm, and the interpretation of interaction. *Psychological Science, 6,* 3–9.

Rosnow, R. L., & Rosenthal, R. (1996a). Computing contrasts, effect sizes, and counternulls on other people's published data: General procedures for research consumers. *Psychological Methods, 1,* 331–340.

Rosnow, R. L., & Rosenthal, R. (1996b). Contrasts and interactions redux: Five easy pieces. *Psychological Science, 7,* 253–257.

Rosnow, R. L., & Rosenthal, R. (1997). *People studying people: Artifacts and ethics in behavioral research.* New York: W. H. Freeman.

Rosnow, R. L., & Rosnow, M. (1998). *Writing papers in psychology: A student guide* (4th ed.). Pacific Grove, CA: Brooks/Cole.

Rosnow, R. L., Rotheram-Borus, M. J., Ceci, S. J., Blanck, P. D., & Koocher, G. P. (1993). The institutional review board as a mirror of scientific and ethical standards. *American Psychologist, 48,* 821–826.

Rosnow, R. L., Skleder, A. A., Jaeger, M. E., & Rind, B. (1994). Intelligence and the epistemics of interpersonal acumen: Testing some implications of Gardner's theory. *Intelligence, 19,* 93–116.

Rosnow, R. L., & Suls, J. M. (1970). Reactive effects of pretesting in attitude research. *Journal of Personality and Social Psychology, 15,* 338–343.

Ross, L., Greene, D., & House, P. (1977). The "false-consensus effect": An egocentric bias in social perception and attribution processes. *Journal of Experimental Social Psychology, 13,* 279–301.

Rossi, P. H., Wright, J. D., & Anderson, A. B. (1983). Sample surveys: History, current practice, and future prospects. In P. H. Rossi, J. D. Wright, & A. B. Anderson (Eds.), *Handbook of survey research* (pp. 1–20). New York: Academic Press.

Rothenberg, R. (1990, October 5). Surveys proliferate, but answers dwindle. *New York Times,* pp. A1, D4.

Rozelle, R. M., & Campbell, D. T. (1969). More plausible rival hypotheses in the cross-lagged panel correlation technique. *Psychological Bulletin, 71,* 74–80.

Rubin, Z. (1974). Jokers wild in the lab. In J. B. Maas (Ed.), *Readings in Psychology Today* (pp. 25–27). Del Mar, CA: CRM Books.

Russell, M. S., & Burch, R. L. (1959). *The principles of humane experimental technique.* London: Methuen.

Sacks, H., Chalmers, T. C., & Smith, H., Jr. (1982). Randomized versus historical controls for clinical trials. *American Journal of Medicine, 72,* 233–240.

Saks, M. J., & Blanck, P. D. (1992). Justice improved: The unrecognized benefits of aggregation and sampling in the trial of mass torts. *Stanford Law Review, 44,* 815–851.

Sartre, J. P. (1956). *Being and nothingness.* New York: Washington Square Press.

Saxe, L. (1991). Lying: Thoughts of an applied social psychologist. *American Psychologist, 46,* 409–415.

Schachter, S. (1968). Obesity and eating. *Science, 161,* 751–756.

Schlaifer, R. (1980). The relay assembly test room: An alternative statistical interpretation. *American Sociological Review, 45,* 995–1005.

Schuler, H. (1982). *Ethical problems in psychological research.* New York: Academic Press.

Schultz, D. P. (1969). The human subject in psychological research. *Psychological Bulletin, 72,* 214–228.

Schuman, H., & Presser, S. (1996). *Questions and answers in attitude surveys: Experiments on Question Form, Wording, and Content.* Thousand Oaks, CA: Sage.

Scott, W. A. (1968). Attitude measurement. In G. Lindzey & E. Aronson (Eds.), *The handbook of social psychology* (2nd ed., Vol. 2, pp. 204–272). Reading, MA: Addison-Wesley.

Scott-Jones, D., & Rosnow, R. L. (1998). Ethics and mental health research. In H. Friedman (Ed.), *Encyclopedia of mental health* (Vol. 2, pp. 149-160). Palo Alto, CA: Academic Press.

Sears, D. O. (1986). College sophomores in the laboratory: Influences of a narrow data base on social psychology's view of human nature. *Journal of Personality and Social Psychology, 51,* 515–530.

Shaw, M. E., & Wright, J. M. (1967). *Scales for the measurement of attitudes.* New York: McGraw-Hill.

Sherman, S. J., Presson, C., & Chassin, L. (1984). Mechanisms underlying the false consensus effect: The special role of threats to the self. *Personality and Social Psychology Bulletin, 10,* 127–138.

Shermer, M. (1997). *Why people believe wierd things: Pseudoscience, superstition, and other confusions of our time.* New York: W. H. Freeman.

Shibutani, T. (1962). *Improvised news: A sociological study of rumor.* Indianapolis, IN: Bobbs-Merrill.

Sidman, M. (1960). *Tactics of scientific research: Evaluating experimental data in psychology.* New York: Basic Books.

Sieber, J. E. (1982a). Deception in social research: 1. Kinds of deception and the wrongs they may involve. *IRB: A Review of Human Subjects Research, 3*, 1–2, 12.

Sieber, J. E. (Ed.). (1982b). *The ethics of social research* (Vols. 1–2). New York: Springer-Verlag.

Sieber, J. E. (1983). Deception in social research: 2. Factors influencing the magnitude of potential for harm or wrong. *IRB: A Review of Human Subjects Research, 4*, 1–3, 12.

Sieber, J. E. (1991). Scientists' responses to ethical issues in science. In W. Shadish (Ed.), *Contributions to social psychology of science*. New York: Guilford.

Sieber, J. E. (1992). *Planning ethically responsible research*. Newbury Park, CA: Sage.

Sieber, J. E., & Saks, M. J. (1989). A census of subject pool characteristics and policies. *American Psychologist, 44*, 1053–1061.

Siegel, S. (1956). *Nonparametric statistics*. New York: McGraw-Hill.

Sigall, H., Aronson, E., & Van Hoose, T. (1970). The cooperative subject: Myth or reality? *Journal of Experimental Social Psychology, 6*, 1–10.

Silverman, D. (1993). *Interpreting qualitative data: Methods for analyzing talk, text, and interaction*. Thousand Oaks, CA: Sage.

Silverman, I. (1977). *The human subject in the psychological experiment*. New York: Pergamon Press.

Singer, E., Von Thurn, D. R., & Miller, E. R. (1995). Confidentiality assurances and response: A quantitative review of the experimental literature. *Public Opinion Quarterly, 59*, 66–77.

Skinner, B. F. (1938). *The behavior of organisms: An experimental analysis*. New York: Appleton-Century-Crofts.

Skinner, B. F. (1948a). Superstition in the pigeon. *Journal of Experimental Psychology, 38*, 168–172.

Skinner, B.F. (1948b). *Walden two*. New York: Macmillan.

Skinner, B. F. (1980). *Notebooks*. (R. Epstein, Ed.). Englewood Cliffs, NJ: Prentice Hall.

Skinner, B. F. (1987). Whatever happened to psychology as a science of behavior? *American Psychologist, 42*, 780–786.

Slife, B., & Rubinstein, J. (Eds.). (1992). *Taking sides: Clashing views on controversial psychological issues* (7th ed.). Guilford, CT: Dushkin.

Slovic, P. (1987). Perception of risk. *Science, 236*, 280–285.

Smart, R. G. (1966). Subject selection bias in psychological research. *Canadian Psychologist, 7a*, 115–121.

Smith, C. (1980). *Selecting a source of local television news in the Salt Lake City SMSA: A multivariate analysis of cognitive and affective factors for 384 randomly-selected news viewers*. Unpublished doctoral dissertation, Temple University School of Communication, Philadelphia.

Smith, M. L., & Glass, G. V. (1977). Meta-analysis of psychotherapy outcome studies. *American Psychologist, 32*, 752–760.

Smith, T. W. (1997, April 20). Punt, pass and ponder the questions. *New York Times*, p. 11.

Snedecor, G. W., & Cochran, W. G. (1989). *Statistical methods* (8th ed.). Ames: Iowa State University Press.

Sobal, J. (1982). Disclosing information in interview introductions: Methodological consequences of informed consent. *Sociology and Social Research, 66*, 348–361.

Sockloff, A. L., & Edney, J. N. (1972, May). *Some extensions of Student's t and Pearson's r central distributions*. Technical Report 72–5. Temple University Measurement and Research Center, Philadelphia.

Solomon, R. L. (1949). An extension of control group design. *Psychological Bulletin, 46*, 137–150.

Solomon, R. L., & Howes, D. (1951). Word frequency, personal values, and visual duration thresholds. *Psychological Review, 58*, 256–270.

Sommer, R. (1968). Hawthorne dogma. *Psychological Bulletin, 70*, 592–595.

Sonneck, G., Etzersdorfer, E., & Nagel-Kuess, S. (1994). Imitative suicide on the Viennese subway. *Social Science and Medicine, 38*, 453–457.

Spearman, C. (1910). Correlation calculated from faulty data. *British Journal of Psychology, 3*, 271–295.

Sperry, R. W. (1968). Hemisphere deconnection and unity in conscious awareness. *American Psychologist, 23*, 723–733.

Spradley, J. P. (1970). *You owe yourself a drunk: An ethnography of urban nomads*. Boston: Little, Brown.

Spradley, J. P. (1980). *Participant observation*. New York: Holt, Rinehart & Winston.

Squire, P. (1988). Why the 1936 *Literary Digest* poll failed. *Public Opinion Quarterly, 52*, 125–133.

Stanley, B., Sieber, J. E., & Melton, G. B. (1987). Empirical studies of ethical issues in research: A research agenda. *American Psychologist, 7*, 735–741.

Stanovich, K. E. (1986). *How to think straight about psychology*. Glenview, IL: Scott, Foresman.

Steering Committee of the Physicians' Health Study Research Group. (1988). Preliminary report: Findings from the aspirin component of the ongoing physicians' health study. *New England Journal of Medicine, 318,* 262–264.

Steinberg, L., Lamborn, S. D., Dornbusch, S. M., & Darling, N. (1992). Impact of parenting practices on adolescent achievement: Authoritative parenting, school involvement, and encouragement to succeed. *Child Development, 63,* 1266–1281.

Sterling, T. D. (1959). Publication decisions and their possible effects on inferences drawn from tests of significance—or vice versa. *Journal of the American Statistical Association, 54,* 30–34.

Stern, S. E., & Faber, J. E. (1997). The lost e-mail method: Milgram's lost-letter technique in the age of the Internet. *Behavior Research Methods, Instruments, and Computers, 29,* 260–263.

Sternberg, R. J. (1985). *Beyond IQ: A triarchic theory of human intelligence.* Cambridge: Cambridge University Press.

Sternberg, R. J. (1990). *Metaphors of mind: Conceptions of the nature of intelligence.* Cambridge: Cambridge University Press.

Sternberg, R. J. (1993). *The psychologist's companion: A guide to scientific writing for students and researchers* (3rd ed.). Cambridge: Cambridge University Press.

Sternberg, R. J., & Detterman, D. K. (Eds.). (1986). *What is intelligence? Contemporary viewpoints on its nature and definition.* Norwood, NJ: Ablex.

Steuer, J. (1992) Defining virtual reality: Dimensions determining telepresence. *Journal of Communication, 42,* 73–93.

Stigler, S. M. (1986). *The history of statistics: The measurement of uncertainty before 1900.* Cambridge: Belknap/Harvard.

Stone, P., Dunphy, D., Smith, M., & Ogilvie, D. (1966). *The General Inquirer: A complete approach to content analysis.* Cambridge, MA: MIT Press.

Street, E., & Carroll, M. B. (1989). Preliminary evaluation of a new food product. In J. M. Tanur, F. M. Mosteller, W. H. Kruskal, E. L. Lehmann, R. F. Link, R. S. Pieters, & G. R. Rising (Eds.), *Statistics: A guide to the unknown* (3rd ed., pp. 161–169). Pacific Grove, CA: Wadsworth & Brooks/Cole.

Strickland, B. R. (1977). Approval motivation. In T. Blass (Ed.), *Personality variables in social behavior* (pp. 315–356). Hillsdale, NJ: Erlbaum.

Strohmetz, D. B., & Rosnow, R. L. (1994). A mediational model of artifacts. In J. Brzeziński (Ed.), *Probability in theory-building: Experimental and non-experimental approaches to scientific research in psychology* (pp. 177–196). Netherlands: Rudopi.

Strunk, W., Jr., & White, E. B. (1979). *The elements of style* (3rd ed.). New York: Prentice Hall.

Suls, J.M., & Miller, R. L. (Eds.). (1977). *Social comparison processes: Theoretical and empirical perspectives.* Washington, DC: Hemisphere.

Suls, J. M., & Rosnow, R. L. (1988). Concerns about artifacts in psychological experiments. In J. Morawski (Ed.), *The rise of experimentation in American psychology* (pp. 163–187). New York: Oxford University Press.

Susman, E. J., Dorn, L. D., & Fletcher, J. C. (1992). Participation in biomedical research: The consent process as viewed by children, adolescents, young adults, and physicians. *Journal of Pediatrics, 121,* 547–552.

Symonds, P. M. (1925). Notes on rating. *Journal of Applied Psychology, 9,* 188–195.

Tan, D. T. Y., & Singh, R. (1995). Attitudes and attraction: A developmental study of the similarity-attraction and dissimilarity-repulsion hypotheses. *Personality and Social Psychology Bulletin, 21,* 975–986.

Tanur, J. M. (Ed.). (1994). *Questions about questions: Inquiries into the cognitive bases of surveys.* New York: Russell Sage Foundation.

Tatsuoka, M. (1993). Effect size. In G. Keren & C. Lewis (Eds.), *A handbook for data analysis in the behavioral sciences: Methodological issues* (pp. 461–479). Hillsdale, NJ: Erlbaum.

Thorndike, R. L. (1933). The effect of the interval between test and retest on the constancy of the IQ. *Journal of Educational Psychology, 24,* 543–549.

Thurstone, L. L. (1929). Theory of attitude measurement. *Psychological Bulletin, 36,* 222–241.

Thurstone, L. L. (1929–1934). *The measurement of social attitudes.* Chicago: University of Chicago Press.

Tolman, E. C. (1959). Principles of purposive behavior. In S. Koch (Ed.), *Psychology: A study of a science* (Vol. 2, pp. 92–157). New York: McGraw-Hill.

Treadway, M., & McCloskey, M. (1989). Effects of racial stereotypes on eyewitness performance: Implications of the real and rumored Allport and Postman studies. *Applied Cognitive Psychology, 3,* 53–63.

Tryfos, P. (1996). *Sampling methods for applied research: Text and cases.* New York: Wiley.

Tukey, J. W. (1977). *Exploratory data analysis.* Reading, MA: Addison-Wesley.

U.S. Department of Health and Human Services. (1983). Protection of human subjects. *Code of Federal Regulations, 45,* 46.115.

Van Maanen, J. (1988). *Tales of the field: On writing ethnography.* Chicago: University of Chicago Press.

Vickers, B. (Ed.). (1996). *Francis Bacon: A critical edition of the major works.* Oxford: Oxford University Press.

Wainer, H. (1972). Draft of Appendix for R. E. Lana & R. L. Rosnow's *Introduction to contemporary psychology.* New York: Holt, Rinehart & Winston.

Wainer, H. (1984). How to display data badly. *American Statistician, 38,* 137–147.

Wainer, H. (1990). *Computerized adaptive testing: A primer.* Hillsdale, NJ: Erlbaum.

Wainer, H., & Thissen, D. (1993). Combining multiple-choice and constructed-response test scores: Toward a Marxist theory of test construction. *Applied Measurement in Education, 6*(2), 103–118.

Walker, C. J., & Beckerle, C. A. (1987). The effect of anxiety on rumor transmission. *Journal of Social Behavior and Personality, 2,* 353–360.

Walker, C. J., & Blaine, B. (1991). The virulence of dread rumors: A field experiment. *Language and Communication, 11,* 291–298.

Walker, H. M., & Lev, J. (1953). *Statistical inference.* New York: Henry Holt.

Wallis, W. A., & Roberts, H. V. (1956). *Statistics: A new approach.* New York: Free Press.

Weaver, C. (1972). *Human listening.* Indianapolis: Bobbs-Merrill.

Webb, E. J., Campbell, D. T., Schwartz, R. F., & Sechrest, L. (1966). *Unobtrusive measures: Nonreactive research in the social sciences.* Chicago: Rand McNally.

Webb, E. J., Campbell, D. T., Schwartz, R. F., Sechrest, L., & Grove, J. B. (1981). *Nonreactive measures in the social sciences* (2nd ed.). Boston: Houghton Mifflin.

Webber, R. A. (1970). Perception of interactions between superiors and subordinates. *Human Relations, 23,* 235–248.

Weber, R. P. (1985). *Basic content analysis.* Beverly Hills, CA: Sage.

Wechler, J. (Ed.). (1978). *On aesthetics in science.* Cambridge, MA: MIT Press.

Weick, K. E. (1968). Systematic observational methods. In G. Lindzey & E. Aronson (Eds.), *The handbook of social psychology* (2nd ed., Vol. 2, pp. 357–451). Reading, MA: Addison-Wesley.

Weick, K. E. (1995). *Sensemaking in organizations.* Thousand Oaks, CA: Sage.

Weinberger, D. A. (1990). The construct validity of the repressive coping style. In J. L. Singer (Ed.), *Repression and dissociation: Implications for personality theory, psychopathology, and health* (pp. 337–386). Chicago: University of Chicago Press.

Weiner, B. (1991). Metaphors in motivation and attribution. *American Psychologist, 46,* 921–930.

Weisberg, R. W. (1994). Genius and madness? A quasi-experimental test of the hypothesis that manic-depression increases creativity. *Psychological Science, 5,* 361–367.

Werner, H. C., & Kaplan, B. (1963). *Symbol formation: An organismic-developmental approach to language and the expression of thought.* New York: Wiley.

Weschler, L. (1988, January 18).Onward and upward with the arts. *New Yorker,* pp. 33–56.

Wheeler, L., Martin, R., & Suls, J. (1997). The proxy model of social comparison for self-assessment of ability. *Personality and Social Psychology Review, 1,* 54–61.

Wickesberg, A. K. (1968). Communication networks in a business organization structure. *Journal of the Academy of Management, 11,* 253–262.

Wiggins, J. S. (Ed.). (1996). *The five-factor model of personality.* New York: Guilford Press.

Wilcox, B., & Gardner, D. (1993). Political intervention in scientific peer review: Research on adolescent sexual behavior. *American Psychologist, 48,* 972–983.

Wolman, B. B. (Ed.). (1977). *International encyclopedia of psychiatry, psychology, psychoanalysis, and neurology* (Vols. 1–12). New York: Van Nostrand Reinhold.

Woodrum, E. (1984). "Mainstreaming" content analysis in social science: Methodological advantages, obstacles, and solutions. *Social Science Research,* *13,* 1–19.

Wyer, R. S., Jr., & Srull, T. K. (Eds.). (1989). *Advances in social cognition:* Vol. 2. *Social intelligence and cognitive assessment of personality.* Hillsdale, NJ: Erlbaum.

Yin, R. K. (1989). *Case study research: Design and methods.* Newbury Park, CA: Sage.

Zajonc, R. F. (1965). Social facilitation. *Science,* *149,* 269–274.

Zechmeister, E. G., & Nyberg, S. E. (1982). *Human memory: An introduction to research and theory.* Monterey, CA: Brooks/Cole.

Zipf, G. K. (1935). *The psycho-biology of language.* Boston: Houghton Mifflin.

Zipf, G. K. (1949). *Human behavior and the principle of least effort.* Reading, MA: Addison-Wesley.

Name Index

Subject Index